W9-AKB-061

Teaching,
Teachers,
& Teacher
Education

Copyright © 1987 by President and Fellows of Harvard College.
All rights reserved. No part of this publication may be reproduced or transmitted in any form
or by any means, electronic or mechanical, including photocopy, recording, or any information storage and retrieval systems, without permission in writing from the publisher.

Library of Congress Card Number 87-80233. ISBN 0-916690-21-0.
Printed by Capital City Press, Montpelier, VT 05602. Typography by Villanti & Sons, Williston,
VT 05495. Cover design by Cyndy Brady (Northlight Studio Press, Barre, VT 05641).

Harvard Educational Review
Longfellow Hall, 13 Appian Way
Cambridge, Massachusetts 02138

Teaching, Teachers, & Teacher Education

Edited by Margo Okazawa-Rey,
James Anderson, and Rob Traver

PART 2   Cultural Critique

PART 3   Teaching Teachers

PART 4   Academics Reflect on Teaching

PART 5   Critical Reviews

Introduction

We as a nation are reexamining our views on teaching. The reform proposals of 1986 have intensified an already growing public interest in the role of teachers, the practice of teaching, and the nature of teacher education. Recognizing that these newly aroused perceptions hold great possibility for change, the editors of the *Harvard Educational Review* wish to introduce the best of its recent published writings on this topic in the form of an anthology. Such an anthology, we believe, will serve many who have a significant stake in the outcome of the debate: the teachers who wish to assess more deeply their role in schools and society; the reform-minded administrators who are seeking to understand the school-life of teachers; the researchers who must develop methods of inquiry relevant to the improvement of teaching; and the teacher educators who are working to understand, describe, and explain teaching to those who would be teachers.

The arrangement of articles reflects two points of departure. First, we have observed certain "common sense" boundaries which will make the anthology a useful reference. Second, we have incorporated a degree of editorial perspective in the grouping and ordering of articles. For example, we believe that one of the major impediments to understanding teachers and their work is the refusal to listen to them carefully when they speak for themselves. Teachers are uniquely qualified to understand, describe, criticize, and modify their own perspective. Their voices are essential to the task at hand. To acknowledge that fact, the anthology positions teacher-authors at the very beginning, in a section titled "Teachers Reflect on Practice."

The authors of the second group of articles, "Cultural Critique," consider the cultural context of teachers and teaching. For them, the teacher is a pivotal figure in influencing the shape, development, and transmission of culture. They are concerned, therefore, with how teachers themselves and the society at large should regard the limits, prospects, and responsibilities of such a role. The understanding and prescriptions that they develop derive from a critical analysis of the culture; they argue that teaching reform is only a dimension of school reform and school reform will only take place when fundamental shortcomings of society are brought to light. Their self-proclaimed task is to provide the necessary illumination.

The papers in the third group, "Teaching Teachers," are written by those working with teachers and with students preparing to be teachers. These teacher educators reflect on their own practice—the programs, methods, sensitivities, and skills which they have found to provoke and support the development of teachers. These authors contribute to the view that no true education of teachers can take place without comprehending the role and the personhood of teachers, without understanding institutional and cultural prospects and constraints, and without reflecting on the pedagogy and curriculum that teacher education has employed in the past.

In the fourth section, "Academics Reflect on Teaching," members of the academic community present their perspectives on teaching. For the most part, these people too are teachers. Many spend a good portion of their time as practitioners in college or university classrooms. Some have taught and administered in primary and secondary schools and have shared at that level in the school-lives of teachers. But the role of an academician is in many ways distinct; it assumes the responsibility of providing general perspective more than it serves the immediate demands of practice. The result of this intended distancing is a different viewpoint and sometimes a different formulation from that of teachers. These different perspectives make an important — though not a privileged — contribution to the discussion.

Finally, we devote the last section, "Critical Reviews," to evaluations of a number of books that we believe deal directly with the purpose of the anthology. This sampling of recent works broadens the discussion still further, presenting the common concern for reform in teaching as it appears in writings focused on a diversity of educational subjects.

All in all, this anthology represents what the editors believe the *Harvard Educational Review* can offer to the extensive and serious contemporary discussion of teachers, teaching, and teacher education. We realize that much of what is said in these pages is in the tone of critique. So be it. The world is not as it should be, and teachers here in the United States have a significant stake in shaping the required reform. What we hope to have presented here, in the interest of that task, is a collection of voices that deserve to be heard and heeded. The questions they raise and seek to answer are abiding ones: What characterizes good teaching? What creates and sustains the good teacher? What is the teacher's role in the life of the community and culture? Admittedly the questions are difficult; these papers offer no easy answers. But we have proposed, at least, a direction for the work that lies ahead. More careful attention must be given to the immediate accounts of the complexity of practice as it is understood and experienced by reflective teachers. It is to teachers that the challenge to develop a better world falls again and again; and it is our great respect for the importance of their work that we hope stands out clearly in these pages.

MARGO OKAZAWA-REY
JAMES ANDERSON
ROBERT TRAVER

Issue Editors

PART 1

Teachers Reflect on Practice

Two Teachers of Letters

MARGARET TREECE METZGER

CLARE FOX

In the face of parental pressure and with the lure of "high status" occupations, a prospective teacher seeks advice and insight from a former, favorite high school English instructor. Her question, "What does teaching mean to you?" brings a clarion reply: It is passion and paradox, love and hate, routine and excitement — and it always matters. After two years of teaching, the young teacher writes again, this time to say that she agrees — teaching does matter — but that she must leave it to try her hand at another career.

Spring 1984

Dear Mrs. Metzger,

I am writing to you as a former student who has just graduated from Brown University and who is considering teaching English next year. I remember you as a compelling and demanding teacher who seemed to enjoy her job. At the moment, you are the only person I know who would support my career choice. Almost everyone else is disparaging about teaching in public schools.

I am told that I didn't have to go to Brown University to become a teacher. I am told that teaching is a "wonderful thing to do until you decide what you really want to do with your life." I am told that it's "nice" that I'm going to be a teacher. Why does it seem that the decision to teach in our society is analogous with the decision to stunt one's growth, to opt out intellectually in favor of long summers off?

But teaching matters. I know that. You mattered to me, and other teachers have mattered to me. I enjoyed student teaching and I look forward to next year. I have imaginary dialogues with the students in my mind. I hear myself articulating my policy on borderline grades, explaining why I keep switching the chairs from circles to rows as I flounder in my efforts to decide what's best, or laughing with the students as I struggle to overcome saying "okay" too often when I lecture. But I wonder how much of teaching is actually an ego trip, a ploy to be liked, accepted, and respected by a group of people who have limited say in the matter. I also know the humiliation of a student's glare. I know there will be problems. Yet I cannot deny the tremendous sense of worth I felt as a student teacher when students offered me their respect and when students worked hard and were proud of their effort.

Harvard Educational Review Vol. 56 No. 4 November 1986, 349-354

I wonder where I would get this sense of worthiness if I were to work in a New York advertising firm or as an engineer at Bell Labs. And yet, going to work for a big corporation — whether an advertising firm, a bank, or a publishing house — impresses me. It would seem "real," "grown-up," as teaching never will. Nobody would tell me that being an engineer is "nice" or a wonderful way to figure out what I "really want to do."

For graduation, my mother and sister gave me a beautiful, sleek attaché case. My reaction was twofold. First, I realized that it would never be large enough to carry the load of an English teacher, and second, I realized that, should I ever decide to leave teaching, it would be perfect for the real world of professional writers and young executives.

My mother doesn't want me to go into teaching. She is afraid I will get "stuck," that my efforts will not be appreciated or rewarded, and that I will not meet men. When I called home from Minneapolis after a long, productive, and exhilarating day interviewing at schools, my mother congratulated me and suggested that I spend the evening putting together a second resumé — a writing resumé — before I forgot everything else I know how to do. She suggested I spend the following day visiting television studios scouting for writing jobs, "just in case."

And my mother has been in public education for almost twenty years! Granted, when she entered Boston College in 1952, she had to choose between teaching and nursing. I, however, have chosen to teach from among many options available to me as a Brown graduate with a strong liberal arts degree.

I write to you, Mrs. Metzger, because you were the first person to excite me about the processes of writing and because your integrity in the classroom has long been an influence on me — and on my decision to teach. You mattered. I am turning to you because you are a professional; and you continue to choose teaching after eighteen years. I welcome any advice, comments, or solace you could offer me.

Sincerely,

Clare Fox

Spring 1984

Dear Clare,

I admire your courage to consider teaching. Your friends and relatives are not alone in their negative opinions about teaching. I'm sure you read the claim in the President's Commission on Education that education is a national disgrace. *Newsweek's* September 1984 cover showed a teacher in a dunce cap with the headline, "Why Teachers Fail — How to Make Them Better." NBC ran a three-hour special on education — an exposé of inadequate schools. At least four blue-ribbon studies have concluded that teacher education is inadequate, that the pay is the lowest of all professions, that schools have deplorable management, and that the job is full of meaningless paperwork.

I know that much of the criticism is valid. However, the reports sensationalize and do not tell the whole truth. I appreciate your letter because you are giving me a chance to defend a profession I love.

Clare, I look forward to teaching. By mid-August I start planning lessons and dreaming about classrooms. I also wonder whether I'll have the energy to start again with new classes. Yet after September gets under way, I wake up in the morning expecting to have fun at work. I know that teaching well is a worthwhile use of my life. I know my work is significant.

I am almost forty years old, and I'm happier in my job than anyone I know. That's saying a lot. My husband, who enjoys his work, has routine days when he comes home and says, "Nothing much happened today—just meetings." I never have routine days. When I am in the classroom, I usually am having a wonderful time.

I also hate this job. In March I wanted to quit because of the relentlessness of dealing with one-hundred antsy adolescents day after day. I lose patience with adolescent issues: I think I'll screech if I have to listen to one more adolescent self-obsession. I'm physically exhausted every Friday. The filth in our school is an aesthetic insult. The unending petty politics drain me. Often I feel undermined on small issues by a school system that supports me well on academic freedom.

Like all jobs, teaching has inherent stresses. As you know from student teaching, you must know how to discipline a roomful of adolescents; you need to have a sense of purpose about what you are teaching; you need to cope with the exhaustion; and as an English teacher you must get the paper grading under control. I am always saddened by the number of excellent teachers who leave teaching because they think these difficult problems are unsolvable.

A curious irony exists. I am never bored at work, yet my days are shockingly routine. I can tell you exactly what I have done every school day for the past eighteen years at 10:15 in the morning (homeroom attendance), and I suspect I will do the same for the next twenty years. The structure of the school day has changed little since education moved out of the one-room schoolhouse. All teachers get tired of the monotonous routine of bookkeeping, make-up assignments, twenty-minute lunches, and study hall duties. I identify with J. Alfred Prufrock when he says, "I have measured out my life with coffee spoons." My own life has been measured out in student papers. At a conservative estimate I've graded over 30,000—a mind-boggling statistic which makes me feel like a very dull person indeed.

The monotony of my schedule is mirrored in the monotony of my paycheck. No matter how well or poorly I teach, I will be paid the same amount. There is absolutely no monetary reward for good job performance, or any recognition of professional growth or acquired expertise. My pay depends on how long I've taught and my level of education. I work in a school district in which I cannot afford to live. I am alternatively sad and angry about my pay. To the outside world it seems that I am doing exactly the same job I did in 1966—same title, same working conditions, same pay scale (except that my buying power is 8 percent less than it was when I earned $5,400 on my first job). To most people I am "just a teacher."

But this is the outside reality. The interior world of the teacher is quite different. Although you have to come to some terms with the outward flatness of the career, I want to assure you that teachers change and grow. So little research has been done on stage development of teachers that the literature recognizes only three categories—intern, novice, and veteran. This is laughably over-simplified. There is life after student teaching; there is growth after the first year. You will some day

5

solve many of the problems that seem insurmountable during your exhilarating student teaching and your debilitating first year.

Sometimes I am aware of my growth as a teacher, and I realize that finally, after all these years, I am confident in the classroom. On the very, very best days, when classes sing, I am able to operate on many levels during a single class: I integrate logistics, pedagogy, curriculum, group dynamics, individual needs, and my own philosophy. I feel generous and good-natured towards my students, and I am challenged by classroom issues. But on bad days, I feel like a total failure. Students attack my most vulnerable points. I feel overwhelmed by paperwork. I ache from exhaustion. I dream about going to Aruba, but I go to the next class.

I keep going because I'm intellectually stimulated. I enjoy literature, and I assign books I love and books I want to read. I expect class discussions and student papers to give me new insights into literature. As you may remember, I tell students that in exchange for my hard work, they should keep me interested and they should teach me. They do.

To me, teaching poses questions worthy of a lifetime of thought. I want to think about what the great writers are saying. I want to think about how people learn. I want to think about the values we are passing on to the next generation. I am particularly interested in teaching thinking. I love to teach writing. I am working now on teaching writing as a tool for thinking. Questions about teaching are like puzzles to me; I can spend hours theorizing and then use my classroom as a laboratory.

I am also intellectually challenged by pedagogical problems. I have learned to follow the bizarre questions or the "wrong answers." Some questions reveal chasms of ignorance. For example, "Where is Jesus' body?" or "Before movies were in color, wasn't the world dull just being in black and white?" Sometimes students make shocking statements which demand careful responses: "All athletic girls are lesbians" or "Sexually abused toddlers probably really enjoy the sex." And every year, new students require new teaching skills—Cambodian boat children who have never been in school and are illiterate even in their own language, or handicapped children such as a deaf Israeli girl who is trying to learn English without being able to hear it.

And then there are all the difficult, "normal" situations: students and parents who are "entitled," hostile, emotionally needy, or indifferent; students who live in chaotic homes, who are academically pressured, who have serious drug and alcohol problems. The list goes on and on. No school of education prepared me for the "Hill Street Blues" intensity and chaos of public schools. I received my combat training from other teachers, from myself, and mostly from the students. You will too.

Sometimes I think I can't do it all. I don't want to be bitter or a martyr, so I am careful to take care of myself. I put flowers on my desk to offset the dreariness of an old school building. I leave school several times a week to run errands or to take walks in order to feel less trapped. Other teachers take courses at local colleges, join committees of adults, talk in the teacher's lounge, or play with computers. In order to give to others, teachers must nurture themselves.

Ultimately, teaching is nurturing. The teacher enters a giving relationship with strangers, and then the teacher's needs must give way to students' needs. I want to work on my own writing; instead I work on students' writing. My days are spent encouraging young people's growth. I watch my students move beyond me, thinking and writing better than I have ever done. I send them to colleges I could never afford. And I must strive to be proud, not jealous, of them. I must learn generosity of heart.

I am a more compassionate person because I have known teachers and students. I think differently about handicaps because I worked with Guy, who is quadriplegic from a rugby accident. Refugee problems have a human face because I've heard Nazmul tell stories about refugee camps in Bangladesh, and I've heard Merhdad tell about escaping from Iran, hidden in a camel's baggage. I have seen the school social worker give suicidal students his home phone number, telling them to call anytime. I have seen administrators bend all the rules to help individual students through personal crises. Every day I hear stories of courage and generosity. I admire other teachers.

Facing every new class is an act of courage and optimism. Years ago, the courage required was fairly primitive. I needed courage to discipline my classes, to get them into line, to motivate them to work. But now I need a deeper courage. I look at each new class and know that I must let each of these young people into my life in some significant way. The issue is one of heart. Can I open my heart to two hundred more adolescent strangers each year? Put bluntly, can I be that loving?

I hope to love my students so well that it doesn't even matter whether they like me. I want to love them in the way I love my own son — full of respect and awe for who they are, full of wanting their growth, full of wonder at what it means to lead and to follow the next generation.

Clare, when you consider a life's work, consider not just what you will take to the task, but what it will give to you. Which job will give self-respect and challenge? Which job will give you a world of ideas? Which job will be intellectually challenging? Which job will enlarge you and give you life in abundance? Which job will teach you lessons of the heart?

With deep respect,

Margaret Metzger

Spring 1986

Dear Mrs. Metzger,

After two years of teaching, I still derive strength and vigor from the letter you wrote me so long ago. Your letter makes me remember all of the best parts of teaching — the self-evaluations written by students who liked their work and the silliness of the class that plotted ways to walk out on me, knowing I would catch up with them and we'd resume class wherever we were — the library, another classroom, the basketball court. I remember lots of laughing. I laugh a lot in the classroom, more than I do in my private life.

And I think a lot, too. There is no better way to learn a book than to teach it, no better way to think through a writing problem than to wrestle through the drafts of a paper, guiding the writer beyond frustration to resolution. I am at my brightest, some moments, in the classroom.

And yet I have decided to leave teaching.

I am feeling too selfish to teach, too possessive of my time and my future. I have decided to work full-time at the publishing company where I have worked afternoons this year, where I work on my own writing with others coaching me, and where my writing is printed, a thousandfold and over. I will earn almost $5,000 less than I would if I taught full-time next year, and I will work all summer with few vacations.

After a strong, satisfying year I left my first teaching job in June because I was afraid of the cycle that had already been established. I taught six classes a day — five writing and one advanced reading — to seventh graders. I taught at an exceptionally demanding, academically rigorous junior high. By February I was exhausted, and by June I had made two friends outside of teaching. Too much of my time outside of school had been spent on papers, or in the library looking for good reasons to teach *Alice in Wonderland*. I spent a lot of time with other teachers from the school — a smart, professional, and fun group of people. But still we talked about school — and our shared exhaustion.

After living for Memorial Day weekend, I found myself with no plans. I realized how completely I'd been absorbed by my job. I also saw myself years from now, a good teacher — better than I am now — but still without plans for a holiday weekend. And each year the kids would move on.

Yet for all my martyrdom, I have never once felt caught up. I have never passed back a set of papers without wondering whom I had disappointed, who had counted on my intuitions and my goodness and not just my editorial skills. And I am only teaching part-time this year — juniors in high school. There is no room for complacency in the classroom; we are forever judged and measured. No matter how achingly we want to do it right, there is always something that could be done better. I could know more about Fitzgerald before I introduce *The Great Gatsby*; I could be more responsive to student needs if I gave up my lunch hour every day. And yet I could struggle for hours over the perfect comment for a student's paper, or the best approach to a piece of literature, and still not know which sentence the student would walk away with.

I hope to teach again some day, when I have more in my life and other investments to balance with teaching. I would like to combine my teaching skills with my own writing, perhaps by coordinating a writing program or working with other teachers to promote writing across the curriculum.

In my heart I think I'll be back. And I think I'll be a better teacher for having stepped out and indulged my selfishness.

Thank you for your support. You have been very important to me.

Sincerely,

Clare Fox

Confessions from a Community College

PHILIP SBARATTA

In this essay Philip Sbaratta reflects upon his interactions as a community college English instructor in Beverly, Massachusetts. These vignettes offer a poignant view of teaching in an institution that has a unique place in the American educational system.

Fall 1975, Basic English. I am using a writing workshop format. Students are meeting with me individually so that I can examine their writing journals and assist them in the revision process. Bob, a tall, blond nineteen-year-old, saunters to where I'm working. He gently lays before me his journal entry. It begins: "The nightmare continues. I go to sleep and die a little more each night. If the terror doesn't stop, I'm going to end it myself."

I've sometimes wondered how I became a teacher—fate, free will, genes, environment? I do remember, however, that when I was asked what I wanted to be, "teacher" was frequently among my replies. The competing careers were doctor and theater usher. I soon learned that I had not the stomach for the medical profession, and ushering—for all the free movies—was a humdrum job.

Whatever the influences, I did become an English teacher. Like most aspiring English teachers, I delved into the intricacies of literature. I agonized over whether *The Adventures of Huckleberry Finn* was the great American novel; I considered the objective correlative in T.S. Eliot's poetry; I experienced the epiphany in James Joyce's fiction; and I delighted in the sprung rhythm of Gerard Manley Hopkins.

But none of this, though I loved it, prepared me for teaching writing and, perhaps more importantly, for dealing with Bob. I did not have to teach writing for long to understand the intimacy of the writing process. The writing teacher promotes and participates in an intellectual triangulation: the writer, the reader, and the written discourse merge in an act of creation moving toward some sense of satisfaction and completion.

Untrained to teach writing, I consulted the experts. I reviewed Richard Braddock's research; I stopped students from writing what Ken Macrorie calls "Engfish"; I incorporated Peter Elbow and Donald Murray's suggestions for working with student writers.[1]

---

[1] Richard Braddock, Richard Lloyd Jones, and Lowell Schoer, *Research in Writing Composition* (Champaign, IL: National Council of Teachers of English, 1963); Macrorie defines the term "Engfish" as phoney, pretentious language in his *Telling Writing* (Rochelle Park, NJ: Hayden, 1970), p. 4; Elbow, *Writing Without Teachers* (New York: Oxford University Press, 1973); and Murray, *A Writer Teaches Writing* (Boston: Houghton Mifflin, 1968).

Harvard Educational Review Vol. 55 No. 3 August 1985, 321–323

And there was Bob, whose "voice" told me about suicide and depression. As I stared at his suicide threat, I felt paralyzed. Suddenly the notions of organization, coherence, and usage seemed absolutely ludicrous. Bob had taken away the safety net, and I was free-falling. After an excruciating silence, I finally suggested, somewhat coldly, that he see me in my office. He did not respond but merely picked up his journal and returned to his seat.

That was the last I saw of Bob. He stopped coming to my class. When I inquired as to his whereabouts, I learned that he had dropped out. To be candid, I was relieved. By his disappearance, Bob had taken me off the hook. But Prufrock's questions still nag at me: "And should I then presume? And how should I begin?"

Spring 1979, Composition 101. I am discussing the use of brainstorming as a way to learn what we know about a subject. While getting students to generate ideas for writing by free association, I notice at the far left of the room two freshman women. They look much like the other women in the class except that they do not watch me. Instead, they follow the intricate finger movements of their sign language interpreter.

The community college seems a distinctively American phenomenon. Its offer of access and its recruitment of nontraditional students gives the community college a special place in the struggle toward the ideal of equal opportunity. So, as a community college instructor, I was not surprised to find two deaf students attempting to comprehend the cajoling of an English teacher. My lack of surprise, however, did not mean I was prepared.

Within a few meetings I became aware, with an extraordinary intensity, of the power and complexity of language. I was faced with two students for whom the world of oral communication was severely limited. The nuance of word choice, the drama of volume and emphasis, the singular effect of pronunciation and diction were no longer teaching tools I could rely on. Here I was trying to teach without the medium to do so. Though I met with the deaf students individually, our conversations seemed like parodies of communication. They nodded their heads, vehemently proclaiming comprehension, but I was never wholly convinced that they understood what I was saying. I thought I knew how to teach, but these two students challenged my complacency. They reminded me of my former students who had drifted through the pages of my gradebook—those who had failed or refused to respond, those who could not keep up, those who had mysteriously disappeared. Perhaps I had not found the medium for teaching them either.

Spring 1984, American Literature. Having completed a discussion on Walt Whitman, I returned to my office. At the doorway appears Sarah, a brilliant student. She is about thirty, a high school dropout and a welfare recipient with two children, who bears the emotional burdens of a brutal marriage and the responsibility of raising children as a single parent. She sits down, and speaking about the circumstances of her life, softly asks, "What am I supposed to do now?"

Research suggests that teachers are motivated by the hope of making a difference. They want to give students the means to take charge of their lives. Both *Pygmalion* and the film *Educating Rita* offer versions of a teacher's motivation. But what are the effects on the students? Both the disenfranchised Eliza Doolittle and the irascible Rita are unalterably transformed by their education; neither can return to her former way of life nor find a place for her new self.

Sarah's decision to attend college seemed to have saved her from a world of narrow hopes and, as Langston Hughes writes, of a "dream deferred." For Sarah, college was an awakening, with a surge of ideas and a bombardment of images and sounds. Her mind grew, and she developed an eagerness to know. Battered professors, tired of unenthusiastic students, felt renewed by Sarah.

I had been impressed with Sarah's analytic thinking and her ability to draw on knowledge acquired in other courses. With other professors, I allowed myself the vanity of taking at least partial credit for her success.

Sarah, whose sad demeanor had surprised me, explained her dilemma. College had opened up the world, yet her situation had not really changed since she had started attending classes—except that she wanted more. Her teachers were encouraging her to transfer to some well-known, competitive college, but her family and financial circumstances were forcing her to attend night school locally or to find a job and give up school for good. Had we encouraged this talented woman to expect more than life would ever offer? Was this another "dream deferred"?

For Sarah there is a happy ending. Through some inquiries and contacts, Sarah gained admission to a prestigious women's college, offering her a special scholarship which provided not only tuition and fees but a stipend and a support network for her children. When Sarah crossed the stage to receive her diploma, we saw a woman who had freed herself from a life of quiet desperation. And we, those who had taught her, had found purpose because her success was our triumph.

What ultimately prompts us to be teachers? Henry Adams, recollecting his education, wrote that a "teacher affects eternity; he can never tell where his influence stops."[2] When teachers step into a classroom, they come to know to what extent students are a part of their education. Perhaps—to quote Archibald MacLeish's definition of a poem—a teacher "should not mean/but be."

[2] Adams, *The Education of Henry Adams,* Modern Library Edition (New York: Random House, 1931), p. 275.

The Torpedo's Touch

DONALD W. THOMAS

In this thoughtful essay Donald Thomas communicates his teaching philosophy through one of his first experiences as a teacher. The setting of his story is the Harvard-Newton summer training program back in 1961 when he was one of four interns assigned to a master teacher and to a single class. The master teacher set the curriculum and the interns were required to teach parts of it. Thomas, now as then, believes in immersing students deeply in education, awakening them to confront the perplexities of life.

Robert Frost once compared education to bringing a load of hay to the barn. The teacher stands on top of the load and the student waits below, ready to receive neat little packets. Instead, the teacher dumps the whole load, shouting, "Look out! Here comes education."

Such a comparison would have been out of fashion when I was learning how to teach. In those days, B. F. Skinner had reached the pinnacle of his influence and had persuaded us to divide instruction into neat little packets, each of which could be duly "reinforced." The timing of such reinforcement was thought to be critical — down to the second, lest for lack of swift praise the implanted learning become extinguished, like so many sparks falling on cold ground. Our method left no room for wonder or perplexity, no place for wisdom or sudden insight, because learning had been acclaimed a science, and science abjured whatever smacked of mysticism or romance.

The first lesson I ever taught fell sadly short of the anticipated ideal. I had been assigned to teach that dark corner of American literature represented by Jonathan Edwards. Faced with the grim preachings of this dour cleric, I decided that his writing would have to be dramatized if it were to stick. The lesson began with a recent newspaper account of a man who had been killed at a crossing by a speeding train. What was now fact, I suggested, might well have been predestined all along; the man and the train aimed to collide at the appointed time, irrespective of their individual traits or wills. Knowing nothing of their futures, the railroad engineer and his victim were powerless to change the inevitable course of events. My seventh graders took that possibility in stride since it had already occurred to them on separate occasions, but they entertained serious doubts about their fate being irremediably prescribed.

The ground being prepared, I now moved to set the scene, drawing the blinds and asking my students to raise their desktops in simulation of high Puritan pews. Reversing my coat and setting a lectern atop the desk, I mounted to deliver in

Harvard Educational Review   Vol. 55   No. 2   May 1985, 220-222

muted Edwardian tones the fire and brimstone of "Sinners in the Hands of an Angry God."

It was a stunning lesson, if I may say so, however flamboyant. When the sermon ended, the students sat gaping and transfixed in their pews. I closed the book, the bell rang, and we were jolted back into our accustomed routines. In my twenty some years of teaching, I do not think I have managed to surpass the impact of that first class. Unfortunately, my supervisors were not so well pleased. There had been no fewer than ten of them sitting at the back of the room, all scribbling madly, anxious to demonstrate their critical training so that they might be authorized to judge rather than to teach. No sooner had the class ended than the arduous critique began.

At first I was cool and confident, secure in the belief that my lesson had hit home. But they were relentless in their queries. What had been my objectives? What had the children learned? How did I propose to measure this learning objectively? Somewhat taken aback, I struggled to explain what had seemed to me self-evident. The students had experienced what it was like to be a Puritan, how ruthless and discomfiting the doctrine of predestination could be, how graphic and powerful Edwards was in describing their predicament. But all of this seemed to no avail, and as the minutes crept by, I began to think that Edwards' congregation had not been so badly off. Sensing my gradual retreat, my inquisitors grew more aggressive. What skills had the students employed and what had been my strategy for reinforcing them? Was I aware that I had used *slang?* They swept aside my halting responses and pressed me hard for answers. "But what did the students learn?" In desperation I cried, "I don't know what they learned, but they'll never forget it." Their victory complete, they let me go.

Recollected in tranquility, the lesson still shines, though its luster has softened considerably over time. Since that day, one of the supervisors still remembers me only as "Jonathan Edwards." I see now that in many ways it was the kind of lesson that only a young teacher might try, valor seeming the better part of discretion, and theatrics the lesser part of precision. Today, it would not occur to me to leap upon a desk, and more's the pity, for in that impulse lay a certain logic that I have since come to appreciate. I shall call it "the torpedo's touch," in honor of its ancient progenitor, Plato.

It was in reading the "Meno"[1] that I first discovered my vindication. There Meno accuses Socrates of casting spells over his adversaries, at once enchanting and bewitching their minds.

> If I may venture to make a jest upon you, you seem to me both in your appearance and in your power over others to be very like the flat torpedo fish, who torpifies those who come near him and touch him, as you have now torpified me, I think.

To which Socrates replies,

> As to my being a torpedo, if the torpedo is torpid as well as the cause of torpidity in others, then indeed I am a torpedo, but not otherwise; for I perplex others, not because I am clear, but because I am utterly perplexed myself.

[1] *The Dialogues of Plato*, trans. B. Jowett, Vol. 1 (New York: Random House, 1937), pp. 359-364.

The fish he refers to is what we now call the electric ray, which has a pair of organs that can deliver enough voltage to stun its victims senseless. These days, of course, the word torpedo suggests far more lethal consequences, like blowing one's students out of the water. Moreover, there are those who take exception to Socrates' notorious method of inquiry, which in the hands of the less facile and perspicacious can induce the kind of perplexity that may be deemed destructive to young minds. Indeed, the public is inclined to view philosophers as those who purport to see perplexity for its own sake where others find only detachment.

In essence, however, Socrates contended that we are better off knowing our ignorance, that the worst kind of ignorance is that which ignores itself. To prove his point, he volunteers to teach one of Meno's young slaves certain geometrical principles. Following his first demonstration, this conversation ensues:

> *Socrates:* If we have made him doubt, and given him the "torpedo's shock," have we done him any harm?
>
> *Meno:* I think not.
>
> *Socrates:* We have certainly, as would seem, assaulted him in some degree to the discovery of truth; and now he will wish to remedy his ignorance, but then he would have been ready to tell all the world again and again that the double space should have a double side.
>
> *Meno:* True.
>
> *Socrates:* But do you suppose that he would ever have enquired into or learned what he fancied that he knew, though he was really ignorant of it, until he had fallen into perplexity under the idea that he did not know, and had desired to know?
>
> *Meno:* I think not, Socrates.
>
> *Socrates:* Then he was better for the torpedo's touch?
>
> *Meno:* I think so.

In teaching we are too often persuaded to be gentle, fearing that we shall damage our children if we immerse them in dissonance or perplexity. We accede to the argument that each successive generation faces increasing complexity in life and so deserves greater sympathy and support to cope with the mounting difficulties that assault from every side — recession, divorce, pollution, addiction, nuclear holocaust. We may argue that the young need not be torpified, but on the contrary require clarity, structure, simplification, reward. In their struggle to patch together the shreds of their identities, they reach out to us for guidance that we dare not withhold.

But perhaps it is we who fear the perplexity and disorder that for them is already intrinsic to life. For my part, I do not believe them to be in any worse straits than my generation. Like us, they long to experience life in all its fullness and measure. They are anxious to engage us in conversation that is real, undiminished, dynamic. Weary of little packets, they want the load.

And so each time I enter class I bring with me some part of the abyss that I plan to reveal. We begin, as Socrates so often does, with pleasantries and talk of surface things. And as they negotiate these waters, splashing amiably about in specifics, I lie in wait for them, ready to deliver the torpedo's touch and pull them under as far as they can go. I want them to leave exhilarated yet perplexed by what they have considered, conscious that we have managed but a glimpse of the depths that surge below. To be educated is to know what depths await us underneath the surface of things, whatever those things may be. To shield our children from life's inevitable perplexities is to leave them at the mercy of their ignorance and to deny them the wonder that is the basis of everything we know.

Thinking about Teachers
and the Curriculum

WILLIAM AYERS

A newborn baby, two parents, and a midwife give William Ayers occasion to reconsider the terms on which students and teachers might meet. What he learns is that unlocking potential and power in students yields personal renewal for teachers.

My friend Aña is a midwife who attended the birth of our first child several years ago. Knowing Aña, watching her work, and talking with her about her professional experiences has stimulated me to think about teachers in a different way — to consider the similarities between midwifery and teaching.

When we first met Aña she explained to us what her role would be in the upcoming labor and delivery of our baby. She talked about some technical aspects of birth, some routine interventions to anticipate, and some of the equipment and backup systems she would have on hand. Finally, she said: "My skills and experiences can help you have the birth you want to have. The things I know can empower you."

Since then I've thought a lot about that statement: "The things I know can empower you." This view of the professional role is dramatically different from the traditionally accepted view. From the traditional standpoint, professionals are the powerful ones, the ones with the special knowledge and training that allow them to control and solve other people's problems. Teachers teach; lawyers litigate; doctors heal. The professionals are the active ones. They bring culture to the masses, remove tumors, and prescribe cures. Their clients receive ministrations and services passively, are educated, acquitted, or cured.

Yet this perspective allowed for little personal interaction. Communication in this view is trivialized and reduced to a tactical question of teaching style or bedside manner rather than being seen as the heart and soul of a relationship that can unlock potential and power. Of course, there are doctors who acknowledge that the action of the body itself is the primary and essential healer, just as there are teachers who base their practice on an understanding that knowledge is acquired through an active process of construction and reconstruction. But it is interesting to consider how much of the language of professionalism is a top-down and inaccessible language of mystification and distance. Rarely is a professional person as

Harvard Educational Review   Vol. 56   No. 1   February 1986, 49–51

clear as Aña was: "My job is to empower you, to help you take active control, to aid you in making the important choices."

Good teachers, like good midwives, empower. Good teachers find ways to activate students, for they know that learning requires active engagement between the subject and "object matter." Learning requires discovery and invention. Good teachers know when to hang back and be silent, when to watch and wonder at what is taking place all around them. They can push and they can pull when necessary—just like midwives—but they know that they are not always called upon to perform. Sometimes the performance is and must be elsewhere; sometimes the teacher can feel privileged just to be present at the drama happening nearby.

Midwives make themselves available to mothers and babies. They do not schedule a birth, and they cannot rely on an abstract timetable. Rather, midwives are "on call," and they assume that in most cases the baby will ring when ready. Teachers also make themselves available to students. They, too, are on call, ready to seize the moment when a child is ready to learn or to grow.

In reference to a birth a midwife may say, "I witnessed a birth," "I attended a birth," or "I helped with a birth," a midwife will not say, "I had another baby." Similarly, good teachers are comfortable enough in their role that they do not confuse the central purpose or the major actors. They understand their own importance in the classroom, and they know that it is their own vital relationship with children that is at the heart of the educational enterprise. And so, without belittling themselves, they are able to communicate to their students in a thousand ways, "you are of central importance here," "your work is honored here," "your discoveries and growth are respected here," and, finally, "you are the very reason we are here."

Does all this prescribe a passive teacher, a teacher who merely observes and approves? Not at all. A teacher who empowers is likewise empowered. He or she becomes an actor and an interactor. Like midwives carrying the black bag of professional tools, teachers bring their constantly developing experiences, their growing sense of themselves and their work, and their ever-widening knowledge of both content and craft to their work. Much of what they bring is learned on the job, for in teaching, as in midwifery, there is only so much you can talk about before immersion in the work itself initiates a never-ending process of training and growing. Teachers accumulate experiences, skills, and techniques. They develop a repertoire that is complex, multilayered, and idiosyncratic.

Teachers, like midwives, must be improvisational and intuitive—no two births are exactly alike, just as no two classes, no two children, and no two learning situations are the same in every detail. Teachers build a reflective practice, a praxis, that matures and develops and deepens. Good teachers seek the proper balance between content and children, between curriculum and students' real-life needs, abilities, concerns, feelings, dreams, and purposes.

I spoke recently with Eliot Wigginton, who is the teacher responsible for the inspirational Foxfire project and books. Wigginton is a teacher fascinated with exploring the world around him and committed to allowing youngsters to find their own voices in that world. Wigginton values the experiences of others, he listens closely and respectfully, but he also brings his knowledge and experiences to bear in the teaching relationship. He extends worlds by introducing different domains

—the study of literature perhaps, or biography, or history—which enrich the tale, the anecdote, the memoir. The overall experience is enlarging for everyone. Yet Wigginton never loses his central regard for the individual voice, the lived life; and, so, for the students there is genuine ownership of the experience.

Teachers, like midwives, are part of an ancient profession, one that is currently undervalued and misrepresented in our society, but one that can trace its roots back through antiquity to the earliest stirrings of civilization—to healers, griots, gurus, and curanderas. In recent years our profession has struggled to base itself more firmly on modern scientific understandings and discoveries. Paradoxically, the more we understand about the science of teaching and learning, the more clearly we see, in the words of Philip Phenix, that it is "embedded in a mystery." The more we hear from the biologist, the geneticist, and the physiologist, the more we see how absolutely incredible birth is. The more we hear from the educational researcher, the learning theorist, and the developmental psychologist, the more we stand in awe of the learner.

When our first child was born and he came slipping and bawling into our world, all of us there that morning were overcome with joy, relief, exhaustion, and hope as we cried and laughed and hugged one another. Aña was crying too. How many births had she seen? Three hundred? Five hundred? And yet she was willing to yield herself to the wonder, the mystery, and the magic of the event. Ours was an intimate relationship—like the relationship with a very special teacher—that would be short-lived and would never again achieve that kind of closeness or greatness. Yet Aña gave the moment its due, she gave herself to its meaning in our lives. This was not just a birth, this was the birth of our first child. And it was the one and only miraculous birth for him, just as there would be only one amazing time when he first rode a bicycle, wrote his name, read a book, invented addition. Aña saw the moment as unique and maintained her awe, reverence, inspiration, and excitement—the very passions, as she once told me, that made her want to become a midwife in the first place.

I think that there is a relationship between Aña's serious dedication to empowerment, her faith in and commitment to others, and her ability to maintain her values and humane perspective on her work. Because she opens herself to surprise and change, she avoids the dulling habits that become the prelude to burnout. Because she assumes a shared world of responsibility and personal meaning, she maintains perspective on accomplishment and fault. I think that meeting people on their own terms is, in part, an act of personal renewal.

Learning in Small Moments

DANIEL MEIER

Teachers are charged with teaching concepts, ideas, methods, information, skills, and ways of thinking. But in a teacher's day-to-day life in the classroom it is often the short and small incident or event that really gets the message across to a student. In this essay, the author looks at the small moments that provide some of the unexpected and surprising beauties in teaching.

Whenever I read a fable to my class of first-grade students, they love to guess the moral. There have been many memorable responses, such as "don't ever take a nap" for "The Tortoise and the Hare" and "don't try for something if it's too high" for "The Fox and the Grapes." But my favorite moral is that "big things sometimes come in small packages" for the mouse who saves the lion in "The Lion and the Mouse." Not only is this a clever response for a seven-year-old, but it applies very well to the small moments in learning.

As a teacher I always face the task of teaching big things like geometry, punctuation, concentration, the relationship between letters and their sounds, sharing, ways of scientific investigation, organization, the culture of a foreign people, and creative writing. In many ways, this teaching requires a very conscious and deliberate effort. When I prepare to teach a lesson, whether it is a twenty-minute lesson on the sound that "oo" makes in *foot* versus *boot* or a two-week unit on the animals of the Amazon River, I always try to make the whole lesson as organized and thorough as possible.

I make sure that the topic is introduced clearly and coherently, that the ideas flow together, and that I am providing enough examples. Whenever possible, I like to know where I am going in a lesson and how I am getting there. Otherwise, I fear that if I am lost, then my students will be also. My lesson plans, whether they are on paper or in my head, all have a beginning, a middle, and an end. They can also include preambles, introductions, asterisks, chapter headings, conclusions, footnotes, and references. Thus, although I teach seven-year-olds, my lessons often read like a graduate school lecture or a college textbook.

But when I look back on a lesson and try to find out what has happened to the big things I have tried to teach, the evidence is limited. There are often only a few clues here and there. There is a spelling mistake, an inaccurate sum, an oral reading error, a beautifully colored graph, an intricate diorama, six children saying, "But I don't get it," a misplaced period, a frown, a smile, a laugh, a groan. Too often I am left with the fragmentary knowledge that at time X, on day Y,

Harvard Educational Review Vol. 56 No. 3 August 1986, 298–300

during lesson Z, I did such and such and then certain children reacted in certain ways. The lesson plan that goes in well organized often comes back out fifteen minutes or an hour later disjointed and beaten out of shape.

When I sense that the ways of learning are too mysterious in my classroom, I often find myself looking back on my own education. Such reminiscing always reminds me that in teaching and learning "big things often come in small packages." It also tells me that I neither learned everything that was presented to me nor fully understood what I had learned. Thus, my remembrances are not of whole books or papers, but rather of bits and pieces of my education. I realize that much of my learning has been in slivers and slices. I call these the small moments in learning. These are times that, like the light of the firefly, are experienced for only a short while. They come and go, and it is impossible to tell when they will appear, disappear, or reappear. Students cannot simply sit back and wait for such moments nor can teachers produce them on cue. They are spontaneous, intuitive, surprising, and unpredictable. They appear here and there, disturbing the normal ebb and flow of classroom life. They may not affect everyone — they are not meant to — nor do they affect every student in the same way.

As a young child I remember listening to *Where the Wild Things Are,* but only taking a fancy to the phrase, "they roared their terrible roars, gnashed their terrible teeth, and showed their terrible claws." In high school I took a course on existentialism and literature, but I remember reading and enjoying only one short story. In college I wrote a thesis on *Great Expectations,* filling it with many quotes and claims and arguments, but only a few parts still stand out. For example, I remember that when Joe finally went to visit Miss Havisham in her house, he addressed Pip as he spoke to Miss Havisham.

Once, in graduate school, I was sitting in my class on adolescent psychology when some children were heard running through the outside hallway. A student in the first row rose to close the door, but the professor motioned for her to sit down. The professor then proceeded to make a point about the children and the student trying to shut the hallway door, instead of continuing with his lecture as I thought he would. He said that the children were only being children and that the noise would go away. It did. He then observed that educators and teachers too often make themselves into policemen, feeling that they must control and manipulate all situations involving children. He argued that this is a mistake, because if more adults would allow children to solve their own affairs, the children would learn to be more independent and would not be cast in a negative light. This whole little incident lasted all of ninety seconds and was highly unexpected, but I will always remember it.

Another time, in another graduate school course on the teaching of reading, the professor stopped reading her lecture, came around to the front of the podium and told us about a television show in which a doctor explained that he used x-rays to confirm or disprove his predictions about a patient's condition. The professor used this story to argue that teachers need to use their own observations about a student's reading ability before passing judgment based on a standardized test. This was another off-the-cuff moment that was set off from the normal and expected flow of the class.

When I was a student teacher, I asked one of my students to read her paper out loud for the class to hear. As she started to read, I moved across the room to close the door. Afterwards, my supervising teacher told me that when I ask a student to read out loud, I should listen attentively. Otherwise, turning my back and moving away may give the student and the class the unconscious message that I do not value what is being read. Ever since this small incident I never move away when I ask a student to read out loud.

These few small moments of learning are sprinkled throughout my education. For both teacher and student, they are incidents and situations that cannot be predicted or planned. They will pop up as a surprise, as a treat, when one least expects it. And often, when these moments arise, they come quietly and subtly. They are not accompanied or preceded by proclamations or warnings, or followed by a double asterisk or an exclamation point.

They are the odd and quirky moments that spin off from a teacher's love of the moment and willingness to improvise, to go on a hunch, to take a risk, to deviate a little, to go with one's teaching intuition. For the student, such moments are like morals to fables. They are short and concise and have a certain pithiness of language. They are quickly absorbed and, being pocket-sized, are easily carried away. They can be hidden in the cracks and crevices of one's education and brought out for reference as one needs them.

Back to Kindergarten Basics

ANNE MARTIN

Anne Martin's impassioned essay assaults teacher-proof curricula and abstract, formal learning theories. Her argument is based on the observation that kindergartners are deeply aware of their own learning needs and will practice the skills and activities necessary to satisfy those needs if allowed to do so. A key element in developing these individualized curricula is an autonomous teacher who has ample time to discover and help with what it is the children are trying to learn on their own.

Kindergarten used to mean brightly colored paintings, music, clay, block building, bursting curiosity, and intensive exploration. Now the kindergarten's exuberance is being muted, its color drained and spirit flattened, leaving us with stacks of paperwork and teacher manuals. No longer even designated "preschool," kindergarten is becoming an adjunct to first grade, with workbooks replacing art materials and formal instruction replacing activities that follow the children's interests. One rationale for this change is that because children grow up more rapidly in the age of TV and computers, they are ready for "skill work" earlier than they used to be. Consequently, much of the day is taken up by whole-class drill in numbers, letters, and phonics, mostly through coloring and filling in commercial workbook pages. In deference to the children's youth, "play time" may still be allowed as a reward for worksheets completed correctly, or in small doses at the beginning and end of the day, but it is clearly separate from the "real work" of the class.

This trend toward a formalized kindergarten curriculum appears to me not only mistaken — a misunderstanding of the way young children learn — but actually counterproductive. Everything I observe in my own kindergarten class contradicts the notion that children need to be corralled at this age into abstract paper and pencil exercises in order to learn. Paperwork is only one path to learning, an inappropriate one for most kindergarten children, narrowing down their options by cutting out a whole range of learning possibilities. For instance, if we want to encourage our gregarious five-year-olds to develop language skills, the last thing we should do is to consign the children to their chairs to work in silent isolation. They should be talking informally and in groups, looking at books and reading together, helping each other write signs and messages, playing out dramatic scenarios, telling stories and listening to others read and tell them.

We must learn to trust children to work at what they need to know. Every day I am impressed by the intensity with which the children practice language, both in soliloquy and with others. Here is Teresa in dress-up clothes — long skirt, flowery hat, and high heels — talking into the toy telephone. I have already given sev-

Harvard Educational Review Vol. 55 No. 3 August 1985, 318–320

eral notices of clean-up time, and she is the only child left in the house corner. I try to signal her to stop talking, but she pretends not to see, pointedly turning her back as she continues her conversation. Finally, rather irritated, I reach my arm around her and hang up the phone, telling her that it is time to end. Teresa is outraged. She flounces out of the house corner to the furthest limits of the room, where she finds an empty spot. There she reaches for an imaginary wall phone, dials into the air, and speaks into her cupped hand. Then she hangs up with an expression of relief and comes back into the group.

I have no idea what Teresa was saying in her call, nor why she was so persistent. I do know, however, that Teresa has grown tremendously in her ability to communicate with other children. At the beginning of the year, she was easily angered, burst into tears when she was questioned or challenged, and sometimes even bit children who disagreed with her. She was upset by these incidents, and I kept reminding her that she had to learn to explain herself to others in *words*. Gradually I could hear Teresa defending her ideas in strong but more reasonable terms, often making herself understood without conflicts. Once she even reenacted a conversation to show me that she was practicing communication. A bright, articulate girl, Teresa would probably do well with worksheets, but she might not have learned to use words effectively with other children without her hours of dramatic play in the house corner. Teresa's increased ability to express her ideas will undoubtedly be an advantage in future academic work. Her choice of activity was directly related to what she needed to learn.

Activity periods, where children make their own choices among a rich selection of materials, are the heart of my kindergarten program, though we also learn through whole-group discussions, storybooks, singing, drama, and outdoor play. It is during activity periods that I can observe individual children and small groups in their use of materials, which gives me clues as to what to provide in the classroom. When I saw Daisuke, a tiny Japanese child who is just beginning to catch on to English, writing numbers day by day and making calendars for himself, I encouraged him to keep on exploring numbers. When I gave him large graph paper and a number chart to use as a model, Daisuke easily wrote out sequenced numbers, first to 100, then to 110, lately to 700. Now he is discovering and pointing out number patterns, something most children would not do until much later in school. Packagers of commercial materials for kindergarten would not include such number explorations, because their expectations for young children are based on an abstract model of what children should learn at each age and the sequence in which concepts should be taught. But Daisuke has a real feel for our number system, which I would never have known if he had not had ample time and opportunity to choose his own activities, and if I had not had the chance to observe him during many informal work periods.

Daisuke's understanding of numbers may be unusual at his age, but his need for long, uninterrupted work time to pursue his interests is not. We have a steady group of block builders who spend more than an hour each day building increasingly complex structures and spinning elaborate fantasies about their creations. Though their buildings frequently bristle with weapons (juxtaposed with dinosaurs and lions) and traps to catch the "bad guys" who steal jewels, this group of active boys (occasionally joined by a girl or two) has achieved a peaceful companionship. They discuss each aspect of the construction and act out the accompanying plot together. The tangible results are often striking, in both technical and artistic terms.

Quality art work, too, requires daily opportunities to experiment with color, line, and form, whether in painting, drawing, collage, printing, or clay. When a variety of open-ended materials are available for a large portion of class time, all the children have a chance to involve themselves in depth, rather than perform a series of short, unrelated tasks. Although each child may pursue particular interests, the excitement about learning is contagious. Just as Daisuke's number charts evoke other children's interest in numbers, so Jerrold's latest marble roll stimulates other experiments with inclined planes; Bertha's pride in reading an easy-reading book brings other children begging to try one; and Keith's eloquent dictated stories lead other children to dictate at the typewriter. In this way, each individual's achievements and explorations, including the teacher's, are brought back into the whole class to enrich us all.

Nothing is too small or too large for the enthusiastic curiosity of five-year-olds. They want to know about ants, worms, cars, boats, water, air, space, foreign countries, letters, machines, trees, colors, families, seeds, rocks. And their deepest concerns, played out in fantasy every day, are the timeless human ones: love, hate, birth, death, friendship, war, peace, cosmic forces, good and evil. The challenges children take on are far deeper and more complex than what is usually presented to them as "basic skills," just as the academic aims of textbooks, workbooks, and expensive learning kits are generally much lower than the aims of the children themselves.

There is a real danger that in the current educational atmosphere, primary classrooms are being reduced in spirit and scope, with rigid curricula and "teacher-proof" materials turning teachers into technicians and children into products. Instead of letting curricula grow organically out of the needs and interests of children as perceived by teachers (and parents), schools are mandating standardized materials that bear little relation to what happens in the classroom. This contradicts everything I have learned from experience: that teaching and learning essentially depend on specific responses of teachers and children to each other, on mutual understanding and acceptance, on valuing children's gifts and creating possibilities for every child to contribute to the classroom community. If children are not trusted to learn without predigested lessons, and teachers are not trusted to search out their own materials and ways of presenting them, classrooms become constricted, teacher morale drops, and the demanding job of teaching will become even harder to fill.

It is extremely difficult for individual teachers to maintain their confidence in themselves and in children's potential in the face of increasing pressures from within and outside the schools. Teachers tend to be isolated in their classrooms, and even the joy of the children's amazing vitality may not be enough to sustain us in the continual battle to preserve the autonomy necessary to maintain a lively, responsive classroom. I think it might not be possible for me to remain in such a stressful job if I did not have the support of a group of colleagues with whom I meet regularly to reflect on children and teaching. Starting with the particulars of our daily experience, we are able to share our insights and open ourselves to new responses. But it is time now for us to raise our voices and participate in the national debate on education. Unless teachers speak up (and are heard) about their own classroom experience, and assert their hard-won understanding of how children learn, the art of teaching may be further eroded, and our children's potential for serious pursuit of knowledge may trickle away while the public rejoices in each decimal-point rise in standardized test scores.

Raising the Teacher's Voice and the Ironic Role of Theory

JOSEPH P. McDONALD

Teachers must often make special efforts to overcome the silences among them — silences enforced by teachers' subordinate roles and the isolation of the classrooms in which they work. Joseph McDonald traces here the progress of a group of teachers from different high schools who meet regularly to discuss and explore together the insights, uncertainties, and paradoxes that arise from their teaching work. He finds that the group has evolved through three phases — the first concerned mainly with collegiality for its own sake; the second notable for an effort to gain some policy power; and the third distinguished by increasing confidence in claiming policy power on the basis of knowledge generated by teaching practice.

This is the story of a group of high school teachers who began to reflect on their practical knowledge as teachers, and who came to understand thereby that practical knowledge can be powerful. It is also the story of the indispensible role that academic theory about teaching played in the raising of these teachers' voices. It is thus an ironic story, since theorists of teaching have long been intimately associated with the suppression of the teacher's voice.[1] One important difference this time is that the teachers managed to stay in charge, and to bring theory into their conversation on their own terms.[2]

The story begins when several high school teachers, who have been meeting by themselves periodically to discuss the work of teaching, invite a theorist to join them one evening and to suggest something they might read. The theorist is

---

[1] For a historical perspective on the role of theoretical expertise in closely defining how the teacher must do his or her work, see Raymond E. Callahan, *Education and the Cult of Efficiency* (Chicago: University of Chicago Press, 1962); also Edward A. Krug, *The Shaping of the American High School, 1920–1941*. Vol. 2. (Madison: University of Wisconsin Press, 1972). Alan Tom in *Teaching as a Moral Craft* (New York: Longman, 1984) examines the long history of confidence among theorists that effective teaching can be empirically verified and thus become the basis for prescriptive school improvement. This confidence is based on an epistemology which, in Tom's words, "assume[s] supremacy of theory over practice" (p. 197); an epistemology which in its severest form splits knowledge about teaching into a creative and an applied phase, assuming the university to be dominant in the first of these and the curriculum supervisor in the second. The effect can be to relegate the teacher to the role of technical operative.

[2] I do not mean to suggest, however, that the teachers' control of the agenda in this group was the only reason why theory enhanced rather than diminished the teachers' voices. Another important reason, I believe, was the presence of several group members, including me, whose work lives are in various proportions split between school and university.

Harvard Educational Review Vol. 56 No. 4 November 1986, 355–378

Theodore Sizer, then at work on *Horace's Compromise*; he suggests that, in preparation for his visit, the group might read Seymour Sarason's *The Culture of the School and the Problem of Change*.[3]

I recall vividly my reaction then as a member of the group to Sarason's book, which has since become important to me: I did not find it interesting or useful. It seemed too theoretical. But I enjoyed our vigorous discussion with Sizer, who took off his jacket and rolled up his sleeves and obviously enjoyed the pizza and beer and our concrete talk about teaching in high school. It did not occur to me at the time, nor, I think, to other members of the group, that his enjoyment was as much professional as personal. Teachers are not used to thinking that they know some things which some theorists, at least, consider valuable.

One result of Sizer's visit was that our group acquired a reading habit. We could not always talk with people like Sizer in the flesh, but we could read their books. That is not to say that we depended on such books thereafter for the whole stuff of our conversation. On the contrary, we produced useful professional conversation in abundance even when we did not have a book to discuss; and when we did have a book to discuss, we often discussed it rather indirectly, even peripherally. We kept reading books, however, because we felt that they offered us some protection against a troublesome tendency we had discovered in our earlier conversations to become insular and self-absorbed. Initially, we had thought it wonderful just to know others who felt the same joys and frustrations in their work that we felt, and to share those joys together and vent those frustrations together. But after a few months of sharing and venting, the wonder wore off, and it seemed that we ought to do something more. In fact, after some meetings, we felt worse about our work than better, as if by complaining about this or that working condition, we had recognized our bitterness and sealed ourselves in it. Reading books, we discovered, seemed to help with this problem.

In the academic year that followed Sizer's visit, our group decided to adopt a rigorous reading schedule. It was the year that saw the publication of a number of widely read and reviewed reports and other works on schools, and we decided to read as many of them as possible.[4] This seemed at the time a simple extension of our reading habit, except that now we had a reading list. In fact, however, the simple extension masked an important transformation in our purpose. We wished not just to learn from these works, but also to critique them. We distrusted the ability of the theorists and polemicists who were writing to get at the truth of schools as we saw them. I think we were intuitively alert to the danger that the then-germinating school policy reform movement might diminish rather than enhance the power of teachers, and hurt children already at risk.[5] The implicit purpose of the reading we assigned ourselves was to enable us to join the policy debate and to help counter these effects.

[3] Sizer, *Horace's Compromise: The Dilemma of the American High School* (Boston: Houghton Mifflin, 1984); Sarason, *The Culture of the School and the Problem of Change* (Boston: Allyn and Bacon, 1971).

[4] See "Symposium on the Year of Reports: Responses from the Educational Community." *Harvard Educational Review, 54* (1984), 1–31.

[5] I use the word intuitively here to suggest that our response at the time was based less on thoughtful analysis, and more on a quick assessment of the political implications of the rhetoric used in such reports as the one issued by the National Commission on Excellence in Education, called *A Nation at Risk: The Imperative for Educational Reform* (Washington, DC: U. S. Department of Education, 1983).

The first work we tackled was Mortimer Adler's *Paedeia Proposal*.[6] In preparation for our discussion of it, one group member, Marshall Cohen, committed some of his thoughts to paper and brought the paper with him to the group. After some of us had read what he had written, we urged him to try to get it published. And some months later it appeared as the back-page essay of *Education Week*.[7]

Marshall's essay seems to me now a symbol of the group's transition from its first phase, distinguished by collegiality for collegiality's sake, to a second phase, distinguished by an effort to gain some policy power. Later, the group entered still a third phase, distinguished by an effort to claim power on the basis of knowledge gained in teaching practice. I think of each of these three phases as steps in the raising of our teachers' voices.

Phase One: Talking to Break the Silence

The EdCo Secondary Study Group began in 1982 as a result of a three-day conference sponsored by the Education Collaborative for Greater Boston (EdCo) and organized by two Newton (Massachusetts) North High School teachers, Paula Evans and Henry Bolter.[8] The topic of the conference was collaboration among teachers in the interest of school improvement. The conference was action-oriented. Its featured speakers were practitioners, not theorists, and it aimed at fostering collaboration — or collegiality — not only among teachers in general, but particularly among the energetic and progressive Boston-area high school teachers in attendance.

I believe that we teachers who were there were attracted to the conference vision of collegiality not only because of our discovery over the course of three days that talking together feels good, but also because we sensed that talking together might offer some protection for our energy and ideals in the face of changing times and our own approaching middle age. Most of us had begun our teaching careers in the late 1960s, eager to do good work and confident that our good work would be appreciated. In the years since, many of us had been innovators in one sense or another, teaching in alternative schools or alternative programs, pioneering courses, teaching for social change. Now, at the start of the 1980s, Massachusetts suddenly had Proposition 2½, a tax limitation plan about to wipe out many of the interstices of the system where experimentation was possible; and the nation

---

In fact, the reform movement may be said indeed to have diminished the power of teachers in that it has generally diminished local control of schools (*Education Week*, 8 May 1985, pp. 1, 24–26). Moreover, a 1985 Louis Harris poll reported that 64 percent of a nationwide sample of teachers said the reforms enacted in their states reflect the views of administrators, while only 43 percent said they reflect the views of teachers; and 63 percent of teachers reported that their views were not sought during the formulation of reforms in their states ("Summary of The Metropolitan Life Survey of the American Teacher," Metropolitan Life Insurance Co., conducted by Louis Harris and Associates, April-June 1985).

As to the effects of the reform movement on "children at risk," see Board of Inquiry Project, *Barriers to Excellence: Our Children at Risk* (Boston: National Coalition of Advocates for Students, 1985).

[6] Adler, *The Paedeia Proposal: An Educational Manifesto* (New York: Macmillan, 1982).

[7] Cohen, "Public Schools Can't Be Reformed from the Top Down: A 'Front-Line' View of the Paedeia Proposal's Shortcomings," *Education Week*, 2 March 1983, p. 24.

[8] The conference was funded by grants from the National Endowment for the Humanities and the Massachusetts Department of Education.

suddenly had Ronald Reagan at the vanguard of a conservative mood and, we feared, an anti-school, anti-teacher attitude.

Faced with what we saw as hard times ahead, we decided to keep our conference going indefinitely, to keep talking with each other in order to support each other. So, with the crucial support of EdCo and its Director of School Services, Judi Sandler, we turned the conference into a group—a monthly dinner club with a nearly invariable menu: pizza, beer, and a rambling but spirited conversation about schools and teaching in them. In the first phase of the group's development (its rough end-marker the publication of Marshall Cohen's essay) our sense of the "teacher's voice" was a relatively simple one: the sound of teachers talking to each other after a long silence.

A sociological perspective helps explain the causes of such silences among teachers. Dan C. Lortie's[9] important work on the sociology of teaching, for example, notes the "cellular" design of schools with their semi-autonomous, semi-detachable teaching "stations." This design has been a structural response to the steady expansion in the student population over many decades and to the commonly high turnover rate among teachers. Cellular design permits a school to grow or diminish by this teacher or that without much organizational consequence. But of course the design itself is of great organizational consequence, including the empowerment of those who coordinate the cells, the subordination of those who inhabit them, and—as Lortie particularly notes—the discouragement of cooperation, inquiry, collegiality, and participation in the fashioning of a school-wide culture.[10] In the cellular school, teachers are severely isolated from each other during the bulk of their working days. As Sarason claims, the problem is not just that they are alone, but that they adapt to being alone.[11] Used to the absence of colleagues, they grow silent. In fact, as several researchers have suggested, teachers may fail even to develop a language in which to talk with each other.[12]

But the silence is more than the pernicious effect of isolation; it is also the protective response to subordination. A concern for autonomy against the threat of curricular tightness and administrative supervision was one of the four most salient themes in the talk of the teachers whom Philip Jackson interviewed in his seminal study, and others have also written about this dimension of teaching life.[13] If, officially, the teacher's views are considered secondary at best to those of others, even on such intimate matters as the allocation of teaching time and the choice of teaching materials and strategies, then at least teachers can close their doors and cultivate their own gardens—and, like Candide, grow silent amid the trumpeting, competing, and relatively irrelevant philosophies around them. Or, like the generation that Voltaire presaged, they can demand some power at last.

---

[9] Lortie, *Schoolteacher: A Sociological Study* (Chicago: University of Chicago Press, 1985), pp. 15–17.

[10] Lortie, *Schoolteacher*, p. 56.

[11] Sarason, *Culture of the School*, p. 106.

[12] See, for example, Philip Jackson, *Life in Classrooms* (New York: Holt, Rinehart and Winston, 1968); Judith Warren Little, "Norms of Collegiality and Experimentation: Workplace Conditions of School Success," *American Educational Research Journal, 19* (1982), 325–340; Harry F. Wolcott, *Teachers Versus Technocrats: An Educational Innovation in Anthropological Perspective* (Eugene, OR: Center for Educational Policy and Management, 1977), p. 63.

[13] Jackson, *Life in Classrooms;* Wolcott, *Teachers Versus Technocrats;* Lortie, *Schoolteacher;* and Sarason, *Culture of the School.*

Phase Two: Taking a Voice in Policy

In its second phase of development, the Secondary Study Group cultivated the teacher's voice not simply to break the long silence and thus gain support through collegiality, but also to gain some say in policy. The group adopted a political aim to sit beside its psychological one — to transform the teacher's role from that of passive recipient of policy *made* to active participant in policy *making*.

One fruit of the group's second phase was the publication of a review of another major work, Ernest Boyer's *High School*.[14] Written by Paula Evans, the review is based on a transcribed conversation among the discussion group. Interestingly, it is a rather scathing review of a book regarded by many as sympathetic to teachers. Boyer seemed, however, to represent for us *all* the policymakers in education, and especially the ones more likely than he to ignore or suppress the teacher's voice:

> *High School's* style and approach to educational reform determine the tone and scope of this book. Boyer has created what one member of our group labeled "a phenomenon," larger than the book — including a film, television and newspaper interviews, and Carnegie School Grants. A media event of such scope is designed to attract attention well beyond the schools. As the foundation of this event, the book itself may have inevitably demanded a generalizing tone. We found it bland, prosaic, ingenuous, and laundered.[15]

Evans told me that she showed an early draft of the review to a friend who is a superintendent of schools. He urged her to soften its criticism in recognition of the fact that Boyer at least acknowledges the need to improve the working conditions of teachers. Why not reserve attacks, her friend suggested, for the reformers whose agendas view teachers as mere tools of those who make and enforce policy?

The group's implicit response to this question, captured in Evans's final draft, was, first of all, political. Voiceless groups loathe those who patronize them at least as much as they loathe those who oppress them; and they deeply resent tokenism.

> Although [Boyer] recognizes the teacher's feeling of powerlessness, he apparently fails to understand its significance, and his suggestions are disappointing. In *High School*, teachers are awarded token power: they are to have a "greater voice in selecting materials appropriate to their own subject areas" (p. 143); they are to control the shaping and the oversight of a career path for teachers; and they are to participate in the design of computer software to be used in schools. But they are accorded minimal participation in the decision-making process. Most of the major decisions concerning priorities, organizational framework, and programs are made by someone outside of the classroom. "Where are we in all of this?" we asked.

Voiceless groups are also particularly wary of those who would seem to support their achievement of voice while subtly undercutting it. "While he cites the need for teachers, parents, and students to become involved in developing their own school plans," Evans's review says at another point, "his 'agenda for action' usurps

---

[14] Boyer, *High School: A Report on Secondary Education in America* (New York: Harper & Row, 1983); Evans's review is entitled "A Dialogue Among Teachers," *Harvard Educational Review*, 54 (1984), 364–371.

[15] Evans, "A Dialogue," p. 366.

their initiative by defining all the priorities and guidelines for change and urging the adoption of his proposals."[16]

The group's reaction to Boyer was covertly epistemological, however, just as it was overtly political. What gives Boyer the right to make recommendations about high schools? What does he really *know* about them? So, for example, the review comments on his knowledge of students:

> His description of students is almost always tied to some notion of their future opportunities or limitations. He divides students into two categories — those who will go on to some form of higher education and those who will go on to work. He seems hardly aware of high school students in the present. They are a complex, demanding lot. We found ourselves asking, "Has he met the beast?"[17]

Although the group was at the time of the review months away from taking it, the step was only a small one from questioning what Boyer knows about high schools to asserting that teachers know quite a lot.

Phase Three: Power through Knowledge

In November 1985 another theorist, David K. Cohen, visited the Secondary Study Group. He came to hear its members' views of a draft of what later became Chapter 5 of *The Shopping Mall High School*.[18] During the conversation he urged the group to find public ways to bring its particular expression of the teacher's voice to the school policy debate.

His implication that what we might publish could fill an important policy void highlighted a writing purpose less evident in group members' earlier works. It suggests that the raising of the teacher's voice is not simply a good solution to a political problem — the subordination of teachers, who are key parties in the schooling process. It is a solution to another kind of problem too: the teacher's voice can contribute to school policy essential knowledge that is available from no other source.

To understand the subtle shift between the group's second or political phase and its third or epistemological one, it helps to add one other cause to the list cited above of the causes of teachers' silence. Apart from the pressures of structural isolation and of hierarchical subordination, certain dynamics inherent in teaching itself tend to limit the teacher's voice. Teaching a class of students is highly complex work. It entails numerous ambiguities, including the fundamental one concerning the relationship between one's teaching efforts and the effects on students' learning.[19] Moreover, teaching is full of what Arthur Bolster calls "unanticipated con-

---

[16] Evans, "A Dialogue," p. 367.

[17] Evans, "A Dialogue," p. 368.

[18] Arthur G. Powell, Eleanor Farrar, and David K. Cohen, *The Shopping Mall High School: Winners and Losers in the Educational Marketplace* (Boston: Houghton Mifflin, 1985).

[19] Jackson in *Life in Classrooms* is among the many who have written about the complexity of teaching in classrooms. He tells us that "the elementary school teacher typically engages in 200 or 300 interpersonal interchanges every hour of her working day" (p. 149). Among those who have examined the fundamental ambiguities of teaching work are Marvin Lazerson, Judith Block McLaughlin, Bruce McPherson, and Stephen K. Bailey in *An Education of Value* (New York: Cambridge University Press, 1985). They write: "Many teachers recognize that teaching is a hit-or-miss affair, that there are no certain scientific methods. Their disappointments are frequent; their doubts that they have done their best are pervasive" (p. 98).

tingencies"; some of these suit one's purpose, some do not, but all must be dealt with.[20] Finally, the dynamics of teaching are inherently volatile because teaching inevitably entails tension, a tension which Paulo Freire regards as "the same tension which exists between theory and practice, between authority and freedom, and perhaps between yesterday and today."[21]

All the complexity, ambiguity, and tension of the work have consequences for the teacher's voice. Jackson suggests that it may account for what he regards as the conceptual simplicity of teachers' talk — its tendency to reveal an uncomplicated view of causality, a high proportion of intuition relative to rationality, an opinionated as contrasted with an open-minded quality, and a narrowness in the use of abstract terms.[22] By the same token, Jackson suggests, the development of a more articulate voice will do nothing to advance the work.

> If teachers sought a more thorough understanding of their world, insisted on greater rationality in their actions, were completely open-minded in their consideration of pedagogical choices, and profound in their view of the human condition, they might well receive greater applause from intellectuals, but it is doubtful that they would perform with greater efficiency in the classroom.[23]

Bolster goes further, suggesting that a teacher might acquire such academic habits only at the cost of impeding his or her urgently required ability, in the face of classroom complexity, to limit choices of action severely, and to discriminate efficiently between cues which must be noticed and cues which can be safely ignored.[24] Thus teachers' silence on matters that they would seem to know a great deal about may at least partially involve their wish to protect their capacity to act. And so they leave inquiry to the theorist, who theorizes without benefit of the teacher's intimate knowledge of practice, and, in time, the resulting theory comes round to the teacher in the form of some policy directive.

But why must it be so? Why should understanding one's work well, and articulating that understanding for the benefit of others who need to know — such as colleagues, parents, politicians, academics — cause one to work less effectively? In fact, as Donald Schön and others maintain, it need not be so.[25] Associating understanding and articulation with less effective action is, according to John Dewey, the result of a habit prevalent in Western thought since Plato — that of associating truth with absolute certainty. The goal of reflection in such light must be to rise above uncertainty, to achieve predictability. Note, for example, the coupling in Jackson's statement above of "thorough understanding of their world" with "greater rationality in their actions." The problem with practice in this regard (and thus with practitioners' knowledge), is that its most distinctive feature is *uncertainty*.

[20] Bolster, "Toward a More Effective Model of Research on Teaching," *Harvard Educational Review*, *53* (1983), p. 299.

[21] Freire, *The Politics of Education: Culture, Power, and Liberation* (South Hadley, MA: Bergin & Garvey, 1985), p. 177. Other contributors to the theory of tension at the heart of teaching include Sarason, in *Schooling in America: Scapegoat and Salvation* (New York: Free Press, 1983); and Willard Waller in his classic *The Sociology of Teaching* (New York: Wiley, 1932).

[22] Jackson, *Life in Classrooms*, p. 144.

[23] Jackson, *Life in Classrooms*, p. 149.

[24] Bolster, "Toward a More Effective Model," p. 300.

[25] Schön, *The Reflective Practitioner: How Professionals Think in Action* (New York: Basic, 1983).

No matter how smart practitioners may be, their "judgment and belief regarding actions to be performed," as Dewey put it, "can never attain more than a precarious probability."[26] Teachers in the United States, like others trained in Western habits of thought, come therefore to regard their own knowledge as inherently provisional — useful perhaps for getting one through a teaching day, but not particularly worth sharing with others, nor even worth articulating to oneself. Discovering uncertainty when certainty is the measure of knowledge can only produce demoralization, and perhaps paralysis of action as well.

But what if teachers, recognizing the uncertainty in their work, raised their voices instead of growing silent? And what if theorists recognized that intimate knowledge of this uncertainty was exactly what was missing from both their theories and the policies these theories provoke?

Helping to achieve this is the principal work of the third phase of the Secondary Study Group's development. This phase, which continues today, concerns the Group's growth into an awareness of voice as *content* rather than just expression, and into an awareness that this content has something to do with what Schön calls the "complexity, uncertainty, instability, uniqueness, and value conflict" which lie at the heart of practice.[27] This growth has been attended by the emergence of a paradox and the group's gradual, tentative acceptance of it. The story of the group's development in its third phase concerns two realizations whose order of occurrence is very important: first, that theorists need teachers; and, second, that teachers need theorists. The paradox is that in cultivating one's own voice, one may learn to value another's.

Finding a Place for Theory

We decided that to explore the content of the teacher's voice in our group, we needed only a means to focus it, a tape recorder to trap it, and a way of presenting it to ourselves and others. During twenty minutes near the end of the meeting that David Cohen attended, we managed the first two of these tasks: we would postpone the reading scheduled for our next meeting (ironically, Schön's *The Reflective Practitioner*), in order to prepare and present to each other reflective "anecdotes" from our teaching practice; and I would bring my tape recorder to document them.[28]

Still, it happened that we spent much of that next meeting on matters of clarification. It was not that we had arrived unprepared to tell anecdotes; but, having prepared, it was as if we then needed to verify that we had prepared in roughly the same way. So, for over an hour, we warmed up our voices.

Marshall said he thought it best to concentrate on unsuccessful teaching moments, while Abby preferred a focus on successful ones. Paul asked the group to consider whether a teaching "moment" was the right unit of analysis, given what

---

[26] Dewey, *The Quest for Certainty* (New York: Minton, Blach, 1929), p. 6.

[27] Schön, *Reflective Practitioner*, p. 14.

[28] I enclose the word anecdotes within quotation marks here in order to emphasize that we chose an angle, not a genre; we had to have a name for what we were about to do, and this seemed as good as any. But we did not mean the word to hem us in — to restrict us to narration without exposition, for example, or to accounts of incidents rather than either more elaborate or less tidy experiences.

the group wished to document, and whether anecdote, with what he suggested was its momentary connotation, was the right means of display. He drew an analogy between teaching and psychotherapy. Many regard the latter, he said, in terms of a series of epiphanies. The problem, he warned, is that therapy is not really like that at all, and neither is teaching. Then, to illustrate the inadequacy of anecdote, he began to tell the evening's first anecdote. The irony in his doing so prefigures the larger irony which is the subject of this essay. Paul was able to use anecdote to illuminate the insufficiency of anecdote just as the group was later to use theory to illuminate the insufficiency of theory. But that is getting ahead of the story.

The setting for Paul's anecdote is a graduation ceremony at which he wished to demonstrate for the benefit of all those assembled — including, undoubtedly, himself — what one particular graduate had accomplished in several years of Paul's remedial math classes. He had no story to tell of a sudden epiphany or break-through — "how the kid was cured after I was able to explain fractions the right way at last" — so he instead took years of this student's math papers and pasted them to a roll of wallpaper. Then, before handing the student his diploma, he let this huge roll of math papers unroll across the stage and down the main aisle of the auditorium.

Paul's anecdote was helpful in clarifying the group's task in that it dramatized its essential difficulty — how to frame a portrayal of teaching that is true at once to its banality and its mystery. Throughout the rest of the session, vision seemed to vie with ordinariness for the role of essential fabric of the anecdotes. When Peggy suggested that the anecdotes might be "missionary stories" designed to re-cruit new teachers, Margaret answered that they must not sacrifice honesty about the drudgery of the work.

During the meeting, Don asked the group to clarify our sense of audience:

> Is the thrust of this that by kind of revealing the heart and soul of teaching — could that be done — that somehow this communication will be received by a waiting public who will be disabused of all the mythology that they have clung to? . . .
> I sort of despair if that is the object.

The public, he added, will never believe what we have to say. "My friends don't believe me," he said. "They simply don't understand what it is I'm doing all the time, why I can't come out to play." Other teachers, he told us, would make a bet-ter audience.

I responded by making the point that teachers need opportunities "outside the rush of teaching" to talk to each other about the work they do. They need to teach each other (as, for example, physicians do) their profession's technical variations and its subtle specialties.

Paula agreed that this is one reasonable function for the anecdotes, but not, she added, the only one. And here she took issue with Don's reluctance to embrace an audience wider than that comprised of other teachers. One very important part of the audience for these anecdotes, she argued, ought to be school district-level policymakers. She was struck, she said, by the oddity of the fact that the city where she lives could presume to decide the important question of how to structure the middle grades — whether in a middle school, junior high, or K–8 configuration — based on criteria that included no perspectives on what it is like to teach or to learn within these same configurations. Teachers can supply such perspectives, she said, and without them, all the other arguments dredged up from the educational literature to guide such decision making, no matter how logically ordered, remain shallow. So her hope for the anecdotes, as she put it, was that they might be a means of "getting into the literature a perspective from teachers."

Paula's argument seems to symbolize the emergence of group consensus on the question of audience: be it resolved that the EdCo Secondary Study Group will experiment with the telling of anecdotes in order to address the larger issue of bringing the teacher's voice to bear on questions of educational policy. The significance of this resolution is that it brings together two senses of the teacher's voice — power and meaning — both the right to a say in policy and the idea that teachers possess unique knowledge.

First Round: Three Anecdotes

I had been keeping a little journal about my teaching since November in which I tried to examine something that I did each day. I was trying to understand what it is that I do. I was just looking over this journal before coming in, and I thought I would tell this anecdote.

"One of the people that I am when I teach."

Joe: It happened the day after Christmas vacation. I was feeling that day-after-Christmas-vacation bewilderment that I get . . . It's shocking, the amount of detail that you typically juggle in a day, and if you haven't been juggling in a while, it's just awful to walk suddenly in and there it's all on you . . . and this particular day, because it had been two weeks since I was last there, some of the details were fresh and some of them were confusing. You know, there were a couple of kids who hadn't taken a test that was taken in the class before, and I was trying to remember to give it to them, and there were some books that hadn't been returned that should have been returned, and there was an assignment to go out, and somebody had asked me a question that I didn't know the answer to, and I had promised to look it up, so I was trying to write myself a note to do that, and in the midst of all this, I just said to a kid, "What?" — you know, have that bewildered look on my face. And a kid said to me, "You should take lecithin. It helps you with your memory."

Now that's the extent of the anecdote, except that I was thinking later . . . that one of the personas that I have in my teaching is to have all these details, to juggle all these things — that's one of the people that I am in my class. And it's because, I think, that by juggling a lot of things, keeping a lot of activity going, I avoid the kids' losing interest. I end up — at least I think this is my strategy — appealing to more kids than I otherwise would.

Abby: Intentional or not, do you think the effect is to make the kids a little more responsible and involved because you don't come across as totally in control of everything?

Joe: I think they like being able to make fun of me, or to laugh when I say something that's . . . You know, it's the way you relate to an eccentric professor or something. You enjoy the eccentricity.

Marshall: Do you do this to all classes the same way? Or just some classes? Are there certain kinds of kids that that persona works better for than for other kids?

In other words, I'm trying to imagine an incredibly intense AP class. Would that be charming to them?

Joe: I'm sure that [it] like everything else, is done in response to the group and how I feel about the group, and how I think they feel about me. If I feel that they're hostile, or that there are pockets of hostility toward me, typically I grow cold and efficient.

Marshall: You're sort of almost intuitively choosing a persona that will over time, you learn, appeal to groups of kids, certain groups of kids in certain situations. And probably, intuitively, you adopt a slightly different persona with different kinds of other classes.

Paula: And depending upon where you are in your teaching career.

"We were having what I thought was a really good discussion."

Paula: I want to tell mine . . . This was when Henry Bolter and I were doing a local history project with kids from Madison Park and kids from Newton . . . We had planned this course very, very, very carefully — weeks of summer workshops. . . . We argued, we fought, we discussed what was appropriate and what wasn't appropriate for these two very different groups of kids, and we started the year out with a long, extensive unit on family and neighborhood history, in which the kids did a lot of sharing with each other about their family history, where they went to three different neighborhoods in Newton and three different neighborhoods in Boston and were led on tours by kids in the class through those different neighborhoods, and so on and so forth.

This was a good two months into the course, and we were having what I thought was a really good discussion one day at Madison Park with just the Madison Park kids. I felt that it was very important to structure the class carefully. These kids were truant a fair amount; and I had folders on each kid — I was using everything I knew — I was checking the homework every single day and they were getting it back the next day; if a kid didn't show up, I'd track the kid all over the building. I had time to do this. We were really on them. And I felt like it was a fairly cohesive group.

We were seated around a table discussing whatever the issue was, and there was an argument going on between two kids. There was some participation from the other kids, and Linda, the other teacher, and I were sort of leading it and facilitating it, and there was five minutes left in the class, and you know, I needed to talk about homework and one thing and another, and I said, "Clearly we haven't finished this discussion, but we need to go on."

This one kid looked at me and he said, very angrily, "I hate this class." He said, "I hate it. You never give us any answers in this class. Everything we ever discuss is always left unfinished. And I hate it."

I said, "David, David, how can you say that?" This particular kid was very talented, and when we went on tours of neighborhoods, he could point out all the different architectural details. He knew the whole history of Roxbury. He was terrific. He couldn't write worth a damn. I was meeting with this kid twice a week to help him with his writing in addition to whatever. I said, "We will finish it. There are lots of things that there aren't answers to."

All of a sudden I looked up and David had walked around to the other side of the table, and he and Chris were arm wrestling. And finally one of them won, and he looked up at me, and he said, "There, I feel much better."

The end of it is that the kid dropped the course at the halfway mark when kids had an option to stay in or go. He said, "I don't like the kind of class that you have. I don't have other classes like this." I have had kids drop classes or tell me they didn't like classes for lots of different reasons, but never for that one . . . You know, I had done all the familiar things that I was used to doing, and that had always worked.

Don: It seems to me that this is somewhat similar to what Joe said. You prefaced this by saying that you were really being goody two shoes about this teaching stuff. I mean, you were really on top of everything. You were so good, that he could not abide you. So in control. I think that's often the problem that Joe's solution — I mean, I don't know whether you gave up and sort of messed up the details at all, and let the homework go for two days instead of one.

Paula: But I don't know. I mean, I felt that I was being quite myself with these kids.

"It was like I was an object."

Paula: Let me just add one little sort of coda to this. . . . They were nagging me at Madison Park all the time about how you're from Newton and you don't know these kids, and so finally I said, "Yeah, give me a class, give me a regular U.S. History class."

So they did, and my God! I prepared for that class for three weeks. I did an enormous amount of research and stuff, because they were using a textbook that had been written for idiots, for people with IQs of 30 or below . . . These kids were juniors; some of them were 19 years old. I walked in and I had Xeroxed up these original documents, and I had this class straight for two weeks. It went fairly well. These kids were really into talking and stuff — they couldn't write at all, but they loved talking and they loved discussing.

But the third day into it, I'm just up there sweating, you know, I'm leading this discussion and I'm trying to pull kids in, making sure the radio's turned off in that corner and one thing and another, and this kid yells out — you know, I think things are going well — and this kid yells out, "Hey, are you a teacher?"

I thought, "What is this? It was like I was an object."

Marshall: Neither cat nor dog.

Paula: But I was trying to get these kids to sort of join me, and I realized I didn't know anything about it.

Peggy: What did you say to the kid?

Paula: I said, "Yeah, I am." He said, "You teach here?" I said, "Yeah, I do." I didn't dare mention Newton at that point . . . He said, "You don't look like one."

Don: It was that Newton tweed.

Paula: Let me think about that. Yeah, in some ways, I probably did look different . . . A lot of teachers dressed up much more than I. I didn't wear pants or anything like that. You know, a skirt, a sweater . . . I remember sort of looking at myself . . . I felt like a beginner all over again.

Second Round: Growing More Theoretical

I present these anecdotes embedded in some of the questions and comments they sparked, because I want to illustrate that we found them *theoretically* interesting. That is, while we enjoyed their rich specificity, we also tried to frame them with generalizations. As our experiment continued, moreover, this urge to theorize grew stronger. Consider, for example, the contrast in theoretical richness between the anecdotes above, even embedded in the comments they aroused, and the following one.

Judy: What we did last time is people shared experiences — not just experience — visions, feelings, whatever. People have very different approaches to it. But something that colored their view of what was the fabric of good teaching for them. And we captured it on tape . . .

Dan: Well, let me give you one. This was a really powerful year for me as far as teaching because I had had a job where I was director of Social Studies. I didn't teach; and this year I'm teaching again. I was out of teaching for three years and now I've gone back to it. It's an unbelievable experience. It's been the most difficult challenge I've ever faced. I'm just now — this week — getting to where I think I know what I'm doing.

Marshall: What were some of the problems?

Dan: My pacing was all screwed up, I was scared of the damn kids, I was scared . . . I had taught for 14 years, but lately if a kid would snicker or smile, I'd fall apart. I was hyper about all the subtlest things that were going on in the class. I was convinced that I forgot every fact I ever knew about American history . . . I couldn't answer questions. Kids would ask very simple questions like, "Who was Andrew Jackson's vice president?" and I wouldn't know. And I'd be embarrassed about it, and I'd say I'll tell you tomorrow. . . .

I was spending nights, up till one in the morning, night after night, preparing, preparing like I've never prepared . . . It was the craziest experience. I can't understand it, I can't explain it, but what it made me appreciate was how complex the teaching act is, and how much I had assumed. I used to be able to jump out of bed, hit the classroom, boom, you know. I was pretty good in the last year I taught. You know, I was confident, I was really hot, the whole thing. I figured I'll get right back into that in a week. I don't know if I'll ever get back to that.

I didn't realize at the time the whole tableau of skills and subtle instincts that it takes to be good in the classroom. But what I've learned from it is every administrator should go back to the classroom. Because it has made my own evaluation process so much more sensitive, because I'm watching teachers do things that I can't do that I used to be able to do, and I watch them and say, whew!

Marshall: Can you help them improve their teaching, though, as a result? I mean, to what end are your evaluations of them better?

Dan: If they're having a problem, I can identify the problem much better because I'm having the same damn problem. . . . So I can't dismiss it as lack of skill. There are lots of problems in a class; teaching is a complicated act. The whole balance of . . . stupid things like how many objective questions do I give? Is this test really valid? Am I doing too much lecturing?

I used to be a great believer in group work. I've only recently started doing group work, and I'm telling my teachers they should be doing more group work, because I was afraid to do groups. I was afraid I was going to lose control of the class. I was feeling like a jerk. I was evaluating people and saying, "You ought to do more group work and interaction," and I think to myself I hope the hell they don't ask me if I do it myself . . . I would've been honest and said, "I'm not up to speed yet, just not up to speed."

Judi: Were you as self-critical before though?

Dan: No, probably not. I must admit I've become a little more conservative now that I'm back in the classroom. I used to do stuff that was . . . I did some fun things when I was teaching that when I look back I see didn't really have any educational agenda. I was sort of cheating a little bit. I cheat a lot less now.

I don't know if you sense what I'm saying. I did a lot of self-delusion when I used to teach. I've come to recognize that. I'm really concerned now that everything I do, every minute, is productive, goes some place, has a reason. And I didn't really have that self-discipline or that self-view before. So I've benefited from being an evaluator that way. Maybe that's why I'm more critical about myself.

Nevertheless, I'm still having a lot of difficulty getting my skill back. I just started to do it this week, just began. I took kids on a field trip today, and that was a real release . . . It was the first time I could relax on the bus and I could talk to the kids, and I think I'll be a lot better tomorrow.

Marshall: That sort of suggests that a lot of the skill that's involved in teaching is not directly cerebral, but more intuitive, and I have noticed that early in the school year, I spend a lot more time preparing than I do later in the school year, and I think it may be partly a function of the fact that over the summer my skills are dulled to the point where I have to over-compensate with preparation, whereas later in the year, it becomes so natural that a lot less preparation suffices, which is actually very lucky because later on there are other things that take up a lot of time . . . evaluating work and stuff like that.

Dan: There's something about momentum. I don't know what it is. I remember the feeling of when it's happening. You know, when the questions are coming [clicks fingers] and the whole thing about getting the kids up to a higher cognitive level, where there's real analysis and interpretation. I'll tell you, I think I hit that once this year, and I can't believe it. I used to hit it at least twice a week before. But I'm just . . . I think I'm going to start getting to where I can do it now. I'm going to be able to use today's field trip to coalesce a lot of that stuff. . . .

You know what it is, it reminds me of skiing. Remember when you started to ski and you felt super clumsy, and you'd watch somebody coming down . . . and that's like effortless teaching.

You know, I was really into being the evaluator. You know, I had all my criteria . . . all the little graphs and the little things that you do, and the timing things, and I was becoming very proficient at it . . . And this kind of thing shook me. Like there's a whole other dimension of teaching that you can't measure with these instruments because it's not measurable — it's artistry.

Marshall: I'm glad Don isn't here because I can tell . . . I went to see one of his classes last year, and he really is incredible. I mean it's a similar kind of thing — he's very low key, and he's sitting there, just sits at his desk, and talks in somewhat of a monotone . . . and it's almost boring, but it's really not. And there's a lot going on beneath, and by the end of the class all these sorts of things come together and the kids are sitting there like they're watching a cobra or something.

He was talking about *Crime and Punishment* that day, and he took a couple of chapters, and he said, "Now what do we notice?" He asked them to list everything they noticed, and then he called their attention to certain other things, and then he wove it together, and by the end of the class it was very clear not only what was going on in the class, but what Dostoevsky was trying to do in the scope of the whole novel by this chapter. I mean, it was really wonderful, and it was the kind of thing that I think some idiot could come in there . . . and say, well, God, he wasn't walking around the classroom, he didn't use the chalkboard once, no visuals. . . .

Jay: In the American history course that I was teaching, there was a different kind of talk sometimes, and I tried to figure out what it was, and I called them after awhile conversations enjoying American history, enjoying some feature like the way that Andrew Jackson was like Ronald Reagan . . . enjoying the drama of it, just taking pleasure in American history the way that you would talk around the dinner table or something like that.

Then there were times when I really wanted the kids to put — more like the Dostoevsky example — to sort of put some things together in order to reach a third level. And so those were much more like what I called discussions. You wanted a mix of them. You didn't necessarily want the conversations to have a particular point because the point was you could really be interested in, you know, Andrew Jackson or Reagan.

Joe: The metaphor you were using — the skiing metaphor — I think of driving a stick shift often. And I think that teaching well often has, you have to have sort of the right rhythm of clutch and gas. But the clutch is as important as the gas, and when you were talking about your concern about how you used to do fun things and now you don't anymore . . . you're more productive . . . it worried me that you were giving too much gas and not letting enough clutch in.

Jay: In your new discipline on yourself and your higher standards, you're not making room for what I call conversations.

Dan: Well, today's field trip. For the first time, kids saw me in my element. I was in the city. I was showing them, Hey, this is my world, guys. And I was really relaxed and I was kidding them, and I have a feeling it's going to be much better tomorrow.

About a month after this meeting, Dan confirmed that the field trip he mentions here had indeed proven to be the turning point he sensed it might be. He set his account of this within a highly theoretical context; clearly what he had had to say at the meeting was part of a larger range of thoughts about his work that he was exploring.

The field trip, he told me, had enabled him to shift "modes."

"Modes?" I asked.

"Modes or poles," he explained. Teaching, he believes, has four of them: curriculum-centered, teacher-centered, student-centered, and institution-centered. No teacher occupies any one of these modes exclusively, as he sees it, but rather everyone favors one mode while employing others on occasion. Dan, for example, favors the curriculum-centered mode, at least at this point in his career. That is, he relates to his work principally as one who engages with students in an exploration of a particular constellation of subject matter. He used to favor the student-centered mode; that is, he related to his work as one who engages with students' lives by means of subject matter. Now, however, this mode tends to be secondary with him. Third for him is the teacher-centered mode: relating to work as one who engages in teaching in order to expand his own interests and extend his own growth. And the institution-centered mode is now last for him: relating to work as one whose principal task is bigger than personal growth — the transmission of culture, the inculcation of political and moral values.

The field trip was an occasion for Dan to shift out of his favorite curriculum-centered mode into a student-centered mode, and the shifting limbered him up. It enabled his students to see him as a student, too. "I was visibly learning." And they saw him seeing them as people:

> Little things, like I made sure they had bathroom facilities, and we spent a lot of time just talking and laughing. It was a climate thing. They enjoyed themselves. We enjoyed each other. When I was last teaching, learning climate was as important to me as curriculum. I remember kids organized a Great Gatsby party. The girls who did it got a lot of status out of that. Now I haven't been in that mode lately. . . . I've been teaching this year a very curriculum-centered mode. But on this trip, there were things like, five kids had to use my umbrella. It was fun. That was an event. There was something about it. And everybody was talking about it the next day.

Third Round: Two Theorists Join the Conversation

There was a poor turnout for our third session of anecdote swapping, held late in May. That was perhaps why, after pizza, the six of us drifted into stories that were not quite the deliberately framed *teaching* stories of earlier sessions. Nor did we acknowledge the readings assigned for the meeting until much later, and then almost by chance. Tricked by the informality of the process, I failed to turn on the tape recorder until halfway through a story by Judi.

It concerns her experience as a young teacher losing control of a group of children on an overnight field trip to northern New England. Among her problems was one boy who ran away, and another who broke all the windows on one side of the lodge where they were staying.

> *Judi*: Oh, it was awful. Everything went wrong. . . . We just didn't know what to do. Even if you knew what to do, you didn't know what to do, because there were things that were totally out of control. We got the kid back; we found the kid I don't know how many hours later. That was the worst worry. And the people who owned the lodge were really good about the windows. . . . They were so nice about it; they empathized with us.

This reminds me of my experiences as a young teacher chaperoning groups of high school students on vacation trips to France and Spain. I start to tell a "horror story" about imagined drug deals in Madrid and real prostitutes in Paris, but I do not take it very far before I uncover an insight that has theoretical implications: it was just at the beginning of my teaching, and I hadn't yet mastered the business of how to control kids. . . .

> *Joe*: I have been reading an old book called *The Sociology of Teaching* by Willard Waller,[29] and he talks often in the book about the dynamic of controlling kids as being at the heart of teaching, and he draws all kinds of implications from it about teaching practice, even about anti-teacher feelings that persist in society long after people are out of school—they have a memory of having been controlled—in a sense, forced to submit to the authority of the teacher.

[29] Waller, *Sociology of Teaching*.

It's an essential part of teaching to be able to get people to submit to you for a larger good, but there's always resentment and tension involved in the process. . . . And I didn't know how to do that very well yet, and here I was in a foreign country where the controls — the external controls — were just simply not there, and so it had to be all *me* doing it, and I couldn't do it. I think I could now.

Judi: But thinking back on it, were you that scared then?

Joe: I wasn't scared.

Judi here introduces a second theoretical perspective that, like Waller's, lingers throughout much of the rest of the evening's conversation. Its immediate application concerns the effect of the teacher's age on his or her willingness to take risks: "I'm a completely different person than I was in my early twenties," Judi says, "I'd do anything then, but not now." This perspective broadens, as our conversation develops, and we discuss a view of human development as stage-like. Its corollary is a view of teacher and student as people naturally out of phase with each other's lives, whose very difference in this respect provides the moral basis for their relationship.

Bill is the first to bring together the perspective on life changes with Waller's perspective on teachers controlling students. Bill describes the audience reaction to a play he has recently seen, *Sister Mary Ignatius Explains It All for You*.[30] Portraying the often grim controls of the Catholic schools of the 1950s, this is a play whose appeal seems to lie largely in its capacity for reminding members of the audience that they are now safely grown up. Bill's mention of it brings another play to Gene's mind — also a play about school, and about control and loss of control.

Gene: Do you remember *Miss Margarida's Way?*[31] At the intermission . . . all these people went down onto the stage and wrote obscenities on the blackboard, and dumped over the wastebasket. . . . It was interesting to see who decided to do it — actually get up and go down on the stage and trash the teacher's desk. She treated the audience like an eighth grade class, and I was teaching high school then. And you felt yourself slipping away, and you wanted to become an eighth grader again, and you knew exactly how to do it, and there was something in what she was doing that made you get into the role opposite her, and we all *knew* — every person in the audience knew the role.

At this point, Judi picks up another thread of our conversation, on ways that people at different life stages can foster one another's growth. She refers with amazement to Margaret's earlier revelation that she and her family have lived communally with nine other families for more than twelve years.

Joe: How has this whole experience affected your teaching career?

Margaret: Watching whole groups of kids grow up . . . watching, for example, kids have issues which are life-time issues, that no individual teacher can intervene and completely change — in the same way that when you have your own kids you realize that kids come out with certain personalities — I mean, it's not as though you've *shaped* them entirely.

[30] Christopher Durang, *Sister Mary Ignatius Explains It All for You*, a play in one act first performed at Playwrights Horizon, New York City, circa Nov. 1981.
[31] Roberto Athayde, *Miss Margarida's Way*, a play first performed at the Public Theater, New York City, circa Oct. 1977.

When I was young I had that sort of sense that parents had either done something right or wrong. . . . I know the issues of these nine families. I know the issues between the siblings . . . and I've watched some of them resolve themselves, but mostly they keep playing out in different ways, and people make adjustments and help them do what they can, but basically these kids are independent critters. But then at the same time to realize that the one I would like this year would be the one I couldn't stand the next year, and that it alternated all the time, and that was really soothing to me as a parent — to really believe in stages in a way I had never really believed it in my gut before. . . .

Joe: And in your teaching too?

Margaret: Yeah, maybe sort of being able to look at kids and see them across a spectrum. When you're really down about teaching, you look at them in all their adolescent melodrama, stubbornness, or all that, and you just feel mired in March sensation. . . . And then when you feel better about kids, you look at them and say . . . in five years, they'll be fine. And next month they'll be better . . . none of us was at our best at fifteen either.

Abby: So does it make you feel in a way that you can have less control?

Margaret: Yes, and more tolerance, I think. And the realization that so much of kids' issues is just who they are, and that it's not that I'm so much doing something wrong or right.

Then Margaret talks about the quality of relationships among the members of the group with whom she lives, and also among members of the group and outsiders. And I ask her once again to relate this to her teaching:

Margaret: I think it made me more trusting of people's ability to work things out in classrooms, more believing that if you assume that everyone will act responsibly, they will. My classes feel to me quite relaxed; if I'm absent, I don't get subs, for example . . . and kids tell me that they feel more trusted. . . . In the high school generally, there's this feeling that you have to keep watching them all the time — that control issue — and my sense is that that's not really true — that they will rise to how you treat them.

I am intrigued by the juxtaposition of the two lessons for teaching that Margaret draws from her communal experience, and the paradox it suggests: (1) teachers cannot control the dynamic of children's growth; (2) teachers can channel growth toward worthy ends by providing their students ample vision of these ends. I struggle to explain the paradox by observing that a teacher's sense of her own limits to affect students' growth need not limit her will to intervene in that growth. "It's just a different kind of intervention," I say, "but I think people outside of teaching typically think that teachers are either on top of kids shaping them, and responsible for whether they're learning or not learning . . . or they're lazy and they're not doing anything." As I speak, I again have in mind a theoretical fragment — Alan Tom's image of the teacher as moral craftsman, who at once must cope with all the ambiguity and obliquity of craft work, yet keep a straight moral vision.[32]

But it happens that my comments suggest to the rest of the group yet another theoretical source — in fact, the evening's official one. Abby and Bill tell me that

[32] Tom, *Teaching As a Moral Craft*.

I sound just like one of our assigned readings, an article entitled "Embracing Contraries in the Teaching Process."[33]

Although at the time I thought I understood the discussion of it which followed my inadvertent introduction, it was only months later that I fully realized the power of its theoretical contribution to the whole evening's conversation. I think now that its perspective fixed our theoretical starting point on this particular evening. It then intersected with both Judi's perspective on life-stages and Waller's perspective on control conflicts at the heart of teaching, and provided the framework on which the conversation was built.

In this article, Peter Elbow maintains that the essential conflict which teachers experience is between, on one side, a commitment to students to nurture and support them in the face of the anxieties that learning entails; and on the other, a commitment to colleagues and society to cherish the great subtleties of knowledge, and to uphold the most exacting definition of what it means to attain knowledge. This is inner conflict — the reflective response to the outer conflict that Waller identifies. It is a conflict between the wish to love in response to an expectation of love on the part of students, and a responsibility to fulfill a most important social function. This theory is turned into flesh with an anecdote.

> *Margaret*: Here's the teaching problem: I gave last fall an assignment for kids to keep a thought journal, and they were to keep it for a whole semester three times a week — a record of what they thought about. They weren't to keep diaries of events, and they weren't to keep a whole lot of emotional stuff — it could be how zippers work or the nature of democracy. And kids wrote wonderful, wonderful things. . . . I'd read and write little comments, and I always felt real privileged, and told them that I felt privileged to read the journals. They were interesting and lively and very enlightening.
>
> Then at the end of the year, kids wrote evaluations of my course — what things I should keep and change — and 95 percent of the kids were enormously enthusiastic about the thought journals. Kids wrote, "You are like a garbage pail — anything we thought about we just threw at you. You were like a therapist — no matter what we were thinking, we'd tell you and you'd listen.
>
> But one girl freaked out on me . . . and had four complaints. . . . The first one was that she was really angry that I knew more about her than she knew about me, and her solution was — and this took two days to work out in class. . . . she thought that I should have passed out my journal to all 46 of my kids. . . .
>
> And there was no way I could say, "Jane, sorry, I'm the adult and you're the kid. That's how this works. There's no getting around that. We're not peers here." And part of my problem in fighting back was that with adolescents, you can't fight back fair. . . . You have to be so fair to them that you're not fair to yourself. . . .
>
> Secondly, she said, "And I don't like that you didn't keep confidences." I said, "What?" The only one I knew was that I reported one child abuse case. And that's the law — we have to do that.
>
> I said, "Jane, I *did*."
>
> She said, "No, no, you didn't. We all know."

[33] Elbow, "Embracing Contraries in the Teaching Process," *College English*, 45 (1983), 327–339; the second assigned reading was also by Elbow, "Critical Thinking Is Not Enough," delivered as the Reninger Lecture, University of Northern Iowa, April 1983.

It turned out after considerable discussion that what she was furious about was that I had said, "Danielle [another student] has the most magnificent imagination that I have run across in years." Danielle was dumpy, poor, fat, and ugly, with an imagination that, you know, rivals Toni Morrison's. . . . She—Jane—is sleek, popular, rich, well dressed, and beautiful, and an only child. I think she has never been not the center of attention.

The real issue was that she was jealous. Who do you love more? And I couldn't say to her, "Damn it, I don't care if Danielle is ugly and fat and poor, she still has more imagination than you do. And that's not doing what you accuse me of. What you *want* to accuse me of is you don't love me as much, but what you accuse me of is breaking confidences."

Joe: Why couldn't you say that to her after class?

Margaret: Because the anger was so great at me, and on sort of multi-levels. That I knew so much about her, and then having known about her, I didn't choose her somehow to be the one that I adored most. And I couldn't make it worse by saying, "I know even more than you think I know. . . . " The only way to deal was to sort of back up and apologize and pretend I had half done this, and to take on guilt I didn't even own.

Abby: Your other option would have been to just say, "Well, we can't talk about it here. It sounds like there are a lot of personal issues, and. . . . "

Margaret: By now, though, she had brought in the whole group. She had started this conversation holding hands with her friends, as if I was such an enemy. And it was clear that they had talked about it in advance. . . . she started by saying the whole class thinks this, and I stopped that, "Wait a minute, wait a minute, how many people agree that . . . ?" And she and her little friend raised their hands and nobody else did.

Joe: Classic teacher trick.

Margaret: Yeah, reality check. Please look around you. You made an assumption that everyone agreed.

Judi: I'm curious to know what she wrote in her thought journal.

Margaret: Oh, that was part of the problem. She had written all year long very, very emotional stuff. I had suggested repeatedly, "Jane, you don't want me to read all this stuff. Get two journals. I'll buy you a second one." I gave her a second one. "Put the emotional stuff in here, and give me ideas. Can you get these two separate? In your papers you don't know the difference between a feeling and a thought. You're emotionally all over the map."

That was a phrase I used with her that months later I heard she was really upset by. Well, she comes in crying half the time and hugging everybody the other half of the time. I mean, she *is* all over the map. So she's angry at the very thing that I've worked all year to get her to stop doing.

This escalates a couple of weeks later . . . to bringing her mother in to talk to me about this.

Gene: What were her other objections?

Margaret: Um . . . [pause] Oh, that this assignment was given for my pleasure and not theirs! I said, "Jane, I've read 5,000 pages of adolescents' thinking, 5,000, count them. And you think that on an evening I'd do that instead of reading a novel?" She said, "Yeah, you basically wanted to snoop into our lives, and you kept telling us how much you liked reading the journals." I did all that to . . .

Bill: Get them to write.

Margaret: Yeah, to encourage them and hold their egos, then it got turned against me.

Joe: There was probably some part of you, though, that was saying — a little tiny voice saying, "She's right on that." I mean even though you know that isn't why you did it.

Judi: Or maybe what she did is she fulfilled the risk that you took when you originally set up the assignment, whatever anxiety or fear you had.

Margaret: The mother comes in and says the same thing to me . . . another adult telling me that 5,000 pages of student thinking could be that fascinating? Only teenagers could think that fascinating.

At this point, Judi temporarily diverts the conversation away from the specifics of Margaret's encounter with Jane and her mother, and toward an examination of a public policy issue which provides an apt backdrop for the anecdote. The issue concerns the efforts of a number of politically conservative activist groups to attach a broad interpretation to a feature of the so-called Hatch Amendment, the 1978 Protection of Pupil Rights Amendment to the General Education Provisions Act. According to its congressional author, Senator Orrin G. Hatch, the feature in question stipulates that federally funded educational programs must seek parents' permission before engaging children in psychological testing or counseling, and that parents may review the materials to be used in such activities before deciding whether to give their consent. The activists' interpretation, by contrast, holds that the feature properly applies to any classroom activity touching upon personal and family values and history, and conducted within a school that receives any part of its financing from federal sources.[34] Judi is upset about what appears to be an effort by the U. S. Education Department to accommodate this broader interpretation, and her passion on the subject unsettles the group. It seems to heighten the intensity of our comradely support for Margaret by setting her predicament within a broader social context — one colored, as Waller put it, by the memory possessed by ex-students of all ages of the hostility felt toward their own teachers.

Judi now turns the focus back to Margaret's problem, but the effect of the digression is noticeable:

Judi: What did you say to this mother? What did the mother say to you?

Margaret: It was one of those things where we talked first, and whatever it was we said somehow defused or made her unable to say. . . .

Judi: We meaning you and the mother talked?

Margaret: No, I and an administrator talking to the mother.

Joe: Did you do that because you suspected there'd be . . . I mean, why didn't you talk alone with her?

Margaret: Because I figured the daughter was really off the wall and I didn't want a conversation without witnesses.

---

[34] The story of the broad interpretation, of Hatch's rejoinder, and of Secretary of Education William Bennett's initial embrace of the interpretation and his later disavowal, is told in Ann Bridgman, "Groups Press Parent-Control Campaign, Get High-Level Support," *Education Week*, 20 Feb. 1985, pp. 1, 36; and also in James Hertling, "Hatch Regulations Misinterpreted, Bennett Asserts," *Education Week*, 6 March 1985, pp. 1, 29.

Joe: Smart move!

Margaret: Also . . . I was in real bad shape at the time. I really went under on this. I felt so attacked on something that I felt like I had given and given and given.

Bill: Yet 98 percent of the kids thought that this was great. Only 2 percent shot you down.

Margaret: Yeah, that feeling that the one kid who complains in class can undermine you totally. How many times has this happened in my life—when kids have been enormously supportive and appreciative, and even verbal about it—been grateful—I mean, not the nature of the beast. And then one kid complains.

I just felt . . . I had visions of never going back to this class. I was trying to figure out how I could claim I had car trouble every morning—there were only so many days before [summer vacation]. I had all these fantasies about never going back to them. I was just completely wiped out by it. I'd worked so hard. . . .

Joe: And had success.

Margaret: It was like Paula's story about working, working, working with that class. . . . What feels so undermining is when you go out on a limb for kids, and even if you know you're in the right. . . .

Judi: But you had all the kids but two.

Margaret: That wasn't enough somehow . . . my reaction was way overreaction. I really didn't want to go back; I'm not exaggerating. I cried and cried about it.

Gene: She sounds like a powerful kid.

Joe: But so much of teaching is that vulnerability.

Our conversation closes, appropriately enough, with some analysis of how Jane's behavior toward Margaret was "closure" behavior—conflict erupting as a defense against the pain of separation. Margaret says that she thinks every class fights with its teacher in the last few weeks of school as a response to the teacher's subtle efforts to terminate their relationship.

Margaret: In fact you have to say goodbye to a class. You have to make room for the next one. You can't just accumulate—you have to say, "I've loved you and I've known you and goodbye."

This remark provokes Judi to remember again an old conflict from her teaching days.

Judi: I remember my getting married, what it did to the kids, the way they dealt with it—people hiding my keys, or one kid tried to burn a building. The day I got married, one of my kids set fire to the blind children's home next to the New England Home for Little Wanderers.

And thus the tape ends where it began—with a story of conflict between Judi and her kids. But this is not a simple "horror story"; it packs knowledge of a subtle paradox—knowledge that is the product not only of experience, but of the evening's effort to collectivize and analyze experience in the light of theory; indeed, I believe, of the group's effort over the course of years to grow in its capacity to do so. The paradox itself is the one Waller identifies: conflict is a fundamental factor in teaching work, yet the work remains constructive. Since both Waller and Elbow were *theoretically* present for this evening's discussion, I have invited them to get nearly the last word in by commenting on this paradox. Waller explains it, while Elbow tells us how we might best cope with the inner conflict that it generates.

> *Waller*: Conflict is a constructive process, and creates as much as it destroys. And conflict unifies as much as it divides; it is one of the greatest group-making factors. Our most meaningful relations are often characterized by antagonistic cooperation. Conflict preserves relations which might otherwise become intolerable. Conflict, further, is a means to peace. Conflict is an essential part of the dialectic of personal growth.[35]

> *Elbow*: How can we manage to do contrary things? Christ said, "Be ye perfect," but I don't think it is good advice to try being immensely supportive and fierce in the same instant, as he and Socrates somehow managed to be. In writing, too, it doesn't usually help to try being immensely generative and critical-minded in the same instant as some great writers are, and as the rest of us sometimes are at moments of blessed inspiration. This is the way of transcendence and genius, but for most of us most of the time there is too much interference or paralysis when we try to do opposites at once. But it is possible to make peace between opposites by alternating between them so that you are never trying to do contrary things at any one moment.[36]

Conclusion

In closing, I want to call special attention to two thematic threads in the anecdotes I have repeated above. One is that the experience of teaching involves a struggle for complex, and ultimately tenuous, control. A second is that as a result of this struggle, there is an inevitable and morally legitimate tension between teachers and students. I believe that this struggle and its tensions are at the heart of what I called above the uncertainty of teaching, its messy practicality, which theorists generally sidestep. Most theory about teaching — and in consequence much policy too — supposes that teaching is at best simply the rational application of means to given ends. In this light, all the ambiguity, irrationality, and conflict which teachers are used to feeling in their bones, if not used to talking about, are simply evidence of teaching failure.

In an essay that documents the role that theory played in raising some teachers' voices, I must one last time acknowledge theory's rapacious history, its missing of the mark. I do so, however, not to dismiss all theory, but to urge that the teacher's intimate knowledge of uncertainty and its central and creative role in practice become as much a cornerstone of theory as it is a reality in the classroom.

In *The Quest for Certainty*, Dewey suggested that joining theory and practice can benefit both. Practitioners who are open to theory gain liberation from what he calls "the bondage of habit which is always closing in on us, restricting our vision both of what is and of what the actual may become."[37] Theorists who are open to practice gain liberation from the expectation that they carry all the burdens of knowledge themselves — not only of its generalities but of its particularities too; not only of its articulation but of its creation. Ironically, by giving up what Dewey

[35] Waller, *Sociology of Teaching*, p. 352.
[36] Elbow, "Embracing Contraries," p. 334.
[37] Dewey, *Quest for Certainty*, p. 310.

calls their monopolistic claims, theorists may also gain greater respect for what they can uniquely contribute to human progress.[38]

But there is a final paradox—the one which Freire notes—that the necessary partnership of theorists and practitioners, like the partnership of teachers and students, authority and freedom, yesterday and today, must be as full of tension as of progress.

[38] Dewey, *Quest for Certainty*, p. 298.

The author wishes to acknowledge the helpful comments of Sara Lawrence Lightfoot and David K. Cohen on earlier drafts of this paper.

Skills and Other Dilemmas
of a Progressive Black Educator

LISA D. DELPIT

In this article the author reflects on her practice as a teacher and as a teacher of teachers. Arguing from her perspective as a product of the skills-oriented approach to writing and as a teacher of the process-oriented approach to writing, she describes the estrangement many minority teachers feel from the progressive movement. Her conclusions advocate a fusion of the two approaches and point to a need for writing-process movement leaders to develop a vocabulary which will allow educators who have differing perspectives to participate in the dialogue.

Why do the refrains of progressive educational movements seem lacking in the diverse harmonies, the variegated rhythms, and the shades of tone expected in a truly heterogeneous chorus? Why do we hear so little representation from the multicultural voices which comprise the present-day American educational scene?

These questions have surfaced anew as I begin my third year of university "professoring" after having graduated from a prestigious university known for its progressive school of education. My family back in Louisiana is very proud about all of that, but still they find me rather tedious. They say things like, "She just got here and she's locked up in that room with a bunch of papers talking about she's gotta finish some article. I don't know why she bothers to come home." Or, "I didn't ask you about what any research said, what do *you* think?!"

I once shared my family's skepticism of academia. I remember asking myself in the first few months of my graduate school career, "Why is it these theories never seem to be talking about me?" But by graduation time many of my fellow minority students and I had become well trained: we had learned alternate ways of viewing the world, coaxed memories of life in our communities into forms which fit into the categories created by academic researchers and theoreticians, and internalized belief systems that often belied our own experiences.

I learned a lot in graduate school. For one thing I learned that people acquire a new dialect most effectively through interaction with speakers of that dialect, not through being constantly corrected. Of course, when I was growing up, my mother and my teachers in the pre-integration, poor black Catholic school that I attended corrected every other word I uttered in their effort to coerce my Black English into sometimes hypercorrect Standard English forms acceptable to black nuns in Catholic schools. Yet, I learned to speak and write in Standard English.

Harvard Educational Review   Vol. 56   No. 4   November 1986, 379–385

I also learned in graduate school that people learn to write not by being taught "skills" and grammar, but by "writing in meaningful contexts." In elementary school I diagrammed thousands of sentences, filled in tens of thousands of blanks, and never wrote any text longer than two sentences until I was in the tenth grade of high school. I have been told by my professors that I am a good writer. (One, when told about my poor community and segregated, skill-based schooling, even went so far as to say, "How did you *ever* learn how to write?") By that time I had begun to wonder myself. Never mind that I had learned — and learned well — despite my professors' scathing retroactive assessment of my early education.

But I cannot blame graduate school for all the new beliefs I learned to espouse. I also learned a lot during my progressive undergraduate teacher training. There, as one of the few black education students, I learned that the open classroom was the most "humanizing" of learning environments, that children should be in control of their own learning, and that all children would read when they were ready. Determined to use all that I had learned to benefit black children, I abandoned the cornfields of Ohio, and relocated to an alternative inner-city school in Philadelphia to student-teach.

Located on the border between two communities, our "open-classroom" school deliberately maintained a population of 60 percent poor black kids from "South Philly," and 40 percent well-to-do white kids from "Society Hill." The black kids went to school there because it was their only neighborhood school. The white kids went to school there because their parents had learned the same kinds of things I had learned about education. As a matter of fact, there was a waiting list of white children to get into the school. This was unique in Philadelphia — a predominantly black school with a waiting list of white children. There was no such waiting list of black children.

I apprenticed under a gifted young kindergarten teacher. She had learned the same things that I had learned, so our pairing was most opportune. When I finished my student teaching, the principal asked me to stay on in a full-time position.

The ethos of that school was fascinating. I was one of only a few black teachers, and the other black teachers were mostly older and mostly "traditional." They had not learned the kinds of things I had learned, and the young white teachers sometimes expressed in subtle ways that they thought these teachers were — how to say it — somewhat "repressive." At the very least they were "not structuring learning environments in ways that allowed the children's intellect to flourish" — they focused on "skills," they made students sit down at desks, they made students practice handwriting, they corrected oral and written grammar. The subtle, unstated message was, "They just don't realize how smart these kids are."

I was an exception to the other black teachers. I socialized with the young white teachers and planned shared classroom experiences with them. I also taught as they did. Many people told me I was a good teacher: I had an open classroom; I had learning stations; I had children write books and stories to share; I provided games and used weaving to teach math and fine motor skills. I threw out all the desks and added carpeted open learning areas. I was doing what I had learned — and it worked. Well, at least it worked for some of the children.

My white students zoomed ahead. They worked hard at the learning stations. They did amazing things with books and writing. My black students played the games; they learned how to weave; and they threw the books around the learning stations. They practiced karate moves on the new carpets. Some of them even learned how to read, but none of them as quickly as my white students. I was doing the same thing for all my kids — what was the problem?

I taught in Philadelphia for six years. Each year my teaching became less like my young white friends' and more like the other black women's who taught at the school. My students practiced handwriting; I wrote on the board; I got some tables to replace some of the thrown-out desks. Each year my teaching moved farther away from what I had learned, even though in many ways I still identified myself as an open-classroom teacher. As my classroom became more "traditional," however, it seemed that my black students steadily improved in their reading and writing. But they still lagged behind. It hurt that I was moving away from what I had learned. It hurt even more that although my colleagues called me a good teacher, I still felt that I had failed in the task that was most important to me — teaching black children and teaching them well. I could not talk about my failure then. It is difficult even now. At least I did not fall into the trap of talking about the parents' failures. I just did not talk about any of it.

In 1977 I left Philadelphia and managed to forget about my quandary for six-and-a-half years — the one-and-a-half years that I spent working in an administrative job in Louisiana and the five years I spent in graduate school. It was easy to forget failure there. My professors told me that everything I had done in Philadelphia was right; that I was right to shun basals; that I was right to think in terms of learner-driven and holistic education; that, indeed, I had been a success in Philadelphia. Of course, it was easy to forget, too, because I could develop new focal points. I could even maintain my political and moral integrity while doing so — graduate school introduced me to all *sorts* of oppressed peoples who needed assistance in the educational realm. There were bilingual speakers of any number of languages, there were new immigrants. And if one were truly creative, there were even whole countries in need of assistance — welcome to the Third World! I could tackle someone else's failures and forget my own.

In graduate school I learned about many more elements of progressive education. It was great. I learned new "holistic" teaching techniques — integrating reading and writing, focusing on meaning rather than form. One of the most popular elements — and one, I should add, which I readily and heartily embraced — was the writing-process approach to literacy. I spent a lot of time with writing-process people. I learned the lingo. I focused energy on "fluency" and not on "correctness." I learned that a focus on "skills" would stifle my students' writing. I learned about "fast-writes" and "golden lines" and group process. I went out into the world as a professor of literacy armed with the very latest, research-based and field-tested teaching methods.

All went well in my university literacy classes. My student teachers followed my lead and shunned limited "traditional" methods of teaching. They, too, embraced holistic processes and learned to approach writing with an emphasis on fluency and creative expression.

But then I returned to Philadelphia for a conference. I looked up one of my old friends — another black woman who was also a teacher. Cathy had been teaching for years in an alternative high school. Most of the students in her school, and by this time in the entire Philadelphia system, were black. Cathy and I had never

Their insistence on skills is not a negation of their students' intellect, as is often suggested by progressive forces, but an acknowledgment of it: "You know a lot; you can learn more. Do It Now!"

I run a great risk in writing this—the risk that my purpose will be misunderstood, the risk that those who subject black and other minority children to day after day of isolated, meaningless, drilled "subskills" will think themselves vindicated. That is not the point. Were this another paper I would explain what I mean by "skills"—useful and usable knowledge which contributes to a student's ability to communicate effectively in standard, generally acceptable literary forms. And I would explain that I believe that skills are best taught through meaningful communication, best learned in meaningful contexts. I would further explain that skills are a necessary, but insufficient aspect of black and minority students' education. Students need technical skills to open doors, but they need to be able to think critically and creatively to participate in meaningful and potentially liberating work inside those doors. Let there be no doubt: a "skilled" minority person who is not also capable of critical analysis becomes the trainable, low-level functionary of dominant society, simply the grease that keeps the institutions which orchestrate his or her oppression running smoothly. On the other hand, a critical thinker who lacks the "skills" demanded by employers and institutions of higher learning can aspire to financial and social status only within the disenfranchised underworld. Yes, if minority people are to effect the change which will allow them to truly progress we must insist on "skills" *within the context of* critical and creative thinking.

But that is for another paper. The purpose of this one is to defend my fellow minority educators at the same time I seek to reestablish my own place in the progressive educational arena. Too often minority teachers' voices have been hushed: a certain paternalism creeps into the speech of some of our liberal colleagues as they explain that our children must be "given voice." As difficult as it is for our colleagues to hear our children's existing voices, it is often equally difficult for them to hear our own. The consequence is that all too often minority teachers retreat from these "progressive" settings grumbling among themselves, "There they go again." It is vitally important that non-minority educators realize that there is another voice, another reality; that many of the teachers whom they seek to reach have been able to conquer the educational system *because* they received the kind of instruction that their white progressive colleagues are denouncing.

What am I suggesting here? I certainly do not suggest that the writing-process approach to literacy development is wrong or that a completely skills-oriented program is right. I suggest, instead, that there is much to be gained from the interaction of the two orientations and that advocates of both approaches have something to say to each other. I further suggest that it is the responsibility of the dominant group members to attempt to hear the other side of the issue; and after hearing, to speak in a modified voice that does not exclude the concerns of their minority colleagues.

It is time to look closely at elements of our educational system, particularly those elements we consider progressive; time to see whether there is minority involvement and support, and if not, to ask why; time to reassess what we are doing in public schools and universities to include other voices, other experiences; time to seek the diversity in our educational movements that we talk about seeking in our classrooms. I would advocate that university researchers, school districts, and teachers try to understand the views of their minority colleagues and constituents, and that programs, including the country's many writing projects, target themselves for study. Perhaps ethnographies of various writing projects, with particular attention given to minority participation and nonparticipation would prove valuable. The key is to understand the variety of meanings available for any human interaction, and not to assume that the voices of the majority speak for all.

I have come to believe that the "open-classroom movement," despite its progressive intentions, faded in large part because it was not able to come to terms with the concerns of poor and minority communities. I truly hope that those who advocate other potentially important programs will do a better job.

Creative Education for Bilingual Teachers

ALMA FLOR ADA

The author prescribes a bilingual teacher-training process that is based on a critique of the current condition of bilingual education and the professional concerns of bilingual teachers. Her approach would enable bilingual teachers to discern and analyze interpersonal, social, and political issues unique to their struggles. She suggests a "creative" approach to teacher training that she believes will strengthen the image of bilingual teachers and, consequently, benefit both teachers and students.

Schools today, and teachers in particular, are under a great deal of criticism. Bilingual teachers, caught between the accepted practices they are required to follow and the sound theories and research that contradict those practices, are especially vulnerable to attack. Most bilingual teachers were not educated in bilingual programs, nor have they had the experience of teaching in bilingual schools that receive full societal support. In many instances they themselves have been victims of language oppression and racism; thus, in order to empower their students to overcome conditions of domination and oppression, they must first be empowered themselves. This paper, based on reflections of bilingual teachers in U.S. schools, will analyze the nature of the teacher training process and propose elements of an empowering process for training bilingual teachers.

All teachers must contend with the uncertainties arising from the lack of societal support for their profession, but the situation is doubly difficult for bilingual teachers.[1] Education in general is often criticized, but its critics talk of improvement, not of elimination. Bilingual education, on the other hand, faces opposition from a large proportion of the population, who would willingly do away with it.

Criticism of bilingual education comes from a variety of sources. Under the pervasive influence of the misused "melting pot" metaphor, some opponents fear that bilingual education will promote divisiveness among the general population. They see the maintenance of home languages as un-American. Other opponents, often members of language minority communities themselves, fear that participation in

[1] Schools in the United States are currently perceived, as noted with considerable insight by Giroux (1986), as instruments of societal reproduction. As such, they are attacked by conservatives and radicals alike — by conservatives for failing to produce adequately trained workers for an increasingly complex technological economy; by radicals for legitimizing the prevailing societal value of the dominant corporate order and perpetuating the existing gender, racial, and class inequalities.

Harvard Educational Review   Vol. 56   No. 4   November 1986, 386–394

bilingual education will segregate and ostracize children and will jeopardize their future societal success.

Subtractive versus Additive Bilingualism

The fear that home-language maintenance will hinder the acquisition of English is not borne out by research. Achieving high-language proficiency in English does not preclude maintaining proficiency in the mother tongue. Despite its widespread acceptance, the subtractive model of bilingualism, in which mastery of the second language is achieved at the expense of proficiency in the first, need not be the framework on which bilingual education rests. Additive bilingualism, in which a second language is acquired while maintaining and continuing to develop the first, is a healthy and viable alternative to subtractive bilingualism (Cummins, 1981, 1986; Dolson, 1985; Lambert & Tucker, 1972; Skutnabb-Kangas, 1984).

The benefits of additive bilingualism are many. Peal and Lambert's (1962) classic study suggested that having a dual repertoire to label and organize reality fosters students' cognitive flexibility. Since then, most research shows that bilingualism contributes positively to the cognitive, linguistic, and psychosocial development of children. Other, more subtle, advantages have been found; for example, enhanced metalinguistic development frequently correlates with bilingualism (for reviews, see Cummins, 1986; Dolson, 1985).

A major benefit, so obvious that it is frequently ignored, is the knowledge of two languages. There is a bitter irony in the fact that an English-speaking student may earn college credit for learning to speak another language, while a language minority child is encouraged not to use, and therefore lose, the same skill.

In addition to preserving a valuable skill, encouraging the maintenance and development of the home language can foster a bilingual student's identity and self-esteem, which tend to correlate with academic success. While it is difficult to determine whether the greater success of students in bilingual programs that emphasize the use of the first language is due to better promotion of cognitive/academic skills in the first language or to the reinforcement of cultural identity provided by the intensive use of the home language, Cummins (1986) states that "considerable research data suggest that, for dominated minorities, the extent to which students' language and culture are incorporated into the school program constitutes a significant predictor of academic success" (p. 25).

Finally, it should be noted that the maintenance of the home language strengthens family and community ties. Home language maintenance enhances communication between generations. When students are encouraged to forget the language of their families and communities, they may lose access to their heritage. Frequently heard comments along the lines of, "my parents made it without bilingual education," disregard the significant changes that have taken place in society, and fail to take into account the grief of immigrants whose sacrifices and efforts are rewarded by estrangement from their grandchildren, with whom communication is limited, at best.

Beyond the Use of Two Languages

I believe the views of Freire (1982a, 1982b) and Aronowitz and Giroux (1985) are correct: schools do hold out the possibility of critical analysis and reconstruction of social reality through meaningful dialogue between teachers and students, by a process termed "transformative education." In this paper I refer to that transformative education process, which differs from the traditional reproductive education, as *creative education*.[2] Through creative education, students learn to understand and appreciate themselves, to use that understanding as a means of valuing the diversity of others, to reflect critically upon their experiences so that these can be a source of growth, and to respond creatively to the world around them. If bilingual students are to have an opportunity to validate their own language and culture — acknowledging both the difficulties faced by their ethnic groups and the possibilities open to them for effecting change and for making positive contributions to society — they must be participants in creative education. Only then will students and teachers be able to reclaim bilingualism as an asset for both individuals and society.[3]

Proponents of bilingual education suggest that the communicative and critical thinking skills that will empower students can best be developed, in the case of dominated minorities, through the utilization of the child's first language (Ada & de Olave, 1986; Cummins, 1986; Skutnabb-Kangas, 1984). These reasoning processes, once developed in the home language, are transferable to the second language, along with learning skills and academic content. Most important, the child's experience with success — a result of an additive approach that builds upon the child's existing knowledge — will create a positive attitude towards learning which will also be transferable to the second language.

However, if creative education is to be viable, teachers themselves must be empowered. Unfortunately, many teacher education programs seem designed to train teachers to accept social realities rather than to question them. Teachers are trained to conform to a mechanistic definition of their role rather than to recognize it as involving a relationship between human beings, with a possibility of growth for both teachers and students. As a result, teachers frequently find themselves trapped in a series of ritualistic activities — taking attendance, maintaining order, creating and following lesson plans, testing and reporting test results — with little opportunity to step back from the reality in which they are immersed in order to analyze it critically and become true agents of transformation. In short, if a creative education is to be brought about, teachers must experience it themselves.

Bilingual Teachers' Unheard Voices

Before something like creative education is introduced to teachers, it is important to know what those teachers' experiences have been. In order to listen to the voices of bilingual teachers, I engaged in dialogue with four groups of them and discussed the problems they face daily and the ways in which teacher education programs

---

[2] For an application of creative methodology to a language arts curriculum, see Ada and de Olave (1986).

[3] The positive value of bilingualism increases as the country moves from an industrial society to a technological/informational one. It is indeed paradoxical that precisely when the country most needs communication skills in order to export its technology to the rest of the world, we should see the appearance of an "English-only initiative" aimed at discouraging the maintenance and development of such skills.

might better address those problems. In all, thirty-eight participants contributed to these reflections.[4]

All the participants welcomed the opportunity to discuss their teacher education. When first asked what their education had given or not given them, they were extremely enthusiastic about engaging in dialogue. Typical comments were quite broad: "We would need a year to discuss everything my teacher education failed to give me"; or "We could write a whole book about what my teacher education didn't provide." Yet, despite the promise of critical reflection that those initial statements held out, when the participants were asked to describe their education, they responded with a series of limited observations: "I wasn't given any preparation for class management"; "We were not told anything about all the bureaucratic requirements, all the forms we would have to fill out"; and "I needed to know how to handle A/V equipment."

As the dialogue came closer to tackling the issues and social realities they faced in their daily lives as teachers, the participants began to look at their experiences in a comprehensive way. As they realized the impact of having been led to look at their profession as a sequence of unrelated tasks, rather than as a vital life project that has impact on society, the teachers expressed recurrent themes of isolation, powerlessness, and insecurity. This realization emerged out of a broad criticism of their teacher-training programs and generated myriad questions that troubled these teachers: If children really benefit from learning in their mother tongue, why should we put a ceiling on how much first-language instruction they receive? What varieties of the home language are acceptable in the classroom? How much of their cultural heritage do children need in order to develop self-esteem? Should education be neutral, free from political implications? Will children not have a better chance of survival if they are taught to be "good Americans" rather than to question the ethics of the country they live in? How will children fare if they are exposed to creative education and helped to develop as critical thinkers for a brief period, and then later forced to return to a traditional style of education?

Although these questions were raised out of concern for the children, the questions by no means applied only to them. The questions had to do as well with the teachers' own identities, their ideologies and beliefs, their use of language, their culture, and the social realities that surrounded them. The concerns they expressed about the children reflected their own concerns about themselves as teachers in schools that often devalue their work because they are members of cultural groups that are often socially invisible.

---

[4] The first group comprised bilingual teachers working with migrant children in the Parajo Valley School District, Watsonville, California; the second group were bilingual teachers in a number of communities between Santa Cruz and Salinas, California; the third group were bilingual teachers from the San Francisco Bay area; the fourth group included principals, counselors, and teacher educators, as well as teachers. Not all those in group four are engaged in bilingual education, but they all work with minority populations in various areas in California. All members of groups two and three are pursuing a Master of Education degree; those in group four are doctoral students. Although approximately 50 percent of them received their teacher education in California, the institutions they attended vary greatly (University of California at Davis, Berkeley, Santa Cruz, and Los Angeles; San Jose State University; Stanford University, University of Southern California). The others studied in Ohio, Michigan, New York, Massachusetts, Florida, and elsewhere.

Isolation

The absence of support for bilingual education in the society at large reinforces the perception of many bilingual teachers that support is flagging within their own schools. Administrators and monolingual teachers, while applying pressure to have language minority students mainstreamed as soon as possible, often attack bilingual teachers for the lack of success of those very children who have been prematurely required to perform in a language whose mastery threshold they have not yet reached (Cummins, 1981).

The importance of peer support was mentioned in every group discussion. The mistaken perception of bilingual education as nonprestigious makes peer support networks among bilingual teachers a necessity. One, in suggesting that teacher-education programs should encourage future teachers to develop such support mechanisms, said that "especially in nonprestigious areas like bilingual education, it is imperative to receive affirmation from one's peers." The lack of peer support—and their being "locked" in classrooms with little interaction with the rest of the school, the district, and the community—results in a feeling of isolation among teachers in general, and bilingual teachers in particular.

All the groups agreed on the need for interaction with parents and community so as to involve them in the educational process. One teacher suggested that teacher education programs should include inservices from community leaders. Another pointed out that the need is twofold: to involve the community in the educational process and to get teachers involved in community action. A third teacher suggested that teacher education programs should include a form of internship in community projects so that teachers might gain a holistic view of the community and become involved in wider societal issues. In addition, all the groups saw education and teaching as political activities, and they considered it desirable for teachers to be politically aware.

Sense of Inadequacy in Language Mastery

Since language performance plays a major role in the perception that others have of us and thus may affect our personal and professional success, feeling inadequate in the use of language is a painful experience. Bilingual teachers may feel inadequate in their language ability because of several factors. Those teachers whose mother tongue is English may not have had the opportunity to acquire full mastery of a second language—a sad reflection on our limited and deficient foreign language teaching. Members of language minorities who chose to become bilingual teachers may also have been victims of language oppression as children, when they were scolded or punished in school for using their home language. Therefore it should not be surprising that many bilingual teachers lack confidence in their literacy skills. Yet if these individuals can acknowledge that the language inadequacy they experience stems from deeply rooted institutionalized oppression and is highlighted by the one-teacher model, they will be better able to understand what their students may be going through.[5] Instead of reproducing a negative outcome, these

---

[5] The elite bilingual schools found in other countries, which include American schools abroad, use a two-teacher model of education. In a single classroom, each of two teachers provides instruction

teachers' past experiences can serve as a positive, constructive example. However, in order to free teachers from feelings of inadequacy, we must examine the reasons for language limitations and then discuss ways to overcome them.

Future bilingual teachers would benefit from an opportunity to live, study, and, perhaps, teach in a country where the language they will be teaching is spoken. Spending a few months in such an environment might be an ideal way to recapture, or to master, their language. This exposure might be beneficial in other ways as well. A successful bilingual teacher in one of the groups said the most valuable part of her teacher training had been the incentive it provided for her to visit and teach in Peru and Mexico. Observing different life styles, interacting with people in other countries, and having to teach under conditions very different from those she had always known gave her greater flexibility and creativity. She stated that she could better innovate because of her first-hand knowledge of diverse situations, and she derives strength from her experiences in unfamiliar places; she also feels the need to adopt a critical outlook because she has a new perception of the sociopolitical reality of the children who come to her classroom.

Powerlessness

The lack of opportunity to explore conflicting issues in a psychologically-safe climate often leads to denial, defensiveness, and, most especially, powerlessness. Indeed, powerlessness was one of the recurring themes in all four discussion groups. Although the participants felt at first that their powerlessness stemmed from isolation and feelings of inadequacy, further examination revealed that the deeper causes were the interactive forces between the schools, the community, and the larger society.

The participants recognized that parents ought to be involved in the educational process because they are genuinely concerned about their children's education. For the most part, however, adequate mechanisms are not in place to facilitate real parent participation. Since parents are often perceived by the school authorities as uneducated and ineffective, they are given a limited role in decision making. In addition, parents sometimes withdraw their support of bilingual programs by choosing to take their children out of them or by discouraging the use of the home language. This lack of support increases the frustration felt by teachers. It is not widely understood by the teachers that parents withdraw support because they have internalized the negative view towards bilingual education that is widespread in society.

Uncertainty Regarding Cultural Identity

To their feelings of powerlessness and language inadequacy many bilingual teachers add their own conflicts regarding their identity. In spite of the fact that the

---

for half the day, speaking only in his or her native language and thus motivating the children to become proficient in that language. In that system, the children, not the teacher, are expected to become fully bilingual. In contrast, the one-teacher model, which is followed in most bilingual programs in the United States, requires a single teacher to teach all subjects in both languages. Yet, few teachers are equally proficient in both languages, precisely because there has not been a tradition of additive bilingual education in this country.

American society claims to respect the ideals of equality, diversity, and inclusion, the reality for language minority people has been inequality, the push for conformity to one standard, and exclusion. One of the greatest contradictions confronting minorities is that society urges them to become mainstream and thereby abandon their language and cultural traditions, but even after they assume the views and behavior of the majority culture in hope of increased acceptance, they often continue to be victimized by the same forces that compelled their conformity.

In the case of some Hispanics, the question of self-identity is doubly complicated. As one teacher explained: "One of the great puzzlements of my childhood was hearing my barrio cousins and friends say in school that they were Spaniards, not Mexicans. Because my father used to tell stories about how cruel and bloodthirsty the Spaniards had been and how they had destroyed the Indian civilizations, I could not believe that any of my classmates would want to call themselves Spaniards. To this day I am troubled by the fact that my home language is Spanish." This painful experience—of having a mixed heritage in which one represents the dominator and the other the dominated—is not uncommon among Hispanics. It is an unresolved issue felt throughout Latin America. Every one of us who has Spanish-speaking parents or grandparents in this hemisphere is a *mestizo*, either ethnically or culturally.

Guillén (1972) proposes a solution in a powerfully poetic image. By accepting his mixed heritage, he manages to unite the shadows of his two grandparents, the Spanish warrior and the African slave.[6] Such an acceptance would help us to keep in mind past inequities and the valuable lessons the knowledge of these past inequities provides. This knowledge would allow us to accept ourselves as a whole and give us the strength to struggle against present-day oppressors, who obviously are not the Spaniards of today.

In any case, these are issues that need to be addressed during the creative education process, since they strongly affect the Hispanic teacher's sense of identity and thus limit the ability to model self-worth for children.

The Need to Integrate Theory and Experience

The participants saw the need for teacher education programs to integrate solid theory and ample experience in a mutually supportive manner. Many of them described their own educational experience as highly mechanistic. According to one teacher, "All we were told was how to set goals and objectives and how to write lesson plans. I wrote more than a hundred lesson plans, but I knew nothing about the classroom." Another teacher's complaint was that "all courses dealt with the ideal student, as if all students would be alike. We never heard anything about the students as real individuals." A third teacher said, "They gave us seminar syndrome. We never had the opportunity to experiment and explore. Now we do the same thing with our students. A lot of teaching goes on, but very little learning."

---

[6] In the poem *Balada de los dos abuelos*, Guillén writes: "Sombras que solo yo veo,/ me escoltan mis dos abuelos./ . . . /Yo los junto./ . . . /Los dos se abrazan./Los dos suspiran. Los dos/las fuertes cabezas alzan;/los dos del mismo tamaño,/bajo las estrellas altas;/los dos del mismo tamaño,/ ansia negra y ansia blanca;/ los dos del mismo tamaño,/ gritan, sueñan, lloran, cantan./ Sueñan, lloran, cantan./ Lloran, cantan./ ¡Cantan!"

This brings us to the most crucial issue. Participants in all groups said that although they were very much concerned about the need to develop critical thinking in their students, they wanted to learn how to empower themselves first. The strongest criticism of teacher education was directed at the discrepancy between what the faculty in the schools of education taught and what they practiced. One participant expressed the shared complaint in this way: "They preached to us to teach creatively, but we were never allowed any creativity. They encouraged us to be good communicators, but the classes they taught were deadly. There was some lip service paid to the need for encouraging children to think, but we were expected to memorize and repeat."

Creative education recognizes that the process of learning is more than the accumulation of information. Some teachers came to this recognition on their own. One teacher said, "My teacher training wasn't great; the content was too remote. But I did get something — I learned myself. I learned how to learn, how to develop learning skills, how to organize my own learning style, and this has been the most useful thing for me." In discussing what a creative teacher education program should provide, another teacher commented, "It would offer the opportunity to look inside, to find their own biases, to learn not to be afraid of sharing intimacies and their own experiences. Students may not learn content, but they learn the teacher; they learn how to emulate the teacher. It is important to provide opportunities to validate the teacher's self-integrity."

Summary

In order to provide creative education for language minority children, bilingual teachers themselves need to experience the liberating forces of this type of education. Teachers need to be validated as human beings, as conscientious, creative, intellectual human beings. They need the power that comes from communicating effectively, both orally and in writing, and the power that is built on solidarity. They need to understand the societal forces that have influenced their cultural and linguistic identity so that they can stop passively accepting their circumstances and become not only agents of their own transformation but also leaders in the world around them.

References

Ada, A. F., & de Olave, M. de P. (1986). *Hagamos caminos.* Reading, MA: Addison Wesley.

Aronowitz, S., & Giroux, H. A. (1985). *Education under siege.* South Hadley, MA: Bergin & Garvey.

Cummins, J. (1981). The role of primary language development in promoting educational success for language minority students. In Office of Bilingual Education (Ed.), *Schooling and language minority students: A theoretical framework.* Los Angeles: California State University.

Cummins, J. (1986). Empowering minority students: A framework for intervention. *Harvard Educational Review, 56,* 18–36.

Dolson, D. (1985). The effects of Spanish home language use on the scholastic performance of Hispanic pupils. *Journal of Multilingual and Multicultural Development, 6*(2), 135–155.

Freire, P. (1982a). *Education for critical consciousness.* New York: Continuum.

Freire, P. (1982b). *Pedagogy of the oppressed.* New York: Continuum.

Giroux, H. A. (1986). *Radical pedagogy and the politics of student voice.* Unpublished manuscript.

Guillén, N. (1972). Balada de los dos abuelos. In *Abra Poetica: 1920–1958.* Havana: Instituto Cubano del Libro, 137–139.

Lambert. W., & Tucker, R. (1972). *Bilingual education of children: The St. Lambert experiment.* Rowley, MA: Newbury House.

Peal, E., & Lambert, W. (1962). The relation of bilingualism to intelligence. *Psychological Monographs, 75,* 1–23.

Skutnabb-Kangas, T. (1984). *Bilingualism or not: The education of minorities.* Clevendon, Eng.: Multilingual Matters.

Discussions at the First Working Conference on Critical Pedagogy held at the University of Massachusetts, Amherst, in February 1986, motivated me to write this paper. I would like to express my appreciation to the participants at this conference. I would also like to thank Paulo Freire, Tove Skutnabb-Kangas, Jim Cummins, Ellen Herda, and Dennis Parker, as well as my students in the Multicultural Program, University of San Francisco, for their enriching dialogue. This paper benefited from the insightful comments of my daughter Rosalma Zubizarreta and my editor and friend, Bernice Randall.

Fifth Graders Respond to a Changed Reading Program

CORA LEE FIVE

Cora Lee Five, a fifth-grade teacher, puts into practice innovative ideas gleaned from the work of other teachers and researchers. She realizes, however, that she must rely on her own observations and questions to test these ideas in her classroom. Five concludes that through her own study of her students' responses to literature she has become more able to follow their development as readers.

How can teachers continue to learn about teaching? This question receives much attention in the current discussion about improving schools. Throughout my teaching career I have attended many university courses and inservice workshops. Usually these are opportunities for teachers to learn about new curricula and teaching approaches. Although these sessions have introduced me to many ideas I would not have come across on my own, I have had to find my own ways to make new ideas work in my classroom.

My own classroom research has helped me understand the impact new approaches have in my own classroom. As a teacher-researcher I welcome the opportunity to test hypotheses and pay attention to what my experiences teach me. Observing, listening, and questioning keep me alert to my students' needs and help me find ways to improve my instruction. Often this means involving the students in the research. I do this by telling them that I, too, want to learn, and by explaining what it is I want to learn. As my students become an active part of my research, we become a community of learners, rather than a teacher-centered classroom. The result is reciprocity in our learning: I learn from my students as they learn from me.

Classroom research helped me improve the way I teach reading. What follows is an account of my efforts to adapt and try out a new reading program with my fifth graders. I will acknowledge the ideas I received from other people who inspired the various changes I attempted. But I will concentrate on what I learned as I made these program changes and how my research enabled me to figure some things out for myself.

Over the past few years, the work of three people — Nancie Atwell, Mary Ellen Giacobbe, and Jerome Harste — has profoundly influenced my teaching of reading. Atwell's (1984, 1985) description of how her eighth graders responded to their reading by writing letters to her in dialogue journals stimulated my own thinking.

Harvard Educational Review Vol. 56 No. 4 November 1986, 395–405

She became involved in students' reactions to books by writing letters back to them. Giacobbe (1985) made me realize that teachers must be responsive to children and their reading. She described ways to hold a quick reading conference with each child every day. Harste (1984, 1985) interested me in viewing children as informants and learning from them. His ideas helped me recognize the benefits of encouraging children to use many strategies to make meaning and of allowing time for collaborative learning—time for students to talk, time for them to think and respond.

Inspired by the insights of these three people, I embarked on a new venture two years ago—the creation of a reading program that would give children time to read and time to make meaning through writing and talking about books. The twenty-five students in my self-contained classroom had a wide range of abilities. The class included children who had learning disabilities and children who spoke English as a second language. I hoped all of these students would turn into readers who loved reading, and I hoped research would help me recognize how that happened.

The first thing I did was the most difficult: With much trepidation, I gave up the reading workbooks. As an alternative, I set up a reading program based primarily on Atwell's approach using dialogue journals. It had worked with her eighth graders; would it work with my ten-year-olds? The answer turned out to be, "Yes." My students became immersed in books—they began to talk books, authors, reading, and writing. And so did I.

As I considered how I wanted to use the ideas of Atwell, Giacobbe, and Harste, I noticed that three crucial elements—time, ownership, and response—made my new approach to teaching reading similar to the process approach to teaching writing. It was essential to increase the amount of school time children had for reading. Each forty-five minute reading period began with a mini-lesson during which the class and I discussed character development, setting, titles, different genres, or various aspects of the reading process. Following this lesson students read books of their own choosing. During this reading time I spoke briefly with each child about his or her book, and then I spent the remainder of the period reading a book of my own choice. We ended the period with either a group sharing-time, often related to the mini-lesson, or discussions among two or three students who talked about some aspect of their books.

The children maintained ownership in this process because they decided what to read. Books from home, from the public and school libraries, and from the classroom all became texts for our reading period. Children read the books they selected, not those assigned by me.

The third element, response, became the focus of my research. Discussions during the reading period were not the only way the students communicated about what they read; they also responded to their reading in a variety of ways in their literature journals. The primary way of responding was a letter to me when they finished a book. I read their journals and wrote letters back to them. They also wrote several letters each month about their books to a friend or partner in the classroom. This written communication following the completion of a book or the arrival of a partner's letter was completed during the reading period.

One of my first observations was of the difference between the oral and written responses. When the students talked to each other, they usually retold the literal details of the story. When they wrote, they apparently used time to reflect, to think. The letters, in particular, fascinated me because I could return to them and read them again. As each child's work accumulated, I could more easily follow the changes and development in their thinking about literature. At the beginning of the year the journal responses resembled the book reports which the students had prepared in their earlier grades. The children summarized plots and offered recommendations about their books. Gradually, the topics addressed in the mini-lessons and in our discussions of the books I read aloud began to appear in the children's journal entries. Their letters to me and to each other eventually included discussions of the following:

— the characters, often making personal connections to them
— the main idea or focus of the book
— the tone or mood
— characteristics of a particular author or techniques used by the author that they wished to apply to their own writing
— the way a certain lead, ending, image or a particular voice or feeling contributed to a story
— their predictions, inferences, and questions based on the books
— their own interpretations of their reading
— their own reading process, and of how they learned to read.

As I collected and compared students' responses and asked myself new questions about how students handled this task and became more involved in their reading, I learned much from Danny. Danny, who did not like reading at the beginning of the year, used one of his journal entries to describe his experience of learning to read.

Dear Miss Five

when I was 4 years old my mom ust to read to me. some times she would let me try. I was pretty pitifull. then in kindergarden I always acted like I was reading and never raised my hand to read out loud. then in first grade we had a reading period and I sat and turned the pages. by this time I was a pro at turning the pages. when the teacher came over I don't know how she noticed but she did and she knew I didnt know how to read and she taugt me how to read. Also the new kid on the block was danish and he didnt know any english so as I taught him I taught myself in a way. . . .

After two months of the school year there were signs of Danny's increasing involvement with books. Here is how he responded at that time to Okimoto's (1982) *Norman Schnurman, Average Person.*

November 27

Dear Miss Five,

This letter is about *Norman Schurnman* — *"Average Person"*. The things I liked best about this book were, feeling and comedy. Especialy feeling. Because when I read the part when he told his Dad he didn't want to play football. I think he desvered "Ten Medals"! Because if I had a Dad like that I would have probably played the whole season even if I was that bad and got hurt alot. Because I wouldnt have the heart to watch him put his head down in dissapointment. And if he did put his head down, I would have felt so guilty I would have came back ten minutes later and said Dad I'll play, No matter how bad it felt. But I guess me and norman are different people. And I thought the author had a good ending because it made you in a way forget about the incident with his Dad.

Truly Yours,
Danny

In my letter back to Danny I commented on the personal connections he was beginning to make with the characters.

November 27

Dear Danny,

I could tell you were really involved with the characters in this book. I agree with you that Norman had a difficult decision to make. It must have been very hard for him to tell his dad, but I imagine it was also very hard for Norman to keep playing on the team. I guess Norman felt he did the best he could do and had to make his own decision.

You made a good point about the ending. Perhaps the author wanted a happy ending, and the ending in the book does make you forget about the situation with his father.

Sincerely,
Miss Five

Four months later Danny loved to read and write and developed an interest in the authors of the books he was reading. He discovered the writer Byars through *Good-bye, Chicken Little* (1979) and began to wonder about the basis for her story.

. . . I thought that this book was so true and this may have happened to a kid. I think I might send a letter to Betsy Byars to see if this book was based on experience. I thought his biggest mistake was fighting with conrad. this book was so good I wish I could read it forever.

That discovery was important to Danny in several ways. He wrote to Byars and treasured the letter he received in return, stapling it into his literature journal. He read all the rest of her books. He also decided to write in his personal journal every night because, as he explained it, "In case I really do become an author, I want to remember all my experiences so I can put them in books for kids my age."

As the year progressed, many students began to experiment, struggling to interpret the ideas in the books they read. Josh described the character Jess in Patterson's (1977) *Bridge to Terabithia.*

Dear Miss Five,

Jess has so many feelings its hard to discribe him. Let's say he had three stages. First, a normal, hardworking stage at the beginning, and feelings, if he had any, would never be shared with anyone else. The second stage, when Leslie came into his life, tured into a kind of magical stage in a way for him. The third stage, when Leslie died, he began to relate to adults. These three stages make him real.

Sincirly,
Josh

69

John, a less able reader, responded to the same book.

Dear Miss Five,

I think that Jess is changing on the inside because of lesslys death. He is starting to undersand not only his father but all gronups and I think that he likes his sister better.

Etay began to interpret and extend his ideas after only a few weeks. His response to Byar's (1974) *After the Goatman* and his other letters showed his developing ability to look beyond the story line.

Oct. 21

Dear Miss Five,

On Thursday I finished *After the Goat Man.* I thought it was better than all the other books I read by Betsy Byars. I think she got the idea of the goat from as goats are supposed to be stubborn and the character is stubborn. I think thats her symbol for the character. I also like the way she puts Harold as a kid still in his fantasys and still dreaming about himself. I like the way she put her characters. There is also something that I liked about an anology about life. Figgy puts life as a spider-web and everybody's all tied up except for him, and he's only tied up by one string which is his grandfather (the Goat Man.)

Etay

Etay found a connection between *The Night Swimmers*, also by Byars (1982), and Patterson's (1977) *Bridge to Terabithia.*

. . . In the end of the book Roy asked his oldest sister "is the Bowlwater plant really a big gigantic plant with bedspreads for flowers" and he went on explaining his fantasy. His oldest sister answered "no." At that moment I thought about the book. I thought maybe that was Roy's bridge (like Bridge to Terabithia) from his fantasy world to reallity world.

Etay

The development of the comments in the letters suggested to me that students become better readers when their early, and perhaps less successful, attempts to search for greater depth in their books are not treated as comprehension problems. Just as experimenting and risk-taking are important in learning to write, they are also important in learning to read. I began to pay more attention to how students found ways to express what certain books meant to them.

In the winter Etay discovered Alexander's (1981) *Westmark* trilogy. When he finished the last of the three books, he wrote a long letter relating the ideas throughout the trilogy. The conclusion of the letter summarized his thoughts.

. . . In the end it wasn't the monarchy that won the war but the people. And the people are the ones who took over everything. I think in this triology Lloyd Alexander shows what happened in England. In the start England's monarchy had power over everything, like in the first book (Westmark). Slowly the power of the monarchy lessened, until now the monarchy has probably no power at all. In *the Beggar Queen*, in the end, the monarchy was overthrown by the people.

Etay

Many students, including David, used their letters to express the joy of finding a wonderful book.

Dec. 17

Dear Miss Five,

Yesterday I finished the best book, called, *The Green Futures of Tycho*. As soon as I read the back of it at the book fair I knew it was the book for me. And I was right, it felt as though it was made especially for me. . . . Ever since I was a little kid, I loved the thought of going into the past & the future, & telling my future, & thinking about all of it.

But David's response was not limited to this personal interest in the book's topic. He also commented on the author's craft.

. . . I like how the author kept changing & making the future & past more exciting. Like in the future he invented things, but didn't tell what they did, he let you figure it out. You should definitely read it to the class.

From
David

The letters to partners raised some new questions about children as responders to literature. Three or four times a month each child would write about his or her book to another child in the class. The understanding was that if they received a letter, they were required to write back. Their letters to each other often differed from the ones they wrote to me; they struck me as having a more casual tone, and the writers seemed less concerned with what they thought I expected them to say in their response. Early in the school year David and Etay started to write to each other.

Oct. 8

Dear Etay,

I just finished *A Wrinkle in Time*. It is great book. I think you should read it again. Some parts of the book are pretty confusng though.

From,
David

Dear David,
I hate science fiction!!!

Etay

By November more of an exchange of ideas appeared.

November 14

Dear Etay,

I am reading a book called *Alice's Adventures in Wonderland*. I don't like it very much. I think it is to *boring*! It seems that it takes forever. I have always liked *Alice in Wonderland*, but I don't like this one. Even thought it is by the original author, Lewis Carrol. I am up to The Mock turtle's story. My favorite parts so far is when she was playing croquet & when she kept growing & shrinking when she ate the mushroom, even though those parts are not so good. I am not going to read, *Trough the Looking Glass*.

David

Dear David,

I can see that you didn't like this book. I didn't like it either. I thought it was just an adventure after an adventure and then all it lead to was a dream. It was written the best way it could but I don't think it was made for our age. I think it was made for smaller kids (who see it as a cute little fantasy) or for grownups (who see it with some meaning). We're in the middle because we're too big to see it as a cute fantasy and we're too small to see it with some meaning.

Etay

The letters my students wrote to me and to each other also made me think about the classroom context needed to support their reading. I realized that they read with greater depth when they selected their own books, ones that appealed to them rather than those that I thought they "should" read. I also realized that they probably took risks to find ways to express themselves because I did not label their comments as "correct" or "incorrect." A classroom environment that accepted and respected what children said about books was necessary for these journal entries and their increased interest in reading. Furthermore, the example of the peer correspondence shows that the acceptance from other students can be as important as the teacher's.

Writing letters was not the only way my students responded to literature. "Mapping" is another strategy. Krim (1985, 1986) uses mapping with her senior high school students. Intrigued with her concept, I decided to try it with my fifth graders. I asked some students to map Patterson's (1977) *Bridge to Terabithia*. Some of their drawings appear on pages 402–404.

Bridge to Terabithia is a story about a fifth-grade boy, Jess, who has difficulty relating to other people. He has no friends until Leslie moves near his home. Together they create Terabithia, a kingdom where Jess is king and Leslie queen. Jess loses his friend when Leslie has a fatal accident in Terabithia. As he tries to adjust to her death, Jess grows and begins to build a closer relationship with his father and others. In the end, Jess is able to give the magic of Terabithia to his younger sister Maybelle.

In his map Josh used lines and numbers to connect his drawings of important events. Although most of the events appear in comparatively small drawings, Josh represented two key points of the story with larger drawings. In one he made a bridge between Jess and his father; in the other he showed Jess rebuilding the magic of Terabithia for his sister Maybelle.

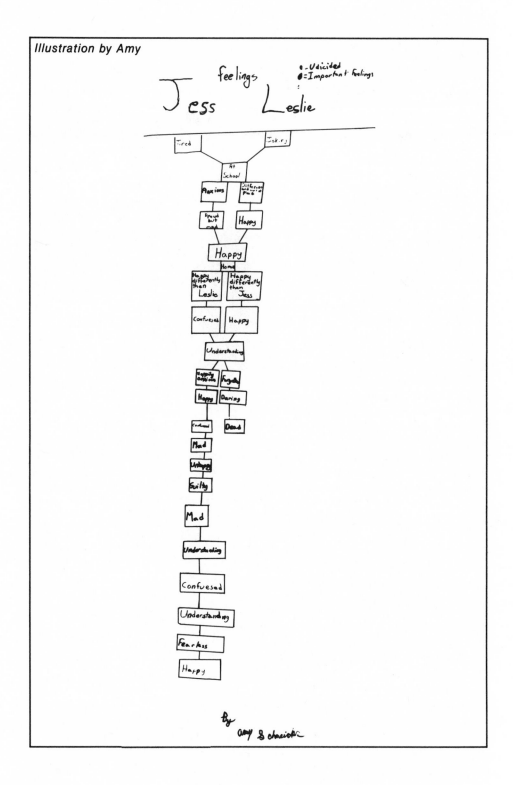

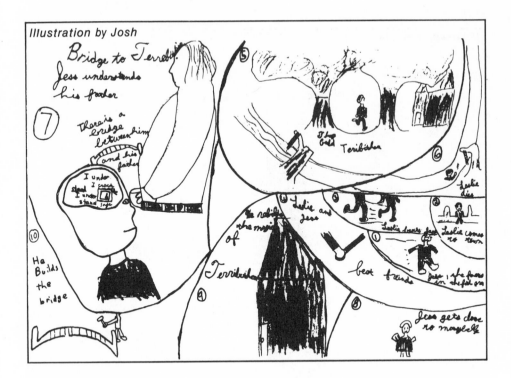

Illustration by Josh

Amy mapped the story in a different way. She saw the book in terms of feelings and made a flow chart with the characters Jess and Leslie at the top. They come together at school, where Jess is at first "anxious" and Leslie feels "different and out of place." "Proud but mad" are Jess's feelings after a specific school experience that made Leslie feel "happy." As their friendship progresses, they are both happy but, as Amy notes, in different ways. Amy follows with other feelings that describe the characters until Leslie's death. Then she continues with the range of emotions Jess experiences as he tries to deal with and accept the loss of his best friend.

Another strategy I used is one suggested by Harste (1985) called Sketch to Stretch. In this approach, as in mapping, the students pick out the most important ideas in their books and combine them in a sketch. This turned out to be a good way to develop sequencing skills as students connected events in a logical order to make a meaningful whole.

David has sketched the important parts of *Good-bye, Chicken Little* and has numbered his sketches to show the order in which they occur: the uncle drowns, Jimmy feels guilty and responsible, he fights with Conrad, they become friends again, and in the last picture David wrote that Jimmy "almost" forgets, and "everything turns out almost perfect."

The effect this kind of reading program had on both my students and me continues to amaze and excite me. By the fourth month of the program I could see children listening to each other and seeking recommendations for their next selections. They wondered about authors and tried to imitate authors' techniques in their own writing. They looked for feelings, for believable characters, and for interesting words, and they were delighted with effective dialogue.

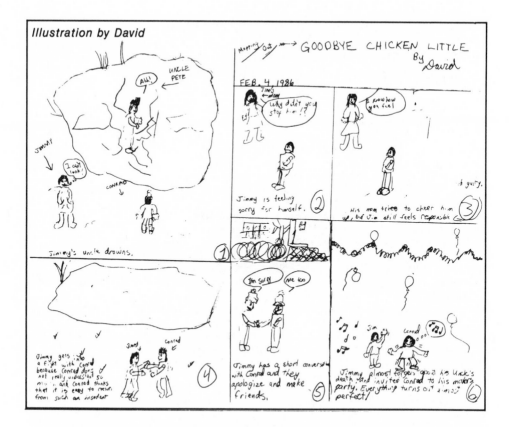

Illustration by David

Another indication of students' interest and joy in reading was the number of books they read during the year. The less able readers, including students with learning disabilities and those for whom English is a second language, read between 25 and 42 books each; the average readers read about 47; and the top readers between 47 and 144 books.

And the new approach had an effect on me. My students and I began to talk books before school, at recess, and at lunchtime; their reading period never seemed to end at twelve, even though the bell had rung. Their enthusiasm was infectious. I was constantly drawn into their discussions and especially their thinking, as I became more and more involved in their reading and their responses. This approach and my researcher's role helped me continue to learn more about these students, their reading processes, and their attitudes. Again and again, I saw the importance of giving them freedom to read and opportunities to experiment with and to explore their own ideas.

By collecting, sorting, reading and rereading their letters, maps, and sketches, I found for myself a much closer view of how children struggle and then succeed to find meaning in books. The process also kept me engaged in learning because it led me to new questions. What do children learn from my mini-lessons? In what situations will children take more risks with interpreting what they read? These new questions might be ones that help me reach more children in the way I reached John.

John, a real hold-out in terms of reading and loving books, a boy who completed reading few books in the fourth grade, could not have given me a greater gift. One day, I found him at at his desk when everyone else had gone to lunch. He was reading. When I walked in he looked up and smiled, saying, "I love this book. I just have to finish this chapter before I go out."

References

Alexander, L. (1981). *Westmark*. New York: Dutton.

Alexander, L. (1982). *The kestrel*. New York: Dutton.

Alexander, L. (1984). *The beggar queen*. New York: Dutton.

Atwell, N. (1984). Writing and reading literature from the inside out. *Language Arts, 61,* 240–252.

Atwell, N. (July, 1985). *Reading, writing, thinking, learning* [course]. Institute on Writing, sponsored by Northeastern University. Martha's Vineyard, MA.

Byars, B. (1974). *After the goatman*. New York: Viking.

Byars, B. (1979). *Good-bye, Chicken Little*. New York: Harper & Row.

Byars, B. (1980). *The night swimmers*. New York: Delacorte.

Giacobbe, M. E. (July, 1985). *Reading, writing, thinking, learning* [course]. Institute on Writing, sponsored by Northeastern University. Martha's Vineyard, MA.

Harste, J. C. , Woodward, V. A. , & Burke, C. L. (1984). *Language stories and literacy lessons*. Portsmouth, NH: Heinemann Educational Books.

Harste, J. C. (July, 1985). *Creativity and intentionality* [course]. Institute on Writing, sponsored by Northeastern University. Martha's Vineyard, MA.

Krim, N. (1986). Where do we go from here? Try mapping. Unpublished manuscript.

Krim, N. (March, 1985). *Integrating reading, writing and critical thinking skills in the teaching of literature: Focus, mapping, and sequencing strategies*. Presentation at the annual spring conference of the National Council of Teachers of English.

Okimoto, J. D. (1982). *Norman Schnurman, average person*. New York: Putnam.

Patterson, K. (1977). *Bridge to Terabithia*. New York: Crowell.

Sleator, W. (1981). *The green futures of Tycho*. New York: Dutton.

On Listening to What the Children Say

VIVIAN GUSSIN PALEY

A growing number of teachers and researchers are collaborating on research projects involving classroom learning; some teachers, however, become their own investigative reporters. Vivian Gussin Paley has developed a method for studying the young child in her classroom that is at the same time a new approach to teaching. In this essay, she explains how the method evolved and describes its effect in the classroom.

Years ago, when I was a young woman in New Orleans, I led a Great Books discussion group that met at the public library. The participants came from many occupations and educational backgrounds, and they were all older and more experienced than I. Whatever advantage I had was contained in the lists of questions provided by the Great Books people, who also sent along the following directive: There are no right or wrong answers. Get everyone talking and then find connections — person-to-person, person-to-book.

The advice was sound: do the required reading, ask most of the questions, and manage to connect a number of the ideas that arise at each meeting. Unfortunately, I did not fare too well; something was missing from my performance — a simple ingredient called *curiosity*. I was not truly interested in the people sitting around the table or curious about what they might think or say. Mainly, I wanted to keep the discussion moving and to avoid awkward silences.

Soon after leading these discussions, I became a kindergarten teacher. In my haste to supply the children with my own bits and pieces of neatly labeled reality, the appearance of a correct answer gave me the surest feeling that I was teaching. Curriculum guides replaced the lists of questions, but I still wanted most of all to keep things moving with a minimum of distraction. It did not occur to me that the distractions might be the sounds of children thinking.

Then one year a high school science teacher asked if he could spend some time with my kindergarteners. His first grandchild was about to enter nursery school, and he wondered what it would be like to teach the youngest students in our school. Once a week he came with paper bags full of show-and-tell, and he and the children talked about a wide range of ordinary phenomena. As I listened, distant memories stirred. "You have a remarkable way with children, Bill," I told him. "They never tire of giving you their ideas, and somehow you manage to use them all, no matter how far off the mark."

Harvard Educational Review   Vol. 56   No. 2   May 1986, 122–131

"The old Socratic method," he said. "I was a Great Books leader once up in Maine. It seems to work as well with kindergarteners as with my seniors."

Of course. That was exactly what he was doing. He asked a question or made a casual observation, then repeated each child's comment and hung onto it until a link was made to someone else's idea. Together they were constructing a paper chain of magical imaginings mixed with some solid facts, and Bill was providing the glue.

But something else was going on that was essential to Bill's success. He was truly curious. He had few expectations of what five-year-olds might say or think, and he listened to their responses with the anticipation one brings to the theater when a mystery is being revealed. Bill was interested not in what he knew to be an answer, but only in how the children intuitively approached a problem. He would whisper to me after each session, "Incredible! Their notions of cause and effect are incredible!" And I, their teacher, who thought I knew the children so well, was often equally astonished.

I began to copy Bill's style whenever the children and I had formal discussions. I practiced his open-ended questions, the kind that seek no specific answers but rather build a chain of ideas without the need for closure. It was not easy. I felt myself always waiting for the right answer — my answer. The children knew I was waiting and watched my face for clues. Clearly, it was not enough simply to copy someone else's teaching manner; real change comes about only through the painful recognition of one's own vulnerability.

A move to a new school in another city and an orientation speech given by Philip Jackson shook me up sufficiently to allow the first rays of self-awareness to seep in. He described a remarkable study done by two Harvard psychologists, Robert Rosenthal and Lenore Jacobson, who deliberately supplied several teachers with misleading information about their students.[1] In random fashion, children were labeled bright or slow by means of fictitious IQ scores. The teachers, I was shocked to find out, consistently asked more questions, waited longer for answers, and followed up more often with additional comments when they were speaking to a "smart" child.

I was shocked because I knew that one of those unsuspecting teachers could have been me, although certainly I listened more to myself than to *any* of the children in the classroom. Suddenly, I was truly curious about my role in the classroom, but there were no researchers ready to set up an incriminating study to show me when — and perhaps why — I consistently veered away from the child's agenda. Then I discovered the tape recorder and knew, after transcribing the first tape, that I could become my own best witness.

The tape recorder, with its unrelenting fidelity, captured the unheard or unfinished murmur, the misunderstood and mystifying context, the disembodied voices asking for clarification and comfort. It also captured the impatience in *my* voice as children struggled for attention, approval, and justice. The tape recordings created for me an overwhelming need to know more about the process of teaching and learning and about my own classroom as a unique society to be studied.

---

[1] Rosenthal and Jacobson, *Pygmalion in the Classroom: Teacher Expectations and Pupils' Intellectual Development.* (New York: Holt, Rinehart & Winston, 1968).

The act of teaching became a daily search for the child's point of view accompanied by the sometimes unwelcome disclosure of my hidden attitudes. The search was what mattered — only later did someone tell me it was research — and it provided an open-ended script from which to observe, interpret, and integrate the living drama of the classroom.

I began using the tape recorder to try to figure out why the chidren were lively and imaginative in certain discussions, yet fidgety and distracted in others ("Are you almost finished now, teacher?"), wanting to return quickly to their interrupted play. As I transcribed the daily tapes, several phenomena emerged. Whenever the discussion touched on fantasy, fairness, or friendship ("the three Fs" I began to call them), participation zoomed upward. If the topic concerned, for example, what to do when all the blocks are used up before you can build something or when your best friend won't let you play in her spaceship, attention would be riveted on this and other related problems: Is it fair that Paul always gets to be Luke Skywalker and Ben has to be the bad guy? And, speaking of bad guys, why should the wolf be allowed to eat up the first two pigs? Can't the three pigs just stay home with their mother?

These were urgent questions, and passion made the children eloquent. They reached to the outer limits of their verbal and mental abilities in order to argue, explain, and persuade. No one moved to end the discussion until Justice and Reason prevailed.

After the discussion, a second, more obvious truth emerged. If the tape recorder was left running, what I replayed later and dutifully transcribed became a source of increasing fascination for me. The subjects that inspired our best discussions were the same ones that occupied most of the free play. The children sounded like groups of actors, rehearsing spontaneous skits on a moving stage, blending into one another's plots, carrying on philosophical debates while borrowing freely from the fragments of dialogue that floated by. Themes from fairy tales and television cartoons mixed easily with social commentary and private fantasies, so that what to me often sounded random and erratic formed a familiar and comfortable world for the children.

In fact, the children were continually making natural connections, adding a structure of rules and traditions according to their own logic. They reinvented and explained the codes of behavior every time they talked and played, each child attempting in some way to answer the question, What is going on in this place called school, and what role do I play?

"Let's pretend" was a stronger glue than any preplanned list of topics, and the need to make friends, assuage jealousy, and gain a sense of one's own destiny provided better reasons for self-control than all my disciplinary devices. A different reality coexisted beside my own, containing more vitality, originality, and wide-open potential than could be found in any lesson plan. How was I to enter this intriguing place, and toward what end would the children's play become my work?

The tape recorder revealed that I had already joined the play. I heard myself always as part of the scene, approving, disapproving, reacting to, being reacted to. The question was not *how* would I enter but, rather, *what* were the effects of my intervention? When did my words lead the children to think and say more about their problems and possibilities, and when did my words circumvent the issue and silence the actors? When did my answers close the subject?

Once again, the decisive factor for me was curiosity. When my intention was limited to announcing my own point of view, communication came to a halt. My voice drowned out the children's. However, when they said things that surprised me, exposing ideas I did not imagine they held, my excitement mounted and I could feel myself transcribing their words even as they spoke. I kept the children talking, savoring the uniqueness of responses so singularly different from mine. The rules of teaching had changed; I now wanted to hear the answers I could not myself invent. IQ scores were irrelevant in the realms of fantasy, friendship, and fairness where every child could reach into a deep wellspring of opinions and images. Indeed, the inventions tumbled out as if they simply had been waiting for me to stop talking and begin listening.

Later, teaching at a nursery school, I found that the unanticipated explanations of younger children bloomed in even greater profusion. The crosscurrents of partially overheard talk lifted my curiosity to new heights. It was similar to watching the instant replay of an exciting baseball moment. Did the runner really touch second base? Did Frederick actually say, "My mother doesn't have no more birthdays"? What does a four-year-old mean by this odd statement made in the doll corner? The next day I am pressed to find out.

"Frederick, I'm curious about something I heard you say in the doll corner yesterday. You said your mother doesn't have birthdays any more." (Frederick knows my tendency to begin informal conversations in this manner, and he responds immediately.)

"She doesn't. How I know is no one comes to her birthday and she doesn't make the cake."

"Do you mean she doesn't have a birthday *party*?"

"No. She really doesn't have a *birthday*."

"Does she still get older every year?"

"I think so. You know how much old she is? Twenty-two."

"Maybe you and your dad could make her a birthday party."

"But they never remember her birthday and when it's her birthday they forget when her birthday comes, and when her birthday comes they forget how old she is because they never put any candles. So how can we say how she is old?"

"The candles tell you how old someone is?"

"You can't be old if you don't have candles."

"Frederick, I'll tell you a good thing to do. Ask mother to have a cake and candles. Then she'll tell you when her birthday is."

"No. Because, see, she doesn't have a mother so she doesn't have a birthday."

"You think because your grandma died your mother won't have any more birthdays?"

"Right. Because, see, my grandma borned her once upon a time. Then she told her about her birthday. Then every time she had a birthday my grandma told. So she knew how many candles to be old."

I turn to Mollie. "Frederick says his mother doesn't have any more birthdays."

"Why doesn't she?" Mollie wants to know.

"Because," Frederick answers patiently, "because my grandma died and my mother doesn't know how many candles old she is."

"Oh. Did your grandfather died, too?"

"Yeah. But he came back alive again."

Mollie stares solemnly at Frederick. "Then your grandma told him. If he whispers it to your mother maybe it's already her birthday today."

"Why should he whisper, Mollie?" I ask.

"If it's a secret," she says.

"I think Mollie has a good idea, Frederick. Why don't you ask your grandfather?"

"Okay. I'll tell him if my mommy could have a birthday on that day that they told her it was her birthday."

Why not just tell Frederick the truth: "*Of course* your mother has a birthday; everyone has a birthday." Tempting as it might be to set the record straight, I have discovered that I can't seem to teach the children that which they don't already know.

I had, in fact, made this very statement—that everyone has a birthday—the previous week in another context. I had brought a special snack to school to celebrate my own birthday, and Frederick and Mollie seemed surprised.

"Why?" they asked.

"Why did I bring the cookies?"

"Why is it your birthday?"

"But everyone has a birthday. Today happens to be mine."

"Why *is* it your birthday?" Mollie insisted, attempting to give more meaning to her question by emphasizing another word.

"Well, I was born on this day a long time ago."

The conversation ended and we ate the cookies, but clearly nothing was settled. Their premises and mine did not match. What, for instance, could it possibly mean to be born on *this* day a long time ago?

A week later, Frederick made cause and effect out of the presence of one's own mother and the occasion of a birthday. The matter is not unimportant, because the phenomenon of birthday looms large. It is constantly being turned around and viewed from every angle, as are the acts of going to bed, going to work, cooking meals, shooting bad guys, calling the doctor or the babysitter—to name just a few of the Great Ideas present in the preschool.

Every day someone, somewhere in the room, plays out a version of "birthday." Birthday cakes are made of playdough and sand, and it is Superman's birthday or Care Bear's birthday or Mollie's birthday. "Birthday" is a curriculum in itself. Besides being a study in numbers, age, birth, and death, it provides an ongoing opportunity to explore the three Fs—fantasy, friendship, and fairness.

"You can't come to my birthday if you say that!"

"You *could* come to my birthday, and my daddy will give you a hundred pieces of gum if you let me see your Gobot."

Any serious observation made about a birthday is worth following up, not in order to give Frederick the facts and close the subject, but to use this compelling material as a vehicle for examining his ideas of how the world works. If I am to know Frederick, I must understand, among many other things, how he perceives his mother's birthday and his grandfather's permanence.

As the year progresses I will pick up the threads of these and other misconceptions and inventions in his play, his conversation, his storytelling, and his responses to books and poems. He will make connections that weave in and out of imagined and real events, and I will let my curiosity accompany his own as he discards old stories and creates new ones.

My samples of dialogue are from the kindergarten and nursery school, the classes I teach. But the goal is the same, no matter what the age of the student; someone must be there to listen, respond, and add a dab of glue to the important words that burst forth.

The key is curiosity, and it is curiosity, not answers, that we model. As we seek to learn more about a child, we demonstrate the acts of observing, listening, questioning, and wondering. When we are curious about a child's words and our responses to those words, the child feels respected. The child *is* respected. "What are these ideas I have that are so interesting to the teacher? I must be somebody with good ideas." Children who know others are listening may begin to listen to themselves, and if the teacher acts as the tape recorder, they may one day become their own critics.

Reading between the lines is both easier and harder when the setting is preschool. It is easier because young children rehearse their lines over and over in social play and private monologues, without self-consciousness; older children have already learned to fear exposing their uncommon ideas. On the other hand, the young child continually operates from unexpected premises. The older student's thinking is closer to an adult's and easier to fathom: the inevitability of birthdays is not an issue in the third grade, and the causal relationship between age and candles has long since been solved. Yet, third graders and high school students struggle with their own set of confusions, fantasies, and opinions that need to be listened to, studied, compared, and connected.

The fact that the thoughts of the teacher and student are furthest apart in preschool makes it a fruitful place for research and practice in the art of listening to what children say and trying to figure out what they mean. My curiosity keeps me there, for I still cannot predict what children of three and four will say and do. One must listen to them over long periods of time. Being their teacher provides me the rare luxury of living with my subjects for two years. Like a slow-motion Polaroid developing its images, piece by piece, over many months, the children's patterns of thought and speech need much time to be revealed.

An early conversation with a group of three-year-olds convinced me that these were the children who would best prove my assumption that the first order of reality in the classroom is the student's point of view, for here the pathways to knowledge lead directly through the doll corner and the building blocks. For me this is where the lessons are to be found.

> Carrie has her own version of hide-and-seek, in which she pretends to hide and pretends to seek. She hides a favorite possession, then asks a teacher to help her find it. She pretends to look for it as she takes the teacher directly to the missing item. "Oh, here's my dolly's brush!" she squeals delightedly. All these games resist the unknown and the possibility of loss. They are designed to give the child control in the most direct way.
>
> Sometimes, however, the child has no control; something is really missing. Then the threes are likely to approach the problem as if the question is "What is *not* missing?" This is exactly what happens when I try to direct the children's attention to an empty space in the playground. Over the weekend, an unsafe climbing

structure has been removed. The doll corner window overlooks the area that housed the rickety old frame.

"See if you can tell what's missing from our playground?" I ask.

"The sandbox."

"The squirrely tree."

"The slide."

"But I can *see* all those things. They're still in the playground. Something else was there, something very big, and now it's gone."

"The boat."

"Mollie, look. There's the boat. I'm talking about a big, brown, wooden thing that was right there where my finger is pointing."

"Because there's too much dirt."

"But what was on top of the place where there's too much dirt?"

"It could be grass. You could plant grass."

Libby and Samantha, four-year-olds, see us crowded around the window and walk over to investigate. "Where's the climbing house?" Libby asks. "Someone stoled the climbing house."

"No one stole the house, Libby. We asked some men to take it down for us. Remember how shaky it was? We were afraid somebody would fall."

The threes continue staring, confused. I should have anticipated their response and urged that the structure be dismantled during school hours.[2]

If my words contain more stories than theories, it may be that I have taken on the young child's perspective, which seems to be organized around the imperative of *story*. I am still listening to what the children say, but since the younger children disclose more of themselves as characters in a story than as participants in a discussion, I must now follow the plot as carefully as the dialogue. School begins to make sense to the children when they pretend it is something else. And teaching, in a way, makes sense to me when I pretend the classroom is a stage and we are all actors telling our stories.

We do more than tell our stories; we also act them out. The formal storytelling and acting that often arise out of and run parallel to the children's fantasy play have become a central feature of our day. The children's stories form the perfect middle ground between the children and me, for they enable us to speak to one another in the same language. Much to my surprise, when I moved from the kindergarten to the nursery school, I found that the storytelling and acting were accepted with equal enthusiasm as the natural order, for nearly everything there takes on more recognizable shape in fantasy.

If, in the world of fantasy play, four- and five-year-olds may be called characters in search of a plot, then the three-year-old is surely a character in search of a character.

Place this three-year-old in a room with other threes, and sooner or later they will become an acting company. Should there happen to be a number of somewhat older peers about to offer stage directions and dialogue, the metamorphosis will come sooner rather than later. The dramatic images that flutter through their

[2] Vivian Gussin Paley, *Mollie is Three* (Chicago: University of Chicago Press, 1986), pp. 69–70. Many of the excerpts from *Mollie is Three* do not conform to the original text. The author has taken the liberty of adding a word or phrase to clarify the extracted passages.

minds, as so many unbound stream of consciousness novels, begin to emerge as audible scripts to be performed on demand.[3]

Possibilities for connecting play and outside events are fleeting, but the teacher who listens carefully has many opportunities to apply the glue. In the following episode, Mollie joins the older girls for a pretend valentine party in the doll corner. Here the play is more real to her than the actual event to come. My task is to help Mollie connect the doll corner reality to the classroom celebration — quite different from the usual procedure of connecting *my* reality to a classroom celebration. This is the doll corner version of the holiday.

"Ding-dong. Ring-ring."
"Come in. Who is it?"
"Trick or treat valentine."
"Don't say trick or treat to our house. The baby is sleeping. Don't ring the bell."
"I'm making valentines for the baby. 'I love you.' This spells 'I love you.' "
"Teacher, can you write 'I love you' on my baby valentines? This is my valentine to get married and have a baby. This is Valentine's Day."
"Are you having a valentine party?" I ask Mollie.
"It's the baby's birthday valentine. I'm giving everyone whoever is nice a valentine."

When Valentine's Day arrives Mollie is surprised that her picture valentines are meant to be given away.

"But Mollie, that's why your mother bought them. You're supposed to give one to each child."
"No, it's for me," Mollie insists, starting to cry. "It says M-O-L-L-I-E."
"Mother wrote your name so the children will know they're from you."
She cries vigorously. "I have to bring them home. My mommy said."
"Okay, Mollie. Let's put them back in the box."

Instantly the tears stop. "I'm telling a valentine story and it has a monkey climbed a tree. Then he fell down on a cushion. Then another monkey came."
"Which is the part about Valentine's Day?"
"The part about the monkey climbed a tree." Mollie looks at her box of valentines, then at the table filled with lacy red hearts. Today's event is controlled by others; she can think only of a monkey climbing a tree.

The image of the doll corner valentine party suddenly fills my mind and I gather the children around me. "I have a valentine story for us to act out. Once upon a time there was a valentine family with a mother, father, sister, brother, and baby. They were all busy making valentines because it was Valentine's Day and the baby's birthday also. 'We have to write "I love you" and give them to all the nice animals who ring our bell,' they said. Ring-ring. Who is it? It's the four bears. Good. Here's your valentines. Ring-ring. Who is it? It's the four squirrels. Oh, good. Here's your valentines. Ring-ring. Who is it? It's the four elephants. Oh, very good. Here's your valentines. Ring-ring. Who is it? It's the four rabbits. Oh, very, very good. Here's your valentines. And all you animals must bring your valentines to the baby's birthday valentine party."

Mollie jumps up. "Wait a minute. I'm the sister. I have to get my valentines. I'm supposed to give them to the animals."

Mollie has an entree into the holiday. Moments earlier she was an outsider, just as she was, in fact, to school itself during the first few weeks. She worked her way

[3] Paley, *Mollie is Three*, p. xvi.

to an understanding of school through the same doll corner fantasies that now illuminate Valentine's Day. And I, the outsider to three-year-old thinking, am learning to listen at the doll corner doorway for the sounds of reality.[4]

A month later, Mollie tells her own valentine story. "Once a time the valentines came to a little girl that was Fire Star. It was her birthday that day they came. Her real birthday."

"And was it also the real Valentine's Day?" I ask.

"It *was* the real valentine's birthday and also the real Fire Star and also the pretend Fire Star."

Mollie struggles with the idea of a real and pretend Fire Star. She will attempt to explain this enigma to herself and others as she acts it out, and my questions will not always be of help. Often, in fact, my questions fall flat or add to the confusion. At such times, my expectations and those of the children may be too far apart — or the children *think* they are too far apart.

> The children cannot always figure out the adults' relation to fantasy play. What powers do we possess that might affect the outcome? Can we, for instance, hear the children's thoughts?
>
> "Why is Leslie doing that?" Mollie asks me. Leslie is her baby sister.
>
> "Doing what?" I ask.
>
> "Crying in my head. Did you listen?"
>
> "Mollie, I can't hear the sounds in your head," I reply.
>
> "Margaret, can you hear Leslie crying in my head?" Mollie asks.
>
> "Yeah, I hear her crying in your house," Margaret says.
>
> "She wants milk from her mama, that's why," Mollie informs her.
>
> "I already knew that," Margaret nods.
>
> I must have misread the question. Did Mollie want me to imagine that Leslie was crying? What do the children think about adults' literal approach to events? . . . Such is the concern, I think, when I unexpectedly appear at the door of the doll corner during a hospital drama.
>
> "Come here, nurse," Libby says impatiently to Mollie. "Come here and undress the baby."
>
> "Are you the mother?" Mollie asks.
>
> "Yes, and Peter is the doctor. I'm sick too. Hurry, put the medicine on me. I cut my knee. Put on the stitches, doctor. Look in my mouth. Say you see bumps. Put us in the x-ray."
>
> "Sh! There's the teacher." Mollie points to me as I pass by. "What if she calls this the doll corner?"
>
> "She can't see us. We're in the hospital. It's far away downtown."
>
> "Sh! She'll think it's the doll corner."
>
> "Get inside the hospital. We're getting far away so she doesn't know where the hospital is."[5]

The vivid image of her sister crying and the equally graphic hospital scene present Mollie with a similar worry. Does the teacher understand the nature of the fantasy and, if not, to what extent do the fantasy and its players exist? When Mollie was two, she did not perceive the boundaries of these internal pictures; by the time

---

[4] Paley, *Mollie is Three*, pp. 92–94.
[5] Paley, *Mollie is Three*, pp. 102–103.

she is six, she will know what can be seen and heard by others. But now she may sometimes flounder in doubt between her reality and mine.

So often I drift around on the edge of their knowing without finding a place to land. Here, for example, is a peanut butter and jelly tale that continues to perplex me.

> Of the eight children at my snack table, six ask for peanut butter and jelly on their crackers, one wants plain peanut butter, and one, plain jelly. My question: What did I make more of, peanut butter and jelly or plain peanut butter? The children stare at me blankly and no one answers.
>
> "What I mean is, did more people ask for peanut butter and jelly or did more want plain peanut butter?" Silence. "I'll count the children who are eating peanut butter and jelly." I count to six. "And only Barney has peanut butter."
>
> "Because Barney likes peanut butter," Mollie explains.
>
> "Yes, but did I make more more sandwiches that have both peanut butter and jelly?"
>
> "Because we like peanut butter *and* jelly," Fredrick responds patiently.
>
> My question has misfired again and this time I can imagine several possible reasons. Since everyone is eating peanut butter and/or jelly, the entire group is included in the peanut butter and jelly category. In addition, "more" could refer to those who asked for more than one sandwich. Perhaps the word "plain" is the stumbling block or they may think I want to know why they chose peanut butter with or without jelly.
>
> Another possibility: Peanut butter and jelly may be akin to Peter and the Wolf, in that the words are not easily separated. Thus, "peanut butter and jelly" also represents plain peanut butter or plain jelly.
>
> . . . I anticipate the obvious response, but the children do not follow my thinking. Perhaps at another time they might have accidently linked their images to mine. Of one thing I am certain: had I put my inquiries into dramatic form and given us roles to play, I would have been understood.[6]

Tomorrow we *will* act it out, but probably not with peanut butter and jelly. Images tend to stay fixed for a long time in the young child's mind. No matter. The proper message has come across: confusion — mine or theirs — is as natural a condition as clarity. The natural response to confusion is to keep trying to connect what you already know to what you don't know.

Next time the children and I may be on the same track, and meanwhile we are getting valuable practice in sending signals. As anyone who attends the theater knows, clues and signals are given all along the way, but the answers are never revealed in the first act. The classroom has all the elements of theater, and the observant, self-examining teacher will not need a drama critic to uncover character, plot, and meaning. We are, all of us, the actors trying to find the meaning of the scenes in which we find ourselves. The scripts are not yet fully written, so we must listen with curiosity and great care to the main characters who are, of course, the children.

[6] Paley, *Mollie is Three*, pp. 91–92.

A Teacher's Quest
for a Child's Questions

KATHE JERVIS

The author, who was an observer for a year in another teacher's classroom, offers a reflection on the unfolding relationship between a teacher's unique philosophy and a child's growth. Detailing both the gradual uncovering of the child's questions and the careful response of the teacher who sees progress where others might see only continued stubbornness and misbehavior, the author emphasizes the significance of those aspects of the teacher's craft that cannot be quantified, but that contribute to the rich environment in which a diversity of children can best develop and learn.

This description of one child in an urban third/fourth-grade public school classroom is really about teaching. I was not the teacher.

Ideally, teachers should write about their own classrooms, but the time and energy demanded by teaching precludes this for all but a small handful of teacher-writers. I have written briefly about my own classroom[1] but in less detail and depth than I would have liked, so when the opportunity arose to write about someone else's classroom, I jumped at it. I had begun working in this classroom under the auspices of the Teachers and Writers Collaborative. The following year the class teacher, Karen (as I am calling her), welcomed me as a note-taking observer from September to June. I was not a participating teacher — we agreed that I would write and she would teach — but I was available to the children for conversation and help. Mine was the luxurious perspective of the undistracted eye.

Teachers know how to make good classroom decisions, but they often do not articulate their reasons. My goal was to understand and make explicit what Karen did in the classroom. We need to know more about how individual teachers operate, how they think about children, and how their philosophy influences what they do. We also need to know more about children's unique patterns.

I did not choose Karen's class at random. Aside from the good fortune of finding someone who welcomed my scrutiny and a principal who didn't prevent it, Karen was a good colleague for such a project. Language is central to her whole life. She writes journals, poetry, complaints, notes to parents, and narrative report cards when checklists would be sufficient. Yet, like most teachers, her decisions are intuitive. My presence forced her to state why she acted as she did.

---

[1] Jervis, *Children's Thinking in the Classroom* (Grand Forks, ND: University of North Dakota Press, 1978).

Harvard Educational Review Vol. 56 No. 2 May 1986, 132–150

Further, her teaching intrigued me. She operates from a particularly strong political and philosophical base; her value system is at the forefront of her classroom vision, influencing her every interaction, relationship, and decision about teaching. She strives resolutely for the goals her values dictate. She has a powerful effect on children, perhaps because she is so unconflicted about what she does.

Karen sees her classroom not in terms of an imposed curriculum, but as a group of individuals in a community. She registers, notes, and reveres nuances of how people relate to her and to each other. Her interventions start from these observations. She has an uncanny sense of when to support, when to insist, when to back off, and when to interpret to the child what she sees.

People with her values are not found frequently enough in the teaching profession. Because she frees children from large amounts of teacher-imposed work and allows them to choose their own activities, they seldom develop feelings of incompetence if they do not read or speak as well as other children. Karen does not praise children for good reading or good speaking. On the contrary, she is on a campaign: she passionately attacks those who overvalue verbal facility. She is vitriolic about teachers who reward children for their ability to speak well. It angers her that less verbal children are frequently ignored and overlooked. She notices and encourages strengths that are often undervalued.

The children in her school are diverse along many dimensions: religion, ethnicity, language, and economic status. Karen welcomes every child in this population, even the most difficult, without complaint. She is the one who takes children no other teachers want, and no one wanted Daryl at the time he entered her class. Some teachers might have recommended him for a special education class, but Karen refused.

While all children are extraordinary, Daryl would stand out in any class. His beginning stance was distancing, mute, and provocative; whatever mattered to him was unrecognized by the school community, as he gave no clue to his real self, his aspirations, or his strengths. Karen's focus on Daryl's "quest" (her word for any child's central concerns)[2] allowed him to move beyond the alienating, confrontational persona he presented at school.

Creating the opportunity to discover each child's own questions (the "quest" that Karen takes so seriously) is Karen's most compelling reason for structuring her teaching as she does. She believes children learn by investigating their own questions, "even though on some level all of our questions are the same; how we go about answering them—in what medium and with what materials—is significant

---

[2] One of Karen's core beliefs is in the existence of a "quest," a serious word in her idiosyncratic lexicon. I didn't see its importance until after my year of note-taking was over. Though I criticized much about her practice and we discussed every facet of her teaching, she never changed her views or flinched under my criticism. She simply said, "You are not seeing children's questions." She was right and the clues were there. An article by Beth Alberty so confirmed what she thought that she excerpted the following paragraph and sent it home as part of a notice on parent conferences and field trips (see "Children's Art: Where Art and Education Meet," *ArtworkersNews, 11*, No. 5 (1982), 20–21):

> [Descriptions of children's artwork] are unfinished and partial, but at least they make more visible to us, as interested adults and especially as educators, a personal intentionality on the part of the child that is a form of questing. It is here, to my mind, that art and education meet in children's art, for in its deepest sense, education, like artmaking, is a quest, an inquiry into the world, self, and others from which personal understanding evolves.

in who we are and who we are going to be" (personal communication, 1985). The purpose of giving children class time to pursue activities of their own choice, as Karen does, is to give them more opportunities to show themselves. The more children are known, the more she as teacher can sense what their questions are. She believes that "once I understand a child's questions, I can see the learning in what the child has chosen, and the activities become more legitimate to me as the teacher. Most of the time children can't articulate their vital concerns. When I see what their questions are, then I can help them recognize what they are about" (personal communication, 1985).

Daryl's questions—Who is in control? Where do I fit in? What are my limits? Who is imposing them? How can I get around them?—are typical questions fourth graders ask as they grow toward autonomy. For some reason we will never know, Daryl needed more latitude to find answers than most children. For the two years he was in her class, Karen saw that he had it.

Daryl: A Child in Need of an Anchor

I first met Daryl in the middle of his third-grade year, when I came to teach drama. My early memories of him are filled with images of leaping or floating. His thin torso was loose and graceful, but his arms, just hanging, were magically attached and seemed unrelated to the rest of him. He appeared not to be anchored to the ground. He seemed to propel himself, gazelle-like, on and off the tables, as if the only way to get from one side of the room to the other was on the tops of furniture—a brown blur bounding through my line of vision on his way to nowhere.

During that third-grade year, the children nearby were as inaccessible to him as the floor beneath his feet. He had no friends and probably spent as much time roaming the halls as he did wafting about the classroom.

One thread, however tenuous, did connect Daryl with various adults. I vividly remember glimpses of him as I moved through the school. He would be standing motionless, silent, sleepy-eyed, an eight-year-old of average height, looking up at the grown figure facing him. The only sign that he was relating to this adult was a certain angular jutting of his chin—as if, despite his overwhelmingly passive body language, this was the one part of him that represented resistance to adult authority. Opposite Daryl's statuelike pose, the adult would be in a position of full-stage alert, rising to maximum stature, eyes flashing, often lecturing, threatening, or confronting. Undeniably, Daryl had difficulty with authority, but the symptoms usually showed up more dramatically in the adult response.

What we gleaned about his life out of school revealed the same detached child we saw in school. He came to school on the bus—a long ride each way—with other black children, none of whom he knew well. Opportunity for him to make friends on the bus was limited; early in the year he had angered the bus driver and was confined to the front seat, where he was admonished to sit silently. Restive under these constraints, he was always on the verge of being kicked off the bus. When he returned home each afternoon, Daryl went to a local after-school program, whose other participants went to neighborhood schools. This program provided no sanctuary. In a rare moment he confided the problem, "Kids at my after-school tease me 'cause I go to this white school." He was estranged from his most natural peer group and felt compelled to defend his "white school." Daryl was caught with no social anchor, uptown or downtown. Once again he was floating.

Karen believed that before Daryl could make any progress, he needed an anchor. He chose to anchor himself to her, characteristically on his own terms. Usually flexible about rules, Karen has one that is almost unbreakable — the classroom door is locked at lunchtime and no children may intrude on her privacy. Daryl, however, after knocking on the door and jumping up high to peek in the window, was reluctantly admitted one day during the sacred lunch period. He began to come up every lunch period on some pretext — he'd forgotten some food, his comic book, his jacket, something essential to his lunch hour welfare. Since no child so careful of his possessions would intentionally "forget," Karen let him in; he would retrieve the item and ask, "What are you eating?" or inform her of his fatigue and wait for her response, then leave. One day he hurt himself on the playground and came up to cry in her presence. Those tears were the first emotional connection he made to Karen; thereafter, lunchtime visits became a ritual, a singular point of relatedness in Daryl's day.

At the end of his third-grade year the entire faculty — except Karen — saw a child who was isolated from peers at home and at school, who was locked in passive battles with white authorities, who thumbed his nose at routines, who abstained from visible work, who exempted himself from group activities, and who, to tighten the noose around his own neck, did poorly on standardized tests.

Daryl's third-grade year, however, was more productive than it appeared on the surface. Though he irritated authorities as soon as he stepped outside the threshold of room 312, inside he had Karen's unconditional acceptance. He formed a solid relationship with Karen, his first attachment to an adult in the school, his first to any white adult authority figure, and maybe even his first important attachment to any adult outside of his family. No other task could have been more crucial. A sense of belonging, whether to the peer group or to part of the hierarchy, is a necessary condition for learning, especially in an institutional setting, and Daryl's relationship with Karen drew him toward the community, reducing his isolation from both children and adults. Karen communicated to Daryl that he was a valued person whether or not he fit into the class.

Daryl in Fourth Grade: Time and Resistance

By fourth grade, Daryl and Karen had a solid relationship, but having him in class was not easy. To a teacher in charge of children in large groups, one of his most exasperating characteristics was the immense quantity of time he took to change from one activity to another. He could run at top speed on a field trip to be the first person across the bridge or at the head of the line walking through Central Park, but he could also be the last, lagging far behind. Then he was like a twig lodged against a rock in the stream of classroom events. Daryl got stuck, though all reason dictated that he should have moved with the rest of the class. The excessive time he needed for adult-dictated transitions was unreasonable for any teacher who had to engineer complicated schedules for children in groups. Whether he was holding onto a shred of autonomy or executing a passive maneuver to make authorities angry, the result was disruptive.

Rather than nagging him to be prompt, Karen accepted his unsynchronized day because she felt he needed to be on the edge of any group, either first or last, so that he could explore the personal and institutional boundaries of which he was so unsure. She felt he was not ready for the conventional discipline which shapes mature classroom behavior.

Karen's attitude of acceptance extended to Daryl's academic work as well. Some researchers correlate time-on-task with measurable learning outcomes. Karen does not. She is unconcerned with children wasting this currency which teachers are always admonishing children not to squander. She believes that lasting significant results occur over the long term, that children cannot be forced to grow like hothouse orchids, and that their growth cannot be quantified. Measurements can identify only trivial, testable gains, but only elusive, not easily enumerated gains matter. And those, she believes, are nourished by an abundance of time. She felt Daryl needed time, measured in months, to make friends, and time, measured in years, to mature. Time would result eventually in more disciplined behavior and more learning. She was not in a hurry to measure progress, and she did not hurry Daryl to learn faster.

In any case, compelling Daryl to meet a classroom timetable would have been fruitless, as he resisted direct instruction. His unwillingness to learn in a group was extreme; sometimes it took all his energy just to conform outwardly and he could do no more than that. From my notes on November 19th:

> At the Metropolitan Museum, his small group stopped to look in detail at Cezanne's *Card Players*, which required all six children to face forward. Daryl refused and sat with his back to the painting. In a rare moment of insistence, Karen took the time to make an issue. "I ask so little of you. Turn around." Moved perhaps by the urgency in her voice, he oriented his body somewhat closer to the painting, but he volunteered nothing and as far as I could tell, looked a million miles away.

Standardized testing is the epitome of necessary compliance. He willfully resisted during the entire week. This is only one example:

> Every test section begins with two sample questions. For five days, three times a day, Daryl marked the answers to the samples where the first real answers were meant to be, making answers out of sequence from the beginning. On Monday it was understandable; by Friday it was willful. Some could be fixed, others couldn't. On one reading test Daryl's score was lower than chance.

Always the effort required to submit drained energy from the work itself:

> On June 4th, Karen asked Daryl to complete the math work on the board. The first problem is 164 x 20, and he has answered 2,128. Karen asks him to do it again and he argues, "But I have so much math. Can't I do it at home?" Karen insists. He protests, "I don't know how." She sets it up for him (100 x 20; 60 x 20; 4 x 20). He does it with her sitting next to him. When he gets the answer, he has a big, satisfied smile. He says, "finished," as if he has been working at hard labor for an hour rather than three minutes on computation.

The case for a steady diet of direct instruction is weak for many children and hopeless for children like Daryl. Assigned classwork only creates an arena for conflict as teachers lament, "I taught him, but he just won't learn." Some children resist learning when they have no control, but because their behavior is less extreme than Daryl's, a settled routine results; they have an unspoken contract with the teacher—"I won't cause trouble if you don't make demands"—and class time is spent copying off the board and completing other nonengaging tasks.

In some classrooms, Daryl's behavior would have been an obstacle rather than the platform on which further growth could take place. Rather than absorbing Daryl into the group and accepting his rhythm, Karen could have silenced him by demands to "hurry up," "be still," "get out," all of which might have kept him where he started: mute and outside the group. Karen accepted Daryl, unregulated as he was. By allowing him to contribute when he was ready and on his own terms, she enabled him to change from a silent isolate into someone about whom she could write in her final report, "Daryl has made enormous social growth this year. He is part of and central to the class. He is not on the outskirts, nor does he want to be."

Karen had an intuitive sense of Daryl's questions, though what they were and how she figured them out remained a mystery to me throughout the year. Only after studying my notes and Daryl's notebooks did I come to understand what Karen had been doing. My constant questions also forced her to articulate why she made the decisions she did. But it was Daryl who yielded evidence that her strategies supported his growth.

Choice, Drawing, and Shared Perspectives

How Daryl got from the outskirts of the class to its center is not one linear story of unimpeded progress. I have recorded dates and told the story chronologically, but Daryl's growth, like everyone's, is not of one piece.

Daryl's attachment to Karen and her acceptance of him were crucial, but their bonds were embedded in her classroom philosophy, especially her attitude toward choice. Karen believes that giving children freedom to choose how they spend classroom time enables them to make their own preferences clearer to themselves and others. The classroom then becomes a community of persons sharing their perspectives.

Karen describes what that means in vivid and idiosyncratic language. What matters to Karen is that children have a "place" (a secure sense of themselves in the group), that they "stand tall" (speak for themselves in the group), and that they do not hide behind masks or retreat from the give-and-take of peers. Nurturing these qualities in school requires a classroom where, as Karen recorded in her journal of December 16, 1980, "Children are getting angry and sharing it, finding solutions on their own without rage, becoming proud of their effort and work. The central theme of my class is living together and sharing perspectives." Karen strives for community, but not unity. The atmosphere in her class is not a medium which cultivates homogeneity. Ensuring a "place" for each child emphasizes diversity; differences make for choices. She does not question children's choices. Daryl chose to draw.

When Daryl gravitated to the drawing table, Karen assumed his reason would eventually be clear to her. The record surrounding Daryl's drawing demonstrates (often to my surprise) that what he drew and what he chose to say and write about drawing confirmed Karen's conviction that he needed extraordinary space to explore boundaries and find his own direction. When given this space, he thrived.

Initially I believed that any slice of the record would document Daryl's undeniable growth, and I chose to look at his drawing because he chose drawing. Now it is clear to me that drawing was crucially intertwined with his development as a person. Close observation at the drawing table turned out to be as important for my understanding as the resulting drawings. Often children's finished work is only a small, though significant, artifact of what transpires while they draw.

Daryl brought to drawing, as he brought to everything, his own style and rituals. He preferred cartooning, and in the beginning he traced characters from comic books. Then he taught himself to copy them and finally executed them freehand, a development which took several months. Persistence with the tracing book and freehand practice required effort. He persevered until he could draw what he called a "cartoon universe." His involved concentration and labor—more than he ever applied to assigned work—ensured a measure of skill and satisfaction. His drawing was a spontaneous outlet for self-expression and an exercise in disciplined self-teaching.

A teacher-chosen art activity might have served a similar community-building purpose, but Daryl's drawing was pressure-free, without any need to bend to group standards and demands. A class mural might have failed, because he would have resisted any external constraints.

Daryl's interest in drawing first surfaced in second grade, but because he refused to put his pens away and move on to other work, his drawing became an arena for confrontation with the teacher rather than a vehicle for growth. In Karen's class, drawing was as legitimate as reading, receiving neither more nor less approval than any other activity.

While Daryl drew, he surveyed the classroom, positioning himself as if he were not going to be there long. From my notes in early September:

> He is perched on a picnic bench, balanced on his knees, which are crossed, leaning far over the table. He never sits solidly and looks as if he could either take flight or be wafted away at any moment. He is drawing in his Drawing Book and has a pencil, provided by Karen at his request. He is not uninvolved with his drawing; his mouth is slightly open in concentration and his expressionless eyes cast downward, but at the same time he is monitoring the action in the rest of the room. Others are drawing congenially in twos and threes, but Daryl is at a table alone.

Is he using drawing as an excuse to observe before participating? "Better to be checking out the action in the room than out in the hallway," Karen said.

Had Daryl been the only one to draw, the social benefits would have been less striking, but drawing is natural for children at this age. They often spend free time drawing at home or in the interstices of a class which permits it, usually after all the teacher-assigned work is finished. In Karen's class, drawing was an appropriate activity which allowed children enough time to focus on each other, meeting a need rarely recognized in most schools. The social nature of drawing enhanced Karen's goal that every child find a "place." Children chatted as they drew, asking each other questions and discussing their views on the world. This is what Karen means by sharing perspectives.

Drawing has two other components which were good for Daryl's growth. First, it anchored him to one physical location. As his noisy disruptiveness made him newly visible, a stationary position at the drawing table gave children the opportunity to make overtures to him that they could not make when he was floating around the room or out in the halls. Second, drawing calmed him and saved him from his old forms of misbehavior. When faced with a new situation, a test, or a transition, he drew. When the music was "scary" at a concert, he took his pens from his back pocket and drew on the program. Before standardized tests, he drew. He found safety in drawing: the act of sitting with pencil and paper helped him cope.

Karen felt Daryl needed exposure to his more social peers through the mutual exchange and conversation which accompanies drawing. He needed to learn to focus on others as he had not the previous year. This leisurely drawing time gave him the chance to be included in a small friendship group and, as Karen said, "learn how it's done."

His socializing developed tentatively. As he reached out to others, his overtures were not hasty. But over the fall I observed a progression. First, Daryl appears in my notes drawing in various places alone; then silently with Jason and Terry; then with Arnie and Jeremy; then with Jason, Arnie, Jeremy, and David. The following excerpt from my notes shows him making a rare, early overture to another child and quickly withdrawing, but in it are the seeds of future friendship:

On October 5th Daryl is at a central table, knees on the bench, body resting on his crossed legs, tracing comic book characters from *Crazy Magazine*. Arnie is sitting next to him. Daryl says, "Play you a game of Space Invaders?" This is the first time I have witnessed such an initiative. Arnie nods, changes his position, gets out a clean piece of paper, and says, partly for my benefit, "I played last year every recess." Daryl adds, "I never played at all last year."

Arnie is the acknowledged class expert at this game. It is played by two or more players and the point is to destroy an opponent's bases. The strategic location of bases can impede attack. The only constraint is a firmly held pencil which is manipulated as a bomb. The distance a bomb can travel is the length of one pencil mark, about 1½ inches.

Daryl and Arnie draw their bases and agree on dividing their paper more or less equally. Daryl is using Karen's personal marker. "Can I use your pencil?" Daryl asks me. I trade with him, but he isn't satisfied (a stalling move?) with my wobbly eraser. He goes ever so slowly across the room to get three new pencils from his briefcase.

Arnie masterfully holds his pencil poised to destroy an asteroid. Daryl is much more tentative and is clearly outclassed.

After two or three rounds, lasting maybe four minutes, Daryl stops. All of a sudden, with no verbal communication, Daryl has retreated, and Arnie is playing alone.

Kamal, who takes the bus with Daryl, sits down next to him and Daryl switches into his performing mode — louder voice, phonier tone. I sense he is playing to an audience. Kamal and Daryl begin to draw on one piece of paper. Kamal draws USA in red on one of Daryl's space ships. Daryl says loudly, "Don't do that." Kamal invites Daryl to draw on his ship. Daryl retorts, "We're playing our way," casting an eye on Arnie's deftly drawn game.

Kamal and Daryl are sitting very close, their bodies touching. There is a cast of silliness to the whole enterprise, but it seems to me a genuine interaction and involvement with each other. Those are rare for Daryl. When Kamal stops drawing to put a Band-Aid on his finger, Daryl wordlessly helps him to get it on properly.

This interaction with Kamal would have been wholly gratifying had it not taken place exactly as Karen announced, "Time to line up for the yard." Daryl and Kamal played while the class complied with Karen's request. Mary, the student teacher, asked Daryl to line up and then grabbed his pencil away in an affectionate physical tussle. He acknowledged her with a smile but didn't move. Finally Kamal said in a parental tone, "Come on, Daryl, do it." But Daryl didn't budge, and Mary put down the pencil and left with the group. Only after more than four minutes of slow-motion organizing was Daryl ready to leave, but Kamal waited for him and they went out together.

Daryl's overtures, when they occurred at all, were usually awkward. They were often disruptive because the time or topic was inappropriate. He needed to learn, almost by successive approximation, how and when to initiate, but his attempts were complicated by his insensitivity to what was going on around him. "Time for him to know and become known," was Karen's prescription for his yet-to-be-developed ability to relate to individual children.

A "black group" formed temporarily in the early fall, and Daryl's inclusion in it helped him cross the line from disruptive performance to more genuine friendship with a smaller group. Ten black children, four of whom were female, stuck together and to the black student teacher, as she put it, "like white on rice." This group spent long hours of uninterrupted time together, collaborating on stories, drawing, finding out about each other's favorite music, testing power relationships, making allies and enemies, computing math problems, and differentiating themselves from the rest of the class in an effort to feel safe in this primarily white environment. Daryl, while not an active force, hung on the fringes of the group and was included by virtue of his color. I saw him watching the wrestling on the gym mats or sitting in the corner reading his *Smurfs*, next to others who were oblivious to him but tolerant of his neutral presence. One day at the end of October, Daryl moved to the center of this group. It was two o'clock, time for writing daily logs. Six children were at the table.

> Easy transition from meeting to work. Daryl sits down with the "black group" who are assembled at a table in the corner of the room. He has written in his log during silent reading (though Karen said he could not), and he is proud of his long, finished entry. He is making a pretense of drawing, but he is really interested in distracting the group, telling elephant jokes and using street language. It is the first time I have seen him funny with words rather than slapstick gestures. Daryl is supplying the energy and a new impetus every time conversation lulls. There is much giggling and camaraderie among the boys. The girls are merely observers, but a crucial audience. Daryl has a kind of uncharacteristic charm, quite unlike his mute presence or the exaggerated ham I have seen before, and is clearly enjoying himself.

When Karen decided this "black group" felt secure enough for unity again, she said to them one afternoon, "What is this? The back of the bus?" Though she continued to ease these children gently back into the larger unit, Daryl took advantage of this ready-made group to begin to develop relationships. But a group could be a vehicle for Daryl's growth only when he contributed appropriately. His skill in drawing gave him a better opening than distracting others; it didn't, however, necessarily encourage better timing, as the following anecdote shows.

Under Karen's direction, the class composed an illustrated book of "Stories and Poems We Made Together" which could be given as a Christmas gift. Daryl volunteered his "friends" to do the illustrating, marking a point in the year when one could say he had a congenial group of peers with whom to draw. But characteristically he contributed on his own terms, insisting that his illustration could be done only during silent reading: "I can't read—I hafta draw another picture to go with Terry's story because my first one got lost." Request granted.

The Christmas book was teacher-organized. By January, Daryl and his friends spontaneously produced a series of collaborative "Joke Books." The idea was to copy jokes from library books, make them up, or get them from classmates' joke books. The jokes were inscribed and then illustrated. "Welcome to the Daryl, Jamel, and Nick Joke Book" reads one, and then below, "Made by the Art and Joke Club." "The Jamel-N-Daryl Drawing-N-Joke Book" is nine pages of drawings and captions, no jokes. The theme of superheroes is emblazoned across each page, accompanied by smaller subtitles: "Justice vs. the Demons," "Justice vs. the Cosmic Craters," and "Justice in Death."

These collaborative efforts were contagious; they spread through the class and absorbed more children than just the "black group." They incorporated even the boys who usually played sophisticated pencil-and-paper war strategy games. As the most prolific of joke book producers, Daryl was becoming known for his cartooning skill and even sought after as a partner. In September he had not been capable of consistent participation—much less leadership—in a class discussion, on the playground, or even in the corridors. But drawing, matching as it did his own preferences, enabled Daryl to test out a more positive role instead of being typed as the class ham or the distracter par excellence.

This spate of joke books coincided with Daryl's beginning to behave differently, at least within the classroom. He communicated more openly, was out of the room less (though he almost always left when a visitor came), and more willingly risked new experience. There was a gradual shift in how he reacted to the rules. He still offered whiny resistance, or complained, "I'm too tired" or "Do I have to?" But he eventually lined up, joined the circle, or otherwise did what he was asked to do. These changes sprang from various corners of life under Karen's tutelage, but his improvement and his new social "place," carved out at the drawing table, seemed connected.

By March the joke book phenomenon had died down, but the pattern was set for shared art. Evidence of this shared activity comes from both the art room and Daryl's journal.

The art room was the only location outside the classroom where he did not invite antagonism. The lunchroom aide was quite specific, telling me one January day, "If you want to give me a nervous breakdown, just send me Daryl," but after lunch Daryl behaved like a "straight kid." During recess at P.S. 135, children can choose among gym activities, outside games, or the art room. The art room was a dream setup for a child like Daryl and provided essential support in much the way Karen did: no direct instruction, no lessons, just materials and a chance to explore. Students from grades K through 5 worked side by side. Daryl could enter and exit at will, float around to see where the action was, momentarily involve himself, and move on. He spent time there every day.

Excerpts from his daily log:

3/31 I went to the art room with Nick and he drew a space picture.

4/4 I went to gym and went to the art room and my friend drew me and my friend a picture.

4/20 . . . Then I went to the art room and drew space ships.

4/22 Then I went to the art room so then my friend drew me a picture.

4/29 Then I went to the art room with my friend and he drew me a Garfield and then I drew in my Drawing Book.

5/6 Then I went to the art room and my friend Hugh drew me a picture.

5/7 Then I went to the art room and drew my friend Tyrone something. Then I drew another picture for my friend Ebbin.

None of the children he mentions, except Nick, were in his class. This group regularly congregated in the art room; they were the school's most passionate artists. The fact that Daryl was a part of their reciprocal gift-giving ritual shows how far he had come out of his social isolation and how much he felt a part of the entire school community. This was major growth.

Pencils, Paper, and Daryl's Drawing Book

Karen and I have radically different attitudes toward classroom materials, so I paid special attention to basic supplies in her classroom. I am constantly provisioning and organizing; Karen leaves it up to the children. But far from being indifferent, her strong teaching values extend to pencils and paper.

In keeping with her philosophy that children need to contribute for the good of their own education, Karen provided few supplies. Supplies were the children's responsibility and, by extension, their parents', who, she believed, should be deeply involved in the classroom. Children were encouraged — even required — to bring in pencils for the whole class. "My own pencil" was not a phrase supportive of Karen's idea of community. Shared materials were the norm, and she considered children's use or abuse of them indicative of how far they had come toward her vision of community. Many teachers in this era of inadequate budgets resort to their own pocketbooks. When Karen contributed, she did so for the whole school. Through her mother's workplace she had access to a seemingly endless quantity of the highest quality eighteen by twenty-four inch white drawing paper, and the entire P.S. 135 population enjoyed that luxury. Her classroom depended on materials donated by its members to be used by everyone.

Daryl brought materials from home, and what he shared and what he hoarded provided an interesting commentary on his growth. He kept his collection of essentials in top condition: thin-tipped pens, a drawing notebook, and a pad of tracing paper. He stored his pencils in his cubby and frequently expressed surprise that anyone would "bring in pencils for the whole class when the class hadn't done nothin' in return." But he rarely used his own pencils, preferring to borrow one from an adult. He never loaned his pens and took such care of them that no one dared to ask. They were kept in his back pocket where he could get to them in a hurry, and he touched them often just to check their whereabouts. He followed the losses of other people's pens carefully, though he never lost his own or became involved in ownership disputes.

He owned an extensive collection of comic books which he brought each day. This meticulously cared-for resource became a necessary prop for his drawing, and possibly smoothed his entry into the class social life. Although he didn't lend his pens, he shared the precious comics; it was the combined activity suggested by comic books and drawing that provided his first collaborative work projects.

That he hoarded pencils and refused to contribute to the class supply, yet lent his comics, was curious. My sense was that he knew the comics were his and he would continue to own them, but he could not reconcile giving up consumables to others without any tangible return. This was true through the end of the year, but Karen says she has confidence that a fond dream of hers will come true—"that somewhere, in a classroom I will never hear about, Daryl will bring ten pencils for the whole class without being asked."

Some children use possessions to engage others in acts of friendship, but Daryl lent comics without ceremony to anyone who was interested. Early in the year he had no investment in any particular children, and those who gravitated to the drawing/cartooning activities were the natural borrowers. Karen was ever alert to children who "buy off" others and would not have allowed the comics to remain had Daryl used them to include and exclude.

Karen organized very little. "How can I organize for children I haven't met?" was Karen's response before school opened to my asking why she didn't devise procedures for organizing materials. Though she appreciated every scrap of writing or drawing and valued the thought and the child who created it, she just didn't value its corporeal manifestation—that it needed a place in the classroom on real shelves with real mechanisms for keeping it in order. As she pointed out in one of our heated discussions of this issue, "Those children for whom organization is important maintain that organization without me." Daryl was one of those children. The environmental chaos did not seem to touch him; he remained meticulously organized all year.

Despite the availability of all Karen's wonderful drawing paper, Daryl chose to draw in a lined composition book. He labeled it "Daryl's Drawing Book" and generally carried it with him or kept it in his cubby. He never left it lying around, nor did he ever misplace it or leave it at home. He did not date the pages but drew on them in order, leaving no pages blank. He never did math or wrote stories in this book (with one important exception), though he occasionally added fragmentary captions.

This Drawing Book was very much a part of him. When I wanted to Xerox it at the end of the year, he could hardly bear to part with it, even for an hour. When I insisted, Karen rushed over. (She would have taken his side had any real dispute developed.) Daryl complained to her, "She thinks it's like a treasure." We both said in unison, "It is." He was pleased enough by my interest to consent to the book's absence during music, if I promised to have it back by recess. However, he had the last word. He pulled a straight-faced joke on me, making me promise not to return his book all white. I agreed without understanding, but when I gave it back to him, he said, "Good. I thought you were going to Clorox it."

The Content of the Drawing Book

The Drawing Book exudes energy and motion. Some figures are fully drawn, others are moving sticks achieved by swiftly dashed-off lines. Explosions pepper most pages. Some pages have captions, some don't. There are no stories or assignments. This is an artist's sketchbook with experiments, doodles, and half-finished work.

Daryl didn't start out drawing in this vivid way. At first he taped tracing paper to comic books and traced characters over and over until he felt ready to draw them freehand. He valued his tracing—and perhaps the confidence it gave him—so much that a substitute teacher once outraged him by insisting his tracing was "babyish." She had passed out tracing paper and colored tissue paper for children to tear up and make scenes of spring. Daryl matter-of-factly refused, saying, "I did this in kindergarten," and proceeded to trace from a book. The substitute continued to argue that tracing was "a crutch, and a mindless activity." His defense was weak—"Karen lets us trace." He was the only one who ever traced, but his use in late May of "us" bespoke his new community feeling. He stopped the tracing, but from that moment on he provoked this woman mercilessly, as only he knew how. Daryl's tracing was important to him; he depended on this safe method of learning that contributed to his pleasure and eventually to his skill.

In the Drawing Book, immobile cartoon characters without Daryl's special stamp are occasionally interspersed with his action drawings. When asked by a teacher to draw during class, he often returns to these stereotyped drawings, but the work he did for himself is much more expressive.

Karen saw his cartooning in a broader context. "Cartoon," she reminded me, "has other meanings, one of which is a preparatory design for a larger work." Daryl's larger work, according to Karen, was to explore his own questions. Looking in detail at one page in his Drawing Book illuminates his unique perspective, as would any slice of his drawing, writing, or behavior.

The drawing I have chosen to describe here was done during February, with a very thin Magic Marker. The nine furiously active figures are suspended in midair like trapeze artists, floating without visible ground to anchor them, but Daryl has supplied an imaginary floor to give them leverage to push or kick. Facial expressions (hard to study in a reproduced version) show anger, exertion, and concentration. Like many of Daryl's drawings, the triangularity stands out: three figures in each of three groups are connected by lines which instinctively cause the viewer to supply a missing hypotenuse. The top third of the page is blank, and these three triangular shapes plus an obscure figure in the lower right form a parallelogram.

Conflict is the subject, and ambiguity reigns. The muscular figures are neither clothed nor naked. Each of them deploys a weapon, superheroic body force, or both. Each emits a laser-like beam, or a defense against it. The essentially parallel lines which connect the figures either begin or end in short radiating bursts which might be devastating explosions or protective shields. Action dominates, but meaning is obscured. Is there a story? Are these the same figures over time? Is there any outcome? Hard to tell.

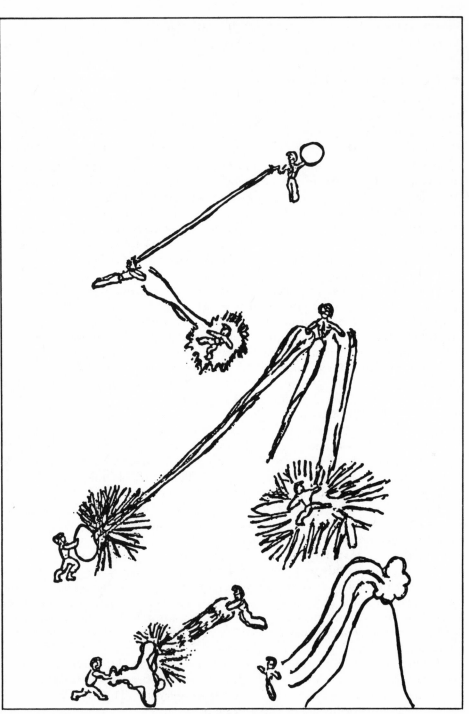

Daryl's Drawing

Power seems to be at issue, but unlike hand-to-hand combat this is power-at-a-distance. Who has the power? Is it two against one? Or one against two? The power is so symmetrical it is impossible to tell. Elegantly balanced, this is a collision of equals; no one conquers, and no one is conquered. The overriding impression is tension among the combatants as they challenge and resist.

Daryl's thought, as in all cartoons, is condensed, abbreviated, and conveyed by parsimonious lines. Cartooning is a tightly-bound medium. This is not the comic book plot of good prevailing over evil, but rather Daryl's perspective on attack and resistance. He has captured the tension between and among his characters without identifying his own viewpoint. This is a place where ambiguity and lack of clarity could exist within tight boundaries, an arena for Daryl's own explorations.

Every child's drawings are uniquely expressive, though some adults find it easy to dismiss children's cartoon-style drawing as trite, unoriginal, and repetitive. For that reason, Daryl's cartoons did not get the attention they deserved during the year from me or any of the other adults in his life, except Karen.[3] She valued his drawings and attended to his self-image as an artist.

Daryl approached institutional life so hesitantly but with such insistence on his own conditions that when he disclosed any part of himself at school, Karen took notice. Daryl first identified himself out loud as an artist when the dance teacher asked children what they were going to be for Halloween. After some coaxing, Daryl answered, "a artist." Though he wore no costume for the traditional school parade, Karen took it that "the thought was in his head."

Except for the Christmas books, Karen's role in how the children spent their free time was characteristically indirect, so any intervention took on a heightened significance. On January 19, sitting next to Daryl as he traced, she said quietly, "I knew someone who made a whole comic book and told a story with tracings. Maybe you could do that." No requirements, no pressure, just a casually tossed-off comment, but her tone conveyed conviction that he could do whatever he wanted to do. Daryl responded as if he were sharing a secret, "I know what I want to be when I grow up," he said, enumerating on his fingers, "a artist and a storyteller."

In January he wrote in his Drawing Book: "Daryl is not a drawer, he is a good drawer." In February he had expertise to share and added a PR touch at the end:

Today kids we're going to draw cartoon people with Daryl.

No. 1 You draw a head with some ears.

No. 2 Then you start to draw some eyes with a nose and a mouth.

---

[3] During the year, though I saw his drawing as a mark of social progress, I did not look carefully at the content. I scooped the Joke Books off the floor, worried that they were casually treated by the children, and marvelled only that there were so many of them, a goodly number not finished. Karen was characteristically unconcerned. I took them, along with the "Cloroxed" Drawing Book, off to the Prospect Summer Institute and left them on my shelf, ignored, until a college-level children's art teacher pounced on them when she came to my room for a chat. We had been discussing her doctoral research, a once-a-week class with children where she determined the agenda. She had photographed and catalogued all the products beautifully, but she was dissatisfied. All the Institute participants had oohed and aahed over her slides, but she felt her children's work was "inauthentic." When she saw Daryl's work, she exclaimed, "This is what I mean by authentic. This work has the stamp of the child all over it. What I wouldn't give to have access to a class that did artwork like this." She made me take another look at what Daryl had invested in his drawing and to pay more attention to how important it was for him to have the opportunity to draw.

No. 3 And then you start to draw the Body with some clothes and some shoes.
No. 4 Then you write your name and tell your friends that you drew it.
And that's all.

In June, modestly but with confidence, he announced to a group of peers, "I am a better drawer than some. In fact I'm a good drawer."

Karen picked up these fleeting references and made them more salient to Daryl, his classmates, and me. Between the art room and the classroom he was becoming known to other children for his cartooning.

In February, when he wrote an undisguised autobiographical story in his Drawing Book (the only composition to appear there), Karen took it as his effort "to make himself more visible to himself and others." She believes one function of written self-expression is to "hear yourself as you write." She said, "Daryl is addressing his family to make them see who he is and understand that he is a strong person in his own right, entitled to his own goals and preferences." This is the composition, corrected for punctuation to make it more readable, but uncorrected for spelling (he made no errors) and grammar.

> Once upon a time there was a boy name Daryl and he like drawing and wanted to be a artist. But his brother said "No, no, no, be a football player." "No, no, no, be a painter," said his mother and then his father said, "Wait a minute now. If Daryl wants to be a artist let him be a artist." "That's right mommy. I'm going on ten and you keep telling me to be a painter," said Daryl. "But don't you want to be like Rembrandt?" "No," said Daryl. "Why?" "Because I like to draw pictures," said Daryl. So one day Daryl made a picture and his father said "Wow, that's great. I'll go and show it to your mother." "No," said Daryl. "She might say 'he shoulda painted it.' " "So what. Don't let that get in your way," said the father. "Okay. She could see it, but I will show it to her." So Daryl showed his mother and his mother saw it and called Kirk and Kirk said "Daryl should be an artist after all," and Daryl got married and been a artist. — The End

The narrator starts out in the powerful language of the storyteller: "Once upon a time there was a boy named Daryl who wanted to be a artist." He names the boy Daryl, but puts some distance between himself and the story by choosing to write in the third person. Fairytale-like, the story begins with a goal for the future, poses obstacles to surmount, and has a happy ending.

Daryl's task is to overcome the "no, no, no's" showered on him by his mother and brother, which are not so much life-threatening as soul-threatening. His father is the enabler who runs interference, the catalyst for Daryl's growth: "Wait a minute now. If Daryl wants to be a artist, let him be a artist." Three times his father intervenes, and each time Daryl stands up for himself and his increasing maturity. Daryl begins to argue for himself, and then, foregoing merely oral argument, he draws a good picture and proves his qualifications. Still, he is not yet strong enough to stand entirely on his own. The final arbiter is his brother Kirk, who gives the needed permission: "Daryl should be an artist after all." Daryl wins out. The story ends romantically despite a plot devoid of romance: "Daryl got married and been a artist."

From the first, Daryl knows what he wants and persists until he engineers an agreement. He is caught in a typical preadolescent dilemma; he depends on his family's approval, even as he resists their advice. He is saying, "I'm going on ten years old and you are still telling me how to run my life." But he still needs their reassurance and approval.

"This composition," Karen says, "is about growing up, making choices, and having aspirations. Daryl is struggling with the coming of age that allows us to get onto the next stage." Karen has protected Daryl against the "no, no, no's" which thwart his own inner direction. She has been an enabler, giving him space and encouragement. In turn, Daryl has adopted one of her most characteristic sayings, "Don't let that get in your way." "If Daryl wants to be an artist, let him be an artist" is exactly how Karen feels about honoring children's preferences.

This writing could easily have been ignored, like his cartoons, or used to demonstrate sticky family politics, limited vocabulary, immature style, or puzzling confusion between painters and artists, rather than as an entry into how he views the world. Karen assumes that each act of self-expression, each spoken word, and each classroom choice is a significant statement and deserves respectful attention. To understand those choices is her quest.

Daryl's Questions

Conversation on June 3rd:

Daryl: I want to be the first and only one on the moon.
Jeremy: But you wouldn't have any friends.
Daryl: But then I'd see what the future is like.

Conversation on June 25th:

Daryl: Hey, what age would you be if you could be any age?
David: I don't know.
Daryl: I'd be old enough to drive. I would drive myself right home.
David: You wouldn't know the way.
Daryl: Yes, I would. I know in my head. I would just get in the car and go right there.

Excerpt from my notes, June 7th:

On the way back to school, Daryl regards the rest of the field trip as his own personal shopping expedition. Even though thirty adults and ninety children are walking together through Midtown, Daryl is stopping at each store window to check it out, comment, fantasize. He runs way ahead, then lags until the group passes him. The adults are concerned that we will lose him if we don't wait, but miss the school bus if we do. I am nominally in charge and visibly exasperated. Just as I was too dizzy from keeping tabs on him to care whether he got lost or not, Karen passed by and without even making eye contact with him, calmly said, "If you miss the school bus, don't ask me for help."

And he did miss the school bus. And he did solve the problem, as Karen knew he would. He didn't call his mother at work or ask anyone for city bus money. He walked thirty blocks to his after-school program, though he had never gone on foot before. He found his way by remembering landmarks. The next day as he retold the story, he was proud of his effort, his good memory, and that "I wasn't even tired." Karen was proud on his behalf.

So much of Daryl's energy went toward deviating from what was expected that his potential had gone unnoticed, as had his startlingly strong sense of self-direction. To school authorities, Daryl appeared to be a classically oppositional child, fighting battles for the sake of fighting. On closer observation, Daryl knew exactly where he wanted to go, and how to find his way. Karen was the first adult in his school life to see this. She knew he needed to travel his own path, and her commitment to supporting him on that journey never wavered. She understood his questions.

When I first came to Karen's class, the image of Daryl floating silently around the classroom overwhelmed any other impression of him. By June he had ceased to float and had revealed his destination: he is bound for the moon, for home, and for his after-school program, all under his own command. He knows the routes and controls how he travels. He is self-reliant, not only in fantasy, but in reality. Karen, if only intuitively, understood all along, but it took me months of studying my notes to see that until he felt autonomous, Daryl was incapable of learning in a conventional classroom setting where institutional strictures and academic demands were beyond his control. As Daryl emerged from his silence, he was no longer an invisible child in danger of falling into the special education track; his deviant presence was no longer a nuisance. He was ready to move on within the mainstream.

Karen believed that had Daryl not been in her class, he would have continued to be "a child who spoke under his breath, never daring to raise his voice." He would have kept himself so enveloped in protective layers that no one would ever have known his true nature. In fact, Daryl changed from a contained, unknown child into a "straight kid" (Karen's word for a typical ten-year-old) whose wit, facility with language, and capacity for intimate friendship came as something of a surprise to everyone but Karen. Her skill was the ability to unite the issues of time, self-direction, and compliance with her acceptance of Daryl.

Daryl's slowness, recalcitrance, and need to ponder the world at his own pace were parts of his personality that Karen made no attempt to change. She insisted that the group include Daryl as he was and stretched the usual school and class rules so he did not feel boxed into situations from which he could not escape.[4] His stony resistance dissolved in part because Karen diluted institutional demands enough so that he began to see himself as a "straight kid," not as a deviant nuisance. Others began to see him more positively, too. Karen mediated external time pressures on Daryl because she felt that he could not yet comply and forcing him would lead nowhere. Even though his behavior could try one's soul, she never expressed distaste for the way he was. On the contrary, she appreciated him and took pleasure in him as his personality emerged over the year. Her willingness to allow Daryl some leeway in conforming gave him a chance to negotiate this unfamiliar school territory at his own pace and in his own way.

Karen understood that Daryl questioned personal, institutional, and physical boundaries. Boundaries obsessed him. He pushed adults to the end of their tolerance. Instinctively he moved to the fringe in any group, always toying on the edge

[4] For my article on her strategies, see "Daryl: Becoming Part of a Group," *Outlook, 49* (Autumn 1983) 3–24.

of the barely permissible. He made tentative contact with his surroundings as if he weren't quite sure walls, chairs, and tables were solid. He chose the tightly bound medium of traced cartoons for his first disciplined activity. At first glance, an obvious teaching strategy would dictate setting firm limits, but any attempt to impose secure boundaries failed. Paradoxically, the more closely drawn the external rules, the more Daryl overstepped them, but the less clear the boundaries were, the more anxious and provocative his behavior became. Karen saw him through this paralyzing conflict. She did not hold him to the rules and tolerated his provocations until they stopped. She created an environment in which he could be himself.

Conclusion

Good teachers are not all alike. Karen's approach is only one possibility among many, but unless teachers have the autonomy to apply their own philosophy and values, schools will continue to miss out on an enormous wealth of talent.

Karen's classroom, though unconventional and incomplete in some ways (the Cusenaire rods on the floor drove me crazy), is a success for many children because she teaches by her own idiosyncratic methods. For some children there is a greater chance of growth in this classroom than in other places in school. There are teachers and administrators who might think that this kind of teaching belongs in special education, but Karen disagrees for the same reason she refused to refer Daryl to special education classes: she believes the labeling and segregation of children is pernicious. She feels that daily, relaxed, sustained interaction among children of different backgrounds and temperaments is crucial to their knowing each other and breaking down the barriers which separate them. This is how understanding is built.

The structure of schooling must encourage differences rather than similarities in teaching styles if schools are ever to meet the needs of the unique children in their care. Schools need teachers like Karen for her passion, her ability to teach hard-to-reach children, her insight, and her acceptance of all children as they are.

I have been helped by talks about Daryl with Karen, with members of my Los Angeles Children's Thinking Seminar, with Lillian Weber, and with numerous Prospect Summer Institute participants, especially Pat Carini, Anne Martin, and Nancy Lambert.

How Do Teachers Manage to Teach? Perspectives on Problems in Practice

MAGDALENE LAMPERT

The author is a scholar of teaching practice and also an elementary mathematics teacher. Her work, like that of her colleagues at the Institute for Research on Teaching, focuses on teaching practice from the point of view of the practitioner. Here, in two case studies, she views the teacher as dilemma manager, a broker of contradictory interests, who "builds a working identity that is constructively ambiguous." To emphasize her conviction that teaching work is deeply personal, the author makes herself the subject of one of these studies. She concludes with an examination of how her view contrasts with prevalent academic images of teachers' work.

In the classroom where I teach fourth-, fifth-, and sixth-grade mathematics, there are two chalkboards on opposite walls. The students sit at two tables and a few desks, facing in all directions. I rarely sit down while I am teaching except momentarily to offer individual help. Thus the room does not have a stationary "front" toward which the students can reliably look for directions or lessons from their teacher. Nevertheless, an orientation toward one side of the room did develop recently in the fifth-grade class and became the source of some pedagogical problems.

The children in my classroom seem to be allergic to their peers of the opposite sex. Girls rarely choose to be anywhere near a boy, and the boys actively reject the girls whenever possible. This has meant that the boys sit together at the table near one of the blackboards and the girls at the table near the other.

The fifth-grade boys are particularly enthusiastic and boisterous. They engage in discussions of math problems with the same intensity they bring to football. They are talented and work productively under close supervision, but if left to their own devices, their behavior deteriorates and they bully one another, tell loud and silly jokes, and fool around with the math materials. Without making an obvious response to their misbehavior, I developed a habit of routinely curtailing these distractions from the lesson by teaching at the blackboard on the boys' end of the classroom. This enabled me to address the problem of maintaining classroom order by my physical presence; a cool stare or a touch on the shoulder reminded the boys to give their attention to directions for an activity or to the content of a lesson, and there was no need to interrupt my teaching.

Harvard Educational Review   Vol. 55   No. 2   May 1985, 178–194

But my presence near the boys had inadvertently put the girls in "the back" of the room. One of the more outspoken girls impatiently pointed out that she had been trying to get my attention and thought I was ignoring her. She made me aware that my problem-solving strategy, devised to keep the boys' attention, had caused another, quite different problem. The boys could see and hear more easily than the girls, and I noticed their questions more readily. Now what was to be done?

I felt that I faced a forced choice between equally undesirable alternatives. If I continued to use the blackboard near the boys, I might be less aware of and less encouraging toward the more well-behaved girls. Yet, if I switched my position to the blackboard on the girls' side of the room, I would be less able to help the boys focus on their work. Whether I chose to promote classroom order or equal opportunity, it seemed that either the boys or the girls would miss something I wanted them to learn.

This first-person account of a particular pedagogical problem is an unusual way to begin an analysis of the work of teaching. Commonly, such inquiries begin with general observations based on a consideration of several instances of teaching practice or with assertions about what teaching can or should be. I have taken a different tack, however, not because I believe these approaches cannot offer useful insights into what it is that teachers do, but because I believe they are incomplete. Efforts to build generalized theories of instruction, curriculum, or classroom management based on careful empirical research have much to contribute to the improvement of teaching, but they do not sufficiently describe the work of teaching.[1] Such theories and research are limited in their capacity to help teachers know what to do about particular problems such as the one I have just described. My intention, however, is not to build another kind of theory which can more adequately guide practice but to describe those elements of practice which are unconsonant with theoretical principles. To do this, I shall use both my experience as a classroom practitioner and the tools of scholarly inquiry.

The special and salient value of descriptions of teaching from the practitioner's perspective has been recognized by scholars and supported by researchers.[2] Moving back and forth between the world of practice and the world of scholarship in order to inquire into the nature of practice fosters in the inquirer a useful sort of

[1] My distinction between theory and practice here follows that developed by Joseph Schwab in his studies of curriculum development. Schwab has observed that the particulars of time, place, person, and circumstance which surround questions of what and how to teach are incongruent with the order, system, economy, and generality required to build a good theory; see Schwab, "The Practical: Arts of Eclectic," in *Science, Curriculum, and Liberal Education: Selected Essays*, ed. Ian Westbury and Neil J. Wilkof (Chicago: University of Chicago Press, 1978), p. 322.

[2] See, for example, Susan Florio and Martha Walsh, "The Teacher as a Colleague in Classroom Research," in *Culture and the Bilingual Classroom*, ed. Henry T. Trueba, Grace P. Guthrie, and Kathryn H. Au (Rowley, MA: Newbury House, 1981), 87–101; Eliot Eisner, "Can Educational Research Inform Educational Practice?" *Phi Delta Kappan, 65* (March 1984), 447–452; and Leslie L. Huling, Myron Trang, and Linda Correll, "Interactive Research and Development: A Promising Strategy for Teacher Educators," *Journal of Teacher Education, 32* (1981), 13–14.

Christopher Clark and Penelope L. Peterson have recently emphasized that descriptive research on how teachers make interactive decisions in the classroom should be done as a basis for further theory building about teacher thinking; see their "Teachers' Thought Processes," Occasional Paper No. 73, Institute for Research on Teaching (East Lansing, MI: Michigan State University, 1984), p. 76.

deliberation; it enriches and refines both the questions one can ask about teachers' work and the attempts one can make to answer them.[3] In this essay, I shall present two cases which first describe teaching problems from the teacher's point of view and then examine, from the scholar's point of view, the work involved in facing them.

The teacher's emphasis on concrete particulars in the description of a classroom problem distinguishes the perspective of practice from the perspective of the theory-builder. This distinction has received considerable attention in the literature on teaching.[4] Another fundamental though less familiar difference involves the personal quality of teaching problems as seen through the eyes of a practitioner.[5] Who the teacher is has a great deal to do with both the way she defines problems and what can and will be done about them.[6] The academician solves problems that are recognized in some universal way as being important, whereas a teacher's problems arise because the state of affairs in the classroom is not what she wants it to be. Thus, practical problems, in contrast to theoretical ones, involve someone's wish for a change and the will to make it.[7] Even though the teacher may be influenced by many powerful sources outside herself, the responsibility to act lies within. Like the researcher and the theoretician, she identifies problems and imagines solutions to them, but her job involves the additional personal burden of doing something about these problems in the classroom and living with the consequences of her actions over time. Thus, by way of acknowledging this deeply personal dimension of teaching practice, I have chosen not only to present the particular details of two teachers' problems but to draw one of these problems from my own experience.

In addition to recognizing the particular and personal qualities of the way teachers understand problems in their work, I would like to consider another distinction between practice and theory building in education. Some of the problems the practitioner is required to do something about might be defined as unsolvable.

---

[3] Schwab describes the value of such "deliberation" as a method for studying the teaching process in "The Practical 4: Something for Curriculum Professors to Do," *Curriculum Inquiry, 13* (1983), 239–265. His notions are expanded, particularly with relation to deliberative exchanges among differing aspects of one's self, by Lee Shulman in "The Practical and the Eclectic: A Deliberation on Teaching and Educational Research," *Curriculum Inquiry, 14* (1984), 183–200.

[4] The "particularistic" nature of the teacher's perspective has been described by Arthur S. Bolster, "Toward a More Effective Model of Research on Teaching," *Harvard Educational Review, 53* (1983), 294–308. The context-specific character of work in classrooms as it appears to practitioners has been examined by Walter Doyle in "Learning the Classroom Environment: An Ecological Analysis," *Journal of Teacher Education, 28* (1977), 51–55, and "Paradigms for Research on Teacher Effectiveness," *Review of Research in Education,* Vol. 5, ed. Lee Shulman (Itasca, IL: Peacock, 1977), 163–198. Philip Jackson compared teachers' propensity for "anecdotal" descriptions of their work with the more abstract quality of academic writing about teaching. See Jackson, "The Way Teachers Think," in *Psychology and Educational Practice,* ed. Gerald S. Lesser (Glenview, IL: Scott, Foresman, 1971), pp. 10–34.

[5] The personal quality of teachers' knowledge is emphasized by Sharon Feiman and Robert Floden. See their "Cultures of Teaching" in *Third Handbook of Research on Teaching,* ed. Merlin C. Wittrock (New York: Macmillan, 1986), pp. 505–526. Gary Fenstermacher argues for considering the effect of the teacher's own concerns and personal history on the decisions she makes in the classroom in "A Philosophical Consideration of Recent Research on Teacher Effectiveness," in *Review of Research in Education, 6,* ed. Lee Shulman (Itasca, IL: Peacock, 1979), pp. 186–215.

[6] I have chosen the feminine gender for pronouns which apply to teachers throughout this manuscript because the majority of teachers are women.

[7] Schwab, "The Practical: A Language for Curriculum," in Westbury and Wilkof, p. 289.

The work required to manage such problems will be the particular focus of my inquiry. It is widely recognized that the juxtaposition of responsibilities which make up the teacher's job leads to conceptual paradoxes.[8] I will argue further that, from the teacher's point of view, trying to solve many common pedagogical problems leads to practical dilemmas.[9] As the teacher considers alternative solutions to any particular problem, she cannot hope to arrive at the "right" alternative in the sense that a theory built on valid and reliable empirical data can be said to be right.[10] This is because she brings many contradictory aims to each instance of her work, and the resolution of their dissonance cannot be neat or simple. Even though she cannot find their right solutions, however, the teacher must do something about the problems she faces.

Returning to my own classroom at this point will serve to explicate more clearly these qualities of a teacher's work. One might think it possible to monitor the boys' behavior in my fifth-grade math class in a way that does not reduce my attention to the girls, or to involve the girls more in the math lesson without reducing my capacity to monitor the boys' behavior. But teaching dilemmas like this are often not so easily resolved in practice. For example, if I were to assign seats mixing the boys and the girls, it might be possible to give equal attention to everyone no matter which blackboard I use, but the silliness that results from proximity to the opposite sex in the fifth grade might then take so much away from the lesson that there would be less of my attention to go around. If I were to leave the boys and the girls where they choose to sit, and walk around the room to spread my attention, then the walking around might cause even greater disruption because it would take me away from the boys who need my presence. It might be possible to use desks instead of tables and seat everyone facing in the same direction as a way of monitoring behavior, but that might make the students' valuable problem-solving discussions with one another impossible. All these possible "solutions" lead to problems. I felt I could not choose a solution without compromising other goals I wanted to accomplish. Yet, I knew that not implementing a solution would have negative consequences too. I was convinced that some action had to be taken.

When I consider the conflicts that arise in the classroom from my perspective as a teacher, I do not see a choice between abstract social goals, such as Excellence versus Equality or Freedom versus Standardization. What I see are tensions between individual students, or personal confrontations between myself and a particular group of boys or girls. When I think about rewarding Dennis's excellent,

---

[8] See, for example, Bryan Wilson, "The Teacher's Role: A Sociological Analysis," *British Journal of Sociology, 13* (1962), 15–32; Charles Bidwell, "The School as a Formal Organization," in *Handbook of Organizations*, ed. James G. March (Chicago: Rand McNally, 1965), pp. 972–1022; and Ann Lieberman and Lynn Miller, "The Social Realities of Teaching," *Teachers College Record, 80* (1978), 54–68.

[9] The language of "dilemmas" to describe classroom problems has also been used by Ann Berlak and Harold Berlak in *The Dilemmas of Schooling: Teaching and Social Change* (London: Methuen, 1981). However, their analysis focuses on cultural contradictions and opportunities for social change as they are manifest in teachers' dilemmas and gives less attention to the practical work involved in managing dilemmas in the classroom.

[10] See Schwab, "The Practical: Arts of Eclectic," p. 318; for a comparison between the knowledge produced by social science research and the knowledge practitioners use in their work, see Charles E. Lindblom and David K. Cohen, *Usable Knowledge: Social Science and Social Problem Solving* (New Haven: Yale University Press, 1979); and also David K. Cohen, "Commitment and Uncertainty," Harvard University, unpublished manuscript, 1981.

though boisterous, contributions to problem-solving discussions, while at the same time encouraging reticent Sandra to take an equal part in class activities, I cannot see my goals as a neat dichotomy and my job as making clear choices. My aims for any one particular student are tangled with my aims for each of the others in the class, and, more importantly, I am responsible for choosing a course of action in circumstances where choice leads to further conflict. The contradictions between the goals I am expected to accomplish thus become continuing inner struggles about how to do my job.

A Pedagogical Dilemma as an Argument with Oneself

The solutions I imagined to restrain the boys' boisterous behavior and to encourage the girls' involvement in class activities were contradictory. I could do neither without causing undesirable consequences, yet both were important to me. One way to think about the dilemma that I faced is to see it as a problem forcing a choice between equally undesirable alternatives. In this view, my job would be to grit my teeth and choose, even though choosing would bring problematic consequences.[11] Another way to think of a dilemma, however, is as an argument between opposing tendencies within oneself in which neither side can come out the winner. From this perspective, my job would involve maintaining the tension between my own equally important but conflicting aims without choosing between them. It may be true that some teachers do resolve their dilemmas by choosing — between excellence and equality, between pushing students to achieve and providing a comfortable learning environment, between covering the curriculum and attending to individual understanding; but I wish to argue that choosing is not the only way to manage in the face of self-contradictory alternatives. Facing a dilemma need not result in a forced choice. A more technical definition of a dilemma is "an argument that presents an antagonist with two (or more) alternatives, but is equally conclusive against him whichever alternative he chooses."[12] This definition focuses on the deliberation about one's alternatives rather than on a choice between them. The conflicted teacher is her own antagonist; she cannot win by choosing.

As I presented my case for leaving the boys' area of the room to be nearer to the girls, my argument for taking such an action was conclusive against me because my students and I would be distracted from our lessons by my need to control overtly the boys' behavior. If I argued, on the other hand, for continuing to teach from the boys' side of the room, I would also lose the argument because I

---

[11] Descriptions of teacher thinking have emphasized choice between alternative courses of action as the outcome of teacher decision making, based on models of cognitive information processing. See, for example, Richard J. Shavelson, "Teachers' Decision Making," in *The Psychology of Teaching Methods, The 75th Yearbook of the National Society for the Study of Education*, Part I, ed. Nathaniel L. Gage (Chicago: University of Chicago Press, 1976), pp. 143–165; John Eggleston, ed., *Teacher Decision Making in the Classroom* (London: Routledge & Kegan Paul, 1979); and Christopher Clark and Robert Yinger, "Research on Teacher Thinking," *Curriculum Inquiry* (1977), 279–304.

[12] *Funk and Wagnalls' Standard College Dictionary* (New York: Harcourt Brace and World, 1963), p. 372. For a psychological description of the contradictory imperatives that can arise within the person of the teacher, see Angelika C. Wagner, "Conflicts in Consciousness: Imperative Cognitions Can Lead to Knots in Thinking," paper presented at the First Symposium of the International Study Association on Teacher Thinking, Tilburg University, The Netherlands, 26–28 Oct. 1983.

would not be giving the girls at least equal amounts of my attention. Instead of engaging in a decision-making process that would eliminate conflicting alternatives and lead to a choice of which problem to solve, I pursued a series of such losing arguments with myself as I considered the consequences of various alternatives. One element of the teacher's work is having an argument with oneself—a speculative argument that cannot be won. The thinking involved in this sort of work is quite different from the kind of thinking that might go into concluding that one can make the correct choice between dichotomous alternatives. My arguments with myself served to articulate the undesirable consequences of each of my alternatives in terms of potential classroom confrontations. In order to hold the conflicting parts of my job and myself together, I needed to find a way to manage my dilemma without exacerbating the conflicts that underlay it.

Pedagogical Dilemmas and Personal Coping Strategies

My argument with myself resulted from a desire to do contradictory things in the classroom. My ambivalence about what to do was not only a conflict of will, however; it was a conflict of identity as well. I did not want to be a person who ignored the girls in my class because the boys were more aggressive in seeking my attention. I think of myself as someone who encourages girls to become more interested and involved in mathematical thinking. At the same time, I did not want to have a chaotic classroom as a result of turning away from the boys' behavior. But neither did I want to appear to have such a preoccupation with order that I discouraged enthusiasm; standing near the boys enabled me to keep them focused without attending to their misbehavior directly. Working out an identity for this situation was more than a personal concern—it was an essential tool for getting my work done. The kind of person that I am with my students plays an important part in what I am able to accomplish with them. Figuring out who to be in the classroom is part of my job; by holding conflicting parts of myself together, I find a way to manage the conflicts in my work.

The self that I brought to the task of managing this classroom dilemma is a complicated one. My personal history and concerns contributed to the judgment that it would not be wise simply to make a choice in this case. I felt sympathy for the girls who were seated in what had inadvertently become the "back of the room" because of the many pained moments I had spent with my raised hand unrecognized at the back of my own predominately male trigonometery class in high school. But I was not of one mind about that experience. Competing for attention with the more aggressive boys in my math class had not been wholly negative; a significant amount of the satisfaction which I derive from my work in mathematics is based on the knowledge that there are few women who are successful in this area. Although I believe girls are entitled to special encouragement in learning mathematics, this belief is entangled with my feeling of accomplishment from having developed an interest in the subject myself despite discouragement. Now, as part of my job, I had to accomplish a balance between these conflicting influences in what I chose to do about this classroom dilemma. There were similarly divergent personal concerns behind how I understood the actions I might take in relation to the boys in the class. In my teaching relationship with them I had to balance my own conflicting yet simultaneous desires for freedom and order.

My capacity to bring disparate aspects of myself together in the person that I am in the classroom is one of the tools that I used to construct an approach to managing my dilemma. Because a teacher is present to students as a whole person, the conflicting parts of herself are not separable, one from another, the way they might be if we think of them as names for categories of persons or cultural ideals, like child oriented versus subject oriented, or democratic versus authoritarian.[13] A teacher has the potential to act with integrity while maintaining contradictory concerns. I did not want to be a person who treated girls unequally, as my high school trigonometry teacher had done. Nor did I want to be someone who gave special attention to girls just because they were girls. I did not want to be a person who had such a preoccupation with order that I discouraged enthusiasm. Nor did I want to try to do my work in a disorderly classroom. The person that I wanted to be — this ambiguous self-definition — became a tool to enable me to accomplish my pedagogical goals.

Constructing Solutions in the Face of Unsolvable Problems

When I met my class the morning after recognizing my dilemma, I had not resolved any of the arguments with myself about what to do, but I did have some sense of who I wanted to be. And that made a difference.

It happened that two of the more offending boys were absent that day, so I was able to leave everyone seated where they were, walk to the other side of the room, and do most of my teaching standing at the blackboard near the girls' table without any major disruptions occurring. I used this hiatus to construct a strategy for managing the conflict that did not involve stark choices.

While I taught the class, my thinking about the boys and the girls merged with my thinking about some other currently pressing matters in the classroom. I was about to begin a new instructional unit which involved using manipulative materials and had been wondering about how to organize the students' activities with those materials. I had also been talking with my student teacher, Sandy, about ways in which she might take on responsibility in the class. We had planned the next unit together, and she was prepared to do some of the teaching. So I divided the class into four small groups (two of girls and two of boys) and put Sandy in charge of instructing and managing one group of boys and one group of girls, while I took responsibility for the other two groups. This strategy depended heavily on specific elements in the context of my classroom. It enabled me to cope with

[13] For example, such dichotomous categories are used to examine teachers' work in Harry L. Gracey, *Curriculum or Craftmanship: Elementary School Teachers in a Bureaucratic Setting* (Chicago: University of Chicago Press, 1972); George Spindler, "Education in a Transforming American Culture," *Harvard Educational Review*, 25 (1955), 145–156; and Mary Haywood Metz, *Classrooms and Corridors: The Crisis of Authority in Desegregated Secondary Schools* (Berkeley, CA: University of California Press, 1978). In contrast, views of the teacher derived from the social psychology of George Herbert Mead and others in "the Chicago School" present a more complex picture: for example, Willard Waller in *The Sociology of Teaching* (New York: Wiley, 1932); and Philip Jackson in *Life in Classrooms* (New York: Holt, Rinehart and Winston, 1968). The Berlaks in *The Dilemmas of Schooling*, p. 133, describe the teacher's job in the face of contradictions as "transformation," by which they mean the invention of a pedagogical process which joins opposing poles of a cultural contradiction; in their view, the teacher has the capacity to be a vehicle whereby "the contending presses of the culture at least for the moment are synthesized and thus overcome."

the surface of my problem while keeping its more general conflicts submerged. It was not a general solution nor a permanent one; it was an act of improvisation, a product of adjusting my ambivalent desires to the particular circumstances in which I was working.

I moved one group of boys to the area near the girls' blackboard and one group of girls to the other side of the room. This helped to avoid the distractions that would result from grouping the boys and girls together, but without geographically dividing the class along gender lines. Furthermore, because there were now two groups of boys and two of girls, both the class and I could identify other criteria for group membership besides gender. Instructing in small groups also meant that neither the teachers nor the students would be performing in front of both boys and girls at the same time, so my attention would be less likely to be judged as preferential toward either the boys or the girls. Paradoxically, because I would be teaching boys only in the company of other boys, and girls only in the company of other girls, I would be able to respond to the children more as individuals than as members of one sex or the other, as I had done when I taught them all together while they were seated at opposite ends of the room.

What can we learn from this case about how a teacher works? I did not choose this strategy because it would solve problems. I managed my dilemma by putting the problems that led to it further into the background and by bringing other parts of my job further to the foreground. Although this meant that the problems remained, my strategy gave me a way to live with them, a temporary respite that would prevent the underlying conflicts from erupting into more serious, distracting discord.

A Second Case: Conflicts over the Nature of Knowledge as Another Source of Classroom Dilemmas

The adversity in my situation arose because of contradictory social goals in my teaching. One might imagine that if I had been able to put problems of social organization aside and had defined my job only in terms of whether my students learned the subject matter, then the dilemmas I described would have disappeared. In fact, some scholars have argued that by using an impersonal "technology of instruction" (more often called a curriculum) teachers can produce subject matter knowledge in students without concern for social problems in or out of the classroom.[14] Others, who understand knowledge as a construction of the individual learner, leave social problems aside and focus on the teacher's work in fostering an individual child's understanding.[15] It may be true that if teaching and learning occur in a one-to-one encounter outside the classroom, the sort of dilemma I have described may not arise, but it is not possible in schools to separate social problems

---

[14] See Carl Bereiter, "Schools Without Education," *Harvard Educational Review, 42* (1972), 390–414; see also John D. McNeil, "A Scientific Approach to Supervision," in *Supervision of Teaching*, ed. Thomas J. Sergiovanni (Alexandria, VA: Association for Supervision and Curriculum Development, 1982), pp. 18–34.

[15] This position is characteristic of those educational reformers whose philosophy of learning is built on theories of individual cognitive development.

from subject-matter knowledge. In the teacher's job, at least as it is now under-stood, a clear distinction between tasks related to social organization and tasks re-lated to instruction is unachievable. The following case study is intended to illus-trate this point. Neither it nor the preceding case, however, is intended in any way to illustrate good or bad, skillful or skill-less teaching. Both cases presume a value in studying common teaching practice, however it may be evaluated, whatever its effects.

Rita Cerone is a fourth-grade teacher in a small, urban public school.[16] In the situation I am about to describe, she was faced with a set of problems which arose out of her use of a workbook to instruct students in science. Her concern for solv-ing these problems led her into a pedagogical dilemma, and what she did to man-age her dilemma raises issues about teachers' work that are similar to those already described.

Science lessons in Rita's classroom often consisted of students reading their workbooks, looking at the drawings and diagrams in them, and then answering questions and checking their answers with the teacher. The topic of one such exer-cise was "The Cycle of Water." The workbook presented the students with a pic-ture of a cloud, and next to it a question: "Where does the water come from?" Rita said it seemed obvious to her from the illustration that the answer was "clouds," and so she had "marked it right" when students gave that answer. (She checked other answers which were not so obvious to her in the teacher's guide before she judged them right or wrong.) Rita was, therefore, a bit perplexed when one of the girls in her class, Linda, came up to have her work corrected and declared with unusual confidence that "the answer to where water comes from is *the ocean*." Rita indicated on the girl's paper that this answer was incorrect, but Linda was sur-prised by this judgment and insisted that she was right.

Rita was hesitant to contradict Linda because the girl was so confident about her answer. Although Rita disagreed with her, she sensed a conflict brewing and wanted to avoid it. So she tried to understand more about what Linda was think-ing. "I said to her: 'Well, I don't understand. Explain it to me.' I was fumbling around and I was trying to figure out what she meant. It finally turned out that she knew, but she couldn't verbalize it for quite a while. After asking her questions and having her look at the workbook page, [Linda] said, 'The clouds pick the wa-ter up. I don't know how, but it puts the water from the ocean back in the clouds.' " Rita decided in this exchange that Linda "knew" what she was supposed to learn from the lesson even though her answer did not match the answer in the teacher's guide.

The potential conflict between perspectives on what it means to "know" some-thing was momentarily resolved when Rita agreed with Linda that her answer was indeed correct. The equilibrium between Linda's understanding and the text-book's standards of knowledge was short-lived, however, when the other students

---

[16] I had the opportunity to observe and work with Rita Cerone over three years as part of the Teacher Development Project in the Division for Study and Research in Education, Massachusetts Institute of Technology. This project is described in my "Teaching about Thinking and Thinking about Teaching," *Journal of Curriculum Studies, 16,* (1984), 1–18. Quotes of Rita's remarks are taken from transcripts of meetings of the teacher participants in that project and transcripts of my individual interviews with Rita, which occurred over a three-year period. The name "Rita Cerone" is a pseudonym, as are all student names used in this manuscript.

in the class took an interest in Rita's judgment. As Rita recalled, "Linda went running back to the rest of the group and told them she wasn't wrong. The other kids started arguing with Linda because they saw it the way I saw it *and* the way the answer book saw it. But Linda could prove she was right." Rita had exacerbated an underlying contradiction in her classroom when she told Linda that her answer was correct. The conflict came to the surface because Linda was a member of a group of students studying the same material. Moreover, they had all been using the teacher's guide as the standard by which to judge the correctness of their answers. Their complaint was that Rita had applied a familiar standard to judging their answers but had used another standard to evaluate Linda's. Unless Rita did something to manage this conflict, it threatened to become a more difficult classroom problem.

One student, Kevin, confident that *his* answer was right because it matched the answer in the teacher's guide and because Rita had told him it was right, led the class in an argument with Linda and, by implication, with their teacher. In Rita's words: "One of the kids, Kevin, said Linda was really dumb because the ocean was where the water started out, and it ended up in clouds just before it rained. It wasn't that he didn't get her explanation, but he just dismissed it because I had told him earlier that his answer was right and he also knew that was the answer the book wanted. That's why she came up to me in the first place: to get confirmation that she was right because Kevin had said she was wrong." Like Rita, Kevin "got" Linda's explanation. Yet, her individual understanding of the matter was not his concern. He "dismissed" Linda's explanation (as Rita herself had done at first) because it did not match what the book and his teacher said was "right," and he began an argument in order to settle the matter. If the teacher and the textbook were to be taken seriously, he argued, Linda could not also be right.

Rita's job here, as in my situation, might be viewed as requiring a choice between dichotomous alternatives. If she were to practice "child-centered" teaching, she would favor defending Linda's way of thinking while rejecting the textbook's authority. If she were to practice "curriculum-centered" teaching, she would judge Linda's knowledge using the written curriculum in the teacher's guide as the standard. Those students whose answers agreed with the book's answer were pushing her toward the latter, while Linda was pushing her toward the former.

Rita's Argument with Herself.
Rita did not represent her work in this situation as making such a forced choice, however. Instead, she reviewed a series of complicated arguments she had with herself on the issues involved. She contended on the one hand that the question in the workbook was not very clear; its ambiguity made her less inclined to trust the answers in the teacher's guide. In addition, by reflecting on her conversation with Linda, she recognized that the girl really understood the "cycle of water," whereas those students who put down "clouds" might only have looked at the illustration in the book. Rita articulated this skepticism about impersonal measures of students' knowledge in a conversation she had with some other teachers about the incident: "I think too often kids get marked wrong for things that really aren't wrong. I mean, if you corrected Linda's paper and she wasn't around to explain her answer, she would never have had the chance to defend herself or say that this

is the way I think. I mean, that's what happens on those Stanford Achievement Tests. They're not given any room for individuality of thought." Rita accepted Linda's answer as a valid representation of the girl's understanding. Yet, she also thought that both she and Linda should concur with the answer in the book. Rita related her thinking about this incident to her first year of teaching; she had read the teacher's guides very carefully that year and "tried to stay one step ahead of the kids" because she was trying to teach material she had not learned before. Even later she relied heavily on the teacher's guide; she typically referred students directly to the "answer book" to check their own work so that she could spend time on helping others who were slower to finish their assignments. Rita argued that if she let Linda "get away with" her nonstandard interpretation of the question in the science book, she might be undermining her students' trust in these books as well as her own ability to guide her students' learning. For this teacher and her students, textbooks carry a great store of meaning about the nature of what is to be learned. So Rita was torn: she could produce good reasons for accepting Linda's answer as correct, and she could also produce good reasons for marking it wrong.

Rita could not win this argument with herself about how to evaluate Linda's answer; like me, she was her own antagonist. Whether she announced to the class that Linda was right and thus implied that what the book said did not matter, or that Linda was wrong because she had interpreted the "cycle of water" in her own way, the consequences would be more overt conflict. While some might see such additional conflict as educationally productive, Rita, in her circumstances, clearly did not.

Rita's Inner Tensions as a Tool of Her Trade

Rita drew on her own conflicted concerns to arrive at her decision about what to do in this situation. Her conviction that she should not choose between Linda and the textbook was based on her personal capacity to value different, potentially contradictory kinds of knowledge. This was part of the "person she wanted to be." She had begun teaching and had been reasonably successful at it without much understanding of science. She had also grown up believing that the people who write books are smarter than she — even smarter than her teachers. The public knowledge she learned in school from books had allowed her to achieve the position of teacher. So she had reason to trust the "rightness" of the knowledge represented by the standard curriculum. At the same time, however, she believed that much of what she knew could not be contained in books or measured by tests. She knew that she understood things she had figured out for herself, and sometimes she saw these ideas more clearly than those she had read in books. Rita was, therefore, concerned about the limitations of standard measures of knowledge, but her concern was not unconflicted.

Several months later Rita expressed the same ambivalent view of knowledge that formed the basis of her deliberations in this case in a conversation about the way a standardized test had been used to assess her own knowledge. She thought the test was not a very good tool for measuring what would make her a successful learner, but she also recognized that the test had some meaning to people who did not know her. She believed it would be "unfair" to deprive students of the instruction they might need to do well on such tests, even while she argued that the tests do not necessarily measure one's capacity for understanding. "If they don't have a serious attitude about tests," she said, "they're never going to make it in college. They have to have some respect for this information because it's controlling where they are going to go in life. I realize that society is not going to change before they get out of my classroom, and I don't want to put my burdens on the kids. You have to respect these tests, as I do, because I had to take them too. It's a ticket for the next place you want to go." Because Rita had not resolved her own feelings about the value of the sort of knowledge represented by scores on standardized tests, she had been in an effective position to use herself to mediate the conflict betwen conventional knowledge and individual understanding in the situation with Kevin and Linda. Her personal conflict about the value of standardized knowledge was a resource she drew upon in order to do her work in this classroom situation.

As the person responsible for settling disputes among her students about who is right, Rita represented the possibility of bringing these potentially contradictory ways of knowing together in the public arena of the classroom. Rather than siding with Kevin or Linda, she told them they were both right. She improvised. "I finally said to Kevin and Linda that they were both right. And I left it at that, and I let them handle it from there. (But I was kind of listening to what they would do.) Linda understood exactly what she was trying to get across. Kevin understood it also. But they understood on two different planes. I understood on a third one. I don't think there was any need for clarification, but there was a need for them to know they were both right."

Rita made no stark choices. She did not throw out the textbook and tell Kevin and Linda it didn't matter, nor did she tell Linda that she was wrong because she did not conform to the book's expectation. She accepted both of their answers on "two different planes" while putting herself on a "third plane," where she could value both Kevin's standards and Linda's divergence from them.

Coping Rather Than Solving.

Rita constructed a way to manage the tension between individual understanding and public knowledge without resolving it. Since she had some authority as the teacher in this situation, Kevin and Linda took her judgment seriously, even though it was ambiguous. Both of them came out with a different, more complex view of knowledge. Kevin was told that the answer in the teacher's guide is not the only right answer in the public setting of the classroom, while Linda was told that the textbook answer has validity even though she sees things differently. Rita managed to deflect the vehement competition between these two students by issuing a more complex set of rules for judging one another's answers.

In my math class, I made it more difficult to draw the line between teaching that favored girls and teaching that favored boys. By muddying the waters with small-group instruction, I pushed the social conflicts that this dichotomy suggested further into the background. Rita did a similar thing in the area of instruction when she said Kevin and Linda were both right. She confused their ability to judge one another's knowledge and thereby mediated the conflict between them. As in my situation, she did not eliminate the original conflict; rather, she avoided it so as to avoid additional conflicts. This way of submerging the conflict below an improvised, workable, but superficial resolution is, of course, quite different from what many cognitive psychologists or curriculum experts would advocate.

Images of Teachers' Work and Their Implications for Improving It

These two stories portray the teacher as an active negotiator, a broker of sorts, balancing a variety of interests that need to be satisfied in classrooms. The teacher in each story initiates actions as solutions to particular environmental problems and defines herself as the locus of various alternative perspectives on those actions. Conflicts among these perspectives arise in the teacher both presently within the classroom and in the way she interprets her own past experience. In order to do her job, the dilemma-managing teacher calls upon this conflicted "self" as a tool of her trade, building a working identity that is constructively ambiguous. While she works at solving society's problems and scholars' problems, she also works at coping with her own internal conflicts. She debates with herself about what to do, and instead of screening out responsibilities that contradict one another, she acknowledges them, embraces the conflict, and finds a way to manage.

What does this image of the teacher as a dilemma manager suggest about the nature of teachers' work and how to improve it? Images of teaching frame our construction of the tasks teachers perform; our sense of the work involved in successfully accomplishing these tasks forms the basis for designing improvements. Whether the actions of the two teachers I have described here should be thought of as typical strategies or be promoted as expedient practices will remain open to question. These stories are intended only to illustrate an image of teachers' work which can help us think about the nature of classroom practice. In order to learn something from the image about how to improve practice, it is necessary to compare it with other images of teachers in the literature and to examine the influence these images have had on the kind of help we give teachers when they face classroom problems.

Most commonly, *teachers are assumed to make choices among dichotomous alternatives:* to promote equality *or* excellence; to build curriculum around children's interests *or* around subject matter; to foster independence and creativity *or* maintain standards and expect everyone to meet them.[17] These choices are thought to enable teachers to avoid dilemmas in their everyday practice. An example of this perspective can be found in the way Mary Haywood Metz analyzed the manner in which a group of teachers responded to the work tensions produced by the desegregation of their schools.[18] Metz defined keeping classroom order and promoting student learning as "contradictory imperatives" for teachers and concluded that those she observed could not both maintain standards of behavior in the classroom and nur-

---

[17] See, for example, Gracey, *Curriculum or Craftsmanship*; Jackson, "The Way Teachers Think"; Bidwell, "The School as a Formal Organization"; and Spindler, "Education in a Transforming American Culture."

[18] Metz, *Classrooms and Corridors*.

ture students' commitment to learning; instead, they divided themselves into opposing camps. Part of the work of these teachers, in this view, was to figure out whether classroom order or students' commitment was more important to their success as teachers, and then to choose between them. Thus it would seem appropriate that help from outsiders appear in the form of arguments to teachers about why they should pay more attention either to classroom order or to student commitment. Much preservice and inservice teacher education today takes this form. Professors and staff developers use evidence from research, rationales drawn from educational philosophy, or personal charisma to convince teachers that one approach is better than its opposite.

Another view of pedagogical work is illustrated by Gertrude McPherson's picture of the "small town" teacher.[19] She describes teachers' conflicts entirely in terms of contradictory external pressures. In this image, *the teacher is a person besieged by other people's expectations.* She cannot teach because of the need to defend herself against the inconsistencies in what students, administrators, colleagues, parents, and public officials expect her to do. Managing conflict is part of the teacher's job, in this view, but it is seen as a source of "unhappiness and frustration" rather than as a means by which the teacher defines herself. McPherson's view carries with it a sense of what must be done to improve teaching practice: there is very little worthwhile work that can be accomplished by the teacher "as long as the goals of our educational system are unclearly defined, . . . internally inconsistent, [and] inconsistent with dominant and often themselves inconsistent values in our larger society."[20] The more current literature on teacher stress takes a similar view: unless the goals of the teacher's job are redefined, the only positive steps a practitioner can take to reduce the harmful effects of the tension produced by conflicting expectations are engaging in regular physical exercise and maintaining a healthy diet.[21] These attitudes toward teaching regard the contradictions in teaching as problems to be solved by altering the way education is organized and conceptualized by society. In this view, society needs to become more consistent about its own goals and what it expects of teachers, and, thus, conflict will be eliminated.

Yet another way of portraying teaching, one which might be thought of as a response to this abstract hope for unified goals, arises out of the work of social science researchers and government policymakers. These problem-solvers have teamed up to find ways to help teachers increase student achievement. They turn away from conflicts that might arise in the classroom and assume that *the teacher is a technical-production manager* who has the responsibility for monitoring the efficiency with which learning is being accomplished. In this view, teaching can be improved if practitioners use researchers' knowledge to solve classroom problems.[22] The teacher's work is to find out what researchers and policymakers say

[19] McPherson, *Small Town Teacher* (Cambridge: Harvard University Press, 1972).
[20] McPherson, *Small Town Teacher*, p. 215.
[21] Kathleen V. Hoover-Dempsey and Earline D. Kendell, "Stress and Coping in Teaching: An Integrative Review of the Literature," paper presented at the annual meeting of the American Educational Research Association, New Orleans, 25 April 1984.
[22] See, for example, Nathaniel L. Gage, "An Analytic Approach to Research on Instructional Methods," in *The Social Psychology of Teaching,* ed. Arnold Morrison and Donald McIntyre (Hammondsworth, Eng.: Penguin Books, 1972); Robert E. Slavin, "Component Building: A Strategy for

should be done with or to students and then to do it. How much time should be spent on direct instruction versus seatwork? How many new words should be in stories children are required to read? If the teacher does what she is told, students will learn. Taking this perspective suggests that practical conflicts can be avoided if researchers' solutions are correctly implemented by teachers.

Some educational scholars reject this image of the teacher as a "black box" through which researchers' knowledge passes into the classroom.[23] In their view, *the teacher has an active role in deciding how to teach*; she makes decisions by putting research findings together with the information available in the classroom environment to make choices about what process will produce the desired objectives. Because cognitive information processing has been used as the model in these studies of teacher decision making, however, a "decision" is seen only as a process of mathematically ordering one's choices on the basis of unequally weighted alternatives.[24] At each point in the thinking process, the decider is assumed to see clearly which of two alternative routes is preferred to reach a given goal.[25] Therefore, improving teaching involves simplifying alternatives by screening out contradictory concerns so that any reasonable person would make the same correct choice using the same information. The process is mechanical, not personal; it is the sort of thinking one can imagine would be done better by unbiased machines than by people.[26] This theory, therefore, cannot help teachers to figure out what to do about the sort of unsolvable conflicts in their work that I have described.[27]

These images of teachers — as cognitive information processors, as implementers of researchers' knowledge about how to produce learning, as stressed and neurotically defensive, and as members of opposing camps — portray the conflicts in teaching as resolvable in one way or another. In contrast, the image of the teacher as dilemma manager accepts conflict as a continuing condition with which persons can learn to cope. This latter view does not replace the idea that the teacher plays conflicting roles in society, or the idea that it is useful to note patterns in the relationship between behaviors and their outcomes in order to make productive decisions; but it puts the teacher in a different problem-solving relationship to the social conflicts and behavioral patterns in her work. It suggests that, in addition to

Research-Based Instructional Improvement," *Elementary School Journal, 84* (1984), 255–269; John D. McNeil, "A Scientific Approach to Supervision"; and Jere Brophy and Thomas Good, *Teacher-Student Relationships: Causes and Consequences* (New York: Holt, Rinehart, and Winston, 1974).

[23] Hilda Borko, Richard Cone, Nancy Russo, and Richard J. Shavelson, "Teachers' Decision Making," in *Research on Teaching: Concepts, Findings and Implications*, ed. Penelope L. Peterson and Herbert T. Walberg (Berkeley, CA: McCutcheon, 1979).

[24] See Shavelson, "Teachers' Decision Making" in Gage, *Psychology of Teaching Methods*; Eggleston, *Teacher Decision Making in the Classroom*; and Clark and Yinger, "Research on Teacher Thinking."

[25] This model is outlined in Clark and Peterson, "Teacher's Thought Processes," pp. 63–69.

[26] The problems with mechanical information processing as the ideal model for describing human decision making in situations fraught with conflict have been cogently outlined in David Braybrooke and Charles Lindblom, *A Strategy of Decision: Policy Evaluation as a Social Process* (New York: Free Press, 1963), pp. 246–247. More recently, Joseph Weizenbaum has argued against assuming that human judgment is comparable to even the most sophisticated computers, in *Computer Power and Human Reason: From Judgment to Calculation* (San Francisco: Freeman, 1976).

[27] Richard Shavelson and Paula Stern, "Research on Teachers' Pedagogical Thoughts, Judgments, Decisions, and Behavior," *Review of Educational Research, 51* (1981), 471.

defending against and choosing among conflicting expectations, she might also welcome their power to influence her working identity. The major difference, then, between the image of the teacher as dilemma manager and the other images I have described is that the dilemma manager accepts conflict as endemic and even useful to her work rather than seeing it as a burden that needs to be eliminated.

There are, of course, many incentives for teachers and scholars to want to eliminate conflict and to think of classroom problems as solvable. If pedagogical problems could be separated one from another rather than entangled in a web of contradictory goals, then they could be solved in some sort of linear progression — shot down like ducks coming up in a row at a penny arcade. Thinking of one's job as figuring out how to live with a web of related problems that cannot be solved seems like an admission of weakness. Sorting out problems and finding solutions that will make them go away is certainly a more highly valued endeavor in our society. Strategies which merely enable us to "cope" or "manage" go against our deep-seated hopes for making progress by gaining control over our interactions with one another. Many people — including teachers — believe that if only scholarship in psychology and the social sciences could come up to the levels achieved by the natural sciences, and if only, with the help of technology, individuals could achieve the ideal of control over the environment represented in such scholarship, then everyone could live happily ever after. The work of managing dilemmas, in contrast, requires admitting some essential limitations on our control over human problems. It suggests that some conflicts cannot be resolved and that the challenge is to find ways to keep them from erupting into more disruptive confrontations.

This connection of limitation with dilemma management needs to be clarified, because we have come to identify classroom management with the teacher's ability to control students' behavior and direct them in learning tasks. This common usage most closely parallels the nonschool definition of a manager as a person who controls or directs the affairs of others. Such control is certainly an essential part of the teacher's job. I use the term "manage" in a different sense, however. To manage to do something can also mean to contrive to do it, implying that the capacity for invention or improvisation is a necessary part of the manager's repertoire. This usage suggests that a manager is one who is able to find a way to do something and that action and invention are fused together in the management process. We might also think of people as managing when they are able to continue to act or even to thrive in adverse circumstances. The teacher's work involves just this sort of invention and action in situations where potential adversity makes solving some kinds of problems inadvisable.

In order to do the work of teaching, as I have portrayed it, one needs to have the resources to cope with equally weighted alternatives when it is not appropriate to express a preference between them. One needs to be able to take advice from researchers but also to know what to do when that advice is contradictory, or when it contradicts knowledge that can only be gained in a particular context. One needs to hold at bay the conflicting expectations of those who have the power to determine whether one can succeed as a teacher or not and at the same time use those expectations as references in self-definition. One can be committed to a particular ideology or its opposite while recognizing the limitations of taking any single-minded view of such complicated processes as teaching and learning in schools. One needs to be comfortable with a self that is complicated and sometimes inconsistent.

Perhaps it is our society's belief in the existence of a solution for every problem that has kept any significant discussion of the teacher's unsolvable problems out of both scholarly and professional conversations about the work of teaching. But there may be other explanations as well. It may be that many teachers are able to carry on with their work as if there were no conflicts in what they are expected to do, or that there are in fact no conflicts in the way they define their jobs. It also may be the case that the sorts of people who become teachers and stay in teaching do not have the intellectual capacity to recognize the complications in the work that I have described.[28] These possibilities certainly deserve our attention.

But if dilemma managing is a significant part of the work of teaching, there are several questions that deserve further examination. First, there are questions about *frequency*. I have argued only that it is possible for teachers to work in ways that suggest that some classroom problems are better managed than solved. How much of a role does this sort of work play in what teachers do? How often do dilemmas of the sort I have described arise in classrooms? How often are they "managed" rather than "resolved"? What are the characteristics of teachers who do more dilemma managing than others? What are the characteristics of classrooms in which dilemma management is common?

A second category of questions can be grouped around understanding and evaluating what teachers actually do when they manage dilemmas. My emphasis in this essay has not been on the particular strategies used by the teachers but on the more general elements of the work involved. What different kinds of *strategies* are used in classrooms to cope with unsolvable problems? How could they usefully be grouped? Are there better and worse ways of keeping classroom conflict under the surface? How do the strategies teachers use compare with those used by other professionals who face dilemmas?

We also need to know more about what kind of *resources* teachers have available to cope with contradictions within themselves and in their work. How do they learn to cope, or that it is an appropriate thing to do? What characteristics of their working environment make dilemma managing more or less possible? How can teachers who have trouble coping with conflict get better at it? What role do supervisors, formal course work, other life experiences, and colleagues play in the development of the teacher's capacity for actively tolerating ambiguity? How are the personal resources required to manage pedagogical dilemmas related to the skills that researchers and policymakers use to address educational problems or the knowledge that scholars use to analyze the tensions in the work of teaching? What resources besides skill and knowledge might teachers bring to this aspect of their work?

Our understanding of the work of teaching might be enhanced if we explored what teachers do when they choose to endure and make use of conflict. Such un-

---

[28] Jackson proposes this possibility in *Life in Classrooms*, pp. 144–148.

derstanding will be difficult to acquire if we approach all of the problems in teaching as if they are solvable, and if we assume that what is needed to solve them is knowledge that can be produced outside the classroom. In order to pursue the questions I have listed here, we shall need to adopt an image of teaching which takes account of the possibility that the teacher herself is a resource in managing the problems of educational practice.

The author would like to acknowledge the helpful comments of Gemmette Reid, Marvin Lazerson, and David K. Cohen on earlier drafts of this paper.

The Passion and Challenge of Teaching

SOPHIE FREUD

Reviewing her years as a student, wife, mother, and psychiatric social worker, Sophie Freud Loewenstein examines issues of concern to many women who try to combine family with career. She discusses her late intellectual maturation, her conflicts with and resolutions of women's double-role dilemmas and her struggle with depression and self-doubt. Feeling that she acquired a sense of identity only when she finally became an educator—a role she has embraced—she describes the challenges and rewards of this role, highlighting the paradoxes faced by professional women who are also wives and mothers.

"A sense of knowing where one is going" is Erikson's definition of identity (1959, p. 118), and it describes precisely how I felt when I found my identity as an educator. It was an identity delayed until midlife, leaving me with a compelling urge to make up for lost years. It was greatly enriched by earlier experiences that I had brought to it, or that had brought me to it. The first forty years of my life were an apprenticeship that led to the goal of becoming an educator. My apprenticeship as social worker, therapist, friend to other women, wife, and mother would become an integral part of the perspective that orders the passion and power, the doubts and challenges of my role as teacher.

My ambitions had progressed from being the best behaved child in Vienna to being the perfect mother, to being the flawless teacher. To reveal this quest for perfection is risky; claiming such successful hurdling of obstacles smacks of hubris. But I believe that my own efforts played only a part in bringing me to a respected position in society. Although striving for control has been a lifelong goal, deep down I agree with Amelie Rorty (1977):

> In truth, the real agents of my life have been, as I believe they are in every life, Time and Chance. Most of the events that were formative were coincidences. . . . Everything crucial might easily have been wholly different. The good things that have happened to me— and there have been many—seem to have been largely a matter of good fortune. I am less convinced that damaging things might have gone otherwise. I do not have the sense of having been at the center of my life, directing its course. (p. 41)

I have decided to risk self-exposure because my students, readers, and audiences belong to my group of "significant others." They give meaning to my identity as an

An earlier version of this paper was presented as part of the Askwith Symposium, Harvard University, April 1979.

Harvard Educational Review   Vol. 50   No. 1   February 1980, 1–12

educator, and consequently I now want to share thoughts about my life with them as a way of repaying my debt for their affirmation and support.

In evaluating my own life, I find many contradictions. Perhaps paradox characterizes a woman's life. For example, I view myself as a woman of power, yet I am dependent on the approval of my students and the recognition of the public. Despite a family of great accomplishment, I had trouble finding my own professional niche in society. Personality characteristics that were strengths in work situations added to my vulnerability as a mother. Although work was an emotional necessity for me, I long denied its significance in my life. My ambitions require solitude, yet I am sustained by my relationships with a community of women. Thus, my life has been neither orderly nor rational.

At the age of forty-two, I suddenly had a vivid image of self-fulfillment: I wanted to teach adults skills and help generate ideas that would enhance their professional competence and enrich their lives and the lives of the people with whom they worked. While I had interesting and challenging jobs before then, they had essentially been ready-made. This time I created my own, designing a course on the parent-teacher relationship for teachers-in-training, which grew out of my experience as a parent and out of my professional work with children and their families. My object was to train teachers in interviewing skills and help them see the parents' reality, because my dealings with my own children's teachers had often been disappointing. Designing this course was, then, really an early, characteristic attempt to master life's frustrations through an intellectual project.

I sent my handwritten labor of love to the department head of a teachers' training college. She was interested in the outline, but offered me only the opportunity to conduct one session as a guest lecturer. It was a crushing defeat. Then, one week before the fall semester began, the person who taught a similar course fell ill and I was asked to give my course. I approached this first teaching job without anxiety or hesitation, confident that I could deliver my important messages with skill and enthusiasm. My background as a psychiatric social worker proved to be ideal preparation for dealing with students in a classroom. Through my encounters with troubled people I had acquired enough practical experience to give flesh and meaning to theoretical content. More importantly, my practice in building positive relationships and my sensitivity to verbal and nonverbal messages were vital bridges between counseling and teaching. The students loved my course and I loved it. I felt that I belonged in a classroom; I had finally come home. Even when I reared my children, I had most enjoyed the teaching aspects of child-rearing. Teaching that course was a glorious experience that united many meaningful aspects of my life.

This opportunity exemplifies that combination of luck and initiative that eventually transformed my working life into a career. The watershed of my own professional life was entrance into the academic world through the official sanction of the Ph.D. degree. It is striking how many years it had taken me to reach professional and intellectual maturity. Levinson's (1978) men entered adulthood with a dream of adult accomplishment that shaped their lives in particular ways. I did not have such a dream. As a young adult, I was more concerned with honorable social and emotional survival than with dreams.

I was born in Vienna and emigrated to Paris at the age of thirteen, a few months after Hitler's Anschluss. Immigrants, especially those who speak the language poorly, have little status in a foreign land. Getting an education assumed a new importance when it was no longer easy or taken for granted. To restore my self-esteem, I sought to become an excellent student. I spent my eighteenth year in Casablanca at a time when Jewish children were not permitted to attend public school. Prohibited from finishing my education in the usual way, I studied at home to pass the high school examination. Not being allowed to go to school was very frightening.

In November 1942, I came to the United States at the age of eighteen. I was accepted at Radcliffe College in February 1943 and graduated three years later. Getting through Radcliffe with only an elementary knowledge of English initially, and no financial resources whatsoever, was clearly a feat. I did it, not with enjoyment and appreciation for learning, but with the grim determination of a survivor. My adolescence was overshadowed by immigration and war. Perhaps life as a European Jewish refugee was too turbulent and unpredictable to sustain an image of the future. More likely, an alternative dream of raising happy, well-adjusted, socially enlightened, and successful children eclipsed all other visions.

As a young mother, I started working part-time because I was restless and because I had noticed that my little daughter was showing telltale signs of my over-involvement with her. I had no sense of building a career, no dreams of glory, no particular sense of personal competence, and no professional goals—a surprising fact in view of a background that had provided unusually strong models and professional expectations.

My mother is an ambitious professional woman. She reached the age of eighty-four before she retired from full-time practice as a speech therapist. In contrast to other ambitious women who, according to research studies and autobiographies (Addams, 1910; Roosevelt, 1939; Hellman, 1969; Chisholm, 1970, Deutsch, 1973; Lozoff, 1973; Hennig, 1973), had especially strong bonds with their fathers, my primary identification, both positive and negative, has been with my mother. She worked throughout my childhood, and I always assumed that I would become a professional woman.

In addition, I was born into as royal a family as a Jewish child could ever claim. My grandfather, Sigmund Freud, was an intellectual king, and there was never any question in my mind that I was a princess. My first ambition was to become *das brautse Kind von Wien*—the best behaved child in Vienna. I cannot decide whether this meant that I was being socialized to be a good little girl, or whether I emphasized the competition and self-abnegation involved in such a goal. In either case, this early image contained both a sense of narcissistic entitlement and an obligation to meet high standards, and I grew up with the feeling that a life without intellectual achievement and public recognition would be worthless.

Even with this compelling script for achievement, conflicting societal expectations interfered with a clear pursuit of professional goals. My latent ambitions found destructive expression through projecting, first on my husband and later on my children, the unfair and absurd expectation that they would fill my needs for fame and glory. I have thus burdened my children with a heritage of delegated, excessive ambition (Stierlin, 1972). These high but unformulated aspirations made me vulnerable to profound self-doubt and recurring depression. In recent years, working fifteen hours a day, seven days a week, I have become more consistently confident that life has meaning and can be managed. Controlling my own life, I have less need to control the lives of others, and can now take responsibility for only my own successes and failures—which is a big relief.

Because I am more satisfied with my life now than I was during my child-rearing years, I often wonder whether I would have had a more productive and fulfilling life if, instead of rearing children, I had discovered and used my talents as an educator in earlier years. I had decided to become a mother, not because I was yearning for a child or had a special love for babies. On the contrary, I had been working at a clinic where I had seen everything that could go wrong with young children. I simply had a child because it never occurred to me that there was a choice. Life was easier in those days.

Motherhood swamped me with an array of intense and heretofore unknown emotions (Chodorow, 1976). My one full-time year at home was unsuccessful. My need always to excel and to be in full control of situations, along with my high energy level—all assets in working situations—interfered with being a relaxed and accepting young mother. Besides, I had an intergenerational debt to pay (Boszormeny-Nagy & Spark, 1973): feeling that I had been ungrateful and unloving toward my mother, I had to keep my emotional bank account balanced by overloving my daughter. I had a passion for my first child, accompanied like all passions by depression. The essence of passion is a fusion of identities; it leaves one powerless, subject to another's whims. I regret that I burdened my oldest child with the intensity of that passion.

I started to work part time when my daughter was one year old and continued to do so while nursing and rearing two more children, gradually increasing my working hours as the family grew older. Splitting my life into the two roles of social worker and mother raised problems of organization and energy, but no major emotional conflicts. I had been reared primarily by *fràuleins* and was quite determined to be the emotional anchor for my own children. Although I had the luxury of household help, I remained my children's primary caretaker and in full charge of the household. My husband was certainly ready to help with the household and rearing the children, but he was pursuing his own career in a more goal-directed way than I, working long hours and supporting our family financially. We had an unspoken agreement that all major decisions regarding our children would be in my hands. I admire and wonder at some of today's young mothers who seem so eager to share child-rearing with their husbands. Although I do not know whether my husband could have arranged his working life differently, I wish I had had the wisdom and generosity of spirit to move in that direction.

I want to bear witness loudly and clearly to the fact that none of my jobs ever approached in difficulty the emotional and intellectual demands of rearing children in our society. My heart beats faster even today when I remember the stress and anxiety of dealing with delayed developmental milestones, prolonged bedwetting, eczemas that must not be scratched, difficulties in reading and spelling, homesickness at summer camp, drug experimentation, refusal to get out of bed in the morning, Valentine's Day without valentines, getting into college and, once there, making it to graduation.

As a psychoanalytically trained mental-health professional, I was convinced that early development, especially the early mother-child interaction, irreversibly sets the stage for later personality formation, and felt guilty whenever I saw my emotional problems reflected in my children. But even worse, I saw each passing developmental problem as a threatening portent, and now I sometimes feel that my background in psychoanalytic theory poisoned my child-rearing years with needless, excessive anxiety. I am now careful to alert my students to newer, less deterministic research in child development (Clarke & Clarke, 1977) and to readings that question some of the expert advice offered to mothers (Wortis, 1971; Ehrenreich & English, 1978).

Researchers have been exploring the still unanswered question of why women are more vulnerable to depression than men (Weissman & Klerman, 1977). My own depressions were often related to child-rearing difficulties. The myth of blissful motherhood has only recently and mercifully been exploded (McBride, 1973; Radl, 1973; Lazarre, 1976; Rich, 1976) and only belatedly have mothers been vindicated by recent research suggesting that rearing young children is a mental health hazard for some women and that employment can be an important mitigator of this stress. This was certainly true for me; work was a salvation then, as it is now. Most men have two major roles, and this increases their chances of finding satisfaction in at least one (Gove & Tudor, 1973). I found this true as well. Having both roles eased rather than increased the strain of rearing children. A major difficulty of my child-rearing efforts was my inability to see my children as separate from myself (Bowen, 1976), a major problem for many mothers. Being a working mother did not protect me from over-involvement with my children; I continued to feel their pains and failures as if they were my own, but more keenly because I felt helpless to protect them from the vicissitudes of life.

Competence as a mother lies, in my opinion, in how successful one is in viewing one's children as separate from oneself. I cherish them and wish them well, but I try to remember that they have their own lives to lead, and must bear their own pain and make their own mistakes. Friends of mine have been destroyed when a major misfortune befell one of their children. I do not know if a mother can continue to lead a good life in this circumstance, but I wish it could be so. As I differentiate myself from my children, I hope that I shall never again become a prisoner of the despairing moods that once corroded my life.

I have come to the conclusion that both my emotional and professional life would have been impoverished had I chosen to remain childless. My deepest intellectual insights ultimately come from my own life experiences. Without feeling the anguish and joys of motherhood, I could never have fully grasped its meaning to others. I could not fully have found my way into other women's hearts and minds. I could never have become a student and teacher of issues relating to women's lives.

My children have been my most compelling teachers. They have helped me first to grow up and then to stay young. They have introduced me to new perspectives and lifestyles, and have helped me to become more tolerant. They were my first students as well, and like all students, they taught me as much as I taught them. They taught me wisdom, compassion, and humility. Although I practiced on them and made many mistakes, they have forgiven me, and now treat me with respect and affection, an unexpected bonanza in midlife.

The choice of working or not working, or working part-time or full-time, is a luxury that was given to middle-class women of my generation. On the one hand, the idea that I worked for pleasure rather than for money was reassuring. Work was less of a compelling duty, and that allowed me the freedom to leave a job when it offered no new challenge. On the other hand, it made work almost a form of self-indulgence, even a luxury, since it propelled us into a higher tax bracket while all my earnings were actually spent on childcare. Although for me work was an emotional necessity, it brought no visible benefits to my family, except insofar as it protected my children, to some small extent, from an overcontrolling mother.

One contradiction I cannot resolve is that work provided me with much satisfaction and yet I long denied its significance in my life. My self-esteem was not derived from competence at work but from my children's well-being. It took me about fifteen years to stop thinking of work as recreation, and even now I have difficulty with our society's strict distinction between work and leisure. I continue to find my greatest pleasure in work. My peak experiences come after teaching an especially good class, or finishing a paper. People have called me a "workaholic" because I am better at working than at playing, but considering one's work a joy strikes me as an asset, not a flaw.

I have always used work to modulate emotional crises in my life; the discipline demanded by work has protected me from excessive absorption with the crisis at hand. In addition, I have converted these crises into intellectual problems to be studied and objectified through theoretical formulations derived from reading, research, and writing. Thus I have used work as the highest form of play and as a way of mastering the problems of living. Perhaps this is why I am known as a person who is invariably cheerful while working. I enjoy working and am keenly conscious of the privilege of leading a life that I find fascinating.

Even while I had young children, I did not let work and parenting interfere with each other. I avoided role conflicts by establishing clear priorities which I seldom transgressed. For example, I organized matters so that I would not need to stay home if the children were sick. I wanted to be a completely dependable worker, and I never missed a day's work. It was another way of being the best behaved child in Vienna. Yet, I was always home for dinner and refused to accept either work or social engagements that would interfere with that routine.

As my job activities expanded, however, other pursuits such as entertaining, hobbies, and housekeeping had to be curtailed. While this did not affect my children, it caused hardship for my husband and I felt guilty for neglecting my role as a wife. My drive to work had gained momentum and had become an irrepressible necessity. My children have confronted me with my shortcomings as a mother, but my unavailability was not one of their complaints. My conflicts as a working mother were manageable only because my part-time social work jobs had well-defined hours. I could never have managed to be a creative college teacher while raising three children.

Even in my early days as a working mother, I had decided to be coldbloodedly protective about my time. I now hoard my time as a miser hoards money, carefully accounting for every moment, but splurging now and then to spend a whole afternoon with a friend. Hoarding time is unwomanly. It is sometimes greeted with consternation and resentment. Only a time hoarder understands another time hoarder; others consider one unfriendly, selfish, or arrogant. Although my good friends assure me that I am always there when they need me, the time problem nevertheless interferes with my feminist wish to be as available as I want to be to other women.

Many women turn to me for information, advice, and help and, once again, as with rearing children, difficult choices must be made. I have had to set priorities as to what claims people will have on my time. Anyone whom I have ever taught has very high priority for me. I take seriously the bond established between us and I have a sense of life-long commitment to students. To some extent, I think about them as I do about my children. I have educated them to the best of my ability and sent them out into the world, but this does not end my responsibility to them or my interest in their growth.

Keeping up with the new books and articles in my fields of human behavior and feminist studies is, of course, an impossible task, making me feel forever behind and in some ways as though I am failing in my duty. But I love teaching precisely because it allows me to live in a world of books. There was a time in my adolescence when I felt that books made life worth living. I now have an official mandate to do what I enjoy doing most — reading books and then sharing my thoughts, perceptions, and feelings with my students. I now read everything with a focus on what can be shared with them, which makes reading even more enriching. I start each of my classes with a warm-up period, seizing the opportunity for impromptu, passionate book reviews. I have an endless list of books to read in retirement, but I wonder if I will enjoy them as much, without an opportunity to share my ideas.

Before I knew what teaching was all about, I used to be afraid that it would lose its challenge after a few years and that I would become arid and stale. To avoid even the possibility of stagnation, I change the content of my old courses every year and I am forever designing new ones. Teaching a new course is an exciting adventure, full of risk and uncertainty. There are days when I am afraid that I cannot keep up with the dramas and challenges that I manage to impose on my life, and I realize now that I shall never fully master the kind of teaching that I do. It continuously forces me to use and stretch all my talents and abilities. The frontiers of teaching and learning are infinitely broad and receding.

Creativity poses another challenge. Nothing demands more inner discipline than self-imposed work. It is done at the expense of seeing friends, going to a movie, sewing, baking a cake, or doing all those other things that are inviting and relaxing. Tillie Olsen (1965) has become the spokesperson for mothers who cannot find the energy or time for creative efforts. At least mothers have a good excuse; we non-mothers or no-longer-mothers have only ourselves to blame for frittering our lives away. It is most difficult to find the solitude needed for creative effort. Miller (1976) points out that "affiliation is both a fundamental strength, and at the same time the inevitable source of many of women's current problems" (p. 89). Some of my women colleagues who are more talented than I have never been able to write scholarly papers because of their inability to work alone. I have been able to master this necessary discipline. During my solitary working hours, I eagerly look forward to being with people at the end of the day.

Both the creative process of writing and the process of recuperating from rejection and failure have been tests of endurance and self-discipline for me. When I first started to send papers for publication, they tended to come back, unaccepted. It would then take me months to send them to another journal, to say nothing of writing another paper. I dreaded looking into the mailbox and finding the large brown manila envelopes which contained rejected papers. When my husband started to worry about the manila envelopes as well, the tension became unbearable. As I reassured him that I could survive the disappointment, I reassured myself — to some extent. With time, I learned to write publishable papers and to become more resilient about setbacks. However, the opportunity to exchange ideas in writing with an international community of educators is deeply satisfying. My first successful paper was as big a building block of my identity as an educator as the first course that I taught.

I have never been attuned to the fear-of-success syndrome (Horner, 1972; Condry & Dyer, 1976). I think it is a male-oriented concept that assumes that anyone who does not want to play the game by the usual rules is troubled. I personally feel torn between wanting public recognition and whatever modest fame comes my way, and despising the empty publicity that sometimes goes with it, fearing the world will encroach upon my life and swallow me up. I am, however, very alive to the fear of failure that success entails. May Sarton (Note 1) tells us how difficult it is for an author to have every new book measured against all her other books. In teaching, too, with every new class, there is the fear of establishing new criteria against which one will be measured in the future. I fear having to live up to ever-increasing and eventually unattainable standards. I fear that a successful class will not be matched next week, and sometimes warn my students that the next one will be less interesting. In the same vein, I receive compliments about a good class uneasily, perceiving them as subtle criticism of prior classes.

I am especially vulnerable to criticism from my students. One critical comment, especially from a respected student, can undermine my self-confidence for days. With increasing self-confidence, I find myself more open to criticism, more able to learn from it, more ready to see it in perspective. I now try to be less devastated by student criticism and more philosophical about not being liked or appreciated by every student. It is rewarding to find that, in the process of becoming more open and vulnerable, I have actually become stronger. I no longer interpret criticism as a total invalidation of my worth, but rather as an issue to be examined.

As a woman, I have been brought up to please others (Miller, 1976, p. 110), and it is hard for me to displease my students or to feel in disharmony with them. Students are not usually aware of the extent to which teaching involves interaction. The mere presence of one or two silently or openly hostile students in a small class inhibits my ability to enjoy the class and to give fully of myself. I am even sensitive to the quality of the response of an audience in a large lecture hall; if it is missing or I cannot elicit it, I am drained of energy and can no longer communicate. I suspect that my characteristically feminine sensitivity to the moods of others (Miller, 1976, p. 61) is both an asset and a liability in my professional life.

I find it difficult to weigh the value of my own goals against the opinion of students when the two clash. There are so many of them and only one of me—how can I be sure I am right? Although teaching is a lonely enterprise most of the time, I feel that great autonomy is one of the most enviable privileges of an educator. Ultimately I can find the key to good teaching within myself: I can use my own power.

Powerful women are still a novel and unwelcome presence in our society. It has been suggested that a woman's power is awesome and aversive to both men and women since it is a traumatic throwback to the absolute power of the mother in early life (Lerner, 1974; Dinnerstein, 1976). In my early years of teaching, some of my students were intimidated by and resentful of my "overbearing" style. I do not know whether my students, for the most part in the last stages of emancipation from their mothers, were justified in their complaints or not. My own self-image as a nurturing and caring teacher who had little sense of personal power clashed with my students' perceptions. It took several years for their reactions to become credible to me. Perhaps, in the process of gaining self-confidence and assertiveness, I confused power as strength, with power as the exercise of influence (Miller, 1976, p. 117). I think I was carried away with the hope of convincing students of my particular viewpoint. Once I fully understood their feelings of vulnerability and powerlessness, I became more cautious about the use of power in the classroom, without relinquishing leadership. Untutored in the use of power (Miller, 1976, pp. 116-124), women teachers have to monitor it carefully.

Eventually I learned to become authoritative rather than authoritarian, and this coincided with starting a large, adult-education class and with giving frequent lectures to big audiences. I would not have been able to project myself to the audience, to present myself with self-assurance, to field friendly and hostile questions with skill and humor if I did not feel myself to be a woman of power.

Although coming into my own power as a woman has sustained me in my midlife years, I continue to question to what extent this power is an integral part of my identity. I have recently, while away from home, become aware of its shifting nature and its dependence on my social context. I hope that I do own some of my power, but I suspect that much of it is bestowed upon me by my affirming human community.

I have been particularly fortunate in the many relationships which have fostered my emotional and intellectual growth and helped me attain my goals. My husband's unflinching respect and his belief in my abilities was an important source of self-confidence in early adulthood. He offered me a financially and emotionally secure base of operation, and accepted me as an equal partner in our struggle to lead a good life. He recognized my relentless drive, and has either encouraged or accepted each new step of my professional journey, even though my total absorption in work sometimes leads us in different directions.

Likewise, I have been supported by women and men in teaching, supervisory, and collegial roles. Most of my female mentors have become close and lifelong friends, while male mentors have become respected colleagues. All through my life, I have had extremely close and loving women friends. We applaud each other's victories and support each other in times of defeat. In recent times I have found a large community of women who sustain me through their belief in me and their interest in my writing and teaching activities.

For a while I was so enchanted with teaching as interpersonal communication that I drifted away from my training as a therapist. Then I realized that the subjects of human behavior, emotions, and women's development had profound meaning for my students. I have come to believe that education is a powerful therapeutic tool. Good teaching is also good therapy, and good therapy involves a great deal of teaching. I have chosen to teach mature adult women who seem to use theoretical knowledge to lead more self-aware and powerful lives. Women who take my courses come into their own power. They feel they can conquer the world. I have returned to my early interest in using teaching as a way of improving people's lives.

Teachers are in an exposed position, scrutinized and judged daily by hundreds of students. There are days when I grow weary of performing, entertaining, and filling up others' emptiness. There are days when I tire of offering stimulation, encouragement, and comfort, and of being the target of my students' unresolved parental loves and hates. But curiously, as the years go by, those days grow fewer, perhaps because along with being more open, I have also become more detached. I used to get angry at students who did not meet my standards, and positively dislike and scorn them. With greater wisdom I have become less narcissistically engaged, both in my praise and criticism. I had to relearn the same lesson that motherhood had taught me. Students, like children, must learn and achieve for themselves, not for their teachers. I must take care that my love and concern for my students, like motherly love and concern, does not become a prison. Sarton (1961) made this dilemma the subject of one of her early novels; it is one familiar to women teachers. The teacher role implies distance, authority, evaluation, and objectivity, as well as warmth and nurturance.

Partly because I am Sigmund Freud's granddaughter, psychoanalytic theory has been imprinted on my thoughts, and my basic perceptions will always bear its stamp. For many years I was a virtual prisoner of its values and assumptions, in my roles as a woman, therapist, wife, and mother. It directed my thoughts to pathology and to the domination of the unconscious, implying individual responsibility, individual blame, and individual helplessness, rather than acknowledging strengths and the influence of fate and social forces. Rejecting the destructive aspects of this framework, which had such intense personal meaning for me, became my own declaration of independence. Most of my papers have been the result of coming to grips, sometimes after many months of reading or research, with some aspect of psychoanalytic theory. My theoretical papers are therefore highly personal documents.

I have thus grown from a passive, eager learner and teacher whose talent was to abstract and explain others' concepts into a person able to evaluate ideas and to build my own values. As a teacher, I have been forced continually to examine my values and ideas because I must state them clearly and defend them well. My acts and words are both very visible. As a model to my students I must live by the values that I teach. Above all, teaching is a way of sharing myself, of making an impact on the world, of making my intellectual and political contribution to society.

It is only in midlife that I have found my current, most genuine and autonomous identity as an educator. Finding this identity has given my life new meaning and new drama. My identity is an integration of my most meaningful roles: enthusiastic student, painfully maturing mother, struggling wife, and empathic social-work counselor. It involves my keen and caring interest in people, and my enjoyment of reading, writing, and teaching. It sanctions my wish to be a lifelong learner. It nurtures my creativity. This identity has helped me to overcome excessive narcissism and its accompanying depression. The public performances in which I often take pleasure, and the recognition which I have received, are both an indulgence and a sublimation of that narcissism. The sheer enjoyment of my work helps to protect me against depression. My work with adult women has forced me to attend to my own maturation and differentiation.

My identity as an educator was neither forged in adolescence nor consolidated through marriage. For me—and I think this is true for many women—the sequential stages of identity, intimacy, and generativity, regardless of the order in which they are proposed (Erikson, 1959; Goethals, 1976), do not describe the order of my life. Self-definition came first through motherhood and later, more autonomously, through work and competence. I had to proceed simultaneously on all fronts to master the complexities of many roles.

I have grown from a sweet and obedient little girl to a woman of passion and power. But the standard of being "the best-behaved child in Vienna" has remained a core aspect of my identity. I used to long to be really bad—just once in my life not to live up to everyone's expectations, especially my own. So far I have not succeeded. I have resigned myself to "being good," which has come to mean doing what I set out to do, to the best of my ability. Above all, it means being self-disciplined.

Although I have led a privileged life and may not be considered a traditional woman, I still expect that many women will recognize themselves in me. I have never spoken to another woman, regardless of how different her life circumstances, without feeling profound kinship with her struggles. A striking feature of my development, one that I share with other women, has been my late intellectual awakening. Although I have worked almost all my life, it was only in my forties that work became emotionally significant and a source of self-esteem, and only in my fifties that my latent ambition found self-expression.

Thus I find myself in midlife with a passion for my work. Like any other passion it is addictive and enslaving. Although a passion for work makes one less dependent on other people, it does not assure invulnerability. I still rely on students, institutions, health, and other circumstances for the opportunity to continue teaching. A passion for teaching, however, seems to be a little more one's own than other passions.

I am beginning to understand that the paradoxes of my life are related to being a student and teacher of topics that intimately touch my own and other people's lives. Such a field demands total devotion to its subject matter, as well as providing rich and varied life experiences. It demands tight self-discipline and loose creativity. It demands openness to people and absorption with ideas, protection of time and energy, as well as endless commitment to students. It demands both solitude and many human encounters. It demands skills of objectivity, observation, and involvement, distance as well as intimacy. It demands self-assurance, power, and humility.

Reference Note

1. Sarton, M. Comments made during a Radcliffe Open Forum, April 4, 1978.

References

Addams. J. *Twenty years at Hull House*. New York: Macmillan, 1910/1966.

Boszormeny-Nagy, I., & Spark, G. *Invisible loyalties*. New York: Harper & Row, 1973.

Bowen, M. Theory in the practice of psychotherapy. In P. Guerin (Ed.), *Family therapy: Theory and practice*. New York: Halsted Press, 1976.

Brown, G. W., Bhrolchain, M. N., & Harris, T. Social class and psychiatric disturbance among women in an urban population. *Sociology*, 1973, **78,** 225–254.

Chisholm, S. *Unbought and unbossed*. Boston: Houghton Mifflin, 1970.

Chodorow, N. Oedipal asymmetries and heterosexual knots. *Social Problems*, 1976, **23,** 454–467.

Clarke, A., & Clarke, A. D. M. *Early experience: Myth and evidence*. New York: Free Press, 1977.

Condry, J., & Dyer, S. Fear of success: Attribution of cause to the victim. *Journal of Social Issues*, 1976, **32** (3), 63–83.

Deutsch, H. *Confrontations with myself*. New York: Norton, 1973.

Dinnerstein, D. *The mermaid and the minotaur*. New York: Harper & Row, 1976.

Ehrenreich, B., & English, D. *For her own good: 150 years of the experts' advice to women*. New York: Anchor Press/Doubleday, 1978.

Erikson, E. The problem of ego identity. *Psychological Issues*, 1959, 1 (1), 101–164.

Goethals, G. W. The evolution of sexual and genital intimacy: A comparison of the views of Erik E. Erikson and Harry Stack Sullivan. *Journal of the American Academy of Psychoanalysis*, 1976, **4** (4), 1-16.

Gove, W. R., & Tudor, J. F. Adult sex roles and mental illness. *American Journal of Sociology*, 1973, **78,** 812-835.

Hellman, L. *An unfinished woman.* Boston: Little, Brown, 1969.

Hennig, M. Family dynamics for developing positive achievement motivation in women: The successful woman executive. *Annals of the New York Academy of Sciences*, 1973, **208,** 77-81.

Horner, M. The motive to avoid success and changing aspirations of college women. In J. Bardwick (Ed.), *Readings on the psychology of women.* New York: Harper & Row, 1972.

Lazarre, J. *The mother knot.* New York: McGraw-Hill, 1976.

Lerner, H. Early origins of envy and devaluation of women: Implications for sex role stereotypes. *Bulletin of the Menninger Clinic*, 1974, **36** (6), 538-553.

Levinson, D. J., with Darrow, C. N., Klein, E. B., Levinson, M. H., & McKee, B. *The seasons of a man's life.* New York: Knopf, 1978.

Lozoff, M. Fathers and autonomy in women. *Annals of the New York Academy of Sciences*, 1973, **208,** 91-97.

McBride, A. B. *The growth and development of mothers.* New York: Harper & Row, 1973.

Miller, J. B. *Toward a new psychology of women.* Boston: Beacon Press, 1976.

Olsen, T. Silences. *Harper's Magazine*, October 1965, pp. 153-161.

Radl, S. *Mother's day is over.* New York: Charterhouse, 1973.

Rich, A. *Of woman born.* New York: Norton, 1976.

Roosevelt, E. *This is my story.* New York: Harper & Row, 1939.

Rorty, A. O. Dependency, individuality and work. In S. Ruddick & P. Daniels (Eds.), *Working it out.* New York: Pantheon Books, 1977.

Sarton, M. *The small room.* New York: Norton, 1961.

Stierlin, H. *Separating parents and adolescents.* New York: Quadrangle, 1972.

Weissman, M. M., & Klerman, G. Sex differences and the epidemiology of depression. *Archives of General Psychiatry*, 1977, **34,** 98-111.

Wortis, R. The acceptance of the concept of the maternal role by behavioral scientists: Its effect on women. *American Journal of Orthopsychiatry*, 1971, **41,** 733-746.

What I Teach and Why

SELWYN R. CUDJOE

*In this article the author chronicles the major movements of Afro-American litera-
ture, demonstrating both its particularity and its universality and depicting the manner in which the content of Afro-American experiences shapes the literary forms
through which it is expressed. Throughout the essay, Selwyn Cudjoe describes the perspective and methodology which underlie his teaching of Afro-American literature.*

I teach Afro-American Literature because I am trained in the area of literature and
because it is the literature of my people. When one speaks of Afro-American
literature, one speaks about the literary expressions of the spiritual and emotional experiences of one of the most oppressed people in the world today. Our oppression has
led to our profound alienation and has involved the malicious attempt to reduce us to
beings concerned only with the satisfaction of our animal desires.[1] Like all great art,
literature is nothing more than a human document which reflects the historical content of a given age. As a pedagogical tool, it is a means of trying to grasp the nature of
physical and emotional reality. As such, Afro-American literature mirrors the life of
Afro-American peoples, showing how they lived, how they were treated by their oppressors, how they have transformed themselves and been transformed over time, and
the various forms which have been used to capture the essential features of their on-
tological being.

I see truth as central to any discussion about pedagogy and the process of arriving at
that truth as a crucial function of my method. Therefore, I begin my teaching with
what I call the threefold synthesis of truth. First of all, I let my students know that I
perceive the world in a particular manner and that because I am a social being I

---

[1] In differentiating between man's purely "animal functions" and his "human functions," I draw upon
Karl Marx. In differentiating between the two processes, Marx made the following observation:

"As a result, therefore [of man's alienation from his own labor], man (the worker) only feels himself freely
active in his animal functions—eating, drinking, procreating, or at most in his dwelling and in dressing up,
etc.; and in his human functions he no longer feels himself to be anything but an animal. What is animal
becomes human and what is human becomes animal.

"Certainly eating, drinking, procreating, etc., are also genuinely human functions. But taken abstractly,
separated from the sphere of all other human activity and turned into sole and ultimate ends, they are
animal functions." Karl Marx and Frederick Engels, *Collected Works,* III (New York: International
Publishers, 1976), 274-275.

This article is adapted from a lecture presented to the Cambridge Forum, First Parish Church, Cambridge, Massachusetts, February 7, 1979.

Harvard Educational Review   Vol. 50   No. 3   August 1980, 362–381

possess certain values: I am neither neutral nor unbiased in my presentation of pedagogical materials. I explain that each society has its own heroes and villains, its own ideals, and affirms its own values within a well-defined aesthetic mode. Moreover, I want my students to understand that the Eurocentric perceptions of what is ideal and beautiful are not the only ones, and that one has to employ a historical methodology to understand the truth of this statement. Sometimes I use the following argument to buttress my case:

> The works of the great Asian, African and American cultures of the Middle Ages form a special aesthetic world apart. They contain a great deal that is strange and un-familiar to the eye of the European who, directly or indirectly, had absorbed the Greco-Roman tradition. One is frequently struck by their expressive power and com-plex symbolism, clearly marked by the influence of primitive magic with its "cryp-tography," a system of taboos, concrete personification and deification of the powers of nature, and cult of guardian spirits, along with the specific socio-historical forms and features of life of the various peoples.[2]

Secondly, I remind my students that truth, as I see it, is an approximation. It is the attempt always to bridge the gap between "is" and "ought," knowing full well that the gap will always be unbridgeable.[3] Because the discovery of truth lies in process, we proceed by dialogue. Together we search to arrive at an approximation of truth, knowing that one of the most important achievements of our time will be finding a methodology, an epistemology, and a perception of being that provide us with a framework for accomplishing that task.

Thirdly, our approach to scholarship is profoundly humanistic. We insist, in the words of Fidel Castro, that artistic creations should be valued in "proportion to what they offer mankind, in proportion to their contribution to the revindication of man, the liberation of man, [and] the happiness of man." As he noted aptly: "There can be no esthetic value in opposition to man. Esthetic value cannot exist in opposition to justice, in opposition to the welfare of or in opposition to the happiness of man. It can-

---

[2] Vladislav Zimenko, *The Humanism of Art* (Moscow: Progress Publishers, 1976), p. 44.

[3] In discussing Georg Lukács's concept of the dialectical interrelation of "ought" ("sollen") and "is," Istvàn Mèszàros makes the following observation: "The dominant note of his [Lukács's] formulations is a 'longing for objectivity' and, in accordance with it, a never ending explicit polemic against 'ought.' Yet Lukács is intensely aware of the problematic character of any cult of objectivity in our age, and therefore qualifies his statements in such a way that the 'overtones' of his analyses to some extent reassert the validity of 'ought' in an indirect form. . . . In an essay written in 1909, after praising [Thomas] Mann's dialectical and artistic powers of seeing 'the connection between all things,' as well as his great sense of objectivity, Lukács makes the general point that 'objectivity can perhaps never exist without a certain irony. The most serious regard for things is always somewhat ironic, for somewhere or other the great gulf between cause and effect, between the conjuring of fate and the fate conjured, must become obvious. . . . The philosopher feels the same dislocation from, and the same longing for, an objective synthesis and unity in a world in which the gulf between 'cause and effect,' 'intention and result,' 'value and reality', appear to be ever-increasing, al-though of course for him [Lukács] 'irony cannot bring a solution' " (p. 42). If truth is to be found in the resolution or the synthesis of these antitheses, one can only take heart from the French epigram which sug-gests that "truth is marching on and the end of ends will not stop it." ("*La verité est lentement en marche et à la fin des fins rien ne l'arrêtera*" (p. 45). The point, of course, is that truth in this case is such that it is never quite achieved nor is it ever fully resolved. See Istvàn Mèszàros, *Lukács's Concept of Dialectic* (Lon-don: Merlin Press, 1972). The concept of the approximation of all truth is confirmed also by modern science. As Fritjof Capra has pointed out, "the basic attitude of modern science [is] that all of its concepts and theories are approximate" (*The Tao of Physics* [New York: Bantam, 1976], p. 123).

not exist."[4] Our pedagogy, therefore, is one of humanism, where people stand as the supreme value—not property, not the sacredness of artificial systems, not the elaborate web of superstitious practices, but human beings in their poeticized wisdom and folly, strength and weakness, beauty and ugliness.

Consistent with this approach to pedagogy, I see the students as the most important presence in my classroom. I am fortunate that my classes never exceed thirty-five students, and so I am able to treat each student individually. During the semester I meet with each student for at least thirty minutes to discuss the lectures, the student's work, and his or her response to what I am trying to convey.

According to the Harvard tradition, each professor is supposed to make a unique contribution to the student's development. Because I seek to cultivate critical minds, all students are required to present a ten-minute paper on an assigned topic to the class, thereby exposing their ideas and interpretation to the rigorous critique of their peers. According to one student evaluation of the course, "most students find this approach very rewarding; others argue that one learns more from the professor than from the students."[5] Whatever the merit of this procedure, I try to encourage my student's participation in the experience of discovering knowledge and truth, and value open criticism of my methods from my students.

In our course, we begin to examine Afro-American literature by establishing the fact that it is a manifestation of the consciousness of Afro-American peoples. Our aesthetic concern is with a particular kind of person—a historic being who has emerged under specific circumstances and whose aesthetic sensibilities have been fashioned by a particular geography, social setting, and economic arrangement. As a teacher and scholar, I wish to find those aesthetic forms which are used to capture the particularity of Afro-American man and woman, through the explication of literary text. I am, therefore, concerned with the dialectical interrelationship of form and content, bearing in mind Hegel's notion that they are interpenetrative.

But literature is a universal phenomenon. To be literature, a piece of work must abide by certain well-defined canons. The literary arts present peculiar difficulties because their subject matter is people and, no matter how radical one becomes, one must always revert to the universality of human existence. As Marx explained: "To be radical is to go to the root of the matter. For man, however, the root is man himself."[6] Afro-American literature is universal in that it abides by the universal canons of literature, and yet specific in that it arises out of a context that is both African and American and that involves both slavery and multinational cooperation. Because culture is fluid and social situations change, a literature which began deeply embedded in one context changes as that culture is transformed by history; in the process, so too does the very nature of literary sensibilities. Thus a literature which began with Africans in a New World was transformed over time into a literature of Afro-Americans in an unfree world.

The development of Afro-American literature has paralleled that of most other forms of Western literature. In it one can see a classical period in which the works of

---

[4] Fidel Castro, quoted in Roberto Fernandez Retemar, "Caliban, Notes Towards a Discussion of Culture in our America," *The Massachusetts Review*, 15, Nos. 1-2 (1974), 60-61.

[5] *CUE (Course Evaluation Guide)*, Committee on Undergraduate Education, Harvard University, 1979, p. 85.

[6] Karl Marx, quoted in Georg Lukács, *History and Class Consciousness* (London: Merlin, 1971), p. 83.

Phillis Wheatley were most conspicuous. William Wells Brown's *Clotel*[7] can be seen as part of a romantic tradition. Brown used the arguments of two scholars of the Enlightenment and the Romantic period, Voltaire and Rousseau, to buttress his condemnation of slavery. In Charles Chesnutt's work, we see a literature of realism, and in the work of Richard Wright we see aspects of naturalism and, later on, of existentialism. In Toni Morrison's writings, we find a complex attempt at what I call sociopsychological realism, which seeks to examine clinically the nature of that psychic dispossession of which Frantz Fanon spoke so eloquently.

There are certain pecularities of form which can be ascribed specifically to Afro-American culture, highlighting the richness of its literature and, thereby, of all American literature. I refer to the brilliant essays of James Baldwin, which seem to derive from the sermonesque-rapping of the Afro-American religious experience, the dialect which Paul Laurence Dunbar introduced into his works, and Chesnutt's skilled integration of the folkloric tradition in his "conjure tales."[8] Indeed, in Chesnutt's work we see the most energetic integration of the particularity of Afro-American literature blended with the universal concerns of world literature. As Karen Myers suggested in her perceptive criticism of *The Conjure Woman:*

> The parallels between Ovid's *Metamorphoses* and Chesnutt's *Conjure Woman* are representative of universal mythic patterns in literature. The similarities are particularly striking because both artists utilize myths of the fall and of transformation to define a relationship between human life and the rest of the natural world and because both find in these ancient patterns an appropriate means of revealing basic psychological patterns and of commenting upon contemporary life. The continuing appeal of such tales suggests both the universality of human experience and the power of creative fiction to engage the imagination in the interest of social progress.[9]

Nowhere else but in the literature of Afro-Americans does one find the very special use of the African elegy as in the works of Phillis Wheatley, the richness of Arabic poetry upon which Claude McKay draws in his poems, the use of jazz rhythms by Langston Hughes, and the particular coolness of Afro-American life-style rapping in the work of Don L. Lee.

These nuances of form were responses to experiences which needed a vehicle of expression. Precisely because Afro-Americans are an oppressed people, the dominant trend of that literature has been a reflection of that oppressed condition. Thus we find that the content of Afro-American literature simultaneously affirms humanistic ideals and is actively committed to the liberation of Afro-American men and women. Therefore, I reject the characterization of Afro-American literature as "protest literature." It exemplifes a cultural arrogance by which others have sought to interpret our reality and to be the sole arbiters of what is, and what should constitute, our reality.

This tradition of affirming our own reality can be seen from the very inception of Afro-American literature. Beginning with the poetry of Phillis Wheatley, around 1770, we first hear the broken strains of this affirmation:

[7] Williams Wells Brown, *Clotel or the President's Daughter, A Narrative of a Slave's Life in the United States* (1853; rpt. New York: Collier, 1970).

[8] See Charles W. Chesnutt, *The Conjure Woman* (1899; rpt. Ann Arbor: Univ. of Michigan, 1972).

[9] Karen Magee Myers, "Mythic Patterns in Charles Waddell Chesnutt's *The Conjure Woman* and Ovid's *Metamorphoses*," *Black American Literature Forum*, 13, No. 1 (1979), 17.

No more, *America* in mournful strain
Of wrongs, and grievance unredress'd complain.
No longer shalt thou dread the iron chain,
Which wanton *Tyranny* with lawless hand
Has made, and with it meant t' enslave the land.
  Should you, my lord, while you peruse my song,
Wonder from whence my love of *Freedom* sprung,
Whence flow these wishes for the common good,
By feeling hearts alone best understood,
I, young in life, by seeming cruel fate
Was snatch'd from *Afric's* fancy'd happy seat:
What pangs excruciating must molest,
What sorrows labour in my parent's breast?
Steel'd was that soul and by no misery mov'd
That from a father seiz'd his babe belov'd:
Such, such my case. And can I then but pray
Others may never feel tyrannic sway?[10]

In 1792, approximately twenty years later, Gustavus Vassa wrote one of the first prose pieces by an Afro-American:

Permit me, with the greatest deference and respect, to lay at your feet the following genuine narrative, the chief design of which is to excite in your august assemblies a sense of compassion for the miseries which the Slave Trade has entailed on my unfortunate countrymen. By the horrors of that trade was I first torn away from all the tender connections that were naturally dear to my heart; but these, through the mysterious ways of Providence, I ought to regard as infinitely more than compensated for by the introduction I have thence obtained as to the knowledge of the Christian religion, and a nation which, by its liberal sentiments, its humanity, the glorious freedom of its government, and its proficiency in arts and sciences, has exalted the dignity of man.[11]

As Edward Scobie pointed out in *Black Brittania*, not only did *The Interesting Narrative of the Life of Olaudah Equiano, the African* "excite . . . a sense of compassion for the miseries which the Slave Trade . . . entailed upon his countrymen," but also, "This vivid personal account of the sufferings of a captured African was widely quoted whenever the motion for abolition was being debated in the House [of Parliament]."[12] In this respect, then, the *Narrative of Olaudah Equiano* accomplishes one of the major functions it was intended to achieve.

One can only understand the manner in which Afro-American reality and its literature came into being by looking at the contradictions within it. On the one hand were the horrors of slavery and the middle passage, while on the other were the possibilities of redemption and the affirmation of humanism promised by Christianity. It was, I suspect, the attempt to synthesize these two polarities that became the modus operandi of the literature. Thus one can argue that the central principle of Afro-American literature derives from the simultaneous negation of the barbarity of slavery

[10] Phillis Wheatley, *Memoir and Poems of Phillis Wheatley, A Native African and a Slave* (1838; rpt. Miami: Mnemosyne, 1969), p. 48.
[11] Olaudah Equiano, *The Interesting Life of Olaudah Equiano or Gustavus Vassa, the African* (Leeds, Eng.: printed for James Nichols; London: Cracock and Joy and W.H. Blackburn, 1814), pp. ii–iv.
[12] Edward Scobie, *Black Brittania* (Chicago: Johnson, 1972), p. 79.

and its consequent horrors, and the affirmation of the progressive aspect of our existence in slavery and capitalism from which the luminous quality of our humanism emerged. Initially, this contradiction attempted to resolve itself within the context of religion. As the literature flowered, it sought resolution within the context of nationalism and, later, of socialism.

The theme of affirmation and negation was picked up by David Walker, who counselled in 1828:

> Never make an attempt to gain our freedom or *natural right*, from under our cruel oppressors and murderers, until you see your way clear—when that hour arrives and you move, be not afraid or dismayed; for be you assured that Jesus Christ the King of heaven and earth, who is the God of justice and of armies, will surely go before you. And those enemies who have for hundreds of years stolen our *rights*, and kept us ignorant of Him and His divine worship, He will remove.[13]

But if Walker was concerned about our oppression by those whom he called our "natural enemies," William Wells Brown stressed the inherent contradictions of the relationship between Afro-Americans and Euro-Americans, illustrating it in concrete detail. He contrasted the pious words and grandiloquent phrases of Thomas Jefferson with his actions. It is in this context that Jefferson's words seem so unflinchingly hypocritical:

> The whole commerce between master and slave is a perpetual exercise of the most boisterous passions; *the most unremitting despotism on the one part, and degrading submission on the other.* With what execration should the statesman be lauded who, permitting one half the citizens thus to trample on the rights of the other, transforms those into despots and these into enemies, destroys the morals of the one part, and the *amor patriae* of the other! For if the slave can have a country in this world, it must be any other in preference to that in which he is born to live and labour for another; in which he must lock up the faculties of his nature, contribute as far as depends on his individual endeavours to the evanishment of the human race, or entail his own miserable condition on the endless generations proceeding from him . . . . I tremble for my country, when I recollect that God is just, and that His justice cannot sleep forever. The Almighty has no attribute that can take sides with us in such a struggle.[14]

Brown contrasts these righteous phrases with the actions of Jefferson in abandoning his daughter, Clotel, to the institution of slavery. Rather than accept the cruelties of this system, Clotel escaped from slavery only to be captured once more in the nation's capital. Brown allowed the drama of *Clotel* to unfold "within plain sight of the President's house and the capital of the Union."[15] Rather than return to slavery, Clotel willingly accepted death when she plunged into the Potomac River in plain sight of the symbols of liberty and justice. Wringing every last drop of romantic emotion from the scene, Brown describes the last minute of Clotel's life in the following manner:

> Her resolution was taken. She clasped her *hands* convulsively and raised *them*, as she at the same time raised her *eyes* towards heaven, and begged for that mercy and com-

[13] David Walker, "Appeal in Four Articles, Together with an Appeal to the Coloured Citizens of the World, But in Particular, and Very Expressly, to Those of the United States of America." In *Chronicles of Black Protest*, ed. Bradford Chambers (New York: New American Library, 1968), p. 57.
[14] Brown, *Clotel*, pp. 122-123.
[15] Brown, p. 177.

passion *there*, which had been denied her on earth; and then, with a single bound, she vaulted over the railings of the bridge, and sunk forever beneath the waves of the river.

Thus died Clotel, the daughter of Thomas Jefferson, a president of the United States; a man distinguished as the author of the Declaration of American Independence, and one of the first statesmen of that country.

Had Clotel escaped from oppression in any other land, in the disguise in which she fled from the Mississippi to Richmond, and reached the United States, no honour within the gift of the American people would have been too good to have been heaped upon the heroic woman. But she was a slave, and therefore out of the pale of sympathy.[16]

Clotel was the first Afro-American novel in which what we may call the American Contradiction was first expressed through a literary character. More important, in this novel we saw the grandiloquent gesture versus the monumental emptiness of America's action. Yet one had to wait until the end of the century to see this question posed in fuller novelistic terms. It was in *The Marrow of Tradition* that Charles Chesnutt suggested that ingrained racism—that antihuman ideology which lay at the very vitals of the national character—was poisoning our national life. He proposed filial reconciliation as the essential ingredient for healing the American spirit. This point is made graphically when Mrs. Carteret pleads with Dr. Miller, the chief protagonist in the novel, to save the life of her white child. Mrs. Carteret, who is white, has refused to acknowledge the existence of Janet Miller, her mulatto half sister (both children of the same father) for twenty-five years. Therefore, before Dr. William Miller attempts to save the life of Mrs. Carteret's only child, he demands that Mrs. Carteret acknowledge her black sister's existence—that is, that Euro-America acknowledge its filial relationship with Afro-America—in order to save the future of the nation which her son represents. Paradoxical as it may seem, however, it is the son of the black doctor who must be sacrificed (Dr. Miller's son is killed when a racial riot breaks out in the town) in order to effect this spiritual reconciliation.

The plea for reconciliation was a persistent theme in the literature. Euro-America, however, chose not to listen. As a consequence, Afro-America recoiled within itself, and, faced with insistent oppression,[17] Afro-Americans had only two choices. They could either pass for white, that is, "sell one's birthright for a mess of pottage,"[18] as did the chief protagonist of *The Autobiography of an Ex-Coloured Man*, or resist, as did Claude McKay, nobly exclaiming:

> If we must die, O let us nobly die,
> So that our precious blood may not be shed
> In vain; then even the monsters we defy
> Shall be constrained to honor us though dead![19]

Yet the very manner in which the choice is posed suggested a grave and fundamental dichotomy in the life and fate of many Afro-Americans—one opted either for spiritual

---

[16] Brown, p. 177.

[17] Within the period from 1890 to 1918, approximately 2500 Afro-Americans were killed by lynch mobs, and an avalanche of racial literature appeared during the first part of this period, 1890-1900.

[18] James Weldon Johnson, *"The Autobiography of an Ex-Coloured Man"* (1912; rpt. New York: Knopf, 1927), p. 211.

[19] Claude McKay, *Selected Poems of Claude McKay* (New York: Bookman, 1953), p. 36.

or physical annihilation. In any case, the future looked very grim for our forebears, and they suggested, through the vehicle of prose and verse, that life was not and would not be any "crystal stair."[20]

Given this choice, one could only be more cautious in one's affirmation. The search for one's origins and authentic being in order to verify one's existence proceeded apace in the 1920s. This search was articulated best by Countee Cullen, whose magnificent poem "Heritage," asked "What is Africa to me?," posing a dilemma faced by so many of our forebears:

> What is Africa to me:
> Copper sun or scarlet sea,
> Jungle star or jungle track,
> Strong bronzed men, or regal black
> Women from whose loins I sprang
> When birds of Eden sang?
> *One three centuries removed*
> *From the scenes his fathers loved,*
> *Spicy grove, cinnamon tree,*
> *What is Africa to me?*
> . . . .
> Quaint, outlandish heathen gods
> Black men fashion out of rods,
> Clay, and brittle bits of stone,
> In a likeness like their own,
> My conversion came high-priced;
> I belong to Jesus Christ,
> Preacher of humility;
> Heathen gods are naught to me.
> . . . .
> Do I play a double part.
> Ever at Thy glowing altar
> Must my heart grow sick and falter,
> Wishing He I served were black,
> . . . .
> Lord, I fashion dark gods, too,
> Daring even to give You
> Dark despairing features where,
> Crowned with dark rebellious hair,
> Patience wavers just so much as
> Mortal grief compels, while touches
> Quick and hot, of anger, rise
> To smitten cheek and weary eyes.
> Lord forgive me if my need
> Sometimes shapes a human creed.[21]

It is this strange dichotomy which presents itself to the Afro-American writer in the twentieth century. Whereas in the eighteenth century both Phillis Wheatley and

---

[20] Langston Hughes, "Mother to Son," in *Selected Poems of Langston Hughes* (New York: Knopf, 1959), p. 187.

[21] Countee Cullen, *On These I Stand* (New York: Harper & Row, 1925), pp. 24-28.

Olaudah Equiano were Africans in America, experiencing New World realities with African sensibilities, the writers of the twentieth century were African-American,[22] faced with trying to reconcile the ambiguous nature of their Africanness with the problematic nature of their Americanness. In striking contrast to Cullen's dilemma, Langston Hughes could say in "Epilogue":

> I, too, sing America.
>
> I am the darker brother.
> They send me to eat in the kitchen.
> When company comes,
> But I laugh,
> And eat well,
> And grow strong.
>
> Tomorrow,
> I'll sit at the table
> When company comes.
> Nobody'll dare
> Say to me,
> "Eat in the kitchen,"
>
> Then.
>
> Besides,
> They'll see how beautiful I am
> And be ashamed —
>
> I, too, am America.[23]

But if the search for roots in Africa and its fusion with newly acquired Americanness represented the passive side of our Afro-Americanness — the plea to be accepted as Americans — the revolutionary awareness and bitterness of our depraved condition both here and in Africa spoke to the impotence and almost blind rage with which we experience our exclusion from the social and political life of America. This lucid vehemence is perhaps best captured by Claude McKay in his sonnet, "Enslaved":

> Oh when I think of my long-suffering race,
> For weary centuries, despised, oppressed
> Enslaved and lynched, denied a human place
> In the great life line of the Christian West,
> And in the Black Land disinherited,

---

[22] The term "Afro-American" was apparently coined by E. J. Waring in 1878. Odessa B. Baker, in her wondrously illuminating thesis on the nature of metaphoric language in Afro-American thought, suggests that, by the use of the term, E. J. Waring "introduces through semantic suggestion the concept of Black rootedness — genically, African, culturally, American; both of which were being intellectually and political- ly denied by the larger society. The designator "Afro-American" is proposed not only to fuse two worlds apart but also to generate (through semantic induction) a new paradigm (or metaphor) of perception in which a more positive image of Blacks would prevail." See Odessa B. Baker, "Metaphor of Self-Identity as Contained in the Black Press from 1827 to the Present," Diss. Harvard Univ. 1978, pp. 82-83. Incidentally, this is by far one of the best works in which the use of the metaphor as a method of self identity within the Afro-American community is examined.

[23] Langston Hughes, "Epilogue," in *Black American Literature,* ed. Darwin Turner (Columbus, Ohio: Merrill, 1970), p. 225.

> Robbed in the ancient country of its birth,
> My heart grows sick with hate, becomes as lead,
> For this my race that has no home on earth.
> Then from the dark depths of my soul I cry
> To the avenging angel to consume
> The white man's world of wonders utterly:
> Let it be swallowed up in earth's vast womb,
> Or upward roll as sacrificial smoke
> To liberate my people from its yoke![24]

And yet all was not vehemence and hate. There was also beauty such as Jean Toomer's *Cane*,[25] which offered lyricism in a wondrous concoction of poetry and prose. Still, there lingered the emotional displacement of his women, who never seemed to find fulfillment in relationships with their men. Was it prophecy? Writing in 1979, half a century later, Michele Wallace, a young black woman, commenting on the sexual politics of black men and black women, argued that

> for perhaps the last fifty years there has been a growing distrust, even hatred, between black men and black women. It has been nursed along not only by racism on the part of whites but also by an almost deliberate ignorance on the part of blacks about the sexual politics of their experience in this country.
>
> As the Civil Rights Movement progressed, little attention was devoted to an examination of the historical black male/female relationship, except for those aspects of it that reinforced the notion of the black man as the sexual victim of "matriarchal" tyranny. The results have been calamitous. The black woman has become a social and intellectual suicide; the black man, unintrospective and oppressive.
>
> It is from this perspective that the black man and woman faced the challenge of the Black Revolution — a revolution subsequently dissipated and distorted by their inability to see each other clearly through the fog of sexual myths and fallacies. They have gone on alternately idealizing and vilifying their relationship, very rarely finding out what they are really made of. This has cost them a great deal. It has cost them unity, for one thing.[26]

I find Wallace's book dangerous because it seeks to simplify very complex realities, and because it is illiterate in the area of sociopolitical analysis. Any work which suggests that "the Black Power Movement was probably one of the most fiercely romantic in America's history,"[27] or that "the black revolutionary of the sixties calls to mind nothing so much as a child who is acting for the simple pleasure of the reaction he will elicit from, and the pain he will cause, his father,"[28] shows quite clearly that the author, despite her posturing, has a woeful lack of understanding of political reality in the contemporary United States.

Nonetheless, I cite the work for the very important reason that it attempts to grapple with the intrasocial and emotional complexities of Afro-American existence to which Jean Toomer alluded in 1923 when he produced *Cane*. In this context, also, I

---

[24] McKay, p. 42.
[25] Jean Toomer, *Cane* (1923; rpt. New York: Harper & Row, 1969).
[26] Michele Wallace, *Black Macho and the Myth of the Superwoman* (New York: Dial, 1979), p. 13.
[27] Wallace, p. 34.
[28] Wallace, p. 75.

presume that when one talks about the special perspective which the Afro-American Studies Department brings to bear upon its subject matter, this is one area—the sexual politics of black male/black female relationships, black male/white female relationships, and the incredible variants of emotional reactions involved—where only the initiated may want to tread. Also, one may regard *Black Macho and the Myth of the Superwoman* as another instance in which Euro-Americans, through the skillful dissemination of ideas, attempt to control our conceptions of our reality by telling us what we should read and how we should feel about ourselves. Nothing else can explain the enthusiastic manner in which the Euro-American literary and cultural establishment has pushed this work, and the amount of publicity its author received when, one year earlier, Jeanne Noble in *Beautiful, Also, Are the Souls of My Black Sisters,*[29] had addressed many of the same issues in a much more sophisticated manner. Noble's book is an illuminating work which traces the history of black woman from the time African women were "a collective force in molding African civilization, particularly the institutional life of marriage and family,"[30] to the present, in which the African-American woman lives, "in the shadow of negative comparisons with white women whose images as ideal feminine women are entrenched in the folklore and myths of America."[31] It is from this historical and cultural perspective, which is so lacking in Wallace's book, that Noble examines the African-American woman and the black revolution of the sixties.

Richard Wright used a naturalistic and existential approach in attempting to sketch the complexities and nuances of Afro-American life. He depicted the sordidness of Afro-American life and sought to introduce certain Marxist premises to interpret our reality. Arguing that the consciousness of the Afro-American writer "had lagged sadly" behind that of black workers, Wright contended that "Negro writing" should mold the lives and consciousness of the Afro-American masses towards new goals and should indeed "create values by which this race is to struggle, live, and die."[32] However, precisely because literature is not simply a photographic reproduction of reality, Wright failed to achieve in his major work, *Native Son,*[33] the depiction of "Negro life in all of its manifold and intricate relationships" which he called for in his "Blueprint for Negro Writing."[34] Instead, even though Wright produced the starkest and most graphic depiction of black reality ever to appear on the literary canvas of the United States, he lacked the overall vision to define the Afro-American in some or all of his complexities, and therein lay his major fault. Ralph Ellison may have been correct in suggesting that "Wright could imagine Bigger, but Bigger could not possibly imagine Richard Wright."[35] Indeed one can argue that Bigger, the protagonist in *Native Son,* was more a reflection of Euro-American perception of Afro-American reality than he was the Afro-American's perception of himself.

---

[29] Jeanne Noble, *Beautiful, Also, Are the Souls of My Black Sisters* (Englewood Cliffs, N.J.: Prentice-Hall, 1978).

[30] Noble, p. 23.

[31] Noble, p. 27.

[32] Richard Wright, "Blueprint for Negro Writing," in *The Black Aesthetic,* ed. Addison Gayle (New York: Doubleday, 1971), p. 321.

[33] Richard Wright, *Native Son* (New York: Harper & Row, 1940).

[34] Wright, "Blueprint," p. 320.

[35] Ralph Ellison, *Shadow and Act* (New York: Vintage, 1972), p. 114.

It was left to Ralph Ellison to develop the Afro-American in all his invisible and indivisible wholeness. In the tradition of the classical epic of Western literature, an unnamed protagonist sets out on a journey, a search for identity, on which depends the future of his race and his nation. From the *Odyssey* to *Sir Gawain and the Green Knight,* amidst superhuman danger, virtue came through the struggle of the hero and his triumph over evil forces. In Ellison's work, these dangers were the forces of capitalism (Mr. Kimbro and the paint factory), communism (the Brotherhood), and nationalism (Ras, the Exhorter).

At the end of this quixotic journey, however, Ellison's protagonist had not yet resolved the paradox of his American identity. Though he discovers the roots of his identity in Harlem, at the end of his journey he still has not discovered "the next phase," as he puts it, and so can only

> denounce and defend, or feel prepared to defend. I condemn and affirm, say no and say yes, say yes and say no. I denounce because though implicated and partially responsible, I have been hurt to the point of abysmal pain, hurt to the point of invisibility. And I defend because in spite of all I find that I love. In order to get some of it down I *have* to love. I sell you no phoney forgiveness, I'm a desperate man—but too much of life will be lost, its meaning lost, unless you approach as much through love as through hate. So I approach it through division. So I denounce and I defend and I hate and I love.[36]

And so he returned underground to contemplate the chaos of his being. The realism of Ralph Ellison is critical in that it examines the causal factors which result in the nexus of relationships that determines our reality, a reality that is problematic, uncertain, and invisible within the context of the United States of America. But this is the only home he knows.

The attempt to reconcile what it means to be negroid and to be American becomes the painful burden of the cutting essays of James Baldwin. He uses his unique gift of language, blending the art of rapping with the terror and brimstone of the Afro-American sermon, which possesses its own peculiar cadences, to orchestrate the intense emotional experiences of Afro-Americans. For Baldwin, of course, this violent synthesis of being negroid and American can only be negotiated successfully if Afro-Americans, like Euro-Americans, accept the total reality of the uniqueness of their Americanness.[37]

The years 1954 and 1957 were important ones for Afro-American people. The former marked the Supreme Court decision that schools in the United States could not be both separate and equal; and the latter marked the independence of Ghana, the first twentieth-century African state. For black people, these events highlighted the intensity of the American Contradiction and ushered in a new era in the social and political consciousness of Afro-Americans. This heightened consciousness was reflected in the literature.

---

[36] Ralph Ellison, *Invisible Man* (New York: Penguin, 1965), pp. 566-567.
[37] See James Baldwin, *Notes of a Native Son* (Boston: Beacon Press, 1955), esp. the essays, "Many Thousands Gone," "Notes of a Native Son," and "Stranger in a Villlage."

Equally as important, in 1952 Frantz Fanon published *Black Skin, White Masks*[38] which, as Irene Gendzier has pointed out, "tend[ed] towards a psychological interpretation of racism."[39] More than any other work in this period, with the possible exception of *The Wretched of the Earth*,[40] this book had a tremendous influence upon the black intellectuals and artists of the black revolution of the sixties and the early seventies. In this work, Fanon delved with great depth and perception into the psychological problems that black people who lived in a white-dominated world had to deal with, and examined the myths and taboos within the collective unconscious of black and white people alike. As he suggested:

> In the United States, as we can see, the Negro makes stories in which it becomes possible for him to work off his aggression; the white man's unconscious justifies this aggression and gives it worth by turning it on himself, thus reproducing the classic schema of masochism. We can now stake out a marker. For the majority of white men the Negro represents the sexual instinct (in its raw state). The Negro is the incarnation of a genital potency beyond all moralities and prohibitions. The women among the whites, by a genuine process of induction, invariably view the Negro as the keeper of the impalpable gate that opens into the realm of orgies, of bacchanals, or delirious sexual sensations.[41]

However one wished to view these theories, it became very clear that the Afro-American, and indeed all colonized peoples, needed new conceptual tools with which to analyze their existence and move beyond the present historical moment. Speaking in Hegelian terms, Fanon ended his discussion with the following prescription:

> No attempt must be made to encase man, for it is his destiny to be set free.
> The body of history does not determine a single one of my actions.
> I am my own foundation.
> And it is by going beyond the historical, instrumental hypothesis that I will initiate the cycle of my freedom.
> The Disaster of the man of color lies in the fact that he was enslaved.
> The disaster and the inhumanity of the white man lie in the fact that somewhere he has killed man.[42]

Herein lay the foundation for building the new Afro-American, and Afro-American writers, radical theorists, and those engaged in "the struggle" latched on to the ideas of Fanon with abiding tenacity.

In 1963 Fanon's *The Wretched of the Earth* became available to English-speaking readers. Published just a few days before Fanon died of leukemia, this work had a profound impact upon Afro-Americans and the entire colonial world. What was Fanon's message in *The Wretched of the Earth* and why was it so appealing to many Afro-Americans? In the first place, Fanon made it very clear that colonialism was a compact built upon violence, and suggested that such a compact could only be broken through reciprocal violence. For Afro-Americans who saw themselves as a colonized society

---

[38] Frantz Fanon, *Black Skin, White Masks* (New York: Grove, 1967).
[39] Irene L. Gendzier, *Frantz Fanon: A Critical Study* (New York: Pantheon, 1973), pp. 46-47.
[40] Frantz Fanon, *The Wretched of the Earth* (New York: Grove, 1963).
[41] Fanon, *Black Skin, White Masks*, pp. 176-177.
[42] Fanon, *Black Skin, White Masks*, pp. 230-231.

within a society and considered their confinement in the ghettoes of the United States as proof of their separateness, this theme had a familiar ring. Indeed, Malcolm X declared that "America is a colonial power. She has colonized 22,000,000 Afro-Americans by depriving us of first-class citizenship, by depriving us of civil rights, actually by depriving us of human rights."[43]

Fanon suggested that the decolonization process taking place in Africa was, by definition, an inherently violent phenomenon which owed its existence to the class of two diverse economic systems. Further, it was a system which destroyed the social forms which existed in the colonies and which would generate reciprocal violence once colonial peoples assumed the burdens of their lives.

The violence which characterized the colonization process was not confined to the social and economic order. It went to the heart of the aesthetic values of the people as well. Thus the process of decolonization becomes a process in which the values of the white master culture must be violently uprooted and expunged. According to Fanon:

> The violence with which the supremacy of white values is affirmed and the aggressiveness which has permeated the victory of these values over the ways of life and of thought of the native mean that, in revenge, the native laughs in mockery when Western values are mentioned in front of him. In the colonial context the settler only ends his work of breaking in the native when the latter admits loudly and intelligibly the supremacy of the white man's values. In the period of decolonisation, the colonized masses mock at these values, insult them and vomit them up.[44]

For Fanon, therefore, decolonization almost invariably demanded the therapeutic necessity of violence as a cleansing force which released colonized people from a sense of inferiority and gave them back their sense of self-worth and dignity. This collective participation in the process of decolonization made the people guard their newly acquired freedom with a passion and made them reject all attempts at trying to mystify the process of liberation. Such analysis and, perhaps more importantly, such rhetoric, found a ready echo in the black American revolution that was gathering momentum at the time that Fanon's book appeared.

In 1964 Malcolm X, the self-proclaimed black nationalist, on breaking away from the Nation of Islam, stated categorically that "it is criminal to teach a man not to defend himself when he is the constant victim of brutal attacks,"[45] and speaking on the black revolution a month later, declared, "this is a year of bloodshed, that the black man has ceased to turn the other cheek, that he has ceased to be non-violent, that he has ceased to feel that he must be confined to all these restraints that are put upon him by white society in struggling for what white society says he was supposed to have had a hundred years ago."[46] Indeed, drawing upon the revolutionary experiences of the United States during its war of independence, Malcolm X not only argued that violence was necessary to achieve the liberation of black people in this country, but also advanced the theory that the Afro-American liberation movement was a part of the world-wide struggle of black people for independence and that these two streams of revolutionary activity would merge eventually.

[43] *Two Speeches by Malcolm X* (New York: Merit, 1969), p. 9.
[44] Fanon, *Wretched of the Earth*, p. 35.
[45] *Two Speeches by Malcolm X*, p. 4.
[46] *Two Speeches by Malcolm X*, p. 7.

For Malcolm X, the national liberation movement of the Third World, which gained in intensity in 1945, gave further impetus to the Afro-American liberation struggle and led Malcolm X to believe that 1964 was the year of revolution in the United States. As Malcolm reminded us,

> Revolutions are never fought by turning the other cheek. Revolutions are never based upon love your enemy, and pray for those who spitefully use you. And revolutions are never waged singing, "We Shall Overcome." Revolutions are based on bloodshed. Revolutions are never compromising. Revolutions are never based on negotiations. Revolutions are never based upon any kind of tokenism whatsoever. Revolutions are never even based upon that which is begging a corrupt society or a corrupt system to accept us into it. Revolutions overturn systems, and there is no system on this earth which has proven itself more corrupt, more criminal than this system, that in 1964 still colonizes 22,000,000 African-Americans, still enslaves 22,000,000 Afro-Americans.[47]

Against this background it is not difficult to understand why the writing of Fanon would find a ready response in the minds and hearts of Afro-Americans. Indeed, as Irene Gendzier was perceptive enough to understand, it was not so much Fanon's theory of violence that was emphasized in *The Wretched of the Earth*, as it was "the analysis of political development in the third world, . . . the penetrating discussion of political organization, and the genesis and degeneration of nationalist movements and parties."[48]

In 1968 Eldridge Cleaver, a young black man in the prisons of white America and an ardent follower of Malcolm X and Fanon, produced his sensational work, *Soul on Ice*. Profoundly influenced by Fanon and struck by the violent assassination of Malcolm X, whom he revered, he was able in his anger to capture the dominant sentiments of America's black men when he asserted: "We shall have our manhood. We shall have it or the earth will be leveled by our attempts to gain it."[49]

In his introduction to *Soul on Ice*, Maxwell Geisman called Eldridge Cleaver one of the distinctive black voices of the age and compared his book very favorably with Richard Wright's *Native Son* and Malcolm's *Autobiography*. More importantly, he saw *Soul on Ice* and Fanon's *Black Skin, White Masks* as proposing the liberation of black people from the spiritual colonization of the white world. Whatever one may have thought of Geisman's placing *Soul on Ice* in such elevated literary company, it is very clear that Cleaver drew much from Fanon and Malcolm, even though he vulgarized much of the more sophisticated psychiatric findings of Fanon (who was a psychiatrist by profession) and issued forth in much more "inauthentic" terms some of the nationalistic concerns of Malcolm X.

Significantly, Cleaver began *Soul on Ice* in 1954, some months after the Supreme Court outlawed segregation. For him this judicial event marked a time when "I began to form a concept of what it meant to be black in white America."[50] For Cleaver, however, this decision had much more epochal significance in American history. It meant that black people could compete equally with white people and assert themselves in all areas of life. Set in such a context, there was always the

[47] *Two Speeches by Malcolm X*, pp. 8-9.
[48] Gendzier, *Frantz Fanon*, pp. 197-198.
[49] Eldridge Cleaver, *Soul on Ice* (New York: Ramparts, 1968), p. 61.
[50] Cleaver, p. 3.

"pathological" motivation of Blacks to be better than whites at all times and the tendency of whites to remove themselves further from Blacks. Like Fanon and Malcolm, Cleaver sought to show the interconnectedness of the African liberation movement with the Black Revolution in America and saw the eradication of white superiority and dominance as the principal tasks of both movements. Even though Cleaver recognized the achievements of European civilization, he felt compelled to protest against the inhumanity of slavery and those who promulgated its virtues. For him the national liberation struggle of the Third World had shattered the illusions of white supremacy which had accumulated over the last two centuries and opened up a new way of looking at history. For Cleaver, the future of America lay in the hands of the Afro-American and Euro-American youth, who together had understood the possibilities which the world-wide struggle for national liberation had opened up for all people.

The influence of Fanon touched all levels of the literature. Even the poets found themselves constrained to invoke the name of Fanon in their art to encourage their young revolutionaries to struggle. According to the poet Sonia Sanchez:

> an u got a
> re vo lu tion
> goin'
>   like.man.program
> us in blk/
>   ness & u'll
> have warrior
>   sons & young
> sistuhs who will take
> what we just rapped
> bout doin'.
>   read us midnite
> poems of Elijahs fanons
> nkrumahs karengas
>   and then
> make us sing they music/
> wisdom by heart
>   to our children
> but. above all.
>   LOVE US.
>   LOVE US.
> LoooooooooOOOVE US
> yo/stereotyped/blk/woman
>   & u got a win![51]

Nikki Giovanni demonstrated the symbolic importance of Fanon when she ridiculed middle-class Blacks who used their acquaintance with Fanon to camouflage their real passivity:

---

[51] Sonia Sanchez, *We a BaddDDD People* (Detroit: Broadside, 1970), p. 68.

> I am the token negro
> I sit in the colored section with Fanon in hand
> (to demonstrate my militancy).[52]

Yet the invocation of Fanon by our poets was used not simply to assuage our grief but to convey a body of truths to transform our spiritual reality and to excoriate the whiteness that blackened our souls. Summing up the impact of Fanon upon black consciousness at the end of the decade and the impetus that his thoughts gave to the black aesthetic movement, Addison Gayle agreed with Fanon that during the time of revolutionary struggle the traditional Western liberal ideals must be vigorously opposed. "The young writers of the black ghetto have set out in search of a black aesthetic, a system of isolating and evaluating the artistic works of black people which reflect the special character and imperatives of black experience."[53] This was the cry of the new black aesthetic movement, which sought to fashion new ideals and idols of beauty for black people. More importantly, this movement sought to articulate the fact that Afro-American peoples are beautiful, capable of creating fine artifacts, and possessed of a reservoir of patience and a capacity for endurance which kept them going from the time they were brought to this country.

The psychological studies of Fanon bore fruit in the seventies, particularly in the writings of black female novelists, who explored what it meant to be a black woman in white America. Writers such as Maya Angelou, Toni Morrison, Toni Cade Bambara, Alice Walker, and Louise Meriwether examined the sociopsychological reality of black women and their relationships with each other, and in the process deepened our understanding of what it meant to be black in America. Mary Helen Washington in her collection of stories by these and other black women, argued that their stories are classic because, "in probing the black woman's experiences with integrity and skill, they offer a vision of black women that has dimension and complexity as well as fidelity to history."[54] More importantly, the presence of these black female writers and the attempt by critics like Washington to place female writers such as Nella Larsen (*Quicksand*),[55] Zora Neale Hurston (*Their Eyes Were Watching God*),[56] and Gwendolyn Brooks (*Maude Martha*),[57] squarely within the tradition of Afro-American letters could not help but broaden the contours of our literature.

The seventies, therefore, was a period in which Blacks dug deeply into themselves, both figuratively and colloquially, in an attempt to understand their inner being. It was at this time that Fanon became the theoretical explicator of our reality. As he said in his chapter, "The Negro and Psychopathology," "Freud and Adler and even the cosmic Jung did not think of the Negro in all their investigations. And they were quite right not to have. It is too often forgotten that neurosis is not a basic element of human reality. Like it or not, the Oedipus complex is far from coming into being among

---

[52] Nikki Giovanni, "The Dance Committee Concerning Jean-Leon Destine," in *Black Feeling, Black Talk, Black Judgment* (New York: Morrow, 1970), p. 43.

[53] Addison Gayle, Jr., ed., *The Black Aesthetic* (New York: Anchor, 1971), p. 8.

[54] Mary Helen Washington, ed., *Black-Eyed Susans* (New York: Anchor, 1975), p. xxxi.

[55] Nella Larsen, *Quicksand* (1928; rpt. New York: Negro Universities Press, 1969).

[56] Zora Neale Hurston, *Their Eyes Were Watching God* (Greenwich, Conn.: Lippincott, 1937).

[57] Gwendolyn Brooks, *Maud Martha* (New York: Harper, 1953).

Negroes."[58] Like it or not, we dug Fanon because he dug us and understood us in our deepest being, and we responded in kind.

In the portals of ivy, Afro-American literature was not a subject to be studied. After all, what did Afro-Americans know about versification, the strophe, or the periphrase? How else could one explain the fact that *The American Tradition in Literature,* one of the standard texts used in American colleges during the 1960s, devoted only two and a half of more than 3000 pages to Afro-American literature?[59] Here was an anthology used by most of the universities and colleges in the United States. The men who edited this text possessed some of the most enviable credentials the Euro-American world could confer upon them. Yet they could only find one Afro-American poet worthy of being anthologized.[60] Was this racism? I leave it to the reader to decide. Yet these are some of the same people who tell us today that we do not need Afro-American literature courses, that the quality of Afro-American literature is not comparable to that of Euro-American literature. If one decides to teach the literature of one's people, one is not a serious scholar; a serious scholar would teach and study the works of Pirandello or Beckett, Shakespeare or Dante, Milton or Chaucer.

American scholars are lauded if they study the works of American authors; Irish critics are honored if they know the intricacies of Joyce. One is called perceptive if one can fathom why Beckett's characters are waiting for Godot,[61] or if indeed Pirandello's characters are really in search of an author or vice versa.[62] One admires Pirandello's technical brilliance and his choice of metaphysical subject matter. Yet if and when one decides that the sociopsychological realism of Toni Morrison is indeed of tremendous literary significance,[63] or that Margaret Walker's fusion of history and literature poses some rather interesting epistemological questions,[64] one is told that one is not a serious scholar and that even the most pedantic and empty scholasticism is superior to Afro-American scholarship if it deals with anything other than the Afro-American experience.

This brings me to another issue—not with or why I teach, but where. In Afro-American Studies, *where* seems always to take precedence over all other questions. At each moment of my academic life, I find myself having to explain why I teach in the "refuse heap of academia," an Afro-American Studies department. Sometimes, overwhelmed by evidence of the most "objective" kind, I, like Aimé Césaire, am forced to "declare my crimes" and confess that "the expanse of my perversity confounds me."[65] I must confess that I love my people and find no other salvation but writing for my

[58] Fanon, *Black Skin, White Masks,* pp. 151–152.

[59] Sculley Bradley, Richard Croom Beatty, and E. Hudson Long, *The American Tradition in Literature,* Vols. I, II, 3rd ed. (New York: Norton, 1966).

[60] The poet anthologized was Le Roi Jones whose poems, "In Memory of Radio," and "An Agony. As Now," appeared as the last two poems in Vol. II of *The American Tradition.* Ironically, however, the biographical notes assert: "Jones is easily the most interesting of the Negro poets, but race is not often an issue in his poetry and does not restrict its appeal" (p. 1721).

[61] Samuel Beckett, *Waiting for Godot* (New York: Grove, 1954).

[62] Luigi Pirandello, "Six Characters in Search of an Author: A Comedy in the Making," in *Naked Masks,* ed. Eric Bentley (New York: Dutton, 1952).

[63] Toni Morrison, *The Bluest Eye* (New York: Pocket Books, 1970).

[64] See Margaret Walker, *Jubilee* (New York: Bantam, 1966).

[65] Aimé Césaire, *Return to My Native Land* (Harmondsworth, Eng.: Penguin, 1970), p. 55.

people, studying with my people, and attempting to share my knowledge with my people.

But yet the haunting question lingers: Why Afro-American Studies? It is because I believe that Afro-American Studies have a special perspective on the quality of our humanity. And was it not Leopold Senghor who, after spending two weeks in New York, exclaimed:

> New York! I say to you: New York let black blood
>   flow into your blood
> That it may rub the rust from your steel joints, like
>   an oil of life,
> That it may give to your bridges the bend of buttocks
>   and the suppleness of creepers.
> Now return the most ancient times, the unit recovered,
>   the reconciliation of the Lion the Bull and the Tree
> Thought linked to act, ear to heart, sign to sense,
> There are your rivers murmuring with scented crocodiles and
>   mirage-eye manatees. And no need to invent the Sirens.
> But it is enough to open the eyes to the rainbow of April
> And the ears, above all the ears, to God who out of the
>   laugh of a saxophone created the heaven and the
>   earth in six days.
> And the seventh day he slept the great sleep of the Negro.[66]

It is this quality of humanity and our immersion in the world that I submit is the unique contribution which we as a people can make to the established disciplines. As Aimé Césaire said, we are "truly the eldest sons of the world open to all the breaths of the world."[67]

More specifically, I teach Afro-American literature because I like to believe that I bring to my students life-giving thoughts. I teach them to hate racial exclusiveness and the shameful exploitation of people. I teach my students that life is the highest value and should not be bought or sold for even the choicest pieces of silver.

I teach Afro-American literature because I believe that when one removes the iron armor of racial identity, all that one finds beneath is the person: puny yet powerful; fragile yet fecund; humble and humane; an individual in all of his or her wonderful and multifarious beauty. The Afro-American shares in this kinship, and so it is that through our images, metaphors, symbols, and the subtle nuances that have been the province of literature from time immemorial, we express the unique and distinctive elements of our humanity.

I teach Afro-American literature because it makes a profound statement about our people and our heritage as it makes itself manifest in historical time. I also teach Afro-American literature because, despite our shortcomings, we are one of the most profoundly creative of all contemporary peoples. In spite of our innocence, we are truly the elders of the world, and when the morrow comes and our adversaries look upon our countenance, they will truly be ashamed and be constrained to say: Indeed, you too are American.

---

[66] Leopold Senghor, "New York," in Gerald Moore and Ulli Beier, *Modern Poetry from Africa* (Baltimore: Penguin, 1963), p. 58.

[67] Césaire, *Return to My Native Land*, p. 75.

PART 2

Cultural Critique

Teacher Education and the Politics of Engagement: The Case for Democratic Schooling

HENRY A. GIROUX
PETER McLAREN

Henry A. Giroux and Peter McLaren argue that many of the recently recommended public-school reforms either sidestep or abandon the principles underlying education for a democratic citizenry developed by John Dewey and others in the early part of this century. Yet, Giroux and McLaren believe that this historical precedent suggests a way of reconceptualizing teaching and public schooling which revives the values of democratic citizenship and social justice. They demonstrate that teachers, as "transformative intellectuals," can reclaim space in schools for the exercise of critical citizenship via an ethical and political discourse that recasts, in emancipatory terms, the relationships between authority and teacher work, and schooling and the social order. Moreover, the authors outline a teacher education curriculum that links the critical study of power, language, culture, and history to the practice of a critical pedagogy, one that values student experience and student voice. As they state, "teacher education programs must assume a central role in reforming public education and, in so doing, must assert the primacy of a democratic tradition in order to restructure school-community relations."

As far back as 1890, a teacher from New England named Horace Willard cogently argued that in contrast to members of other professions, teachers lived "lives of mechanical routine, and were subjected to a machine of supervision, organization, classification, grading, percentages, uniformity, promotions, tests, examination."[1] Nowhere, Willard decried, was there room in the school culture for "individuality, ideas, independence, originality, study, investigation."[2] Forty years later Henry W. Holmes, dean of Harvard University's new Graduate School of Education, echoed these sentiments in his criticism of the National Survey of the Education of Teachers in 1930. According to Holmes, the survey failed to support teachers

---

[1] Arthur G. Powell, "University Schools of Education in the Twentieth Century," *Peabody Journal of Education, 54* (1976), 4.
[2] Powell, "University Schools," p. 4.

Harvard Educational Review Vol. 56 No. 3 August 1986, 213–238

as independent critical thinkers. Instead, it endorsed a view of the teacher as a "routine worker under the expert direction of principals, supervisors, and superintendents."[3] Holmes was convinced that if teachers' work continued to be defined in such a narrow fashion, schools of education would eventually respond by limiting themselves to forms of training that virtually undermined the development of teachers as critically-minded intellectuals.

At different times both of these noteworthy critics of American education recognized that any viable attempt at educational reform must address the issue of teacher education. Most important was their conviction that teachers should function professionally as intellectuals, and that teacher education should be inextricably linked to critically transforming the school setting and, by extension, the wider social setting.

In the early part of the century, a number of experimental teacher education programs managed to shift the terrain of struggle for democratic schooling from a largely rhetorical platform to the program site itself. One such program was organized around New College, an experimental teacher training venture affiliated with Columbia University, Teachers College between 1927 and 1953. Spokespersons from New College proclaimed "that a sound teacher education program must lie in a proper integration of rich scholarship, educational theory, and professional practice."[4] Furthermore, New College embarked on a training program based on the principle that "it is the peculiar privilege of the teacher to play a large part in the development of the social order of the next generation."[5] The College's first announcement claimed that if teachers were to escape from the usual "academic lock step . . . [they] required contact with life in its various phases and understanding of it — an understanding of the intellectual, moral, social, and economic life of the people."[6]

The idea that teacher education programs should center their academic and moral objectives on the education of teachers as critical intellectuals, while simultaneously advancing democratic interests, has invariably influenced the debates revolving around the various "crises" in education over the last fifty years.[7] Moreover, it has been precisely because of the presence of such an idea that a rationale eventually could be constructed which linked schooling to the imperatives of democracy and classroom pedagogy to the dynamics of citizenship. This is not to suggest, however, that either public education or teacher training programs were overburdened by a concern for democracy and citizenship.[8] Nevertheless, the historical precedent for educating teachers as intellectuals and developing schools as

---

[3] George Counts, quoted in Powell, "University Schools," p. 4.

[4] As quoted in Lawrence A. Cremin, David A. Shannon, and Mary Evelyn Townsend, *A History of Teachers College, Columbia University* (New York: Columbia University Press, 1954), p. 222.

[5] Cremin, Shannon, and Townsend, *A History*, p. 222.

[6] As quoted by George Counts in Cremin, Shannon, and Townsend, *A History*, p. 222.

[7] For an interesting discussion of this issue, see Ira Katznelson and Margaret Weir, *Schooling for All: Class, Race, and the Decline of the Democratic Ideal* (New York: Basic Books, 1985).

[8] See esp. the work of the revisionist historians of the 1960s. Among the representative works are Michael B. Katz, *The Irony of Early School Reform: Educational Innovation in Mid-Nineteenth Century Massachusetts* (Boston: Beacon Press, 1968); Colin Greer, *The Great School Legend* (New York: Basic Books, 1972); and Clarence J. Karier, Paul Violas, and Joel Spring, *Roots of Crisis: American Education in the Twentieth Century* (Chicago: Rand McNally, 1973).

democratic sites for social transformation might begin to define the way in which public education and the education of teachers *could* be appropriately perceived today. We wish, in other words, to build upon this precedent in order to argue for the education of teachers as transformative intellectuals. We use the term "intellectual" in the manner described by Frank Lentricchia:

> By "intellectual" I do not mean what traditional Marxism has generally meant — a bearer of the universal, the political conscience of us all. Nor do I mean "a radical intellectual" in the narrowest of understandings of Antonio Gramsci — an intellectual whose practice is overtly, daily aligned with and empirically involved in the working class. By intellectual I refer to the *specific intellectual* described by Foucault — one whose radical work of transformation, whose fight against repression is carried on at the specific institutional site where he finds himself and on the terms of his own expertise, on the terms inherent to his own functioning as an intellectual.[9]

By the term "transformative intellectual," we refer to one who exercises forms of intellectual and pedagogical practice which attempt to insert teaching and learning directly into the political sphere by arguing that schooling represents both a struggle for meaning and a struggle over power relations. We are also referring to one whose intellectual practices are necessarily grounded in forms of moral and ethical discourse exhibiting a preferential concern for the suffering and struggles of the disadvantaged and oppressed. Here we extend the traditional view of the intellectual as someone who is able to analyze various interests and contradictions within society to someone capable of articulating emancipatory possibilities and working towards their realization. Teachers who assume the role of transformative intellectuals treat students as critical agents, question how knowledge is produced and distributed, utilize dialogue, and make knowledge meaningful, critical, and ultimately emancipatory.[10]

We argue in this paper that within the current discourse on educational reform[11] there exists, with few exceptions,[12] an ominous silence regarding the role that both teacher education and public schooling should play in advancing democratic practices, critical citizenship, and the role of the teacher as intellectual. Given the legacy of democracy and social reform bequeathed to us by our educational forebears, such as John Dewey and George Counts, this silence not only suggests that some of the current reformers are suffering from political and historical amnesia; it also points to the ideological interests that underlie their proposals. Regrettably,

---

[9] Lentricchia, *Criticism and Social Change* (Chicago: University of Chicago Press, 1983), pp. 6–7.

[10] See Stanley Aronowitz and Henry A. Giroux, *Education under Siege: The Conservative, Liberal, & Radical Debate over Schooling* (South Hadley, MA: Bergin & Garvey, 1985).

[11] We are using the term "discourse" to mean "a domain of language use subject to rules of formation and transformation," as quoted in Catherine Belsey, *Critical Practice* (London: Methuen, 1980, p. 160). Discourses may also be described as "the complexes of signs and practices which organize social existence and social reproduction. In their structured, material persistence, discourses are what give differential substance to membership in a social group or class or formation, which mediate an internal sense of belonging, and outward sense of otherness," as quoted in Richard Terdiman, *Discourse-Counter-Discourse* (New York: Cornell University Press, p. 54).

[12] Aronowitz and Giroux, *Education under Siege*; and Ann Bastian, Colin Greer, Norm Fruchter, Marilyn Gittel, and Kenneth Haskins, *Choosing Equality: The Case for Democratic Schooling* (New York: New World Foundation, 1985).

such interests tell us less about the ills of schooling than they do about the nature of the real crisis facing this nation—a crisis which, in our view, not only augurs poorly for the future of American education, but underscores the need to reclaim a democratic tradition presently in retreat. Bluntly stated, much of the current literature on educational reform points to a crisis in American democracy itself.

The discourse of recent educational reform characteristically excludes certain proposals from consideration. For instance, missing from the various privileged discourses that have fashioned the recent reform movement, and absent among the practices of public school teachers whose participation in the current debate on education has been less than vigorous, are concerted attempts at democratizing schools and empowering students to become critical, active citizens. This reluctance on the part of teachers has had a particularly deleterious effect, since the absence of proposals for rethinking the purpose of schools of education around democratic concerns has further strengthened the ideological and political pressures that define teachers as technicians and structure teacher work in a demeaning and overburdening manner. Kenneth Zeichner underscores this concern when he writes:

> It is hoped that future debate in teacher education will be more concerned with the question of which educational, moral and political commitments ought to guide our work in the field rather than with the practice of merely dwelling on which procedures and organizational arrangements will most effectively help us realize tacit and often unexamined ends. Only after we have begun to resolve some of these necessarily prior questions related to ends should we concentrate on the resolution of more instrumental issues related to effectively accomplishing our goals.[13]

The current debate provides an opportunity to critically analyze the ideological and material conditions—both in and out of schools—that contribute to teacher passivity and powerlessness. We also believe that recognition of the failure to link the purposes of public schooling to the imperatives of economic and social reform provides a starting point both for examining the ideological shift in education that has taken place in the 1980s and for developing a new language of democracy, empowerment, and possibility in which teacher education programs and classroom practices can be defined. Our central concern is in developing a view of teacher education that defines teachers as transformative intellectuals and schooling as part of an ongoing struggle for democracy. In developing our argument, we will focus on four considerations. First, we will analyze the dominant new conservative positions that have generated current educational reforms in terms of the implications these viewpoints hold for the reorganization of teacher education programs. Second, we will develop a rationale for organizing teacher education programs around a critical view of teacher work and authority, one that we believe is consistent with the principles and practices of democracy. Third, we will present some programmatic suggestions for analyzing teacher education as a form of cultural politics. Finally, we will argue for a critical pedagogy that draws upon the many-sided conversations and voices that make up community life.

[13] Zeichner, "Alternative Paradigms of Teacher Education," *Journal of Teacher Education*, *34* (1983), 8.

Education Reform and the Retreat from Democracy

Underlying the educational reforms proposed by the recent coalition of conservatives and liberals, conveniently labeled "the new conservatives," is a discourse that both edifies and mystifies their proposals. Capitalizing upon the waning confidence of the general public and a growing number of teachers in the effectiveness of public schools, the new conservatives argue for educational reform by faulting schools for a series of crises that include everything from a growing trade deficit to the breakdown of family morality.[14] As is the case with many public issues in the age of Ronald Reagan, the new conservatives have seized the initiative by framing their arguments in a terse rhetoric that resonates with a growing public concern about downward mobility in hard economic times, that appeals to a resurgence of chauvinistic patriotism, and that points toward a reformulation of educational goals along elitist lines. Such a discourse is dangerous not only because it misconstrues the responsibility schools have for wider economic and social problems—a position that has been convincingly refuted and need not be argued against here[15]—but also because it reflects an alarming ideological shift regarding the role schools should play in relation to society. The effect of this shift, launched by the new right's full-fledged attack on the educational and social reforms of the 1960s, has been to redefine the purpose of education so as to eliminate its citizenship function in favor of a narrowly defined labor market perspective. The essence and implications of this position have been well documented by Barbara Finkelstein.

> Contemporary reformers seem to be recalling public education from its traditional utopian mission—to nurture a critical and committed citizenry that would stimulate the processes of political and cultural transformation and refine and extend the workings of political democracy. . . . Reformers seem to imagine public schools as economic rather than political instrumentalities. They forge no new visions of political and social possibilities. Instead, they call public schools to industrial and cultural service exclusively. . . . Reformers have disjoined their calls for educational reform from calls for a redistribution of power and authority, and the cultivation of cultural forms celebrating pluralism and diversity. As if they have had enough of political democracy, Americans, for the first time in a one hundred and fifty-year history, seem ready to do ideological surgery on their public schools—cutting them away from the fate of social justice and political democracy completely and grafting them onto elite corporate, industrial, military, and cultural interests.[16]

[14] Some of the more representative writing on this issue can be found in Diane Ravitch, *The Troubled Crusade: American Education 1945–1980* (New York: Basic Books, 1983); John H. Bunzel, ed. *Challenge to American Schools: The Case for Standards and Values* (New York: Oxford University Press, 1985); Ravitch, *The Schools We Deserve: Reflections on the Educational Crises of Our Time.* (New York: Basic Books, 1985); and Edward Wynne, "The Great Tradition in Education: Transmitting Moral Values," *Educational Leadership*, 43 (1985), 7.

[15] Some of the best analyses are Lawrence C. Stedman and Marshall S. Smith, "Recent Reform Proposals for American Education," *Contemporary Education Review*, 53 (1983), 85–104; Walter Feinberg, "Fixing the Schools: The Ideological Turn," *Issues in Education*, 3 (1985), 113–138; Edward H. Berman, "The Improbability of Meaningful Educational Reform," *Issues in Education*, 3 (1985), 99–112; Michael Apple, "National Reports and the Construction of Inequality," *British Journal of Sociology of Education*, 7 (1986), 171–190; and Aronowitz and Giroux, *Education under Siege*.

[16] Finkelstein, "Education and the Retreat from Democracy in the United States, 1979–198?," *Teachers College Record*, 86 (1984), 280–281.

It is important to recognize that the new conservative attack on the reforms of the last decade has resulted in a shift away from defining schools as agencies of equity and justice. There is little concern with how public education could better serve the interests of diverse groups of students by enabling them to understand and gain some control over the sociopolitical forces that influence their destinies. Rather, via this new discourse, and its preoccupation with accountability schemes, testing, accreditation, and credentializing, educational reform has become synonymous with turning schools into "company stores." It now defines school life primarily by measuring its utility against its contribution to economic growth and cultural uniformity. Similarly, at the heart of the present ideological shift is an attempt to reformulate the purpose of public education around a set of interests and social relations that define academic success almost exclusively in terms of the accumulation of capital and the logic of the marketplace. This represents a shift away from teacher control of the curriculum and toward a fundamentally technicist form of education that is more directly tied to economic modes of production. Moreover, the new conservatives provide a view of society in which authority derives from technical expertise and culture embodies an idealized tradition that glorifies hard work, industrial discipline, domesticated desire, and cheerful obedience. Edward Berman has deftly captured the political nature of this ideological shift.

> Architects of the current reform have, to their credit, dropped the rhetoric about the school as a vehicle for personal betterment. There is little pretense in today's reports or the resultant programs that individual improvement and social mobility are important concerns of a reconstituted school system. The former rhetoric about individual mobility has given way to exhortations to build educational structures that will allow individual students to make a greater contribution to the economic output of the corporate state. There are few rhetorical flourishes to obfuscate this overriding objective.[17]

The ideological shift that characterizes the current reform period is also evident in the ways in which teacher preparation and classroom pedagogy are currently being defined. The rash of reform proposals for reorganizing schools points to a definition of teacher work that seriously exacerbates conditions which are presently eroding the authority and intellectual integrity of teachers. In fact, the most compelling aspect of the influential reports, especially the widely publicized *A Nation at Risk*, *Action for Excellence*, and *A Nation Prepared: Teachers for the 21st Century*, is their studious refusal to address the ideological, social, and economic conditions underlying poor teacher and student performance.[18] For example, as Frankenstein and Louis Kampf point out, public school teachers constantly confront conditions

[17] Berman, "Improbability," p. 103.

[18] We are using the term "influential" to refer to those reports that have played a major role in shaping educational policy at both the national and local levels. These include The National Commission on Excellence in Education, *A Nation at Risk: The Imperative for Educational Reform* (Washington, DC: GPO, 1983); Task Force on Education for Economic Growth, Education Commission of the States, *Action for Excellence: A Comprehensive Plan to Improve Our Nation's Schools* (Denver: Education Commission of the States, 1983); The Twentieth Century Fund Task Force on Federal Elementary and Secondary Education Policy, *Making the Grade* (New York: The Twentieth Century Fund, 1983); Carnegie Corporation, *Education and Economic Progress: Toward a National Education Policy* (New York: Author, 1983); and Carnegie Forum on Education and the Economy, *A Nation Prepared: Teachers for the 21st Century* (Hyattsville, MD: Author, 1986).

"such as the overwhelming emphasis on quantification (both in scoring children and keeping records), the growing lack of control over curriculum (separating conception from execution) and over other aspects of their work, the isolation from their peers, the condescending treatment by administrators, and the massive layoffs of veteran teachers."[19]

Instead of addressing these issues, many of the reforms taking place at the state level further consolidate administrative structures and prevent teachers from collectively and creatively shaping the conditions under which they work. For instance, at both the local and federal levels, the new educational discourse has influenced a number of policy recommendations, such as competency-based testing for teachers, a lockstep sequencing of materials, mastery learning techniques, systematized evaluation schemes, standardized curricula, and the implementation of mandated "basics."[20] The consequences are evident not only in the substantively narrow view of the purposes of education, but also in the definitions of teaching, learning, and literacy that are championed by the new management-oriented policymakers. In place of developing critical understanding, engaging student experience, and fostering active and critical citizenship, schools are redefined through a language that emphasizes standardization, competency, and narrowly defined performance skills.

Within this paradigm, the development of curricula is increasingly left to administrative experts or simply adopted from publishers, with few, if any, contributions from teachers who are expected to implement the new programs. In its most ideologically offensive form, this type of prepackaged curriculum is rationalized as teacher-proof and is designed to be applied to any classroom context regardless of the historical, cultural, and socioeconomic differences that characterize various schools and students.[21] What is important to note is that the deskilling of teachers

---

Also considered are other recent reports on teacher education reform: The National Commission for Excellence in Teacher Education, *A Call for Change in Teacher Education* (Washington, DC: American Association of Colleges in Teacher Education, 1985); C. Emily Feistritzer, *The Making of a Teacher* (Washington, DC: National Center for Education Information, 1984); "Tomorrow's Teachers: A Report of the Holmes Group" (East Lansing, MI: Holmes Group, Inc., 1986); and Francis A. Maher and Charles H. Rathbone, "Teacher Education and Feminist Theory: Some Implications for Practice," *American Journal of Education, 101* (1986), 214-235. For an analysis of many of these reports see Catherine Cornbleth, "Ritual and Rationality in Teacher Education Reform," *Educational Researcher, 15*, No. 4 (1986), 5-14.

[19] Frankenstein and Kampf, "Preface," in Sara Freedman, Jane Jackson, and Katherine Boles, "The Other End of the Corridor: The Effect of Teaching on Teachers," *Radical Teacher, 23* (1983), 2-23. It is worth noting that the Carnegie Forum's *A Nation Prepared* ends up defeating its strongest suggestions for reform by linking teacher empowerment to quantifying notions of excellence.

[20] Stedman and Smith, "Recent Reform Proposals," pp. 85-104.

[21] We are not automatically opposed to all forms of curricular software and technologies, such as interactive video disks and computers, as long as teachers become aware of the limited range of applications and contexts in which these technologies may be put to use. Certainly, we agree that some prepackaged curricula are more salient than others as instruments of learning. Too often, however, the use of such curricula ignores the contexts of the immediate classroom situation, the larger social milieu, and the historical juncture of the surrounding community. Furthermore, classroom materials designed to simplify the task of teaching and to make it more cost-efficient often separate planning or conception from execution. Many of the recent examples of predesigned commercial curricula are largely focused on competencies measured by standardized tests, precluding the possibility that teachers and students will be able to act as critical thinkers. See Michael W. Apple and Kenneth Teitelbaum, "Are Teachers Losing Control of Their Skills and Curriculum?" *Journal of Curriculum Studies, 18* (1986), 177-184.

appears to go hand-in-hand with the increasing adoption of management-type pedagogies.

> Viewing teachers as semiskilled, low-paid workers in the mass production of education, policymakers have sought to change education, to improve it, by "teacher-proofing" it. Over the past decade we have seen the proliferation of elaborate accountability schemes that go by acronyms like MBO (management by objectives), PBBS (performance-based budgeting systems), CBE (competency-based education), CBTE (competency-based teacher education), and MCT (minimum competency testing).[22]

The growing removal of curriculum development and analysis from the hands of teachers is related to the ways technocratic rationality is used to redefine teacher work. This type of rationality increasingly takes place within a social division of labor in which thinking is removed from implementation and the model of the teacher becomes that of the technician or white-collar clerk. Likewise, learning is reduced to the memorization of narrowly defined facts and isolated pieces of information that can easily be measured and evaluated. The significance of the overall effects of this type of rationalization and bureaucratic control on teacher work and morale has been forcefully articulated by Linda Darling-Hammond. She writes:

> In a Rand study of teachers' views of the effect of educational policies on their classroom practices, we learned from teachers that in response to policies that prescribe teaching practices and outcomes, they spend less time on untested subjects, such as science and social studies; they use less writing in their classrooms in order to gear assignments to the format of standardized tests; they resort to lectures rather than classroom discussions in order to cover the prescribed behavioral objectives without getting "off the track"; they are precluded from using teaching materials that are not on prescribed textbook lists, even when they think these materials are essential to meet the needs of some of their students; and they feel constrained from following up on expressed student interests that lie outside of the bounds of mandated curricula. . . . And 45 percent of the teachers in this study told us that the single thing that would make them leave teaching was the increased prescriptiveness of teaching content and methods—in short, the continuing deprofessionalization of teaching.[23]

The ideological interests that inform the new conservative proposals are based on a view of morality and politics that is legitimated through an appeal to custom, national unity, and tradition. Within this discourse, democracy loses its dynamic character and is reduced to a set of inherited principles and institutional arrangements that teach students how to adapt rather than to question the basic precepts of society. What is left in the new reform proposals is a view of authority constructed around a mandate to follow and implement predetermined rules, to transmit an unquestioned cultural tradition, and to sanctify industrial discipline. Couple these problems with large classes, excessive paperwork, fragmented work

[22] Darling-Hammond, "Valuing Teachers: The Making of a Profession," *Teachers College Record, 87* (1985) 209–218.
[23] Darling-Hammond, "Valuing Teachers," p. 209.

periods, and low salaries, and it comes as no surprise that teachers are increasingly leaving the field.[24]

In effect, the ideological shift at work here points to a restricted definition of schooling, one that almost completely strips public education of a democratic vision where citizenship and the politics of possibility are given serious consideration. When we argue that the recent conservative or "blue-ribbon" reform recommendations lack a politics of possibility and citizenship, we mean that primacy is given to education as economic investment, that is, to pedagogical practices designed to create a school-business partnership and make the American economic system more competitive in world markets. A politics of possibility and citizenship, by contrast, refers to a conception of schooling in which classrooms are seen as active sites of public intervention and social struggle. Moreover, this view maintains that possibilities exist for teachers and students to redefine the nature of critical learning and practice outside of the imperatives of the corporate marketplace. The idea of a politics and project of possibility is grounded in Ernst Bloch's idea of "natural law" wherein "the standpoint of the victims of any society ought to always provide the starting point for the critique of that society."[25] Such a politics defines schools as sites around which struggles should be waged in the name of developing a more just, humane, and equitable social order both within and outside of schools.

We have spent some time analyzing the new conservative discourse and the ideological shift it represents because in our view the current reforms, with few exceptions, pose a grave threat to both public schooling and the nature of democracy itself. The definition of teaching and learning provided by this discourse ignores, as we have pointed out, the imperative of viewing schools as sites of social transformation where students are educated to become informed, active, and critical citizens. The gravity of this ideological shift is hardly ameliorated by the fact that even public schooling's more liberal spokespersons have failed to develop a critical discourse that challenges the hegemony of dominant ideologies. For example, the highly publicized reports by John Goodlad, Theodore Sizer, Ernest Boyer, and others neither acknowledge nor utilize the radical tradition of educational scholarship.[26] While the liberal position does take the concepts of equality of opportunity and citizenship seriously, we are, nevertheless, left with analyses of schooling that lack a sufficiently critical understanding of the ways in which power has been used to favor select groups of students over others. In addition, we are given only a cursory treatment of the political economy of schooling, with its scattered history of

[24] For an excellent theoretical analysis of this issue, see Freedman, Jackson, and Boles, "The Other End of the Corridor. For a more traditional statistical treatment, see Darling-Hammond, *Beyond the Commission Reports: The Coming Crisis in Teaching,* R–3177–RC (Santa Monica, CA: Rand Corporation, July 1984); National Education Association, *Nationwide Teacher Opinion Poll, 1983* (Washington, DC: Author, 1983); and American Federation of Teachers, *School As a Workplace: The Realities of Stress,* Vol. I (Washington, DC: Author, 1983).

[25] Dennis J. Schmidt, "Translator's Introduction: In the Spirit of Bloch," in Ernst Bloch, *Natural Law and Human Dignity,* trans. Dennis J. Schmidt (Boston: MIT Press, 1986), p. xviii.

[26] Goodlad, *A Place Called School: Prospects for the Future* (New York: McGraw-Hill, 1983); Sizer, *Horace's Compromise: The Dilemma of the American High School* (Boston: Houghton Mifflin, 1984); and Boyer, *High School: A Report on Secondary Education in America* (New York: Harper & Row, 1983).

dishonorable linkages to corporate interests and ideology. Furthermore, we are provided with little understanding of how the hidden curriculum in schools works in a subtly discriminating way to discredit the dreams, experiences, and knowledges associated with students from specific class, racial, and gender groupings.[27]

In the absence of any competing critical agenda for reform, the new conservative discourse encourages teacher education institutions to define themselves primarily as training sites that provide students with the technical expertise required to find a place within the corporate hierarchy. Thomas Popkewitz and Allan Pitman have characterized the ideology underlying the current reform proposals, moreover, as betraying a fundamental elitism since it basically adopts a perspective of society that is undifferentiated by class, race, or gender. The logic endemic to these reports, the authors argue, demonstrates an attachment to possessive individualism and instrumental rationality. In other words: "Quantity is seen as quality. Procedural concerns are made objects of value and moral domains. The teacher is a facilitator . . . or a counselor. . . . Individualization is pacing through a common curriculum . . . . Flexibility in instruction is to begin 'where the student is ready to begin' . . . . There is no discussion of what is to be facilitated or the conceptions of curriculum to guide procedures."[28]

Furthermore, Popkewitz and Pitman see a distinctive shift from a concern with equity to a slavish regard for a restricted notion of excellence. That is, the concept of excellence that informs these new reports "ignores the social differentiations while providing political symbols to give credibility to education which only a few can appreciate."[29] What is rightly being stressed is that the concept of excellence fashioned in the reports is designed to benefit "those who have already access to positions of status and privilege through accidents of birth."[30]

Given the context in which teaching and learning are currently being defined, it becomes all the more necessary to insist on an alternative view of teacher education, one which, in refusing to passively serve the existing ideological and institutional arrangements of the public schools, is aimed at challenging and reforming them.

Teacher Education: Democracy and the Imperative of Social Reform

We want to return to the idea that the fundamental concerns of democracy and critical citizenship should be central to any discussion of the purpose of teacher education. In doing so, we will organize our discussion around two arguments. The first represents an initial effort to develop a critical language with which to reconstruct the relationship between teacher education programs and the public schools, on the one hand, and public education and society on the other. The second, and more detailed, argument presents a view of authority and teacher work

---

[27] For an overview and critical analysis of this literature, see Henry A. Giroux, "Theories of Reproduction and Resistance in the New Sociology of Education: A Critical Analysis," *Harvard Educational Review,* 53 (1983), 257–293.

[28] Popkewitz and Pitman, "The Idea of Progress and the Legitimation of State Agendas: American Proposals for School Reform," *Curriculum and Teaching,* 1 (1986), p. 21.

[29] Popkewitz and Pitman, "The Idea of Progress," p. 20.

[30] Popkewitz and Pitman, "The Idea of Progress," p. 22.

that attempts to define the political project we believe should underlie the purpose and nature of teacher education programs.

If teacher education programs are to provide the basis for democratic struggle and renewal in our schools, they will have to redefine their current relationship to such institutions. As it presently stands, schools of education rarely encourage their students to take seriously the imperatives of social critique and social change as part of a wider emancipatory vision. If and when education students begin to grapple with these concerns at the classroom level, it is invariably years after graduation. Our own experiences in teacher education institutions—both as students and as instructors—have confirmed for us what is generally agreed to be commonplace in most schools and colleges of education throughout the United States: that these institutions continue to define themselves essentially as service institutions which are generally mandated to provide the requisite technical expertise to carry out whatever pedagogical functions are deemed necessary by the various school communities in which students undertake their practicum experiences.[31] In order to escape this political posture, teacher education programs need to reorient their focus to the critical transformation of public schools rather than to the simple reproduction of existing institutions and ideologies.[32]

One starting point would be to recognize the importance of educating students in the languages of critique and possibility; that is, providing teachers with the critical terminology and conceptual apparatus that will allow them not only to critically analyze the democratic and political shortcomings of schools, but also to develop the knowledge and skills that will advance the possibilities for generating curricula, classroom social practices, and organizational arrangements based on and cultivating a deep respect for a democratic and ethically-based community. In effect, this means that the relationship of teacher education programs to public schooling would be self-consciously guided by political and moral considerations. Dewey expressed well the need for educators to make political and moral considerations a central aspect of their education and work when he distinguished between "education as a function of society" and "society as a function of education."[33] In simple terms, Dewey's distinction reminds us that education can function either to create passive, risk-free citizens or to create a politicized citizenry educated to fight for various forms of public life informed by a concern for justice, happiness, and equality. At issue here is whether schools of education are to serve and repro-

---

[31] Zeichner, "Alternative Paradigms"; and Jesse Goodman, "Reflections on Teacher Education: A Case Study and Theoretical Analysis," *Interchange*, 15 (1984), 7–26. The fact that many teacher education programs have defined themselves as synonymous with instructional preparation has often given them a debilitating practical slant, leading to a limited conception of teaching as exercises in classroom management and control. Isolated courses on classroom management have had a tragic effect on how teachers are able to critically interrogate the political implications of curricular decision-making and policy development. This predicament can be traced to a history of the academic politics that grew out of the separation of colleges of education from the liberal arts tradition and the arts and sciences faculty; see Donald Warren, "Learning from Experience: History and Teacher Education," *Educational Researcher*, 14, No. 10 (1985), 5–12.

[32] For an excellent analysis of this issue, see National Coalition of Advocates for Students, *Barriers to Excellence: Our Children at Risk* (Boston: Author, 1985).

[33] As quoted in Lentricchia, *Criticism and Social Change*; see also Dewey, *Democracy and Education* (New York: Free Press, 1916) and *The Public and Its Problems* (New York: Holt, 1927).

duce the existing society or to adopt the more critical role of challenging the social order so as to develop and advance its democratic imperatives. Also at issue is developing a rationale for defining teacher education programs in political terms that make explicit a particular view of the relationship between public schools and the social order, a view based on defending the imperatives of a democratic society.

Public Schools as Democratic Public Spheres

Our second concern is directed to the broader question of how educators should view the purpose of public schooling. Our position echoes Dewey in that we believe public schools need to be defined as democratic public spheres. This means regarding schools as democratic sites dedicated to self- and social empowerment. Understood in these terms, schools can be public places where students learn the knowledge and skills necessary to live in a critical democracy. Contrary to the view that schools are extensions of the workplace or front-line institutions in the corporate battle for international markets, schools viewed as democratic public spheres center their activities around critical inquiry and meaningful dialogue. In this case, students are given the opportunity to learn the discourse of public association and civic responsibility. Such a discourse seeks to recapture the idea of a critical democracy that commands respect for individual freedom and social justice. Moreover, viewing schools as democratic public spheres provides a rationale for defending them, along with progressive forms of pedagogy and teacher work, as agencies of social reform. When defined in these terms, schools can be defended as institutions that provide the knowledge, skills, social relations, and vision necessary to educate a citizenry capable of building a critical democracy. That is, school practice can be rationalized in a political language that recovers and emphasizes the transformative role that schools can play in advancing the democratic possibilities inherent in the existing society.[34]

Authority and Intellectuals: Rethinking the Nature and Purpose of Teacher Work

Redefining the notion of authority in emancipatory terms is central to understanding and legitimating teacher work as a critical practice. The importance of such a task can be made clearer by highlighting the significance of authority as part of the fundamental discourse of schooling.

First, as a form of legitimation, authority is inescapably related to a particular vision of what schools should be as part of a wider community and society. Thus, questions about school and teacher authority help to make both visible and problematic the presuppositions of the officially sanctioned discourses and values that legitimate the institutional and social arrangements constituting everyday life in schools. For example, questions might be raised about the nature and source of the authority which legitimates a particular type of curriculum, the way school time is organized, the political consequences of tracking students, the social division of labor among teachers, and the patriarchal basis of authority. In this way,

---

[34] Dewey, "Creative Democracy—The Task Before Us," in *Classic American Philosophers*, ed. Max Fisch (New York: Appleton-Century-Crofts, 1951), pp. 389–394; and Richard J. Bernstein, "Dewey and Democracy: The Task Ahead of Us," in *Post-Analytic Philosophy*, ed. John Rajchman and Cornell West (New York: Columbia University Press, 1985) pp. 48–62.

the concept of authority raises issues about the ethical and political basis of schooling. That is, it calls into serious question the role that school administrators and teachers play as intellectuals in both articulating and implementing their particular views or ideologies. In short, the category of authority reinserts the primacy of the political into the language of schooling by highlighting the social and ideological function that educators serve in elaborating, enforcing, and legitimating schooling as a particular form of social life, that is, as a particular set of ideas and practices that occur within historically defined contexts.

Second, if the concept of authority is to provide a legitimating basis for rethinking the purpose and meaning of teacher education, it must be reconstituted around a view of community life in which morality in everyday existence is fundamental to the meaning of democracy.[35] A form of *emancipatory* authority needs to be developed, one that can illuminate the connection and importance of two questions that teacher education programs should take as a central point of inquiry in structuring the form and content of their curricula. These are: What kind of society do educators want to live in? What kind of teaching and pedagogy can be developed and legitimated by a view of authority that takes democracy and critical citizenship seriously? Authority, in this view, rests on the assumption that public schooling should promote forms of morality and sociality in which students learn to encounter and engage social differences and diverse points of view. In addition, schools should prepare students for making choices regarding forms of life that have morally different consequences. This means that educators must replace pedagogical practices which emphasize disciplinary control and one-sided character formation with practices that are based on an emancipatory authority, ones which enable students to engage in critical analysis and to make choices regarding what interests and knowledge claims are most desirable and morally appropriate for living in a just and democratic state. Equally important is the need for students to engage in civic-minded action in order to remove the social and political constraints that restrict the victims of this society from leading decent and humane lives.

A reconstituted notion of emancipatory authority suggests, in this case, that teachers are bearers of critical knowledge, rules, and values through which they consciously articulate and problematize their relationship to each other, to students, to subject matter, and to the wider community. This view of authority exposes and challenges the dominant view of teachers as primarily technicians or public servants whose role is to implement rather than to conceptualize pedagogical practice. Moreover, the category of emancipatory authority dignifies teacher work by viewing it as an intellectual practice with respect to both its formal characteristics and the nature of the content discussed. Teacher work becomes a form of intellectual labor opposed to the pedagogical divisions between conception and practice, and production and implementation, that are currently celebrated in a number of educational reforms. The concept of teacher as intellectual carries with it the political and ethical imperative to judge, critique, and reject those approaches to authority that reinforce a technical and social division of labor that

---

[35] Henry A. Giroux, "Authority, Intellectuals and the Politics of Practical Learning," *Teachers College Record*, *88* (1986), 22–40.

silences and disempowers both teachers and students. In other words, emancipatory authority is a concept which demands that teachers and others critically confront the ideological and practical conditions which enable or constrain them in their capacity as transformative intellectuals.

It is important to stress that the concept of emancipatory authority provides the theoretical basis for defining teachers not merely as intellectuals but, more specifically, as transformative intellectuals. The distinction is important because transformative intellectuals are not merely concerned with empowerment in the conventional sense, that is, with giving students the knowledge and skills they will need to gain access to some traditional measure of economic and social mobility in the capitalist marketplace. Rather, for transformative intellectuals, the issue of teaching and learning is linked to the more political goal of educating students to take risks and to struggle within ongoing relations of power in order to alter the oppressive conditions in which life is lived. To facilitate this goal, transformative intellectuals need to make clear the nature of the appeals to authority they are using to legitimate their pedagogical practices. In other words, educators need to specify the political and moral referents for the authority they assume in teaching particular forms of knowledge, in taking stands against forms of oppression, and in treating students as if they ought also to be concerned about social justice and political action.

In short, this reconstituted version of authority is important because it contains elements of a language of both criticism and possibility. As part of the language of critique, the notion of emancipatory authority provides a discourse through which educators can critically examine views of authority often used by conservatives and others to link the purpose of schooling to a reductionist view of patriotism and patriarchy. As part of the language of possibility, authority as an emancipatory practice provides the scaffolding with which one can connect the purpose of schooling to the imperatives of what Benjamin Barber calls a "strong democracy," a democracy characterized by citizens capable of seriously confronting public issues through ongoing forms of public debate and social action.[36]

In our view, the most important referent for this particular view of authority rests in a commitment to address the many instances of suffering that characterize the present society. This suggests a recognition and identification with "the perspective of those people and groups who are marginal and exploited."[37] In its practical dimension, such a commitment represents a break from the bonds of isolated liberal individuality and a desire to engage with others in political struggles that challenge the existing order of society as being institutionally repressive and unjust. It is important to note that transformative intellectuals can serve to act, as Welch points out, as bearers of dangerous memory.[38] This means that such intellectuals can link knowledge to power by bringing to light and teaching the subjugated histories, experiences, stories, and accounts of those who suffer and struggle within conditions that are rarely made public or analyzed through the official discourses of public schooling. Thus, we can point to the histories of women, blacks,

---

[36] Barber, *Strong Democracy: Participating Politics for a New Age Theology of Liberation* (Berkeley: University of California Press, 1984).

[37] Sharon Welch, *Communities of Resistance and Solidarity* (New York: Orbis Press, 1985), p. 31.

[38] Welch, *Communities of Resistance*, p. 37.

working-class groups, and others whose histories challenge the moral legitimacy of the structures of society and therefore contain knowledge too "dangerous" to make visible. Of course, teachers of "dangerous memory" must do more than excavate historical reason and subjugated knowledge; they must also make clear that people are called to struggle, that political alternatives do in fact exist, and that such buried knowledge needs to be appropriated in the interest of creating more critically democratic societies.

Rethinking the Nature of Teacher Education

We would like to bring the foregoing discussion to bear on the more practical mission of reconstructing teacher education programs around a new vision of democratic schooling and teaching for critical citizenship. Consequently, we shall devote the remainder of our discussion to outlining, in more detailed and programmatic terms, what we feel are some essential components and categories for a teacher education curriculum and a critical pedagogy for the schools.

As we have argued, most teacher education programs have been, and continue to be, entirely removed from a vision and a set of practices dedicated to the fostering of critical democracy and social justice. A repeated criticism made by educators working within the radical tradition has been that, as it currently exists, teacher education rarely addresses either the moral implications of societal inequalities within our present form of industrial capitalism or the ways in which schools function to reproduce and legitimate these inequalities.[39]

Usually when classroom life is discussed in teacher education programs, it is presented fundamentally as a one-dimensional set of rules and regulative practices, rather than as a cultural terrain where a variety of interests and practices collide in a constant and often chaotic struggle for dominance. Thus, prospective teachers frequently receive the impression that classroom culture is essentially free from ambiguity and contradiction. According to this view, schools are supposedly devoid of all vestiges of contestation, struggle, and cultural politics.[40] Furthermore, classroom reality is rarely presented as if it were socially constructed, historically determined, and reproduced through institutionalized relationships of class, gender, race, and power. Unfortunately, this dominant conception of schooling vastly contradicts what the student teacher often experiences during his or her practicum or fieldsite work, especially if the student is placed in a school largely populated by economically disadvantaged and disenfranchised students. Yet, student teachers are nevertheless instructed to view schooling as a neutral terrain devoid of power and politics. It is against this transparent depiction of schooling that prospective teachers, more often than not, view their own ideologies and experiences through a dominant theoretical and cultural perspective that remains largely unquestioned. Most important, teachers in this situation have no grounds upon which to question the dominant cultural assumptions that shape and structure the ways in which they respond to and influence student behavior.

[39] Zeichner, "Alternative Paradigms"; Henry A. Giroux, *Ideology, Culture, and the Process of Schooling* (Philadelphia: Temple University Press, 1981); and John Sears, "Rethinking Teacher Education: Dare We Work Toward a New Social Order?" *Journal of Curriculum Theorizing,* 6 (1985), 24–79.

[40] Of course, this is not true for all teacher education programs, but it does represent the dominant tradition characterizing them; see Zeichner, "Alternative Paradigms."

Consequently, many student teachers who find themselves teaching working-class or minority students lack a well-articulated framework for understanding the class, cultural, ideological, and gender dimensions that inform classroom life. As a result, cultural differences among students often are viewed uncritically as deficiencies rather than as strengths, and what passes for teaching is in actuality an assault on the specific histories, experiences, and knowledges that such students use both to define their own identities and to make sense of their larger world. We use the term "assault" not because such knowledge is openly attacked — but because it is devalued through a process that is at once subtle and debilitating. What happens is that within the dominant school culture, subordinate knowledge is generally ignored, marginalized, or treated in a disorganized fashion. Such knowledge is often treated as if it did not exist, or treated in ways that disconfirm it. Conversely, ideologies that do not aid subordinate groups in interpreting the reality they actually experience often pass for objective forms of knowledge. In this process, prospective teachers lose an understanding of the relationship between culture and power as well as a sense of how to develop pedagogical possibilities for their students from the cultural differences that often characterize school and classroom life. In the section that follows, we will discuss the elements we feel should constitute a new model of teacher education, one that addresses the above issue more specifically.

Teacher Education as Cultural Politics

Our concern here is with reconstituting the grounds upon which teacher education programs are built. This means developing an alternative form of teacher education curriculum that supports what we call the construction of a cultural politics. In our view, such a programmatic approach to teacher education conceptualizes schooling as taking place within a political and cultural arena where forms of student experience and subjectivity are actively produced and mediated. In other words, we wish to stress the idea that schools do not merely teach academic subjects, but also, in part, produce student subjectivities or particular sets of experiences that are in themselves part of an ideological process. Conceptualizing schooling as the construction and transmission of subjectivities permits us to understand more clearly the idea that the curriculum is more than just an introduction of students to particular subject disciplines and teaching methodologies; it also serves as an introduction to a particular way of life.[41]

At this point, we must forego a detailed specification of teaching practices and instead attempt to briefly sketch out particular areas of study crucial to the development of a reconceptualized teacher education curriculum. We assign the term "cultural politics" to our curriculum agenda because we feel that this term permits us to capture the significance of the sociocultural dimension of the schooling process. Furthermore, the term allows us to highlight the political consequences of interaction between teachers and students who come from dominant and subordi-

[41] See John Ellis, "Ideology and Subjectivity," *in Culture, Media, Language*, ed. Stuart Hall, Dorothy Hobson, Andrew Lowe, and Paul Willis (Hawthorne, Australia: Hutchinson, 1980), pp. 186–194; see also Julian Henriques, Wendy Hollway, Cathy Urwin, Couze Venn, and Valerie Walkerdine, *Changing the Subject* (New York: Methuen, 1984).

nate cultures. A teacher education curriculum as a form of cultural politics assumes that the social, cultural, political, and economic dimensions are the primary categories for understanding contemporary schooling.[42] Within this context, school life is conceptualized not as a unitary, monolithic, and ironclad system of rules and regulations, but as a cultural terrain characterized by varying degrees of accommodation, contestation, and resistance. Furthermore, school life is understood as a plurality of conflicting languages and struggles, a place where classroom and street-corner cultures collide and where teachers, students, and school administrators often differ as to how school experiences and practices are to be defined and understood.

The imperative of this curriculum is to create conditions for student self-empowerment and self-constitution as an active political and moral subject. We are using the term "empowerment" to refer to the process whereby students acquire the means to critically appropriate knowledge existing outside of their immediate experience in order to broaden their understanding of themselves, the world, and the possibilities for transforming the taken-for-granted assumptions about the way we live. Stanley Aronowitz has described one aspect of empowerment as "the process of appreciating and loving oneself."[43] In this sense, empowerment is gained from knowledge and social relations that dignify one's own history, language, and cultural traditions. But empowerment means more than self-confirmation. It also refers to the process by which students are able to interrogate and selectively appropriate those aspects of the dominant culture that will provide them with the basis for defining and transforming, rather than merely serving, the wider social order.

The project of "doing" a teacher education curriculum based on cultural politics consists of linking critical social theory to a set of stipulated practices through which student teachers are able to dismantle and critically examine preferred educational and cultural traditions, many of which have fallen prey to an instrumental rationality that either limits or ignores democratic ideals and principles. One of our main concerns focuses on developing a language of critique and demystification that is capable of analyzing the latent interests and ideologies that work to socialize students in a manner compatible with the dominant culture. We are equally concerned, however, with creating alternative teaching practices capable of empowering students both inside and outside of schools. While it is impossible to provide a detailed outline of the courses of a curriculum for cultural politics, we want to comment on some important areas of analysis that should be central to such a program. These include the critical study of power, language, culture, and history.

Power

A pivotal concern of a teacher education curriculum that subscribes to a cultural politics approach is to assist student teachers in understanding the relationship between power and knowledge. Within the dominant curriculum, knowledge is often

---

[42] Henry A. Giroux and Roger Simon, "Curriculum Study and Cultural Politics," *Journal of Education, 166* (1984), 226–238.

[43] Stanley Aronowitz, "Schooling, Popular Culture, and Post-Industrial Society: Peter McLaren Interviews Aronowitz," *Orbit, 17* (1986), 18.

removed from the issue of power and is generally treated in a technical manner; that is, it is seen in instrumental terms as something to be mastered. That such knowledge is always an ideological construction linked to particular interests and social relations generally receives little consideration in teacher education programs. An understanding of the knowledge/power relationship raises important issues regarding what kinds of knowledge educators can provide to empower students, not only to understand and engage the world around them, but also to exercise the kind of courage needed to change the social order where necessary. Of considerable concern, then, is the need for student teachers to recognize that power relations correspond to forms of school knowledge that both distort the truth and produce it. That is, knowledge should be examined not only for the ways in which it might misrepresent or mediate social reality, but also for the ways in which it actually reflects peoples' experiences and, as such, influences their lives. Understood in this way, knowledge not only reproduces reality by distorting or illuminating the social world; it also has the more concrete function of shaping the day-to-day lives of people through their felt, relatively unmediated, world of commonsense assumptions. This suggests that a curriculum for democratic empowerment must not only examine the conditions of school knowledge in terms of how it is produced and what particular interests it might represent, but should also scrutinize the effects of such knowledge as it is lived day-to-day. In short, prospective teachers need to understand that knowledge does more than distort, it also produces particular forms of life. Finally, in Michel Foucault's terms, knowledge contains hopes, desires, and wants that resonate positively with the subjective experience of a particular audience, and such knowledge needs to be analyzed for the utopian promises often implicit in its claims.[44]

Language

In traditional and institutionally legitimated approaches to reading, writing, and second-language learning, language issues are primarily defined by technical and developmental concerns. While such concerns are indeed important, what is often ignored in mainstream language courses in teacher education programs is how language is actively implicated in power relations that generally support the dominant culture. An alternative starting point to the study of language recognizes the significance of Antonio Gramsci's notion that every language contains elements of a conception of the world. It is through language that we come to consciousness and negotiate a sense of identity, since language does not merely reflect reality, but plays an active role in constructing it. As language constructs meaning, it shapes our world, informs our identities, and provides the cultural codes for perceiving and classifying the world. This implies, of course, that within the available discourses of the school or the society, language plays a powerful role because it serves to "mark the boundaries of permissible discourse, discourage the clarification of social alternatives, and makes it difficult for the dispossessed to locate the source of their unease, let alone remedy it."[45] Through the study of language

[44] Foucault, "The Subject of Power," in *Beyond Structuralism and Hermeneutics*, ed. Hubert Dreyfus and Paul Rabinow (Chicago: University of Chicago Press, 1982), p. 221.

[45] T. J. Jackson Lears, "The Concept of Cultural Hegemony: Problems and Possibilities," *American Historical Review*, 90 (1985), 569–570.

within the perspective of a cultural politics, prospective teachers can gain an understanding of how language functions to "position" people in the world, to shape the range of possible meanings surrounding an issue, and to actively construct reality rather than merely reflect it. As part of language studies, student teachers would become more knowledgeable about and sensitive to the omnipresence and power of language as constitutive of their own experiences and those of their potential students.[46] Student teachers would also benefit from an introductory understanding of European traditions of discourse theory and the textual strategies that characterize their methods of inquiry.[47] Furthermore, through an exposure to the semiotics of mass and popular cultures, students could at least learn the rudimentary methods of examining the various codes and meanings that are constitutive of both their own personal constructions of self and society and those of the students they work with during their practicum or on-site sessions.

History

The study of history should play a more expansive role in teacher education programs.[48] A critical approach to history would attempt to provide student teachers with an understanding of how cultural traditions are formed; it would also be designed to bring to light the various ways that curricula and discipline-based texts have been constructed and read throughout different historical periods. Furthermore, such an approach would be self-consciously critical of the problems surrounding the teaching of history as a school subject, since what is conventionally taught overwhelmingly reflects the perspectives and values of white, middle-class males. Too often excluded are the histories of women, minority groups, and indigenous peoples. This exclusion is not politically innocent when we consider how existing social arrangements are partly constitutive of and dependent upon the subjugation and elimination of the histories and voices of those groups marginalized and disempowered by the dominant culture. In addition, the concept of history can also help illuminate what kinds of knowledge are deemed legitimate and promulgated through the school curriculum. Conventional emphasis on chronological history "which traditionally saw its object as somehow unalterably 'there,' given, waiting only to be discovered"[49] would be supplanted by a focus on how specific educational practices can be understood as historical constructions related to the economic, social, and political events of a particular time and place. It is primarily through this form of historical analysis that students can recover what we referred to previously as "subjugated knowledges."[50] Our use of this term directs

[46] Gary Waller, "Writing, Reading, Language, History, Culture: The Structure and Principles of the English Curriculum at Carnegie-Mellon University." Unpublished manuscript, Carnegie-Mellon University, 1985, p. 12.

[47] We are primarily referring to the French school of discourse theory, as exemplified in the writings of Foucault; see his *The Archaeology of Knowledge*, trans. A. M. Sheridan Smith (London: Tavistock; see also the following works by Foucault: *Language, Counter-Memory, Practice: Selected Essays and Interviews*, Donald F. Bouchard, trans. Donald F. Bouchard and Sherry Simon (Ithaca: Cornell University Press, 1979); and "Politics and the Study of Discourse," *Ideology and Consciousness*, *3* (1978), 7–26.

[48] Waller, "Writing, Reading, Language," p. 12.

[49] Waller, "Writing, Reading, Language," p. 14.

[50] Foucault, "Two Lectures," in *Power/Knowledge*, ed. Colin Gordon (New York: Pantheon, 1980), pp. 78–108.

us to those aspects of history in which criticism and struggle have played a significant role in defining the nature and meaning of educational theory and practice.
For example, students will have the opportunity to examine critically the historical
contexts and interests at work in defining what forms of school knowledge become
privileged over others, how specific forms of school authority are sustained, and
how particular patterns of learning become institutionalized.

Within the format of a curriculum as a form of cultural politics, it is also necessary that the study of history be theoretically connected to both language and reading. In this context, language can be subsequently studied as "the bearer of history" and history can be analyzed as a social construction open to critical examination. The important linkage between reading and history can be made by
emphasizing that "reading occurs within history and that the point of integration
is always the reader."[51] In analyzing this relationship, teachers can focus on the
cultural meanings that students use to understand a text. Such a focus will better
equip student teachers to understand how the process of reading occurs within a
particular student's cultural history and in the context of his or her own concerns
and beliefs. This will also assist student teachers to become more critically aware
of how students from subordinate cultures bring their own sets of experiences, as
well as their own dreams, desires, and voices to the reading act.

Culture

The concept of culture, varied though it may be, is essential to any teacher education curriculum aspiring to be critical. We are using the term "culture" here to signify the particular ways in which a social group lives out and makes sense of its
"given" circumstances and conditions of life.[52] In addition to defining culture as
a set of practices and ideologies from which different groups draw to make sense
of the world, we also want to refashion the ways in which cultural questions become the starting point for understanding the issue of who has power and how it
is reproduced and manifested in the social relations that link schooling to the wider
social order. The link between culture and power has been extensively analyzed
in radical social theory over the past ten years. It is therefore possible to offer three
insights from that literature that are particularly relevant for illuminating the political logic that underlies various cultural/power relations. First, the concept of
culture has been intimately connected with the question of how *social relations are
structured* within class, gender, and age formations that produce forms of oppression and dependency. Second, culture has been analyzed within the radical perspective not simply as a way of life, but as a *form of production* through which different groups in either their dominant or subordinate social relations define and
realize their aspirations through asymmetrical relations of power. Third, culture
has been viewed as a *field of struggle* in which the production, legitimation, and cir-
culation of particular forms of knowledge and experience are central areas of conflict. What is important here is that each of these insights raises fundamental questions about the ways in which inequalities are maintained and challenged in the
sphere of culture.

[51] Waller, "Writing, Reading, Language," p. 14.
[52] Henry A. Giroux, *Ideology Culture, and the Process of Schooling* (Philadelphia: Temple University
Press, 1981).

The study of cultures—or, more specifically, what has come to be known as "cultural studies"—should become the touchstone of a teacher education curriculum. We feel this to be the case because cultural studies can provide student teachers with the critical categories necessary for examining school and classroom relations as social and political practices inextricably related to the construction and maintenance of specific relations of power. Moreover, by recognizing that school life is often mediated through the clash of dominant and subordinate cultures, prospective teachers can gain some insight into the ways in which classroom experiences are necessarily intertwined with their students' home life and street-corner culture. This point is meant to be more than a rallying cry for relevance; rather, it asserts the need for prospective teachers to understand the meaning systems that students employ in their encounters with forms of dominant school knowledge and social relations. It is important, therefore, that student teachers learn to analyze expressions of mass and popular culture, such as music videos, television, and film. In this way, a successful cultural studies approach would provide an important theoretical avenue for teachers to comprehend how ideologies become inscribed through representations of everyday life.

Towards a Critical Pedagogy for the Classroom

In the previous sections we have highlighted the importance of viewing schools as social and political sites involved in the struggle for democracy. In addition, we have reconsidered the relationship between authority and teacher work and have attempted to develop the theoretical rudiments of a program in which teacher education would be viewed as a form of cultural politics. In this final section, we shift the focus from questions of institutional purpose and teacher definition to the issues of critical pedagogy and student learning. In so doing, we point to some of the fundamental elements that we believe can be used to construct a critical pedagogy, one in which the issue of student interests or motivation is linked to the dynamics of self- and social empowerment. We wish to underscore here that the public schools shape and reinforce the attitudes that prospective teachers bring to their clinical experiences. By focusing on some of the theoretical elements that constitute a critical pedagogy, we attempt to clarify the link between our notion of a teacher education curriculum as a form of cultural politics and the actual dynamics of classroom pedagogy. With this in mind, we will now sketch out the rudiments of a critical discourse that defines classroom pedagogy within the parameters of a political project centering around the primacy of student experience, the concept of voice, and the importance of transforming schools and communities into democratic public spheres.

The Primacy of Student Experience

The type of critical pedagogy we are proposing is fundamentally concerned with student experience insofar as it takes the problems and needs of the students themselves as its starting point. On the one hand, a pedagogy of student experience encourages a critique of dominant forms of knowledge and cultural mediation that collectively shape student experiences; on the other hand, it attempts to provide students with the critical means to examine their own particular lived experiences and subordinate knowledge forms. This means assisting students in analyzing

their own experiences so as to illuminate the processes by which they were produced, legitimated, or disconfirmed. R. W. Connell and his associates in Australia provide a cogent direction for this type of curricular approach in their formulation of the kinds of knowledge that should be taught to empower working-
class students when they suggest:

> that working-class kids get access to formal knowledge via learning which begins
> with their own experience and the circumstances which shape it, but does not stop
> there. This approach neither accepts the existing organization of academic knowl-
> edge nor simply inverts it. It draws on existing school knowledge and on what
> working-class people already know, and organizes this selection of information
> around problems such as economic survival and collective action, handling the
> disruption of households by unemployment, responding to the impact of new
> technology, managing problems of personal identity and association, understand-
> ing how schools work and why.[53]

Student experience is the stuff of culture, agency, and identity formation and must
be given preeminence in an emancipatory curriculum. It is therefore imperative
that critical educators learn how to understand, affirm, and analyze such experience. This means not only understanding the cultural and social forms through
which students learn how to define themselves, but also learning how to engage
student experience in a way that neither unqualifiedly endorses nor delegitimates
such experience. This suggests that, first of all, knowledge has to be made meaningful to students before it can be made critical. School knowledge never speaks
for itself; rather, it is constantly filtered through the ideological and cultural experiences that students bring to the classroom. To ignore the ideological dimensions
of student experience is to deny the ground upon which students learn, speak, and
imagine. Judith Williamson addresses this issue well.

> Walter Benjamin has said that the best ideas are no use if they do not make some-
> thing useful of the person who holds them; on an even simpler level, I would add
> that the best ideas don't even exist if there isn't anyone to hold them. If we cannot
> get the "radical curriculum" across, or arouse the necessary interest in the "basic
> skills," there is no point to them. But in any case, which do we ultimately care
> more about: our ideas, or the child/student we are trying to teach them to?[54]

Students cannot learn "usefully" unless teachers develop an understanding of the
various ways in which student perceptions and identities are constituted through
different social domains. At stake is the need for student teachers to understand
how experiences produced in the various domains and layers of everyday life give
rise to the different voices students employ to give meaning to their worlds and,
consequently, to their existence in the larger society. Of course, not all student experiences should be unqualifiedly affirmed or rendered legitimate since some of

---

[53] Robert W. Connell, Dean J. Ashenden, Sandra Kessler, Gary W. Dowsett, *Making the Difference:
Schools, Families, and Social Division* (Winchester, MA: Allen & Unwin, 1982), p. 199; see also Peter
McLaren, *Schooling as a Ritual Performance: Towards a Political Economy of Educational Symbols and Gestures*
(London: Routledge & Kegan Paul, 1986).

[54] Williamson, "Is There Anyone Here from a Classroom?," *Screen, 26* (Jan./Feb. 1984), 24; see
also Henry A. Giroux, "Radical Pedagogy and the Politics of Student Voice," *Interchange, 17* (1986),
48–69.

them undoubtedly will draw from an uncritical categorization and social construction of the world (as in racist and sexist stereotyping, for example). In this case, teachers must understand student experience as arising from multiple discourses and subjectivities, some of which must be interrogated more critically than others. It is crucial, therefore, that educators address the question of how aspects of the social world are experienced, mediated, and produced by students. Failure to do so will not only prevent teachers from tapping into the drives, emotions, and interests that give students their own unique voice, but will also make it equally difficult to provide the momentum for learning itself.

While the concept of student experience is being offered as central to a critical pedagogy, it should also be recognized as a central category of teacher education programs. This suggests that student practicums should be seen as sites where the question of how experience is produced, legitimated, and accomplished becomes an object of study for teachers and students alike. Unfortunately, most student practicums are viewed as either a rite of passage into the profession or merely a formal culminating experience in the teacher education program.

Student Voice and the Public Sphere

The concept of voice constitutes the focal point for a theory of teaching and learning that generates new forms of sociality as well as new and challenging ways of confronting and engaging everyday life. Voice, quite simply, refers to the various measures by which students and teachers actively participate in dialogue. It is related to the discursive means whereby teachers and students attempt to make themselves "heard" and to define themselves as active authors of their worlds. Displaying a voice means, to cite Mikhail Bakhtin, "retelling a story in one's own words."[55] More specifically, the term "voice" refers to the principles of dialogue as they are enunciated and enacted within particular social settings. The concept of voice represents the unique instances of self-expression through which students affirm their own class, cultural, racial, and gender identities. A student's voice is necessarily shaped by personal history and distinctive lived engagement with the surrounding culture. The category of voice, then, refers to the means at our disposal — the discourses available to us — to make ourselves understood and listened to, and to define ourselves as active participants in the world. However, as we have stressed previously, the dominant school culture generally represents and legitimates the voices of white males from the middle and upper classes to the exclusion of economically disadvantaged students, most especially females from minority backgrounds.[56] A critical pedagogy takes into account the various ways in which the voices that teachers use to communicate with students can either silence or legitimate them.

The concept of voice is crucial to the development of a critical classroom pedagogy because it provides an important basis for constructing and demonstrating the fundamental imperatives of a strong democracy. Such a pedagogy attempts to organize classroom relationships so that students can draw upon and confirm

[55] As quoted in Harold Rosen, "The Importance of Story," *Language Arts*, *63* (1986), 234.
[56] For a thorough analysis of this, see Arthur Brittan and Mary Maynard, *Sexism, Racism and Oppression* (New York: Blackwell, 1984).

those dimensions of their own histories and experiences which are deeply rooted in the surrounding community. In addition, by creating active links with the community, teachers can open up their classrooms to its diverse resources and traditions. This presupposes that teachers familiarize themselves with the culture, economy, and historical traditions that belong to the surrounding community. In other words, teachers must assume a pedagogical responsibility for attempting to understand the relationships and forces that influence their students outside of the immediate context of the classroom. This responsibility requires teachers to develop their curricula and pedagogical practices around those community traditions, histories, and forms of knowledge that are often ignored within the dominant school culture. This can, of course, lead to a deeper understanding on the part of both teachers and students of how both "local" and "official" knowledges get produced, sustained, and legitimated.

Teachers need to develop pedagogical practices that link student experiences with those aspects of community life that inform and sustain such experiences. For example, student teachers could compile oral histories of the communities in which they teach, which could then be used as a school and curricula resource — particularly in reading programs. In addition, they could work in and analyze how different community social agencies function so as to produce, distribute, and legitimate particular forms of knowledge and social relations. This would broaden their notion of pedagogical practices and help them to understand the relevance of their own work for institutions other than schools. Similarly, prospective teachers could develop organic links with active community agencies such as business, religious organizations, and other public spheres in an attempt to develop a more meaningful connection between the school curriculum and the experiences that define and characterize the local community. The concept of voice can thus provide a basic organizing principle for the development of a relationship between knowledge and student experiences and, at the same time, create a forum for examining broader school and community issues. In other words, teachers must become aware of both the transformative strengths and structures of oppression of the community-at-large and develop this awareness into curriculum strategies designed to empower students toward creating a more liberating and humane society. In short, teachers should be attentive to what it means to construct forms of learning in their classrooms that enable students to affirm their voices within areas of community life, that is, within democratic public spheres needing constant criticism, safeguarding, and renewal.

Steve Tozer is worth quoting at length on this issue.

> The process of fitting students for community life, then, is an effort to prepare students both for the existing community and to bring them to understand and to appreciate the historical values and ideas which point to a more ideal community than the one that exists . . . the teacher's duty is to recognize the historical ideals which make community life worth living, ideals upon which the larger society is founded: ideals of human dignity and equality, freedom, and mutual concern of one person for another. . . . This is not to say that teachers should prepare students for some nonexistent utopia. Rather, teachers must develop an understanding of the community as it exists *and* an understanding of what kind of people will be required to make it better. They can try to develop for themselves an ideal

of the community their students should strive for, and they should help their students with the knowledge, the values and the skills they will need if they are to be resilient enough to maintain high standards of belief and conduct in an imperfect society.[57]

It is an unfortunate truism that when communities are ignored by teachers, students often find themselves trapped in institutions that not only deny them a voice, but also deprive them of a relational or contextual understanding of how the knowledge they acquire in the classroom can be used to influence and transform the public sphere. Implicit in the concept of linking classroom experiences to the wider community is the idea that the school is best understood as a polity, as a locus of citizenship. Within this locus, students and teachers can engage in a process of deliberation and discussion aimed at advancing the public welfare in accordance with fundamental moral judgments and principles. To bring schools closer to the concept of polity, it is necessary to define them as public spaces which seek to recapture the idea of critical democracy and community. In effect, we want to define teachers as active community participants whose function is to establish public spaces where students can debate, appropriate, and learn the knowledge and skills necessary to live in a critical democracy.

By public space we mean, as Hannah Arendt did, a concrete set of learning conditions where people come together to speak, to engage in dialogue, to share their stories, and to struggle together within social relations that strengthen rather than weaken possibilities for active citizenship.[58] School and classroom practices should, in some manner, be organized around forms of learning which serve to prepare students for responsible roles as transformative intellectuals, as community members, and as critically active citizens outside of schools.[59]

Conclusion

We began this essay by arguing that teacher education should be seriously rethought along the lines of the critical democratic tradition, a tradition which, regrettably, has been all but excluded from the current debates on American schooling. We have argued that this tradition provides the basis for rethinking the relationship of schooling to the social order and for restructuring the education of prospective teachers so as to prepare them for the role of transformative intellectual. Moreover, we have argued that teacher education programs must assume a central role in reforming public education and, in so doing, must assert the primacy of a democratic tradition in order to restructure school-community relations.

---

[57] Tozer, "Dominant Ideology and the Teacher's Authority," *Contemporary Education*, *56* (1985), 152–153.

[58] Arendt, *The Human Condition* (Chicago: University of Chicago Press, 1958).

[59] Attempts to link classroom instruction to community contexts is nowhere more important than during teachers' clinical experiences. On these occasions, prospective teachers should be assisted in making connections with progressive community organizations, especially those affiliated with local governmental council meetings and to interview community leaders and workers in various community agencies linked to the school. This enhances the possibility that prospective teachers will make critically reflective links between classroom practices and the ethos and needs of the surrounding social and cultural milieu.

In our view, the search for a creative democracy undertaken at the beginning of the century by Dewey and others is presently in retreat, having been abandoned by liberals and radicals alike. This situation presents a dual challenge to critical educators: there is now an urgent need not only to resurrect the tradition of liberal democracy, but to develop a theoretical perspective that goes beyond it. In the current age of conservatism, public education must analyze its strengths and weaknesses against an ideal of critical democracy rather than the current corporate referent of the capitalist marketplace. Similarly, public education must fulfill the task of educating citizens to take risks, to struggle for institutional and social change, and to fight *for* democracy and *against* oppression both inside and outside of schools. Pedagogical empowerment necessarily goes hand-in-hand with social and political transformation.

Our position is indebted to Dewey but attempts to extend his democratic project. Dewey's struggle for democracy was primarily pedagogical and largely failed to develop an extended analysis of class relations and historically conditioned inequalities in society. Conversely, our position accentuates the idea that schools represent only one important site in the struggle for democracy. It is different from Dewey's view because it perceives the self- and social empowerment of students as involving not just the politics of classroom culture, but also political and social struggle outside of school sites. Such an approach acknowledges that critical pedagogy is but one intervention — albeit a crucial one — in the struggle to restructure the ideological and material conditions of everyday life. We are convinced that teacher education institutions and public schools can and should play an active and productive role in broadening the possibilities for the democratic promise of American schooling, politics, and society.

Equality Is Excellence: Transforming Teacher Education and the Learning Process

IRA SHOR

Ira Shor suggests that conservative economic and school policy is responsible for a decline in the quality of teaching since the 1960s. He bases his analysis on a close observation of the current reform wave which, he points out, too often focuses only on student and teacher "mediocrity" and on the need for higher standards of "excellence." While refuting the conservative perspective, Shor proposes that the liberal critique needs to further infuse educational reform with an egalitarian overview and with the notion of change-agency. He suggests that teacher education must be critical, multicultural, student-centered, oriented toward equality, and desocializing, if it is to prepare teachers who can inspire students.

> Teacher education programs are disturbingly alike and almost uniformly inadequate. . . . This nation cannot continue to afford the brief, casual, conforming preparation now experienced by those who will staff its classrooms. . . . We will only begin to get evidence of the potential power of pedagogy when we dare to risk and support markedly deviant classroom procedures. (Goodlad, 1983, pp. 249, 315, 317)

> Only a few teachers used the difficult decade of the 1970s to teach themselves and their students with some new methods. . . . It is easy to claim that a radical restructuring of society or the system of education is needed for the kind of cultural bridging reported in this book [*Ways With Words*] to be large scale and continuous. (Heath, 1983, pp. 363, 369)

> Far too many teachers give out directions, busy work, and fact-fact-fact lectures in ways that keep students intellectually passive, if not actually deepening their disregard for learning and schooling. (The Holmes Group, 1986, p. 29)

> It is astonishing that so few critics challenge the system. . . . When one considers the energy, commitment, and quality of so many of the people working in the schools, one must place the blame [for school failure] elsewhere. The people are better than the structure. Therefore the structure must be at fault. (Sizer, 1984, pp. 29, 30)

Reform in the Name of Authority since 1983

Wisdom says that where there is light there is heat, but experience shows the opposite is not always true. The current wave of school reform, "the great school de-

Harvard Educational Review   Vol. 56   No. 4   November 1986, 406–426

bate" chronicled by many educators, has created the context for examining teacher education.[1] But the reform movement so far has generated more heat than light. Perhaps it is understandable that discussion of root causes and forward-looking solutions languishes in these conservative years. The Reagan administration commissioned *A Nation at Risk*, the report of the National Commission on Excellence in Education (1983), which accuses students and teachers of an alarming "mediocrity." According to the report, this "mediocrity" has helped Japan and Germany outpace our economy and has even threatened our national security. The recommended antidote fits the regressive tenor of the times—more traditional courses, more mechanical testing, a lust for "excellence," and a token glance at equality.

The influential Education Commission of the States (1983b) fired a second major salvo in its report, *Action for Excellence*. Highlighting "the teacher gap"—that is, the shortage of qualified teachers and the lower achievement of those entering the profession—this report echoed the White House alarm about the decline of schools. Many other studies and documents were released in that same year: *Academic Preparation for College* (The College Entrance Examination Board, 1983), *Making the Grade* (Twentieth Century Fund Task Force, 1983), *Educating Americans for the 21st Century* (The National Science Board, 1983), and *America's Competitive Challenge* (Task Force of the Business-Higher Education Forum, 1983). This great wave from above provoked statewide legislation and reviews of curriculum, and eventually swept the sad condition of teacher education into its nets.

Fishy Nets: Why the Authorities Launched their Reforms

Unhappy with the costs and the outcomes of schooling, the highest policymakers turned their attention after 1983 to curricular reform, to restructuring their management of the teaching profession, and to teacher education. Business and the military complained about the quality of graduates entering the workforce and the service, especially in regard to literacy and to discipline in the workplace.[2] From another perspective, the new arms race and the high-tech boom in the economy during the early 1980s created an undersupply of computer workers and engineers (estimated at 40,000 a year by the Task Force of the Business-Higher Education Forum, 1983). In response to this labor shortage, the curriculum tipped towards technology and computer studies. Unfortunately, by 1986 sectors of the electronics industry were laying off workers in a period of economic recovery, sorry news for students who rushed to computer majors and for college planners who promoted business needs through curriculum.

Still another labor factor brought curriculum and teacher education into the spotlight. By 1984 the teacher surplus of the 1970s had become a teacher shortage. Although education programs had grown by 113 in number since 1973, by the 1980s they were producing 53 percent fewer teachers (see Feistritzer, 1984).

---

[1] See Gross and Gross (1985), Passow (1984), Education Commission of the States (1983a, 1983b), Task Force on Education for Economic Growth (1983). For a summation that includes some critique, see Cross (1984, pp. 167–172).

[2] See National Commission on Excellence in Teacher Education (1983, pp. 9–10), Task Force on Education for Economic Growth (1983, pp. 17–19), and Panel on Secondary School Education for the Changing Workplace (1984, pp. xi–xii, 17–19) for commentary on the business-military perception of literacy and work discipline in young graduates.

Schools were experiencing disruptive spot shortages of teachers, especially in math, science, and foreign languages. Inner-city schools had unusually high turnover rates in their staffs each year. Substantial portions of the teacher corps were teaching out-of-license (for example, music majors instructing math courses) in nominally temporary arrangements that became a permanent and irrational way of life. The teacher supply problem is expected to grow worse in the coming decade. This has prompted "manpower" strategies to overhaul the professional pipeline training new teachers and to reorganize teaching in order to get more from current staff.

With few exceptions, the official reports explained away the real issues in the teacher shortage and in the decline of education. They chose instead "blaming-the-victim" formulas such as student-teacher "mediocrity," the need for "excellence" and higher "standards," the softness in a "cafeteria-style" high school curriculum, and the "breakdown of discipline" in school and the family.[3] In reality, the current crisis resulted from budget cuts that left class sizes too large, school buildings shabby, instructional materials in short supply, education programs unable to afford careful mentoring of student teachers, and aging academic departments deprived of new blood. Further, conservative educational policy in the 1970s imposed depressing programs of careerism and back-to-basics, making intellectual life in the classroom dull, vocational, and over-supervised.[4] These new curricula discouraged creativity and liberal education. They invited gifted teachers to leave the profession, while they dissuaded students from thinking of education as an exciting career. Also in the 1970s, the job market for liberal arts majors and for teachers collapsed at the same time that the number of business and computer majors expanded wildly. This vocational imbalance in college curriculum steered a generation of students away from education as a career; for those teachers already in service, fiscal austerity since the Nixon administration has led to wage losses and to decay in their schools. These depressing public-sector conditions are characteristic of the recent conservative era.

Two other factors contributed to the teaching crisis: higher wages in the private sector for some college graduates, and the appearance of a new baby boom. First, wages for technical-scientific graduates are better in the private sector than in education or in public-sector jobs. This difference draws labor to industry, attracting

[3] One exception to the routine assertions of the 1983 reform wave is *High Schools and the Changing Workplace* (National Academy Press, 1984), which did not wax grandiloquent on high-tech and computers, as did the other reports. Stanford economist Levin was on the panel producing this report, and its cool assessment of high-tech may reflect his research into the marginal impact computers would have on wages, opportunities, and employment in the future job market. Another exceptional source is the "Background Paper" by Peterson (1983), attached to the Twentieth Century Fund (1983) report, *Making the Grade*. Peterson's research found no educational crisis or collapse to justify the official claims of 1983. His lengthy study showed positive outcomes from federal equity programs in the 1960s, thus reversing the report's majority statement in favor of more emphasis on "excellence" and less on equality. A third exception is the California Commission on the Teaching Profession's (1985) report, *Who Will Teach Our Children?*, which recommended ending state regulation of teacher education programs, thus allowing each campus to experiment. Goodlad (1983) was on this commission, and this unusual recommendation reflected at least one concern in his study, *A Place Called School*.

[4] See Shor (1986, chap. 2, on career education, and chap. 3 on the literacy crisis). For more background on the depressant political effects of vocationalism in the 1970s, see Karabel (1972) and Grubb and Lazerson (1975). An illuminating study of the economics of the 1970s and 1980s can be found in Bowles, Gordon, and Weiskopf (1983). Another spacious survey was done by Bowles and Gintis (1982) and the aggressive conservative politics of this age were studied by Piven and Cloward (1982).

teachers out of low-paying education jobs into better-paying corporate ones. In an economy kept unbalanced by high military spending there is a domestic "brain drain" of math, science, and engineering teachers out of education into the booming military and electronics sectors of the job market.[5]

Second, the rising birthrate made its predictable impact on the elementary grades by 1984, creating a demand for new teachers after a decade of economic and social policy that undermined public education. This sudden demand for labor is as much a crisis in education as in any other labor-short part of the economy. The $130 billion-a-year school system will need about one million new teachers in the coming decade, according to the National Institute of Education (NIE, 1984a) report, *The Condition of Education*.

Evading criticism of economic policy and the arms race, the "excellence" reformers promised that renewal would come from high technology, greater emphasis on traditional subjects, more required testing, career ladders in the teaching profession, and something called "education for economic growth." Such proposals hid the causes of school decline, which included budget cuts, withdrawal of federal support for equality, redirection of funds from social services to the military, and the dramatic failure of the corporate job market to inspire graduates with employment equal to their educations.[6] Only a few years before the White House initiative in 1983, educators were debating the terrible predicament of "the overeducated American." Along with Freeman's (1976) book of that name, studies by Berg (1970), NIE (1983), Braverman (1974), and Levin and Rumberger (1983) pointed to a work force that was becoming more educated while the job market *deskilled* work through automation and *raised* the credentials needed to get routine jobs. The official reports were silent on the bizarre phenomenon of "overeducation" turning so quickly into "mediocrity." In reality, students are not overeducated, and are not mediocre. Such mystifications merely explain away the root causes of the current crisis. The stagnant economy of this conservative era cannot distribute equality or prosperity, the two legs of the American dream on which the corporate system stands. Myths of overeducation and mediocrity distract attention from the systemic causes of decline.

The System of Silence: Pushing Liberal Values to the Margins

By ignoring uncomfortable political questions, the recent reform wave has prompted a remarkably unbalanced debate and legislative season. Official commissions, legislative groups, and the media have followed a narrow line of traditional frameworks and authoritarian remedies.[7] These "get tough" approaches

[5] For some analysis of the domestic brain drain, see Levin (1985). Levin's research points out that from 15–50 percent of all scientific personnel are employed directly or indirectly by the Defense Department.

[6] For a discussion of the job market's impact on school performance, see National Coalition of Advocates for Children (1985). For another consideration of how economic decline after the 1960s affected student learning, see Levin (1981); for a discussion of businesses' tilting of curriculum in the 1980s, see Spring (1984).

[7] For a sample of the restricted debate in the mass media, see the following cover stories on the education crisis: "The bold quest" (1983), "Can the schools be saved?" (1983, May 9), "Why teachers fail" (1982), and "What makes schools great" (1984).

caused visible dismay in out-of-favor liberal circles. Boyer (1983, p. 5; 1984) complained that proponents of the new regimens forgot that "education is to enrich the living individual" while Sizer declared that the current reform wave lacked the compassion for students that characterized earlier periods of change ("The bold quest," 1983, p. 66). Boyer, Sizer, and other skeptics like Goodlad (1983) and Howe (1985a, 1985b) doubted the claims of the "excellence" camp with regard to illiteracy, the SAT decline, and the need for heavy doses of back-to-basics.[8] The liberal dissenters noted the strident emphasis on more testing of teachers and students, more required courses, fewer electives, a reduced federal role in guaranteeing equity, and the call for standard English over bilingual teaching.

The liberal perspective deserved more attention than it received in a period dominated by conservatism. In addition to that in Boyer (1983), liberal departures can be found in Sizer's (1984) *Horace's Compromise* and Darling-Hammond's two studies, *Beyond the Commission Reports* (1984a) and *Equality and Excellence: The Educational Status of Black Americans* (1984b). Early liberal statements made by Kohl (1982) and Maeroff (1982) included a critique of the conservative politics behind the back-to-basics movement. These got far less attention than Adler's (1982) traditional *paideia* program. Also among the liberal departures, Heath (1983) offered a nontraditional ethnographic model of teaching and learning which unfortunately had no impact on state legislation or on district-wide curricular policies. In addition, Richardson, Fisk, and Okun (1983) did not blame working-class students for their learning deficits, but offered another pedagogical challenge. Richardson pointed to mechanical teaching styles, state under-funding of mass higher education, and the vocational bias of the community-college system as the principal obstacles to the development of "critical literacy" needed by working students.

Other meagerly discussed reports from this dissenting group were the NIE's (1984) *Involvement in Learning*, the New World Foundation's (Bastian et al.,1985) *Choosing Equality*, the Association of American Colleges' (AAC, 1985) *Integrity in the College Curriculum*, and Goodlad's (1983) monumental *A Place Called School*. These documents presented policy and pedagogical alternatives to the conservative tide of the 1980s. *Choosing Equality* boldly recommended egalitarian federal funding, public economic development to create jobs, and student/teacher/parent "empowerment" as the foundations for educational reform. It was one "grass-roots" correction to the "excellence" mystification launched by *A Nation at Risk* (National Commission, 1983) and *Action for Excellence* (Education Commission of the States, 1983b), and promoted by "excellence" networkers such as Finn and Ravitch (1984).[9]

Those taking an egalitarian perspective matched policy issues with presentations of alternative pedagogy. Heath's work in the Carolina Piedmont area of the East Coast demonstrated the power of student-centered teaching to break the tra-

[8] Less discussed critiques of the post–1983 school reforms can be found in Leonard (1984), Hacker (1984), and Karp (1985).

[9] Finn and Ravitch set up the National Network for Excellence in Education in 1984, and edited a compendium with Fancher. See Finn and Ravitch's (1984) "Conclusions and Recommendations: High Expectations and Disciplined Effort," for their traditional curricular position in the great debate. See Finn (1981, 1983) for his conservative view on educational policy. A liberal response to the elite impact of the "excellence" reforms is in Toch (1984).

ditional separation of school and community. The NIE (1984a, 1984b) and AAC (1985) reports took stands for an interactive, interdisciplinary curriculum. Goodlad (1983) supported experimental, participatory pedagogy in contrast to the traditional teacher-talk which dominated the thousand classrooms visited by his researchers. Sizer (1984), Boyer (1983), and Goodlad (1983) all acknowledged the failure of the regular school syllabus to address the needs and themes of adolescents. Darling-Hammond (1984b) discussed the unequal curriculum offered to black students. The NIE and AAC reports acknowledged the failure of traditional curricula to serve the educational needs of college students whose learning was hindered by the academy's departmental sectarianism, preference for lecture methods, and rewarding of professors for narrow research instead of teaching.[10] This dissenting body of literature did not support "get tough" programs to solve the school malaise.

The Heart in the Dissenting Body: An Egalitarian Synthesis

The liberal dissenters in this antiliberal period occupied marginal ground. Their defense of student-centered, egalitarian, and interactive values was a heroic holding action. Education as a change-agent, however, constituted one undeveloped value in this dissenting margin. *Choosing Equality* (Bastian et al., 1985) stands out for its advocacy of community empowerment and community-based school reform. This report called for including parents in school policy-making and for linking education to local leadership and existing community organizations. Even farther out in the margins, energetic networks of "participatory researchers" and adult or community educators developed a vision of the educator participating in social change.[11]

Besides greater attention to the idea of change-agency, the dissenting body of literature needs an egalitarian overview. Such a synthesis is too important to leave implicit or unrecognized. I suggest the following framework as one way to pose egalitarianism and change-agency in education: *Equality is excellence and inequality leads to alienation.* Excellence without equality produces only more inequality. Inequality leads to learning deficits and to resistance in the great mass of students. Alienation in schools is the number-one learning problem that depresses academic performance and elevates student resistance. Student resistance to intellectual life is socially produced by inequality and by authoritarian pedagogy in school,

[10] The NIE (1984b) report deals more with learning process than does the AAC (1985) report. AAC focused on curricular policy for higher education, promoting interdisciplinary and critical themes, in a desire to reorient a research professoriat back toward teaching.

[11] Some networks supporting community-based, participatory, or change-agency education include the Institute for Responsive Education (Boston), the Public Education Information Network (St. Louis), The Association for Community-Based Education (Washington, DC), Basic Choices (Madison, WI), the Participatory Research Group (Toronto), the Center for Popular Economics (Amherst, MA), the Lindeman Center (Chicago), the Highlander Center (New Market, TN), and the Labor Institute (New York City). See, for example, Adams and Horton (1975), The Labor Institute (1982), and The Institute for Responsive Education (1984). For one experience in community-based, change-oriented education, see Minkler and Cox (1980).

[12] In *The 1984 Metropolitan Life Survey of the American Teacher* (Harris and Associates, 1984), teachers ranked lack of student interest as the most serious problem in the classroom, with budget cuts running a close second.

worsening the literacy problem and the crisis in teacher burnout.[12] Teacher burnout and student resistance are social problems of an unequal system and cannot be fully addressed by teacher-education reforms or by classroom remedies alone. Participatory and critical pedagogy, coupled with egalitarian policies in school and society, can holistically address the education crisis.

I am proposing that the education crisis is thus an expression of social inequality. Equality empowers people and raises aspirations in school and society. Power and hope are sources of motivation to learn and to do. Motivation produces student involvement, and involvement produces learning and literacy. Such participation also supports teacher morale, makes the hard work of teaching attractive and rewarding, and decreases burnout. Teacher and student morale will be increased from the heightened joy of learning; this morale will in turn inspire more people to choose teaching as a career — and to stay in teaching once there, thus easing the teacher shortage. Inspiring classroom experiences can also encourage teachers and students to take themselves more seriously as intellectuals who can critically grasp any issue, technical process, body of knowledge, moment in history, or political condition in society. Teachers and students oriented to debate and critical study will be better able to act as citizens democratically transforming society. Democratic participation in society may include action against the arms race and budget cuts, which could potentially shift spending priorities from guns to learning, and consequently improve the quality and appeal of intellectual life in schools.

My egalitarian perspective, outlined and synthesized above, simply recognizes that economics, community life and literacy, commercial mass culture, and political action outside the classroom grossly influence the fate of education. Apart from the billions of dollars spent on weapons, the most glaring social inequity is the greater amount of money invested in the education of richer students at all levels. Years after the landmark *Serrano v. Priest* (1971) decision against unequal school funding, children of poor and working-class families still have much less invested in their educations, according to Fiske (1981) and Sizer (1984, p. 36).[13] This inequality is only the tip of the iceberg because the daily lives, the language, and the job opportunities of poor and working-class students can also work against success in traditional classrooms.[14] This citing of the "arms race" and "inequality" to explain the school crisis did not appear in the official reports because it blames the business world and its educational subsystem, that is, the function of schools to socialize students for their places in the corporate economy. Rather, the reports chose to point haughty fingers at student-teacher "mediocrity," at "spongy" courses in high school, at open admissions to college, or at the alleged breakdown of discipline in the family. But the corporate education system itself gutted public education and invited students and teachers to go on a performance strike.

---

[13] The study by Jencks et al. (1972) is the watershed document on this issue; see also Bowles and Gintis (1976, esp. pp. 4, 33, 133).

[14] Heath's (1983) *Ways With Words* is an illuminating study of how community literacy and school literacy conflict. She examines how the idioms of black and white non-elite schoolchildren in the Carolina Piedmont clashed with elite usage favored by the schools. For another excellent study of the clash between language and culture in the schools, see Willis (1981).

Performance Anxiety: Why Teaching Matters

While factors beyond the classroom greatly affect education, what goes on in school makes an important difference. This is true not only with respect to the quality of a student's life and learning, but also to the possible transformation of students, teachers, and the society that sets the curriculum. The strongest potential of teaching lies in studying the politics and student cultures that affect the classroom. It is politically naive or simply "technocratic" to see the classroom as a separate world where inequality, dominant ideology, and economic policy do not affect learning. It is equally damaging to think pessimistically that nothing good can be achieved in the classroom until the economic system and society are changed. Similarly, it is also a mistake to believe that education by itself can change society one classroom at a time.

Individual classrooms cannot change an unequal social system; only political movements can transform inequality. In working for transformation, egalitarian pedagogy can interfere with the disabling socialization of students. Schools are one large agency among several which socialize students; they can confirm or challenge socialization into inequality. Teachers can reinforce student alienation from critical thinking by confirming the *curricular* disempowerment of their intelligence, or teachers can employ critical pedagogy to counter the disabling character of students' prior educational experiences. As a dependent sector of society, schools can either play a role in reproducing alienated consciousness or they can challenge inequality through a curriculum critical of the dominant culture that offers such a disabling mass education.

When pedagogy and curricular policy reflect egalitarian goals, education can be empowered *to oppose dominant socialization with critical desocialization*. This involves developing critical consciousness in preference to commercial consciousness and transforming society rather than reproducing inequality. Efforts at critical desocialization could serve to illuminate the myths that support the elite hierarchy of society, to invite students to reflect on their own conditions, and to challenge them to consider how the limits they face might be overcome. Critical literacy programs and participatory courses can also raise awareness about the values expressed through language in daily life. They would further serve to distribute research skills and censored information useful for investigating power and policy in society.

Critical pedagogy recasts education as an opposition to the purpose of traditional curriculum, which is the reproduction of inequality (Apple, 1982; Bowles & Gintis, 1982; Carnoy & Levin, 1985; Giroux, 1983; Jencks et al., 1972; Willis, 1981; and others). Several roads can lead to critical classrooms that oppose the reproduction of subordinate consciousness in school. A number of educators have experimented, for example, with Freire's methods and approaches (Finlay & Faith, 1979; Fiore & Elsasser, 1982; Frankenstein, 1983; Shor & Freire, 1986; Shor, in press; Wallerstein, 1983). Heath (1983) tested an ethnographic model; Kohl (1982) offered a humanistic language program similar to Judy's (1980) proposals; and Pattison (1982) suggested a "bi-idiomatic" approach to teaching colloquial and formal discourse simultaneously. When we discuss teacher education programs or curriculum at any level of schooling, we can pose the questions of critical pedagogy and desocialization. Once we accept that education's role is to challenge inequality and dominant myths like student "mediocrity" or the alleged neutrality of "standards," rather than to socialize students into the status quo, we have set the foundation needed for inventing practical methods of desocialization.

Desocialization thus builds on the terrain already staked out by the liberal dissenters. Pattison (1982), for example, refused to define "correct usage" as a universal standard of excellence, referring to it simply as the idiom of the triumphant middle classes, useful for supporting authoritarian societies as easily as democratic ones (see esp. chaps. 5,6,7). Boyer (1983) asserted that equality constitutes an unfinished agenda for education. Darling-Hammond (1984b) reflected Boyer's view in her study of the education of black students whose progress toward equality during the 1960s has eroded since 1975. Further, Darling-Hammond (1984c) saw state-mandated testing and syllabi as depressing the performance of teachers.[15] Sizer (1984) acknowledged that social class has a great impact on educational choices but that class as a theme was not included in school curricula. Heath (1983) suggested reaching out into everyday life in an effort to build on the existing literacy of any school population. Her work was a refreshing break from routine assertions that students were "mediocre" or "illiterate." Goodlad (1983) offered the most systematic critique of traditional teaching, including the tendency for minority students to be placed in vocational tracks in school. Lastly, the AAC (1985) report strongly criticized the remoteness of college professors from teaching.

The liberal agenda and the aims of desocialization may yet make the more important contribution to education reform, if only because an authoritarian approach — memorization, mechanical testing, teacher-talk and student silence, abstract subjects remote from student interest, standardized syllabi, balkanized faculties, and Byzantine administrations — cannot solve the current school crisis. This is the regime which produced student alienation and teacher burnout in the first place. By proposing solutions that caused the problem, the commissions and legislatures offer water to a drowning school system. Conservative regimens will only intensify the dilemmas faced by teachers and students in school. The authorities are inviting a more severe crisis down the road;[16] at that point, in the vacuum of Reagan-era reforms, liberal humanists may find that their program is an idea whose time has come.

Cleaner Vacuums: The Reform Wave Washes over Teacher Education

In the spinoff debate on reforming teacher education, liberal dissent once again has been overshadowed by conservative policy. Some of Goodlad's (1983) comments on teacher education, and Heath's (1983) teaching model, stand out from business-as-usual. Goodlad recommends experimental schools in each district, where future teachers would train to enter the profession. Teacher-apprentices would spend two years as interns in these experimental schools, learning their craft in settings that model student-centered pedagogy. This would introduce them to teaching through a participative approach rather than a traditional one. Heath's model of having both teachers and students engaged in ethnographic research is another alternate method for teacher training. Teachers would be ethnographers

---

[15] See also Darling-Hammond's (1984c) critique of the testing craze in the 1983 reform wave.
[16] Cuban (1984) wisely assessed the potential for failure in a mechanical reform program.

of their students' communities and cultures, while students would be trained as local ethnographers, studying scientifically the language and habits they had previously only experienced. Through such a pedagogy, students and teachers would teach and learn from one another. This mutual education also offers students a certain distance from reality and models the critical habit of mind, which can be defined as the habit of analyzing experience and questioning received knowledge. Heath's program collapses the wall between classroom and community, between research and teaching, and between research and living. It is an example of the experiential/conceptual approach to learning that Dewey (1900/1956, 1902/1956, 1938/1956) proposed.

In contrast, official reports after 1983 defined the teaching and learning crisis in ways that evaded the real needs of the classroom. One evasion focused on managing the profession — teacher testing, certification requirements, merit pay — while bypassing the three big-ticket items that most concern teachers: higher wages across the board, smaller class sizes, and lighter course loads. A second evasion concerned the learning process. The official view posed teaching and learning in terms of the "Great Books," a fixed authority based on standard reading lists. Accordingly, the teacher functioned as a delivery system in a one-way transfer of information and skills to students. This mechanical notion of education sought traditional material for its core curriculum: the American Heritage and Western Civilization.[17] Such rejections of the multicultural diversity that emerged from the 1960s are reflected by Hirsch (1985, pp. 8–15), who defines "cultural literacy" as a 130–page reading list of Eurocentric works.[18] Hirsch suggests that this list can be reduced, for curriculum purposes, to a more manageable size, but he maintains that without familiarity with these works — written predominantly by white, male, Western authors — a person could not be considered literate. Similarly, Adler's (1982, 1983) bookish *paideia* program posed another canonical thrust which endorsed the teaching of "classics" through a lecture-based pedagogy.

The notion of a core curriculum based on traditional values and classical texts appealed also to Finn, who, as assistant secretary of education in the Reagan administration, prepared a gray booklet called *What Works: Research About Teaching and Learning* (1986). This volume exhorts the family to do more at home for education. It insists that hard work and self-reliance, not social policy or school funding, are the heart of student success. Finn's traditional bent, as a key "excellence" spokesperson, was borne out by the many quotations from ancient and pre–1800 sources sprinkling the text, as well as by recommendations to teach a "shared" heritage to students that would instill national pride. This myth of a neutral, shared, national history reduces the critical and multicultural potentials of education.

The traditional models of Hirsch, Adler, and Finn informed legislative action. They denied the student-centered and experiential values of Goodlad (1983) and

---

[17] These were the curricular emphases in California's reform legislation Senate Bill 813 and in New York's Regents Action Plan with its Part 100 Regulations. Secretary of Education Bennett (1984) also took up these themes in his report.

[18] Hirsch's (1985) quantitative canon is discussed in his essay. Cuban (1984) also offers a concise critique of the mechanical approach to learning. For some historical perspective on the politics of literacy, see Donald (1983). Donald offers an illuminating look at the literacy debate in 19th-century Britain, when state-sponsored literacy in official schools helped reduce dissent. For another fine discussion of literacy, see Ohmann (1985).

Heath (1983), and of Silberman (1971), who, during the upheavals of the 1960s, defined a community *paideia* (pp. 5, 49). Goodlad also referred to *paideia* as education in a whole community, not as a school-bound event alone. The house of authority, however, heard only Adler's *paideia*.

One lesson from this debate is that the learning process itself is a form of politics and ideology, not a neutral realm of activity. Another lesson is that the learning process we set for the schools is the model that socializes future teachers in how to teach. By reasserting an elite canon and a mechanical menu of testing and teacher-talk, the official commissions and legislative bodies after 1983 also reimposed a model of teaching. In-service teachers now feel great pressure to teach to the tests, while future teachers receive passive canonical instruction in high school, in collegiate liberal arts, and in their academic majors. A passive pedagogy that utilizes dismal texts and traditional reading lists is the curriculum modeled to students, including that fraction who will one day be teachers. This is why all of schooling is actually "teacher education," a *paideia* socializing teachers in how to teach and what to learn. To segregate "pedagogy" courses as *the* place to study teaching is one way to hide the authoritarian, mechanical ideology embedded in the standard curriculum.

Cannons Aimed at Canons: The Culture War over the Learning Process

For over a century, mechanical, factory models of teaching and learning have been at war with critical, interactive education.[19] The quality of the learning process was an issue for liberal dissenters after 1983, heirs as they are to the Deweyan side in the long culture war over curriculum. On the managerial side of this debate, a number of official reports from around the nation fail to give adequate attention to the learning process.[20] Instead of providing a systematic discussion of learning, these reports focus on managing the profession, on certification of teachers, on merit pay schemes and career ladders, on alternate routes to the profession, and on time spent in collegiate programs. The documents do acknowledge the importance of student teaching, and the California (1985) report, with Goodlad on the commission, does recommend deregulating teacher education in order to allow colleges to experiment. Their discussion, however, omits examination of the learning process and leaves intact the mechanical pedagogy that dominates teacher education as much as it dominates other classrooms.

While the reports differ in style and emphasis, they display a compatibility and a consensus. A policy agenda from this group could be synthesized as follows:

The teaching profession needs higher standards for training and licensure.

Teacher education programs should be more selective; in-service teachers need to

---

[19] In a heated reform year Gibboney (1983, pp. 55–56) wrote a cheerful counter to the conservative agenda and a pointed reminder of the long debate over curriculum. He discussed Colonel Parker's reversal of educational decline in the Quincy, Massachusetts, schools in the 1870s through "progressive" pedagogy. For a substantial history of the Progressive movement, see Cremin (1964).

[20] See the Southern Regional Education Board (1985), Galambos (1985), Oregon State System of Higher Education (1984), California Commission on the Teaching Profession (1985) policy study, New York Education Department (1985), Feistzritzer (1984), and the most prominent of all, the National Commission for Excellence in Teacher Education (1985).

meet more rigorous standards. Admissions and graduation standards in college programs should be raised.

Teachers need more in-service development. Veteran classroom teachers can train new teachers in school and future ones in campus programs.

Salaries need improvement, especially at entry-level, and career ladders should be instituted to give teachers incentives.

Teachers should be assigned fewer noninstructional duties, granted more autonomy in their classrooms, and included more in administrative and policy decisions.

More care and funds should be given to student teaching in college programs. Teacher preparation should include at least a one-year student-teaching internship.

The training of teachers should remain primarily on college campuses with some alternate, off-campus routes into the profession (a choice made by a number of states, most notably New Jersey and its alternate certification plan).

Education majors need more liberal arts courses in college.

For certification, new teachers should have to pass exams in subject matter, basic skills, and knowledge of pedagogy, in addition to completing successfully a one-year internship in student teaching.

Efforts should be made to attract the brightest students, especially high-achieving minority candidates, to teaching.

Research on teaching needs to be more widely disseminated in education courses and in public schools.

A five-year undergraduate teacher education program is needed. This would require liberal arts, a concentration in an academic major, education courses, and an internship in student teaching, all of which could not be completed within the current four-year degree programs.

A five-year undergraduate program was recommended by the National Commission for Excellence in Teacher Education (1983), by the California Commission on the Teaching Profession (1985), and by the NIE (1984b) statement. The heads of both teacher unions, Shanker of the American Federation of Teachers (AFT) and Futrell of the National Education Association (NEA), served on the National Commission, and strongly endorsed the recommendation for a five-year baccalaureate program. The five-year undergraduate education program is one way to paint yourself into a corner if you lose sight of the quality of a learning process. I will return to this point shortly to discuss "time" fallacies in mechanical approaches to learning.

Faults aside, this consensual agenda does suggest items beneficial to the teaching profession: higher pay, more classroom autonomy for teachers, carefully mentored internships, in-service development, and veteran schoolteachers serving as adjunct faculty in college programs (see Shanker, 1985).[21] The California Commission even recommended the teacher's nightly wish: reduced class size. The agenda, however, was undemocratically developed and imposed, with little or no

---

[21] Shanker (1985) proposed hiring veteran teachers as mentors and adjunct faculty in teacher-education programs and confirmed his support of a national teacher-testing program and career ladders, including a category of "transient" teacher at the entry-level position.

input from teachers. The first high-profile reforms to be pushed through have suggested more testing and more required courses in the syllabus. Very little debate has focused on the learning process in teacher education or in the colleges and schools.

The Proof of the Pudding Is in the Process: If More Liberal Arts Is the Answer, What Is the Question?

One repeated claim in the major reports is that education courses are soft on content while liberal arts courses are hard. Therefore, future teachers who need a better grasp of the canon should study more academic courses. Future secondary teachers already spend the largest part of their credits in liberal arts (natural sciences, social sciences, and literature courses) and only about 20 percent of their baccalaureate hours in education courses.[22] Still, the information mystique of the liberal arts reappears at a time when mechanical pedagogy fits the needs of authoritarian reform.

The humanities curriculum should be admired when it generates critical thought in students and inspires them to be interactive learners. Academic studies should not be bodies of knowledge consumed in gulps by information-hungry students. Liberal arts courses should develop conceptual habits of mind, critical methods of inquiry, and in-depth scrutiny that displays the relationship between intellect, politics, values, and society. Sending future teachers to liberal arts courses where they are lectured at and made passive recipients of information socializes them into an inadequate model of learning and teaching. The validity of every liberal arts course rests on how much critical thinking it generates, how much participation it mobilizes, and how it relates its body of knowledge to other disciplines and to the larger conditions of society. It should be noted that these are the pedagogical responsibilities of any course, not merely liberal arts.

Soul Repository: The Spirit of Qualitative Learning

In proposing a qualitative process instead of mechanical learning, I want to suggest a pedagogy that is participatory, critical, values-oriented, multicultural, student-centered, experiential, research-minded, and interdisciplinary. Such a pedagogy focuses on the quality of an activity, not on the quantity of skills or facts memorized, or on the quantity of hours or credits spent on a task. Further, the quality approach addresses a major myth in the recent discussion of teacher education, that undergraduate preparation of teachers requires *five* years instead of *four*. Another myth is that teacher education should be done at the graduate level only. These are mechanical fallacies in the reports, which can nevertheless be credited for speaking of the need to make teacher education more clinical, more in touch with research, and more open to minorities (even though the new teacher tests are producing high minority failure rates).

Because the reforms propose a one- or two-year internship in student teaching prior to entering the profession, the four-year baccalaureate programs run out of

---

[22] How an education major spends her or his credits at the undergraduate level is discussed in the National Commission for Excellence in Teacher Education (1985, p. 13).

time, not to mention money, in the limited budgets usually allocated to education schools. A seriously mentored internship requires more money and more faculty attention on campus and in the cooperating school than is likely to be invested. Clinical settings in real schools are the best places to learn a teacher's craft, but when the reports favor *more* subject-matter specialization and *more* liberal arts at the undergraduate level, they wind up adding a *fifth* year to squeeze in a teacher internship. This is the sad result of the quantitative approach to learning. If you measure knowledge by minutes, hours, courses, credits, semesters, and years, you are ruled by the clock, not by the intellect. Instead, the focus should be on the kind of learning and teaching modeled at every level of education. If a passive, authoritarian model of pedagogy dominates all levels of school and college classrooms, what good is it for future teachers to spend an extra year being socialized in the worst model of teaching? Four years of bad models will not be remedied by adding a fifth.

The Holmes Group (1986) understood this need for interactive pedagogy. But four years of good models—critical, participatory learning—will also make the Holmes call for graduate teacher-training far less urgent. The challenge here is the same one made to the information myth of the liberal arts. What kind of learning and teaching is modeled at every year and level of education? If the learning process is interactive and critical, then four years is enough to prepare future teachers. If the learning process models equality and critical thought on school and society, then teacher education will be a serious enterprise at the undergraduate level. If a curriculum at any degree level, for any number of years, is dominated by teacher talk, didactic lectures, canonical reading lists, commercial textbooks, and standardized testing, then five or six years of undergraduate work, or two years of graduate study, will not develop the teachers needed to inspire learning. Further, even the best teacher education will have limited results as long as low pay, large classes, heavy work loads, administrative oversupervision, standardized testing, and shabby conditions dominate the classroom.

It will be useful for teacher education reformers to confront the time fallacy. Concerns about more time in liberal arts, a five-year baccalaureate, or a two-year M.A.T. pale in comparison to the question of the learning process. The socializing power of any experience is greater in its quality than in its quantity, greater in the quality of social relations than in the quantity of statements or rules. A desocializing, egalitarian, and critical pedagogy is a quality process which can invite teachers and students to take their educations seriously. It is one not being modeled now. To help define a desocializing model for teacher education, I want to offer an agenda of themes for the learning process.

Modeling New Fashions: Egalitarian Teacher Education

Dialogic Teaching

The dialogic method discussed by Freire (1970, 1973) is one way to reduce student withdrawal and teacher-talk in the classroom. A dialogic class begins with problem posing and critical discussion. This interactive opening sends powerful signals to students that their participation is expected and needed to solve problems of mutual interest. It will not be easy to learn the arts of dialogue because education now offers so little critical discussion and so few constructive peer exchanges. Dialogue is the art of intervention and the art of restraint, so that the verbal facility of a trained intellectual (the teacher) does not silence the verbal styles of unscholarly students.

Practice in leading long dialogic inquiries in class will require making the curriculum itself dialogic. It also suggests study in group dynamics, the social relations of discourse, and the linguistic habits of students in their communities, in relation to their sex, class, race, region, age, and ethnic origin.

Critical Literacy

Literacy that provokes critical awareness and desocialization will involve more than minimal competency. It will require critical literacy across the curriculum and will ask that all academic subjects develop habits of reading, writing, thinking, speaking, and listening, in order to provoke conceptual inquiry into self, society, and the discipline itself. This means that future teachers in every subject specialization, from biology to architecture, will learn how to pose problems in an effort to develop thinking and language skills.

Critical literacy invites teachers and students to "problematize" all subjects of study — that is, to understand existing knowledge as an historical product deeply invested with the values of those who developed such knowledge. A critically literate person does not stay at the empirical level of memorizing data, or at the impressionistic level of opinion, or at the level of dominant myths in society, but goes beneath the surface to understand the origin, structure, and consequences of any body of knowledge, technical process, or object under study. This model of literacy establishes teaching and learning as forms of research and experimentation. It calls on us to test hypotheses, examine evidence and artifacts, and finally to question what we know. In addition, teaching/learning as research suggests that teachers constantly observe students' learning in order to make pedagogical decisions, while students are also researching their language, their society, and their own learning.

Situated Pedagogy

This goal asks teachers to situate learning in the students' cultures — their literacy, their themes, their present understandings, their aspirations, their daily lives. The goal is to integrate experiential materials with conceptual methods and academic subjects. Grounding economics, nursing, engineering, mathematics, or biology in student life and literacy will not only connect experience with critical thought, but will also demonstrate that intellectual work has a tangible purpose in our lives. Further, only a situated pedagogy can bring critical study to bear on the concrete conditions of life, which critical learning may help recreate.

Ethnography and Cross-Cultural Communication

A teacher's academic program needs components in ethnography and cultural anthropology. To situate critical literacy and dialogue inside the language, themes, and cognitive levels of the students, a teacher needs to study the population he or she is teaching. This study can be carried out using the ethnographic methods described by Heath (1983), the sociolinguistics demonstrated by Hoggart (1957) and

Bisseret (1979), and the grounded-theory approach to research discussed by Glaser and Strauss (1967).

Further, experience in cross-cultural communications will be valuable for teachers who are likely to lead classrooms with diverse student populations. Bidialectalism and bilingualism in schools are academic themes that invite learning about the communication problems of teaching in a multicultural society. A final anthropological feature of teacher education is the need to study literatures outside the official canon, from labor culture, ethnic groups, and women's writings.

Change-Agency

To be egalitarian change-agents, teachers need to study community analysis and models of community change.[23] How do communities structure themselves? How do they change? How do outsiders identify and work with local leaders? How can classroom instruction model itself on key issues of community life?

Teachers will also need to study school organization, school-based curriculum design, the legislative environment for education, and professional politics. Inside the institution of a school or college, political methods for change can include staff-development seminars, community-school linkages, faculty committees and assemblies, internal publications, political lobbying, and union organization. Future teachers can benefit from studying histories of organizing change in the classroom, in schools or colleges, and in communities.

Inequality in School and Society

This academic interest can be studied through courses in sociology, economics, history, and psychology. How do inequalities in race, sex, and class influence school outcomes and expenditures? How did the current school system emerge in relation to the politics of each preceding age? What impact have egalitarian movements had on school and social policy? How have nontraditional, egalitarian programs affected student performance?[24]

Performance Skills

Teachers can benefit from voice and drama training to enhance their skills in problem posing and discussion leading. To be a creative problem poser in the classroom, drama and voice skills are helpful. The teacher needs to think of herself or himself as a creative artist whose craft is instruction. An exciting instructor is a communications artist who can engage students in provocative dialogue. Also, performing skills can habituate new teachers to the intimidating challenge of standing up each hour in front of a large group and taking charge of the session. Lastly, a dramatic teacher models the aesthetic joy of dialogue, the pleasure of thinking out loud with others.

This agenda of themes is meant to be suggestive rather than exhaustive. Each study item does not require a separate course; an ethnography class can demonstrate dialogic methods of teaching as well as provide background on literacy sit-

---

[23] For a well-defined program in community education, see Harris (1982).

[24] For an informative survey of the unknown successes in non-traditional programs, see Jennings and Nathan (1977); see also Nathan (1983).

uated in student culture, which can be studied for the impact of social inequality on daily life and learning. The above program can be coordinated with student teaching. Further, there are other subjects worthy of study: child psychology and adolescent development, the history of pedagogical thought, international education, immigrant patterns of assimilation, a second language (preferably Spanish, for U.S. teachers), and survival during the teacher's first year in the classroom. The most valuable element is participatory learning, which mobilizes critical thought and democratic debate.

In conclusion, I would emphasize that learning is not the transfer of skills or information from a talking teacher to a passive student. Education is different from narrow training in business careers. These are negative recipes which will produce even more student alienation and teacher burnout.

A teacher must aspire to be much more than a talking textbook, more than a mere functionary who implements standardized tests and mandated syllabi. Teaching should offer an illumination of reality which helps all of us grasp the social limits that constrain us. Critical learning does not define students as empty vessels to be filled with packaged bits of facts and figures. Teachers must oppose the mechanical pedagogy and the unequal tracking that take some students to success and most others to low wages and underemployment, to despair and anti-intellectualism. Learning which is more than job training and more than socialization into subordinate lives involves the critical study of society. Such education is a charmingly utopian challenge to inequality and to authoritarian methods. It aims to foster a humorous, rigorous, and humanizing dialogue, with the April hope of lowering student resistance and teacher burnout, and the August desire of reknowing ourselves and history, within that vast arena of culture war called education.

References

Academy for Educational Development. (1985). *Teacher development in schools: A report to the Ford Foundation.* New York: Author.

Adams, F., & Horton, M. (1975). *Unearthing seeds of fire: The idea of highlander.* Winston-Salem, NC: Blair.

Adler, M. (1982). *The paideia proposal: An educational manifesto.* New York: Macmillan.

Adler, M. (1983). *Paideia problems and possibilities.* New York: Macmillan.

Apple, M. (1982). *Cultural and economic reproduction in education.* London: Routledge & Kegan Paul.

Association of American Colleges. (1985). *Integrity in the college curriculum.* Washington, DC: Author.

Bastian, A., Fruchter, N., Gittell, M., Greer, C., & Haskins, K. (1985). *Choosing equality: The case for democratic schooling.* New York: New World Foundation.

Bennett, W. (1984). *To reclaim a legacy: A report on the humanities in higher education.* Washington, DC: U.S. Government Printing Office.

Berg, I. (1970). *Education and jobs: The great training robbery.* New York: Praeger.

Bisseret, N. (1957). *Education, class language, and ideology.* London: Routledge & Kegan Paul.

The bold quest for quality. (1983, October 10). *Time,* pp. 58–66.

Bowles, S., & Gintis, H. (1976). *Schooling in capitalist America: Educational reform and the contradictions of economic life.* New York: Basic Books.

Bowles, S., & Gintis, H. (1982). The crisis of liberal democratic capitalism in the case of the United States. *Politics and Society, 2*(2), 51–93.

Bowles, S., Gordon, D., & Weiskopf, T. (1983). *Beyond the wasteland: A democratic alternative to economic decline.* New York: Anchor.

Boyer, E. L. (1983). *High school: A report on secondary education in America.* New York: Harper & Row.

Boyer, E. L. (1984). Reflections on the great debate of '83. *Phi Delta Kappan, 65*, 525–530.

Braverman, H. (1974). *Labor and monopoly capital.* New York: Monthly Review.

California Commission on the Teaching Profession. (1985). *Who will teach our children? A strategy for improving California's schools.* Sacramento: Author.

Can the Schools be Saved? (1983, May 9). *Newsweek* [Shaping Up], pp. 50–58.

Carnoy, M., & Levin, H. (1985). *Schooling and work in the democratic state.* Stanford: Stanford University Press.

The College Entrance Examination Board. (1983). *Academic preparation for college: What students need to know and be able to do.* New York: Author.

Commission for Excellence in Teacher Education. (1985). *A call for change in teacher education.* Washington, DC: Author.

Cremin, L. (1964). *The transformation of the school.* New York: Vintage. (Original work published in 1961)

Cross, K. P. (1984). The rising tide of school reform reports. *Phi Delta Kappan, 66*, 167–172.

Cuban, L. (1984). School reform by remote control: SB 813 in California. *Phi Delta Kappan, 66*, 213–215.

Darling-Hammond, L. (1984a). *Beyond the commission reports: The coming crisis in teaching.* Santa Monica: Rand Corporation.

Darling-Hammond, L. (1984b). *Equality and excellence: The educational status of black Americans.* New York: College Entrance Examination Board.

Darling-Hammond, L. (1984c, January 8). Mad-Hatter tests of good teaching. *New York Times,* II-2.

Dewey, J. (1956). *The school and society.* Chicago: University of Chicago Press. (Original work published in 1900)

Dewey, J. (1956). *The child and the curriculum.* Chicago: University of Chicago Press. (Original work published in 1902)

Dewey, J. (1956). *Experience and education.* New York: Collier. (Original work published in 1938)

Donald, J. (1983). How illiteracy became a problem (and literacy stopped being one). *Journal of Education, 165*, 33–52.

Education Commission of the States. (1983a, November). *A summary of major reports on education.* Denver: Author.

Education Commission of the States, Task Force on Education for Economic Growth. (1983b). *Action for excellence: A comprehensive plan to improve our nation's schools.* Denver: Author.

Feistritzer, C. E. (1984). *The making of a teacher: A report on teacher education and certification.* Washington, DC: National Center for Education Information.

Finlay, L. S., & Faith, V. (1979). Illiteracy and alienation in American colleges: Is Paulo Freire's pedagogy relevant? *Radical Teacher, 16*, 28–40.

Finn, C. E., Jr. (1981). Why public and private schools matter. *Harvard Educational Review, 52*, 510–514.

Finn, C. E., Jr. (1983, April). The drive for educational excellence: Moving toward a public consensus. *Change, 15*, pp. 15–22.

Finn, C. E., Jr. (1986). *What works: Research about teaching and learning.* Washington, DC: U.S. Department of Education.

Finn, C. E., Jr., & Ravitch, D. (1984). Conclusions and recommendations: High expectations and disciplined effort. In Finn, C. E., Jr., Ravitch, D., & Fancher, R. T. (Eds.).

Against mediocrity: The humanities in America's high schools. (pp. 237-262). New York: Holmes & Meier.

Fiore, K., & Elsasser, N. (1982). Strangers no more: A liberatory literacy curriculum. *College English, 44*(2), 115-128.

Fiske, E. B. (1981, October 27). Court invalidates school financing in New York State. *New York Times,* p. II-3.

The Ford Foundation. (1985). *Teacher development in schools.* New York: Author.

Frankenstein, M. (1983). Critical mathematics education: An application of Paulo Freire's epistemology. *Journal of Education, 165,* 315-339.

Freeman, R. (1976). *The overeducated American.* New York: Academic Press.

Freire, P. (1970). *Pedagogy of the oppressed.* New York: Seabury.

Freire, P. (1973). *Education for critical consciousness.* New York: Seabury.

Galambos, Eva C. (1985). *Teacher preparation: The anatomy of a college degree.* Atlanta: Southern Regional Education Board.

Gibboney, R. A. (1983). Learning: A process approach from Francis Parker. *Phi Delta Kappan, 65,* 55-56.

Giroux, H. A. (1983). *Theory and resistance in education.* South Hadley, MA: Bergin & Garvey.

Glaser, B. G., & Strauss, A. L. (1967). *The discovery of grounded theory: Strategies for qualitative research.* Chicago: Aldine.

Goodlad, J. I. (1983). *A place called school: Prospects for the future.* New York: McGraw-Hill.

Gross, R. & Gross, B. (1985). *The great school debate: Which way for American education?* New York: Simon and Schuster.

Grubb, W. N., & Lazerson, M. (1975). Rally round the workplace: Continuities and fallacies in career education. *Harvard Educational Review, 45,* 451-474.

Hacker, A. (1984, April 12). The schools flunk out. *New York Review of Books,* pp. 35-40.

Harris, I. M. (1982). An undergraduate community education curriculum for community development. *Journal of the Community Development Society, 13,* 69-82.

Harris, L., & Associates. (1984). *The 1984 Metropolitan Life survey of the American teacher.* New York: Author.

Heath, S. B. (1983). *Ways with words.* New York: McGraw-Hill.

Hirsch, E. D. (1985). Cultural literacy and the schools. *American Educator, 9,* pp. 8-15.

Hoggart, R. (1957). *The uses of literacy.* London: Chatto & Windus.

The Holmes Group. (1986). *Tomorrow's teacher: A report of The Holmes Group.* East Lansing, MI: Author.

Howe, H. (1985a). Let's have another SAT score decline. *Phi Delta Kappan, 66,* 599-602.

Howe, H. (1985b). Education moves to center stage: An overview of recent studies. *Phi Delta Kappan, 67,* 167-172.

The Institute for Responsive Education. (1984). *Action for educational equity: A guide for parents and members of community groups* (Order No. 16C). Boston: Author.

Jencks, C., Smith, M., Acland, H., Bane, M. J., Cohen, D., Gintis, H., Heyns, B., & Michelson, S. (1972). *Inequality: A reassessment of the effect of family and schooling in America.* New York: Basic Books.

Jennings, W., & Nathan, J. (1977). Startling/disturbing research on school program effectiveness. *Phi Delta Kappa, 41,* 568-572.

Judy, S. (1980). *The ABCs of literacy.* New York: Oxford.

Karabel, J. (1972). Community colleges and social stratification. *Harvard Educational Review, 42,* 521-562.

Karp, W. (1985, June). Why Johnny can't think: The politics of bad schooling. *Harper's,* pp. 69-73.

Kohl, H. (1982). *Basic skills.* New York: Bantam Books.

The Labor Institute (1982). *What's wrong with the U.S. economy? A popular guide for the rest of us.* Boston: Southend.

Leonard, G. (1984, April). The great school reform hoax. *Esquire,* pp. 47-56.

Levin, H. (1981). Back-to-basics and the economy. *Radical Teacher, 20,* 8–10.

Levin, H. (1985). Solving the shortage of mathematics and science teachers. *Education evaluation and policy analysis, 7,* 371–382.

Levin, H., & Rumberger, R. (1974). *The educational implications of high technology.* Institute for Research on Education Finance and Governance: Stanford University.

Maeroff, G. (1982). *Don't blame the kids: The trouble with America's schools.* New York: McGraw-Hill.

Minkler, M., & Cox, K. (1980). Creating critical consciousness in health. *International Journal of Health Services, 10,* 311–322.

Nathan, J. (1983). *Free to teach: Equity and excellence in schools.* New York: Pilgrim.

National Academy Press. (1984). *High schools and the changing workplace: The employers' view.* Washington, DC: Author.

National Coalition of Advocates for Children. (1985). *Barriers to excellence: Our children at risk.* Boston: Author.

The National Commission for Excellence in Teacher Education. (1985). *A call for change in teacher education.* Washington, DC: Author.

The National Commission on Excellence in Education. (1983). A *Nation at Risk: The Imperative for Educational Reform.* Washington, DC: U.S. Department of Education.

National Institute of Education. [Chaired by J. O'Toole]. (1983). *Work in America.* Washington, DC: Department of Health, Education and Welfare.

National Institute of Education. (1984a). *The condition of education.* Washington, DC: Author.

National Institute of Education. (1984b). *Involvement in learning.* Washington, DC: U.S. Department of Education.

The National Science Board Commission on Preschool Education in Mathematics, Science, and Technology. (1983). *Educating Americans for the 21st Century.* 2 vols. Washington, DC: National Science Foundation.

New York State Education Department. (1985). *Strengthening teaching in New York State.* Albany: Author.

Ohmann, R. (1985). Literacy, technology, and monopoly capital. *College English, 47,* 675–684.

Oregon State System of Higher Education. (1984). *Quality assurance: Teacher education in the Oregon State System of Higher Education.* Eugene: Author.

Panel on Secondary School Education for the Changing Workplace. *High school and the changing workplace: The employers' view.* (1984). Washington, DC: National Academy Press.

Passow, A. H. (1984). Tackling the reform reports of the 1980s. *Phi Delta Kappan, 65,* 674–683.

Pattison, R. (1982). *On literacy: The politics of the word from Homer to the age of rock.* New York: Oxford.

Peterson, P. E. (1983). (Background paper attached to *Making the grade.*) New York: Twentieth Century Fund.

Pincus, F. (1980). The false promise of community colleges: Class conflict and vocational education. *Harvard Educational Review, 50,* 332–361.

Piven, F., & Cloward, R. (1982). *The new class war: Reagan's attack on the welfare state.* New York: Pantheon.

Richardson, R. C., Fisk, E. C., & Okun, M. K. (1983). *Literacy in the open-access college.* San Francisco: Jossey Bass.

Serrano v. Priest. (1971). 5 Cal. 3d 584, 487 P. 2d 1241, 96 Cal. RPTR 601.

Shanker, A. (1985). *The making of a profession.* Washington, DC: American Federation of Teachers.

Shor, I. (1986). *Culture wars: School and society in the conservative restoration, 1969–1984.* New York: Routledge & Kegan Paul.

Shor, I. (1987). *Critical teaching and everyday life* (3rd ed.). Chicago: University of Chicago Press.

Shor, I., & Freire, P. (1986). *A pedagogy for liberation*. South Hadley, MA: Bergin & Garvey.

Silberman, C. (1971). *Crisis in the classroom*. New York: Vintage.

Sizer, T. R. (1984). *Horace's compromise: The dilemma of the American high school*. Boston: Houghton Mifflin.

Southern Regional Education Board. (1985). *Improving teacher education*. Atlanta: Author.

Spring, J. (1984, April). From study hall to hiring hall. *The Progressive, 46*, 30–31.

Task Force of the Business-Higher Education Forum. (1983). *America's competitive challenge*. Washington, DC: Author.

The Twentieth Century Fund Task Force on Federal Elementary and Secondary Education Policy. (1983). *Making the grade*. New York: Twentieth Century Fund.

Toch, T. (1984). The dark side of the excellence movement. *Phi Delta Kappan, 65*, 173–176.

Wallerstein, N. (1983). *Language and culture in conflict: Problem-posing in the ESL classroom*. NJ: Addison-Wesley.

What makes great schools great. (1984, August 27). *U.S. News and World Report*, pp. 46–51.

Why teachers fail: How to make them better. (1984, September 24). *Newsweek*, pp. 64–70.

Willis, P. (1981). *Learning to labor: How working class kids get working class jobs*. New York: Columbia University Press.

A Discourse Not Intended for Her: Learning and Teaching Within Patriarchy

MAGDA LEWIS
ROGER I. SIMON

The overwhelming experience of women in a society dominated by men is that of being silenced. Feminist writers have shown that women are often silenced everywhere they turn, including in the classroom. Magda Lewis and Roger I. Simon, one as female student and the other as male teacher, describe and analyze the process of silencing as it occurred in their graduate seminar designed to explore the relationship between language and power.

> Listen to the voices of the women and the voices of the men; observe the space men allow themselves, physically and verbally, the male assumption that people will listen, even when the majority of the group is female. Look at the faces of the silent, and of those who speak. Listen to a woman groping for language in which to express what is on her mind, sensing that the terms of academic discourse are not her language, trying to cut down her thought to the dimension of a discourse not intended for her. (Rich, 1979, pp. 243-244)

In the spring of 1985 the two of us participated in a graduate seminar, one as faculty/teacher, the other as a student; one of us is a man, the other a woman. Our common interest in this seminar was in exploring questions concerning the relation between text and discourse seen in light of a consideration of the relation between language and power.[1] Although our interests were common, our experience of the class was very different. This paper tells of this difference as it emerged and as it continues to be understood by us. We struggled over finding a common voice in this shared — yet different — experience. But the results of our search for a single voice were never satisfactory, as one or the other of us was unintentionally but inevitably silenced. As our dialogue continued, it became clear to us that the difficulty we were having in our attempt to speak with a single voice had not so much

---

[1] "Discourse" refers to particular ways of organizing meaning-making practices. Discourse as a mode of governance delimits the range of possible practices under its authority and organizes the articulation of these practices within time and space although differently and often unequally for different people. Such governance delimits fields of relevance and definitions of legitimate perspectives and fixes norms for concept elaboration and the expression of experience. "Text" refers to a particular concrete manifestation of practices organized within a particular discourse. In everyday life, meaning-

Harvard Educational Review   Vol. 56   No. 4   November 1986, 457-472

to do with us as individuals but rather more powerfully with our different relations to those social, political, and economic practices that make possible the privilege of men over women: patriarchy.

In her now classic article, Hartmann (1984) defines patriarchy as a social system characterized by "the systematic dominance of men over women" (p. 194). It emerges as a "set of social relations between men, which have a material base, and which, though hierarchical, establish or create interdependence and solidarity among men that enable them to dominate women. Though patriarchy is hierarchical, and men of different classes, races, or ethnic groups have different places in the patriarchy, they also are united in their shared relationship of dominance over their women: they are dependent on each other to maintain that domination" (p. 197). Hartmann goes on to say that *"patriarchy is not simply hierarchical organization* but hierarchy in which *particular* people fill particular places. It is in studying patriarchy that we learn why it is women who are dominated and how" (p. 199).

Patriarchy so defined has the potential to obliterate the will, desire, and capacity of particular individuals, be they women or men, to form personal and collective relationships that are not based on an acceptance of male prerogative. We do not minimize the importance of such struggles. Nonetheless, what we sometimes think of as our private lives are not separable from the social forms within which they are constituted. Patriarchy is a social form that continues to play on and through our subjectivities, affecting conceptually organized knowledge as well as elements that move us, without being consciously expressed. It continues to provide us with different vantage points, and positions us differently within relations of power. For this reason we have decided to keep our voices separate, not in order to provide a dialogue but to juxtapose our differences as the ground on which we could formulate a reconstructed practice that would counter patriarchy.

We realize that women constitute only one of many disadvantaged social groups that include people of color, people of racial and ethnic minorities, people in countries dominated politically and economically by imperialist powers, and people who must work in exploitative relations of wage labor or commodity exchange, all of whom suffer disempowerment and silencing. Within this paper we do not discuss race and class dynamics, not because we think such concerns less important than gender or that gender relations can be understood outside the context of other social relations, but because the specific events we speak about in this essay occurred among a homogeneous group of people with respect to race and class. Our discussion of patriarchy, however, is clearly linked to other forms of domination and we would argue that counter-patriarchic practices have a strong relevance to other struggles against unjust social relations.

Magda Lewis

The overwhelming experience of women in a society dominated by men is that of being silenced.[2] This has not only been shown over and over again by a growing

---

making does not exist in isolation, but forms complexes that are organized contingently through time and space. Examples of text include written passages, oral communication, nonverbal communication accomplished through body movement and expression, and visual forms of representation such as paintings, photographs, and sculpture. For further elaboration of these concepts, see Terdiman (1985).

[2] For discussions of various forms of such silencing, see Rich (1979), Smith (1978), and Spender (1980, 1981).

number of feminist writers but can be graphically documented in the daily lives of all women. The search for examples does not have to be long or intensive. A woman I sat next to on a recent train trip summed it up exquisitely. After the conductor, the steward, and the railroad's public relations representative overlooked her in their various dealings with the passengers, she turned to me and said, "Sometimes I think I must be invisible. People don't see me. They don't hear me. Sometimes I wonder if I am really here." This was a woman, a grandmother, a secretary, who had never read Spender's (1982) *Invisible Women*. I passed on that reference along with a couple of others and she promised to read at least one of them. But she admitted feeling reluctant to buy books with titles like *Sex, Gender and Society* (Oakley, 1972), or *Women's Oppression Today* (Barrett, 1980). *Invisible Women*, she thought, sounded sufficiently like the title of a science fiction novel that she could smuggle it into the house without arousing her husband's suspicion. She implied that if her husband were aware of its subject, the book would surely be banned from the house and her reading even more closely monitored.

Is this an extreme example? I don't think so. It is simply a particular manifestation of a general social condition that is played out among men and women on a daily basis in a variety of forms and places.[3] The example is instructive, however, in that it uncovers the power relations within which men's lives and interests circumscribe those of women. I equivocate deliberately on the word "interest" for I do indeed intend both meanings of the word—what interests men as well as what is in their interest.

As we parted company, my seatmate said, "You younger women have it made. You know what you want and you are so outspoken, people listen to you. Women my age never had a chance." Had there been time I could have explained; I could have told her what I am about to say here, that she and I inhabit the same world, that we are both engaged in the collective struggle to claim our voice, to be heard, to become visible.

Roger Simon

The department we are in consists largely of male faculty members. While this department is not the most extreme example of the male character of academic institutions, it is important to make this point simply to highlight the fact that women graduate students are familiar with the negotiations and accommodations that are required of them in order to survive in the world of male academia.[4] Shaped by the political/theoretical discourse of socialist feminism and critical pedagogy, my daily experiences in this context have fed my interest in the project of feminist pedagogy.[5] What has made me most uneasy is the growing realization of my complicity in the practice of gender domination, which is constructed on the one hand through the relationship between language use and nonverbal practices, and on the other, through the moral regulation of people that results from the limi-

---

[3] Radway (1984) documents the extent to which men are not tolerant of women's reading, particularly if it can be construed as a challenge to the balance of power in a marriage.

[4] For a detailed first-person analysis of such negotiations, see Finn (1982).

[5] No single perspective defines the notion of feminist pedagogy. For a variety of discussions see, for example, Bunch and Pollock (1983), McVicker, Belenky, Goldberger, and Tarule (1985), and Thompson (1983).

tation of what are considered appropriate forms of thought, expression, and behavior.

In the spring of 1985 I developed and taught a new graduate course entitled "Discourse, Text, and Subjectivity." This course was designed to explore questions concerning the relation between language and power. I intended that the participating students would develop with me a way of framing questions that explore the relation between language and the enhancement of human possibility; for example, how language enters into such questions as who we are and what we are able to be and do. It is an issue that begins to crystallize when we ask how language can be not only a vehicle for learning but, in Foucault's terms, a form of "government" as well.[6] Foucault allows this word the broad meaning it had in the sixteenth century. "Government" referred then not only to political structures or to the management of states, but, in addition, to the way in which the conduct of individuals or groups might be directed: the government of children, of souls, of communities, of families, of the sick. To govern, in this sense, is to structure the possible field of human action. To think in these terms is to ask how language is linked to the freedom of women and men, a question which points to a concern with discourse as the concrete process of morally regulated expression and the central component of the production of subjectivity.

Magda Lewis

While all of us — students and teacher, women and men — came to this new course for a variety of personal and professional reasons, we also came with an intact social repertoire. We came carrying the baggage of our governed selves. For the women this meant that we already knew that what we said and how we said it was not quite as important to our male colleagues as the fact that we spoke at all. In a set of social relations where women's ideal discursive state within patriarchy has been defined as silence, a woman speaking is itself a political act (Spender, 1980). Under these conditions the very act or intention of speaking becomes an intrusion and a potential basis for a violent reaction on the part of those who have decreed our silence. Ultimately for individuals who transgress the limits of patriarchy, the forces of regulation are without a doubt swift, sure, and relentless.

As we began to take up the first of the assigned readings, the interesting and significant work by Dorfman, *The Empire's Old Clothes* (1983), the social dynamics in the class were aggravating but not unusual: the men monopolized not only the speaking time but the theoretical and social agenda as well. They sparred, dueled, and charged at each other like gladiators in a Roman arena. Yet their camaraderie intensified with each encounter. Throughout this exchange, the women were relegated to the position of spectators. When a woman speaks, it means that a man cannot speak, and when a man cannot speak it means that the social relations among the men are disrupted. Women, therefore, have no place on this playing field. Independently, we felt our exclusion more and more intensely the more we struggled to find room for our voices and to locate ourselves in the discourse.

---

[6] Corrigan (1984) points out that the English translation of the concept to which Foucault (1982) refers is better expressed as *governance* not government. For explicit discussion of how governance works within patriarchic social forms, see Fox-Genovese (1982).

Roger Simon

For several weeks I held discussions after class with a few students on how to break the discursive monopoly. I felt I had to do something to alter the situation, and so I became more and more of a "gatekeeper," trying to make room in the discussion for people who were not speaking. At one point we thought that introducing literature on men's dominance of conversation in mixed gender groups might help, but I resisted this as I thought it too much of a "diversion" from my planned agenda. I held to the steady but not very successful path of "space-making": asking for comments from those women who had not yet spoken, repositioning myself at the table so that I could see most of the women and perhaps through eye contact and body language encourage their entry into the conversation, noticing when a woman did try to speak, and cutting off those men who had been speaking most often.

Of course, these tactics did nothing to alter the deeply sedimented forms of inequality at work in the class. These tactics simply shifted the focus from a masculine discursive monopoly to women's silence. What I missed here was the fact that the women knew (despite my efforts) that it was not a safe place to speak. Women know that being allowed to speak can be a form of tyranny.[7] I was and still am unsure of why I backed away from confronting this fact—and my complicity in the situation. Knowing, however, that one cannot donate freedom, I deliberately imposed one limit on myself. I knew that as a male teacher I could not, from my position of authority (a position established by my being a man and a professor), overtly name and make topical the oppressive relations in the class. Perhaps this was partly the reason for my reluctance to introduce special readings in the course as a vehicle for raising the issue of the gender relations of the class. Retrospectively, what was needed was not a pedagogy that itself structured not "women as the question" but rather a practice wherein women could "enunciate the question" (Felman, 1981).

Magda Lewis

The feeling of being in a space that is not one's own is familiar to women in a society marked fundamentally by patriarchy.[8] It is not that there were not ideological differences among the men in how they took up the agenda of the class or in how they envisioned its pedagogical implications. In many instances, there was more in common both pedagogically and ideologically between groups of men and women than between people of the same gender. But since the overriding issue in this class was not the politics of curriculum but rather the politics of gender, ideological differences among the men were obliterated by the desire to structure gender solidarity.

Because patriarchy organizes the political and economic forms within which we must survive, regardless of our gender, class, or racial and ethnic identification, all men can benefit in some way from belonging to the dominant group. At the most mundane level, this means that, for men, the boundaries of social relations are so extended that a whole range of social behaviors that is seen to be acceptable

[7] My thanks to Ann-Louise Brookes for pointing this out to me.
[8] For an excellent discussion of this issue see Imray and Middleton (1983).

for them is deemed to be inappropriate for women, irrespective of their social class or ethnic and racial origin.

In the context of our course this meant that the men were allowed to speak at length — and did. Their speaking was seldom if ever interrupted. When a woman and a man began speaking at the same time, the woman always deferred to the man. Women's speaking was often reinterpreted by the men through phrases such as "what she *really* means. . . ." More than just a few times the actual talk of women was attributed in a later discussion by a man to a man. Women's ideas — sometimes reworded, sometimes not — were appropriated by men and then passed off as their own. Whenever a woman was able to cut through the oppressive discourse, the final attempt at silencing took the form of aggressive yelling. It became clear to us that the reversal of this dynamic would have been totally unacceptable to those who held the power of legitimation.

Gender solidarity is not rooted first and foremost in some vague notions about sociality but rather in the politics and economics of patriarchy. This is not to say, however, that "homosociality" is not an important strategic position from which to maintain and reinforce male dominance, or that such homosociality does not have extremely effective and deeply felt results.[9] Rather, men's political and economic advantage continues to be confirmed, supported, and legitimized through a social discourse that arises from their particular relations to one another.

Women have found legitimation only to the extent that we have been able or willing to appropriate the male agenda, a particularly self-violating form of escape from domination which in the end turns out to be no escape at all. The price we pay for this appropriation is the disclaiming of our collective experience of oppression, an act that forfeits our voice and gives overt support to the dominant social, political, and economic forms. We, as women, have appropriated to a large extent the terms of our own subjection. This is not a case of false consciousness. Rather, we have accepted the powerlessness of these terms to define a discourse within which we can speak partly because we are powerless to do otherwise. While many feminists are clear about the need for women to legitimate each other and thereby begin to break away from the patriarchic stranglehold, it is also clear that intellectual assault is just one of many forms of violation that act in concert to disempower women. Given the complexity of the relationships between physical, emotional, psychological, and intellectual abuse, it is clearly not easy for women to subvert this assault.

Roger Simon

From the beginning I had planned to use Radway's *Reading the Romance* (1984) as a key text in the course. At the time I had no idea how pivotal a text it would be. In this book Radway examines extensively both the production and consumption of mass-marketed popular romance novels. Radway's work is unique in that she not only develops an ideological critique of the novels she examines, but she also analyzes empirically and theoretically the reading of these books as part of the discursive practices of a particular group of women. She not only identifies the way they use and read romance novels, but also gives us an understanding of how

[9] The concept of homosociality is introduced and discussed in Morgan (1981).

packaged forms of romance are integrated into daily lives that are historically and structurally constituted within patriarchic social practices of courtship, sexuality, and marriage. Radway questions how, why, by whom, and with what purposes and meanings such books are read. In examining the readings produced by the women she studies, Radway reveals contradictory constructions of resistance and regulation. Hence, she shows how we can investigate the reading of a text as a form of social practice that can be examined for the work it does in organizing subjectivity. What provoked me to rethink my pedagogy was not our examination of women reading romance but the experience of the women students' reading Radway's text under the determinant conditions of our graduate seminar.

Magda Lewis

Despite conversations and discussions that took place between small groups of women as the course proceeded, by the time we came to Radway's book the women in the class had been all but muted. Either because we had been oppressed into silence or because we had made a conscious decision to refrain from the discussion as a form of resistance to being silenced — how ironic that the result in both cases should be the same — we had become prisoners or exiles within a wall of silence. In part the reason the text of the book enraged us was the context within which we read it and our realization that what was going on with the women in Radway's study was precisely what was going on with us in the classroom. Her study demanded a response. As the male-defined resistance to the formulation of our response intensified, it became clearer to us (the women) that what we were engaged in in this class was a struggle not just for ourselves but for all women — including those women who are reading the romance.

Had we not been required to read Radway's study in this context we might never have been pushed to the outer limits of our marginality. While we could doubt ourselves, our capabilities, our understanding, and even our experiences within the context of most male-defined academic discourse, in this instance the disjunction between content and process became obvious. We knew we had not only an experiential base from which to take up Radway's agenda, but a lived theoretical framework from which to understand it as well.

Women are politically disempowered, economically disadvantaged, and socially delegitimated, not as individuals (although it is as individuals that the effects are felt most often and most brutally) but as a group. We occupy particular positions in our homes, in our employment, and in the street that lead to experiences different from those of groups who are more advantageously positioned. The material basis of women's and men's lives, therefore, plays a major role not only in how they are positioned but also in how their particular social perspective arises. What is often forgotten by both women and men but is important to remember is that this process is man-made — although not without a struggle — and therefore neither natural nor neutral.

We needed to understand that what we were experiencing was indeed a collective experience, and we needed to know what this collective experience was about. Our reading of Radway's *Reading the Romance* was the catalyst that enabled us to understand the divisive and individualizing process embedded in the taken-for-granted prerogative of male discourse.[10] As a collective we could more easily challenge the oppressive boundaries and limited interpretations imposed through such discourse.

It is important to understand that the disjunction between male and female discourse does not arise out of the distinction between objective knowledge on the one hand and subjective knowledge on the other. Rather it is reflective of the disparity in the relations of power between men and women. This implies that women's experience and discursive forms are defined by men as illegitimate *within the terms of men's experience and men's discursive forms*. The assertion that women's knowledge is based on personal experience while men's knowledge is based on objective grounds obliterates, first and foremost, the relationship between education, personal experience, and politics. The only education that can have meaning is education that is personal and therefore political. The ingenuousness of an educational process that attempts to obliterate the personal and political is profoundly silencing.

Roger Simon

With the introduction of *Reading the Romance* into the course more was at stake than just the struggle for "air-time." I did not realize at the time that Radway's book, as a text dealing with how particular women named their own experience within patriarchy, would have the capacity to crystallize a perception of past events in the class in a way that made the present visible as a "revolutionary moment" (Buck-Morss, 1981).

What was about to happen has subsequently become a significant episode in my attempt to clarify the basis of a counter-patriarchic pedagogy. Being clear about the concrete conditions that prefigure this episode seems to require an elaboration of what it means to be "muted." Being muted is not just a matter of being unable to claim a space and time within which to enter a conversation. Being muted also occurs when one cannot discover forms of speech within conversation to express meanings and to find validation from others.

As we began the discussion of *Reading the Romance*, the majority of male students in the class and I defined the issues raised within the text in an abstract and distanced language. In my authoritative position as instructor I validated and legitimated this "preferred" theoretical discourse insofar as I encouraged it and — more important — participated in it. Through this very particular and academic form of homosociality, we simultaneously excluded and silenced the women sitting among us. This is not at all to say that the women in the class were incapable of full participation in our theoretical mode of conversation. Rather it is to acknowledge that women experiencing patriarchy not only in our class but also at home, at work, and in the streets would have something different to say about Radway's text from that which is abstractly constructed by men.

---

[10] Individualizing refers to a process of constructing the "self" so that a person views herself or himself as the unique proprietor of one's thoughts, capacities, and feelings. It is a construction basic to the historically constituted political formation which has arisen in Canada and the United States since 1850. For an extensive discussion, see MacPherson (1962).

Within the frame of patriarchy, the men in the class could not speak any other way about the substance of this text. While our own lives do not preclude our considering female oppression, for us it can only be the experience and situation of an Other. We can discuss this experience and situation, we can analyze it, and it can become a provocation for our moral anger. But if we alone take up women's experience of patriarchy, it will be within a discourse that is distanced and abstract. The double problem in this case was that my own objective for the course included the development of a "theoretical fluency," which meant, in part, legitimating and *encouraging* the meaningful use of what for many of the students were new terminology and concepts. I had wanted to use *Reading the Romance* as an example of how we could understand the relation between language, power, and subjectivity. It was to this end that I was encouraging a discussion of Radway in abstract terms, appropriating her text to my agenda of introducing students to a new theoretical position. But at this moment the women did not wish to engage in these abstractions. Thus the lived relations of patriarchic power which specified who controlled how we would study mediated our "difference" into inequality. Worse, with the women silenced, we were doing what I said earlier should never be done, enunciating women's problems.

Magda Lewis

Silence can turn into rage when we realize that who "speaks" and whose authority governs that speaking cannot be disassociated from those relations of power that mark the structures within which individuals live their daily lives. How we knew that the occasion we chose to cast aside our silence was the right one demands an articulation of "soft" data about body language and a profound sensibility to nonverbal discourse that at times becomes the only means of communication between and among members of oppressed groups. As women in the class, we knew we had to confront our silencing concretely.

It is important to signal that what happened to the women in this class was not just consciousness-raising—as important as that is—but, more important, it was a moment of politicization. This always implies collective action and, to the extent that it challenges the status quo, such action is always revolutionary and difficult. Suddenly and forcefully the revolutionary moment became concrete. While we were waiting for the elevator during one of our breaks, a moment of solidarity was precipitated by what may have seemed an offhand comment made to me by one of the other women: "I can't go back into that room."

I responded with an invitation to talk. The usual practice during breaks had been for the men and women students to sit together—a time of informal discussion during which the same dominant discourse prevailed. The two of us took our coffee and tea and moved to a private space. Other women noticed and joined us. Some went to get the rest of the women until all but one of us were gathered. The possibility of this action was facilitated by the deliberate practice of the instructor to absent himself during our breaks. Our gathering was not unnoticed by the male students, whose body language and joking demands to know "what's going on" punctuated our construction as the Other. Only one of the men asked if he could join us, in a show of solidarity. While his gesture was appreciated, his presence, however unobtrusive, would have been silencing. We said no. Our meeting was seen to be and was an overtly political act. As we talked, the anger came in floods.

Without jeopardizing personal confidences, I want to relate some of the discussion that took place during our break:

> "I don't understand what they [the men] are talking about. I feel like I'm not as well educated as them. I haven't done too much reading in this area. They know so much more than I. I just feel that if I said anything they'd say, what is she doing in this class, she doesn't know anything, so I keep my mouth shut."

> "I haven't got the right language so I always feel like such a dummy. I don't really want to talk because if I do they [the men] will realize how stupid I am."

> "I feel very angry and uncomfortable in that room. They have no right to talk about us like that. I feel so embarrassed. It's like men passing around pornographic pictures. I don't think it's appropriate."

> "I've talked a few times, but nothing I say seems to make a difference. What I say never gets taken up. It's like I hadn't said anything. So I've given up. Why bother?"

> "They talk about those women [in Radway's study] as if they were me. I don't sit at home reading junk like that. I've worked all over the world and have done many interesting things. In this class it's like none of that counts. You're a woman so you must sit at home reading cheap romance novels. That life isn't my life, and I resent being compared to them. But then I get angry at myself for saying that. Why do I want to distance myself from those women? We are no different, they and I."

> "I always have the feeling you get when people are talking about you as if you don't exist but in fact you're sitting right there. It's the way people talk about children or mental incompetents."

> "You know, they are just like little boys, always demanding attention and monopolizing all the time. I just sit back and think, let them have their say. Sometimes I think it's quite funny."

It was now not as individuals but as a group that we uncovered the perspective from which the men in the class discussed Radway's work, drawing as they did on their own version of what women were supposed to be like. Thus we were able to discern the subtleties of how they twisted the analysis until the subjects of Radway's study fit the image that was required to sustain the notion of male superiority. We came to understand the oppressive relation within which women become the subjects of male discourse. It became clear that the only difference between us and the women in Radway's study was that as graduate students we lived out and contested the patriarchic social relations under different circumstances. The oppression was no less felt, and the struggle was no less difficult. We were the women in Radway's study. The women in Radway's study were us. In a moment of collective insight we understood that we are our history, and our history is laid within patriarchy. To deny that we are a collective body is to deny not only our history but the possibilities for healing and recovery. Realizing our identity with the women in Radway's study was the first step in releasing us from the bonds of patriarchy.

When we connected with, talked, and listened to each other we became a viable political force in this context. We reappropriated our voice, found support in each other, and were able (for a short time and certainly not completely) to lift the oppression. Our act of refusing silence produced a moment of speaking. After our extended break we returned to the class, each of us prepared to make a statement. What we could never have accomplished individually became possible for us as a group. We disrupted the male agenda and appropriated our space.

But this is not altogether a happy story. On the one hand it was clear that, as the term continued, a true sense of equality and understanding was achieved on occasion between some of the women and some of the men. On the other hand this was not a miraculous transformation of patriarchy. The men became conscious of their own speaking and began to monitor themselves and each other. Moreover, being "given" time and space had its own oppressive moments in that the power of control over such time and space had not changed. Nonetheless, the power dynamics were made explicit.

I suspect all women, like those of us in this class, have lived this struggle, have felt anguish in response to the strength-sapping power of the oppressor pushing us to the edge and demanding us to conform, and felt terror and rage welling up from the depths of our being when sometimes in hopelessness we think that conforming would be so much easier. Most of the time the strength is there to keep up the struggle. But when it seeps away, it is these golden touchstones, the reference points signifying a collective struggle, that enable us to say we are not alone.

Roger Simon

It is ironic to realize in retrospect that we were producing concretely a "textbook" example of how the privileged use of language can be an act of domination and an occasion for resistance, while I strove to show the class that same point through reading Radway's book. This course met for two-and-one-half hours a week for thirteen weeks. Within this constraint I had an agenda which I thought gave form and justification to naming our collective weekly meetings as a credit course in a graduate department of education. My agenda is most simply described as the systematic discussion of an assigned set of readings (supplemented by lectures and assignments) examining various aspects of the relation between language and power. I have long felt that an important purpose of graduate teaching is to empower students through the development of the practical competence that is inherent in theorizing. Theorizing has meant to me exploring ways of comprehending and thinking about situations. What I had to offer was the possibility of a discourse which might clarify and critique existing educational practices and create new possibilities.

How this agenda is to be accomplished so that it might work to empower all our students remains a central teaching problem. Barthes (1982) has emphasized that "what is oppressive in our teaching is not, finally, the knowledge or the culture it conveys, but the discursive forms through which we propose them. Since our teaching has as its object taken in the inevitability of power, *method* can really bear only on the means of loosening, baffling or, at the very least, lightening this power." Corrigan (1984) agrees with this point and emphasizes that "we face a plenitude of naming claims which erase, by mentalizing, our very bodies. Language embodies power never more strongly as where it renders bodies powerless. We have been colonized (and subsequently have become the colonizer) through the enforced modalities of a required, encouraged, rewarded discursivity" (p. 8).

We must beware of discursive forms which colonize and silence bodies—all bodies.[11] Forms of discourse that do not allow an answer to the question, "Where is *my body* in that text?" silence us.

I am trying to understand how particular discursive forms— those social, political, and economic relations extended over space and time in concrete practices— subjugate the experiences of some people. This happens when a particular text is taken to be *the* text and therefore the locus of silence and terror. Discourse becomes the assertion of certainty when it naturalizes a specific regime of truth manifested in patriarchy as the Law of the Father, God, Nature, or any other form of rule.

We must ask ourselves: Does our teaching, our use of particular sets of practices and forms of discussion, subjugate? It is clear to me that mine sometimes does. As an example, read the words of one of my doctoral students. I had suggested that she read some of Foucault's work in light of the problems she had in analyzing her thesis data. After reading the text she wrote me a short note:

> To sort out the content from how Foucault projects it is impossible for me. He is disembodied, disassociated, beyond knowledge, beyond human frailty, a single phallus waving in the breeze, frightened of the breeze and certainly wretchedly ambivalent about the need for communication imposed by writing. To read Foucault means entering that space, becoming part of it (because of the inseparability of content/context of utterance) which is very destructive for me, despite the possibilities Foucault holds out for what I am trying to study.

Now I do not read Foucault that way. I cannot dismiss the type of discourse associated with Foucault. It always seems so rich to me and teaches me so much about the very issues we have been writing about here. Within the political/ethical project out of which I teach, I identify it as a discourse that can make an important difference in how we understand our world and our lives so as to make possible practices of justice, caring, and solidarity. This is a crucial paradox for any male teacher within patriarchy. What can we offer that will not become a form of malefic generosity?

Towards Counter-Patriarchic Practice

Aided by our juxtaposed reflections, what can we say together about teaching and learning within patriarchy that encourages a collective educative practice bound by a politics of solidarity rather than opposition? We pose this question in particular reference to mixed-gender education. This is not to deny the importance of recent feminist reconsiderations of the value of all-female learning situations,[12] but rather to pose the possibility of a counter-patriarchic pedagogy in the mixed gender institutions within which we work and study.

We begin by suggesting several qualities required by a counter-patriarchic form of teaching and learning, qualities for which both students and teachers must take

---

[11] There is an extensive body of literature about the issue of language colonizing bodies in the context of discussions of racism and colonialism. See, for example, Fanon (1967).

[12] See, for example, the discussion of feminist proposals for sex-segregated schools and classes in Shaw (1980) and Howe (1984).

responsibility. The first is the embodied quality of discourse: the fact that oppression is enacted not by theoretical concepts but by real people in concrete situations. Put most simply, this means that theories don't oppress, people do. In that people are differentially placed socially, politically, and economically, there can be no text that one can claim as displaying a rational, neutral, androgynous form. To the extent that academic discourse appears objective and distanced (and is understood and privileged in this way) it becomes a vehicle for domination. It devalues alternative perspectives, understanding, and articulation of experience. It denies the lived reality of difference as the ground on which to pose questions of theory and practice. It favors one set of values over others as they are generated by the multiplicity of human experiences.

It is the experience of the reality of lived difference that critical pedagogic practice must claim as the agenda for discussion. This means that both students and teacher must find space within which the experience of their daily lives can be articulated in its multiplicity. In practice this always implies a struggle — a struggle over assigned meaning, a struggle over discourse as the expression of both form and content, a struggle over interpretation of experience, and a struggle over "self."[13] But it is this very struggle that forms the basis of a pedagogy that liberates knowledge and practice. It is a struggle that makes possible new knowledge that expands beyond individual experience and hence redefines our identities and the real possibilities we see in the daily conditions of our lives. The struggle is itself a condition basic to the realization of a process of pedagogy: it is a struggle that can never be won — or pedagogy stops. It is the struggle through which new knowledge, identities, and possibilities are introduced that may lead to the alteration simultaneously of circumstances and selves.

We emphasize that our position does not require teachers either to suppress or abandon what and how they know — essential aspects of what they bring to teaching. Indeed, the struggle over meaning-making is lessened without such resources. However, teachers and students must find forms within which a single discourse does not become the locus of certainty and certification. In particular, teachers must ask how they can help create a space for the mutual engagement of lived difference that is not framed in oppositional terms requiring the silencing of a multiplicity of voices by a single dominant discourse.

It is clear from the separate accounts of the episode we have written about that such a meeting must rest on a politics of solidarity which requires the contestation of patriarchic relations. What does this mean? If social relations are to change, it is not enough for women to be explicit about their experience of oppression. It is necessary for those men who believe that liberating politics and practices can truly humanize our world to question the privileged status of their own practices. Men have to resist using male prerogative to shape social relations and set the historical agenda. Women's struggles are not just against the silence imposed from within and without: they are also against the silence created by our failure to make explicit men's experience of the practice of domination. We need to understand the

---

[13] We take the notion of "self" to be nonunitary and multiple. A struggle over self refers to the situation where one is confronted with multiple, often contradictory, discursive possiblities for naming and claiming one's identities.

meaning of this powerful form of male silence. An emancipatory pedagogy requires that explicitness be taken up as a political position by men as well as women. This questioning of one's privileged practices is not a call for declarations of guilt but rather for the unequivocal acknowledgement that one's embodiment as "man" accrues privileges and prerogatives that are not equally available to all and which therefore must be refused. It requires that we understand that emancipation is not just freedom from power over us but also freedom from our power over others. Hence, men need to be located differently not just in relation to women but in relation to themselves.

Irigaray (1985) has suggested that "the first question to ask is . . . how can women analyze their own exploitation, inscribe their own demands, within an order prescribed by the masculine? Is a woman's politics possible within that order?" (p. 81). This is neither the first nor the only question to ask. As our colleague Ann-Louise Brookes has suggested, we must simultaneously ask the following: "In an order prescribed by the masculine, how might men analyze the methods of exploitation which they use to inscribe and make legitimate their claims about human freedom? How might men move from a voice of authority to a voice of questioning in their attempt to freely speak about exploitation?"

In the context of our seminar, what could men have done differently that would have rejected the assumption of male privilege? First of all, it would have been necessary for them not to see the women's developing political protest as individual moments of hysteria, for which the cure was the calming hand of the Father. Second, it would have been necessary for them to take equal responsibility for naming patriarchy as an immorally oppressive social form that denies freedom and human possibility. There is no easy answer to how this could have been done. If men are to participate in the emancipatory project, they can neither assume the burden of providing women's freedom and legitimacy nor enjoy the luxury of remaining silent in the face of oppression. To declare solidarity with women under either of these conditions can be rightly challenged as insincere. Learning how to listen, how to hear, how to see, and how to watch is a precondition to becoming fully aware. But this is insufficient. The men needed to risk more than a comfortable indignation that declares solidarity with women without requiring action on their conviction. Men need to embody forms that do not express and construct masculinity as defined within patriarchy. One cannot simply donate freedom from a position that does not challenge privilege. As is the case for any oppressor group, for men to ally themselves with the oppressed, they must understand the power of their privilege and the privilege of their power, and self-consciously divest themselves of both. It is important to note that emancipatory practices are only truly emancipatory when they challenge our own privilege, whether we accrue such privilege by the color of our skin, our class position, our age, or our gender.

In the context of our seminar, what was required was a position from which a man could say, "While I have had complicity with and benefit from what is happening here, it has become offensive and is no longer acceptable to me." The precondition is that men accept that no single voice can speak for our multiple experiences; that no simple understanding of how things are and how they ought to be can derive from a limited perspective; and that ultimately, in the push and pull of social and political relations, they might have to yield.

We are arguing here for a pedagogical project that allows a polyphony of voices, a form which legitimates the expression of difference differently. To struggle for a practice supportive of the equality of possibility we need to speak on our own terms, ones framed by *our desire for solidarity and freedom*. But such desire cannot be taken for granted. We must ask and ask again, who needs to listen?

References

Barrett, M. (1980). *Women's oppression today*. London: Verso Editions.

Barthes, R. (1982). Inaugural lecture, Collège de France. In S. Sontag (Ed.) *A Barthes reader* (pp. 457–478). New York: Hill & Wang.

Buck-Morss, S. (1981, July–August). Walter Benjamin — Revolutionary writer. *New Left Review, 128*, 50–75.

Bunch, C., & Pollack, S. (Eds.). (1983). *Learning our way: Essays in feminist education*. Trumansburg, NY: Crossing Press.

Corrigan, P. (1984). *The body of intellectuals/the intellectual's body*. Unpublished manuscript.

Dorfman, A. (1983). *The empire's old clothes: What the Lone Ranger, Babar, and other innocent heroes do to our minds*. New York: Pantheon Books.

Fanon, F. (1967). *Black skins, white masks*. New York: Grove Press.

Felman, S. (1981). Re-reading femininity. In *Feminist readings: French texts/American contexts* (pp. 19–44). (From *Yale French Studies, 62*).

Finn, G. (1982). On the oppression of women in philosophy, or whatever happened to objectivity? In A. Miles and G. Finn, *Feminism in Canada: From pressure to politics* (pp. 145–173). Montreal: Black Rose Books.

Foucault, M. (1982). The subject and power. *Critical Inquiry, 8*, 777–789.

Fox-Genovese, E. (1982, May–June). Placing women's history in history. *New Left Review 133*, 5–29.

Hartmann, H. (1984). The unhappy marriage of Marxism and feminism: Towards a more progressive union. In R. Dale, G. Esland, R. Ferguson, & M. McDonald (Eds.), *Education and the state: Politics, patriarchy, and practice* (Vol. 2, pp. 191–210). Sussex: Falmer Press.

Howe, F. (1984). *Myths of co-education*. Bloomington: Indiana University Press.

Imray, L., & Middleton, A. (1983). Public and private: Marking the boundaries. In E. Gamarnikow, D. Morgan, J. Purvis, & D. Taylorson (Eds.), *The public and the private* (pp. 12–27). London: Heinemann.

Irigaray, L. (1985). *This sex which is not one*. Ithaca: Cornell University Press.

MacPherson, C. B. (1962). *The political theory of possessive individualism*. Oxford: Clarendon Press.

McVicker, C., Belenky, M., Goldberger, N., & Tarule, J. (1985). Connected education for women. *Journal of Education, 167*, 28–45.

Morgan, D. (1981). Man, masculinity, and the process of sociological inquiry. In H. Roberts (Ed.), *Doing feminist research* (pp. 83–113). London: Routledge & Kegan Paul.

Oakley, A. (1972). *Sex, gender, and society*. London: Temple Smith.

Radway, J. (1984). *Reading the romance: Women, patriarchy, and popular literature*. Chapel Hill: University of North Carolina Press.

Rich, A. (1979). *On lies, secrets, and silence: Selected prose, 1966–1978*. New York: Norton.

Shaw, J. (1980). Education and the individual: Schooling for girls, or mixed schooling — A mixed blessing? In R. Deem (Ed.), *Schooling for women's work* (pp. 66–75). London: Routledge & Kegan Paul.

Smith, D. (1978). A peculiar eclipsing: Women's exclusion from man's culture. *Women's Studies International Quarterly, 1*, 281–295.

Spender, D. (1980). *Man made language*. London: Routledge & Kegan Paul.

Spender, D. (Ed.). (1981). *Men's studies modified: The impact of feminism on the academic disciplines*. Toronto: Pergamon Press.

Spender, D. (1982). *Invisible women: The schooling scandal*. London: Writers & Readers Publishers.

Terdiman, R. (1985). *Discourse/counter-discourse: The theory and practice of symbolic resistance in 19th century France*. Ithaca: Cornell University Press.

Thompson, J. (1983). *Learning liberation: Women's response to men's education*. London: Croom Helm.

We acknowledge Ann-Louise Brooks and Phillip Corrigan for their insightful comments during the completion of this article and thank them for their courageous participation in emancipatory pedagogy.

Cultural Myths in the Making of a Teacher: Biography and Social Structure in Teacher Education

DEBORAH P. BRITZMAN

Deborah Britzman believes that recent theoretical discussions of the role of education in the reproduction of the social system, while illuminative, need to be grounded in descriptions of particular aspects of the educative process. The author addresses this need by drawing on her experiences as a teacher/educator to offer an analysis of the reproductive mechanisms at work in teacher education. She describes the way in which teachers' personal histories interact with common myths of our culture to maintain current teaching practices. By becoming conscious of these mechanisms, Britzman argues, student teachers can gain a critical perspective and, hence, control of the social mechanisms which otherwise tend to control them.

Student teaching is routinely considered the ritual bridge between the student's world and the teacher's world. Fresh from university course work, the student teacher enters the classroom and attempts simultaneously to experience, incorporate, and interpret the teacher's perspective. Presumably, student teaching should be a time when the student teacher's practice begins to become informed by educational theory and where the metamorphosis from the role of student to that of teacher begins. Indeed, the dominant model of teacher education is organized on this implicit theory of immediate integration: the university provides the theories, methods, and skills; schools provide the classroom, curriculum, and students; and the student teacher provides the individual effort; all of which combine to produce the finished product of professional teacher. This training model, however, ignores the role of the social and political context of teacher education while emphasizing the individual's effort. Here, the social problem of becoming a teacher is reduced to an individual struggle. Furthermore, this problem is exacerbated by the dominant cultural view of the teacher as rugged individualist (Waller, 1961). Understanding the complex process of learning to become a teacher, however, requires a qualitatively different perspective on the context within which learning to teach occurs. Student teachers need to understand how the interaction between time, place, people, ideas, and personal growth contributes to the process of professional development. Critical consideration must be given to what happens when

Harvard Educational Review   Vol. 56   No. 4   November 1986, 442–472

the student teacher's biography, or cumulative social experience, becomes part of the implicit context of teacher education.

The sense of time and place in which teacher education is currently rooted reflects its nineteenth-century origins. Then, as now, teacher education was largely designed as vocational training, based on an apprenticeship model of education (Gordon, 1985). Inherent in this apprenticeship model is a behavioristic view of learning: learning is achieved through imitation of working teachers and repeated practice. This model, however, ignores the cultural baggage carried by new student teachers: the mass experience of compulsory education has made teaching one of the most socially familiar professions in the United States. We have all played a role opposite teachers for a large part of our lives. It is taken for granted that we all know what a teacher is and does. Prospective teachers, then, bring to their teacher education more than their desire to teach. They bring their implicit institutional biographies—the cumulative experience of school lives—which, in turn, inform their knowledge of the student's world, of school structure, and of curriculum. All this contributes to well-worn and commonsensical images of the teacher's work and serves as the frame of reference for prospective teachers' self-images. But the dominant model of teacher education as vocational training does not address the hidden significance of biography in the making of a teacher, particularly as it is lived during student teaching.

The apprenticeship of student teaching is routinely considered in contradictory terms. It is both a time of "getting one's feet wet" and a "sink-or-swim" experience. This contradiction between gradual and abrupt experience reveals the tensions of learning to teach amid the immediate demands of classroom life. But learning to teach requires more than attending to the immediate present. The hidden work of the student teacher really involves negotiating past and present demands. While the student teacher's past informs her/his present teaching, the present generates its own constraints. The student teacher must try to understand his or her own institutional biography, as it is evoked by the return to classroom life, while at the same time educating others and learning the teacher's world. Throughout student teaching, the tensions between biography, practice, and structure create a cacophony of conflicting demands. How does the student teacher make sense of them?

This article explores what prospective secondary teachers ostensibly learn about the work of teachers as they combine their own experience in compulsory education and teacher education with their student teaching practice. The words of two student teachers will be used to illustrate how they made sense of the dilemmas they confronted. I argue that the underlying values which coalesce in one's institutional biography, if unexamined, propel the cultural reproduction of authoritarian teaching practices and naturalize the contexts which generate such a cycle. My analysis rests upon the assumption that teacher education, like any education, is an ideological education. It promotes particular images of power, knowledge, and values by rewarding particular forms of individual and institutional behavior. The ways that prospective teachers understand and experience power throughout teacher education shape their acceptance or rejection of the status quo. Similarly, teacher education's conception of knowledge can promote a view of the teacher as either technician or intellectual, and the extent to which values are rendered explicit can either inhibit or encourage a more critical pedagogy. By situating the problem of becoming a teacher within a political and ideological framework, we can better understand how past teaching models are reproduced during student teaching, and the consequences of cultural reproduction in the lives of those learning to teach.

The Structure of Experience and the Experience of Structure

To understand that school provides the context within which compulsory education occurs calls for an awareness of the power of its structure. Three important facts commonly shape our views and experiences of secondary school teaching and learning. First, social control is a significant dynamic in classroom life. Second, curriculum is compartmentally organized. Finally, schools are hierarchically ordered. While these statements appear simply to characterize the organization or the structure of experience, their consequences are ultimately political in that this structure supports particular social, economic, and ideological interests of the dominant society (Apple, 1982).

Within the United States, public education is compulsory. While the desirability of compulsory education is not disputed here, the influence of the compulsory context on the ways that students are organized accounts for many antagonisms between students and teachers. Within this context, power struggles are inevitable, and teachers are required to spend an inordinate amount of time orchestrating the practice of social control. It is the teacher's work to control large groups of students in order to get through classroom routine. This part of the teacher's work is so common as to be characterized by teachers as "mob-control." Yet what dominates the perceptions of both teachers and students is the individual teacher's ability to control the class rather than the institutional mandate to control. Indeed, for students, this structural feature of the teacher's work often appears as an extension of the teacher's personality (Everhart, 1983; Payne, 1984; Waller, 1961).

The compartmentalization of curriculum defines classroom structure, our images of knowledge, and the work, status, and roles of teachers and students. Curricular organization is fragmented into instructional activities reduced to discrete blocks of time, thereby isolating subject areas and decontextualizing skills. This process of fragmentation severs knowledge from its sociopolitical context and consequences, and obscures relationships which connect the student to her/his social world. For example, in studying the United States Constitution, students may memorize its structural features without acquiring an awareness of their own civil rights. Knowledge takes on the appearance of a product, something unrelated to the learner's experience and empowerment; as Freire's (1981) work demonstrates, it is as if the teacher "banks" education into the passive vessel of the student. As a product which is socially distributed by the teacher, it is privately acquired by the student.

While the hierarchical order of school creates and sustains specific institutionalized roles of unequal power and status, in the eyes of students, the teacher's place in this hierarchy is often obscured by her/his seemingly autonomous classroom presence. Since students are segregated from the behind-the-scenes world of teachers and administrators and have no power to effect organizational change, they often reduce school hierarchy to that of classroom life. To students, school hierarchy looks more like a teacher's personal decision than a structural feature of the school (Everhart, 1983; Payne, 1984).

For students and teachers who remain in the same classroom day after day, the classroom does indeed take on the appearance of a separate and private world. Its relationship to school structure is taken for granted and thus becomes invisible, as do the underlying values of social control, hierarchical authority, and knowledge as external to the knower. Structure becomes personified by the teacher, since the teacher is the most accessible authority figure and distributor of school knowledge. The teacher's classroom appearance, however, as autonomous, charismatic and in control (Descombe, 1982), tends further to cloak school structure by glorifying individual effort. But while the classroom represents the teacher's mandated authority, it also represents the teacher's isolation. Despite the reality that teachers share collective problems, in this individual world, asking for help is viewed as a sign of weakness. Within the culture of teachers, the combination of isolation and an emphasis on the value of autonomy functions to promote an "ethos of privacy" (Descombe, 1982, p. 257). As shared concerns become individualized as private concerns, privacy becomes valued as a source of teacher autonomy.

Within this context of school structure students construct images of the teacher's world. In an ethnographic study of junior high school students, Everhart (1983) describes how students understand the work of teachers.

> From the student point of view, there was little else involved in what teachers did in the classroom other than represented in this simple 'factory model' of learning; that is, the teacher's pouring in the facts and the students pouring them back in the form of papers and tests. . . . The student picture of teachers provided little room for emotion, with the exception of that associated with student violation of school standards. The teacher's world, in the student's eyes, was straightforward and linear, hardly complex at all. (p. 74)

This simplification of the teacher's work is a direct consequence of the hierarchical context from which this work is viewed. Since students rarely have any structural mechanism for sharing decision-making power in determining school hierarchy, curriculum, or pedagogical style, they experience these factors as an accomplished fact. On the classroom level, it is a rare teacher who lends students insight into her/his own teaching struggles. Consequently, what students tend to observe is a pattern that results from the hidden influences of teacher preparation, school policy, curricular mandates, and state law. Beyond students' recognition that teachers have more police-like power in the classroom, students perceive the teacher's work as similar to their own work, and, as such, reduce it to mere classroom performance.

Years of classroom experience allow students to have very specific expectations of how teachers should act in the classroom. Students, for example, expect the teacher to maintain classroom control, enforce rules, and present the curriculum. Students expect teachers to be certain in both their behavior and in their knowledge, and students articulate these expectations if the teacher in any way deviates from this traditional image. In this sense, students do coach their teachers in ways which reinforce school structure and, as such, constitute an immediate source of teacher socialization (Britzman, 1985). So, while teachers are socializing the students, students are also socializing teachers.

Practical Experience and Remote Theory

Prospective teachers enter teacher education with practical theories about the work and stance of teachers. Grounded in their student perspectives, constructed from their prolonged experience of compulsory classroom life, their view of the teacher's work is incomplete insofar as it is simplified to mere classroom performance. Yet this partial view is a significant factor in shaping prospective teachers' desires for a practical training experience (Beyer, 1985; Buchmann & Schwille, 1983; Descombe, 1982). The problem, however, is not so much their desire for practical methods as it is their understanding, usually legitimated by vocational models of teacher education, of methods as ends rather than as means. The "methods as ends" model of teaching reduces the complexity of pedagogical activity to a technical solution (Beyer, 1985).

Emphasis on a utilitarian approach reinforces present school structure and legitimates the existing school reality as the only possible reality. Consequently, the dominant organization of teacher education which presupposes an acceptance of the way things are, tends also to reinforce the ideas and images of education that prospective teachers bring to their training. It is a cycle which powerfully affects prospective teachers' understanding of the relationship between pedagogical practice and theory. Prospective teachers, then, want and expect to receive practical things, automatic and generic methods for immediate classroom application. They bring to their teacher education a search for recipes, and, often, a dominant concern with methods of classroom discipline, because they are quite familiar with the teacher's role as social controller. Education course work which does not immediately address "know-how" or how to "make do" with the way things are, appears impractical and idealistic. Real school life, then, is taken for granted as the measure of a teacher education program, and, as such, the student teaching semester is implicitly valued as the training ground which will fill the void left by theoretical course work.

These implicit needs and expectations of prospective teachers help determine which education courses are seen to be meaningful during student teaching. Courses in pedagogical theory, child psychology, educational history, and sociology generally do not inform the student teacher's practice, particularly if these courses are organized in lecture format (Iannaccone, 1963; Maddox, 1968; Seiferth & Purcell, 1980). Maddox's findings, based on sixty-two graduate student teacher interviews, reveal, for example, that student teachers depend more on learning by intuitive trial-and-error during student teaching than on knowledge presented in teacher education.

Indeed, theory informs only a small portion of the pedagogical practice that takes place during the student teaching experience. This theoretical void is commonly explained by pointing to the nature of student teaching. Many researchers contend that student teachers are more concerned with survival than with theory (Fuller & Brown, 1975; Popkewitz, 1978). Because survival becomes a "sink-or-swim" situation, student teachers are more likely to consider what works in the classroom while ignoring the reasons for and consequences of activities which appear to work (Hooper & Johnson, 1973). What works in the classroom is usually congruent with bureaucratic expectations and norms. So when 162 student teachers in Sorenson's (1967) study were asked to list for their best friends the things one must do in order to get an "A" in student teaching, the following advice was frequently offered: do as you are told without question, be well organized, and keep your class under control. As for theory, these student teachers warned their friends not to attempt to apply it (Sorenson, 1967).

The remoteness of educational theory, however, is not limited to the condition of student teaching. Within school settings, university theory counts for little. That is, teachers are usually evaluated on their ability to orchestrate classroom control rather than to articulate pedagogical theory (Descombe, 1982). In my own study on secondary student teacher socialization all participants viewed their education courses as a waste of time (Britzman, 1985). In the words of two student teachers:

> I had instructional planning, which I despised. Instructional planning, I felt, could have merged with a methods course, or leave it to on-the-job training. . . . But I would rather just have gotten the information and go do it. Teacher training doesn't compare to actually being in school and learning. And I don't know how much help all those education classes gave me. (p. 120)

> They're all theory courses, outside of the one where you develop something. None of the courses are like, this is how you fill out a grade book, or this is how you teach. I think it's something I'm going to learn how to do myself. I don't think you learn to be a teacher by going to the university. You have to rely on your experience, develop your own style. (p. 255)

The apprenticeship model of teacher education implicitly encourages student teachers to look to on-the-job training regardless of whether or not schools are designed to facilitate teacher education. In each of the above cases, education courses were not considered as real experience. Instead, in the minds of these student teachers, their education courses failed to demonstrate the value of theory, or even to shed light on their pragmatic needs.

The learning expectations brought to teacher education by these student teachers resembled the images of learning cultivated in their compulsory school lives. There, learning took the form of a concrete product, something acquired, possessed, and immediately applied. Consequently, the university-promoted theories, often dispensed in a language separate from the student teaching reality, appeared more like speculative idealism than concrete realism. Repeatedly, student teachers do leave their university course work with a concept of theory as abstract and untenable. Moreover, the student teacher's over-reliance on and glorification of practical first-hand experience tends to devalue theory even before it is encountered. Instead, student teachers internalize the pervasive cultural belief that experience makes the teacher. So while first-hand classroom experience is a prerequisite to understanding the complex work of teachers, experience, like teaching methods, is a means for understanding rather than an end in itself. (Feiman-Nemser & Buchmann, 1985). Unless teaching experience is critically analyzed in

✳ *closing*

relation to educational theory, experience that is taken for granted tends to reinforce prospective teachers' commonsensical perspectives brought to their teacher
education.

Telling Experience and the Stuff of Myths

The student teacher enters the apprenticeship classroom armed with a lifetime of
student experience. This institutional biography tells the student teacher how to
navigate through the school structure and provides a foundation for the stock responses necessary to maintain it. Additionally, implicit in these stock responses
are particular images of the teacher, mythic images which tend to sustain and
cloak the very structure which produces them.

Early on, the student teacher learns that teaching is a lonely endeavor. The student teacher's isolation simultaneously suggests an overwhelming burden of responsibility as well as the promise of individual power. But while the structure of
the teaching experience is characterized by isolation, it is also sustained and obscured by the value placed on individual effort. As structure fades into the background of daily activity and is "forgotten," the teacher's individualized effort appears as the sole determinant of educational matters. Consequently, while the
teacher is a significant actor in the educational drama, the valorization of individual effort sustains a view of the teacher as the only actor. With this view, individual effort takes on mythic proportion.

Throughout the course of my study of secondary student teacher socialization,
student teachers and the professionals who surrounded them held shared views
about the work and power of teachers (Britzman, 1985). Evoked to somehow illustrate and explain their teaching intentions, these views, or what I have come to
call cultural myths, tended to rationalize and legitimize the existing school structure as well as to provide a semblance of order, control, and certainty in the face
of the uncertainty of the teacher's world. Given the emphasis on social control in
the school context, order and certainty are significant psychological and institutional needs. In the case of the student teacher, cultural myths contribute to the
student teacher's taken-for-granted views of power, authority, and knowledge,
while serving to mystify school structure. Cultural myths, then, provide a set of
ideal images, definitions, justifications and measures for thought and activity, and
sustain a naturalized view of the reality it seeks to encode. As Barthes (1985) observed, a myth, as a language for codifying what a culture values, serves contradictory functions: "it points out and it notifies, it makes us understand something
and it imposes it on us" (p. 117).

Three recurring cultural myths emerged throughout the course of my study: (1)
everything depends on the teacher; (2) the teacher is the expert; and (3) teachers
are self-made. While each cultural myth concerns a social aspect of the teacher's
work—control, curriculum and the presentation of self—they are all stated in
highly individualistic terms. These myths valorize the individual and make incon-
sequential the institutional constraints which frame the teacher's work. The
teacher is depicted as a self-contained world. Such myths transform the teacher's
actual isolation into a valued autonomy which, in turn, promotes the larger social
value of rugged individualism.

Everything Depends on the Teacher

Both teachers and students implicitly understand two rules governing the hidden tensions of classroom life: unless the teacher establishes control there will be no learning, and, if the teacher does not control the students, the students will control the teacher. This power struggle, predicated upon the institutional expectation that teachers individually control their classes, equates learning with control. Additionally, outside aid in controlling the class is perceived as a sign of professional incompetency (Descombe, 1982). Teachers tend to judge themselves, and others tend to judge them, on the basis of their success with this individual struggle. Everything—student learning, the presentation of curriculum, and social control—is held to be within the teacher's domain, while the teacher's isolated classroom existence is accepted as the norm.

Isolation thus creates a strong pressure to replace students' real learning with social control. This pressure is especially problematic for the student teacher, who is also engaged in his or her own process of learning. While spontaneity and the unexpected should be significant features of a student teacher's own learning experiences, the classroom requirement to present a stable appearance tends to make student teachers view the unexpected as a "bind" rather than as an opportunity for learning. The fact is, most student teachers hardly understand their own learning processes, and therefore find it difficult to understand them in others. In the words of two prospective teachers:

> Today was the day when I really didn't know what to expect. It seems as a teacher, you're going to have to react then and there. (p. 345)

> Quick thinking . . . getting myself out of the bind I'm in seems like a requirement in teaching. To be able to know, what next, what next. If something isn't working, or to make those transitions really fast to avoid unpleasant silences. (p. 207)

The student teachers who made these statements believe they must master the art of premonition and instantaneous response—both of which depend on the teacher's ability to anticipate and contain the unexpected—to insure control as a prerequisite for student learning. Yet within the push to control learning, the student teacher also devalues her/his power to explore and be open to unknown teaching territory. Consequently, in classroom situations, the student in each student teacher often becomes repressed and denied.

The pressure to control learning, however, affects more than the student teacher's immediate activity. As we saw above, it also sustains implicit views of learning and the learner. When the double pressures of isolation and institutional mandates to control force teachers to equate learning with social control, the teacher's role becomes one of merely instilling knowledge rather than engaging learners. Moreover, this pressure denies the webs of mutual dependency and the power relationships which characterize and give shape to classroom life. As such, student and teacher negotiations, an essential interaction throughout student teaching, are ignored when the student teacher feels compelled to predict, contain, and thus control student learning. A teacher-centered approach to learning is implicitly sustained since this myth assumes that students are incapable of leadership, insight, or learning without a teacher's intervention. When everything depends on the teacher, the teacher's role is confined to controlling the situation. Consequently, the cultural myth that everything depends on the teacher compels the teacher to exert institutional authority. In the case of both the teacher and the student teacher, social control is the measure of establishing competency.

The Teacher As Expert

The fear most commonly articulated by prospective teachers is that they will never know enough to teach. Behind this fear is the larger cultural expectation that teachers must be certain in their knowledge. Teachers are supposed to know the answers. The stance of the expert is particularly problematic for the student teacher simultaneously being educated as a student while educating others. In the words of two student teachers:

> The pressure is there to know, whether it's from yourself, or the students or other teachers. I mean there's a category on the teacher certification evaluation form: Is this person knowledgeable in her field? But when you're in the classroom, initially you're trying to prove yourself, and you want to know. And then someone asks a question. There is that tug. "Gee, why don't I know? I should know that." (p. 219)

> I didn't have much of a background in history and felt just a few pages ahead of the students. It was kind of strange to be put into a position where I'm supposed to know something to teach people and I don't know it myself and I have to hurry up and learn it so I could teach them. (p. 313)

While these student teachers felt the pressure to know and the corresponding guilt in not knowing, classroom performance prevented the deeper epistemological issues — about the nature of knowing and the values which knowledge promotes — from being explored. Instead, knowledge was reduced to a set of discrete and isolated units to be acquired, while not knowing — and indeed, any condition of uncertainty — became a threat to the teacher's authority.

Having been students themselves, teachers have internalized a view of knowing shaped by classroom life and governed by the compartmentalization of curriculum. The combined effects of compulsory school- and university-education have naturalized the image of the teacher as expert. Knowing answers appears to demonstrate the teacher's ability to "think on her/his feet," a seemingly significant ingredient in the making of a teacher. From the student teacher's point of view, the veteran teacher appears to know the material backward and forward. Knowledge, from this perspective, resides between the covers of textbooks and presumably becomes familiar with years of use. Many student teachers, then, tend to approach the problem of knowing, not as an intellectual challenge, but as a function of accumulating classroom experience. Acquiring classroom experience and therefore becoming an "expert" becomes the key to controlling knowledge and imposing it on students as a means for classroom control.

The view of the teacher as expert also tends to reinforce the image of teacher as autonomous individual. From this perspective, teachers seem to have learned everything, and consequently have nothing to learn; knowledge appears as finite and unchanging. As a possession, knowledge also implies territorial rights, which become naturalized by the compartmentalization of curriculum. Knowledge as private property denies the emotional and social changes which accompany the process of reflective understanding. The cultural myth of teachers as experts, then, contributes to the reification of both knowledge and the knower. In the case of the student teacher, any condition of uncertainty is viewed as a threat to becoming an expert.

Teachers Are Self-Made

The third cultural myth, that teachers are self-made, serves seemingly contradictory functions since it supports the conflicting views that teachers form themselves and are "born" into the profession. This myth provides a commonsense explanation to the problem of how teachers are made. It is a highly individualistic explanation which reinforces the image of the "natural teacher." This natural teacher somehow possesses talent, intuition, and common sense, all internal and implicit features which combine to heighten the power of the subjective self. The value placed on these internal qualities diminishes recognition of the importance of social forces and institutional contexts in the teacher's process of growth.

More than any other cultural myth, the dominant belief that teachers "make" themselves functions to devalue teacher education, educational theory, and the social process of making value systems explicit. Here, since the teacher appears as a completed product, there is no need to change or even explain one's activity. This myth structures a suspicion of theory, which takes the form of anti-intellectualism. So while this myth may be a response to teachers' real alienation from their first-hand experience with the decontextualized theory so often dispensed in teacher education programs, a larger consequence concerns the rejection of any concept of theory. Instead of critiquing, generating, or grounding theory, there is a pervasive expectation that the individual generates everything that makes a teacher. For example, one student teacher remarked: "I think teaching is something that I'm going to learn how to do myself. Nobody is going to be able to teach me. You have to rely on your own experience. I think you have to do it and develop your own style." Sentiments like this, which reflect only a part of the reality, are distorted by cultural myth to occupy the whole picture of teacher education.

In the supposedly self-made world of the teacher, pedagogy becomes a product of one's personality. As such, pedagogy is replaced by teaching style. This teaching style, viewed as an extension of one's personality, functions to distinguish one teacher from the next and is valued as an important source of establishing one's individuality and autonomy (Descombe, 1982). Indeed, many in the field of teacher education promote the view that teaching style cannot be taught, but is considered a self-constructed product, mediated only by personal choice. In the case of the student teacher learning to teach, the problem is not so much that teaching style can reflect something about the individual as it is the mystification of the process whereby teaching style develops.

The professional legitimation of teaching style over pedagogy denies both the social basis of teaching and the institutional pressure for teachers to exert social control. In reality, the activity of teaching is significantly influenced by the mutual social relationship between teachers and students. Within this compulsory relationship, both conflict and social dependency are inevitable features, creating an arena of struggle within which teaching style becomes subject to social negotiation.

Teaching style, then, turns out to be not so much an individually determined product as it is a complex movement between the teacher, the students, the curriculum, and the school culture. Thus the myth that teachers are self-made serves to cloak the social relationships and the context of school structure by exaggerating personal autonomy. Like the other myths, this one provides the final brush strokes on the portrait of the teacher as rugged individual: if one cannot make the grade, one is not meant to be a teacher.

Uncovering Biography

Mills (1959) argued that the individual has the capacity to understand critically his/her life experiences and present dilemmas by situating herself/himself within history. This connection allows the individual critical insight into both the nature of her/his relationships to individuals, institutions, cultural values, and political events, and the ways in which these social relationships contribute to the individual's identity, values, and ideological perspectives. In this way, individuals do have the capacity to participate in shaping and responding to the social forces which directly affect their lives. In the case of student teachers, uncovering biography can empower student teachers through a greater participation in their own process of becoming a teacher and move them beyond the sway of cultural authority.

Exploring the internal world of prospective teachers requires a journey into biography and an understanding of the contexts through which the future teacher progresses. One such context is the historical experience of lives lived in compulsory education, since it is there that prospective teachers first experience the classroom life to which they return as student teachers. As previously described, life in the classroom is characterized by routine as well as disruption. Student teachers expect both, and have had years of observing teachers' responses to these situations. But while the situations are familiar, experiencing these tensions from the teacher's role is not. Indeed, the emotional world of the teacher is a new encounter. This is the difficult process of making sense of, and acting within, self-doubt, uncertainty, and the unexpected, while assuming a role which requires confidence, certainty, and stability. It is a painful experience, often carried out in a state of disequilibrium.

While disequilibrium is a necessary condition for transformation, the student teacher tends to deal with disequilibrium as a threatening experience. That is, given the immediacy of classroom life, student teachers often reduce conflicts in a way which minimizes the complexity of their work. The way we interpret a situation influences our response to that situation. The cultural myths previously described should be considered as a way to come to terms with such dissonance: they are not so much mechanical recipes as they are culturally provided ways of seeing the teacher's world, and guidelines for interpreting the teacher's stance. There may not be a direct correspondence between each myth and a specific pedagogy, but the underlying values which each myth supports encourage compliance to bureaucratic expectations while obscuring the more messy process of living these expectations.

Certainly cultural myths promote a view of the teacher as rugged individual, a stance which bestows valor on the lonely process of becoming a teacher, but at the same time obscure the social forces which individualize this struggle. While individual effort is, of course, a necessary prerequisite to learning to teach, so too are social negotiation, interaction, and social dependence. However, the image of the teacher as rugged individual stigmatizes negotiation and views social dependency as a weakness while it promotes autonomy as a strength. The image of the rugged individual represents a familiar and admired legend in the dominant culture, a lesson, so to say, in the possibility of overcoming difficult circumstances through sheer ingenuity and individual effort. Usually, this lesson is used to illustrate economic success in the sense of the individual's ability to rise from "rags to riches." For the rugged individual, any context — be it history, race, class, sex, or society — is viewed as a mere handicap to be individually overcome. In this view, the rugged individual becomes competitive and possessive, uninterested in social change and obsessed with getting ahead. The ideology which supports this notion of the rugged individual is used to justify success or failure, social class, and social inequality. This brand of individualism infuses the individual with both undue power and undue culpability. Ryan (1971), in his analysis of how social problems become individualized while social context and history are trivialized, aptly termed the ideology fueling this individualistic stance as "blaming the victim." Propelled by the belief that the individual is responsible for what is in fact a product of complex social circumstances, the ideology of blaming the victim ignores the influence of social relationships and historical progression. In the case of learning to teach, the cultural myth of the self-made, isolated, expert teacher supports the ideology of blaming the victim and ultimately promotes a simplistic understanding of the operation of power in educational life.

What does it mean to individualize the process of becoming a teacher? Teaching is fundamentally a social relationship, characterized by mutual dependency, social interaction, and social engagement. Individualizing the social basis of teaching dissolves the social context, establishing instead the supposed autonomy and very real isolation of the teacher in the current school structure. Once the student teacher is severed from the social context of teaching, the tendency is to reproduce rather than to challenge her or his institutional biography. The values embedded in the institutional biography become sedimented, and serve as the foundation for the cultural myths which legitimize a hierarchical image of authority, a reified view of knowledge, and a rugged individualist stance. Each of these particular views of power helps maintain the institutional push for social control. The value of individualism, inherent in each of these myths, requires an over-reliance on the self, which actually mandates an over-dependence on one's institutional biography. Consequently, a significant social outcome of the individualization of learning to teach is the reproduction of school structure through world view and teaching style.

Furthermore, this dynamic of cultural reproduction is made insidious by its involuntary nature. Student teachers don't set out to collude with authoritarian pedagogical principles. Just the opposite: they usually begin with intentions of enhancing the human potential of their students and find this intention thwarted by the socially patterned school routines. Student teachers often describe their involuntary collusion with authoritarian pedagogy as "learning what not to do." Their intentions about teaching are contradicted by their daily teaching activity. For example, student teachers may very well intend to create a participatory classroom, but are at a real loss as to how to proceed. They possess no comparative perspective, and lack either prior experience in, or institutional support for, challenging the status quo, and understanding how institutional constraints become lived practice. Student teachers thus see no way out of the reproductive cycle. The irony of this dynamic is that cultural myths are evoked to serve not only as an "ideological escape," in that they function to preserve a facade of power in a seemingly powerless situation, but also as an "ideological trap," in that they preserve the teacher's isolation and naturalize the institutional press for social control.

In exploring the relationship between institutional biography and school structure, I have identified three hidden contradictions which operate within teacher education: (1) the presentation of teaching as an individual act when it is necessarily a social relationship; (2) the reification of knowledge, which obscures the existential, social, and political problems of knowing; and (3) the internalization of school structure in what appears to be a personally determined practice of pedagogy. Each of these problems encompasses the movement between school structure, the social self, and curriculum. Yet, while these problems are experienced as individual predicaments, they are socially generated. The presuppositions of individualism, buttressed by the tacit acceptance of social control in a compulsory setting, result in the individualization of contradictions that are collective in origin.

Throughout this article, I have argued that making critical sense of educational experience in the process of learning to teach requires more than simply the prospective teacher's return to the classroom and assumption of the teacher's role. While experience is always instructive, the issue is whether the instruction empowers human agency or replicates the status quo. Prospective teachers need to participate in developing critical ways of knowing which can interrogate school culture, the quality of students' and teachers' lives, school knowledge, and the particular role biography plays in understanding these dynamics. Without a critical perspective, the relationships between school culture and power become "housed" in prospective teachers' biographies and significantly impede their creative capacity for understanding and altering their circumstances. Moreover, without a critical understanding of how forms of knowledge, commonsensical categories, and cultural myths provide the ideological foundations for hierarchical authority and social control, prospective teachers will continue to be naively trapped in a cycle of cultural maintenance without the means to challenge such a painful circumstance.

In this vein, Aronowitz and Giroux's (1985) concept of the teacher as transformative intellectual can enable prospective teachers to reconsider the cultural images which student teachers bring to their teacher education. The teacher as transformative intellectual can provide a significant counter-framework for envisioning what is possible rather than merely accepting what is probable. Moreover, when prospective teachers become concerned with possibilities, they are able to theorize critically about how their teaching experience shapes their construction of explanations used to inform pedagogical decision making and problem posing. Understanding the work of the teacher as transformative intellectual can empower prospective teachers to "examine their own histories, those connections to the past which in part define who they are and how they mediate and function in the world" (Aronowitz and Giroux, 1985, p. 160). But for this reconception of the teacher to have any import in teacher education, we can no longer view or organize it as a technical education producing technicians (Giroux, 1985). In order for prospective teachers to experience becoming a teacher as an activity of human agency, the structure of teacher education must begin in a social environment which enables prospective teachers to engage in their professional development as students and teachers.

References

Apple, M. (1982). *Education and power*. New York: Routledge & Kegan Paul.

Aronowitz, S., & Giroux, H. A. (1985) *Education under siege: The conservative, liberal & radical debate over schooling*. South Hadley, MA: Bergin & Garvey.

Barthes, R. (1985). *Mythologies*. New York: Hill & Wang.

Beyer, L. (1985). Aesthetic experience for teacher preparation and social change. *Educational Theory, 35*, 385–397.

Britzman, D. (1985). *Reality and ritual: An ethnographic study of student teachers*. Doctoral Dissertation, University of Massachusetts, Amherst.

Buchmann, M., & Schwille, J. (1983). Education: The overcoming of experience. *American Journal of Education, 92*, 30–51.

Descombe, M. (1982). The hidden pedagogy and its implications for teacher training. *British Journal of Sociology of Education, 3*, 249–265.

Everhart, R. (1983). *Reading, writing and resistance*. New York: Routledge & Kegan Paul.

Feinman-Nemser, S., & Buchmann, M. (1985). Pitfalls of experience in teacher preparation. *Teachers College Record, 57*, 53–66.

Freire, P. (1981). *Pedagogy of the oppressed*. New York: Continuum.

Fuller, F., & Brown, O. (1975). Becoming a teacher. In K. Ryan (Ed.), *Teacher Education: The Seventy-fourth Yearbook for the Study of Education: Part 2* (pp. 25–52). Chicago: University of Chicago Press.

Giroux, H. A. (1985). Critical pedagogy and the resisting intellectual, Part 2. *Phenomenology & Pedagogy, 3*(2), 84–97.

Gordon, B. (1985). Teaching teachers: "Nation at risk" and the issue of knowledge in teacher education. *Urban Review, 17*, 33–46.

Hopper, D., & Johnson, T. (1973). Teaching practice: Training or social control? *Education for Teaching, 92*, 25–30.

Iannaccone, L. (1963). Student teaching: Transitional stage in the making of a teacher. *Theory into Practice, 2*, 73–80.

Maddox, H. (1968). A descriptive study of teaching practice. *Educational Review, 20*, 177–190.

Mills, C. W. (1981). *The sociological imagination*. New York: Oxford University Press.

Payne, C. (1984). *Getting what we ask for*. Westport, CT: Greenwood Press.

Popkewitz, T. (1978). Educational reform and the problem of institutional life. *Educational Researcher, 8*, 3–8.

Ryan, W. (1971). *Blaming the victim*. New York: Vintage.

Seiferth, B., & Purcell, T. (1980). Student teachers' perceptions of their preparation for student teaching. *Association for the Study of Perception, 15*, 17–23.

Sorenson, G. (1967). What is learned in practice teaching. *Journal of Teacher Education, 18*, 173–178.

Waller, W. (1932). *The sociology of teaching*. New York: Wiley.

This article originated from a paper given at the First Working Conference on Critical Pedagogy in Amherst, MA, February 1986. Special thanks must go to Marilyn Stocker and Laura Lamash for their critical suggestions and encouragement.

In Search of a Critical Pedagogy

MAXINE GREENE

Maxine Greene discusses the primacy of developing a critical pedagogy appropriate for education in this country. The author asserts that because the problems of education are great and educators' notions of the possibilities for change limited by a constrained discourse, it is often difficult merely to envision more humane, more just, and more democratic alternatives. Yet, without that vision, one cannot develop a critical pedagogy. She therefore suggests ways educators can begin to reappropriate our cultural heritage in order to create conditions for a pedagogy which is meaningful to the American experience.

In what Jean Baudrillard describes as "the shadow of silent majorities"[1] in an administered and media-mystified world, we try to reconceive what a critical pedagogy relevant to this time and place ought to mean. This is a moment when great numbers of Americans find their expectations and hopes for their children being fed by talk of "educational reform." Yet the reform reports speak of those very children as "human resources" for the expansion of productivity, as means to the end of maintaining our nation's economic competitiveness and military primacy in the world. Of course we want to empower the young for meaningful work, we want to nurture the achievement of diverse literacies. But the world we inhabit is palpably deficient: there are unwarranted inequities, shattered communities, unfulfilled lives. We cannot help but hunger for traces of utopian visions, of critical or dialectical engagements with social and economic realities. And yet, when we reach out, we experience a kind of blankness. We sense people living under a weight, a nameless inertial mass. How are we to justify our concern for their awakening? Where are the sources of questioning, of restlessness? How are we to move the young to break with the given, the taken-for-granted — to move towards what might be, what is not yet?

Confronting all of this, I am moved to make some poets' voices audible at the start. Poets are exceptional, of course; they are not considered educators in the ordinary sense. But they remind us of absence, ambiguity, embodiments of existential possibility. More often than not they do so with passion; and passion has been called the power of possibility. This is because it is the source of our interests and our purposes. Passion signifies mood, emotion, desire: modes of grasping the appearances of things. It is one of the important ways of recognizing possibility, "the presence of the future as *that which is lacking* and that which, by its very ab-

---

[1] Baudrillard, *In the Shadow of Silent Majorities* (New York: Semiotexte, 1983).

Harvard Educational Review   Vol. 56   No. 4   November 1986, 427–441

sence, reveals reality."[2] Poets move us to give play to our imaginations, to enlarge the scope of lived experience and reach beyond from our own grounds. Poets do not give us answers; they do not solve the problems of critical pedagogy. They can, however, if we will them to do so, awaken us to reflectiveness, to a recovery of lost landscapes and lost spontaneities. Against such a background, educators might now and then be moved to go in search of a critical pedagogy of significance for themselves.

Let us hear Walt Whitman, for one:

> I am the poet of the Body and I am the poet of the Soul,
> The pleasures of heaven are with me and the pains of
> hell are with me.
> The first I graft and increase upon myself, the latter I
> translate into a new tongue.
>
> I am the poet of the woman the same as the man,
> And I say it is as great to be a woman as to be a man,
>
> . . . .
>
> I chant the chant of dilation or pride.
> We have had ducking and deprecating about enough,
> I show that size is only development.
>
> Have you outstript the rest? are you the President?,
> It is a trifle, they will more than arrive there every one,
> and still pass on.[3]

Whitman calls himself the poet of the "barbaric yawp"; he is also the poet of the child going forth, of the grass, of comradeship and communion and the "en masse." And of noticing, naming, caring, feeling. In a systematized, technicized moment, a moment of violations and of shrinking "minimal" selves, we ought to be able to drink from the fountain of his work.

There is Wallace Stevens, explorer of multiple perspectives and imagination, challenger of objectified, quantified realities — what he calls the "ABC of being . . . the vital, arrogant, fatal, dominant X," questioner as well of the conventional "lights and definitions" presented as "the plain sense of things." We ought to think of states of things, he says, phases of movements, polarities.

> But in the centre of our lives, this time, this day,
> It is a state, this spring among the politicians
> Playing cards. In a village of the indigenes,
> One would still have to discover. Among the dogs
> and dung,
> One would continue to contend with one's ideas.[4]

One's ideas, yes, and blue guitars as well, and — always and always — "the never-resting mind," the "flawed words and stubborn sounds."

And there is Marianne Moore, reminding us that every poem represents what Robert Frost described as "the triumph of the spirit over the materialism by which we are being smothered," enunciating four precepts:

[2] Jean-Paul Sartre, *Search for a Method* (New York: Knopf, 1968), p. 94.
[3] Whitman, *Leaves of Grass* (New York: Aventine Press, 1931), pp. 49–50.
[4] Stevens, *Collected Poems* (New York: Knopf, 1963), p. 198.

Feed imagination food that invigorates.
Whatever it is, do with all your might.
Never do to another what you would not wish done to yourself.
Say to yourself, "I will be responsible."
Put these principles to the test, and you will be inconvenienced by being over-trusted, overbefriended, overconsulted, half adopted, and have no leisure. Face that when you come to it.[5]

Another woman's voice arises: Muriel Rukeyser's, in the poem "Käthe Kollwitz."

What would happen if one woman told the truth about her life?
The world would split open[6]

The idea of an officially defined "world" splitting open when a repressed truth is revealed holds all sorts of implications for those who see reality as opaque, bland and burnished, resistant both to protest and to change.

Last, and in a different mood, let us listen to these lines by Adrienne Rich:

A clear night in which two planets
seem to clasp each other   in which the earthly grasses
shift like silk in starlight
                              If the mind were clear
and if the mind were simple   you could take this mind
this particular state   and say
This is how I would live if I could choose:
this is what is possible[7]

The poem is called "What Is Possible," but the speaker knows well that no mind can be "simple," or "abstract and pure." She realizes that the mind has "a different mission in the universe," that there are sounds and configurations still needing to be deciphered; she knows that the mind must be "wrapped in battle" in what can only be a resistant world. She voices her sense of the contrast between the mind as contemplative and the mind in a dialectical relation with what surrounds.

They create spaces, these poets, between themselves and what envelops and surrounds. Where there are spaces like that, desire arises, along with hope and expectation. We may sense that something is lacking that must be surpassed or repaired. Often, therefore, poems address our freedom; they call on us to move beyond where we are, to break with submergence, to transform. To transform what — and how? To move beyond ourselves — and where? Reading such works within the contexts of schools and education, those of us still preoccupied with human freedom and human growth may well find our questions more perplexing. We may become more passionate about the possibility of a critical pedagogy in these uncritical times. How can we (decently, morally, intelligently) address ourselves both to desire and to purpose and obligation? How can we awaken others to possibility and the need for action in the name of possibility? How can we communicate the importance of opening spaces in the imagination where persons can reach beyond where they are?

[5] Moore, *Tell Me, Tell Me* (New York: Viking Press, 1966), p. 24.
[6] Rukeyser, "Käthe Kollwitz," in *By a Woman Writt*, ed. Joan Goulianos (New York: Bobbs Merrill, 1973), p. 374.
[7] Rich, *A Wild Patience Has Taken Me This Far* (New York: Norton, 1981), p. 23.

Poets, of course, are not alone in the effort to make us see and to defamiliarize our commonsense worlds. The critical impulse is an ancient one in the Western tradition: we have only to recall the prisoners released from the cave in *The Republic*, Socrates trying to arouse the "sleeping ox" that was the Athenian public, Francis Bacon goading his readers to break with the "idols" that obscured their vision and distorted their rational capacities, David Hume calling for the exposure of the "sophistries and illusions" by which so many have habitually lived. In philosophy, in the arts, in the sciences, men and women repeatedly have come forward to urge their audiences to break with what William Blake called "mind-forg'd manacles." Not only did such manacles shackle consciousness; their effectiveness assured the continuing existence of systems of domination — monarchies, churches, land-holding arrangements, and armed forces of whatever kind.

The American tradition originated in such an insight and in the critical atmosphere specific to the European Enlightenment. It was an atmosphere created in large measure by rational, autonomous voices engaging in dialogue for the sake of bringing into being a public sphere. These were, most often, the voices of an emerging middle class concerned for their own independence from anachronistic and unjust restraints. Their "rights" were being trampled, they asserted, rights sanctioned by natural and moral laws. Among these rights were "life, liberty, and the pursuit of happiness," which (especially when joined to justice or equity) remain normative for this nation: they are goods *to be* secured. Liberty, at the time of the founding of our nation, meant liberation from interference by the state, church, or army in the lives of individuals. For some, sharing such beliefs as those articulated by the British philosopher John Stuart Mill, liberty also meant each person's right to think for himself or herself, "to follow his intellect to whatever conclusions it may lead" in an atmosphere that forbade "mental slavery."[8]

The founders were calling, through a distinctive critical challenge, for opportunities to give their energies free play. That meant the unhindered exercise of their particular talents: inventing, exploring, building, pursuing material and social success. To be able to do so, they had to secure power, which they confirmed through the establishment of a constitutional republic. For Hannah Arendt, this sort of power is kept in existence through an ongoing process of "binding and promising, combining and covenanting." As she saw it, power springs up between human beings when they act to constitute "a worldly structure to house, as it were, their combined power of action."[9] When we consider the numbers of people excluded from this process over the generations, we have to regard this view of power as normative as well. It is usual to affirm that power belongs to "the people" at large; but, knowing that this has not been the case, we are obligated to expand the "wordly structure" until it contains the "combined power" of increasing numbers of articulate persons. A critical pedagogy for Americans, it would seem, must take this into account.

For the school reformers of the early nineteenth century, the apparent mass power accompanying the expansion of manhood suffrage created a need for "self-

---

[8] Mill, "On Liberty," in *The Six Great Humanistic Essays* (New York: Washington Square Press, 1963), p. 158.
[9] Arendt, *On Revolution* (New York: Viking Press, 1963), pp. 174–175.

control" and a "voluntary compliance" with the laws of righteousness.[10] Without a common school to promote such control and compliance, the social order might be threatened. Moreover, the other obligation of the school — to prepare the young to "create wealth" — could not be adequately met. Even while recognizing the importance of providing public education for the masses of children, we have to acknowledge that great numbers of them were being socialized into factory life and wage labor in an expanding capitalist society. Like working classes everywhere, they could not but find themselves alienated from their own productive energies. The persisting dream of opportunity, however, kept most of them from confronting their literal powerlessness. The consciousness of objectively real "open" spaces (whether on the frontier, "downtown," or out at sea) prevented them from thinking seriously about changing the order of things; theoretically, there was always an alternative, a "territory ahead."[11] It followed that few were likely to conceive of themselves in a dialectical relation with what surrounded them, no matter how exploitative or cruel. As the laggard and uneven development of trade unions indicates, few were given to viewing themselves as members of a "class" with a project to pull them forward, a role to play in history.

The appearance of utopian communities and socialist societies throughout the early nineteenth century did call repeatedly into question some of the assumptions of the American ideology, especially those having to do with individualism. The founders of the experimental colonies (Robert Owen, Frances Wright, Albert Brisbane, and others) spoke of communalism, mental freedom, the integration of physical and intellectual work, and the discovery of a common good. Socialists called for a more humane and rational social arrangement and for critical insight into what Orestes Brownson described as the "crisis as to the relation of wealth and labor." He said, "It is useless to shut our eyes to the fact and, like the ostrich, fancy ourselves secure because we have so concealed our heads that we see not the danger."[12] Important as their insights were, such people were addressing themselves to educated humanitarians whose good offices might be enlisted in improving and perfecting mankind. Critical though they were of exploitation, greed, and the division of labor, they did not speak of engaging the exploited ones in their own quests for emancipation. No particular pedagogy seemed required, and none was proposed, except within the specific contexts of utopian communities. Once a decent community or society was created, it was believed, the members would be educated in accord with its ideals.

There were, it is true, efforts to invent liberating ways of teaching for children in the larger society, although most were undertaken outside the confines of the common schools. Elizabeth Peabody and Bronson Alcott, among others, through "conversations" with actual persons in classrooms, toiled to inspire self-knowledge, creativity, and communion. Like Ralph Waldo Emerson, they were all hostile to the "joint-stock company" that society seemed to have become, a company "in

[10] Horace Mann, "Ninth Annual Report," in *The Republic and the School: Horace Mann on the Education of Free Men*, ed. Lawrence A. Cremin (New York: Teachers College Press, 1957), p. 57.
[11] Mark Twain, *The Adventures of Huckleberry Finn* (New York: New American Library, 1959), p. 283.
[12] Brownson, "The Laboring Classes," in *Ideology and Power in the Age of Jackson*, ed. Edwin C. Rozwenc (Garden City, NY: Anchor Books, 1964), p. 321.

which the members agree, for the better securing of his bread to each shareholder, to surrender the liberty and culture of the eater."[13] Like Emerson as well, they were all hostile to blind conformity, to the ethos of "Trade" that created false relations among human beings, to the chilling routines of institutional life. It is the case that they were largely apolitical; but their restiveness in the face of an imperfect society led them to find various modes of defiance. Those at Brook Farm tried to find a communal way of challenging the social order: Fuller found feminism; Emerson, ways of speaking intended to rouse his listeners to create their own meanings, to think for themselves.

The most potent exemplar of all this was Henry David Thoreau, deliberately addressing readers "in the first person," provoking them to use their intellects to "burrow" through the taken-for-granted, the conventional, the genteel. He wanted them to reject their own self-exploitation, to refuse what we would now call false consciousness and artificial needs. He connected the "wide-awakeness" to actual work in the world, to projects. He knew that people needed to be released from internal and external constraints if they were to shape and make and articulate, to leave their own thumbprints on the world. He understood about economic tyranny on the railroads and in the factories, and he knew that it could make political freedom meaningless. His writing and his abolitionism constituted his protests; both *Walden* and *On Civil Disobedience* function as pedagogies in the sense that they seemed aimed at raising the consciousness of those willing to pay heed. His concern, unquestionably, was with his "private state" rather than with a public space; but he helped create the alternative tradition in the United States at a moment of expansion and materialism. And there are strands of his thinking, even today, that can be woven into a critical pedagogy. Whether building his house, hoeing his beans, hunting woodchucks, or finding patterns in the ice melting on the wall, he was intent on *naming* his lived world.

There were more overtly rebellious figures among escaped slaves, abolitionists, and campaigners for women's rights; but the language of people like Frederick Douglass, Harriet Tubman, Sarah Grimke, Susan B. Anthony, and Elizabeth Cady Stanton was very much the language of those who carried on the original demand for independence. The power they sought, however, was not the power to expand and control. For them — slaves, oppressed women, freedmen and freedwomen — the idea of freedom as endowment solved little; they had to take action to *achieve* their freedom, which they saw as the power to act and to choose. Thomas Jefferson, years before, had provided the metaphor of *polis* for Americans, signifying a space where persons could come together to bring into being the "worldly structure" spoken of above. Great romantics like Emerson and Thoreau gave voice to the passion for autonomy and authenticity. Black leaders, including Douglass, W. E. B. Du Bois, the Reverend Martin Luther King, and Malcolm X, not only engaged dialectically with the resistant environment in their pursuit of freedom; they invented languages and pedagogies to enable people to overcome internalized oppression. Struggling for their rights in widening public spheres, they struggled also against what the Reverend King called "nobodiness" as they marched and en-

---

[13] Emerson, "Self-Reliance," in *Emerson on Education*, ed. Howard Mumford Jones (New York: Teachers College Press, 1966), p. 105.

gaged in a civil disobedience grounded in experiences of the past. Du Bois was in many ways exemplary when he spoke of the "vocation" of twentieth-century youth. Attacking the industrial system "which creates poverty and the children of poverty . . . ignorance and disease and crime," he called for "young women and young men of devotion to lift again the banner of humanity and to walk toward a civilization which will be free and intelligent, which will be healthy and unafraid."[14] The words hold intimations of what Paulo Freire was to say years later when he, too, spoke of the "vocation" of oppressed people, one he identified with "humanization."[15] And the very notion of walking "toward a civilization" suggests the sense of future possibility without which a pedagogy must fail.

Public school teachers, subordinated as they were in the solidifying educational bureaucracies, seldom spoke the language of resistance or transcendence. It is well to remember, however, the courageous ones who dared to go south after the Civil War in the freedmen's schools. Not only did they suffer persecution in their efforts to invent their own "pedagogy of the oppressed" — or of the newly liberated; they often fought for their own human rights against male missionary administrators and even against the missionary concept itself.[16] It is well to remember, too, the transformation of the missionary impulse into settlement house and social work by women like Jane Addams and Lillian Wald. Committing themselves to support systems and adult education for newcomers to the country and for the neighborhood poor, they supported union organization with an explicitly political awareness of what they were about in a class-ridden society. They were able, more often than not, to avoid what Freire calls "malefic generosity" and develop the critical empathy needed for enabling the "other" to find his or her own way.

For all the preoccupations with control, for all the schooling "to order," as David Nasaw puts it,[17] there were always people hostile to regimentation and manipulation, critical of constraints of consciousness. Viewed from a contemporary perspective, for example, Colonel Francis Parker's work with teachers at the Cook County Normal School at the end of the nineteenth century placed a dramatic emphasis on freeing children from competitive environments and compulsions. He encouraged the arts and spontaneous activities; he encouraged shared work. He believed that, if democratized, the school could become "the one central means by which the great problem of human liberty is to be worked out."[18] Trying to help teachers understand the natural learning processes of the young, he was specifically concerned with resisting the corruptions and distortions of an increasingly corporate America. In the Emersonian tradition, he envisioned a sound community life emerging from the liberation and regeneration of individuals. And indeed, there were many libertarians and romantic progressives following him in the presumption that a society of truly free individuals would be a humane and sustaining one.

---

[14] Du Bois, *W. E. B. Du Bois: A Reader*, ed. Meyer Weinberg (New York: Harper Torchbooks, 1970), pp. 153–154.

[15] Freire, *Pedagogy of the Oppressed* (New York: Continuum, 1970), pp. 27 ff.

[16] Jacqueline Jones, "Women Who Were More Than Men: Sex and Status in Freedmen's Teaching," *History of Education Quarterly, 19* (1979), 47–59.

[17] Nasaw, *Schooled to Order* (New York: Oxford University Press, 1981).

[18] Parker, *Talks on Pedagogics* (New York: Harper, 1894).

This confidence may account for the contradictions in the American critical heritage, especially as it informed education within and outside the schools. Structural changes, if mentioned at all, were expected to follow the emancipation of persons (or the appropriate molding of persons); and the schools, apparently depoliticized, were relied upon to effect the required reform and bring about a better world. If individual children were properly equipped for the work they had to do, it was believed, and trained to resist the excesses of competition, there would be no necessity for political action to transform economic relations. The street children, the tenement children, those afflicted and crippled by poverty and social neglect, were often thrust into invisibility because their very existence denied that claim.

John Dewey was aware of such young people, certainly in Chicago, where he saw them against his own memories of face-to-face community life in Burlington, Vermont. Convinced of the necessity for cooperation and community support if individual powers were to be released, he tried in some sense to recreate the Burlington of his youth in the "miniature community" he hoped to see in each classroom.[19] In those classrooms as well, there would be continuing and open communication, the kind of learning that would feed into practice, and inquiries arising out of questioning in the midst of life. Critical thinking modeled on the scientific method, active and probing intelligence: these, for Dewey, were the stuff of a pedagogy that would equip the young to resist fixities and stock responses, repressive and deceiving authorities. Unlike the libertarians and romantics, he directed attention to the "social medium" in which the individual growth occurred and to the mutuality of significant concerns.

Even as we question the small-town paradigm in Dewey's treatment of community, even as we wonder about his use of the scientific model for social inquiry, we still ought to be aware of Dewey's sensitivity to what would later be called the "hegemony," or the ideological control, implicit in the dominant point of view of a given society. He understood, for instance, the "religious aureole" protecting institutions like the Supreme Court, the Constitution, and private property. He was aware that the principles and assumptions that gave rise even to public school curricula were so taken for granted that they were considered wholly natural, fundamentally unquestionable. In *The Public and Its Problems*, he called what we think of as ideological control a "social pathology," which "works powerfully against effective inquiry into social institutions and conditions." He went on, "It manifests itself in a thousand ways: in querulousness, in impotent drifting, in uneasy snatching at distractions, in idealization of the long established, in a facile optimism assumed as a cloak, in riotous glorification of things 'as they are,' in intimidation of all dissenters — ways which depress and dissipate thought all the more effectually because they operate with subtle and unconscious pervasiveness."[20] A method of social inquiry had to be developed, he said, to reduce the "pathology" that led to denial and to acquiescence in the status quo. For all his commitment to scientific method, however, he stressed the "human function" of the physical sciences and

---

[19] Dewey, "The School and Society," in *Dewey on Education*, ed. Martin Dworkin (New York: Teachers College Press, 1959), p. 41.
[20] Dewey, *The Public and Its Problems* (Athens, OH: Swallow Press, 1954).

the importance of seeing them in human terms. Inquiry, communication, "contemporary and quotidian" knowledge of consequence for shared social life: these fed into his conceptions of pedagogy.

His core concern for individual fulfillment was rooted in a recognition that fulfillment could only be attained in the midst of "associated" or intersubjective life. Troubled as we must be fifty years later by the "eclipse of the public," he saw as one of the prime pedagogical tasks the education of an "articulate public." For him, the public sphere came into being when the consequences of certain private transactions created a common interest among people, one that demanded deliberate and cooperative action. Using somewhat different language, we might say that a public emerges when people come freely together in speech and action to take *care* of something that needs caring for, to repair some evident deficiency in their common world. We might think of homelessness as a consequence of the private dealings of landlords, an arms build-up as a consequence of corporate decisions, racial exclusion as a consequence of a private property-holder's choice. And then we might think of what it would mean to educate to the end of caring for something and taking action to repair. That would be *public* education informed by a critical pedagogy; and it would weave together a number of American themes.

Certain of these themes found a new articulation in the 1930s, during the publication of *The Social Frontier* at Teachers College. An educational journal, it was addressed "to the task of considering the broad role of education in advancing the welfare and interests of the great masses of the people who do the work of society — those who labor on farms and ships and in the mines, shops, and factories of the world."[21] Dewey was among the contributors; and, although it had little impact on New Deal policy or even on specific educational practices, the magazine did open out to a future when more and more "liberals" would take a critical view of monopoly capitalism and industrial culture with all their implications for a supposedly "common" school.

In some respect, this represented a resurgence of the Enlightenment faith. Rational insight and dialogue, linked to scientific intelligence, were expected to reduce inequities and exploitation. A reconceived educational effort would advance the welfare and interests of the masses. Ironically, it was mainly in the private schools that educational progressivism had an influence. Critical discussions took place there; attention was paid to the posing of worthwhile problems arising out of the tensions and uncertainties of everyday life; social intelligence was nurtured; social commitments affirmed. In the larger domains of public education, where school people were struggling to meet the challenges of mass education, the emphasis tended to be on "life-adjustment," preparation for future life and work, and "physical, mental, and emotional health."

There is irony in the fact that the progressive social vision, with its integrating of moral with epistemic concerns, its hopes for a social order transformed by the schools, was shattered by the Second World War. The terrible revelations at Auschwitz and Hiroshima demonstrated what could happen when the old dream of knowledge as power was finally fulfilled. Science was viewed as losing its innocence in its wedding to advanced technology. Bureaucracy, with all its impersonal-

---

[21] Lawrence A. Cremin, *The Transformation of the School* (New York: Knopf, 1961), pp. 231–232.

ity and literal irresponsibility, brought with it almost unrecognizable political and social realities. It took time, as is well known, for anything resembling a progressive vision to reconstitute itself; there was almost no recognition of the role now being played by "instrumental rationality,"[22] or what it would come to signify. On the educational side, after the war, there were efforts to remake curriculum in the light of new inquiries into knowledge structures in the disciplinary fields. On the side of the general public, there were tax revolts and rejections of the critical and the controversial, even as the McCarthyite subversion was occurring in the larger world. Only a few years after the Sputnik panic, with the talent searches it occasioned, and the frantic encouragement of scientific training, the long-invisible poor of America suddenly took center stage. The Civil Rights Movement, taking form since the Supreme Court decision on integration in 1954, relit flames of critical pedagogy, as it set people marching to achieve their freedom and their human rights.

Viewed from the perspective of a critical tradition in this country, the 1960s appear to have brought all the latent tendencies to the surface. The Civil Rights Movement, alive with its particular traditions of liberation, provided the spark; the war in Vietnam gave a lurid illumination to the system's deficiencies: its incipient violence; its injustices; its racism; its indifference to public opinion and demand. The short-lived effort to reform education and provide compensation for damages done by poverty and discrimination could not halt the radical critique of America's schools. And that many-faceted critique — libertarian, Marxist, romantic, democratic — variously realized the critical potentialities of American pedagogies. Without an Emerson or a Thoreau or a Parker, there would not have been a Free School movement or a "deschooling" movement. Without a Du Bois, there would not have been liberation or storefront schools. Without a social reformist tradition, there would have been no Marxist voices asking (as, for instance, Samuel Bowles and Herbert Gintis did) for a "mass-based organization of working people powerfully articulating a clear alternative to corporate capitalism as the basis for a progressive educational system."[23] Without a Dewey, there would have been little concern for "participatory democracy," for "consensus," for the reconstitution of a public sphere.

Yes, the silence fell at the end of the following decade; privatization increased, along with consumerism and cynicism and the attrition of the public space. We became aware of living in what Europeans called an "administered society";[24] we became conscious of technicism and positivism and of the one-dimensionality Herbert Marcuse described.[25] Popular culture, most particularly as embodied in the media, was recognized (with the help of the critical theorist Theodor Adorno) as a major source of mystification.[26] The schools were recognized as agents of "cultural reproduction," oriented to a differential distribution of knowledge.[27] Numer-

---

[22] Jürgen Habermas, *Knowledge and Human Interests* (Boston: Beacon Press, 1972).

[23] Bowles and Gintis, *Schooling in Capitalist America* (New York: Basic Books, 1976), p. 266.

[24] Marcuse, "Some Social Implications of Modern Technology," in *The Essential Frankfurt School Reader*, ed. Andrew Arato and Eike Gebhardt (New York: Urizen Books, 1978), pp. 138–162.

[25] Marcuse, *One-Dimensional Man* (Boston: Beacon Press, 1966).

[26] Adorno, "Cultural Criticism and Society," in *Prisms* (London: Neville Spearman, 1961), pp. 31–32 ff.

[27] See Pierre Boudieu and Jean-Claude Passeron, *Reproduction* (Beverly Hills: Sage, 1977).

ous restive educational thinkers, seeking new modes of articulating the impacts of ideological control and manipulation, turned towards European neo-Marxist scholarship for clues to a critical pedagogy. In an American tradition, they were concerned for the individual, for the subject, which late Marxism appeared to have ignored; and the humanist dimension of Frankfurt School philosophies held an unexpected appeal. Moreover, what with its concern for critical consciousness and communicative competence, Frankfurt School thinking held echoes of the Enlightenment faith; and, in some profound way, it was recognized.

There is, of course, an important sense in which the Frankfurt School has reappropriated philosophical traditions (Kantian, Hegelian, phenomenological, psychological, psychoanalytical) which are ours as well or which, at least, have fed our intellectual past. But it also seems necessary to hold in mind the fact that European memories are not our memories. The sources of European critical theory are to be found in responses to the destruction of the Workers' Councils after the First World War, the decline of the Weimar Republic, the rise of Stalinism, the spread of fascism, the Holocaust, the corruptions of social democracy. As climactic as any contemporary insight was the realization that reason (viewed as universal in an Enlightenment sense) could be used to justify the application of technical expertise in torture and extermination. Europeans saw a connection between this and the rationalization of society by means of bureaucracy, and in the separating off of moral considerations long viewed as intrinsic to civilized life. The intimations of all this could be seen in European literature for many years: in Dostoevsky's and Kafka's renderings of human beings as insects; in Musil's anticipations of the collapse of European orders; in Camus's pestilence, in Sartre's nausea, in the Dionysian and bestial shapes haunting the structures of the arts. We have had a tragic literature, a critical literature, in the United States. We need only recall Twain, Melville, Crane, Wharton, Hemingway, Fitzgerald. But it has been a literature rendered tragic by a consciousness of a dream betrayed, of a New World corrupted by exploitation and materialism and greed. In background memory, there are images of Jeffersonian agrarianism, of public spheres, of democratic and free-swinging communities. We do not find these in European literature, *nor* in the writings of the critical theorists.

One of the few explicit attempts to articulate aspects of the Western tradition for educators has been the courageous work of Freire, who stands astride both hemispheres. He has been the pioneer of a pedagogy informed by both Marxist and existential-phenomenological thought; his conception of critical reflectiveness has reawakened the themes of a tradition dating back to Plato and forward to the theologies of liberation that have taken hold in oppressed areas of the Western world. His background awareness, however, and that of the largely Catholic peasants with whom he has worked, are not that of most North Americans. It must be granted that his own culture and education transcend his Brazilian origins and make him something of a world citizen when it comes to the life of ideas. Like his European colleagues, however, he reaches back to predecessors other than Jefferson and Emerson and Thoreau and William James and Dewey; his social vision is not that of our particular democracy. This is not intended as criticism, but as a reminder that a critical pedagogy relevant to the United States today must go beyond — calling on different memories, repossessing another history.

We live, after all, in dark times, times with little historical memory of any kind. There are vast dislocations in industrial towns, erosions of trade unions; there is little sign of class consciousness today. Our great cities are burnished on the surfaces, building high technologies, displaying astonishing consumer goods. And on the side streets, in the crevices, in the burnt-out neighborhoods, there are the rootless, the dependent, the sick, the permanently unemployed. There is little sense of agency, even among the brightly successful; there is little capacity to look at things as if they could be otherwise.

Where education is concerned, the discourse widens, and the promises multiply. The official reform reports, ranging from *A Nation at Risk* to the Carnegie Forum's *A Nation Prepared*, call for a restructuring of schools and of teacher education to the end of raising the levels of literacy in accord with the requirements of an economy based on high technology.[28] The mass of students in the schools, including the one third who will be "minorities," are to be enabled to develop "higher order skills" in preparation for "the unexpected, the nonroutine world they will face in the future."[29] The implicit promise is that, if the quality of teachers is improved (and "excellent" teachers rewarded and recognized), the majority of young people will be equipped for meaningful participation in an advanced knowledge-based economy wholly different from the mass-production economy familiar in the past.

On the other hand, there are predictions that we will never enjoy full employment in this country, that few people stand any real chance of securing meaningful work. If the military juggernaut keeps rolling on, draining funds and support from social utilities, daycare centers, arts institutions, schools and universities, we will find ourselves devoid of all those things that might make life healthier, gentler, more inviting and more challenging. At once we are reminded (although not by the authors of the educational reports) of the dread of nuclear destruction (or of Chernobyls, or of Bhopal) that lies below the surface of apparent hope for the future. This dread, whether repressed or confronted, leads numbers of people to a sense of fatalism and futility with respect to interventions in the social world. For others, it leads to a sad and often narcissistic focus on the "now." For still others, it evokes denial and accompanying extravagances: consumerism increases; a desire for heightened sensation, for vicarious violence, grows. And for many millions, it makes peculiarly appealing the talk of salvation broadcast by evangelists and television preachers; it makes seductive the promise of Armageddon.

As young people find it increasingly difficult to project a long-range future, intergenerational continuity becomes problematic. So does the confidence in education as a way of keeping the culture alive, or of initiating newcomers into learning communities, or of providing the means for pursuing a satisfying life. Uncertain whether we can share or constitute a common world, except in its most fabricated and trivialized form, we wonder what the great conversation can now include and whether it is worth keeping alive. Michael Oakeshott spoke eloquently of that con-

---

[28] The National Commission on Excellence in Education, *A Nation at Risk: The Imperative for Educational Reform* (Washington: U.S. Department of Education, 1983); and Carnegie Forum on Education and the Economy, *A Nation Prepared: Teachers for the 21st Century* (New York: Carnegie Forum, 1986).

[29] Carnegie Forum, *A Nation Prepared*, p. 25.

versation, "begun in the primeval forests and extended and made more articulate in the course of centuries." He said it involves passages of argument and inquiry, going on in public and in private, that it is an "unrehearsed intellectual adventure. . . ." Education, for him, "is an initiation into the skill and partnership of this conversation," which gives character in the end "to every human activity and utterance."[30] We know now how many thousands of voices have been excluded from that conversation over the years. We know how, with its oppositions and hierarchies, it demeaned. As we listen to the prescriptions raining down for "common learnings" (which may or may not include the traditions of people of color, feminist criticism and literature, Eastern philosophies) and "cultural literacy," we cannot but wonder how those of us in education can renew and expand the conversation, reconstitute what we can call a common world.

Yes, there are insights into humane teaching in the latest reports; but, taking the wide view, we find mystification increasing, along with the speechlessness. We have learned about the diverse ways we Americans interpret our traditions: about those who identify with the old individualism, those who yearn for old communities, those who seek new modes of justice, those who want to lose themselves in a cause.[31] We know something about the persistence of a commitment to freedom, variously defined, and to the idea of equity. At once, we are bound to confront such extremes as a moral majority usurping talk of intimacy and family values, while neoliberals seek out technocratic, depersonalized solutions to quantified problems and speak a cost-benefit language beyond the reach of those still striving for public dialogue.

People have never, despite all that, had such vast amounts of information transmitted to them — not merely about murders and accidents and scandals, but about crucial matters on which public decisions may some day have to be made: nuclear energy, space vehicles, racism, homelessness, life-support systems, chemotherapies, joblessness, terrorism, abused children, fanatics, saints. There are whole domains of information that arouse frustration or pointless outrage. All we need to do is think of the persecution of the sanctuary-movement leaders, of children living in shelters, of the *contras* in Honduras, of adolescent suicides, of overcrowded jails. At the same time, no population has ever been so deliberately entertained, amused, and soothed into avoidance, denial, and neglect. We hear the cacophonous voices of special interest groups; we hear of discrete acts of sacrifice and martyrdom; we seldom hear of intentionally organized collaborative action to repair what is felt to be missing, or known to be wrong.

Complacency and malaise; upward mobility and despair. Sometimes we detect feelings of shame and helplessness perceived as personal failure. To be dependent, to be on welfare, is to be certified as in some manner deviant or irresponsible since good Americans are expected to fend for themselves. Even as oppressed peasants internalize their oppressors' images of them as helpless creatures, so unsuccessful Americans (young or old) internalize the system's description of them as ineffectual. They are unable to live up to the culture's mandate to control their own lives

---

[30] Oakeshott, *Rationalism in Politics and Other Essays* (London: Methuen, 1962), pp. 198–199.

[31] Robert N. Bellah, Richard Madsen, William M. Sullivan, Ann Swidler, and Steve M. Tipton, *Habits of the Heart: Individualism and Commitment in American Life* (Berkeley: University of California Press, 1985).

and contribute to the productivity of the whole. Our institutional responses are ordinarily technical (and we are drawn to technical solutions out of benevolence, as well as out of helplessnesss). Yet we know that to think mainly in terms of techniques or cures or remedies is often to render others and the earth itself as objects to be acted upon, treated, controlled, or used. It is to distance what we believe has to be done (efficiently, effectively) from our own existential projects, from our own becoming among other incomplete and questing human beings. It is to repress or deny the prereflective, tacit understandings that bind us together in a culture and connect us to our history.

Having said all this, I must ask again what a critical pedagogy might mean for those of us who teach the young at this peculiar and menacing time. Perhaps we might begin by releasing our imaginations and summoning up the traditions of freedom in which most of us were reared. We might try to make audible again the recurrent calls for justice and equality. We might reactivate the resistance to materialism and conformity. We might even try to inform with meaning the desire to educate "all the children" in a legitimately "common" school. Considering the technicism and the illusions of the time, we need to recognize that what we single out as most deficient and oppressive is in part a function of perspectives created by our past. It is a past in which our subjectivities are embedded, whether we are conscious of it or not. We have reached a point when that past must be reinterpreted and reincarnated in the light of what we have learned.

We understand that a mere removal of constraints or a mere relaxation of controls will not ensure the emergence of free and creative human beings. We understand that the freedom we cherish is not an endowment, that it must be achieved through dialectical engagements with the social and economic obstacles we find standing in our way, those we have to learn to name. We understand that a plurality of American voices must be attended to, that a plurality of life-stories must be heeded if a meaningful power is to spring up through a new "binding and promising, combining and covenanting." We understand that the Enlightenment heritage must be repossessed and reinterpreted, so that we can overcome the positivism that awaits on one side, the empty universalism on the other. But we cannot and ought not escape our own history and memories, not if we are to keep alive the awarenesses that ground our identities and connect us to the persons turning for fulfillment to our schools.

We cannot negate the fact of power. But we can undertake a resistance, a reaching out towards becoming *persons* among other persons, for all the talk of human resources, for all the orienting of education to the economy. To engage with our students as persons is to affirm our own incompleteness, our consciousness of spaces still to be explored, desires still to be tapped, possibilities still to be opened and pursued. At once, it is to rediscover the value of care, to reach back to experiences of caring and being cared for (as Nel Noddings writes) as sources of an ethical ideal. It is, Noddings says, an ideal to be nurtured through "dialogue, practice, and confirmation,"[32] processes much akin to those involved in opening a public sphere. We have to find out how to open such spheres, such spaces, where a better state of things can be imagined; because it is only through the projection of a bet-

---

[32] Noddings, *Caring: A Feminine Approach to Ethics and Moral Education* (Berkeley: University of California Press, 1984).

ter social order that we can perceive the gaps in what exists and try to transform and repair. I would like to think that this can happen in classrooms, in corridors, in schoolyards, in the streets around.

I would like to think of teachers moving the young into their own interpretations of their lives and their lived worlds, opening wider and wider perspectives as they do so. I would like to see teachers ardent in their efforts to make the range of symbol systems available to the young for the ordering of experience, even as they maintain regard for their vernaculars. I would like to see teachers tapping the spectrum of intelligences, encouraging multiple readings of written texts and readings of the world.

In "the shadow of silent majorities," then, as teachers learning along with those we try to provoke to learn, we may be able to inspire hitherto unheard voices. We may be able to empower people to rediscover their own memories and articulate them in the presence of others, whose space they can share. Such a project demands the capacity to unveil and disclose. It demands the exercise of imagination, enlivened by works of art, by situations of speaking and making. Perhaps we can at last devise reflective communities in the interstices of colleges and schools. Perhaps we can invent ways of freeing people to feel and express indignation, to break through the opaqueness, to refuse the silences. We need to teach in such a way as to arouse passion now and then; we need a new camaraderie, a new en masse. These are dark and shadowed times, and we need to live them, standing before one another, open to the world.

PART 3

Teaching Teachers

Notes on the Context for Learning

KIYO MORIMOTO
with Judith Gregory and Penelope Butler

The author and his assistants examine some of the personal constraints in the teaching and learning process. Teachers need to learn the difficult skill of listening to discover students' real concerns. They must recognize that making decisions nearly always involves giving up options and therefore entails some ambivalence; and that the change learning involves is difficult and slow and must be supported even in its smallest steps. The authors suggest that teachers aware of these aspects of the learning context are more able to respond to students as human beings.

All of us who engage in the process of education—who are involved in the process of helping others to learn—do so, I feel, through various ranges and depths of intimate personal relationships. Learning emerges out of some sense of relationship or connection or engagement, whether it be with a book, a teaching machine, or a person.

What I hope to do in the following pages is to share with you some of what I have found to be involved in an individual's effort to learn. These thoughts have emerged from my experiences working with students, teachers, and administrators in school and university settings.

If we look upon teaching as essentially an interpersonal experience, then it seems that our central concern must be the development of interpersonal skills in line with an understanding of how people learn and change. Any effort to define the responsibilities and functions of a teacher inevitably spills over into a discussion of one's philosophy of teaching and of learning. The question then becomes how that philosophy is articulated in practice.

I have been concerned with helping the individual teacher achieve a fuller realization of his or her own professional and personal resources with the hope that these may become more available to students in their efforts to learn. While individual consultation is often invaluable, working with teachers in groups seems to offer special opportunities. Such a setting invites teachers to explore the various perspectives from which they view their teaching worlds. Through discussion, each teacher can compare issues of central concern to him or herself with issues of importance to his or her colleagues, and come to understand individual differences in desires, assumptions, and purposes. This can lead to the consideration of a variety of approaches or addresses to any one issue. The group leader serves as a catalyst and a resource in the learning process, rather than as a final authority or judge of what teachers "should" learn.

As soon as group members come together, what I call a *context for learning* begins to develop. Words such as "atmosphere" or "climate" mean much the same thing, but I prefer the word context. "Context" derives from a word meaning "to weave": patterns, continuities, and various threads run through a particular setting, forming a kind of fabric of interchange and exploration. These threads are in large part defined by the assumptions that the leader and the various group members bring with them — assumptions about how learning occurs and what relationship teachers and students have to this process.

In creating this context for learning, I make certain assumptions. I believe that an individual is ultimately separate and alone, that he is a meaning-making organism, and that his dignity and his urge to survive are intimately tied in with the ways in which he makes meaning out off his experiences through the use of his intellect, his feelings, and his knowledge. I am primarily interested in helping the individual teacher to discover this capacity to make meaning, and in helping him to claim fully and to expand this capacity. One aspect of the discovery is the recognition that what a teacher knows is meaningful because it is viewed from a particular perspective, and that this same data or experience looked at from a different perspective can take on an entirely different meaning, opening up alternatives and consequences that lead to new understanding. In creating such a context for learning, then, I consider it fundamental to provide opportunities for the individual to explore and come to understand and appreciate the perspectives from which he views any data that is being discussed. As one teacher put it, " 'Listening in' on other teaching experiences helped me to put my own in perspective and made me more aware of my own developing techniques, assumptions, attitudes, and expectations."

The teaching-learning process is complex and, to enhance the students' learning, calls for particular skills and understandings on the part of the teacher. Among these are the skill of listening and the understanding of the concept of ambivalence and the experience of change.

Listening

Listening is crucial in creating a context for learning. When we speak of the importance of listening to one another, we sometimes overlook the complexity and the discipline involved: listening requires more than a warm and accepting attitude. Concern and caring are indeed important parts of listening: concern for the other's integrity and dignity as an individual, caring for his unique efforts to make meaning and to communicate that meaning. Our concern and caring are affected and influenced by our individual biases and values. It is important, then, that we understand as fully as possible the nature and extent of these influences on our capacity to listen.

What does the discipline of listening involve? The levels of meaning expressed by an individual may be myriad and subtle. We cannot claim to understand or address all of them, especially in the immediate moment. So we make choices, we select, we decide to focus on particular areas or levels of meaning in our listening.

This selection process can be a powerful instrument in the hands of a group leader or a teacher, for to a great extent it shapes and determines the nature of the dialogue and the context that develop. For example, if the task of a group is to solve some particular problem, or to make specific decisions, as in committees, listening tends to be directed toward the relevance or usefulness of participants' contributions to the problem to be solved or the decision to be made.[1]

In teaching as in counseling, I find myself listening very carefully to what each individual is saying, at several levels at once. The word, the content, is one thing. Beyond the content and the sequence — that is, the kinds of words that he puts together — what I hear generates in me the effort to try to understand what assumptions he is defining or trying to communicate to me about the situation he is describing. The assumptions are perhaps an expression of very deep yearning or longing of some kind. The very fact that they are expressed indicates to me that the assumptions are there, or some kind of yearning or some kind of longing or maybe some kind of pain.

A student talking about a paper assignment said to her teacher: "Well, I started reading it and then when I had trouble is when I tried to figure out religious meanings, and I — I didn't have anything to refer to." I might respond, for example, "And that left you feeling kind of helpless." I think perhaps this recognizes several things. It recognizes and it honors the experience that she has gone through. It also recognizes her as the individual who is feeling that it was an experience of helplessness in that moment. And so there are two people, really, because the person who is telling the experience may be outside it now, and she's addressing it with compassion that comes out of a deep sense of caring for herself. I think it's that sense of caring for herself as a whole person that has to be recognized, a recognition that comes through acknowledgment by another.

Listening to the individual and communicating respect for his effort to make sense is something totally outside of our day-to-day experiences of talking to people. In many of our conversations, people tend to take positions and they retreat into giving advice: "You should do this, because —" and, they specify the consequences to justify the advice. Whoever is giving the advice is somehow sure in his own mind that it is workable, and that certain consequences follow certain actions almost automatically. Then in other kinds of dialogue, when we're talking theoretically, we may be exchanging ideas and there is opportunity for disagreement. One person may say, "Well, that isn't true. That isn't my interpretation of this thing." This can lead to discussions that dishonor consideration of the individual's struggle with his feelings.

One of the most difficult things to learn is to listen and in some way see the world as the other person sees it, not just conceptually, but also experientially and emotionally. It has always bothered me to presume that anyone can put himself in the position of the other person completely. What I try to do is listen as totally

---

[1] Leadership, tension release, maintaining harmony, maintaining and sustaining positions in the group, and the way these processes function to get the job done, often become concerns in the problem-solving group. For detailed elaboration of group process from this perspective, see Robert F. Bales, *Interaction Process Analysis* (Cambridge, Mass.: Addison-Wesley Press, 1950). For additional perspectives on listening in groups, see Irwin D. Yalom, *The Theory and Practice of Group Psychotherapy* (New York: Basic Books, 1970).

as I can to what the individual is saying and recognize each of his feelings experientially with him, without placing any priority on one or the other but knowing that every one of his feelings — no matter how contradictory or how far out of how shameful — is legitimate because he feels it. Until he has been heard in this way and knows, somehow, that he has been heard, he'll be reluctant to share openly.

I endeavor to recognize these feelings and as a part of this recognition I endeavor to recognize also the hopes that go along or the pain that accompanies these particular feelings. This involves maintaining a kind of openness within myself and trusting the other person to make meaning out of his feelings, trusting that he will discover that he has the capacity to make meaning out of them. I think what makes it possible for me to trust that he can make meaning out of them is the fact that he is experiencing them. If he cannot experience his feelings, then he cannot make meaning out of them. The capacity to make meaning is one of the things that people begin to discover when they are heard. I find, too, that my responses are always in terms of the immediate context, of where the individual is in the moment.

Ambivalence and Our Responses

When we engage in learning, we experience a variety of feelings that enhance or stand in the way of our learning. Common and troublesome, yet little understood, is the feeling of ambivalence. Learning is an emergent process involving choices which call upon the exercise of our discipline and judgment. We are exhilarated in moments when we feel wholly involved; we become integrated and confirmed in our ability to make sense. At other times choices are accompanied by feelings of ambivalence. We feel torn and split, unsure whether to believe, to trust, to be open to learning. Our sense of wholeness is lost, and we feel threatened with the loss of autonomy. Intense experiences of ambivalence are felt to confirm our weakness and immaturity, our inability to choose, to care, to make commitments and to engage in learning fully. We can be left feeling confused, doubtful of our beliefs, and also impotent. The yearning for a sense of wholeness is thwarted and we can act with only partial involvement.

There is an urge in us all of resolve ambivalence. We attempt to cope with the internal feeling of being split by abandoning one part of ourself, rendering it helpless or meaningless, or considering it unworthy. We feel that in order to act we must shut off a part of our caring.

I see ambivalence as a natural part of living, a positive, integrating experience. By denying or refusing to respect our ambivalence, we negate our caring. When we have to act, we often feel that the only alternatives are to care less deeply or to abandon one aspect of what we care about, thus abandoning a part of ourselves. Action of any kind demands the choice and honoring of priorities. The experience of simultaneous urges and yearnings results in the desire to stop time, to postpone commitment and action until we are sure. In moments of choice we inevitably close off opportunities, and experience a sense of loss. By embracing this sense of loss as a legitimate experience, we confirm our caring and honor our feelings of ambivalence. We thus remain whole and more fully present and engaged in our choice, living in time rather than through time.

Roles

One way we try to manage feelings of ambivalence is through the use of roles. By retreating into a prescribed concept of a role, we absolve ourselves of responsibility for the consequences of behavior and actions that fall outside our expectations.

I asked a biology professor how things were going in his laboratory sessions. He said, "Great! But I don't know whether I'm doing things right or not. Do you think it's all right for me to be so enthusiastic about what I'm doing? Maybe I shouldn't be." His ambivalence arose out of his concept of his role as a professional. He seemed to be saying: "Maybe by being so enthusiastic and involved in my subject, I'm being seductive, and I'm brainwashing these students. I'm not being professional." He was worried about not maintaining his proper role and his status in relation to his students.

Preoccupation with a role can interfere with sharing with the students in the process of learning. By recognizing that we teach through our person and not through our role, we assume full responsibility for our choices and their consequences. We are less prone to blame the students for their boredom in our classroom; and we understand through our senses and judgment the context we are creating that legitimizes boredom as a viable response. We can become more responsible and whole persons, whether teacher or student, by examining the assumptions that follow from thinking of ourselves in roles. Subtle and insidious processes through which we absolve ourselves of feelings of ambivalence are often revealed if we have the courage to venture into such explorations.

From the beginning of one of her classes, a math teacher noticed a student looking at the ceiling and staring out the window. When a teacher is trying to conduct a discussion with thirty students, such a response is obvious, even glaring. This teacher chose to ignore the girl, glancing obliquely at her once or twice during the class, all the while feeling uncomfortable. After the period she discussed with her colleagues how frustrated and helpless this student left her feeling. When asked what had led her to ignore the student rather than call on her, the teacher said she was sure the student would feel ashamed and become angry. Then she would have to "take the student on." The alternative was to ignore her.

In speculating about what the student's response in the class might mean, one colleague said she believed looking at the ceiling is a plea to be noticed or acknowledged in some way, because it is so obvious. If that is the plea, by ignoring the student the teacher is saying, "You don't count," or "As far as I'm concerned right now you don't exist." If one is seen as nonexistent, there is no point in assuming responsibility for one's behavior.

The student's behavior can be seen as arising from several competing emotions. She may yearn to be recognized and included and, in addition, be ambivalent about expressing this yearning. At the same time she may be seeking to avoid the shame of exposing her lack of knowledge or her inability to articulate clearly. Any direct recognition by others around her makes her feel vulnerable in a number of ways. The safest response is to avoid eye contact as a way of avoiding responsibility.

The teacher is also ambivalent. She yearns to be open, receptive, and caring, and she wants to honor the students' autonomy, choice, and initiative. She also has the responsibility of teaching her students math. She has invested much time and energy in the study of mathematics and has been hired to teach it. The expectations of her administrators — and to some extent her own expectations — are that she will cover a specific amount of material in any given day. To fall behind is failure. She feels the pressures mount to get on with "teaching."

In deciding to act, we often feel as though we must choose to honor one value and abandon the others. It feels safer to ignore the person and save everyone time and embarrassment. Teachers often fear that if disruptive behavior is recognized, the class will get out of hand. This means that the locus for maintaining decorum so that learning can occur resides only in the teacher. Such an assumption can arise out of a feeling that students are incapable of assuming responsibility. To cope with this condition, the effort of the teacher becomes directed toward working up a better and more interesting curriculum or lesson plan to get and maintain the students' attention. This can take up most of a teacher's time.

One of the reasons teachers often give for not recognizing or responding to certain behavior in the classroom is that they feel they wouldn't know how to respond — or what the consequences would be should they respond in particular ways. In other words, they have no *available* vocabulary of response to engage with the students in a dialogue that serves the students' learning — either of the subject matter or of any other kind.

A high school geometry teacher found himself feeling trapped in his class because one of the girls was endlessly raising questions. Her questions seemed always to be relevant, but in many instances he felt that she already knew the answers. The questions seemed to serve as a way for her to establish and maintain a personal relationship with him. He wanted to continue to maintain her interest in geometry and to increase all the students' learning, but he felt caught in a bind. To continue to answer her questions would result in almost exclusive attention to her (which she seemed to crave) and a neglect of other students in the class. To the girl, learning geometry was secondary or even incidental. Her desire for continual attention seemed insatiable. To ignore her might result in her feeling abandoned, ashamed, and somehow unworthy. He thought of speaking to her after class as a way of helping her realize how her personal need for attention from him interfered with his conduct of the class.

Eventually, he chose to ask other students in the class to assist him in answering each of her questions. This made it possible for him to focus on the learning of geometry by all the students, including the girl. What seemed to be disruptive, attention-getting behavior was in this instance turned into an opportunity for students to engage in helping each other and to learn through such engagement.

To ignore a student who is, for instance, gazing off into space, is in effect saying to him that he doesn't exist or doesn't count or is not as important a person as others who do pay attention. When we recognize a person as existing and present, we recognize also his capacity to assume responsibility for his behavior. To recognize is to communicate to the other person respect for him and for his actions as the expression of his dignity so that he experiences the feeling of being included and received as a person in his own right.

The Problem of Authority

Taking a position without apology is necessary to define one's responsibility as an authority. An authority creates a context for continuing dialogue by assuming personal responsibility for institutional functioning. Retreat into a position of authority as a means of asserting and justifying control and power, however, results in inaccessibility to negotiation and thwarts mutual learning.

When control and power become issues of central concern in a learning situation, the emphasis shifts from an open examination of assumptions. Argument, justification, and subterfuge become the predominant responses, because maintaining one's position becomes the concern that directs participation. Each person's integrity becomes invested in his or her position of authority. Ideas and knowledge become possessions over which one must exert control because maintaining one's status is the focus, rather than sharing one's discoveries, meanings, and speculations. The style of our address to the concerns of each individual determines the central focus in the relationship — whether it be the acquisition or maintenance of power or "authority," or the extension of understanding of the process of learning. In both instances learning will occur, but the nature of the learning in each will be different.

A teacher's doubts about and preoccupation with his or her authority can have a profound effect on the context he or she creates in a classroom. If we assume that authority means we must be able to answer any question or must have some intelligent comment to offer, our need for complete control increases. To admit that we do not know can be experienced as a loss of respect and of control. We can feel that once students discover our vulnerable areas they will no longer respect us or listen to us. To command respect, then, we exert more rigid structure and control. We heighten our sense of authority by reminding the students that the power to grade resides in our hands.

The most frequent way teachers attempt to assist students in their learning is by asking questions. Learning requires thinking on the part of the learner, and questions are designed to assist the student to clarify, to formulate, to draw on and use knowledge more effectively — to learn to use his head. Implicit in all this is the development of the student's skill in the exercise of his or her judgment. Perhaps the handiest and most overworked single word relied upon by teachers to serve these intentions and hopes is the word "why." We seem to take it for granted that it always helps to ask "why" questions. There has been little, if any, careful examination of the context created by such questions and of the way that context is related to learning and to what is learned.

In asking "why," we seek an explanation, cause, purpose, or reason. The focus is on rationality. In attempting to respond to a "why" question, students are likely to feel put on the spot. The internal experience often is that there must be a "right" answer and that one's answer will be judged against it. The immediate urge is to justify, rationalize, and defend one's answer because one's integrity is at stake, and the impulse may be to apoligize, retract, or plead ignorance in order to save oneself.

An alternative address that creates a different context is a question like: "In what sense do you mean that?" Attention is then directed toward listening to the process of thinking and feeling involved in coming to the particular answer offered by the student. That is, what is revealed is the student's answer in context, his or her meaning-making process. Some risk of failure and shame remains, yet it seems that opportunities for students to learn from each other are increased by sharing their efforts to make sense. The focus of participation is on learning as process rather than on knowing the answers.

When we feel that either we do or we should know all the answers, we become unavailable as active participants with the students in the learning process. When we retreat into omnipotence, we abandon opportunities to learn from our students as well as to provide a context for them to discover what they know. When we retreat into humility, we rob the student of opportunities to learn from us and we negate our own knowledge and expertise. Both positions can be seen as ways of managing our feelings of ambivalence about being placed in a position of authority and power.

A more viable position is one of honesty — embracing the limits of our knowledge. The recognition that our knowledge is limited and thus tentative keeps open the necessity for continued exploration and groping. Our expertise then becomes a resource for consideration in a context of trust in the emergence of mutually created learnings.

Frames of Reference

All of us draw on various forms in the effort to make sense out of subtleties and complexities. By forms I means theories, standards, or values by and through which we discover and create meaning. In the process of putting experiences into forms, we run the risk of entrenching them in categories that do not allow for other perspectives or possibilities, and that kill the real life of the process of discovery. We assume that if we can stabilize our world, then we have control over it. I think a different sense of control itself emerges through the discovery of the capacity to make meaning. The subtle changes that occur offer opportunities for innovation, creativity, and learning. This emergent process requires continual examination, redefinition, and renewal of the forms we hold. Trust in this emergent process sustains engagement in continued learning.

Some teachers see their training in terms of the assumption: "If I get enough techniques under my belt, then I'll have full control over the classroom and I can move it in the direction that I feel will be valuable for the students' learning." The imposition of such a form forces the learner to respond in terms of a formula rather than in terms of his or her person. The form in which the teacher addresses a student can restrict his or her responses. Often students respond to their sense of the restriction rather than to the expectations defined by the forms, and then behave in ways that are unexpected. When students are recognized as persons with forms of their own, and when their forms are understood in their own terms, they are more willing to participate actively in their own learning. When students respond contrary to or obliquely to the expectations, it might well be because what is felt to be sacred by the teacher is his or her form and not the student as a person.

That is, unless the student's response fits into one of the teacher's forms, the response is not considered legitimate. The effort to "psych out the teacher," to discover his or her sacred forms, becomes the focus of attention, and learning is restricted or inhibited.

The internal experience for the student can be that he or she is bad or stupid and that the teacher does not care. He may feel alienated and desperately alone and ashamed. He may then be willing to abandon his integrity and meekly adhere to the prescribed expectations so as not to feel the sense of aloneness and badness.

Forms can inhibit very highly trained intuitive and open responses. By discovering each other's ways of experiencing and making sense, we are more likely to recognize the whole person. Legitimacy is then recognized as residing in the *response* of the person and not in the form of his or her response. It then becomes possible to draw upon forms as a way of making sense out of responses. It becomes possible for the teacher and student together to consider the values — and the potential for understanding the topic under discussion — that are inherent in different forms. Thus the search and exploration become mutual. Participants become responsible for their own learning through sharing. Forms are then resources for discovering meaning from which action can emerge with integrity and trust in one's person.

In some respects the leader, like a gardener, helps to create conditions that generate growth. The plant selects what it needs for growth, but too little fertilizer causes the plant to wither from lack of nutrition, while too much fertilizer causes the plant to burn up. The delicate balance between these two extremes is what we are seeking to establish. This optimal blend is the *context for learning*.

In a way, the airing and adjusting of the various hopes and expectations of group members resemble the negotiation of a complex and flexible contract. The more adequately this contract comes to reflect the expectations of everyone, the more learning occurs.

Change

Implicit in any concept of learning is the notion of change. If we learn something, we change some part of ourselves: attitude, behavior, values, assumptions, or perhaps the amount of knowledge we have. The change may mean a rejection or an alteration of previously accepted beliefs or behavior, or it may mean an expansion or extension of them (or a combination of several of these processes). Change, or the idea of change, can be frightening — threatening to rob us of the safety and legitimacy of our own, often cherished, position, especially since maintaining this position has helped us to survive. When change is advocated or demanded by another person, we feel threatened, defensive, and perhaps rushed. We are then without the freedom and the time to understand and to affirm the new learning as something desirable, and as something of our own choosing. Pressure to change, without an opportunity for exploration and choice, seldom results in experiences of joy and excitement in learning.

The capacity to recognize when change has taken place, and to acknowledge it, involves recognition of the courage it takes to change, and an appreciation of how important and difficult it is to take even seemingly very small steps. So often we want and ask for such blatant changes because we do not recognize subtle shifts, nor do we appreciate how difficult it is to make changes, and how much courage and risk it requires on the part of the person who is endeavoring to make the change.

When talking about teaching and learning, we often speak of drawing ideas, thoughts, or answers out of students. The hope implicit in this way of speaking is to force them to learn, on the assumption that if we can only ask the "right" kinds of questions, then people will learn in the ways we think are most meaningful for their well-being. The caring and hope out of which this effort arises are not to be demeaned or denied, because the effort is honorable. There are, however, different ways in which we might assist in this process of helping another in his creativity. As a young, eager child on the farm, I had an experience that helped me to come to trust nature and its processes. We had a young heifer with calf. As she neared calving time, her udder indicated she would be a fine milk producer. We watched her carefully.

One bright morning I looked into the pasture and noticed the heifer lying on her side. I ran out to her and sure enough she was in labor. As a matter of fact, two hooves of the calf were already visible. But the young heifer seemed to be experiencing difficulty. Since it was her first calf, I assumed she needed help. I called to my younger brother to bring a rope. We tied a rope to the exposed hooves, and each time the heifer had a contraction we pulled with complete empathy and care. It took only a couple of contractions, with our help, for the calf to come scooting out, healthy and kicking. The heifer, like a good mother, struggled to her feet after a few moments and began licking the calf to cleanse it. When we inspected the heifer, we found hanging from her what we thought to be the afterbirth. We tried to remove it by tugging at it, but found it was firmly attached to the heifer. We had the good sense to call the veterinarian. He informed us that in our effort to be helpful we had inverted the heifer's uterus. He washed it carefully with disinfectant, replaced it, and trussed her up for a couple of days. She went on to have three additional calves with no difficulty — and no help from us.

As I recount this experience, it raises for me the importance of continuing to examine the ways in which I am trying to serve the learning of my students. Several times over the years I have been confronted, almost accused, by people whom I have endeavored to help. They have gained the perspective to be able to talk about their own concerns differently — which means they have expanded their capacity to perceive things from several different positions. This complicates the process of decision-making, and they become *furious* at me for robbing them in some way of the limited view of reality that has provided them with a kind of stability. I become ambivalent because I wonder if learning is worthy of that much anguish. Am I doing them a service by providing a context that has increased their pain, especially through the discovery of their own limits? Generally, I feel that at least any decision they make or any action they take will be from a basis of being better informed, and that they are in motion and engaged in learning. Ultimately the choice is theirs to make.

Teaching As Research

ELEANOR DUCKWORTH

After an extended account of two features which she considers to be the essence of teaching, Eleanor Duckworth describes how such teaching can, at the same time, be seen as a form of research. In conclusion, she proposes a vision of teachers as significant participants in theoretical and pedagogical discussions on the nature and development of human learning.

What I love to do is to teach teachers. I like to stir up their thoughts about how they learn; about how on earth anyone can help anyone else learn; and about what it means to know something. I like to help them feel that any aspect of human endeavor is accessible to them and that they can make it accessible to any person that they teach. I like to try to find ways into a subject that will catch everybody's interest; to find out what people think about things and to find ways to get them talking about what they think; to shake up things they thought they knew; to get people wrapped up in figuring something out together without needing anything from me; to help build their fascination with what everybody else thinks, and with the light that other people's thinking might shed on their own. I like to see the most productive of questions get born out of laughter, and the most frustrating of brick walls give way to an idea that has been there all along.

But there are two main reasons that I love to teach teachers in particular. One is that teachers are as interested as I am in how people learn, so the dialogue is deeply felt. The second is that I always learn from them in return, when I see the endless variations on how they use what they learn in their own teaching. This paper is about how I teach, how teachers respond to it, and what one can learn through teaching in such a way.

It was a conviction about learning that got me started teaching the way I do. As a student of Piaget, I was convinced that people must construct their own knowledge and must assimilate new experiences in ways that make sense to them. I knew that, more often than not, simply telling students what we want them to know leaves them cold.

So what is the role of teaching if knowledge must be constructed by each individual? In my view there are two aspects to teaching. The first is to put students into contact with phenomena related to the area to be studied — the real thing, not books or lectures about it — and to help them notice what is interesting; to engage them so they will continue to think and wonder about it. The second is to have the students try to explain the sense they are making, and, instead of explaining things to students, to try to understand their sense. These two aspects are, of

Harvard Educational Review   Vol. 56   No. 4   November 1986, 481–495

course, interdependent: when people are engaged in the matter, they try to explain it and in order to explain it they seek out more phenomena that will shed light on it.

Engaging with Phenomena: The First Aspect of Teaching

Since I am teaching about teaching and learning, the phenomena with which I must engage my students must entail teaching and learning.[1] Rather than reading and hearing lectures, the students must learn and teach or watch people learn and teach, and somehow I must make these experiences interesting and different enough to intrigue them and raise new questions which they had not thought of before.

There are three major kinds of teaching and learning experiences with which I try to engage the students. Within each — circles within circles — we find both of the aspects of teaching which I mentioned above; since I am here teaching about teaching, the phenomena I present are themselves composed of the two aspects.

The first kind of experience is that of demonstrations with one or two children or adolescents. I attempt to engage the children with some problem or activity (first aspect), and I attempt to understand their explanations (second aspect). I try to show that the children have reasons for thinking what they think, and that it is possible to find out what these reasons are.

The second kind of experience consists of the students' own attempts to carry out a similar inquiry with one or two people at a time, outside class. They are instructed to present some phenomenon (for example, a particular reflection in a mirror) in a manner that engages people, and to try to understand their explanations of it.

The third kind of experience for the students in this course is to learn as a group about a particular subject other than teaching and learning: for example, about pendulums, or floating and sinking, or mathematical permutations. I try to engage the students in the subject (first aspect) and encourage them to explain how they are thinking about it (second aspect). It is this third activity, learning something together as a group, that I would like to discuss at greater length in this paper.

Work with this other subject of study, which I shall call the secondary subject, proceeds on two levels. On the one hand, I am trying to help them learn about whatever this subject is that we are studying together. On the other hand, I am trying to help them learn about teaching and learning.

As far as teaching and learning are concerned, there is a great range in my classes in what people think they know. I can, however, count on the fact that they are interested in the topic. The secondary subject, on the other hand, is one which no one has chosen to study, so the challenge of finding ways to engage the student is even greater. Furthermore, most of the students know very little, while a few know, or they think that they know, a great deal. It is an awkward distribution.

---

[1] In the course referred to in this paper, I usually have about forty-five students in a class, including experienced classroom teachers, undergraduates seeking teacher certification, and professionals from other careers who have chosen to switch into teaching. Their teaching interests cover all subject matters, dramatic arts through geography, and all ages, preschool through adult. I have done similar work with groups of urban public school teachers, and with undergraduates in a teachers' college.

But my focus on what they themselves *see* and how they make sense of it goes a long way toward providing a common ground. Often those who are knowledgeable know theories and formulas, rather than the complexities of phenomena we encounter in the world. Part of what I have learned to do is to find phenomena which, familiar as they are and simple as they seem, do not lend themselves to satisfactory explanations by distant theories. My other approach for the more knowledgeable class members is to count on their interest in the teaching-and-learning part of the course, to invite them to put their efforts into trying to elicit and understand someone else's explanation. I point out that it serves nobody's purpose to declare something if you are sure of it. It does serve a purpose to propose a tentative idea — because then people can help you think it through.

Of the many different secondary subjects I have used to engage teachers, the example I will use in this paper is the study of the habits of the moon.[2] The first job is to engage the students with the subject. This is just as difficult to accomplish in the case of something they have not bargained for and do not particularly care to learn about (the moon) as it is for something they believe they know about already (teaching and learning). In both cases I go about it in approximately the same way. I look for some phenomenon to draw their attention to, counting on it to do the work of engaging them. I make sure there is always something to do or to watch and to make sense of so that everybody can have something to say, even if it is only to say what they saw.

The students keep and bring to each class a separate notebook in which they make an entry every time they see the moon — when and where they see it and what it looks like. Before we start, I usually ask them when they last saw the moon, what it looked like, when they think they'll see it next and what it will look like then. Sometimes this preliminary discussion gives rise to some conflicting ideas, so some students find themselves immediately engaged. Once, for example, one person said she saw it this way ☾ the previous night and another said she saw it this way ☽. The class was about evenly divided among those who thought they both could have seen what they said they saw, those who thought at least one person must be mistaken, and those who had no idea whether it was possible or not, so we found ourselves right away with an unanswered question.

More often, there is no discord at the start, and thus no preliminary engagement. In these cases some people accept it as a rather flaky assignment that they will do because it does not seem too complicated. Some accept it solemnly because they have been asked to do it. Some resist it as an imposition and a waste of time. Some like the idea right from the start. By the first week's reporting time, at least some people have something to say — have started to get interested, and to have questions to look for the in the following week. Little by little, the assignment gets changed from one that is flaky, arbitrary, or easy, to one that is absorbing and serious (although there always remains an air of playfulness).

The following excerpts from retrospective accounts that students wrote late in the term, exemplify this range of responses. Some of the writers include quotes from their daily moon notebooks.

---

[2] Engaging students in moon-watching as a way into astronomy is an approach I learned from Donald Ford, a fellow staff member at the Elementary Science Study, in 1965 when he was preparing a moon-watching teacher's guide (Elementary Science Study, 1968).

I guess the major question I had going into this experiment was, Is she serious? In fact the requirement almost stopped me from taking this class — I really thought it was silly. I also thought it would be a lot of tedious work. I was wrong.

I keep [my notebook] on my bedside table and every night it's there to remind me to look out the window. . . . It only takes two or three minutes to write down my observations and draw my pictures, but later, when I sit down and read several weeks' notes all together, I can spend 15–20 minutes just generating questions and checking answers. I get excited when the moon moves across the sky just the way I thought it would, and I'm so disbelieving when it does something unexpected that I check my notes again and again. . . .

My observations formed my questions, which caused the focus of my observations to change. I'm now concentrating on the path of the moon each night, not on its color or shape, although I'm still shaky enough to always note those, too. . . . Everything . . . is expanding — my questions and observations are getting broader. . . .

My biggest problem in this class [is] forgetting about being a teacher and relearning how to be a learner. This [notebook] is a big help. I can make hypotheses, and they can be *wrong* — that's OK. . . . I can share observations and theories and be proud when someone says, "Ah, that's good. Tell me how it turns out." I can move at my own pace and ask my own questions. I like it.

* * *

My knowledge of the moon has become internalized. It is not what someone is trying to "teach" me. Rather, it is an area of interest I choose to explore. . . . That change has not occurred suddenly. The following excerpts from my journal may help to illustrate that transformation:

9/25 Moonwatching is proving difficult. I am never in the same place at the same time and in any event, I can't see it from my house. Irritating.

9/29 I'm finally succeeding at my moonwatching. I was looking too early in the evening and in the wrong direction. . . . Now that I've found it, I can watch it. [Little did I realize that once found is not always found!]

10/7 Even though being able to watch the moon is the most difficult part, I know I've already learned some things. (1) It isn't always the same color. (2) It goes from ☾ to ☽. (3) It rises and sets at different times. (4) It comes up in different places.

10/8 Learning about the moon is . . . like I have a bunch of unconnected facts — a puzzle. It's fun to think about it without being punished.

10/20 I have found the moon again. Yea!! It shines mostly during the day right now. Before this, even though I saw it sometimes during the day, I really thought it only shone at night.

10/22 I thought the moon had changed tilt and now I know it does. . . .

10/26 I am having a wonderful time learning about the moon. I can't believe how much it changes in just two days. . . .

The evolution from student to learner occurred over time as a change of perspective. In September, I saw the moon and its habits as external pieces of knowledge which were somehow requirements of the course. I now see them as orienting devices, a way of looking at learning.

* * *

At the beginning I didn't want to watch the moon. I felt that being required to do so was an imposition without any sense. Why did I have to watch the moon? Why did I have to write about it? I felt that in doing so I was being conducted to a new relationship with nature, that I was being told to relate with nature in a predetermined way. . . . During the first weeks of classes, I looked at the moon without allowing myself to get too much involved. I was trying to understand the course, trying to grasp what was really happening. Little by little things were getting clarified. But there was still one piece missing: The moon . . . I was still resisting to watch it. I wanted to understand, but I couldn't. I hadn't yet realized that in order to really learn about the moon . . . I had to watch it.

I must say that during this period, I did look at the moon more frequently than before. The discussions in class, my thought about the course, and mirrors [another subject of study] led me to an increasing curiosity: "There must be something in this moon-watching." And then I began to catch myself looking at it, thinking about it. . . .

Then, questions began to arise from this "casual watching". . . . The questions led to new questions, to new curiosities and, also, to new surprises. I'm still a beginner as a moon-watcher and I have thousands of questions: How do changes in shape occur? Why do I see it sometimes "here" and sometimes "there"? Does it move always at the same pace? Where does it go when I don't see it?

* * *

During my first observations of the moon was when I realized that my understanding of the moon had nothing to do with the theory, and that in fact I am very ignorant about the movement of it. I thought that the moon was sufficiently high and for that reason you could see it from every angle. I also thought that the moon was at the same place every night. This was my first discovery (to understand that my understanding of the moon was wrong).

* * *

October 10: *The Morning Moon*
"6:00 A.M. What! The moon is where it was at 7:30 P.M. last time I saw it. It's early morning. What time did it rise? Why? Is there a connection between its waning and its rising time?"

October 11–16: *The Moon Turns Around (or seems to)*
During this five-day period, I am intent upon systematically measuring the angle of the moon in the sky. I am also checking whether or not I can see it well into the morning. I record the moon on the 11th as shaped like this:

7:00 A.M. ☾

Then, between the 13th and 15th I lose it, don't see it at all.

One evening coming out of Longfellow Hall, 6:15 P.M., I see it right up Appian Way towards the Charles. As if that's not astonishing enough, I notice and record (thank goodness) that the *direction of the horns has changed*. I commented on it in my diary, but had thought little more of it until right now.

6:15 P.M. ☽

* * *

I like a lot of things about the moon watching. I seem to connect with other things in the sky. I look up and observe the stars. I also watch the sun — especially when it sets.

I also like the idea that friends of mine are getting interested in the moon watching idea and discuss things with me. One friend called me up two weeks ago at 4:15 A.M. and told me to look at the huge moon in the western sky!

* * *

I felt that I knew a great deal about the moon (I'd thought about the moon as part of a unit in astronomy with sixth graders [I thought I had]). I knew things about orbits and distance and reflected light and was very comfortable that my familiarity with my friend the moon was an intimate one. The first class discussion clued me in to the fact that my knowledge of the moon falls far short of an understanding. My knowledge was one from a perspective way out in space looking in. It was always easy to think about these three objects in space and their interactions (sun, moon, earth). With this new perspective I had many questions without answers. . . .

Not knowing can be so much more fun than knowing. It's opened my eyes to look for understanding. I curse whatever it was that led me to believe this puzzle was solved.

The Students Explain: The Second Aspect

Having the students watch the moon corresponds to the first of the two aspects of teaching that I mentioned: it engages them in contact with phenomena. It serves this purpose at two levels. With regard to engaging with the solar system, it puts them in touch with the motions of the moon (and, it always turns out, of other heavenly bodies). With regard to engaging with teaching and learning, it puts them in touch with themselves and each other as learners, and with what I am doing as a teacher.

Similarly, the second aspect is brought into play at both of these levels. With regard to the motions of the moon, I continually ask them what they notice and what they make of it, and I encourage them to do the same with each other. The questions that we ask over and over again in class are: "What do you mean?" "Why do you think that?" "I don't quite get it." "Is that the same as what [someone else] thought they saw?" We also talk about what sense they are making of the primary subject of teaching and learning—what do they notice about this experience as learners and what do they make of that? The students also keep journals of their thoughts, their reactions, and the sense they are making of the discussions.

In some ways, it is easier to understand how this works with respect to teaching and learning than with respect to the solar system. After all, what one believes about teaching and learning is complicated, large-scale, hard to define, and close to the soul. If one stops to think about it, it is hard to imagine students learning about teaching and learning *other than* by working out for themselves what they think. Of course, when I say "working out for themselves" I do not rule out presenting people with material for them to make sense of, as I try to describe here—experiences in which they learn, try to explain what they are learning, watch others learn, try to help other people explain, and hear other people's ideas. But it is the *students* who make sense of all of this. It could not be otherwise. And they make sense by trying out their own ideas, by explaining what they think and why, and seeing how this holds up in other people's eyes, in their own eyes, and in the light of the phenomena they are trying to understand.

In other matters less close to the soul I believe that it works the same way. Whatever it is that a person believes and understands, it is *that person* who believes and understands it. Paley (1986), engaged in a very similar exercise in her teaching of three-year-olds, observed, "Why not just tell Frederick the truth: '*Of course* your mother has a birthday; everybody has a birthday.' Tempting as it might be to set the record straight, I have discovered that I can't seem to teach the children that which they don't already know" (p. 126). The best Paley can do is to accept the children's perspectives and to draw attention to some aspects they might think about at the same time. When older children or adults are struggling to make sense, they might be more inclined than Frederick to repeat what I have told them, but I have found that they are no more likely to have integrated it; I have not "set the record straight." Evidence to this effect comes up time and time again, whether the subject be the habits of the moon, a foreign language, fractions, photosynthesis, reading, or poetry.

Instead of explaining to the students, then, I ask them to explain to me what they think and why. I find the following results. (See Jones, 1977, and Moise, 1965, for similar views of teaching advanced mathematics.) First, in trying to make their thoughts clear for other people, students achieve greater clarity for themselves. Much of the learning is in the explaining. (Why should the teacher monopolize occasions for trying to make herself clear?) Second, the students themselves determine what it is they want to understand. It is not only the explanations which come from them, but also the questions. Third, people come to depend on themselves: they are the judges of what they know and believe. They know why they believe it, what questions they still have about it, the degree of uncertainty about it, what they want to know next about it, how it relates to what other people think. Any other "explanation" that they encounter must establish its place within what they know. Fourth, students recognize the powerful experience of having their ideas taken seriously, rather than simply screened for correspondence to what the teachers wanted. One student, an elementary school principal, speaks to these third and fourth points.

> Moon watching has been a profound experience for me. From the beginning, I was thoroughly engaged by the activity. . . . I wrote in my journal, "One of the things I love about moon-watching is this—as a non-scientific person, I have finally been afforded the opportunity to learn about a 'scientific' phenomenon without feeling dumb and unscientific because I don't know the scientific answers. Hurray . . . !"
>
> Here was a profound difference from my previous experience with science. Why? In this case, no premium was placed on "quick right answers." Instead, totally mistaken notions were not only accepted, but honored. . . . How could I feel dumb when whatever I was thinking was accepted with respect?
>
> Do I understand the moon now? I understand a great deal more than I did four months ago, but I feel fairly certain that some of what I "know" is probably wrong, and there's still a lot I don't begin to understand. Why doesn't that bother me? I no longer think I'm dumb if I don't know the "quick right answer". . . . What I do know about the moon is mine forever.

Fifth, students learn an enormous amount from each other:

> Class discussions have helped out a lot. Often people see the moon at different times than I do, and they can tentatively fill in some of my gaps in knowledge (the gaps won't really be filled in until *I* see things for myself). I also like to hear other people's hypotheses, because they give me other avenues and ideas to check out. I especially like it when I can't believe what someone else has seen — it makes me slow down and reevaluate my own notes and theories.

Finally, learners come to recognize knowledge as a human product, since they have produced their own knowledge and they know that they have. What is written in a book becomes viewed as somebody else's creation, a creation produced just as they produced their own. Its origin is not of another order. (By contrast, most students — adults and children — believe "knowledge" to be an absolute, which some people have caught on to, and which they, if they are smart enough, will be able to learn from someone who has caught on.) The following excerpt speaks to this point.

> I had seen the moon changing shape in regular ways, but I never thought of trying to make sense of this, to see it in connection to how the moon and sun and earth work. It's this connection that's been so exciting, this realizing that the moon that we see in our visible world can tell us about a larger world which I thought before was only to be found in classroom and libraries, that we can watch the world and begin to understand how it works. . . .
>
> It's exciting! It's opened up a way of thinking and learning about the world, a potential to slowly make sense of what I see and know and for this visible, familiar world to teach me about things I don't see or understand.

While the major burden is on the students to explain what they think, I actually do try to say much of what I myself believe on the subject of teaching and learning. I often remark on what I see in our work together and I try to say what I think about issues that students raise. (After all, I too am grateful for the occasion to learn from trying to say clearly what I think.) Yet, I have no illusions that what I say will mean the same thing to others as it does to me, nor that the students will, in general, give credence to what I say. But what I say does add to the assortment of things they have to think about.

However, in the case of the secondary subject in which they have as yet little interest and about which they have few ideas of their own (the moon, in this instance), I do not usually say what I think. My efforts are centered on enabling people to see that their own ideas are perfectly reasonable and, in fact, are the best starting points. It would be all too easy, if I were to give my account, for people to sit back, stop thinking, and assume that they understand what I am saying and that what I say is right — not to mention the likelihood that the topic will cease to hold any interest for them if they are simply listening to what I think. I do, though, offer ideas for consideration if I can see a different point of view that no one else has mentioned. Sometimes such an idea is one that I believe in, and sometimes it is not. In either case, I do not present it as a "right" idea, but simply as another one that should be considered. (I usually introduce it by saying, "Some people say . . . .") If discussion gets to a point where I am not at all sure what I think, then I might enter with my own tentative thoughts, acknowledged as mine.

The essential element of having the students do the explaining is not the withholding of all the teacher's own thoughts. It is, rather, that the teacher not consider herself/himself the final arbiter of what the learner should think, nor the creator of what the learner does think. The important job for the teacher is to keep trying to find out what sense the students are making. This sometimes involves what have come to be called in my classes "monkey wrenches" — some idea or evidence that raises some question about what a learner has just said, even if that might be something I agree with. "Throwing a monkey wrench," instead of "reinforcing the right answer" (as the common wisdom of the trade goes) at first seems a perverse teaching practice. Yet it is *because* of the basic concerns of a teacher — *because* of wanting to be sure that students understand — that one remains noncommittal, resists early acceptance of a student's understanding, and searches for any soft spots that require more thinking.

There is one other important aspect to having students do the explaining. I try to have all the students share with me the responsibility of making sure they understand each other. This is tough for many people. For one thing, it is often hard to admit to oneself that one does not understand. Second, many (in fact, most) of the adults I have taught assume that if they have not understood what has been said, the shortcoming is their own. Few think that the speaker said it unclearly, and even fewer, that the speaker might not have been clear in his or her own mind.

The following excerpt indicates how significant it is even for competent adults to take this step.

> [We paid] careful attention . . . to the understanding of each other's understanding, as well as our own. . . . For the first time in my life, I heard myself say to a fellow classmate, in front of approximately fifty others, "I don't think I understand what you mean. Could you please say that again?" Never before had I experienced the self-confidence, the freedom and, perhaps, the comfort necessary to do such a thing. What is significant, however, is that such an honest statement on my part was able to lead to further explanation and exploration of the other's thoughts, thereby raising issues in his own mind to be shared with the others as he experienced them, himself. In a journal entry . . . I wrote the following:
>
>> For the first time, I was able to examine another's thoughts at work. Simultaneously, it seemed, I could examine my own. Excitement! I feel like a supercharged machine, discovering realms of my own capacities which I'd never know were there! What other worlds within worlds within me exist?
>
> Such euphoria was certainly not the norm, but what joy to experience! I felt as though my eyes and ears were operating at heights never before reached — certainly not within a classroom.

Teaching As Research

My view of teaching suggests an analogy to the work of a psychotherapist with a research interest. She is both a practitioner and a researcher. She could not possibly learn anything significant about psychodynamics if she were not genuinely engaged in the therapeutic process. It is only because she knows how to do her job as a practitioner that she is in a position to pursue her questions as researcher. I would like to propose that similarly, through teaching, one is in a position to pursue questions about the development of understanding that one could not pursue in any other way. If as a researcher one is interested in how people build their understanding, then the way to gain insight is to watch them do it, and try to make sense of it as it happens (to paraphrase Armstrong, cited in Engel, 1984).

When I speak of "teaching," I do not necessarily mean school teaching. By "teacher" I mean someone who engages learners, who seeks to involve each person wholly — mind, sense of self, sense of humor, range of interests, interactions with other people — in learning. And, having engaged the learners, she finds her questions to be the same as those that a researcher into the nature of human learning wants to ask, What do you think and why? While the students learn, she learns, too. And it helps if, like Paley (1986), she is *curious* about her students' thoughts. How do other people really think about these matters? Which ideas build on which others and how? Which interests build on other interests? Which ideas get in the way of other ideas? What seem to be, in Hawkins's (1978) phrase, the "critical barriers" in this field? How does an idea get modified? How does a firmly-held conviction influence how a person reads an experience? What is the range of conceptions covered by a "right-sounding" work or phrase? In what circumstances is a person confused by/deaf to/helped by another person's thoughts? What factors keep interest high? How does a specific representation of one's thoughts influence how the thoughts develop further? How does a new idea lead to a new question, and vice versa? (See, for example, Armstrong, 1980; Bussis et al., 1985, Duckworth, 1986; Duckworth, in press; Duckworth, Julyan, & Rowe, 1985; Paley, 1986.)

This kind of research need not take place in a classroom. But it does require as researcher a teacher who knows ways into a subject matter well enough to engage a great variety of learners, and to keep them going as they ask and answer further questions.

After her experience in the course just described, Delaney (1986a), a high school teacher of government on leave from her classroom, did some pilot research of this kind. As she stated in the project proposal, "I am attempting to understand how two high school students [Mark and Tim] . . . make sense of the presidency. In so doing, I would like to be able to identify questions and problems that interest people and prompt them to take notice of their own understanding and to elaborate on it. I am especially interested in . . . four aspects of the presidency: the powers of the president, the restrictions on these powers, the relationship between the president and other government institutions (particularly Congress), and the relationship between the president and the electorate. These four aspects of the presidency seem to be sufficiently broad so that I might be able to glimpse how the national government is understood. Yet they are sufficiently focused so that we have specific problems and issues to explore" (p. 1). Each of her students kept a notebook (equivalent to the moon-watching notebook) in which they recorded each day at least one observation of the president, taken from news broadcasts, papers, or magazines.

Even though she was "attempting to understand," her primary interest in the project was in being a teacher. "The most important goal of this project for me was that [they] learn to think about some aspect of the president in some new way" (Delaney, 1986a, p. 4). She did succeed in "engaging" the students, the first aspect of teaching described above. At the end of the study, she wrote, "The most amazing aspect of this project . . . has been how engaged both Mark and Tim stayed. Every time I called them [to confirm the meetings], they wanted to tell me what they thought of some event and ask what I thought." The following excerpts from one of her field reports further show how the two, research and teaching, are one. Tim was sick this day, and the following session took place with Mark alone.

> Mark rarely hesitates in stating his opinions or thoughts. If his statements seem contradictory to me and I ask him to explain, he calmly states each statement again, not bothering to reconcile the contradiction. (Delaney, 1986a, p. 20)
>
> In our last session, when I asked Mark if a person is disloyal to the country when he or she disagrees with the president, he replied: "No. You have to distinguish between two things. A president is gonna base his decision on two things: either on what the majority of the people like *or* on what he knows best. . . . If he decides to rule by his feelings on a subject on which he knows more than the public then you can't say those people are un-American. Not every American knows in-depth."
>
> Because I did not understand this explanation, I asked Mark about it again [in this session]. I read to him what he had said. He said, "Yeah, I know you didn't really understand all that. . . . " He explained: "People that do [know] as much as Reagan, they still disagree. Because on a particular subject, if they didn't agree . . . Now you got me stuck." "Good. . . . " Mark was truly stuck. He was hesitant from "particular subject" on. He does not like being stuck. When I replied "good," we both laughed. I could see him relax. (Delaney, 1986b, pp. 1–2)

Delaney chose to back off from that question for the time being, in order to put him at ease. Later she returned to it. This passage is particularly interesting in enabling us to see the kinds of decisions Delaney is making throughout this work.

> I asked him to explain once again his notions of the two ways presidents can make decisions. He said, "Well, first of all, it's not just the president. All politicians have that choice. . . . It would be good if politicians in order to get into office tell people what they want to hear, but once they're in just do what they think is best. . . . If what they're doing is right that's OK."
>
> My mind went in two different but related directions: (1) What if what the politicians do is wrong? and (2) who determines what is right and wrong, and how . . . For some time I had suspected that Mark's view of decision-making rested on an assumption that decisions could be classified into either right or wrong decision . . . [I asked him:] "How do you determine if a decision is right?"
>
> "What would benefit overall the people?"
>
> "How do you decide what would benefit the people overall?"
>
> "I'm not sure."
>
> "Let's look at an example that we've talked about. . . . "
>
> "Okay."
>
> "Contra aid. In the public opinion polls, the majority of the American people seem to oppose aid to the contras. Yet the president supports it. How does he decide that the majority is wrong and he is right?"
>
> " . . . You don't know that. The majority could be people who just don't like it. Some people know. Some don't."
>
> From this statement I realized that Mark probably thought of the "majority" as one huge chunk—a monolithic entity holding the same views for the same reasons. . . . I suggested that we make up a poll. . . . I asked: "This 52% represents

624 individuals and this 48% represents 576 individuals. Had you thought of that?"

"Yes."

"Okay, how do you know if these 624 individuals know or do not know about the contra aid issue?"

He responded: "I could say the majority don't know or I could say the minority don't know. You would have to do a very in-depth study."

"Knowing" to Mark seems to be directly linked to "right" and "not knowing" to wrong. In this session and the last . . . he uses "right" and "knowing" interchangeably. To know is to be right. . . . I asked if it might be possible that some people in the majority be misinformed and some be informed? "It's hard to say . . . because some people just base it on what they saw in the news and not on what's real."

In this last statement we have plenty of questions for another [session]. . . . What's the difference between the news and "what's real?" Bypassing this for a moment, I decided to rephrase my question using his terminology. "Is it possible that some people in the majority base their decisions on the news and others on what's real?" Silence. Mark was thinking — *hard*. I could practically hear his brain working when he said, "Wow, I never thought of that before."

"What?"

"That a majority could have different reasons why they're on that side." (Delaney, 1986b, pp. 4–6).

Here was confirmation of her hunch about how Mark was thinking (Delaney as researcher) and at the same time, a great new idea on his part (Delaney as teacher). The session had to come to an end shortly after this. Delaney asked Mark to watch the news "for examples of how people on the same side of an issue . . . may agree for different reasons," and for "more data on how the president decides."

Among her several comments on the session is this one, where she uses the insight gained into Mark's thinking to help her understand something that had puzzled her since the first session:

From our last session, I had suspected that Mark's notion of decision-making rested on a belief that absolutely right and absolutely wrong decisions were possible, and that part of the president's job was to identify *the* right decision. He said in our first session, "It's wrong to change your opinion. You can't just change it like that." This seems a curious statement at first glance, and the juxtaposition of the statements seems even more curious. However, if you believe that your opinion is right then both statements and their relationship begin to make sense: If you *are* right then changing your opinion *is* wrong. (Delaney, 1986b, p. 9)

What, then, has Delaney learned as a researcher? On the face of it, it might look as if what she learned were particulars about Tim and Mark. Of course that *is* what she learned, and at one level we could say that what she learned helped her make specific decisions about how to go further with them. But there are other levels where her learning goes far beyond her work with Tim and Mark. She contributes to our knowledge of what is involved in an understanding of how the American government works, and how such understanding can evolve.

In her final report, she uses Hawkins's (1978) notion of "critical barriers" in discussing two factors she found to characterize Tim and Mark's ideas about the workings of the government. One factor was what she called "single-group nouns" —"majority," "public," and, also, "White House" (in referring vaguely to the president and/or his staff)—which the boys used, as she put it, to "communicate a single entity and obscure the diversity inherent in them." The second factor is their tendency to view the presidency in what she called "bipolar terms"—characterized by making "right" and "wrong" decisions. She points out that the first of these barriers makes it difficult, for example, to appreciate the central importance of diversity in a democracy. The second makes it difficult, for example, to appreciate why a democracy limits the powers of its leaders.

Even from this exceedingly small-scale study there seem to be countless questions for further teaching-research into what is involved in order for people to come to understand the workings of a democratic government. That is one kind of contribution this approach to research makes.

Furthermore, in shedding light on the growth of understanding about a democratic government, such research also sheds light on the growth of understanding in general. Oversimplifying single-group nouns and viewing situations as bipolar are both widespread characteristics of human thinking and their study is a lively concern of psychologists (see Basseches, 1984). Just as specifics can only be understood through generalities, so generalities can only be understood through specifics: it is helpful to think of bipolar thinking as a critical barrier; at the same time, it is only possible to understand what critical barriers are when we see instances of them.

I believe there is yet another kind of knowledge to which this research contributes—namely, knowledge of curriculum possibilities. Delaney's attempts to learn how these youngsters understand government seem to me to indicate ways to *teach* youngsters about government. This almost seems like a tautology—the procedures which result in people getting involved enough to want to talk about what they think are the very procedures which result in people getting involved enough to learn. But if it is a tautology, it certainly has not been much recognized. In any event, she has also learned and written about how to approach the teaching of government in a way that I think would certainly be helpful to other classroom teachers. If we take "curriculum" to be ways of engaging students in giving thought to those matters which we think important, then she has started to develop curriculum.

School Teaching

Delaney did not carry out this research while working full-time as a school teacher. She used her capacities as a teacher, but in a less pressured situation. It is a rare school teacher who has either the freedom or the time to think of her teaching as research, since much of her autonomy has been withdrawn in favor of the policies set by anonymous standard setters and test givers.

But even given the terrible constraints, and even if no resources are available to make known what they learn, there is some opportunity—and I think great need—for teachers to listen to their students explain what they think (for another perspective on this point, see Nussbaum & Novich, 1982).

A student in the course, who was at the same time teaching science in a middle school, did a project with small groups of students from her class (Young, 1986).

The following are some of her comments about this work and her regular teaching job.

> I chose to center my field work around the topic of pulse as an avenue to understanding the . . . circulatory system (a curriculum which I was supposed to "cover"). Initially, I was doubtful about how far we could get with our investigation. I had never given pulse much thought and imagined that it offered a few tactile experiences but might not turn out leading the students on to more questions. . . . I was amazed to discover how much investigation was generated from the pulse work.
>
> My research on students' understanding of pulse is entwined with my . . . teaching. . . . The teacher is researching the student and his understanding and then trying to help that student move on to more unknown territory. My bent is to apply my small group work to my classes. . . . This is the ultimate challenge. The task appears so immense and fragile with one or two people, that the prospect of applying the same concentration to a large group is overwhelming. I do think that it is possible though with some modifications.
>
> If nothing else . . . the teacher would be more sensitive to listening, observing and then talking with her students rather than at them. Although I did not initially link my research with what I do in room 126 at the Middle School, I now see a crucial relationship. . . . My research has become and hopefully will remain a vital element in my teaching. I realize that my understanding of myself as a learner weighs heavily on how I perceive the understanding of other learners. So, we in room 126 are all learners.

Conclusion

I am not proposing that school teachers single-handedly become published researchers in the development of human learning. Rather, I am proposing that teaching, understood as engaging learners in phenomena, and working to understand the sense they are making, might be the sine qua non of such research.

This kind of researcher would be a teacher in the sense of caring about some part of the world and how it works enough to want to make it accessible to others; she would be fascinated by the questions of how to engage people in it and how people make sense of it; she would have time and resources to pursue these questions to the depth of her interest, to write what she learned, and to contribute to theoretical and pedagogical discussions on the nature and development of human learning.

And then, I wonder—why should this be a separate research profession? There is no reason I can think of not to rearrange the resources available for education so that this description defines the job of a public school teacher.

So this paper ends with a romance. But then, it began with passion.

References

Armstrong, M. (1980). *Closely observed children*. London: Writers and Readers Publishing.

Basseches, M. (1984). *Dialectical thinking and adult development*. Norwood, NJ: Ablex.

Bussis, A., Chittenden, E., Amarel, M., & Klausner, E. (1985). *Inquiry into meaning*. Hillsdale, NJ: Erlbaum.

Delaney, M. K. (1986a). *Understanding the presidency: Final report.* Unpublished manuscript, Harvard University, Graduate School of Education, Cambridge.

Delaney, M. K. (1986b). *Protocol 5, 4/28/86.* Unpublished manuscript, Harvard University, Graduate School of Education, Cambridge.

Duckworth, E. (1986). *Inventing density.* Grand Forks: North Dakota Study Group on Evaluation.

Duckworth, E. (in press). Some depths and complexities of elementary arithmetic. *Journal of Mathematical Behavior.*

Duckworth, E., Julyan, C., & Rowe, T. (1985). *Understanding equilibrium: The study of complex systems.* Final Project Report. Cambridge: Harvard University, Educational Technology Center.

Elementary Science Study. (1968). *Where is the moon?* [Prepared by D. Ford]. New York: Webster Division, McGraw-Hill.

Engel, B. (1984). Interview with Michael Armstrong. *Elementary School Journal, 84,* 350–356.

Hawkins, D. (1978). Critical barriers to science learning. *Outlook, 29,* 3–23.

Jones, F. B. (1977). The Moore Method. *American Mathematical Monthly, 84,* 273–278.

Moise, E. E. (1965). Activity and motivation in mathematics. *American Mathematical Monthly, 72,* 407–412.

Nussbaum, J., & Novich, S. (1982). Alternative frameworks, conceptual conflict and accommodations: Toward a principled teaching strategy. *Instructional Science, 11,* 183–200.

Paley, V. (1986). On listening to what the children say. *Harvard Educational Review, 56,* 122–131.

Young, L. (1986). *Teacher as learner in research and the classroom.* Unpublished manuscript, Harvard University, Graduate School of Education, Cambridge.

This article will appear in a book by Eleanor Duckworth, titled *"The Having of Wonderful Ideas" and Other Essays on Teaching and Learning,* to be published by Teachers College Press, 1987.

Reflections on Teacher Empowerment and Teacher Education

MARGARET YONEMURA

Margaret Yonemura discusses the development of her concept of empowerment and its current expression in a teacher education program. The author has been influenced by the Malting House School and its Deweyan focus on the whole child actively generating knowledge out of daily experiences, guided by a teacher who helps connect it with the disciplines. She explores three ways in which she works to empower students in teacher training: through the invention of curriculum, through ongoing peer relations, and through child study. The author joins Jean Piaget, Paulo Freire, and others in suggesting that humans beings can and must shift educational perspectives in the direction of emancipation.

At the first working conference on "Critical Pedagogy," I was impressed by the many different paths we the participants had taken to arrive at a concept of empowerment.[1] Various meanings and interpretations of empowerment grow out of our life experiences and, as a person who works with children and teachers, I bring my own meanings and interpretations to the concept. In this paper I trace the roots of my beliefs about empowerment and the ways in which these beliefs find expression in my work as a faculty member in a master's degree program preparing teachers of young children.

As an undergraduate at the University of London almost forty years ago, I did not know which of my studies would stay with me or why. But looking back I see that the work of Susan Isaacs provided me with one of my earliest understandings of empowerment; it influenced the ways I taught children and continues to influence my work with teachers. In 1924 Isaacs started the Malting House School in Cambridge, England, for about twenty middle-class children aged two through eight. She was interested in seeing how far children could develop intellectually in a Deweyan environment that was responsive to their varied interests and energies. Her book, *Intellectual Growth in Young Children*, is a testament to children and teachers mutually engaged in learning within a curriculum that ranged from geography to pathology, leading the teacher to new understandings about children's intellects.[2]

---

[1] The First Working Conference on Critical Pedagogy, University of Massachusetts, Amherst, February 21–22, 1986.

[2] Isaacs, *Intellectual Growth in Young Children* (London: Lowe & Brydone, 1966).

Harvard Educational Review Vol. 56 No. 4 November 1986, 473–480

Isaacs carried out her work from 1924 to 1927, when the view that children were to obey adults unquestioningly was common. Isaacs, however, revealed a choice that parents and other adults could make in how they saw and responded to children: either in relationships fostering dependence and subservience or in ones based on reciprocity between persons at different developmental stages. Isaacs stepped outside of the role set for teachers in her time. She created perspectives on the curriculum and teaching that opened up choices for liberating children as persons and expanding their decision-making powers. She showed that original designs for classroom life could actively involve everyone in the school, including the teacher. To read the vivid accounts of teaching and learning in that school is to rediscover the satisfaction and empowerment which derive from the adventures of minds that are freed to think.

One brief example may serve to give the flavor of life in Isaacs's school. One day an airplane flew overhead, which was an exciting event in the twenties. When the children saw the airplane, they called for it to come down. One child wondered whether the airplane pilot could see them. When another child asked what the pilot could see and what the children looked like from the plane, Isaacs suggested making a model of the garden as it looked to the pilot. Some of the children climbed as high up on a ladder as they could to see for themselves how the garden and its occupants looked. "One boy of four-and-a-half realized spontaneously that from the plane only the tops of their own heads would be seen, and he dotted a number of small, flat ovals over the paths of the model. 'That's the children running about.' "[3] These beginnings of aerial mapping provided the children with the roots of the discipline of geography, experienced not "as if it were a matter of something already done, constituted, completed, and finished,"[4] but as a form of knowledge to which adults and children could contribute out of their own backgrounds.

During the ten years that I taught in and directed a school serving largely black and Puerto Rican children from New York City, I found that Isaacs's way of working transcended race and social class. The children with whom I worked enthusiastically seized opportunities to make sense of their world and to learn about their environment. They were active inquirers, and were able to join in writing the script of their own education by making as well as absorbing knowledge. They learned to model the Hudson River and Tarrytown as Isaacs's children had moved on to model the River Cam and Cambridge.

My students were inner-city children from a population often described as needing structure—but the structure frequently advocated is highly teacher-dominated. Ironically, the children who so desperately need to experience control and power are often deprived of it. They become passive memorizers of educational scripts to which they make no original contribution, and which do not expand and enrich their day-to-day experiences. The neglect of children's experiences and the denial of the relevance of those experiences to established fields of knowledge stunts children's intellectual growth and diminishes who they are and what they can become. Children can learn universal geographic concepts even as they focus upon the Hudson, the Cam, or other landmarks of the environment. As partici-

---

[3] Isaacs, *Intellectual Growth*, p. 37.
[4] Paulo Freire, *Education for Critical Consciousness* (New York: Continuum, 1973), p. 153.

pants in forming knowledge, they bring feelings of autonomy, initiative, and energy to formal aspects of the discipline. They can bring all of themselves to the task of learning.

From Isaacs, Caroline Pratt, Lucy Sprague Mitchell, Emma Sheehy, and other educators I have come to understand that child empowerment is an outcome of teacher empowerment.[5] I have seen that children *and* teachers learn best when they are viewed as people rather than locked into *pupil roles* or *teacher roles* and are thus freed to bring themselves and their views to the classroom world. Teachers free to be themselves are not threatened by children; they move with, not against, the energy released when children find their own answers.

Consequently, in my work in teacher education I try to help students become familiar with the role teachers play, without being absorbed by that role. I try to help students remain themselves even as they learn to draw on new inner resources in order to teach well. I encourage them to hold on to their own voices rather than adopt the "teacher" voice to which many of us are addicted. I try to help them see themselves as generators of knowledge as well as recipients of the knowledge of the profession. And I try to give them a sense of their own power as learners and teachers.

I use three approaches to empower the students with whom I work. First, in their classroom placements students invent curricula which will permit them to share with children their own experiences and personal meanings. Second, the students work together in pairs as often as possible to support a belief that all of us generate knowledge. Third, students are given opportunities to study and work with children and to see them as active, knowledgeable, and fully human. Through these three approaches, I give students a chance to see that they have power and that the settings of school and classroom are not "inescapable reality," but are transformable.[6]

The program serves about thirty-six graduate students, some of whom are teachers with undergraduate degrees in education, seeking master's degrees for permanent certification, while others are liberal arts graduates in a two-year full-time program of study. The students form a heterogeneous group and they hold varied and complex views about children, the curriculum, and teaching. But for the most part, they have been strongly influenced by teacher- and curriculum-dominated classrooms.

Some of the liberal arts graduates have taken an undergraduate course in applied behavioral science with a practicum in which they — the teachers — function as technicians who enact clipboard programs written elsewhere. They are as highly controlled as the children whom they direct. Even as they observe that "it works," this distancing between teacher and children paradoxically concerns the students. Though they fulfill their very real hopes of teaching children and gain

---

[5] Caroline Pratt founded City and Country School in New York City during the 1930s. Her most noted work is *I Learn from Children* (New York: Cornerstone Library, 1970). Lucy Sprague Mitchell started the Bank Street College of Education, and wrote *Young Geographers: How They Explore the World and How They Mark the World*, rev. ed. (New York: Bank Street College of Education, 1971).

[6] Erik Erikson refers to "the grim determination of 'adults to play roles'—that is, to impersonate to the point of no return their places in a cast forced on them by what they consider inescapable reality" in his *Toys and Reasons: Stages in the Ritualization of Experience* (New York: Norton, 1976), p. 18.

a measure of confidence from using a script written by an expert, these committed young people are nonetheless generally discomforted by their manipulative role.

Understandably, students are searching for ways to anchor themselves in the world of work, to become the experts who write the programs, with all the attendant status and recognition. I have to remind myself about students' expectations and hopes in order to withstand the anger and anxiety that surface when it first becomes clear that they are not going to receive scripts from me. I try to help them realize that I will support them in their own invention of the education script and help them respond confidently and creatively to the question most of them ask themselves about their own knowledge: "What do *I* know?" We have all heard a strongly insistent message in our culture: there are the cognoscenti, and then there are the rest of us. That message was clear, for example, when Merce Cunningham was scorned by critics for daring to introduce his modern dance movement without the expected music and story.

But there are those in the culture who reject the notion of children — and teachers — as empty vessels. In my own life, several teachers helped me become aware of my strengths and knowledge. In particular, I recall a graduate course in music education taught by Sheehy, which I took very reluctantly as part of the master's degree program at Teachers College, Columbia University. I brought a long personal history to music, having grown up in Wales, which thinks rightly of itself as the land of song. Despite music lessons, I emerged as a young adult with a perception that music and I were a poor match. Sheehy had written a book, *There's Music in Children*, and she based her course on the thesis that we were all musically endowed.[7] In such an atmosphere of acceptance, I learned to play the guitar — not well, but well enough. I felt disproportionately pleased about that and about the free explorations of sound in which we engaged. I even made my own drum, an arduous task since we were to produce an honest instrument, not a toy. One result of these experiences was that as a teacher and director of schools for young children, I perceived children as having music within them to be explored in their own way on the piano and other musical instruments. It was easier to guide children to the varieties of music in our culture because I felt they were bringing themselves as musicians to the task. Many students and teachers do not teach music or art because they lack extraordinary talent and therefore feel they have nothing within themselves to draw upon. Of course, I needed to draw on music and art specialists, but Emma Sheehy taught me that I could also draw on myself.

I bring to my work with students a belief that they have within themselves resources for contributing to the education program. Part of my work is to elicit these resources. Time for doing this is built into the advising process, based on the model at the Bank Street College of Education. Each student becomes a member of a small conference group which meets with a faculty member for several hours each week for two semesters. This faculty member makes visits to student placements regularly, and at least once a month students and faculty members confer formally. Reflection on practice and its meanings for the students is the agenda for these seminars and conferences.

A low faculty-student ratio in our program and the time purposefully set aside allow for reflection and for musing together. Most students need these conditions

[7] Sheehy, *There's Music in Children* (New York: Holt, 1946).

in order to reveal their deeply held interests and knowledge, especially since they usually come to the program with a sense that these are peripheral to their teaching. A project developed by students in one of my conference groups may illustrate how these personal interests can illumine teaching.

These students are at the end of the master's program, which means they are completing their integrative projects in lieu of theses, as well as meeting the requirements of the conference group and their classroom teaching. For their integrative projects, three of the ten students in the group have chosen to take part in planning for a city-wide celebration of the arts. They have had the chance to see how they can serve as resource people for a number of community agencies which work together.

We were discussing this integrative project at the beginning of a seminar when Lynn, one of the trio, pointed out that he had worked on a community-wide project before: he and his brother had organized the first sports car race through the streets of Binghamton, New York. He recalled preparing the city streets for the race by surrounding the bases of the buildings with old tires, and the general excitement of the event. He spoke with pride about his car, "no ordinary small car — a red 1954 MG Midget with the front of a bug-eyed Sprite." Brenda, director of an early childhood program, jokingly asked Lynn if he would bring the car to her school. She was planning to take the children to a new museum where an old automobile was being displayed.

When Brenda and Lynn met later to discuss procedures, they decided to design Lynn's visit to meet one of the requirements of a reading course that they were taking; they would videotape the event and present it with follow-up activities as a language-experience approach to the teaching of reading. Later, Lynn and Brenda brought the videotape of the visit to a conference group seminar for us to view. The five-year-olds had been captivated as each took a turn buckling up, steering, and wearing Lynn's red protective helmet. Lynn had listened to their ideas about racing cars — based on television and on direct experiences — and had elicited thoughtful questions. To judge by the children's dictated stories and free crayoned drawings, Lynn had indeed awakened the children's interest in the general concept of speed. In this way, Lynn's knowledge of cars and racing found an outlet in Brenda's educational program.[8]

Opening up curriculum so that student teachers can join in its creation is one way of empowering them. Students need placements where they are allowed to generate knowledge from their own lives and bring it to the children. There is a set of challenges in finding such placements, but I will return to that issue later.

Another way of helping students value their own meanings and knowledge is to provide opportunities for them to explore the question, "What do people like me, my peers, know?" Time is built into the program for pairs of students to work and reflect together. For example, in the final seminar the students pair up in a series of conferences to explore each other's values and beliefs about children, the curriculum, and teaching. Each pair writes and tape-records its discussions and brings extracts to the seminar. They observe one another's teaching and compare espoused and enacted values. Prior to their observations, I have spent a morning

[8] I am indebted to Lynn Little and Brenda Testani for permitting me to use this illustration.

in each of their classrooms gathering non-judgmental data. This information forms the starting point of the conference that follows between the student and me. The classroom data are used to stimulate memory for further details and to determine how the events of the classroom — as we each saw them — accorded with expressed values and beliefs. In our conference, we search for ways to close the inevitable gaps between espoused and enacted values.

The conference group is a forum designed to validate as well as test the personal-professional knowledge we have all acquired. These reflections are honored with *time* because they are as significant as any component in the graduate program. In this way, then, opportunities are built into the program for students to learn to value their own knowledge and experiences, as well as those of their peers.

As a third strategy toward empowerment, we give students opportunities to explore the question, "What do children know?" When we come to see children as knowledgeable, hard at work making meanings, and fully human, we can see ourselves in a new and revealing light. Derived from the psychology of B. F. Skinner, our conventional view of children holds that they are empty vessels; their actions are explained in behavioristic terminology. While my students are often not satisfied with the explanatory power of behaviorism, they do not see the barriers such conceptual schemes put between them and children. The behaviorist framework conceals from them the power of their sensitively tuned relationships with children. It renders invisible the teacher's daily responsiveness and thought. Worst of all, this framework diminishes children: they become mechanisms incapable of making complex meanings, decisions, or choices to change their ways of acting. The teacher educator's challenge is to offer students the chance to examine critically their conceptual framework and the consequences of their beliefs, while presenting alternative ways to perceive children as active, not only reactive, organisms.

One graduate course in the master's program centers on studying children. I make no claims for the originality of this course; it is a standard requirement in most undergraduate and graduate teacher education programs. In the thirteen years I have taught it, however, the course has acquired a different set of foci for me. I have moved from thinking primarily about the individual child to a much more ecological perspective, heeding Gregory Bateson's warning that to focus on one spot in the web is to miss the nature of its interconnectedness.[9] I now see the course as one more place where students, children, and I can come to know what we know, and to examine critically what we know in terms of values, beliefs, and choices.

Students in the course do focus on one child, but they do so within a classroom group in which they play an interactive role. Students do not take the teacher and classroom setting for granted as "inescapable reality," but bring them to center stage periodically to be examined and demystified. The study involves participant observation so that the students can see child growth and development partially as a function of what they themselves do and experience, not simply as professionals, but as persons.

---

[9] Bateson, *Steps to an Ecology of Mind* (San Francisco: Chandler, 1972).

Some students are surprised that I encourage them to perceive the children as persons from whom they can learn, not just as objects of study, but as active inquirers into the meanings they are making collaboratively and uniquely as part of classroom life. Barry Wadsworth points out that "surprise always contains . . . a cognitive element of prediction or expectancy that is *not confirmed*."[10] The surprise is explored for its deeper meanings, which are often connected to the view that children really have nothing to teach us. Since many people do not adequately recognize the knowledge and experience of teachers and students, it is not surprising that they are reluctant to view children as knowledgeable.

Having presented the idea that children have knowledge, we explore ways to gain access to that knowledge. The students learn how to interview children using Piaget's clinical design. For some it is the first time that they have really listened to a child. The children's responses to Piagetian tasks invariably interest most of the class. My hope is that through this experience the students will come to value and respect the knowledge we make from our earliest years on through life.

Students draw on their own observations, their conversations, and their games with the children, and they come to see themselves as gatherers of valuable data. Over the semester I ask them to bring into class portfolios of a particular child's artwork. I encourage them to look at the work of all the children, and to study that one child's work in depth. Most of the students express satisfaction at this immersion in one child's life. Students supplement the description of the child's life in the classroom with various data emerging from tests and other evaluations, but these are presented only as a secondary source of information about the child.

Other aspects of the assignment surprise some of the students because they violate what seems like a "natural" way of behaving. When I point out that they will need to obtain the child's permission in order to do the study, two submerged beliefs surface for exploration. One is that adults do not need to ask children's permission because children are not old enough to know what is good for them. The other belief is that teachers can choose to ask children's permission because teachers hold the power.

A few of the students are also surprised that the children are expected to take part in what is usually referred to as the parent-teacher conference, which therefore becomes a parent-teacher-child conference. These few have not considered that as teachers they have the power to decide whether or not to view the child as part of the conference group. Often they have not been given a chance to reflect on the underlying values and beliefs about childhood that dehumanize young children, which is a common outcome of treating classroom life as if it were "inescapable reality."

What occurs in classrooms is not "inescapable reality," but modifying what happens can be slow and discouraging. It is not easy to find placements that meet my requirements for students. The students sometimes work with teachers who devalue their own knowledge and cling to the rigid structure of a set curriculum. My task is to work toward empowering both the cooperating teacher and the student. I try to avoid ritualistic scripts when we talk together, and I try to listen to the teacher's views so that we may jointly create the best possible learning experience for students.

[10] Wadsworth, *Piaget for the Classroom Teacher* (New York: Longman, 1978), p. 90.

To sum up, I have identified three approaches to the empowerment of teachers and children: through the invention of curriculum, through the fostering of peer relationships, and through study that promotes shifts in perspectives about children. How effective are these approaches? Some students and teachers come into the program already committed to empowerment. I hope to reaffirm their beliefs, and perhaps, with my colleagues and their peers, to offer broader options for acting upon them. Some students grow in understanding before my eyes, and that is encouraging indeed. Some, I know, leave the program as they entered, uncommitted and occasionally hostile to empowerment. On these occasions I am disappointed and sometimes daunted.

Yet I am buoyed by what I have learned about human development. Jean Piaget has shown that right from the start we shift our perspectives in ways that expand our lives. Toddlers live in a world of tactile-kinesthetic awareness, all centered on their own bodies. But Piaget states that "at about eighteen months, through a shift of perspective (decentration) truly comparable to the Copernican revolution, space becomes a single homogeneous container in which all objects are situated, including one's own body."[11] Another liberation and major shift in perspective occurs when a child realizes that her sister has a sister and it is she. The world of social relations expands and opens up. Human beings of all ages struggle all their lives to shift perspectives in order to gain wider worlds.

Piaget also points out that in the struggle for liberating perspectives we move backwards as well as ahead. We do not acquire new knowledge merely by addition, but by the reformulation of previously held viewpoints. These changes can be turbulent and unsettling, and can cause us to regress to safer territory for a time. Paulo Freire urges us toward the struggle in a similar vein when he says that "education is a permanent act of cognition. . . . It means making a new effort, in a new situation, in which new aspects which were not clear before are clearly presented to the educatee."[12] In my own work I interpret this to mean that the cooperating teachers, the students, and I must be ready to take time to talk together and be ready for the backward as well as the forward movement that is inevitably part of a valuable shift of perspective.

[11] Piaget, *Comments* (Cambridge: MIT Press, 1962), p. 4.
[12] Freire, *Education for Critical Consciousness*, p. 151.

Teaching Student Teachers to Reflect

KENNETH M. ZEICHNER
DANIEL P. LISTON

Conventional teacher education programs follow an apprenticeship model and, in so doing, aspire to provide student teachers with pedagogical skills and techniques derived from a pre-existing body of knowledge. In this contribution to HER's special series, "Teachers, Teaching, and Teacher Education," Kenneth M. Zeichner and Daniel P. Liston argue that the conventional approach inhibits the self-directed growth of student teachers and thereby fails to promote their full professional development. Illustrating an alternative model, the authors describe and assess the elementary student teaching program at the University of Wisconsin, Madison — a program oriented toward the goals of reflective teaching, greater teacher autonomy, and increasing democratic participation in systems of educational governance.

> The concern of teacher educators must remain normative, critical, and even political — neither the colleges nor the schools can change the social order. Neither the colleges nor the schools can legislate democracy. But something can be done to empower teachers to reflect upon their own life situations, to speak out in their own ways about the lacks that must be repaired; the possibilities to be acted upon in the name of what they deem decent, humane, and just. (Greene, 1978, p. 71)

Conceptual Orientation of the Program

The stated goals of the elementary student-teaching program at the University of Wisconsin, Madison, emphasize the preparation of teachers who are both willing and able to reflect on the origins, purposes, and consequences of their actions,[1] as well as on the material and ideological constraints and encouragements embedded in the classroom, school, and societal contexts in which they work. These goals are directed toward enabling student teachers to develop the pedagogical habits and skills necessary for self-directed growth and toward preparing them, individually and collectively, to participate as full partners in the making of educational policies. Underlying these goals is a metaphor of *liberation*. A liberated person, according to Siegel (1980), is one who is "free from the unwarranted control of unjustified beliefs, unsupportable attitudes, and the paucity of abilities which can prevent that person from completely taking charge of his or her life" (p. 16).

---

[1] The term "action" is based on Mead's (1938) notion of the "act" and implies a concern with both teacher cognitions and behaviors and their interconnections.

Harvard Educational Review Vol. 57 No. 1 February 1987, 1–22

It is our belief that learning, for both pupils and teachers, is greater and deeper when teachers are encouraged to exercise their judgment about the content and processes of their work and to give some direction to the shape of schools as educational environments.

The program literature draws upon the work of Dewey and makes a distinction between reflective and routine action. *Reflective action* entails the active, persistent, and careful consideration of any belief or supposed form of knowledge in light of the grounds that support it and the consequences to which it leads. *Routine action* is guided primarily by tradition, external authority, and circumstance.

Utilizing Dewey's (1933) concept of reflective action as the organizing principle of its curriculum, the program literature expresses a desire to develop in student teachers those *orientations* (toward open-mindedness, responsibility, and wholeheartedness) and *skills* (of keen observation and reasoned analysis) which lead to reflective action. The continuing development of technical skill in teaching is also addressed, but only within this broader context of reflective action. Since the program is concerned primarily with the growth and development of student teachers in teaching roles, the term *reflective teaching* is used to identify this central goal of the curriculum.

In addition to this emphasis on reflective teaching, the program literature distinguishes between different forms of reflection[2] by drawing upon the work of Van Manen (1977) and his conception of "levels of reflectivity."[3] Van Manen identifies three levels of reflection, each one embracing different criteria for choosing among alternative courses of action. At the first level of technical rationality (also, see Schön, 1983), the dominant concern is with the efficient and effective application of educational knowledge for the purposes of attaining ends which are accepted as given. At this level, neither the ends nor the institutional contexts of classroom, school, community, and society are treated as problematic.

A second level of reflectivity, according to Van Manen, is based upon a conception of practical action whereby the problem is one of explicating and clarifying the assumptions and predispositions underlying practical affairs and assessing the educational consequences toward which an action leads. At this level, every action is seen as linked to particular value commitments, and the actor considers the worth of competing educational ends.

The third level, critical reflection, incorporates moral and ethical criteria into the discourse about practical action. At this level the central questions ask which educational goals, experiences, and activities lead toward forms of life which are mediated by concerns for justice, equity, and concrete fulfillment, and whether

[2] Roemer (1983) argues that if the attainment of rationality as an educational goal is to be more than socialization into current conventions of thought and behavior, then independent norms of rationality need to be established which distinguish the exercise of reason from merely following standard modes of thought. While not claiming to have established an independent theory of rationality to replace the culturally-bound technical rationality which we seek to go beyond, the adaptation of Van Manen's (1977) notion of "levels of reflectivity" for specifying alternative criteria of rationality represents a beginning effort in this direction.

[3] Van Manen's (1977) "levels of reflectivity" and Tom's (1985) "arenas of the problematic" are highly similar. In both cases the degree of comprehensiveness in what is considered problematic distinguishes one level/arena from another. In fact, the three points which Tom (1985) identifies on his continuum of arenas correspond very closely to Van Manen's (1977) three levels of reflectivity, and are also analogous to Fenstermacher and Berliner's (1983) delineation of three aspects of evaluation: success, merit, and worth.

current arrangements serve important human needs and satisfy important human purposes (Tom, 1985). Here both the teaching (ends and means) and the surrounding contexts are viewed as problematic—that is, as value-governed selections from a larger universe of possibilities.

The curricular plan for the student-teaching program at the University of Wisconsin, Madison, is designed to stimulate reflection about teaching and its contexts at all three levels. The program literature defines a "reflective teacher" as one who assesses the origins, purposes, and consequences of his or her work at all three levels. However, because of the historically dominant concern with technical rationality and with instrumental criteria of success (Beyer & Zeichner, 1982; Lanier, 1982) in teacher education programs, a particular emphasis is placed here on encouraging reflection that employs educational and moral criteria.

This goal of enabling students to reflect about their teaching and its contexts at all three levels has been linked to a statement of the kind of teacher we hope would emerge from the program. In 1979 the elementary-area faculty adopted a statement which specifies the qualities it seeks to develop in its students: (1) technical competence in instruction and classroom management—knowledge concerning the content to be taught and competence in the skills and methods necessary for the realization of their classroom intentions; (2) ability to analyze practice—to see how classroom and school behavior (including their own actions) flows from or expresses purposes and goals both anticipated and unanticipated; (3) awareness of teaching as an activity that has ethical and moral consequences, and ability to make defensible choices regarding their classroom and school behavior; and (4) sensitivity to the needs of students with diverse intellectual, racial, physical, and social characteristics and ability to play an active role in developing a respect for individual differences within their classrooms and schools.

This statement of the qualities that the program seeks to develop in its students has been further refined and extended since 1979 and is now presented in the student-teaching handbook as a set of criteria for evaluating the work of student teachers. Since 1979 greater attention has been given to specifying the elements of these four qualities more precisely (for example, the fostering of education that is multicultural) and to the student teacher's role in curriculum development. It is important to note that "reflective teaching" is not viewed as synonymous with any particular changes in teacher behaviors. The program seeks to help student teachers become more aware of themselves and their environments in a way that changes their perceptions of what is possible. The hope is that these expanded perceptions and an enhanced "cultural literacy" (Bowers, 1984) will affect the degree of "reflectiveness" expressed in student teacher actions, and that more reflective teacher actions will lead to greater benefits for the teacher and for all of his or her pupils.

An underlying concern of the program is to enable prospective teachers, both individually and collectively, to develop the desire and ability to assume greater roles in determining the direction of classroom and school affairs according to purposes of which they are aware and which can be justified on moral and educational grounds, as well as on instrumental grounds. The hope is that graduates of the program will be able to exert more control over the content and processes of their own work than is now the case in many schools (Lanier & Little, 1986) and can participate as full partners with parents, administrators, and, in some cases, students in the making of educational policy within more democratically organized decision-making structures.

The conceptual orientation of this program has developed over a number of years and is still being revised and refined as our experience in the program and studies of the program reveal its inadequacies and limitations. We have moved from very general notions of what was wrong with the program (see Tabachnick, Popkewitz, & Zeichner, 1979–1980), to fairly general notions of the kinds of teachers we hope to prepare in the program ("reflective"), to finer and more detailed descriptions of the kinds of criteria we hope our students employ during the process of reflection (technical, educational, ethical), to statements of the specific characteristics and qualities of the teachers we hope to prepare.

This continual evolution of the program in response to experience and research is probably its most important characteristic. There is no more important need for an inquiry-oriented program than to model the processes of self-directed growth and continuing self-renewal that it seeks to engender in its students. If an inquiry-oriented program is to be successful in meeting its goals, then its staff, curriculum, and institutional environment must express these qualities of reflectiveness and self-renewal.

Commonplaces of Teaching

The educational platform of this program can be summarized by employing Schwab's (1978) heuristic of the "commonplaces of teaching." For teaching to occur, someone (a teacher) must be teaching someone (a student) about something (a curriculum) at some place and some time (a milieu). In the present context, school- and university-based *teacher educators* (teachers) work with *student teachers* (students) in *university and school classrooms* (milieu) teaching a curriculum that is concerned with both the student teacher's *teaching* and with the various *contexts* in which the teaching is embedded (curriculum). Each of the four commonplaces can be described along a continuum of alternatives and the program's platform can be identified in relation to each commonplace.

Students

First, with regard to the commonplace of students, the program seeks to prepare students of teaching who view knowledge and situations as problematic and socially constructed rather than as certain. Here the concern is with the degree to which student teachers view the knowledge which is taught in the program itself and the knowledge which is appropriated in student teachers' classrooms as value-governed selections from a larger universe of possibilities. The program is also concerned with the degree to which students treat the institutional form and social contexts of teacher education and schooling as problematic.

These students would also view the role of teacher as one of moral craftsperson (Tom, 1984) rather than as one of simply craftsperson or of technician. These three conceptions of the teacher's role are analogous to Van Manen's (1977) three levels of reflectivity. The teacher as technician would be concerned primarily with the successful accomplishment of ends decided by others. The craftsperson teacher would consider the educational justification for classroom actions and how well the educational goals are being accomplished. The teacher as moral craftsperson would also be concerned with the moral and ethical implications of his or her actions and with the moral and ethical implications of particular institutional arrangements.

Curriculum

Second, the curriculum of the program should reflect in its form and content a view of knowledge as socially constructed rather than as certain. This requires a curriculum for student teaching that is reflexive rather than received. The dimension of received-reflexive (Eggleston, 1977) refers to the degree to which the curriculum of a program is specified in advance. On the one hand, a curriculum that follows a received perspective presents knowledge with the intent that student teachers accept it as predominantly non-negotiable. Student teachers are to be relatively passive recipients of that which is imparted, whether the source is the wisdom of experienced practitioners or the latest findings of research on teaching. On the other hand, a reflexive curriculum does not totally predetermine that which is to be learned but makes provisions for the self-determined needs and concerns of student teachers as well as the creation of personal meaning by students. A reflexive curriculum also includes provisions for the negotiation of content among teachers and learners.

Finally, in terms of the epistemology of the curriculum, the program seeks to draw upon the practical knowledge of student teachers and experienced practitioners, as well as upon insights and concepts generated within the realm of theoretical knowledge. The flow of knowledge is in both directions. For example, it is common practice for student teachers in their seminars to read papers that clarify the goals of reflective teaching and then to discuss, analyze, and evaluate this programmatic goal. Attempts are made to bring the conceptual basis of the program into focus and to provide diverse conceptual frameworks for analyzing the work of the teacher. These frameworks are then employed by student teachers to analyze, understand, and evaluate their practical situations. The student teachers are not passive in this process. They are encouraged actively to respond to and criticize the concepts that underlie the program and the frameworks introduced in seminars to help them examine their situations. They use the conceptual tools to understand and alter their actions in the classroom and in turn to react to the usefulness of the concepts for helping them analyze and interpret their situations. As Shulman (1984) points out, "a danger intrinsic to such examinations is dogmatic dominance of the examination by a single principle or point of view." Deliberate efforts are made by supervisors in the program to establish an interaction between the theoretical and the practical, such that both the concepts and the practical experience of the students gain "richness and clarity from the incursion of the other" (p. 185).

A third characteristic of the curriculum of the program is its relatively broad scope. As will be described below, the curriculum is concerned with teaching in its broadest sense (for example, with the teacher as curriculum developer) as well as with inquiry about teaching and its contexts. It thus stands in opposition to those programs concerned primarily with the teacher's instructional role within a classroom and with the reproduction of valued teaching behaviors (for example, an apprenticeship).

Milieu

The milieu of the program should be *inquiry oriented* rather than "traditional" in relation to the authority relationships which exist between student teachers and teacher educators. According to McIntosh (1968), a traditional environment for clinical education is one that places a high value on "precision in following orders" and does not provide students with opportunities for independent decisionmaking with regard to their own education and that of their pupils. Alternatively, an inquiry environment elicits and rewards initiative and critical thought at all levels of the organization and provides students with opportunities for independent decisionmaking with regard to their education and teaching. Thus, in an inquiry environment, authority relations are more collaborative than in a traditional environment, and attempts are made to break down some of the rigid hierarchical lines which typify traditional programs.

A second characteristic of the milieu of this program is its intent to be self-renewing. Both students and teachers in the program should continually reexamine its curriculum, organization, pedagogy, and authority relationships, and work toward ongoing improvement of the program based on knowledge gained from experience and research or evaluation. The alternative to a self-renewing program is one that remains static and fixed, whatever its orientation, and closed to further growth and revision.

Teachers

Finally, the school- and university-based teacher educators in the program should ideally be living models of the moral craftsperson teacher. These teacher educators' views of knowledge and institutional contexts, as well as of the curriculum and environment in their seminars and supervision, should reflect the biases and emphases identified above. Figure 1 summarizes the characteristics of the program in relation to the four commonplaces.

The Instructional Plan: Program Organization and Curricular Components

The elementary student-teaching program at the University of Wisconsin, Madison, is the final stage in a four-semester sequence of professional education courses leading to certification in one or more of the following areas: kindergarten, grades 1–8, and bilingual education. The required sequence of professional education courses follows two years of course work outside of the School of Education (including a 12–credit area of concentration) and includes an introductory course in elementary education; methods courses in reading and language arts which are integrated with an 80–hour field experience; methods courses in mathematics, science, and social studies which are integrated with a second 80–hour field experience; and a supervised student teaching experience which includes a weekly campus seminar.

FIGURE 1

Aims of the Elementary Student Teaching Program in Relation to the Four Commonplaces of Teaching

		Desired Aims	*As Opposed to:*
Students	View knowledge and situations as	Problematic	Certain
	View the teacher role as	Moral craftsperson	Technical craftsperson
Curriculum	Form	Reflexive	Received
	Epistemology	Practical knowledge Theoretical knowledge	Theoretical knowledge only
	Scope	Broad (teaching and inquiry components)	Narrow (apprenticeship)
Milieu	Authority relationships	Inquiry-oriented	Hierarchical
		Self-renewing	Static
Teachers		Moral craftspersons	Technical craftspersons
		Self-renewing	Static

Additionally, students select from a variety of courses in educational psychology and educational policy studies, and must complete four required methods courses in the creative and performing arts, a course in mainstreaming, and a course in health information for teachers. By the time students enter the student teaching program, they have completed 27 credits of methods courses in various content areas and 160 hours of field experience in elementary and middle/junior high school classrooms. This program is typical of programs for the preparation of elementary school teachers in the United States (Zeichner, 1985a) in terms of its balance between general and professional education, its emphasis on content-specific rather than general methods courses, and its use of student teaching as the final step in a series of planned field experiences in K–8 classrooms.

During the student teaching semester, each elementary education major spends four-and-one-half days per week in one or more public or private school classrooms for an entire university semester (approximately 15 weeks) and approximately two hours per week in a required campus seminar (Seminar in Elementary Classroom Teaching). Preschool and kindergarten majors spend four or five half-days per week in a kindergarten classroom for a full university semester and two hours per week in the required campus seminar. Each student teacher is visited by a university supervisor (a graduate student in the Department of Curriculum and Instruction) at least six times per semester with at least five visits including an observation of the student's teaching and at least one follow-up conference.

Consistent with the program's intent to establish an "inquiry-environment" which elicits and rewards initiative and critical thought at all levels of the organization and which gives students choices with regard to tasks they do and how they do them (McIntosh, 1968), student teachers actively participate in the selection of their placement sites. During the semester prior to student teaching, each student observes and meets with at least two potential cooperating teachers who are assigned to students from a list of teachers approved by the program directors. These observations and discussions occur after an initial interview with university personnel in which students are asked to articulate their perspectives toward teaching and their preferences for a placement site. Students and teachers are required to reach mutual agreement regarding a "match" before a final placement is assigned.

Teaching

Five curricular components comprise the student-teaching program. First, a teaching component ensures the exposure of student teachers to all aspects of the teacher's role in and out of the classroom. As in most programs, over the course of the semester each student teacher is expected gradually to assume responsibility for all aspects of the classroom teacher's role (for example, instruction, classroom management, curriculum development, and pupil evaluation) and to take full responsibility for the classroom program for a minimum of two weeks.

Although most student teaching programs include this same notion of increasing responsibility for a classroom, the focus is frequently on instruction and classroom management and does not always include the student teacher's responsible participation in other aspects of the teachers' role, such as curriculum development and pupil evaluation. The program under discussion particularly emphasizes the student teachers' role in curriculum development and the concept of the teacher as a "user-developer" of curriculum — one who is both aware of critical choice points in curriculum development and who is skilled in curriculum development (Ben-Peretz, 1984). Although student teachers are expected generally to follow the curriculum guidelines of their schools and the curricular programs in their classrooms, they are also expected to be aware of and be able to articulate the assumptions embedded in curricula that are adopted with little or no modification (assumptions about learners and the role of the teacher); to show evidence of adapting and modifying curricular plans and materials for specific situations; and to make original contributions to the classroom program by creating new and varied instructional activities and materials beyond those specified in a given set of materials.

Consistent with a view of the program's curriculum as "reflexive" rather than as "received," all of the specific requirements for student teachers relating to their increasing responsibility for the teacher's role are negotiated by the student teacher, cooperating teacher, and university supervisor. During the first few weeks of the semester a formal contract, or "Letter of Expectations," is drawn up in order to delineate the specific experiences that each student is expected to have during the semester in relation to all aspects of the teacher's role (Grant, 1975). This "letter," which is periodically revised throughout the semester, is used to monitor the student teacher's progress in assuming responsibility and provides, in part, the criteria employed to assess the student teacher's work.

Inquiry

Second, an inquiry component seeks to help students situate schools, curricula, and pedagogy within their socio-historical contexts; to emphasize the socially constructed nature of school knowledge and of schools; and to assist students in becoming more proficient at skills of inquiry. Somewhat more specifically, this component is intended to promote student teachers' understanding of the contemporary cultures of their classrooms and schools, of the relationships between these educational contexts and the surrounding social, economic, and political milieux, and of the historical development of these settings. The goal of this component is to have the classroom and school serve as social laboratories for study rather than as merely models for practice. It seeks to reinforce the view that student teaching is a time for continued learning about teaching and schooling and for establishing pedagogical habits of self-directed growth, rather than a time merely for the application and demonstration of previously acquired knowledge and skills. It also seeks to reinforce the view that teachers can be creators as well as consumers of educational knowledge.

There are several different elements in the inquiry component of the program. First, all students are required to complete at least three observations outside of their "home" classrooms. These observations, which at times may include the viewing of protocol materials rather than live classrooms, are structured for particular purposes by each supervisor and are analyzed and discussed either by the group during a seminar session or by each student individually in writing. These observations have been used by supervisors to accomplish a wide variety of purposes, including: (1) having students compare different general approaches to teaching at a given grade level; (2) having students examine different approaches to teaching in a given content area; and (3) helping students analyze the theories-in-use evident in particular kinds of classrooms.

In addition to carrying out these classroom observations, all students complete at least one of the following: an *action research project*, an *ethnographic study*, or a *curriculum analysis project*. Although each supervisor is given some leeway in how to approach this component, all supervisors develop assignments for student teachers that require the utilization of at least one of these approaches.

The action research projects completed by student teachers involve the adaptation of a framework for conducting classroom action research developed at Deakin University in Australia (Kemmis & McTaggart, 1982). This framework includes the following stages: reconnaissance, planning, acting, observing, and reflecting. Projects are written up by students and shared in the seminar groups. Some students have experimented in the classroom with different grouping strategies in order to assess their effects on maintaining pupil involvement; for example, some have examined a student teacher's behavior toward high- and low-ability groups in reading, while other student projects involved experimentation with different teaching methods. These included an automatic reading program designed to supplement a basal program, and a math program, based primarily on concrete and manipulative materials, for pupils showing little success with the standard math curriculum. Many of these projects were planned collaboratively and carried out by student teachers and other staff in their schools.

One alternative to classroom action-research projects in some of the seminar sections requires students to conduct limited ethnographic studies in their classrooms, schools, and school communities. These projects, examples of which are discussed in some detail in Zeichner and Teitelbaum (1982) and in Gitlin and Teitelbaum (1983), have focused on such topics as studies of the allocation of resources among students of varying abilities and backgrounds, studies of school from the pupil's perspective, examinations of types of questions asked in different classrooms, and examinations of the implications of the language used by school staff.

A final option for the inquiry component in some of the seminar sections is for students to conduct analyses of school curricula and of the processes of curriculum development in the settings in which they work. In addition to projects which examine the values and assumptions embedded in particular curriculum materials and programs (for example, assumptions about learners and teachers, resolutions of particular "dilemmas" of schooling), students have conducted studies of the history and context of curriculum development in their settings in particular content areas. Here students address such questions as who made particular decisions about the curriculum, why certain decisions were made, and how particular institutional factors affected the processes of curriculum development.

The variety of action research, ethnographic studies, and curriculum analysis projects completed by students in the program is very great, but *all* student teachers are required to spend at least a portion of their time in schools formally studying and conducting inquiries related to their practices as teachers and to the settings in which they work. An important element of the inquiry component is the preparation that students receive for conducting their school-based inquiries. In each of the seminar groups some time is spent helping the students to master the tools they will need successfully to carry out an inquiry project. Students are evaluated during the semester on the quality of these inquiries as well as on the quality of their classroom teaching.

Seminars

The student-teaching seminar is the third component of the program and is taught by the university supervisor. The content of each seminar is planned by the supervisor and students in each group within a set of broad program parameters, and most of the assignments that students complete are linked in some way to the students' current classroom experiences. While this course is related to, and in fact builds upon, the students' classroom experiences, it is not intended to provide students with specific methods and techniques for direct application to specific classrooms; nor is it to serve as a forum for the discussion of only classroom-specific experiences. The seminar is designed to help students broaden their perspectives on teaching, consider the rationales underlying alternative possibilities for classrooms and pedagogy, and assess their own developing perspectives toward teaching.

One current emphasis in several of the seminar sections is to have students employ Berlak and Berlak's (1981) "Language of Dilemmas" in the analysis of their own perspectives toward teaching and the teaching of others (Hursh & Zeichner,

1984). Another theme in several of the seminar sections concerns the critical assessment of educational research. Students read and critique studies that present different points of view on selected topics (for example, studies on classroom management or ability grouping) and then discuss the implications of the studies for their own development as teachers. Participants in all of the seminars attempt to establish a collaborative approach to problem solving and inquiry; students are frequently encouraged to conduct collaborative projects and to make joint presentations to their seminar groups. (For a more detailed account of the structure and content of the student teaching seminar, see Zeichner, 1981.)

Journals

Additionally, student teachers are required to keep a journal according to a specific set of guidelines provided by their supervisors. These journals, which record students' development over the semester, are shared on a regular basis with the supervisors, who respond in writing to student teacher entries. The journals are intended to provide the supervisors with information about the ways in which their students think about their teaching and about their development as teachers, with information about classroom, school, and community contexts; as well as to provide student teachers with a vehicle for systematic reflection on their development as teachers and on their actions in classroom and work contexts. The journals are viewed as an integral part of the supervisory process.

Supervisory Conferences

Finally, the supervisory conferences that follow the formal observations of student teachers are considered to be an important learning context for student teachers and an opportunity for supervisors to raise issues related to specific actions and settings which have been considered at a more general level in the seminars. These conferences focus on both the classroom lessons that have been observed and the more general development of student teacher perspectives over the course of the semester.

The form of supervision employed in the program is similar to the dominant model of "clinical supervision" (Goldhammer, Anderson, & Krajewski, 1980) in its structure and its emphasis on the "rational analysis" of classroom instruction. Each visit by a university supervisor, for example, includes a preconference, observation, analysis and strategy, and a postconference. During the observation supervisors compile detailed narrative notes which are used to document patterns and critical incidents in classroom instruction. Supervision in this program departs from the "clinical" model, however, in the following ways:

1. In addition to focusing on observable behaviors, supervision includes analysis and consideration of student teacher intentions and beliefs. Moreover, it emphasizes the analysis of relationships between intentions and the theoretical commitments which are embedded in classroom actions.
2. Since the supervisor seeks to develop the rational analysis of teaching at all three levels of reflection described above, the institutional form and social context of teaching are frequently viewed as problematic and as legitimate topics for analysis.

3. The supervisor gives explicit attention to the content of what is taught in addition to analyzing teaching processes (for example, direct and indirect behaviors). Questions related to the justification of particular content for specific groups of children are of primary concern.
4. The supervision goes beyond consideration of whether or not the student teachers' objectives have been achieved, and places an emphasis on the analysis of unanticipated outcomes and the "hidden curriculum" of the classroom. Here the concern is with understanding those dispositions and attitudes which are fostered (often as "side effects") by particular forms of curriculum, classroom social relations, and instructional practices.

While none of these elements are necessarily excluded from the "clinical" model,[4] the model does not make explicit commitments to particular kinds of rational analysis, nor are commitments made regarding the necessity of addressing instructional content, the "hidden curriculum," or the relationships between student teacher intent and the theoretical commitments embedded in their actions. Thus, while the model of supervision employed in this program can be viewed as consistent with the clinical form, it is shaped to reflect the conceptual·orientation of the program and to imbue the supervisory process with a spirit of "critical inquiry" (Smyth, 1983). Figure 2 summarizes the five components which make up the curricular substance of the student teaching program.

As is the case in most student teaching programs, adopting the teaching role occupies most of the students' time. The critical difference between this program and many others lies in two areas: (1) its relatively broad definition of the teaching role, with its particular emphasis on curriculum development; and (2) the way in which various program components encourage student teachers to employ technical, educational, and ethical criteria in order to reflect systematically about their development as teachers, their actions in the classrooms, and the contexts in which their classroom actions are embedded. All of the various program components are designed to help students learn from their experiences as student teachers and to develop habits of self-directed growth, but the program also seeks to help students overcome the limits of first-hand experience (Buchmann & Schwille, 1983) through utilization of various conceptual tools and skills of inquiry which can help them see beyond the immediate circumstances of their situation.

Studies of the Program's Curriculum-in-Use

A number of studies have focused on Wisconsin's inquiry-oriented elementary education student teaching program. The research includes analyses of the effects of student teaching on student teachers' perspectives toward teaching, examinations of the degree of emphasis placed by student teachers on a view of education

---

[4] Although some advocates of "clinical supervision" include elements in their interpretations of the model which are similar to the emphasis in the Wisconsin program (for example, Sergiovanni, 1976), most of the literature either makes some commitments which are in conflict with the goals of this program (for example, Cogan, 1973) or is not specific with regard to the quality of rational analysis which is to be promoted through use of the model. See Zeichner and Tabachnick (1981) and Zeichner and Liston (1985) for further discussion of this issue.

FIGURE 2
Curricular Components of the Elementary Student Teaching Program

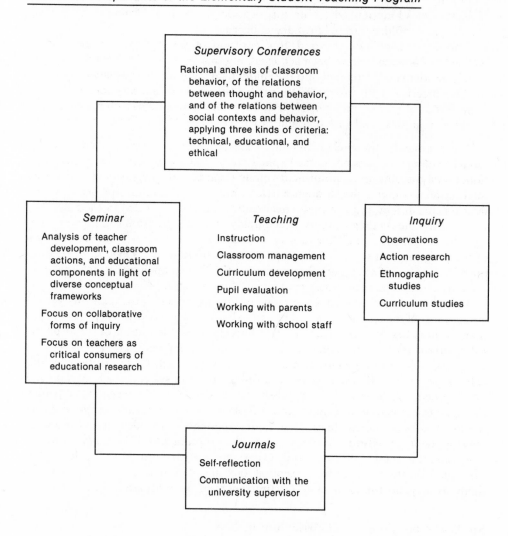

as multicultural, and studies of the university supervisors' perspectives and actions. The studies tend to focus on whether student teachers perceive themselves as technicians, craftspersons, or moral craftspersons; whether student teachers view their contexts and the program's curricula as problematic or certain; and the role that supervisors play in this process. If the program achieved all of its goals, students would perceive themselves as moral craftspersons and view both the curricula and their contexts as problematic. The results show, as might be expected, that the program achieves some but not all of its goals.

Two studies specifically examine the effect of the student teaching experience on the development of student teachers' perspectives toward teaching. Tabachnick and Zeichner (1984) report the results of a study which examined the development of student teachers' perspectives toward knowledge and curriculum, student diversity, teacher-pupil relationships, and the teacher role. They also attempted to identify the relative contribution of personal and institutional factors to this development. They found that student teachers entered the program "with different teaching perspectives and that significant differences among students remained at the end of the semester" (p. 33). Student teaching did not significantly alter the student teachers' views about teaching. Instead, after the semester-long experience, students, for the most part, became more skillful in articulating and implementing the perspectives that they possessed in less developed forms at the beginning of the experience. Ten of the thirteen student teachers studied followed this pattern. The other three student teachers appeared to comply with the demands of their student-teaching situation but maintained strong, private reservations about these demands. The perspectives of these three student teachers did not develop over the semester. Generally, it can be said that if students entered the program with what we would consider a technical- or moral-craft outlook toward the teacher's role, they left at the end of their student teaching experience with essentially the same perspective, albeit a more refined one.

In a second study reported by Zeichner and Grant (1981), a similar finding was noted. Using Hoy and Rees's (1977) pupil-control ideology construct, Zeichner and Grant examined whether student teachers became more custodial toward pupils during the semester, and whether the orientation of the cooperating teacher had any influence on the student teacher's development. They identified one group of student teachers whose views on pupil control were more humanistic than those of their cooperating teachers and another group whose initial views were more custodial than those of their cooperating teachers. At the end of the student-teaching semester, Zeichner and Grant found that "although the pupil-control ideologies of student teachers in both groups were initially significantly different from the pupil-control ideologies of their cooperating teachers, neither group of students altered their views on pupil control by the end of the experience" (p. 305).

Both Tabachnick and Zeichner's (1984) and Zeichner and Grant's (1981) studies are subject to interpretation in a number of ways, but at least two interpretations stand out. On the one hand, these studies show that this inquiry-oriented student teaching program had little effect on student teachers' perspectives toward teaching. Students came into the program with initial perspectives and beliefs about the role of the teacher and the curriculum, and left with those same beliefs essentially intact. The program did not foster the development of teachers who viewed themselves as moral craftspersons. On the other hand, some studies of the student-teaching experience show a significant change from an initially humanistic orientation to a custodial view toward the tasks of teaching (Zeichner, 1980). Given this frequently noted shift toward a more custodial orientation, it could be argued that both Wisconsin studies indicate that the inquiry-oriented student teaching program stems the onrushing move toward a more custodial view. Yet, still another position is possible. It may be that the effects of the student teaching experience are not apparent during or at the end of student teaching. If this is the case, there is a need for longitudinal studies that follow student teachers into their early years of teaching. One such longitudinal study suggests that student teachers who leave the experience with a craft perspective maintain that perspective through the first year of their teaching under certain conditions (Tabachnick & Zeichner, 1985; Zeichner & Tabachnick, 1985). If an inquiry-oriented student teaching program is to be effective, it seems reasonable to expect its impact to endure beyond student teaching. Clearly, further longitudinal studies to illuminate these issues are in order.

In a second set of studies by Grant (1981) and Grant and Koskela (1985), the authors evaluate the degree to which the preservice teacher education students encounter and then implement a view of education that is multicultural (EMC). These studies provide one avenue to assess whether or not instructors provide and student teachers receive a view of the teacher as a moral craftsperson. In a program that presents a perspective on education that is multicultural, the craft and moral emphases are highlighted when students are encouraged to alter existing curricula to provide for cultural differences and to recognize and rectify the injustices connected to these differences. The perspective of EMC differs from the notion of multicultural education. In EMC, teachers recognize the role schools play in furthering the inequalities and injustices of current society and infuse the entire curriculum with a respect for cultural diversity. In a standard multicultural approach, the role of schooling in reproducing inequalities and injustices is not emphasized, and the multicultural curricular units are viewed as additions to an already established "standard" curriculum.

In the initial study by Grant (1981) and the later replication by Grant and Koskela (1985), the authors report findings which identify how the EMC concept was received and implemented at various stages of the elementary education program. In both studies the findings are essentially the same. Grant and Koskela (1985) report that "student teachers attempted and accomplished very little EMC" (p. 14). Grant and Koskela's assessment is based on observational data and the self-reported activities of eleven student teachers. When these student teachers were asked if they did "anything to affirm or implement EMC" in their classrooms during student teaching, seven responded positively (p. 13). Although these seven students reported being engaged in units on Mexico, discussions of sex roles, or designing a bulletin board for International Day, given the definition of EMC, such activities do not represent attempts to implement education that is multicultural. Rather, they serve as additions to a preexisting curriculum. Essentially, Grant (1981) and Grant and Koskela (1985) found little evidence of any attempt during student teaching to implement a view of education that is multicultural.

If retaining and implementing a view of EMC is one aspect of the moral craftsperson outlook, it might be concluded that the student teaching program fails to emphasize it. It could be argued, however, that both the multicultural approach and the view of education that is multicultural represent alternative routes for the morally oriented craftsperson. And, in addition to these two alternatives, other avenues exist. What these two studies do show is that one route, the EMC approach, is presented to students in an initial course in their preservice education program but that it is not implemented during their student teaching.

In studies by Zeichner and Tabachnick (1982) and Zeichner and Liston (1985) the emphasis is on the supervisory aspect of the program. Zeichner and Tabachnick (1982) analyze the various ways supervisors in the inquiry-oriented program gave meaning to their work with student teachers. The authors indicate that the programmatic emphasis on reflective teaching exerted pressures upon supervisors to raise particular kinds of questions — such as, Why are you doing what you are doing with your children? — and to encourage their student teachers to evaluate classroom practices in terms of moral criteria rather than solely in terms of technical criteria. Nevertheless, they found that supervisors implemented the student teaching program goals in various ways. Out of the nine supervisors studied, the authors characterized three as emphasizing a technical-instrumental point of view, four others as utilizing a personal-growth-centered approach, and the remaining two as practicing a critical perspective. Briefly, the technical-instrumental approach focused on the practices and techniques of teaching that enabled the student teacher to transmit an "approved" curriculum to the students in a creative manner. The personal-growth-centered orientation encouraged the development of the student teacher's chosen goals and an emphasis on the educational rationales for actions within the classroom. The critical perspective emphasized the discovery of linkages between the actions in the classroom and institutional characteristics, as well as between classroom behavior and the social forces in the community; moreover, it focused on the use of moral criteria to evaluate classroom action. While all of the supervisors were identified as basically utilizing one of these approaches, Zeichner and Tabachnick (1982) noted that each supervisor employed aspects of all three.

In Zeichner and Liston's (1985) study, the authors assessed the degree of congruence between the expressed goals of the program and the quality of discourse between university supervisors and student teachers in post-observation conferences. The authors distinguished four types of discourse: factual, prudential, justificatory, and critical. In short, factual discourse is concerned with what occurred in a teaching situation or with what will occur in the future. Prudential discourse revolves around suggestions of what to do or evaluations of what has been accomplished. Justificatory discourse focuses on the reasons employed when answering questions of the form, Why do this rather than that? And critical discourse assesses the adequacy of justifications offered for pedagogical activities and examines the values and assumptions embedded in the content of the curriculum and instructional practices. From these categories a reflective teaching index (RTI) was constructed to represent the proportion of discourse most closely related to the program's goals. Using this index, the authors attempted to assess the degree to which the program's reflective orientation was present in conferences between supervisors and student teachers. They found, that of the total 260 minutes of discourse analyzed, 19.6 percent represented attention to reflective forms of communication. Furthermore, they found that the student teachers' conceptual levels appeared to affect the degree of reflective discourse occurring in supervisory conferences. The higher the student teacher's conceptual level, the more often reflective discourse occurred. This finding likely reflects the supervisors' attempts to respond to the cognitive levels of the student teachers. Thus, the student teachers appeared to have a "pulling effect" on the level of discourse occurring in post-observation supervisory conferences.

In both the Zeichner and Tabachnick (1982) and the Zeichner and Liston (1985) studies, it is difficult to determine whether or not the results indicate successful implementation of the program's goals. Without a sound basis for comparison, the interpretations are highly tentative. A few comments, however, can be made. Zeichner and Tabachnick's finding, that of nine supervisors only three employed the technical-instrumental approach, seems positive. Given the conventional emphasis on technical orientations in supervision, this finding suggests a move toward the program's reflective orientation. (Furthermore, as noted earlier, even these three supervisors employed practices associated with the other two orientations.) Zeichner and Liston's report of an RTI of 19.6 percent also appears to reflect a partial implementation of the program's goals. In fact, the authors were surprised by the frequency of reflective discourse. It seems that discussions analyzing the educational rationales for classroom practices could be perceived as "threats" by the cooperating teacher. Supervisors might prefer to leave aside such questions in order to avoid conflict and maintain smooth relationships with school staff. Additional data from a program at another university with a more conventional student teaching program are now being analyzed so as to achieve a better understanding of these findings.

A summary of the pertinent research must also include two other works: Koskela's (1985) study of reflective communication in two student teaching seminar groups and Ullrich's (1985) analysis of student teachers' psychosocial development in an inquiry-oriented program. Koskela's research employs the case study method and examines the presence and effects of reflective communication during student teaching seminars. She defines reflective communication as statements indicating the presence of critical thinking or problem solving, the attitudes of open-mindedness, wholeheartedness, or responsibility, and the skills used for self-analysis. Koskela found that reflective communication occurred during the student teaching seminar and was encouraged by it; moreover, she found that the degree of reflective communication varied within single seminar groups of student teachers over time and between seminar groups. What is most striking about her study, however, are the cases illustrating reflective communication. During one of the observed seminar meetings, a curriculum coordinator responded to the student teachers' questions and concerns about their schools and classrooms. The student teachers had asked about the use of worksheets and had spoken of teacher frustration and student boredom. One result of this meeting was that the curriculum coordinator began questioning teachers about curricular policies and practices which, in turn, stimulated discussions among teachers in the school. Also, as a result of this meeting and the resulting communication, Koskela indicates, one student observed that "institutions could change," individuals could initiate those changes, and, as a result of this process, teachers and student teachers could change their practices in the classroom. Although this type of discussion and related action were not evident in all of the seminar sessions studied, there appears to be some indication that as a result of their seminar, student teachers viewed their school contexts as problematic.

Ullrich's (1985) study concerns an analysis of student teachers' psychosocial development in the Wisconsin inquiry-oriented student teaching program. Specifically, Ullrich investigated whether an experimental small-group-oriented seminar would encourage student teachers to define and act collaboratively on issues of authority and autonomy within the small group. Although his results are tentative,

Ullrich's analysis indicates that none of the seven student teachers who were studied acted in a collaborative manner to define or resolve these issues. Instead, students acted in an individualistic manner and withdrew from discussions related to authority and autonomy. For our purposes, Ullrich's findings indicate that the inquiry-oriented student teaching program may need to pay more attention to collaborative interaction. However, since Ullrich's seminar was atypical in that it focused on the dynamics of small-group interaction, his findings may have limited applicability.

In summary, the research examining Wisconsin's inquiry-oriented elementary education student teaching program has focused on student teachers' views of the teacher's role, on student teachers' understanding of their contexts and the program's curricula, and on the role that the supervisors and seminars play in the education of student teachers. The program attempts to educate student teachers in a reflective manner: to view their knowledge and their contexts as problematic; to view the teacher as a moral craftsperson; to approach the knowledge offered in the program reflexively; and to interact with their fellow student teachers, instructors, and supervisors in a collaborative fashion. There is some evidence that the program encourages students to view their student-teaching context as problematic (Koskela, 1985; Zeichner & Liston, 1985), to see teachers as moral craftspersons (Zeichner & Liston, 1985), and to clarify their own chosen perspectives concerning the teacher's role (Tabachnick & Zeichner, 1984; Zeichner & Grant, 1981). There is also some indication that the program may need to encourage more collaborative interactions among the participants (Ullrich, 1985), and that certain views of the moral craftsperson are not implemented (Grant, 1981; Grant & Koskela, 1985). While these findings may be of some use and interest to the larger teacher-education community, they also provide information and feedback for the program's participants. The program's coordinators, supervisors, and student teachers have examined aspects of these studies and, as a result, have altered certain practices.

Factors Impeding the Realization of the Program's Goals

Although the studies described above do not provide a complete picture of how successful the program has been in accomplishing its goals, it is still possible to speculate on the variety of material and ideological constraints, both within and outside of the program, which "work against" the program's stated aspirations. Although gaps between program rhetoric and reality are an inevitable consequence of the complexity and inherent uncertainty of human affairs (Tabachnick, 1981), it is important for teacher educators to examine the ways in which their own situations influence the character of their programs. This is especially important when a program seeks to encourage "reflective teaching." We will now examine a number of individual and structural factors at three different levels which we feel need to be addressed more adequately in the future.

First, within the student teaching program itself, the historically dominant and commonsense view of student teaching as an exercise in apprenticeship (Stones, 1984) has made it difficult for program personnel to establish the legitimacy of inquiry and reflection within the student teaching program. Efforts have been made to work closely with cooperating school personnel to build an acceptance of, involvement with, and support for the more unconventional aspects of the program. Much time has been spent in justifying and establishing the legitimacy of reflective teaching. And yet, despite these efforts, the commonsense view of student teaching as a time for the "final" demonstration of previously learned instructional skills, together with students' understandable desire to create favorable impressions of their instructional competence in "the here and now" (Haas & Shaffir, 1982), have served to undermine, to some degree, the program's concerns with inquiry and reflection.

Several strategies have been employed to reduce the still prevalent attitude among student teachers that time spent on inquiry and reflection is time "taken away from" the more important tasks of applying and demonstrating knowledge and skills. For example, the inquiry assignments are coordinated with students' gradual assumption of the teaching role in a way which seeks to minimize pressures on students and to maximize the chances for the acceptance of what are not typically viewed as legitimate concerns for student teachers. Specifically, the inquiry assignments are typically heaviest toward the beginning of the semester, when students' teaching responsibilities are the lightest, and then gradually taper off as students assume more and more responsibility for the teaching role.

Deliberate efforts have also been made to include the quality of inquiry and reflection as part of the criteria by which students are evaluated, and to conduct the supervision of students in a manner that encourages and reinforces a reflective orientation to the teaching role. Despite these and other efforts to legitimize inquiry and reflection by student teachers, some student teachers and cooperating teachers still do not actively support these unconventional goals for student teaching and exert various pressures to focus the attention of program participants upon the more narrow concerns characteristic of an apprenticeship. Although much progress has been made over the years in generating more active support from both students and cooperating teachers for these goals (for example, by introducing the concept of reflective teaching in the program's courses and by including discussion of this broader view of student teaching in courses and workshops for cooperating teachers and in school advisory group meetings), the problem of expectations for an apprenticeship still persists.

One possible reason for the continued resistance of some student teachers to devoting serious attention to reflection and inquiry is that when students' total life experiences as pupils and as citizens in our culture are taken into account, the student teaching experience represents a very small portion of their formal preparation for teaching and an even smaller part of their socialization to teaching. There is little doubt that students' experiences outside the boundaries of formal programs exert a great deal of influence on their dispositions toward the teaching role and toward schooling (Feiman-Nemser, 1983). Although students within this program are bright, articulate, and for the most part do not fit the characterizations of teacher education students recently portrayed in the national media (see University of Wisconsin System, 1984), they do not enroll in the Wisconsin program because of its expressed emphasis on reflective teaching. Indeed, prior to student teaching, they have had relatively little experience with the kinds of reasoned analysis and problematic stance toward practice that are emphasized in the program.

Our experience has taught us that much unlearning has to go on before most students are willing to accept the need for a more reflective approach to teaching. The time devoted to this task, within a 15–week semester, may be far too brief to overcome the influence of prior experience and commonly-held expectations regarding the purposes of student teaching.

Another factor which has served to obstruct the realization of program goals is the ways in which the roles of university supervisor and cooperating teacher have been structured. For example, although a supervisor visits each of his or her students on the average of once every other week and has weekly contact with all of his or her students in the seminar, the provisions made in the program for supervisor-student contact are far fewer than those which are necessary to accomplish the ambitious goals set for supervisors. The limited resources allocated to the program, which reflect the relatively low status of clinical teacher education within a university context (Clark & Marker, 1975), lead to heavy workloads for supervisors (who are also full-time graduate students). This serves to make it difficult for supervisors to develop and nurture the kinds of relationships with their students which are needed for the accomplishment of their goals.

The problem is clearly a result of much more than the heavy workloads of supervisors (see Diamonti & Diamonti, 1975; Diorio, 1982). The limited contact between supervisors and student teachers, as well as the lack of formal authority supervisors and students have over the curricular and instructional practices in the student teachers' classrooms, inhibit student teachers from raising the kinds of questions about classroom and school routines which the program seeks to encourage. It is true that some cooperating teachers actively encourage students to question the reasons and rationales for educational practices and provide opportunities for students to create and implement materials and practices which go beyond the routine. Given the formal authority relationships between student teachers and cooperating teachers, however, student teachers are not encouraged to question classroom practices or to implement alternative approaches. For example, although the intent of inquiry and reflection is not to have students criticize particular teachers and their motives, discussions of the rationales for particular classroom practices and of the strengths and limitations of teachers' choices can be seen as potential threats to cooperating teachers, who are ultimately responsible for all that goes on in their classrooms.

Additionally, the supervisors in the program are graduate students in the Department of Curriculum and Instruction who spend anywhere from one to five years working in the program. From our experience, it takes a few semesters to prepare supervisors to work in a program such as this, and particularly for them to develop the expertise to be effective in implementing the inquiry and reflective aspects of the program. Frequently, as soon as supervisors have begun to make sufficient progress in the development of supervisory and pedagogical strategies, they leave, and work must begin to prepare a new group of individuals for supervisory roles. We have tried to counterbalance the frequent coming and going of university supervisors by attempting to establish a stable corps of cooperating teachers who are supportive of the program's goals, but the transitory nature of the supervisory role on long-term program development has remained a persistent problem.

Structural limitations in the cooperating teacher's role have also served to impede the realization of program goals. Although we have been somewhat successful in generating more active support from cooperating teachers for the goals of inquiry and reflection, and although many cooperating teachers are able to help students analyze the rationales underlying classroom and school routines, teachers assume the role of cooperating teacher in addition to their full responsibility over a classroom of children. Little provision has been made within the program to provide cooperating teachers with the recognition, rewards, time, and reduced teaching loads which are necessary for them to be able to work with student teachers in the way that the program desires. In many of the schools with which we work, little has been done to support cooperating teachers' involvement in inquiry and reflection with regard to their own work as well. To some degree, both student teachers and cooperating teachers work within a set of "ecological" parameters and a structural context which work against the goals of the program.

Another set of constraints comes into view when attention is focused on the elementary teacher preparation program as a whole. The Wisconsin program, as is clearly the case for many programs of its size, can be best characterized by its ideological eclecticism and structural fragmentation (Zeichner, 1985a). Although the goals regarding inquiry and reflection are evident in the intentions of those who work with student teachers and in a few other segments of the program, the program as a whole does not represent a coherent and well-coordinated effort to prepare "reflective teachers" according to a set of commonly agreed upon interpretations of this goal.

Each segment of the program is under the control of different faculty members who, in addition to their affiliation with the program, are also affiliated with one or more disciplinary areas (for example, social studies, education, mathematics). A recently completed external evaluation of the program initiated by the elementary faculty found that there was only limited discussion by faculty, students, and cooperating teachers of the program as a whole and concluded that the lack of coherence in the total program and the lack of attention to the shared enterprise of teacher education across content-area boundaries is a major issue that our faculty needs to address (Perrone et al., 1983). Students experience the program in relation to all of its various parts, but few faculty members who work in the program have an overall perspective on the entire enterprise. Most see themselves as primarily affiliated with a particular program component. Although efforts have been made subsequent to this review to focus more of the faculty's attention on issues related to the program as a whole, the organization of the faculty into disciplinary areas (a desirable attribute in relation to the graduate program) works against the establishment of a coherent and well-coordinated program of teacher education that provides continuity of experience for students.

Finally, when we move from the teacher education program as a whole to consider the teaching roles that our students observe as they spend time in classrooms and schools, both before and during their formal preparation for teaching, another important issue emerges. Specifically, a great deal of inconsistency exists between the role of teacher as professional decisionmaker, a role our program encourages students to assume, and the dominant role of teacher as technician, one our society and its institutions seek to maintain. Numerous analyses of recent policies directed at teachers, conducted from a variety of perspectives, have concluded that the effect of these policies is to promote greater control over the content, processes, and outcomes of the teacher's work and to encourage conformist orientations to self and society, as well as technical orientations to the teacher's role (Apple, 1983; Lanier & Little, 1986; Sykes, 1983; Wise, 1979). While it is clear that many teachers do not passively carry out the directives contained in these "technical controls" (see Zeichner, 1985b), it is also clear that most schools do not actively encourage teachers to engage in the kinds of practices that our student teaching program seeks to promote. To some extent we may be preparing student teachers for a teaching role that does not now exist, or does not have the sanction of the institutions in which teachers now work.

Clements (1975) points out an obvious but important condition of improvement: "We cannot improve teacher education in isolation from the conduct of schooling. Improved teachers must go into existing schools" (p. 164). While there is some evidence that the nature of university undergraduate education as a whole and the university-based components of teacher education contribute to furthering the role of teacher as technician (Lanier & Little, 1986; Zeichner & Tabachnick, 1981),[5] it is also clear that changes in the status, recognition, and responsibilities given teachers must occur before an inquiry-oriented teacher education program will have a chance of making any lasting impact.

Shulman (1983), in his *Handbook of Teaching and Policy*, concludes:

> Papers in this volume . . . have painted poignant portraits of the lives of teachers and their attempts to influence the system in which they work. . . . The conditions of teaching set severe limits on the potential for reform. The descriptions of teaching have helped us to appreciate the strains of the working teacher, the frustrations of the profession that foster burnout, and the even more insidious charring that slowly eats away at a teacher in the performance of her duties. Without an improvement of those conditions or a massive shift in the expectations that make them commonplace, talk of improvements in the teacher education process . . . seems pointless. (p. 502)

Short of fundamental changes in the occupation of teaching and in related social and economic conditions, there is clearly much that can be done to improve the quality of the Wisconsin program and those like it. For example, we at Wisconsin need to do a much better job than heretofore of confronting our own "contexts." More material and moral support must be given to the supervisors and teachers who work with our students. Further attention needs to be paid to creating a more coherent and coordinated professional education component. And we need to work more closely with our colleagues outside of the School of Education so as to provide a greater continuity of experience for our students and the kinds of institutional support and structure which are consistent with our pedagogical goals. Our greatest failure has probably been this lack of attention to the implications of our own institutional milieu and the lack of strategies which seek to alter factors out-

---

[5] See Powell (1976) and Palmer (1985) for accounts of the university's historical role in creating graduate programs that have had the effect of undermining the dignity of the classroom teacher's role.

side of the program's boundaries. Unless these efforts at the university, however, are accompanied by massive and fundamental changes in the conditions of the teacher's work and in the expectations and contexts that make such changes acceptable, we will continue to pedal wildly and go nowhere.

It should be noted that we do not hold an overly romantic view of the benefits to be gained from giving teachers a more central role in the making of classroom, school, and educational policies and more relative autonomy over the content, processes, and actions of their work. We recognize the problematic aspects of the notion of professionalism (for example, Larson, 1977), the complexities of the issue of teacher autonomy (for example, Buswell, 1980; Mohrman, Cooke, & Mohrman, 1978), and the mixed benefits which have been shown to accrue from more democratic decision-making structures within schools and their communities (Duke, Showers, & Imber, 1980). We also recognize that more democratic structures of school governance which accord teachers, individually and collectively, more integral roles in the policy-making process, both within the classroom and beyond, do not even begin to address the concentration of power and authority in "the invisible centers of private power" (such as testing agencies and textbook publishers) whose personnel are neither elected nor accountable to anyone who is elected (Cohen, 1978). Finally, we also recognize that these changes do not directly confront the underlying social and economic causes of our problems (for example, division of labor and resources). The kinds of changes which we are working for within teacher education and schooling clearly represent only a beginning toward what will ultimately be necessary for the creation of a more sane, just, and humane society.

Conclusion

In this paper, we have sketched the goals and concepts undergirding the Wisconsin elementary student teaching program, described aspects of its organizational structure and curricular plan, and summarized findings from eight studies which reveal aspects of the program's curriculum-in-use. We have also noted several of the individual and contextual factors which "work against" the accomplishment of the program's goals. From all of this, we can conclude that some of our goals are achieved rather well, others are only partially achieved, and still others appear to be neglected in practice. We recognize that programmatic gaps, conceptual weaknesses, and internal and external contradictions exist with regard to the program, but we continue to examine, to clarify, and to act toward improving the quality of both theory and practice within the program. For unless we can begin to prepare teachers who are willing to assume more central roles in shaping the direction of their own work and school environments, the kinds of changes which may be on the horizon with regard to the occupation of teaching will continue to maintain the familiar pattern of "change but no change." The preparation of reflective student teachers is a necessary first step for those of us who work in university programs of teacher education.

References

Apple, M. (1983). Curricular form and the logic of technical control: The building of the possessive individual. In M. Apple & L. Weis (Eds.), *Ideology and practice in education* (pp. 143-166). Philadelphia: Temple University Press.

Ben-Peretz, M. (1984). Curriculum theory and practice in teacher education. In L. Katz & J. Raths (Eds.), *Advances in teacher education: Volume 1* (pp. 9-27). Norwood, NJ: Ablex.

Berlak, A., & Berlak, H. (1981). *Dilemmas of schooling: Teaching and social change*. London: Methuen.

Beyer, L., & Zeichner, K. (1982). Teacher education and educational foundations: A plea for discontent. *Journal of Teacher Education, 33*(3), 18-23.

Bowers, C. A. (1984). *The promise of theory: Education and the politics of cultural change*. New York: Longman.

Buchmann, M., & Schwille, J. (1983). Education: The overcoming of experience. *American Journal of Education, 91*, 30-51.

Buswell, C. (1980). Pedagogic change and social change. *British Journal of Sociology of Education, 1*, 193-206.

Clark, D., & Marker, G. (1975). The institutionalization of teacher education. In K. Ryan (Ed.), *Teacher education* (pp. 53-86). Chicago: University of Chicago Press.

Clements, M. (1975). Alternatives in teacher education. *Curriculum Theory Network, 5*, 161-167.

Cogan, M. (1973). *Clinical supervision*. Boston: Houghton Mifflin.

Cohen, D. (1978). Reforming school politics. *Harvard Educational Review, 48*, 429-447.

Dewey, J. (1933). *How we think*. Chicago: Regnery.

Diamonti, M., & Diamonti, N. (1975). An organizational analysis of student teacher supervision. *Interchange, 6*, 27-33.

Diorio, J. (1982). Knowledge, autonomy, and the practice of teaching. *Curriculum Inquiry, 12*, 257-282.

Duke, D., Showers, B., & Imber, M. (1980). Teachers and shared decision making: The costs and benefits of involvement. *Educational Administration Quarterly, 16*, 93-106.

Eggleston, J. (1977). *The sociology of the school curriculum*. London: Routledge & Kegan Paul.

Feiman-Nemser, J. (1983). Learning to teach. In L. S. Shulman & G. Sykes (Eds.), *Handbook of teaching and policy* (pp. 150-170). New York: Longman.

Fenstermacher, G., & Berliner, D. (1983). *A conceptual framework for the analysis of staff development*. Santa Monica, CA: Rand Corporation.

Gitlin, A., & Teitelbaum, K. (1983). Linking theory and practice: The use of ethnographic methodology by prospective teachers. *Journal of Education for Teaching, 9*, 225-234.

Goldhammer, R., Anderson, R., & Krajewski, R. (1980). *Clinical supervision* (2nd ed.). New York: Holt, Rinehart & Winston.

Grant, C. (1975, February). *The role of the letter of expectations in facilitating communication in the student teaching experience*. Paper presented at the annual meeting of the Wisconsin Educational Research Association, Baraboo, WI.

Grant, C. (1981). Education that is multicultural and teacher preparation: An examination from the perspectives of preservice students. *Journal of Educational Research, 75*, 95-101.

Grant, C., & Koskela, R. (1985, April). *Education that is multicultural and the relationship between preservice campus learning and field experiences: A report of a study*. Paper presented at the annual meeting of the American Educational Research Association, Chicago.

Greene, M. (1978). The matter of mystification: Teacher education in unquiet times. In M. Greene (Ed.), *Landscapes of learning* (pp. 53-73). New York: Teachers College Press.

Haas, J., & Shaffir, W. (1982). Ritual evaluation of competence. *Work and Occupations, 9*, 131-154.

Hoy, W., & Rees, R. (1977). The bureaucratic socialization of student teachers. *Journal of Teacher Education, 28,* 23–26.

Hursh, D., & Zeichner, K. (1984, January). *Using the "language of dilemmas" in an "inquiry-oriented" student teaching program: A case study.* Paper presented at the annual meeting of the Association of Teacher Educators, New Orleans.

Kemmis, S., & McTaggart, R. (1982). *The action research planner.* Victoria, Australia: Deakin University Press.

Koskela, R. (1985). *A search for reflective thought in the student teaching seminar: A case study.* Doctoral dissertation, University of Wisconsin, Madison.

Lanier, J. (1982). Teacher education: Needed research and practice for the preparation of teaching professionals. In D. Corrigan, D. Palmer, & P. Alexander (Eds.), *The future of teacher education* (pp. 13–36). College Station: Texas A & M University.

Lanier, J., & Little, J. W. (1986). Research on teacher education. In M. Wittrock (Ed.), *Handbook of research on teaching* (3rd ed., pp. 527–569). New York: Macmillan.

Larson, M. (1977). *The rise of professionalism: A sociological analysis.* Berkeley: University of California Press.

McIntosh, R. G. (1968, February). *An approach to the analysis of clinical settings for teacher education.* Paper presented at the annual meeting of the Association for Student Teaching, Chicago.

Mead, G. H. (1938). *The philosophy of the act.* Chicago: University of Chicago Press.

Mohrman, A., Cooke, R., & Mohrman, S. (1978). Participation in decision making: A multidimensional perspective. *Educational Administration Quarterly, 14*(1), 13–29.

Palmer, J. (1985). Teacher education: A perspective from a major public university. In C. Case & W. Matthews (Eds.), *Colleges of Education* (pp. 51–70). Berkeley: McCutchan.

Perrone, V., Clifford, S., Feiman-Nemser, S., Fiedler, R., Miller, M., Spodek, B., & Yatvin, J. (1983). *Elementary teacher education: University of Wisconsin-Madison.* (Report prepared for the University of Wisconsin Board of Regents).

Powell, A. (1976). University schools of education in the twentieth century. *Peabody Journal of Education, 54,* 3–20.

Roemer, R. (1983). Pedagogy and rationality. *Educational Theory, 33,* 167–177.

Schön, D. (1983). *The reflective practitioner.* New York: Basic Books.

Schwab, J. (1978). Part III: On curriculum-building. In I. Westbury & N. J. Wilkof (Eds.), *Science, curriculum, and liberal education* (pp. 275–384). Chicago: University of Chicago Press.

Sergiovanni, T. (1976). Toward a theory of clinical supervision. *Journal of Research and Development in Education, 9,* 20–29.

Shulman, L. S. (1983). Autonomy and obligation: The remote control of teaching. In L. S. Shulman & G. Sykes (Eds.), *Handbook of teaching and policy* (pp. 484–504). New York: Longman.

Shulman, L. S. (1984). The practical and the eclectic: A deliberation on teaching and educational research. *Curriculum Inquiry, 14,* 183–200.

Siegel, H. (1980). Critical thinking as an educational ideal. *Educational Forum, 45,* 7–23.

Smyth, J. (1984). Toward a "critical consciousness" in the instructional supervision of experienced teachers. *Curriculum Inquiry, 14,* 425–436.

Stones, E. (1984). *Supervision in teacher education.* London: Methuen.

Sykes, G. (1983). Contradictions, ironies, and promises unfulfilled: A contemporary account of the status of teaching. *Phi Delta Kappan, 65*(2), 87–93.

Tabachnick, B. R. (1981). Teacher education as a set of dynamic social events. In B. R. Tabachnick, T. Popkewitz, & B. Bszekely (Eds.), *Studying teaching and learning: Trends in Soviet and American research* (pp. 76–86). New York: Praeger.

Tabachnick, B. R., Popkewitz, T., & Zeichner, K. (1979–1980). Teacher education and the professional perspectives of student teachers. *Interchange, 10,* 12–29.

Tabachnick, B. R., & Zeichner, K. (1984). The impact of the student teaching on the development of teacher perspectives. *Journal of Teacher Education, 35,* 28–42.

Tabachnick, B. R., & Zeichner, K. (1985). The development of teacher perspectives: Conclusions from the Wisconsin studies of teacher socialization. *Dutch Journal of Teacher Education, 3*, 117–124.

Tom, A. (1984). *Teaching as a moral craft.* New York: Longman.

Tom, A. (1985, April). *Inquiring into inquiry teacher education.* Paper presented at the annual meeting of the American Educational Research Association, Chicago.

Ullrich, W. (1985). *Will and circumstance in a small group: Orientation to authority, coping/defense and their relationship in the development of reflective student teachers.* Doctoral dissertation, University of Wisconsin, Madison.

University of Wisconsin System. (1984). *Benchmarks of excellence: Recommendations of the University of Wisconsin system task force on teacher education.* Madison: Author.

Van Manen, M. (1977). Linking ways of knowing with ways of being practical. *Curriculum Inquiry, 6*, 205–228.

Wise, A. (1979). *Legislated learning: The bureaucratization of the American classroom.* Berkeley: University of California Press.

Zeichner, K. (1980). Myths and realities: Field-based experiences in preservice teacher education. *Journal of Teacher Education, 31*, 237–244.

Zeichner, K. (1981). Reflective teaching and field-based experience in teacher education. *Interchange, 12*, 1–22.

Zeichner, K. (1985a). Preparation for elementary school teaching. In P. Burke & R. Heideman (Eds.), *Teacher competence: Issues in career-long teacher education* (pp. 62–97). Springfield, IL: Thomas.

Zeichner, K. (1985b). Individual and institutional factors related to the development of teacher perspectives. In L. Katz & J. Raths (Eds.), *Advances in teacher education* (Vol. 2, pp. 135–163). Norwood, NJ: Ablex.

Zeichner, K., & Grant, C. (1981). Biography and social structure in the socialization of student teachers. *Journal of Education for Teaching, 1*, 298–314.

Zeichner, K., & Liston, D. (1985). Varieties of discourse in supervisory conferences. *Teaching and Teacher Education, 1*, 155–174.

Zeichner, K., & Tabachnick, B. R. (1981). Are the effects of university teacher education "washed out" by school experience? *Journal of Teacher Education, 32*(3), 7–11.

Zeichner, K., & Tabachnick, B. R. (1982). The belief systems of university supervisors in an elementary student teaching program. *Journal of Education for Teaching, 8*, 34–54.

Zeichner, K., & Tabachnick, B. R. (1985). Social strategies and institutional control in the socialization of beginning teachers. *Journal of Education for Teaching, 11*, 1–25.

Zeichner, K., & Teitelbaum, K. (1982). Personalized and inquiry-oriented teacher education. *Journal of Education for Teaching, 8*, 95–117.

PART 4

Academics Reflect on Teaching

Knowledge and Teaching:
Foundations of the New Reform

LEE S. SHULMAN

Lee S. Shulman builds his foundation for teaching reform on an idea of teaching that emphasizes comprehension and reasoning, transformation and reflection. "This emphasis is justified," he writes, "by the resoluteness with which research and policy have so blatantly ignored those aspects of teaching in the past." To articulate and justify this conception, Shulman responds to four questions: What are the sources of the knowledge base for teaching? In what terms can these sources be conceptualized? What are the processes of pedagogical reasoning and action? and What are the implications for teaching policy and educational reform? The answers — informed by philosophy, psychology, and a growing body of casework based on young and experienced practitioners — go far beyond current reform assumptions and initiatives. The outcome for educational practitioners, scholars, and policymakers is a major redirection in how teaching is to be understood and teachers are to be trained and evaluated.

Prologue: A Portrait of Expertise

Richly developed portrayals of expertise in teaching are rare. While many characterizations of effective teachers exist, most of these dwell on the teacher's management of the classroom. We find few descriptions or analyses of teachers that give careful attention not only to the management of students in classrooms, but also to the management of *ideas* within classroom discourse. Both kinds of emphasis will be needed if our portrayals of good practice are to serve as sufficient guides to the design of better education. Let us examine one brief account.

> A twenty-five-year veteran English teacher, Nancy, was the subject of a continuing study of experienced teachers that we had been conducting. The class was nearing the end of the second week of a unit on *Moby Dick*. The observer had been well impressed with the depth of Nancy's understanding of that novel and her skill as a pedagogue, as she documented how Nancy helped a group of California high school juniors grasp the many faces of that masterpiece. Nancy was a highly active teacher, whose classroom style employed substantial interaction with her students, both through recitations and more open-ended discussion. She was like a symphony conductor, posing questions, probing for alternative views, drawing out the shy while tempering the boisterous. Not much happened in the classroom that

did not pass through Nancy, whose pacing and ordering, structuring and expanding, controlled the rhythm of classroom life.

Nancy characterized her treatment of literature in terms of a general theoretical model that she employed.

Basically, I break reading skills into four levels:

Level 1 is simply translation. . . . It is understanding the literal meaning, denotative, and frequently for students that means getting a dictionary.

Level 2 is connotative meaning and again you are still looking at the words. . . . What does that mean, what does that tell us about the character? . . . We looked at *The Scarlet Letter*. Hawthorne described a rose bush in the first chapter. Literal level is: What is a rose bush? More important, what does a rose bush suggest, what is it that comes to mind, what did you picture?

Level 3 is the level of interpretation . . . . It is the implication of Levels 1 and 2. If the author is using a symbol, what does that say about his view of life? In *Moby Dick*, the example I used in class was the boots. The boots would be the literal level. What does it mean when he gets under the bed? And the students would say, he is trying to hide something. Level 3 would be what does Melville say about human nature? What is the implication of this? What does this tell us about this character?

Level 4 is what I call application and evaluation and I try, as I teach literature, to get the students to Level 4, and that is where they take the literature and see how it has meaning for their own lives. Where would we see that event occur in our own society? How would people that we know be behaving if they are doing what these characters are doing? How is this piece of literature similar to our common experiences as human beings? . . . So my view of reading is basically to take them from the literal on the page to making it mean something in their lives. In teaching literature I am always working in and out of those levels. (Gudmundsdottir, in preparation)

Nancy employed this conceptual framework in her teaching, using it to guide her own sequencing of material and formulation of questions. She taught the framework explicitly to her students over the semester, helping them employ it like a scaffolding to organize their own study of the texts, to monitor their own thinking. Although as a teacher she maintained tight control of the classroom discourse, her teaching goals were to liberate her students' minds through literacy, eventually to use great works of literature to illuminate their own lives. Whichever work she was teaching, she understood how to organize it, frame it for teaching, divide it appropriately for assignments and activities. She seemed to possess a mental index for these books she had taught so often — *The Red Badge of Courage, Moby Dick, The Scarlet Letter, The Adventures of Huckleberry Finn* — with key episodes organized in her mind for different pedagogical purposes, different levels of difficulty, different kinds of pupils, different themes or emphases. Her combination of subject-matter understanding and pedagogical skill was quite dazzling.

When the observer arrived at the classroom one morning, she found Nancy sitting at her desk as usual. But her morning greeting elicited no response from Nancy other than a grimace and motion toward the pad of paper on her desktop. "I have laryngitis this morning and will not be able to speak aloud," said the note. What's more, she appeared to be fighting the flu, for she had little energy. For a teacher who managed her classroom through the power of her voice and her manner, this was certainly a disabling condition. Or was it?

Using a combination of handwritten notes and whispers, she divided the class into small groups by rows, a tactic she had used twice before during this unit. Each group was given a different character who has a prominent role in the first chapters of the novel, and each group was expected to answer a series of questions about that character. Ample time was used at the end of the period for representatives of each group to report to the whole class. Once again the class had run smoothly, and the subject matter had been treated with care. But the style had changed radically, an utterly different teaching technology was employed, and still the students were engaged, and learning appeared to occur.

Subsequently, we were to see many more examples of Nancy's flexible style, adapted to the characteristics of learners, the complexities of subject matter, and her own physical condition. When learners experienced serious problems with a particular text, she self-consciously stayed at the lower levels of the reading ladder, helping the students with denotative and connotative meanings, while emphasizing literary interpretations somewhat less. When teaching *Huck Finn*, a novel she saw as less difficult than *Moby Dick*, her style changed once again. She gave much more autonomy to the students and did not directly run the classroom as much.

> For *Huck Finn*, she abandoned the stage early on and let the students teach each other. She had the students working independently in eight multi-ability groups, each group tracing one of eight themes: hypocrisy; luck and superstition; greed and materialism; romantic ideas and fantasy; religion and the Bible; social class and customs; family, racism, and prejudice; freedom and conscience. There were only two reading checks at the beginning and only two rounds of reporting. Once the groups were underway, Nancy took a seat at the back of the class and only interacted with students when she was called upon, and during group presentations. (Gudmundsdottir, in preparation)

Thus Nancy's pattern of instruction, her style of teaching, is not uniform or predictable in some simple sense. She flexibly responds to the difficulty and character of the subject matter, the capacities of the students (which can change even over the span of a single course), and her educational purposes. She can not only conduct her orchestra from the podium, she can sit back and watch it play with virtuosity by itself.

What does Nancy believe, understand, and know how to do that permits her to teach as she does? Can other teachers be prepared to teach with such skill? The hope that teaching like Nancy's can become typical instead of unusual motivates much of the effort in the newly proposed reforms of teaching.

The New Reforms

During the past year the U.S. public and its professional educators have been presented with several reports on how to improve teaching as both an activity and a profession. One of the recurring themes of these reports has been the professionalization of teaching — the elevation of teaching to a more respected, more responsible, more rewarding and better rewarded occupation. The claim that teaching deserves professional status, however, is based on a more fundamental premise:

that the standards by which the education and performance of teachers must be judged can be raised and more clearly articulated. The advocates of professional reform base their arguments on the belief that there exists a "knowledge base for teaching"—a codified or codifiable aggregation of knowledge, skill, understanding, and technology, of ethics and disposition, of collective responsibility—as well as a means for representing and communicating it. The reports of the Holmes Group (1986) and the Carnegie Task Force (1986) rest on this belief and, furthermore, claim that the knowledge base is growing. They argue that it should frame teacher education and directly inform teaching practice.

The rhetoric regarding the knowledge base, however, rarely specifies the character of such knowledge. It does not say what teachers should know, do, understand, or profess that will render teaching more than a form of individual labor, let alone be considered among the learned professions.

In this paper, I present an argument regarding the content, character, and sources for a knowledge base of teaching that suggests an answer to the question of the intellectual, practical, and normative basis for the professionalization of teaching. The questions that focus the argument are: What are the sources of the knowledge base for teaching? In what terms can these sources be conceptualized? What are the implications for teaching policy and educational reform?[1]

In addressing these questions I am following in the footsteps of many eminent scholars, including Dewey (1904), Scheffler (1965), Green (1971), Fenstermacher (1978), Smith (1980), and Schwab (1983), among others. Their discussions of what qualities and understandings, skills and abilities, and what traits and sensibilities render someone a competent teacher have continued to echo in the conference rooms of educators for generations. My approach has been conditioned, as well, by two current projects: a study of how new teachers learn to teach and an attempt to develop a national board for teaching.

First, for the past three years, my colleagues and I have been watching knowledge of pedagogy and content grow in the minds of young men and women. They have generously permitted us to observe and follow their eventful journeys from being teacher education students to becoming neophyte teachers. In this research, we are taking advantage of the kinds of insights Piaget provided from his investigations of knowledge growth. He discovered that he could learn a great deal about knowledge and its development from careful observation of the very young—those who were just beginning to develop and organize their intelligence. We are following this lead by studying those just learning to teach. Their development from students to teachers, from a state of expertise as learners through a novitiate as teachers exposes and highlights the complex bodies of knowledge and skill needed to function effectively as a teacher. The result is that error, success, and refine-

---

[1] Most of the empirical work on which this essay rests has been conducted with secondary-school teachers, both new and experienced. While I firmly believe that much of the emphasis to be found here on the centrality of content knowledge in pedagogy holds reasonably well for the elementary level as well, I am reluctant to make that claim too boldly. Work currently underway at the elementary level, both by Leinhardt (1983) and her colleagues (for example, Leinhardt & Greeno, 1985; Leinhardt & Smith, 1986) and by our own research group, may help clarify this matter.

Moreover, those who hold with bifurcating content and teaching processes have once again introduced into policy what had been merely an act of scholarly convenience and simplification in the research. Teaching processes were observed and evaluated without reference to the adequacy or accuracy of the ideas transmitted. In many cases, observers were not expected to have content expertise in the areas being observed, because it did not matter for the rating of teacher performance. Thus, what may have been an acceptable strategy for research became an unacceptable policy for teacher evaluation.

In this paper I argue that the results of research on effective teaching, while valuable, are not the sole source of evidence on which to base a definition of the knowledge base of teaching. Those sources should be understood to be far richer and more extensive. Indeed, properly understood, the actual and potential sources for a knowledge base are so plentiful that our question should not be, Is there really much one needs to know in order to teach? Rather, it should express our wonder at how the extensive knowledge of teaching can be learned at all during the brief period allotted to teacher preparation. Much of the rest of this paper provides the details of the argument that there exists an elaborate knowledge base for teaching.

A View of Teaching

I begin with the formulation that the capacity to teach centers around the following commonplaces of teaching, paraphrased from Fenstermacher (1986). A teacher knows something not understood by others, presumably the students. The teacher can transform understanding, performance skills, or desired attitudes or values into pedagogical representations and actions. These are ways of talking, showing, enacting, or otherwise representing ideas so that the unknowing can come to know, those without understanding can comprehend and discern, and the unskilled can become adept. Thus, teaching necessarily begins with a teacher's understanding of what is to be learned and how it is to be taught. It proceeds through a series of activities during which the students are provided specific instruction and opportunities for learning,[2] though the learning itself ultimately remains the responsibility of the students. Teaching ends with new comprehension by both the teacher and the student.[3] Although this is certainly a core conception of teaching,

---

[2] There are several aspects of this formulation that are unfortunate, if only for the impression they may leave. The rhetoric of the analysis, for example, is not meant to suggest that education is reduced to knowledge transmission, the conveying of information from an active teacher to a passive learner, and that this information is viewed as product rather than process. My conception of teaching is not limited to direct instruction. Indeed, my affinity for discovery learning and inquiry teaching is both enthusiastic and ancient (for example, Shulman & Keislar, 1966). Yet even in those most student-centered forms of education, where much of the initiative is in the hands of the students, there is little room for teacher ignorance. Indeed, we have reason to believe that teacher comprehension is even more critical for the inquiry-oriented classroom than for its more didactic alternative.

Central to my concept of teaching are the objectives of students learning how to understand and solve problems, learning to think critically and creatively as well as learning facts, principles, and rules of procedure. Finally, I understand that the learning of subject matter is often not an end in itself, but rather a vehicle employed in the service of other goals. Nevertheless, at least at the secondary level, subject matter is a nearly universal vehicle for instruction, whatever the ultimate goal.

[3] This formulation is drawn from the teacher's perspective and, hence, may be viewed by some readers as overly teacher-centered. I do not mean to diminish the centrality of student learning for the process of education, nor the priority that must be given to student learning over teacher compre-

it is also an incomplete conception. Teaching must properly be understood to be more than the enhancement of understanding; but if it is not even that, then questions regarding performance of its other functions remain moot. The next step is to outline the categories of knowledge that underlie the teacher understanding needed to promote comprehension among students.

Categories of the Knowledge Base

If teacher knowledge were to be organized into a handbook, an encyclopedia, or some other format for arraying knowledge, what would the category headings look like?[4] At minimum, they would include:

— content knowledge;

— general pedagogical knowledge, with special reference to those broad principles and strategies of classroom management and organization that appear to transcend subject matter;

— curriculum knowledge, with particular grasp of the materials and programs that serve as "tools of the trade" for teachers;

— pedagogical content knowledge, that special amalgam of content and pedagogy that is uniquely the province of teachers, their own special form of professional understanding;

— knowledge of learners and their characteristics;

— knowledge of educational contexts, ranging from the workings of the group or classroom, the governance and financing of school districts, to the character of communities and cultures; and

— knowledge of educational ends, purposes, and values, and their philosophical and historical grounds.

Among those categories, pedagogical content knowledge is of special interest because it identifies the distinctive bodies of knowledge for teaching. It represents the blending of content and pedagogy into an understanding of how particular topics, problems, or issues are organized, represented, and adapted to the diverse interests and abilities of learners, and presented for instruction. Pedagogical content knowledge is the category most likely to distinguish the understanding of the content specialist from that of the pedagogue. While far more can be said regarding the categories of a knowledge base for teaching, elucidation of them is not a central purpose of this paper.

Enumerating the Sources

There are at least four major sources for the teaching knowledge base: (1) scholarship in content disciplines, (2) the materials and settings of the institutionalized educational process (for example, curricula, textbooks, school organizations and finance, and the structure of the teaching profession), (3) research on schooling, social organizations, human learning, teaching and development, and the other

---

hension. But our analyses of effective teaching must recognize that outcomes *for teachers* as well as pupils must be considered in any adequate treatment of educational outcomes.

[4] I have attempted this list in other publications, though, admittedly, not with great cross-article consistency (for example, Shulman, 1986b; Shulman & Sykes, 1986; Wilson, Shulman & Richert, in press).

social and cultural phenomena that affect what teachers can do, and (4) the wisdom of practice itself. Let me elaborate on each of these.

Scholarship in content disciplines. The first source of the knowledge base is content knowledge — the knowledge, understanding, skill, and disposition that are to be learned by school children. This knowledge rests on two foundations: the accumulated literature and studies in the content areas, and the historical and philosophical scholarship on the nature of knowledge in those fields of study. For example, the teacher of English should know English and American prose and poetry, written and spoken language use and comprehension, and grammar. In addition, he or she should be familiar with the critical literature that applies to particular novels or epics that are under discussion in class. Moreover, the teacher should understand alternative theories of interpretation and criticism, and how these might relate to issues of curriculum and of teaching.

Teaching is, essentially, a learned profession. A teacher is a member of a scholarly community. He or she must understand the structures of subject matter, the principles of conceptual organization, and the principles of inquiry that help answer two kinds of questions in each field: What are the important ideas and skills in this domain? and How are new ideas added and deficient ones dropped by those who produce knowledge in this area? That is, what are the rules and procedures of good scholarship or inquiry? These questions parallel what Schwab (1964) has characterized as knowledge of substantive and syntactic structures, respectively. This view of the sources of content knowledge necessarily implies that the teacher must have not only depth of understanding with respect to the particular subjects taught, but also a broad liberal education that serves as a framework for old learning and as a facilitator for new understanding. The teacher has special responsibilities in relation to content knowledge, serving as the primary source of student understanding of subject matter. The manner in which that understanding is communicated conveys to students what is essential about a subject and what is peripheral. In the face of student diversity, the teacher must have a flexible and multifaceted comprehension, adequate to impart alternative explanations of the same concepts or principles. The teacher also communicates, whether consciously or not, ideas about the ways in which "truth" is determined in a field and a set of attitudes and values that markedly influence student understanding. This responsibility places special demands on the teacher's own depth of understanding of the structures of the subject matter, as well as on the teacher's attitudes toward and enthusiasms for what is being taught and learned. These many aspects of content knowledge, therefore, are properly understood as a central feature of the knowledge base of teaching.

Educational materials and structures. To advance the aims of organized schooling, materials and structures for teaching and learning are created. These include: curricula with their scopes and sequences; tests and testing materials; institutions with their hierarchies, their explicit and implicit systems of rules and roles; professional teachers' organizations with their functions of negotiation, social change, and mutual protection; government agencies from the district through the state and federal levels; and general mechanisms of governance and finance. Because teachers necessarily function within a matrix created by these elements, using and being used by them, it stands to reason that the principles, policies, and facts of their functioning comprise a major source for the knowledge base. There is no need to claim that a specific literature undergirds this source, although there is certainly abundant research literature in most of these domains. But if a teacher has to "know the territory" of teaching, then it is the landscape of such materials, institutions, organizations, and mechanisms with which he or she must be familiar. These comprise both the tools of the trade and the contextual conditions that will either facilitate or inhibit teaching efforts.

Formal educational scholarship. A third source is the important and growing body of scholarly literature devoted to understanding the processes of schooling, teaching, and learning. This literature includes the findings and methods of empirical research in the areas of teaching, learning, and human development, as well as the normative, philosophical, and ethical foundations of education.

The normative and theoretical aspects of teaching's scholarly knowledge are perhaps most important. Unfortunately, educational policymakers and staff developers tend to treat only the findings of empirical research on teaching and learning as relevant portions of the scholarly knowledge base. But these research findings, while important and worthy of careful study, represent only one facet of the contribution of scholarship. Perhaps the most enduring and powerful scholarly influences on teachers are those that enrich their images of the possible: their visions of what constitutes good education, or what a well-educated youngster might look like if provided with appropriate opportunities and stimulation.

The writings of Plato, Dewey, Neill, and Skinner all communicate their conceptions of what a good educational system should be. In addition, many works written primarily to disseminate empirical research findings also serve as important sources of these concepts. I count among these such works as Bloom's (1976) on mastery learning and Rosenthal and Jacobson's (1968) on teacher expectations. Quite independent of whether the empirical claims of those books can be supported, their impact on teachers' conceptions of the possible and desirable ends of education is undeniable. Thus, the philosophical, critical, and empirical literature which can inform the goals, visions, and dreams of teachers is a major portion of the scholarly knowledge base of teaching.

A more frequently cited kind of scholarly knowledge grows out of the empirical study of teaching effectiveness. This research has been summarized recently by Gage (1978, 1986), Shulman (1986a), Brophy and Good (1986), and Rosenshine and Stevens (1986). The essential goal of this program of research has been to identify those teacher behaviors and strategies most likely to lead to achievement gains among students. Because the search has focused on generic relationships — teacher behaviors associated with student academic gains irrespective of subject matter or grade level — the findings have been much more closely connected with the management of classrooms than with the subtleties of content pedagogy. That is, the effective-teaching principles deal with making classrooms places where pupils can attend to instructional tasks, orient themselves toward learning with a minimum of disruption and distraction, and receive a fair and adequate opportunity to learn. Moreover, the educational purposes for which these research results are most relevant are the teaching of skills. Rosenshine (1986) has observed that effective teaching research has much less to offer to the teaching of understanding, especially of complex written material; thus, the research applies more to teaching a skill like multiplication than to teaching critical interpretations of, say, the *Federalist Papers*.

There are a growing number of such generic principles of effective teaching, and they have already found their way into examinations such as the National Teachers Examination and into state-level assessments of teaching performance during the first teaching year. Their weakness, that they essentially ignore the content-specific character of most teaching, is also their strength. Discovering, explicating, and codifying general teaching principles simplify the otherwise outrageously complex activity of teaching. The great danger occurs, however, when a general teaching principle is distorted into prescription, when maxim becomes mandate. Those states that have taken working principles of teaching, based solely on empirical studies of generic teaching effectiveness, and have rendered them as hard, independent criteria for judging a teacher's worth, are engaged in a political process likely to injure the teaching profession rather than improve it.

The results of research on learning and development also fall within the area of empirical research findings. This research differs from research on teaching by the unit of investigation. Studies of teaching typically take place in conventional classrooms. Learning and development are ordinarily studied in individuals. Hence, teaching studies give accounts of how teachers cope with the inescapable character of schools as places where groups of students work and learn in concert. By comparison, learning and development studies produce principles of individual thought or behavior that must often be generalized to groups with caution if they are to be useful for schoolteaching.

The research in these domains can be both generic and content-specific. For example, cognitive psychological research contributes to the development of understanding of how the mind works to store, process, and retrieve information. Such general understanding can certainly be a source of knowledge for teachers, just as the work of Piaget, Maslow, Erikson, or Bloom has been and continues to be. We also find work on specific subject matter and student developmental levels that is enormously useful; for example, we learn about student misconceptions in the learning of arithmetic by elementary school youngsters (Erlwanger, 1975) or difficulties in grasping principles of physics by university and secondary school students (for example, Clement, 1982). Both these sorts of research contribute to a knowledge base for teaching.

Wisdom of practice. The final source of the knowledge base is the least codified of all. It is the wisdom of practice itself, the maxims that guide (or provide reflective rationalization for) the practices of able teachers. One of the more important tasks for the research community is to work with practitioners to develop codified representations of the practical pedagogical wisdom of able teachers. As indicated above, much of the conception of teaching embodied in this paper is derived from collecting, examining, and beginning to codify the emerging wisdom of practice among both inexperienced and experienced teachers.

The portrait of Nancy with which this paper began is only one of the many descriptions and analyses of excellent teaching we have been collecting over the past few years. As we organize and interpret such data, we attempt to infer principles of good practice that can serve as useful guidelines for efforts of educational reform. We attempt to keep the accounts highly contextualized, especially with respect to the content-specificity of the pedagogical strategies employed. In this manner we contribute to the documentation of good practice as a significant source for teaching standards. We also attempt to lay a foundation for a scholarly literature that records the details and rationales for specific pedagogical practice.

One of the frustrations of teaching as an occupation and profession is its extensive individual and collective amnesia, the consistency with which the best creations of its practitioners are lost to both contemporary and future peers. Unlike fields such as architecture (which preserves its creations in both plans and edifices), law (which builds a case literature of opinions and interpretations), medicine (with its records and case studies), and even unlike chess, bridge, or ballet (with their traditions of preserving both memorable games and choreographed performances through inventive forms of notation and recording), teaching is conducted without an audience of peers. It is devoid of a history of practice.

Without such a system of notation and memory, the next steps of analysis, interpretation, and codification of principles of practice are hard to pursue. We have concluded from our research with teachers at all levels of experience that the potentially codifiable knowledge that can be gleaned from the wisdom of practice is extensive. Practitioners simply know a great deal that they have never even tried to articulate. A major portion of the research agenda for the next decade will be to collect, collate, and interpret the practical knowledge of teachers for the purpose of establishing a case literature and codifying its principles, precedents, and parables (Shulman, 1986b). A significant portion of the research agenda associated with the Carnegie program to develop new assessments for teachers involves the conducting of "wisdom-of-practice" studies. These studies record and organize the reasoning and actions of gifted teachers into cases to establish standards of practice for particular areas of teaching.[5]

A knowledge base for teaching is not fixed and final. Although teaching is among the world's oldest professions, educational research, especially the systematic study of teaching, is a relatively new enterprise. We may be able to offer a compelling argument for the broad outlines and categories of the knowledge base for teaching. It will, however, become abundantly clear that much, if not most, of the proposed knowledge base remains to be discovered, invented, and refined. As more is learned about teaching, we will come to recognize new categories of performance and understanding that are characteristic of good teachers, and will have to reconsider and redefine other domains. Our current "blueprint" for the knowledge base of teaching has many cells or categories with only the most rudimentary place-holders, much like the chemist's periodic table of a century ago. As we proceed, we will know that something can be known in principle about a particular aspect of teaching, but we will not yet know what that principle or practice entails. At base, however, we believe that scholars and expert teachers are able to define, describe, and reproduce good teaching.

---

[5] It might be argued that the sources of skilled performances are typically tacit, and unavailable to the practitioner. But teaching requires a special kind of expertise or artistry, for which explaining and showing are the central features. Tacit knowledge among teachers is of limited value if the teachers are held responsible for explaining what they do and why they do it, to their students, their communities, and their peers

The Processes of Pedagogical Reasoning and Action

The conception of teaching I shall discuss has emerged from a number of sources, both philosophical and empirical. A key source has been the several dozen teachers whom we have been studying in our research during the past three years. Through interviews, observations, structured tasks, and examination of materials, we have attempted to understand how they commute from the status of learner to that of teacher,[6] from being able to comprehend subject matter for themselves, to becoming able to elucidate subject matter in new ways, reorganize and partition it, clothe it in activities and emotions, in metaphors and exercises, and in examples and demonstrations, so that it can be grasped by students.

As we have come to view teaching, it begins with an act of reason, continues with a process of reasoning, culminates in performances of imparting, eliciting, involving, or enticing, and is then thought about some more until the process can begin again. In the discussion of teaching that follows, we will emphasize teaching as comprehension and reasoning, as transformation and reflection. This emphasis is justified by the resoluteness with which research and policy have so blatantly ignored those aspects of teaching in the past.

Fenstermacher (1978, 1986) provides a useful framework for analysis. The goal of teacher education, he argues, is not to indoctrinate or train teachers to behave in prescribed ways, but to educate teachers to reason soundly about their teaching as well as to perform skillfully. Sound reasoning requires both a process of thinking about what they are doing and an adequate base of facts, principles, and experiences from which to reason. Teachers must learn to use their knowledge base to provide the grounds for choices and actions. Therefore, teacher education must work with the beliefs that guide teacher actions, with the principles and evidence that underlie the choices teachers make. Such reasons (called "premises of the practical argument" in the analysis of Green, 1971, on which Fenstermacher bases his argument) can be predominantly arbitrary or idiosyncratic ("It sure seemed like the right idea at the time!" "I don't know much about teaching, but I know what I like."), or they can rest on ethical, empirical, theoretical, or practical principles that have substantial support among members of the professional community of teachers. Fenstermacher argues that good teaching not only is effective behaviorally, but must rest on a foundation of adequately grounded premises.

When we examine the quality of teaching, the idea of influencing the grounds or reasons for teachers' decisions places the emphasis precisely where it belongs: on the features of pedagogical reasoning that lead to or can be invoked to explain pedagogical actions. We must be cautious, however, lest we place undue emphasis upon the ways teachers reason to achieve particular ends, at the expense of attention to the grounds they present for selecting the ends themselves. Teaching is both effective and normative; it is concerned with both means and ends. Processes of reasoning underlie both. The knowledge base must therefore deal with the purposes of education as well as the methods and strategies of educating.

---

[6] The metaphor of commuting is not used idly. The journey between learner and teacher is not one-way. In the best teachers, as well as in the more marginal, new learning is constantly required for teaching.

This image of teaching involves the exchange of ideas. The idea is grasped, probed, and comprehended by a teacher, who then must turn it about in his or her mind, seeing many sides of it. Then the idea is shaped or tailored until it can in turn be grasped by students. This grasping, however, is not a passive act. Just as the teacher's comprehension requires a vigorous interaction with the ideas, so students will be expected to encounter ideas actively as well. Indeed, our exemplary teachers present ideas in order to provoke the constructive processes of their students and not to incur student dependence on teachers or to stimulate the flatteries of imitation.[7]

Comprehension alone is not sufficient. The usefulness of such knowledge lies in its value for judgment and action. Thus, in response to my aphorism, "those who can, do; those who understand, teach" (Shulman, 1986b, p. 14), Petrie (1986) correctly observed that I had not gone far enough. Understanding, he argued, must be linked to judgment and action, to the proper uses of understanding in the forging of wise pedagogical decisions.

Aspects of Pedagogical Reasoning

I begin with the assumption that most teaching is initiated by some form of "text": a textbook, a syllabus, or an actual piece of material the teacher or student wishes to have understood. The text may be a vehicle for the accomplishment of other educational purposes, but some sort of teaching material is almost always involved. The following conception of pedagogical reasoning and action is taken from the point of view of the teacher, who is presented with the challenge of taking what he or she already understands and making it ready for effective instruction. The model of pedagogical reasoning and action is summarized in Table 1.

Given a text, educational purposes, and/or a set of ideas, pedagogical reasoning and action involve a cycle through the activities of comprehension, transformation, instruction, evaluation, and reflection.[8] The starting point and terminus for the process is an act of comprehension.

Comprehension. To teach is first to understand. We ask that the teacher comprehend critically a set of ideas to be taught.[9] We expect teachers to understand what they teach and, when possible, to understand it in several ways. They should understand how a given idea relates to other ideas within the same subject area and to ideas in other subjects as well.

---

[7] The direction and sequence of instruction can be quite different as well. Students can literally initiate the process, proceeding by discovering, inventing, or inquiring, to prepare their own representations and transformations. Then it is the role of the teacher to respond actively and creatively to those student initiatives. In each case the teacher needs to possess both the comprehension and the capacities for transformation. In the student-initiated case, the flexibility to respond, judge, nurture, and provoke student creativity will depend on the teacher's own capacities for sympathetic transformation and interpretation.

[8] Under some conditions, teaching may begin with "given a group of students." It is likely that at the early elementary grades, or in special education classes or other settings where children have been brought together for particular reasons, the starting point for reasoning about instruction may well be at the characteristics of the group itself. There are probably some days when a teacher necessarily uses the youngsters as a starting point.

[9] Other views of teaching will also begin with comprehension, but of something other than the ideas or text to be taught and learned. They may focus on comprehension of a particular set of values, of the characteristics, needs, interests, or propensities of a particular individual or group of learners. But some sort of comprehension (or self-conscious confusion, wonder, or ignorance) will always initiate teaching.

TABLE 1
A Model of Pedagogical Reasoning and Action

Comprehension
Of purposes, subject matter structures, ideas within and outside the discipline

Transformation
Preparation: critical interpretation and analysis of texts, structuring and segmenting, development of a curricular repertoire, and clarification of purposes

Representation: use of a representational repertoire which includes analogies, metaphors, examples, demonstrations, explanations, and so forth

Selection: choice from among an instructional repertoire which includes modes of teaching, organizing, managing, and arranging

Adaptation and Tailoring to Student Characteristics: consideration of conceptions, preconceptions, misconceptions, and difficulties, language, culture, and motivations, social class, gender, age, ability, aptitude, interests, self concepts, and attention

Instruction
Management, presentations, interactions, group work, discipline, humor, questioning, and other aspects of active teaching, discovery or inquiry instruction, and the observable forms of classroom teaching

Evaluation
Checking for student understanding during interactive teaching

Testing student understanding at the end of lessons or units

Evaluating one's own performance, and adjusting for experiences

Reflection
Reviewing, reconstructing, reenacting and critically analyzing one's own and the class's performance, and grounding explanations in evidence

New Comprehensions
Of purposes, subject matter, students, teaching, and self

Consolidation of new understandings, and learnings from experience

---

Comprehension of purposes is also central here. We engage in teaching to achieve educational purposes, to accomplish ends having to do with student literacy, student freedom to use and enjoy, student responsibility to care and care for, to believe and respect, to inquire and discover, to develop understandings, skills, and values needed to function in a free and just society. As teachers, we also strive to balance our goals of fostering individual excellence with more general ends involving equality of opportunity and equity among students of different backgrounds and cultures. Although most teaching begins with some sort of text, and the learning of that text can be a worthy end in itself, we should not lose sight of the fact that the text is often a vehicle for achieving other educational purposes. The goals of education transcend the comprehension of particular texts, but may be unachievable without it.

Saying that a teacher must first comprehend both content and purposes, however, does not particularly distinguish a teacher from non-teaching peers. We expect a math major to understand mathematics or a history specialist to comprehend history. But the key to distinguishing the knowledge base of teaching lies at the intersection of content and pedagogy, in the capacity of a teacher to transform

327

the content knowledge he or she possesses into forms that are pedagogically powerful and yet adaptive to the variations in ability and background presented by the students. We now turn to a discussion of transformation and its components.

Transformation. Comprehended ideas must be transformed in some manner if they are to be taught. To reason one's way through an act of teaching is to think one's way from the subject matter as understood by the teacher into the minds and motivations of learners. Transformations, therefore, require some combination or ordering of the following processes, each of which employs a kind of repertoire: (1) preparation (of the given text materials) including the process of critical interpretation, (2) representation of the ideas in the form of new analogies, metaphors, and so forth, (3) instructional selections from among an array of teaching methods and models, and (4) adaptation of these representations to the general characteristics of the children to be taught, as well as (5) tailoring the adaptations to the specific youngsters in the classroom. These forms of transformation, these aspects of the process wherein one moves from personal comprehension to preparing for the comprehension of others, are the essence of the act of pedagogical reasoning, of teaching as thinking, and of planning—whether explicitly or implicitly—the performance of teaching.

Preparation involves examining and critically interpreting the materials of instruction in terms of the teacher's own understanding of the subject matter (Ben-Peretz, 1975). That is, one scrutinizes the teaching material in light of one's own comprehension and asks whether it is "fit to be taught." This process of preparation will usually include (1) detecting and correcting errors of omission and commission in the text, and (2) the crucial processes of structuring and segmenting the material into forms better adapted to the teacher's understanding and, in prospect, more suitable for teaching. One also scrutinizes educational purposes or goals. We find examples of this preparation process in a number of our studies. Preparation certainly draws upon the availability of a curricular repertoire, a grasp of the full array of extant instructional materials, programs, and conceptions.

Representation involves thinking through the key ideas in the text or lesson and identifying the alternative ways of representing them to students. What analogies, metaphors, examples, demonstrations, simulations, and the like can help to build a bridge between the teacher's comprehension and that desired for the students? Multiple forms of representation are desirable. We speak of the importance of a representational repertoire in this activity.[10]

Instructional selections occur when the teacher must move from the reformulation of content through representations to the embodiment of representations in instructional forms or methods. Here the teacher draws upon an instructional repertoire of approaches or strategies of teaching. This repertoire can be quite rich,

---

[10] The centrality of representation to our conception of pedagogical reasoning is important for relating our model of teaching to more general approaches to the study of human thinking and problem solving. Cognitive psychologists (for example, Gardner, 1986; Marton, 1986; Norman, 1980) argue that processes of internal representation are key elements in any cognitive psychology. "To my mind, the major accomplishment of cognitive science has been the clear demonstration of the validity of positing a level of mental representation: a set of constructs that can be invoked for the explanation of cognitive phenomena, ranging from visual perception to story comprehension" (Gardner, 1986, p. 383). Such a linkage between models of pedagogy and models of more general cognitive functioning can serve as an important impetus for the needed study of teacher thinking.

including not only the more conventional alternatives such as lecture, demonstration, recitation, or seatwork, but also a variety of forms of cooperative learning, reciprocal teaching, Socratic dialogue, discovery learning, project methods, and learning outside the classroom setting.

Adaptation is the process of fitting the represented material to the characteristics of the students. What are the relevant aspects of student ability, gender, language, culture, motivations, or prior knowledge and skills that will affect their responses to different forms of representation and presentation? What student conceptions, misconceptions, expectations, motives, difficulties, or strategies might influence the ways in which they approach, interpret, understand, or misunderstand the material? Related to adaptation is tailoring, which refers to the fitting of the material to the specific students in one's classrooms rather than to students in general. When a teacher thinks through the teaching of something, the activity is a bit like the manufacture of a suit of clothing. Adaptation is like preparing a suit of a particular style, color, and size that can be hung on a rack. Once it is prepared for purchase by a particular customer, however, it must be tailored to fit perfectly.

Moreover, the activity of teaching is rarely engaged with a single student at a time. This is a process for which the special term "tutoring" is needed. When we speak of teaching under typical school circumstances, we describe an activity which brings instruction to groups of at least fifteen — or more typically, twenty-five to thirty-five — students. Thus, the tailoring of instruction entails fitting representations not only to particular students, but also to a group of a particular size, disposition, receptivity, and interpersonal "chemistry."

All these processes of transformation result in a plan, or set of strategies, to present a lesson, unit, or course. Up to this point, of course, it is all a rehearsal for the performances of teaching which have not yet occurred. Pedagogical reasoning is as much a part of teaching as is the actual performance itself. Reasoning does not end when instruction begins. The activities of comprehension, transformation, evaluation, and reflection continue to occur during active teaching. Teaching itself becomes a stimulus for thoughtfulness as well as for action. We therefore turn next to the performance that consummates all this reasoning in the act of instruction.

Instruction. This activity involves the observable performance of the variety of teaching acts. It includes many of the most crucial aspects of pedagogy: organizing and managing the classroom; presenting clear explanations and vivid descriptions; assigning and checking work; and interacting effectively with students through questions and probes, answers and reactions, and praise and criticism. It thus includes management, explanation, discussion, and all the observable features of effective direct and heuristic instruction already well-documented in the research literature on effective teaching.

We have compelling reasons to believe that there are powerful relationships between the comprehension of a new teacher and the styles of teaching employed. An example, based on the research of Grossman (1985), will illustrate this point.

> Colleen had completed a master's degree in English before entering a teacher education program. She expressed confidence in her command of the subject matter and began her internship with energy and enthusiasm. Her view of literature and its teaching was highly interpretive and interactive. She saw fine literature as lay-

ered communication, capable of many diverse readings and interpretations. Moreover, she felt that these various readings should be provided by her students through their own careful reading of the texts.

Colleen was so committed to helping students learn to read texts carefully, a habit of mind not often found among the young or old, that she constructed one assignment in which each student was asked to bring to school the lyrics of a favorite rock song. (She may have realized that some of these song lyrics were of questionable taste, but preferred to maximize motivation rather than discretion in this particular unit.) She then asked them to rewrite each line of the song, using synonyms or paraphrases to replace every original word. For many, it was the first time they had looked at any piece of text with such care.

When teaching a piece of literature, Colleen performed in a highly interactive manner, drawing out student ideas about a phrase or line, accepting multiple competing interpretations as long as the student could offer a defense of the construction by reference to the text itself. Student participation was active and hearty in these sessions. Based on these observations, one would have characterized Colleen's teaching style with descriptors such as student-centered, discussion-based, occasionally Socratic, or otherwise highly interactive.

Several weeks later, however, we observed Colleen teaching a unit on grammar. Although she had completed two university degrees in English, Colleen had received almost no preparation in prescriptive grammar. However, since a typical high school English class includes some grammar in addition to the literature and writing, it was impossible to avoid teaching the subject. She expressed some anxiety about it during a pre-observational interview.

Colleen looked like a different teacher during that lesson. Her interactive style evaporated. In its place was a highly didactic, teacher-directed, swiftly paced combination of lecture and tightly-controlled recitation: Socrates replaced by DISTAR. I sometimes refer to such teaching as the Admiral Farragut style, "Damn the questions, full speed ahead." Students were not given opportunities to raise questions or offer alternative views. After the session, she confessed to the observer that she had actively avoided making eye contact with one particular student in the front row because that youngster always had good questions or ideas and in this particular lesson Colleen really didn't want to encourage either, because she wasn't sure of the answers. She was uncertain about the content and adapted her instructional style to allay her anxiety.[11]

Colleen's case illustrates the ways in which teaching behavior is bound up with comprehension and transformation of understanding. The flexible and interactive teaching techniques that she uses are simply not available to her when she does not understand the topic to be taught. Having examined the processes of pedagogical reasoning and performance that are prospective and enactive in nature, we now move to those that are retrospective.

Evaluation. This process includes the on-line checking for understanding and misunderstanding that a teacher must employ while teaching interactively, as well

---

[11] In no way do I wish to imply that effective lectures are out of place in a high school classroom. On the contrary, good lecturing is an indispensable teaching technique. In this case I am more interested in the relationship between knowledge and teaching. It might be suggested that this teaching style is more suited to grammar than to literature because there is little to discuss or interpret in a grammar lesson. I do not agree, but will not pursue the matter here. In Colleen's case, the rationale for a linear lecture was not grounded in such an argument, but quite clearly in her concern for limiting the range of possible deviations from the path she had designed.

as the more formal testing and evaluation that teachers do to provide feedback and grades. Clearly, checking for such understanding requires all the forms of teacher comprehension and transformation described above. To understand what a pupil understands will require a deep grasp of both the material to be taught and the processes of learning. This understanding must be specific to particular school subjects and to individual topics within the subject. This represents another way in which what we call pedagogical content knowledge is used. Evaluation is also directed at one's own teaching and at the lessons and materials employed in those activities. In that sense it leads directly to reflection.

Reflection. This is what a teacher does when he or she looks back at the teaching and learning that has occurred, and reconstructs, reenacts, and/or recaptures the events, the emotions, and the accomplishments. It is that set of processes through which a professional learns from experience. It can be done alone or in concert, with the help of recording devices or solely through memory. Here again, it is likely that reflection is not merely a disposition (as in, "she's such a reflective person!") or a set of strategies, but also the use of particular kinds of analytic knowledge brought to bear on one's work (Richert, in preparation). Central to this process will be a review of the teaching in comparison to the ends that were sought.

New comprehension. Thus we arrive at the new beginning, the expectation that through acts of teaching that are "reasoned" and "reasonable" the teacher achieves new comprehension, both of the purposes and of the subjects to be taught, and also of the students and of the processes of pedagogy themselves. There is a good deal of transient experiential learning among teachers, characterized by the "aha" of a moment that is never consolidated and made part of a new understanding or a reconstituted repertoire (Brodkey, 1986). New comprehension does not automatically occur, even after evaluation and reflection. Specific strategies for documentation, analysis, and discussion are needed.

Although the processes in this model are presented in sequence, they are not meant to represent a set of fixed stages, phases, or steps. Many of the processes can occur in different order. Some may not occur at all during some acts of teaching. Some may be truncated, others elaborated. In elementary teaching, for example, some processes may occur that are ignored or given short shrift in this model. But a teacher should demonstrate the capacity to engage in these processes when called upon, and teacher education should provide students with the understandings and performance abilities they will need to reason their ways through and to enact a complete act of pedagogy, as represented here.

Knowledge, Teaching Policy, and Educational Reform

The investigations, deliberations, and debates regarding what teachers should know and know how to do have never been more active. Reform efforts are underway: they range from raising standards for admission into teacher education programs, to establishing state and national examinations for teachers; from insisting that teacher preparation require at least five years of higher education (because there is so much to learn), to organizing elaborate programs of new-teacher induction and mentoring (because the most important learning and socialization can occur only in the workplace).

Most of the current reforms rest on the call for greater professionalization in teaching, with higher standards for entry, greater emphasis on the scholarly bases for practice, more rigorous programs of theoretical and practical preparation, better strategies for certification and licensure, and changes in the workplace that permit greater autonomy and teacher leadership. In large measure, they call for teaching to follow the model of other professions that define their knowledge bases in systematic terms, require extended periods of preparation, socialize neophytes into practice with extended periods of internship or residency, and employ demanding national and state certification procedures.

Implicit in all these reforms are conceptions of teacher competence. Standards for teacher education and assessment are necessarily predicated on images of teaching and its demands. The conception of the knowledge base of teaching presented in this paper differs in significant ways from many of those currently existing in the policy community. The emphasis on the integral relationships between teaching and the scholarly domains of the liberal arts makes clear that teacher education is the responsibility of the entire university, not the schools or departments of education alone. Moreover, teachers cannot be adequately assessed by observing their teaching performance without reference to the content being taught.

The conception of pedagogical reasoning places emphasis upon the intellectual basis for teaching performance rather than on behavior alone. If this conception is to be taken seriously, both the organization and content of teacher education programs and the definition of the scholarly foundations of education will require revision. Teacher education programs would no longer be able to confine their activity to the content-free domains of pedagogy and supervision. An emphasis on pedagogical content knowledge would permeate the teacher preparation curriculum. A national board examination for teachers would focus upon the teacher's ability to reason about teaching and to teach specific topics, and to base his or her actions on premises that can bear the scrutiny of the professional community.

We have an obligation to raise standards in the interests of improvement and reform, but we must avoid the creation of rigid orthodoxies. We must achieve standards without standardization. We must be careful that the knowledge-base approach does not produce an overly technical image of teaching, a scientific enterprise that has lost its soul. The serious problems in medicine and other health professions arise when doctors treat the disease rather than the person, or when the professional or personal needs of the practitioner are permitted to take precedence over the responsibilities to those being served.

Needed change cannot occur without risk, however. The currently incomplete and trivial definitions of teaching held by the policy community comprise a far greater danger to good education than does a more serious attempt to formulate the knowledge base. Nancy represents a model of pedagogical excellence that should become the basis for the new reforms. A proper understanding of the knowledge base of teaching, the sources for that knowledge, and the complexities of the pedagogical process will make the emergence of such teachers more likely.

References

Baxter, J. (in preparation). *Teacher explanations in computer programming: A study of knowledge transformation*. Unpublished doctoral dissertation in progress, Stanford University.

Ben-Peretz, M. (1975). The concept of curriculum potential. *Curriculum Theory Network, 5,* 151–159.

Berliner, D. (1986). In pursuit of the expert pedagogue. *Educational Researcher, 15*(7) 5–13.

Bloom, B. S. (1976). *Human characteristics and school learning.* New York: McGraw-Hill.

Brodkey, J. J. (1986). *Learning while teaching: Self-assessment in the classroom.* Unpublished doctoral dissertation, Stanford University.

Brophy, J. J., & Good, T. (1986). Teacher behavior and student achievement. In M. C. Wittrock (Ed.), *Handbook of research on teaching* (3rd ed., pp. 328–375). New York: Macmillan.

Carnegie Task Force on Teaching as a Profession. (1986). *A nation prepared: Teachers for the 21st Century.* Washington, DC: Carnegie Forum on Education and the Economy.

Clement, J. (1982). Students' preconceptions in introductory mechanics. *American Journal of Physics, 50,* 67–71.

Dewey, J. (1904). The relation of theory to practice in education. In C. A. McMurry (Ed.), *The relation of theory to practice in the education of teachers* (Third Yearbook of the National Society for the Scientific Study of Education, Part I). Bloomington, IL: Public School Publishing.

Erlwanger, S. H. (1975). Case studies of children's conceptions of mathematics, Part I. *Journal of Children's Mathematical Behavior, 1,* 157–283.

Fenstermacher, G. (1978). A philosophical consideration of recent research on teacher effectiveness. In L. S. Shulman (Ed.), *Review of research in education* (Vol. 6, pp. 157–185). Itasca, IL: Peacock.

Fenstermacher, G. (1986). Philosophy of research on teaching: Three aspects. In M. C. Wittrock (Ed.), *Handbook of research on teaching* (3rd ed., pp. 37–49). New York: Macmillan.

Gage, N. L. (1978). *The scientific basis of the art of teaching.* New York: Teachers College Press.

Gage, N. L. (1986). *Hard gains in the soft sciences: The case of pedagogy.* Bloomington, IN: Phi Delta Kappa.

Gardner, H. (1986). *The mind's new science: A history of cognitive revolution.* New York: Basic Books.

Green, T. F. (1971). *The activities of teaching.* New York: McGraw-Hill.

Grossman, P. (1985). *A passion for language: From text to teaching* (Knowledge Growth in Teaching Publications Series). Stanford: Stanford University, School of Education.

Gudmundsdottir, S. (in preparation). *Knowledge use among experienced teachers: Four case studies of high school teaching.* Unpublished doctoral dissertation in progress, Stanford University.

Hashweh, M. Z. (1985). *An exploratory study of teacher knowledge and teaching: The effects of science teachers' knowledge of subject-matter and their conceptions of learning on their teaching.* Unpublished doctoral dissertation, Stanford University.

The Holmes Group (1986). *Tomorrow's teachers: A report of the Holmes Group.* East Lansing, MI: Author.

Leinhardt, G. (1983). Novice and expert knowledge of individual student's achievement. *Educational Psychologist, 18,* 165–179.

Leinhardt, G., & Greeno, J. G. (1986). The cognitive skill of teaching. *Journal of Educational Psychology, 78,* 75–95.

Leinhardt, G., & Smith, D. A. (1985). Expertise in mathematics instruction: Subject matter knowledge. *Journal of Educational Psychology, 77,* 247–271.

Marton, F. (1986). *Towards a pedagogy of content.* Unpublished manuscript, University of Gothenburg, Sweden.

Norman, D. A. (1980). What goes on in the mind of the learner? In W. J. McKeachie (Ed.), *New directions for teaching and learning: Learning, cognition, and college teaching* (Vol. 2). San Francisco: Jossey-Bass.

Petrie, H. (1986, May). *The liberal arts and sciences in the teacher education curriculum.* Paper presented at the Conference on Excellence in Teacher Preparation through the Liberal Arts, Muhlenberg College, Allentown, PA.

Richert, A. (in preparation). *Reflex to reflection: Facilitating reflection in novice teachers*. Unpublished doctoral dissertation in progress, Stanford University.

Rosenshine, B. (1986, April). *Unsolved issues in teaching content: A critique of a lesson on Federalist Paper No. 10*. Paper presented at the meeting of the American Educational Research Association, San Francisco, CA.

Rosenshine, B., & Stevens, R. S. (1986). Teaching functions. In M. C. Wittrock (Ed.) *Handbook of research on teaching* (3rd ed., pp. 376–391). New York: Macmillan.

Rosenthal, R., & Jacobson, L. (1968). *Pygmalion in the classroom*. New York: Holt, Rinehart & Winston.

Scheffler, I. (1965). *Conditions of knowledge: An introduction to epistemology and education*. Chicago: University of Chicago Press.

Schwab, J. J. (1964). The structure of the disciplines: Meanings and significances. In G. W. Ford & L. Pugno (Eds.), *The structure of knowledge and the curriculum*. Chicago: Rand McNally.

Schwab, J. J. (1983). The practical four: Something for curriculum professors to do. *Curriculum Inquiry, 13*, 239–265.

Shulman, L. S. (1986a). Paradigms and research programs for the study of teaching. In M. C. Wittrock (Ed.), *Handbook of research on teaching* (3rd ed., pp. 3–36). New York: Macmillan.

Shulman, L. S. (1986b). Those who understand: Knowledge growth in teaching. *Educational Researcher, 15*(2), 4–14.

Shulman, L. S., & Keislar, E. R. (Eds.). (1966). *Learning by discovery: A critical appraisal*. Chicago: Rand McNally.

Shulman, L. S., & Sykes, G. (1986, March). *A national board for teaching?: In search of a bold standard* (Paper commissioned for the Task Force on Teaching as a Profession, Carnegie Forum on Education and the Economy).

Smith, B. O. (1980). *A design for a school of pedagogy*. Washington, DC: U.S. Department of Education.

Sykes, G. (1986). *The social consequences of standard-setting in the professions* (Paper commissioned for the Task Force on Teaching as a Profession, Carnegie Forum on Education and the Economy).

Wilson, S. M., Shulman, L. S., & Richert, A. (in press). "150 different ways" of knowing: Representations of knowledge in teaching. In J. Calderhead (Ed.), *Exploring teacher thinking*. Sussex, Eng.: Holt, Rinehart & Winston.

Preparation of this paper was made possible, in part, by grants to Stanford University from the Spencer Foundation for the project, Knowledge Growth in a Profession, and from the Carnegie Corporation of New York for research on the development of new modes of assessment for teachers, Lee S. Shulman, principal investigator. Suzanne Wilson, Pamela Grossman, and Judy Shulman provided criticism and counsel when it was most needed. A longer version of this paper will be available from the Carnegie Forum on Education and the Economy. The views expressed are the author's and are not necessarily shared by these organizations or individuals.

Toward a More Effective Model of Research on Teaching

ARTHUR S. BOLSTER, JR.

Classroom teachers wish to improve their craft and educational researchers want to generate useful knowledge, yet educational research seldom influences classroom teaching. Reflecting on twenty years' experience as a junior high school teacher and as a university professor involved in formal studies of classroom teaching, Arthur S. Bolster, Jr. examines the genesis and perpetuation of the divergent perspectives of teachers and educational researchers concerning how knowledge is formulated and determined. He advocates a sociolinguistic ethnographic approach as the research methodology most likely to generate knowledge that is both intellectually rigorous and helpful in teacher development.

For the past twenty years I have worked as a faculty member in two surprisingly separate and distinct worlds, a graduate school of education at a prestigious university and a public secondary school. From this experience I have learned that teaching, when compared to other professions such as business, medicine, law, dentistry, and public health, is least affected by the findings of professional research. In my own district, as in the larger world of education, relations between theorists and practitioners of pedagogy have generally been neither close nor highly productive.[1] Professors of education and the courses they offer are not highly respected by my fellow teachers, with the single exception of practice teaching, which typically is supervised by classroom teachers, not university professors. Moreover, as I reflect upon my own teaching and observe that of my public school colleagues, I find it hard to identify any fundamental changes in classroom practice that have been the direct result of specific advances in educational theory. More commonly, innovations in the organization of materials and methods of instruction, such as "open education" and curricula based on the "structure of the disciplines," derive from theory that at most could be called "middle level," or applied theory. These new practices typically enjoy a brief vogue in the schools and then are gradually overpowered by the more persistent techniques of traditional pedagogy.

---

[1] After an extensive on-site examination of leading schools of education in the United States, the British scholar, Harry Judge, notes the puzzling paradox that, although this country's top graduate schools of education "bask in national and international favor," they display "glaring symptoms of insecurity and self-doubt," and "by deliberate choice have tended to distance themselves from both the task of training teachers for elementary and secondary schools and from addressing the problems and needs of those schools." See *American Graduate Schools of Education: A View from Abroad* (New York: Ford Foundation, 1982), pp. 5-6.

Harvard Educational Review   Vol. 53   No. 3   August 1983, 294–308

It does not seem reasonable to account for this lack of connection between formal pedagogical research and school instruction by claiming that teachers do not want sound knowledge on which to base their practice, or to argue that research on teaching has produced no valid, reliable theory. On the contrary, most public school teachers I know are constantly seeking greater understanding of their craft, and from my own perspective, at least, much educational theory is relevant in day-to-day classroom concerns.[2]

Why then has basic research on teaching had so little influence on practice? The major reason, in my opinion, is that most such research, especially that emanating from top-ranked schools of education, construes teaching from a theoretical perspective that is incompatible with the perspective teachers must employ in thinking about their work. In other words, researchers and schoolteachers adopt radically different sets of assumptions about how to conceptualize the teaching process. As a result, the conclusions of much formal research on teaching appear irrelevant to classroom teachers — not necessarily wrong, just not very sensible or useful. If researchers are to generate knowledge that is likely to affect classroom practice, they must construe their inquiries in ways that are much more compatible with teachers' perspectives. I would like to elaborate this proposition, in the hope that my university colleagues may reconceptualize some of their inquiries to make their scholarly efforts more credible and useful to those who teach in schools.

The Analytic Framework

As I reflect on my work over the past two decades, I recognize that there are two critical differences between how teachers and academic researchers understand the activity of teaching. The first difference lies in how teaching is *formulated*: how knowledge about teaching is perceived, discovered, and structured. This involves how pieces of information and principles of action are logically and conceptually related to one another so that they may be applied to an understanding of practice. The second difference lies in how knowledge about teaching is *determined*: how it is verified or proved.[3] These two dimensions of knowing — discovery and verification — are interrelated; neither my university colleagues seeking valid and reliable theory nor my fellow teachers seeking dependable knowledge upon which to base pedagogy discover significant principles of action at one point in time and validate them at another. Events do not become significant merely because they occur but only when they are noted and organized into a coherent pattern. What one believes to be significant, therefore, depends not only upon what previous experience has taught one to consider important, but also upon beliefs about the most trustworthy way to validate the evidence. Since teachers' and researchers' assump-

[2] Several examples come easily to mind. The basic postulates developed by Ned S. Flanders in *Analyzing Teaching Behavior* (Reading, Mass.: Addison-Wesley, 1970), clearly allow making predictions about the most prevalent classroom activity, verbal interaction; see also Edmund Amidon and John Hough, eds., *Interaction Analysis: Theory, Research, and Application* (Reading, Mass.: Addison-Wesley, 1967). Jacob Kounin has persuasively articulated a number of propositions about one of the most salient concerns of teachers, classroom management, in *Discipline and Group Management in Classrooms* (New York: Holt, Rinehart and Winston, 1970). Michael Dunkin and Bruce Biddle in *The Study of Teaching* (New York: Holt, Rinehart and Winston, 1974), reviewed nearly 500 studies which they classified as research on teaching.

[3] I first encountered these two concepts in the writings of the late Morris Cohen; see his *Reason and Nature: An Essay on the Meaning of Scientific Method* (Glencoe, Ill.: Free Press, 1931).

tions about how knowledge is both formulated and determined differ so markedly, discontinuities of belief are inevitable.

How Teachers Come to Know About Teaching

How, then, do teachers formulate and determine their knowledge about teaching? How do they develop the principles that undergird their viewpoints about the best way to teach? Careful reflection on my own pedagogy and countless hours of conversation with my teacher-colleagues have convinced me that the most important influence on teachers' knowledge of their craft is that it is formulated and determined in a classroom that demands specific categories of knowledge derived from the uses it must serve. The structure of the teaching environment—typically one instructor with twenty-five to thirty-five young people in a classroom—requires that teachers function consistently as *situational decisionmakers*; the knowledge that they deem most important will be derived from that process.[4] Necessarily, teachers will perceive themselves as primarily responsible for managing the classroom situation in such a way that students will achieve specific—usually cognitive and skill-oriented—outcomes.

By conventional wisdom, the teaching process follows a sequence of operations. First, instruction must be planned before the class meets. This requires that instructional objectives be defined at a sufficiently precise level, and that tasks be organized carefully so that their completion by the students will lead to the desired outcomes. When the class meets, the planned tasks must be assigned to the students and the classroom activity managed in such a way as to facilitate their accomplishment. Although student teachers are usually taught that it is critical to specify behavioral objectives as the starting-point of their lesson plan, in actual practice the process of teaching is often not so carefully sequenced. Veteran teachers do not plan class sessions in neat detail. Instead they tend to focus on efficiently directing a stream of activities; systematic thought about outcomes functions more as a rationalization than as a rationale for instruction.

In either process, productive situational decisionmaking is the touchstone of the teaching craft. In the course of their work, competent teachers make an amazing number of decisions based on predictions about the probable effect of their actions on students' task accomplishment. When teachers are planning, these predictions are anticipatory and based largely on beliefs acquired from previous experience. In classroom sessions, the predictions are made more existentially through a process of giving and receiving cues. This process can be seen by the following example. As the class begins, the teacher gives the students instructions concerning the task assignment and appropriate social behavior. Frequently these instructions are given in the form of verbal directives, but they may be communicated nonverbally as well, and more likely there will be some combination of these modes. (By gently laying a hand on the head of a little boy who has begun writing, the teacher signals the impropriety of beginning an assignment before listening to all the directions.) Students interpret these teacher initiatives as cues to determine expected behavior and respond verbally and nonverbally. (The impatient little

---

[4] Situational thinking is also seen as critical to the teaching process by Louis M. Smith and William Geoffrey; see their *An Analysis Toward a General Theory of Teaching: Complexities of an Urban Classroom* (New York: Holt, Rinehart and Winston, 1968).

boy puts down his pencil and stares blankly off into space.) The teacher reads these responses, selecting one or more of them as cues to determine the extent of progress. (Being turned off by a mild rebuke is not like Billy, the teacher muses. She wonders if he is frustrated by the assignment or if some extraneous event is upsetting him.) On the basis of this analysis, the teacher selects and issues one or more "remedial cues" designed to move the students' activity and social behavior closer to the desired outcomes. ("You may begin now," she announces to the class. "While you're working, I'll be around to see how each of you is doing. Billy, why don't I begin with you? Let me see how you've started your paper.") The remedial cues in turn elicit further student response and the complicated interaction process continues until the class session ends.

As this cue-exchanging process is repeated over a number of class meetings, a mutually defined classroom culture emerges which, like all cultures, demands that participants conform to certain norms.[5] The specific elements of the culture vary from classroom to classroom, but the process of its development is always the same. Indeed, more than any other influence, it is this universal definition of teaching that, I believe, causes the underlying "sameness" that all classrooms appear to have to the casual observer. It is my assumption that most teachers' knowledge of teaching is achieved by this continual participation in the situational decisionmaking process and the classroom culture which results from interaction between teacher and students. The beliefs, values, and norms — that is, the knowledge — that teachers come to have the most faith in and use most frequently to guide their instructional behavior are those consistent with predictions that have "worked" in the complex and demanding classroom arena.

Several implications of this conception of teaching as situational decisionmaking help explain the dissonance between researchers' and teachers' views of instruction. First, teachers' views of teaching derive largely from "interactive problem-solving." It is through this process, as Charles Lindblom and David Cohen note in their perceptive analysis of social inquiry, that most "ordinary" social knowledge is achieved. Because of the derivation of teachers' knowledge of teaching, then, it appears to be more "everyday" and "commonsensical" both in form and in structure, than highly specialized and theoretical.[6] Second, contrary to the opinion I have heard expressed on more than one occasion in the halls of academe, it is not reasonable to conclude from this that schoolteaching is a relatively simple-minded professional activity. In fact, in my conceptualization of situational decisionmaking, teaching emerges as a highly complex and intellectually demanding task, and its effective accomplishment clearly requires superior intelligence. Finally, it seems logical that skill in situational decisionmaking would improve, at least up to a point, as one acquires additional experience. Implicit recognition of this fact, I believe, largely accounts for both the widespread belief among teachers that experience is the *sine qua non* of teacher effectiveness, as well as the corollary belief that it is practice teaching rather than knowledge of educational theory which is critical to teacher preparation.

---

[5] My definition of the teaching process has much in common with, and doubtless owes something to, the "classroom ecology paradigm" delineated by Walter Doyle in "Paradigms for Research on Teacher Effectiveness," in *Review of Research in Education*, ed. Lee S. Shulman (Itasca, Ill.: Peacock, 1977), p. 176.

[6] Lindblom and Cohen, *Usable Knowledge: Social Science and Social Problem Solving* (New Haven: Yale Univ. Press, 1979), pp. 18-29.

The Characteristics of Teachers' Knowledge of Teaching

Teachers' knowledge of teaching has two basic characteristics from which other attributes flow. First, it is *idiographic* in origin and therefore *particularistic* in character; that is, this knowledge arises from the need to comprehend the complexity of a particular context with sufficient accuracy to be able to act efficaciously in it. Such knowledge derives not so much from a systematic comparison of a number of similar situations as it does from an intuitive analysis of a specific context in which many important qualities are assumed to be unique. Every teacher, in fact, "knows" that although there are many similarities between classes, each group has its own special characteristics, and that successful teaching requires the recognition and acknowledgement of this uniqueness. Second, teachers' knowledge of teaching is validated pragmatically. Principles are believed to be true when they give rise to actions that "work." For example, when I began teaching eighth grade after a dozen years as a university instructor, I experienced success only when I stopped trying to derive my instructional strategies from theories of early adolescence and curriculum development, and began basing them on what had and had not been effective in previous class sessions.

Four other attributes of teachers' knowledge of teaching are correlates of its particularistic and pragmatic characteristics. First, knowledge that works in a classroom involves tacit consensus between the teacher and students about their mutual expectations. The task which U.S. society imposes on a teacher might, I think, be labeled "instrumental acculturation." Over and over again teachers are publicly and professionally reminded that they are expected to teach all of their students at least some portion of what they need to know to become competent adults. Typically, this task is accomplished in a self-contained classroom. Teachers, therefore, come to believe that they must already possess what each child needs to acquire and that they are expected to guide, monitor, and evaluate each student's progress. While each child is assumed to have unique needs and abilities, teachers' expectations and techniques, to be credible, must be acceptable variants of a general pattern of professional behavior called "teaching." For teachers, therefore, successful classroom management demands understanding the varied ways in which each child interprets and responds to classroom events. The child's successful negotiation of the classroom environment requires comprehending the teacher's expectations and responding to them in acceptable, and therefore rewardable, ways.

Those who work in schools realize that teaching and learning become more efficient as the participants in the classroom become aware of its particular characteristics. A very skillful junior high teacher once explained his effectiveness to me by claiming that his instructional efforts during the first three weeks of each school year were devoted entirely to making his particular expectations "crystal clear" to his students. From then on, he maintained, everything else was relatively easy. It is also this particularistic quality of classrooms that underlies the accurate conventional wisdom among students that the way to succeed in school is to "psyche out" the teachers. While writing this article I received a letter from a former eighth grade student who currently is enrolled in a private school. He informed me that he now types all of his assignments at ten characters per inch instead of twelve to make his teachers think his papers are longer than they actually are. "Don't worry," he wrote me, "I never did that in your class because I found out that what you cared about was quality not length."

Second, valid knowledge of teaching must be based on a holistic conception of the classroom which assumes multiple causation of events. From a teacher's viewpoint, children are not the "passive recipients of instructional treatments."[7] Rather, what a teacher decides to do at any one moment in a class session is very likely to depend on an assessment of what has just occurred. Any single event, therefore, may have several meanings depending on variations of person or circumstance, a characteristic of classrooms that helps explain the not uncommon experience among secondary school teachers of having a carefully planned lesson proceed smoothly with one class at 9:00 A.M. and yet be largely ineffective with an apparently similar group an hour and a half later.

Third, valid knowledge upon which to base teaching must allow for unanticipated contingencies, some of which may be entirely beyond the teacher's control. Although effective teaching clearly requires maintaining reasonable order in the classroom, there are severe limits on the degree to which control can be imposed. Not only do the varying needs of each student make it impossible to predict accurately, and thus control each child's behavior at any given moment, but the fact that each classroom is embedded in a larger school structure makes it frequently subject to the influence of outside events. Every experienced teacher is well aware of the pronounced influence that unannounced fire drills, upcoming athletic and social events, or playground accidents can have on the most artfully designed lesson plan.

Finally, and most importantly, teachers' knowledge of teaching, once achieved, tends to be highly resistant to change. Principles of practice, honed in the demanding arena of the classroom, are not easily discarded or revised, even in the face of conflicting evidence from the most careful experimental studies. Teachers, in fact, appear to have a high degree of mistrust of knowledge about education that is expressed in the specialized language of social science. I recall one teacher defining social science as a "remarkably complicated way of talking about remarkably commonsense notions." To some extent, this distrust of formalized knowledge is similar to the suspicion most people have when problematic situations in their daily lives are explained to them in technical terms by experts. Yet teachers' resistance to modifying their teaching based on the findings of educational research is more than just a matter of semantics; a more important factor is the effect of the teaching role on the stability of beliefs. Classrooms, I have noted, are complex environments requiring rapid and effective responses to a potentially bewildering multiplicity of events. One novice teacher explained to me why she had not made her responses to her class conform more to what she knew about child psychology: "With all that reality crashing in on me, I don't have time to think."

In the practice of teaching, there is an urgency to establish comprehensive principles of action that will severely limit the range of available choices and that will allow the teacher to distinguish those cues likely to be significant from the many others that can be ignored. Moreover, as in all professional behavior, teaching tends to become institutionalized. Schooling is one of the universal experiences in our society, and it engenders a set of widely held expectations that broadly define appropriate teacher behavior. Students carry these societal and institutional expectations as they move from classroom to classroom. Although there are important variations among teachers' responses to these ex-

---

[7] I have borrowed this highly descriptive phrase from Walter Doyle, "Classroom Tasks and Student Abilities," in *Research on Teaching: Concepts, Findings, and Implications*, ed. Penelope L. Peterson and Herbert J. Walberg (Berkeley: McCutchan, 1979), p. 203.

pectations, they establish the outer limits of allowable variance. Teachers, having to practice their craft in a hierarchically structured organization alongside their professional peers, will tend to adhere to superordinate standards of belief with which all acceptable professional knowledge must agree.[8]

Under such circumstances, knowledge tends to become objectified—that is, beliefs, norms, and values will typically be perceived as inherent in the particular work situation and consequently not easily subject to change.[9] Teachers, for example, believe that to maintain order in a junior high school classroom, they must establish formal relationships with students at the beginning of the academic year. "Don't smile until Christmas" is only a slight exaggeration of this widely held norm. This principle rests not on careful analysis of classroom interaction over time but on the widely held assumption that adolescents naturally tend to resist authority and therefore need to have limits specified and reinforced. When teachers, acting on that assumption, are deliberately formal in their classroom demeanor at the beginning of the year, a self-fulfilling prophecy is established. Students come to expect teachers to treat them formally; should they encounter an instructor whose demeanor is highly informal, they will tend to behave deviantly, thereby demonstrating their "natural" tendency to resist authority.

Clearly, however, logic does not reside in events occurring in the classroom but rather in the conclusions participants reach when they reflect on the meaning of those events. Teachers act, observe responses to their actions, and interpret the meaning of those responses. The beliefs, norms, and values which guide their teaching behavior are the generalized results of these reflections. In this sense, the principles underlying teaching practice are "man-made" and should be subject to change in the light of disconfirming evidence. The fact that formal research results rarely encourage teachers to question these generalizations can be accounted for by the radically different characteristics of research knowledge. It is to the researchers' process of generating knowledge that I now turn.

How Researchers Find Out About Teaching

The wellspring of the researcher's knowledge of teaching is not the arena of experience but the tradition of academic social science. I became especially aware of this when, having returned from a morning's teaching in the junior high school, I was asked by university colleagues to comment on their classroom-related research. In spite of their claims to the contrary, I came to believe that researchers do not enter classrooms with a neutral methodology, aiming to discover and verify fundamental principles which explain the processes of teaching and learning. Rather, they come as accredited scholars whose perspectives derive from formal disciplines.[10] Both the substantive principles

[8] The apparent high degree of similarity of professional beliefs among teachers at different levels of the school system—elementary, junior high, and senior high—owes much to the distinctive ways in which schools are organized as well as to the differing ages of the children within each school level.

[9] My theory on the derivation and stability of teachers' beliefs owes a great deal to Peter L. Berger and Thomas Luckmann, *The Social Construction of Reality: A Treatise in the Sociology of Knowledge* (Garden City, New York: Doubleday-Anchor, 1967), esp. ch. 2, "Society as Objective Reality."

[10] The conventional definition of objectivity in research is the condition under which any unbiased observer would reach the same conclusion given the same evidence. The term *unbiased*, however, does not mean that observers approach the inquiry with no frame of reference. It would be more accurate to say that the observers agree to share an identical bias—at least, methodological—about the process to be used in arriving at valid conclusions.

which inform their interests and sensitize their perceptions of what is important — how knowledge will be formulated — and the acceptable canons of proof — how knowledge will be determined — have already been firmly established by their formal training, thus constraining the results of the inquiry.

Moreover, like schoolteaching, academic social science is an institutionalized profession, organized to ensure that its members will maintain common standards of achievement. I remember thinking during my dogged pursuit of a Ph.D. in history that, in view of its highly meritocratic character, the usual pattern of doctoral training seemed partially an "initiation rite" intended to socialize scholar-apprentices like myself into accepting the intellectual standards of our masters. Later, when as a young professor I began to submit manuscripts to professional journals, I realized that the conventional apparatus by which the writings of scholars are evaluated by their peers before and after publication has exactly the same effect. The merits of a researcher's conclusions are not formally determined by practitioners of the profession under inquiry, but by colleagues in the investigator's academic discipline. The worth of the conclusions will consequently be judged primarily by how effectively the procedural and substantive criteria of social science were employed in achieving them. Under these conditions, as is the case with teachers, the perspectives through which researchers learn about teaching are apt to be stable and unlikely to be changed — even in the interest of increasing the practical utility of the resultant knowledge.[11] To explain why the results of social science-based inquiries into classrooms so rarely seem useful to teachers, therefore, we must understand how that knowledge is formulated and determined and the extent to which it is qualitatively different from the knowledge teachers acquire through their experience in classrooms.

The major characteristics of social science research knowledge derive from the epistemological premises that provide its foundation. First, conventional social science is *nomothetic* in aim and *universalistic* in character; that is, social scientists seek to establish general principles about classes of human objects. Their aim is not to explain a particular situation in as much depth as possible, but rather to define and demonstrate the systematic operation of principles across like situations. Second, knowledge is considered valid when it is produced according to the criteria of experimental science. Principles formulated at one place and time must be verified at another. Thus, an inquiry which produces significant explanations about a particular situation must be replicated in other like situations before the results can be judged valid and reliable.

Knowledge of teaching generated according to these premises is conceptually very different from the knowledge derived from practice. In contrast to the teachers' holistic perspective of the classroom, the researchers' will more likely be reductionist. Since the traditional aim of social science has been to establish principles that operate across a range of similar situations, its method is to look at a limited number of variables in a given situation, and to control for others. Formal research in classrooms, therefore, is more likely to try to predict the consistent relationship between discrete classes of teacher and student behavior than to explain the complexity of the process of teaching as a whole.[12] Antecedent and consequent conditions are treated as distinct from one an-

---

[11] Like all such tales, the apocryphal anecdote about the toast raised at the annual meeting of a mathematics association exaggerates a kernel of truth: "Here's to more elaborate and elegant mathematical theory. May it always be of absolutely no use to anyone."

[12] Theoretically, the complexity of the teaching process as a whole could be explained only after all of the most salient of these discrete relationships had been isolated and predicted.

other and as linear and additive in relationship. The most influential behaviors are assumed to be those that occur most frequently. Furthermore, social science researchers generally use only external, observable events as basic data. Usually these are in the form of objective measures of students' and teachers' performance. Each event is normally construed to have only one meaning. The physical and social structure of the classroom may be discounted, and the differing perceptions of teachers and students ignored or neutralized, presumably on the assumption that they are consistent with or irrelevant to the conceptual definitions implicit in the research design. Similarly, formal inquiry into classrooms seeks to filter out the effects of unanticipated contingencies on teaching and learning since the validity and reliability of scientific predictions assume consistency across situations. Often researchers seem to assume that the most significant actions of teachers and students are responses to classroom conditions over which teachers potentially have complete control.[13]

Most important of all, much social science research on teaching assumes that causation in classrooms operates unilaterally from the teacher to the students. Especially in studies of teacher effectiveness, learning is construed as student achievement resulting from the process of teaching which, in turn, is defined in terms of teacher initiatives which stimulate student responses. These initiatives may be seen as directly provoking specific student reactions, or, in some research on the effects of teaching, may be construed as prompting definable forms of information processing which in turn produce learning. In either case, teaching is viewed exclusively in terms of the influence instructors have on pupils; the reciprocal effects of students on teachers or of students on students, and then on teachers, are thought to be either nonexistent or not of central consequence.

Essentially, then, most formal research on teaching conceptualizes teaching not as a process, but as an achievement. Teaching is what happens when students learn. The way to build the most useful and reliable knowledge about teaching is thought to entail identifying those specific behaviors of teachers that, under specified conditions, will universally produce identifiable "learning outcomes" in pupils. It is this underlying conceptualization that is so incompatible with the teachers' perspectives of their work because it fails to take into account the elements of the particular classroom situation — the raw materials of the teachers' craft.

Toward a More Effective Model of Research on Teaching

If the conceptual underpinnings of conventional social science research make its conclusions seem irrelevant to teachers, is it possible to structure formal classroom inquiries in ways that are compatible with teachers' perspectives while maintaining the intellectual rigor that systematic scholarship could add to the revision of pedagogy? Can we in universities whose interest and expertise is in the analysis of teaching produce knowledge that satisfies the scholarly canons of social science and at the same time seems sensible and is therefore useful to schoolteacher-colleagues? Upon what epistemological assumptions would such research have to be based, and how would these assumptions differ from those implied in most present research on teaching?

---

[13] Brian Fay, in *Social Theory and Political Practice* (London: Allen & Unwin, 1975), p. 94, makes this criticism of much formal social science.

I believe that the fundamental requirement of any inquiry which hopes to be conso-nant with the teachers' perspective on teaching is that it must view human behavior as reflexive. People must be considered as both the creators and the products of the social situations in which they live. The basic premises from which this postulate stems are those underlying symbolic interactionism: people act on the basis of the meanings events have for them; the meaning of events arises out of social interaction; and each person "selects, checks, suspends, regroups and transforms the meanings in the light of the sit-uation in which he is placed and the direction of his action."[14] In all our activities, we act on the basis of intent, observe the reaction of others to our behavior, and act purpose-fully again. The most important elements of any social situation are the shared mean-ings which participants take from the process of interaction and which ultimately shape their behavior. Significant knowledge of any social situation, therefore, consists of an awareness of the emerging meanings that participants are developing and the specific ways that these meanings are functioning to shape their endeavors and thus the charac-teristics of the situation itself.

Applied to the process of teaching, the assumption of reflexivity requires envisioning each classroom as a small culture created by teacher and students as they work together over a period of time. The basic elements of the process of teaching in such a conceptual-ization are not defined as specific teacher initiatives which cause students to master skills or process information in predictable ways, but rather as the constant demands that a specific classroom environment places on those who work in it. The ultimate purpose of research based on this view of teaching is not to generate universal propositions that pre-dict teacher effectiveness, but rather to build and verify a coherent explanation of how a particular classroom works.[15] The resultant knowledge will not be expressed as nostrums to improve teacher competence, but as systematic and reliable information which teachers can use to shed light on their own pedagogical situations.

Such research would consist of *thick, critical descriptions* of what is naturally and characteristically occurring as teacher and students go about their daily business in a specific classroom. *Thick, critical description* is loaded with concrete detail about what participants do and say in the setting and is deliberately interpretive, identifying salient patterns of events and generating propositions that explain their interrelationships. The emphasis in these descriptions is on function and process: how what people are saying and doing is being used to make the classroom operate as a unit. The achievement of such knowledge requires that the classroom be construed as a social system character-ized by reciprocity among participants and between the participants and the physical setting. The complex interrelationships among place, roles, and activities are thus cen-tral in explaining the meaning of behavior.[16]

The methodology for such an inquiry would be ethnographic, with data gathered largely by participant-observation. This is therefore qualitative research, consisting of

[14] Herbert Blumer, quoted in Jerold Heiss, *The Social Psychology of Interaction* (Englewood Cliffs, N.J.: Prentice Hall, 1981), pp. 2-3. The theoretical formulation of social interaction stems largely from the thought of George Herbert Mead; see esp. his *Mind, Self, and Society* (Chicago: Univ. of Chicago Press, 1934). Ann and Harold Berlak also argue persuasively for a reflexive perspective in their *Dilemmas of Schooling: Teach-ing and Social Change* (New York: Methuen, 1981), pp. 10-18; 111-119.

[15] Doyle, "Paradigms for Research on Teacher Effectiveness," elaborates this contention effectively.

[16] A useful outline of the epistemology of this kind of research can be found in Uri Bronfenbrenner, "The Experimental Ecology of Education," *Educational Researcher*, 5 (1976), 5-15.

systematic and detailed observations of the physical properties of the setting and the behavior of people in it related to specific information about the meanings participants are assigning to classroom events.[17] Major explanatory propositions would be "grounded" in these observations, and the discovery and verification of hypotheses—that is, the formulation and determination of the research—would take place reciprocally, as the researchers constantly compare the relationship between salient patterns of events and the emergent meanings being assigned to them over time.[18] The researchers would enter the classroom as self-consciously open and broadminded as possible. The question which would initially guide the inquiry is merely, "What's going on here?" As they systematically define the properties of the classroom, observe events in it, and listen to people talk about them, patterns of the events and the interrelationships among them would begin to emerge. The investigators would treat these as hypotheses, defining the relationships as specifically as possible and noting the contextual properties associated with them so that they could be "tested" in future observations. These patterns would be elaborated and revised in the face of new data. Given the assumptions of symbolic interactionism, the eventual critical description would be validated in two ways: *referentially*—the explanatory generalizations must be consistent with repeated patterns of events recorded in the observational data; and *situationally*—the explanatory framework must be consistent with the meanings teachers and students draw from and impose upon the classroom situation.[19]

Prototypes of the mode of research I am suggesting already exist in the growing number of ethnographic studies of classrooms which have been appearing since the mid-1970s. Stemming from the disciplines of sociolinguistics and anthropology, and based on assumptions underlying symbolic interactionism, these studies have typically attempted to describe how communication functions to establish and maintain the norms which shape behavior in specific classrooms. Employing the procedures of ethnomethodological research, such studies incorporate student and teacher interpretations of what is occurring with direct observations of events, from which interpretations arise in fashioning descriptions of the classroom culture. Owing to the research design, these studies are both detailed and complex. Rather than attempting to analyze the entire classroom culture, such studies usually focus on selected aspects, though always from a holistic perspective. As a whole, however, carefully implemented research of this type can generate descriptions of the distinctive nature of specific classrooms.[20]

---

[17] Since the inquiry seeks to describe relationships among the many contextual properties of the classroom, quantitative methodologies do not appear to be highly useful, although, as Richard Light and David Pillemer note, quantitative measures are potentially very effective in identifying relationships that are not apparent from visual observation. See their "Numbers and Narrative: Combining Their Strengths in Research Reviews," *Harvard Educational Review*, 52 (1982), 1-26.

[18] Barney G. Glaser and Anselm L. Strauss, *The Discovery of Grounded Theory: Strategies for Qualitative Research* (New York: Aldine, 1976), chs. 1-5.

[19] I believe it is unprofitable to argue about whether ethnographic research is "scientific." As Dell Hymes notes in *Language in Education: Ethnolinguistic Essays* (Washington, D.C.: Center for Applied Linguistics, 1980), p. 105, the skills needed to produce effective ethnography are enhancements of skills we all use in everyday life. Moreover, as Elliot Eisner observes in *The Educational Imagination: On the Design and Evaluation of School Programs* (New York: Macmillan, 1979), ch. 11, the ability to formulate the subtle qualities of a setting is closely akin to the skill required of a literary artist. Certainly the research I have in mind would be both thought about and expressed in everyday language.

[20] There is a growing body of ethnographic research on classroom contexts too extensive to cite completely. The research of Frederick Erickson and his present and former students is particularly illustrative of the points

In the past five years I have attempted to apply this sociolinguistic, ethnomethodological model of research as a strategy for teacher development. The more I became aware of and experienced with this methodology, the more I became convinced that of all the models of research I knew, this model has the greatest potential for generating knowledge that is both useful and interesting to teachers. Unlike the more conventional quantitative modes of social science inquiry into teaching, the basic conceptualization of this approach is consistent with teachers' perspectives on their craft. Its basic stance is idiographic; its goal is to provide an in-depth understanding of the complexity of a particular classroom rather than the experimental derivation of a selected number of elements whose relationship can be replicated elsewhere. Similarly, this approach focuses on situated meanings which incorporate the various reactions and perspectives of students. In common with the teachers' perspective, it assumes the multiple causation of events: the classroom is viewed as a complex social system in which both direct and indirect influences operate. Unanticipated contingencies potentially illuminate rather than confound understanding since reaction to the unexpected often highlights the salient meanings assigned to what is normal.

Most important of all, symbolic interactionist research in classrooms necessarily relies heavily on the teacher's interpretation of events. The relationship between teacher and researcher as colleagues, therefore, is more perceptive than political, and each has individual and professional motivations for nourishing and extending it. As I have noted, the teacher's efficacy as a situational decisionmaker largely depends upon the ability to make accurate predictions about the relationships between classroom variables and students' task and social behavior. Correspondingly, the symbolic interactionist researcher must comprehend and accept the teacher's views, not merely as a conventional requirement of professional courtesy or to facilitate access to data, but because understanding the meanings the teacher is imposing on classroom events is vital to the research conclusions.[21] The researcher's observations are thus a potentially valuable source of information to the teacher, and can be used to reduce the unexplained complexity of classroom events, thereby facilitating the achievement of the teacher's instructional aims. Moreover, the interactionist assumption that classrooms are inherently complex and the methodological obligation to describe that complexity as precisely as possible — rather than to identify what instructional behaviors are causing or preventing desirable student

made here. See esp. Susan Florio, *Learning to Go to School: An Ethnography of Interaction in a Kindergarten/First Grade Classroom*, Occasional Paper No. 26 (East Lansing, Mich.: Michigan State Univ., Institute for Research on Teaching, 1979); Frederick Erickson and Jeffrey Schultz, "When Is a Context? Some Issues and Methods in the Analysis of Social Competence," *Quarterly Newsletter for Comparative Human Development*, 1 (1977), pp. 5-10; Peter V. Owens, *Narrative Chaining, Discourse Conflict, and Conceptual Strain in Freshman Writing and Speech: A Study in the Teaching and Learning Processes of Basic Writing and Expository Composition*, Diss. Harvard Univ. 1982. See also Hugh Mehan, *Learning Lessons: Social Organization in the Classroom* (Cambridge, Mass.: Harvard Univ. Press, 1979).

[21] Much contemporary writing on school-university collaboration in research misses this point, I think, tending to emphasize political variables like differences in power and prestige or the issue of who controls the definition of research problems. Such writings tend to ignore what I perceive as the fundamental perceptual differences between most researchers and teachers. See, for example, Leslie L. Huling, Myron Trang, and Linda Correll, "Interactive Research and Development: A Promising Strategy for Teacher Educators," *Journal of Teacher Education*, 32 (1981), 13-14. After reviewing literature on a number of collaborative projects, this paper concludes that it is critical to involve practitioners in research "so that the persons who are affected by the change can participate in every phase of the change."

learning—seem likely to diffuse at least some of the anxiety that leads teachers to resist inquiries designed to evaluate and improve their effectiveness.

Both my own experience and that of my colleagues who have employed symbolic interactionist ethnographic research as a strategy for teacher development have borne out these predictions. For teachers, it has proved to be both useful and interesting. Teachers in whose classrooms we have worked have almost always been willing to invest many hours discussing observational data with researchers and have retrospectively reported that the experience was both professionally productive and intellectually stimulating. There is direct evidence in the analysis of taped conversations with investigators that those teachers who participate in such research tend to develop more differentiated and reflective views of their teaching. They testify that they have achieved insights into problematic dimensions of their instruction that they believe would otherwise have been unavailable to them. Further, identifiable changes in several teachers' pedagogy can be traced directly to specific research findings.[22] Such results are not extraordinary. We teachers nearly always act rationally in attempting to achieve our instructional goals but, as we soon discover, to behave rationally is not necessarily to act correctly.[23] Thus, it is not surprising that the classroom teachers with whom I have worked have often extolled the researcher's "extra pair of eyes and ears" that provided otherwise unavailable information on the immediate effects of instruction.

Yet there are two clear limitations of symbolic interactionist ethnographic research on teaching. One is conceptual, the other pragmatic. Conceptually, this type of research assumes that the most crucial knowledge about teaching is context-specific. As a consequence, no matter how carefully formulated and determined they may be, inquiries of this type have no demonstrable generalizability.[24] Since they are inherently in-depth studies of a single classroom, there is no way of knowing whether even these studies' most carefully documented explanatory hypotheses are applicable to other classrooms. Thus, the very quality that makes this mode of research highly useful to individual teachers severely limits its utility for the profession as a whole.

The severity of this limitation is not absolute, however. Carefully implemented ethnographic studies of the teaching process can identify ways in which instruction is affected by variables in a particular classroom. Granting the importance of contextual variables to specific outcomes, it seems reasonable to assume that there are broad areas of similarity among classroom environments, especially at the same grade levels. Consequently, when a sizeable body of ethnomethodological descriptions accumulates, we will have strong indications of how teaching effects occur in various types of settings.[25] It may ap-

---

[22] Teachers' reactions to participation in ethnographic research in their own classrooms are evident in formal evaluations of this research undertaken over a four-year period in some two dozen classes in several undergraduate colleges. See Arthur S. Bolster, Jr., "Preparing Graduate Students to Teach in College: Report on a New Harvard Course in Higher Education," unpublished manuscript, 1980. See also Susan Florio and Martha Walsh, *The Teacher as a Colleague in Classroom Research*, Occasional Paper No. 4 (East Lansing, Mich.: Michigan State Univ., Institute for Research on Teaching, 1978).

[23] Heiss makes this same point in *Social Psychology of Interaction*, p. 14.

[24] An eminent university colleague was apparently alluding to this point when he commented after reading one of my ethnographic studies in this mode that it was very illuminating but "it's really not social science scholarship. It's more like a first-rate consultant's report."

[25] Walter Doyle makes this same claim in "Research on Classroom Contexts," *Journal of Teacher Education*, 32 (November-December 1981), 3-5; Lindblom and Cohen's contention that knowledge resulting from professional social inquiry is best seen as an increment to other knowledge may also be relevant. See their *Usable Knowledge*, p. 52).

pear paradoxical to claim that what ethnographers perceive as significant are the particularistic qualities of the classroom but also that such research may spawn universal propositions about teaching. On the other hand, it would be simplistic to argue that all classroom variables are inherently unique to their particular setting or have no significance except in that specific configuration. Thus, qualitative methodologies should be especially useful in research on teaching, since they allow for specifying and elaborating the nature of relationships that apparently hold across settings.[26] Even if generalizability is accepted as a necessary criterion of useful academic research, naturalistic case study inquiries are a reasonable and necessary first step in this direction. Once a significant number of careful case studies have been completed and published, it should be possible to cross-compare their results in order to identify potentially significant variables whose validity and reliability could then be verified by experimental research.

The pragmatic limitation of symbolic interactionist ethnographic research — that it is highly labor-intensive — is more serious. The holistic perspective implicit in the research design requires that the researcher become immersed in the classroom over a considerable period of time. Many hours of observation are normally needed to gather the requisite data. Although videotaping can facilitate the data-gathering process, its use tends to increase rather than decrease the amount of time required to complete an inquiry.[27] Pairs or small teams of researchers can also be used to divide the hours of observation, and have the additional advantage of providing multiple perspectives on the same classroom. As with videotaping, however, this tends to increase rather than decrease the amount of labor, since a considerable amount of conference time is required to compare perspectives and establish inter-observer reliability. There seems to be no way of avoiding the fact that a substantial investment of time by skilled observers is normally required to produce firmly grounded naturalistic studies of classroom teaching.

This limitation, however, is by no means insurmountable. One way to provide a substantial pool of appropriately skilled observers is to organize courses at major universities that use contextual case studies of classrooms in nearby schools as a vehicle for teaching qualitative research skills. In fact, a substantial portion of the studies cited in this article originated from just this kind of arrangement.[28] To be effective, such courses must be carefully organized and supervised by faculty scholars so that the apprentice-researchers acquire the requisite observational and analytic skills in sufficient depth to generate worthwhile studies. Creating these conditions, however, has proved not only to be possible but to have unanticipated advantages. Experienced teachers seeking to increase their expertise through advanced graduate study testify that participation in this intensive mode of research is the best training experience they have ever had. Their empathy with the teacher's role generally makes them especially acute and sensitive observers; almost without exception they are able to produce competent and often insightful descriptions of the classrooms in which they work. Moreover, the need to define and supervise

---

[26] For a perceptive elaboration of this point, see Light and Pillemer.

[27] Videotaping supplements rather than replaces live observation. Even if one discounts the selectivity of the taping process — the person filming decides what to record — the tape itself must be viewed and analyzed after it is made. Given the tremendous amount of data that is captured on a well-made tape, this is a very time-consuming process. Videotaping can be useful, however, as a check on live observations. When played back to a teacher it can also be an effective stimulus to the recall of forgotten perceptions of classroom events.

[28] The project is detailed in Bolster, "Preparing Graduate Students to Teach."

the implementation of worthwhile studies has proved intellectually valuable to faculty interested in classroom research because it has forced them to constantly reexamine their assumptions about what knowledge of teaching is most worthwhile and how one goes about acquiring it.

The answers to these questions have appeared far too obvious to those of us who share responsibility for the advancement of such knowledge. The minimal effect that university-sponsored research has had on classroom practice is itself a forceful argument that our traditional modes of inquiry are inappropriate to the production of knowledge that teachers will believe in and use. If we wish to achieve that knowledge, we must first rephrase our questions to ask what teachers genuinely need to know. But we must also be sure that our search for answers retains the systematic rigor that only careful scholarship can bring to the understanding of everyday affairs. Both the conceptual structure of symbolic interactionist ethnographic research on teaching and our success thus far in using it suggest that this mode of inquiry has great potential for meeting these needs.

Merit Pay and the Evaluation Problem: Why Most Merit Pay Plans Fail and a Few Survive

RICHARD J. MURNANE

DAVID K. COHEN

Richard J. Murnane and David K. Cohen use the framework of microeconomics to account for the short lives of most merit pay plans. They demonstrate that teaching is not an activity that satisfies the conditions under which performance-based pay is an efficient method of compensating workers. They then show that merit pay plans survive in a few school districts, in part because the districts are special and in part because the merit pay plans are quite different from conventional notions of performance-based pay.

Designing a compensation system that provides strong incentives for employees to pursue organizational goals is a challenge every organization faces. Merit pay for teachers is often suggested as a compensation system that will enable public school systems to meet this challenge. Yet the promise of merit pay is dimmed by knowledge of its history; most attempts to implement merit pay for public school teachers over the last seventy-five years have failed.

The first part of this paper uses microeconomics, the intellectual home of merit pay, to explain the failures of most merit pay plans. We show that merit pay, even taken on its own terms, does not provide a solution to the problem of motivating teachers. The second part of the paper investigates why merit pay survives in a very few school districts in the United States. The analysis is based on interviews we conducted with a great many teachers and administrators in six school districts with enduring merit pay plans. We explain that in these special districts, merit pay contributes to the solution of problems quite different from the problem of motivating teachers.

Compensation of Public School Teachers

More than 99 percent of public school teachers in the United States work in districts that employ uniform salary scales.[1] Under such contracts, a teacher's salary is determined exclusively by educational credentials and years of teaching experience. All teachers with the same credentials and experience receive the same sal-

[1] The 99 percent figure was derived from data presented by Calhoun & Protheroe (1983).

Harvard Educational Review Vol. 56 No. 1 February 1986, 1–17

ary, irrespective of subject specialty or perceived performance. Typically, each school district sets its own salary scale or negotiates it with the local teachers' union through collective bargaining.

The limitations of uniform salary scales have been well documented; there is no financial reward for superior performance and no financial penalty, short of dismissal, for inferior performance (Hanushek, 1981). Many critics of uniform salary schedules argue that improving the quality of education offered by public schools requires a change from uniform salary schedules to a compensation scheme that bases a teacher's compensation on performance, as measured either by gains in student test scores or by supervisors' evaluations of the teacher's actions in the classroom. Such performance-based compensation plans are typically called merit pay.

Merit pay is an old idea. In 1918, 48 percent of U.S. school districts sampled in one study used compensation systems that they called merit pay (Evendon, 1918, as reported in Johnson, 1984). Little is known about these early plans, except that most did not last. In 1923 the National Education Association (NEA) reported that 33 percent of sampled districts used merit pay (NEA, 1923, p. 52), and a subsequent NEA survey reported that 18 percent of districts surveyed awarded merit pay (NEA, 1928, pp. 230–240).

Interest in merit pay waned during the 1940s and early 1950s as the vast majority of public school districts in the United States adopted uniform salary schedules. Between 1939 and 1953 the number of school systems in cities with populations of more than 30,000 that used merit pay fell from 20 to 4 percent (Porwoll, 1979, p. 26).

Sputnik rekindled interest in merit pay by raising questions about the effectiveness of American schools. During the 1960s approximately 10 percent of U.S. school districts had merit pay plans, most of which fared no better than their predecessors. By 1972 the number of districts using merit pay had fallen to 5.5 percent (Porwoll, 1979). A 1978 survey of the 11,500 U.S. school districts with enrollments of 300 or more found only 115 with merit pay plans (that is, 4 percent of the districts that responded to the survey and 1 percent of the districts to whom the questionnaire was sent). Moreover, the majority of districts that reported having tried and dropped merit pay indicated that their plans lasted less than five years (Porwoll, 1979, p. 41).

Thus, the history of merit pay suggests that while interest in paying teachers according to merit endures, attempts to use merit pay do not. Moreover, teacher union resistance cannot account for the demise of most merit pay plans, for most plans predated unions or failed in nonunion districts. We must search for other explanations. We believe that the most powerful ideas for understanding why merit pay plans fail can be found in the literature of economics. Specifically, we turn to economic analyses of employment contracts, a growing field within microeconomics.

Why Most Merit Pay Plans Fail

The Contracts Literature: A Framework for Analysis

One branch of microeconomics, which we will call the contracts literature, examines the costs and benefits associated with using different types of employment contracts to compensate workers engaged in particular kinds of production activities. The following assumptions underlie this literature:

1. Workers' preferences are not completely consonant with the employing organization's goals. Workers prefer to work less hard than the organization would like if there are no adverse consequences for them.
2. Monitoring the output or actions of individual workers is costly.
3. Imperfect monitoring will induce workers to attempt behavior that makes them appear productive relative to other workers but in fact is contrary to the goals of the organization. Williamson (1975, p. 9), an important contributor to the contracts literature, labels this behavior "opportunistic" and defines it as "self-interest seeking with guile."

As seen from the perspective of the contracts literature, the type of employment contract an organization should adopt depends on the type of work employees perform. This is because the cost of evaluating workers' output, the cost of evaluating workers' actions, and the potential for opportunistic behavior all depend on the nature of the production activity.

The perspective provided by the contracts literature is helpful in analyzing merit pay for three reasons. First, this literature takes seriously the evaluation problem. It explicitly acknowledges that evaluating worker performance is costly for management and that imperfect evaluations—defined as less than perfect knowledge of all worker actions—may elicit unpredicted and potentially destructive responses from workers. It is this evaluation problem that has plagued most attempts to introduce merit pay into public education.

Second, the contracts literature emphasizes the importance of trade-offs between the gains from providing incentives for employees to work hard and the costs of various ways of evaluating workers' contributions. Implicit in this emphasis on trade-offs is the often neglected recognition that a merit pay system that brings about modest increases in teachers' effort levels might not be worthwhile if the costs of the measures taken to evaluate teacher performance are extremely high.

Third, the contracts literature focuses attention on the nature of the production activity in which workers are engaged. It explains why an analysis of the production activity provides the best clues to the responses that particular compensation plans will elicit. We will argue that compelling explanations for the failure of most merit pay plans must focus on the nature of teachers' work. In the following sections we use the framework provided by the contracts literature to explain why neither "new style merit pay" nor "old style merit pay" is an effective strategy for motivating teachers to achieve high performance levels.

New Style Merit Pay: A Piece-Rate Compensation System
"New style merit pay" (Bacharach, Lipsky, & Shedd, 1984), also called "payment by results" (Coltham, 1972), bases individual teachers' merit pay bonuses on their students' test score gains. The attractiveness of this strategy is that the evaluation problem is solved by actually measuring certain dimensions of each teacher's output, thereby avoiding the subjective quality of evaluations conducted under old style merit pay, in which bonuses are based on supervisors' evaluations of teachers' performance. There are only a few documented cases of school districts that have

used new style merit pay, although merit pay plans that compensate teachers on the basis of student test score gains have recently been supported by several state legislatures.[2] In this section we show that new style merit pay is very much like what economists know as a piece-rate compensation system, and that teaching does not satisfy the conditions under which this type of compensation is efficient.

Approximately 30 percent of U.S. workers in manufacturing are employed under piece-rate contracts, the most common form of payment by results (Pencavel, 1977; Seiler, 1984). Piece-rate contracts work well when the actual contribution of the individual worker to the firm's output can be measured at relatively low cost. Commercial laundries' contracts with workers who iron shirts provide an example. The number of shirts ironed is a relatively accurate measure of the worker's contribution to the firm. Consumer complaints provide a check on quality. Multiple dimensions of output can be managed by providing a schedule of piece rates for different types of clothing.

Piece-rate contracts do sometimes elicit opportunistic behavior. For example, workers may neglect the maintenance of the machines on which they work since they are not rewarded for machine maintenance (see Pencavel, 1977). For many types of work, however, the costs of such opportunism are outweighed by the advantages that piece-rate contracts have over contracts that attempt to control opportunism by monitoring worker actions. In particular, piece-rate contracts provide a strong incentive for workers to find the most rapid way to iron shirts. High productivity results in immediate rewards; a drop in output results in immediate penalty.

Why haven't merit pay plans that compensate teachers on the basis of their output, as measured by student test score gains, become popular? One reason concerns the nature of the incentives that such a compensation system provides. Any explicit list of pay rates for specific levels of student test score gains (economists would refer to such a list as a payment algorithm) creates a specific price—a piece rate—for each student's test score gain in each subject area. For example, an algorithm that bases compensation solely on gains in average reading scores implicitly places a zero price on student gains in other subject areas. Moreover, it places an equal weight on each student's gain. If teacher time is viewed as a private good (time spent with one student reduces time available for other students), then this algorithm creates incentives for teachers to allocate time so that the last minute of time spent with any child yields the same expected test score gain. This means that there are incentives for teachers to minimize the time they spend with children whose test scores will not respond to modest increases in attention.

There is limited evidence that teachers do respond to payment by results by allocating their time to specific subject areas and individual children. For example, in the middle of the nineteenth century in England, elementary school teachers worked under a payment-by-results plan that based their compensation on the number of children who acquired a set of narrowly defined skills. This led to a narrowing of the curriculum to exclude all nontested subjects, including many that were perceived to be important—for example, history and geography—but were difficult to test (Coltham, 1972, p. 24).

[2] See U. S. Department of Education (1984, p. 45) for a reference to legislation that provides state financial support to school districts that adopt new style merit pay plans.

Other evidence comes from the experiments sponsored by the Office of Economic Opportunity in the early 1970s, in which private firms provided reading instruction to public school children, with the firms' compensation dependent on student test score gains. In at least one of the sites, teachers concentrated their time on children in the middle of the test score distribution, neglecting those at the top who would advance well on their own (test score gains above a threshold were not rewarded), and those at the bottom, whose test scores would not respond to modest additional amounts of teacher time (Gramlich & Koshel, 1975).

Several readers of early drafts of this paper argued that the evidence presented above, in fact, provides support for the usefulness of new style merit pay as a strategy for motivating teachers. They pointed out that the evidence demonstrates that teachers do change their behavior in order to respond to the incentives they face. All that is needed, these readers argue, is to fine-tune the payment algorithm, for example, by giving weight to skill development in more subject areas and perhaps by weighting achievement gains of some children more than those of others. We believe that the proposed technical solution of fine-tuning the payment algorithm neglects two critical problems: the lack of consensus about the appropriate weights, and the nature of teachers' work. We consider each problem in turn.

Most policy debates about public education avoid the divisive topic of weights, which is, at its core, a discussion about whose education, or what sort of education, matters the most. Instead of explicitly debating what the weights should be, it is common in public education to delegate decisions on resource allocation to teachers and administrators, with the inoperable admonition that they provide every student with the opportunity to fulfill his or her potential. Such delegation is not consistent with the design of contracts that pay teachers on the basis of their output, for teachers' different decisions about weights mean that they are each trying to produce a somewhat different mix of outputs.

If the public schools' lack of consensus on weights were the only problem in paying teachers on the basis of their students' progress, one would expect to see more extensive use of such compensation schemes in private schools, where, according to Erickson (1982), family choice leads to greater agreement on school goals. The limited available evidence suggests, however, that performance-based pay for teachers is relatively rare in private schools. In 1983 only 7 percent of Catholic high schools reported that they used any form of merit pay, and none of those schools based pay differentials on student test score gains (National Catholic Education Association, 1985).

Why aren't teachers paid on the basis of their students' test score gains, even in organizations where there is relatively high consensus on goals, union power is negligible, and management can unilaterally decide how teachers will be compensated? We believe that the answer lies in the nature of the work in schools. Even where there is a high level of consensus on goals, the goals are multidimensional—for example, raise the average reading level in each class, teach all students to embrace democratic values, help each student realize his or her potential, and eliminate drugs and violence from the school. While it may be reasonable to attribute progress toward certain goals, such as raising reading scores, to individual teachers working behind closed classroom doors, it is not possible to measure each teacher's contribution to the attainment of other school goals. For example, eliminating violence and drugs from a school requires that teachers open their classroom doors and work *as a team* to monitor students' actions outside the classroom. If teachers really do work as a team, it is not possible to measure each teacher's contribution to the group output — in this case, a lower level of drugs and violence in the school (Alchian & Demsetz, 1972). Consequently, individual teachers' contributions to achieving this school goal cannot play a role in determining their compensation under new style merit pay.

If teachers' pay is based solely on success in raising reading scores, there are strong incentives for teachers to keep their classroom doors closed and neglect the teamwork that contributes to the accomplishment of other school goals. Moreover, the strategy used by some firms to combat this form of opportunism — hiring workers to perform the tasks neglected by piece-rate workers (maintaining the machinery, for instance, in our laundry example) — does not work well in schools. Teachers, who work with students every day in class and know students' names and personalities, are likely to be more effective in eliminating drugs and violence from a school than are specialized security officers.

School principals as well as teachers realize that much of the important work in schools must be done by teachers working together — for example, some maintain quiet in halls and libraries while others teach. Compensation algorithms that reward only those dimensions of performance for which each teacher's contribution can be measured could create perverse incentives, inducing teachers to abandon hall and library duty, for instance. This may explain why paying teachers on the basis of their students' test scores is extraordinarily rare in American education.

It is important to note that our discussion of the problems posed by merit pay rests on the nature of teachers' work and the incentives that piece-rate compensation schemes provide. This is quite different from the typical objection to new style merit pay, which emphasizes the inadequacies of standardized tests. While it is true that standardized tests of, say, students' reading skills often do not provide an accurate measure of students' skills, and consequently of the fruits of teachers' work, the inadequacy of tests is not the fundamental problem with new style merit pay. Even if tests were developed that provided accurate measures of students' skills in particular subject areas, incentives to allocate time strategically to particular students and particular subject areas and to neglect aspects of the job not measurable by standardized tests would still remain.

Old Style Merit Pay

The significance of teamwork and the presence of school principals who have direct supervisory functions suggest the feasibility of basing teachers' compensation on principals' evaluations. In fact, such old style merit pay is the common model. In this section we explore the extent to which the contracts literature helps us understand why most experiments with old style merit pay have failed.

The lessons from the contracts literature (see Alchian & Demsetz, 1972; Williamson, 1975) regarding the conditions under which it is efficient to base the compensation of individual workers on supervisors' assessments of their performance can be easily summarized. Merit pay is efficient when the nature of the activity in which workers are engaged is such that supervisors can provide relatively convincing answers to these two questions posed by workers:

1. Why does worker X get merit pay and I don't?
2. What can I do to get merit pay?

Unloading boxes from a truck is often suggested as an activity where supervisors can answer workers' questions about performance-based pay differentials. Supervisors can state that worker X was paid more than other workers because he carried two boxes at a time, while other workers carried one at a time. Workers are likely to accept this answer because they recognize that carrying two boxes at a time is, in fact, productive. They also recognize that the nature of the activity gives worker X few possibilities for opportunistic behavior—that is, for actions that make him appear productive but in fact do not contribute to the work at hand. Supervisors can answer workers' second question by stating that they too can earn higher pay by carrying two boxes at a time. Workers are likely to find this answer acceptable because the required action is something they can do if they so choose.

Teachers' work is, by its nature, very different from work such as unloading a truck. As is true for workers in any field, some teachers are more effective than others—hence the call for merit pay. Most analysts agree, however, that effective teaching cannot be characterized as the consistent use of particular well-defined techniques.[3] In other words, there is no analog to carrying two boxes on every trip.

One consequence of the imprecise nature of the activity of teaching—where this expression denotes the loose relationship between particular teacher actions and student learning—is that supervisors cannot answer convincingly when teachers ask why teacher X received merit pay and they did not. As one of the administrators we interviewed commented: "I know who the good teachers are. They're so and so, so and so, and so and so. Why are they good teachers? Well, I don't know, they are just good teachers; but I know who they are." Many teachers who are denied merit pay find this answer unsatisfactory. One reason is that they are aware that the nature of teaching, with its closed classroom doors and its network of relationships among teachers and between teachers and parents, provides great potential for opportunistic behavior. In other words, there are many things that a teacher could do to impress a principal and to suggest that he or she was more effective than his or her colleagues. Examples might include using friendships with parents to spread rumors about other teachers' incompetence, and refusing to share materials that could help other teachers. Thus, teachers have reason to question whether merit pay is awarded to teachers who are in fact the most productive or to those who are most facile in impressing supervisors.

A second consequence of the imprecise nature of teaching is that supervisors cannot answer convincingly the teacher's second question, What can I do to earn merit pay? In other words, supervisors cannot suggest specific actions that the teacher can undertake which both teacher and supervisor recognize will enhance

---

[3] See Wise et al. (1984, p. 10) for a discussion of the claims and refutations concerning the role of specific teacher actions in fostering student learning.

the teacher's effectiveness. Without an unequivocal answer to this second question, teachers may have little incentive to change their behavior in pursuit of higher income. What is worse, teachers may learn that concealing their problems and playing up to evaluators is what the organization rewards — dramatically complicating managers' evaluation problem.

In effect, the lesson from the contracts literature is that the problems with old style merit pay are more fundamental than careless implementation or inadequate training of evaluators — to name but two of the explanations often given for the failure of merit pay plans. The problem lies in the nature of the teaching activity itself. Specifically, it is the lack of a blueprint for effective teaching that prevents supervisors from providing convincing answers to teachers' two primary questions about merit pay.

What the contracts literature does not reveal is exactly what problems arise under merit pay that have led most school districts to drop this type of compensation system after a brief trial. While our research was not designed to address this question, we did learn some interesting facts about the problems caused by merit pay, particularly from teachers and administrators in two districts that have had merit pay for more than twenty years and have altered their plans several times to deal with perceived problems. The comments of these participants are informative in understanding what happens when supervisors cannot answer teachers' questions about why some teachers receive merit pay and others do not.

One theme that ran through our interviews was a perception on the part of administrators that merit pay could easily backfire, since teachers who received evaluation ratings lower than they felt were fair might respond by working less hard. This theme is exemplified in the story one former principal told about a fine teacher whose work he rated "excellent." Unfortunately, excellent was the second highest rating in the system, and the teacher firmly believed she deserved the top rating, "outstanding." She responded to the principal with, "If that's all you care, then that's all you'll get," and, indeed, he reported that her work "fell off."

Another theme we discerned from our field notes was that past experiences conditioned teachers' expectations about their evaluations. No teacher expected to be given a rating lower than the one he or she had received in the previous rating period. Rarely do discussions of merit pay focus on the *repetitive* nature of the evaluation process. Yet teachers see their "merit" ratings in terms of what they and others have been told by supervisors in the past. Being demoted is difficult for anyone, but it would be particularly hard if supervisors could not pinpoint what was wrong and explain how the situation could be remedied.

Several administrators cited negative consequences that arose from giving a teacher a lower rating than the teacher had received in the past. One principal mentioned a teacher with no better than adequate performance to whom he gave a rating lower than the rating given by his predecessor. The teacher, who had planned to retire at the end of the year, was so infuriated by this rating that she postponed her retirement for two years. The principal was left with a teacher he did not want; moreover, the teacher had become angry and recalcitrant as a result of her evaluation rating. The key point here is that even an evaluation system that produces valid and reliable performance ratings is not enough to guarantee the success of merit pay. If teachers feel that the ratings are unjust, and evaluators cannot convince them to the contrary, their reactions to the ratings may undermine the education students receive.

A third theme in our interviews was that merit pay tended to interfere with school principals' efforts to build effective instructional teams in their schools. Several school principals commented that, prior to the introduction of merit pay, they often gave teachers ratings higher than they actually deserved and then encouraged them to live up to the high ratings. The principals reported that this was the most effective strategy for stimulating many teachers to improve their performance, because it built teachers' confidence and established trust in the principals. While this evaluation strategy produced ratings that were not objectively valid, the principals felt it promoted teacher morale and better teaching performance. Principals felt that this approach allowed them to focus on the specific problems a teacher was struggling with, whereas more objective evaluations produced an adversarial atmosphere and could create incentives for teachers to conceal problems.

Many of these same principals worried that the use of merit pay would restrict their ability to pursue the strategy of encouraging teachers through the use of high ratings. One reason they worried was that the school district administration was pressing principals to be objective in their ratings and to standardize ratings across schools. A second cause for concern had to do with school board complaints of an excessive number of high ratings; administrators were being pressed to lower ratings and to provide a stronger defense of the top ratings they did give. At the same time, principals felt pressure from teachers to explain why they had not been given the top rating while the teacher in the next classroom had. As one principal stated, "Merit pay turns my job from being a coach into being a referee." He further implied that his teachers no longer saw him as a helpful coach but as a critical referee — and this threatened his ability to motivate the teachers to higher levels of effort.

Some readers may conclude that one of the *benefits* of merit pay is that it pressures principals into actually evaluating teachers objectively, one of the most important parts of their job. There is some truth to this argument; certainly, many of the principals we interviewed felt this pressure. There is more to be said, however. The principal's primary job is to ensure that the children who pass through his or her school learn as much as possible. Yet the principal doesn't teach students; teachers do that work. The principal's success, therefore, depends to a large extent on his or her success in encouraging teachers to work hard and work together. When a principal gives a lower evaluation to a teacher than he or she had previously received, the teacher may lose some money, but the principal may lose the cooperation needed to make the school work. Our field notes contain many stories from principals describing the distressing consequences of giving lower ratings than the teachers expected.

Many principals saw merit pay as making their job more difficult by increasing both the tensions surrounding the formal evaluation process and the intensity with which teachers asked why they did not get the top rating and what they could do to receive a better rating—questions that principals could not answer convincingly. In fact, the general thrust of the principals' comments, with a few notable exceptions, is quite consistent with the survey evidence indicating that low morale and "problems of administration" are the primary reasons school districts drop merit pay (see Calhoun & Protheroe, 1983).

Our evidence leads us to emphasize the importance of the imprecise nature of teachers' work as a factor contributing to the demise of old style merit pay. One of the readers of an early draft of this paper commented that, if we were correct and the problem were not simply poor public sector management, we should expect that old style merit pay would not be common in for-profit educational institutions. While an in-depth exploration of this proposition was beyond our resources, we did attempt to respond to this comment by learning about the compensation policies of the Stanley H. Kaplan Educational Center, a large, nationwide for-profit firm specializing in preparing students to take standardized tests such as the SAT.

Stanley Kaplan does monitor the performance of its teachers closely, in part by observing them in the classroom and, to an even greater extent, by soliciting student evaluations of each teacher's performance. In fact, Kaplan's students are quick to complain when the quality of instruction does not justify the cost of the course. Kaplan uses the feedback from students in deciding which teachers to dismiss, but does not use this information in determining individual teacher's compensation. In fact, teachers who work for Kaplan are paid in much the same manner that public school teachers are paid. All teachers are paid according to a salary scale that bases compensation on experience, that is, on the number of courses taught. There are no bonuses for superior performance.

We asked the personnel director of Kaplan why the firm does not use performance-based pay. Her answer included these points: all Stanley Kaplan teachers are effective; those who are not are dismissed. There are some teachers who are superstars, and the firm has considered paying bonuses to them. This plan was rejected because of management's perception that the positive impact of bonuses on the performances of the superstars would be more than offset by negative effects on the performances of effective teachers who do not receive bonuses, do not know why they were passed over, and cannot be told how to become superstars.

In the context of this paper, the Kaplan evidence can be interpreted as implying that even when management feels it can make relatively accurate, fine-tuned distinctions among teachers, it would not be able to convince the merely good teachers of the superior performance of some of their coworkers. As a result, the responses to the pay differentials would not further the goals of the organization. Thus, the imprecise nature of teaching prohibits evaluators from answering the hard questions teachers pose about old style merit pay and leads a successful profit-making firm to base compensation on experience. It is important to add that Stanley Kaplan uses evaluation aggressively, even without merit pay, both to dismiss ineffective teachers and to offer useful advice to effective teachers. This approach is obviously similar to that taken by administrators in many public schools.

Why Some Merit Pay Plans Survive

If merit pay is not an effective strategy for improving teachers' performance, why do merit pay plans survive in a few districts? Are the districts atypical? Are the provisions of the merit pay plans atypical? Did merit pay in these districts help to solve problems other than that of motivating teachers?

We began our search for the answers to these questions by identifying school districts that have used merit pay for a number of years. Two Educational Research Service publications were helpful in this regard. The first (Porwoll, 1979) identified 115 school districts in the United States that used merit pay in 1978. The second (Calhoun & Protheroe, 1983) reported the results of a survey that inquired whether each of these 115 districts was still using merit pay in 1983, and if not, why not. The 47 districts that reported in the 1983 survey that they were still using merit pay formed the population from which we selected districts for study.

Within the population we looked first for urban districts with ongoing merit pay plans. Since many urban districts are thought to have particularly serious problems with poor teaching quality and low teacher morale, an analysis of enduring merit pay plans in such districts might provide important insights into the factors that contribute to the success of performance-based contracts. However, we found no urban districts with long-lived merit pay plans. In fact, we could not find even one documented case of a large, once troubled school district that had successfully used merit pay to improve its performance. On the contrary, one of the striking aspects of the list of districts with enduring merit pay was the large percentage of very small districts serving relatively homogeneous student populations. Moreover, these districts tended to use very small amounts of money as merit pay bonuses.

We then looked for districts that had used merit pay for at least five years and had either used pay differentials of at least $1,000 or served more than 10,000 students. We found seven districts that met these criteria. We spent several days in six of these districts interviewing teachers and administrators with the goal of learning how each merit pay plan worked and how teachers and administrators reacted to these plans.

Characteristics of the Six Districts

The six districts we studied vary in size from 2,500 to 60,000 students. Three are located in the Southwest, one in the Northeast, one in the Mid-Atlantic region, and one in the North Central region of the country. Two districts have collective bargaining; the union role in the other four is insignificant.

Part of the reason merit pay plans persist in the six districts has to do with their unusual working conditions. All of the six districts are considered to be among the best in their geographical areas — places where teachers like to work and where high housing prices reflect, in part, the desirability of the public schools. In evaluating the role merit pay plays in contributing to these districts' accomplishments, it is important to focus first on attributes other than merit pay that these districts have in common.

All of the districts have salary schedules, to which merit pay is added, that are above average for their geographical areas. The high salaries and good working conditions permit these districts to be selective in choosing applicants for teaching positions. None of these districts adopted merit pay as a response to the idea that there was not enough money to pay all teachers well so they would at least pay a few good teachers well. In fact, several administrators made comments such as, "No merit pay system would ever work without salaries at a point that teachers can live on."

None of these districts use merit pay as a strategy to give negative signals to teachers perceived to be ineffective. However, using evaluation practices that are in principle unrelated to merit pay, they do dismiss teachers judged to be incompetent and are pressured by parents to do so. These practices have not been resisted by teachers' unions in the two districts with relatively powerful unions. The union leaders in these districts stated that they made sure due process was observed but that it was not in the union's interest to protect incompetent teachers. One lesson to be learned from examining the characteristics of school districts with long-lived merit pay plans is that attractive working conditions may be a prerequisite for the survival of merit pay.

Characteristics of the Enduring Merit Pay Plans

Working conditions do not provide the whole answer to why merit pay survives in a few districts. In fact, merit pay has been dropped by a great many districts that appear similar to the six we studied. Thus, to explain the survival of merit pay in our districts we must look at the plans themselves.

The six merit pay plans that we analyzed differ in many respects. However, in every case the plan incorporates a strategy for dealing with the two questions, already noted, that many teachers ask about merit pay. The strategies consist of varying combinations of four themes: extra pay for extra work, making everyone feel special, making the program inconspicuous, and legitimation through participation. These strategies represent adaptations of the merit pay idea that eliminated those conflicts between merit pay and the nature of teachers' work that we discussed above. However, they turn merit pay into something else. In fact, we regard each of these adaptations as evidence supporting the theme developed in the first part of this essay, namely, that teachers' work does not satisfy the conditions under which performance-based compensation is an effective means of motivating workers to high performance levels. In the analysis that follows, we stress the ways in which each district changed one or more crucial aspects of the merit pay idea. While these districts still refer to their plans as merit pay, economists would not view them as examples of performance-based compensation.

Extra pay for extra work. One common element in the long-lived merit pay plans is that the definition of performance is altered so as to reduce emphasis on classroom teaching and increase emphasis on completion of tasks outside the classroom. For example, the numerical rating system used by one district to determine merit pay awards gives school and community service the same weight as classroom performance. Another district requires that a teacher complete six outside activities to be eligible for merit pay. As one teacher commented, "This isn't merit pay; it's how you get the yearbook done."

A complementary practice is to make the *teacher* responsible for documenting that he or she is worthy of merit pay. As part of the merit pay application process in several districts, teachers had to prepare lengthy documents describing their accomplishments and providing evidence in the form of testimonials from colleagues and parents. One teacher commented, "When I finished this last time, I had a volume no less than three inches thick of evidence, arguments, and materials."

These practices, which we call extra pay for extra work, provide one set of relatively convincing answers to the two questions teachers raise about merit pay. Administrators can clearly state that teacher X received merit pay because he or she devoted time to organizing a variety of activities and to documenting his or her accomplishments, both in and out of the classroom. If another teacher wants merit pay, he or she can do these same things.

This approach to merit pay relieves administrators of the impossible task of discerning and defending differences in the quality of teachers' classroom instruction. But this approach also means that the school districts using it have effectively given up any effort to relate financial rewards to the core of the teacher's job— namely, classroom instruction. The use of this approach underscores our earlier argument that merit pay is ill-suited to teaching.

Make everyone feel special. A second theme is to quietly award merit pay to almost all teachers. This strategy is most pronounced in one district in which a numerical rating system is used to determine whether teachers receive no award or an award of $500, $1,000, $1,500, or $2,000. Only teachers who had worked in this district for at least six years were eligible for merit pay. Eligible teachers could choose not to participate in the merit pay plan, and this choice spared them from documenting their accomplishments and undergoing the merit pay review process. Only a very few teachers chose not to participate in this merit pay plan, however.

Teachers whom we interviewed in this district were unaware of the distribution of actual awards but typically were pleased that they each received a substantial award. In fact, every teacher who participated in the voluntary merit pay program (over 90 percent of eligible teachers in the district) received an award; 85 percent of the teachers received either $1,500 or $2,000. We suspect that the bunching of the ratings at the top of the scale and the relatively small monetary differential between the top two awards is important in minimizing ill feeling on the part of teachers in schools headed by hard-grading principals. In this district, if a principal is a hard grader, the effective teacher receives an annual bonus of $1,500 instead of $2,000.

In effect, the "make everyone feel special" strategy deals with teachers' potentially destructive questions about merit pay by reducing the number of teachers who ask. We find it interesting that this theme was particularly evident in the two districts in our sample that have had merit pay for more than twenty years. But if this approach deals effectively with teachers' questions, it does so by rewarding everyone, cutting off questions by cutting off the reasons for asking them. One idea behind merit pay, however, is to use differential financial rewards to improve worker performance. If most teachers receive the top reward or an amount close to it, then there will be little difference in the incentives and thus little chance that the differences will affect teacher performance. Once again, this approach to implementing merit pay provides additional evidence of the poor fit between this type of compensation scheme and teachers' work.

Make merit pay inconspicuous. In several districts, the design of the merit pay system is such that the incentives are of little interest to a large percentage of the teachers. For example, in one district, eligibility for merit pay requires ten years of service, completion of six activities outside the classroom, and satisfactory performance evaluations. The reward for fulfilling these requirements is $600 (somewhat more if coupled with advanced degrees). Only 40 percent of the teachers in this district who do fulfill the length of service requirement choose to participate in the voluntary merit pay plan. In another district, teachers can apply for one of four different award levels, each level having different requirements. While the award levels are sizable — $1,000 for level one, $4,000 for level four — the requirements are so demanding that only 12 percent of the teachers apply for any level (two-thirds of these teachers receive awards). The level four requirements include a master's degree and thirty hours of graduate credits, superior teaching skills as demonstrated, for example, by "representing the district at the state or national level as a resource person, chairperson, or committee member," and superior professional contributions, as demonstrated, for example, by serving "in an official capacity in the management of the professional associations or organizations related to a specific field of study."[4] For the vast majority of the teachers in this school district, the financial awards do not justify the extra work.

In all six districts, merit pay has a low profile. In part, this stems from the perception that merit pay is something almost any teacher could earn but that the financial rewards do not justify the extra work. Another element is that, in five of the six districts, teachers are urged not to discuss with colleagues either who receives merit pay or the amount of the awards. In these districts, where most teachers like their jobs, the primary effect of secrecy seems to be to reduce teachers' interest in merit pay and thereby to reduce the number of teachers who ask the hard questions about why some teachers get merit pay and others do not. But whatever the reasons for the low profile, this common approach to implementation is further evidence that our districts tended to turn merit pay into something else. If the aim of a differential compensation system is to stimulate better performance, then it would be important for workers to know who did the better job, and why. But the districts we visited built barriers against the acquisition of this information.

Legitimation through participation. The final attribute of merit pay uncovered in our districts concerns the process by which the programs were designed. In all of the districts, teachers played a significant role in the design of the merit pay plans. Moreover, in each of the two districts that have had merit pay for more than twenty years, the system has been revised several times in response to teacher complaints. We believe that teachers' participation in the design and redesign of the plans contributes to the plans' longevity. One reason for this effect is that the process of participation reveals information about teachers' preferences that is extremely difficult to collect unless teachers volunteer it. This information, moreover, is critical in enabling supervisors to predict teachers' responses to incentives. Participation gives teachers a reason to volunteer information and a mechanism for doing so. A second reason that participation contributes to the longevity of merit pay plans is that it creates the impression that merit pay is not a system thrust upon teachers but rather one they helped to create. Seen as such, teachers may still ask why some teachers get merit pay and others do not, but the intensity with which they ask is diminished. Teachers recognize that if many of them find the program objectionable, they can change it.[5]

One could view teachers' participation as an example of workers' self-protective behavior. In this case, however, workers' objections to merit pay were shared by

---

[4] These quotations are taken from the school district's description of its performance-based compensation plan.

[5] The importance of voice as a mechanism for improving the performance of organizations is elegantly developed by Hirschman (1970).

management. We therefore view worker participation as yet another effort by management and workers to redefine a compensation system that has great potential for doing damage.

Is There a Role for Merit Pay?

The schemes we studied, then, were not merit pay, at least if this term denotes performance-based compensation. But the six districts nonetheless seemed quite convinced that their compensation plans were useful. We wondered why. Did these plans have some desirable effect on the scholastic performance of students in these districts? Did the plans help the districts to resolve problems that they faced?

On the first question, merit pay in the districts we studied does not appear to have affected the quality of teaching; neither administrators nor teachers offered any evidence that merit pay had a significant impact on the way teachers teach. This is not surprising given the attributes of the enduring plans. This conclusion is also compatible with the theme developed above: the nature of teachers' work is such that basing individual teachers' pay on assessments of their performance is unlikely to motivate teachers to work harder.

If merit pay does not motivate teachers to work harder, why do a very few districts retain it? Our interviews with teachers and administrators suggest that merit pay has helped these six districts solve problems quite different from the problem of motivating teachers. These problems include (1) how to support good teachers who differ in their relative needs for income and free time, (2) how to encourage meaningful dialogue between teachers and administrators about difficult issues, such as the quality of the evaluation process, (3) and how to build community support for the public schools.

In the districts we visited, merit pay contributes to solutions to these problems in the following ways:

1. Extra pay for extra work provides opportunities for teachers with greater financial needs to augment their incomes by spending time on school-related activities.

2. The ongoing discussions of how merit pay works, what its problems are, and what changes are needed provide forums for meaningful dialogue between teachers and administrators concerning difficult issues, such as the nature of the evaluation process.

3. The merit pay plans contribute to the perception that teachers are accountable. As one teacher commented on why members of the community supported merit pay for teachers, "The people out there who are paying taxes want to make sure that in the area of teacher pay, those who are doing the real work are the ones who get the rewards, above and beyond the standard." This perception of accountability increased the willingness of communities to pay teachers well. One administrator remarked that merit pay "has meant a lot of money for a lot of teachers that would otherwise not have been provided, knowing the Board of Education."

We do not mean to imply that merit pay is necessary to solve the problems of satisfying teachers' varied needs, encouraging dialogue, and promoting community support for the schools. In fact, a far greater number of school districts solve these problems without merit pay. For example, many districts meet some teachers' needs for additional income through extra pay for extra work without calling this merit pay, or through small grants competitions.[6] Many districts use the collective bargaining process to promote meaningful dialogue between teachers and administrators (see Freeman & Medoff, 1984). Others promote community support through volunteer programs, public/private partnerships, and outreach activities.

What we do want to suggest is a different way of looking at merit pay. This is useful because, if the past is any guide to the future, the current, perhaps waning wave of interest in merit pay will not be the last time that educators feel pressure to adopt this type of compensation plan. In thinking about merit pay in the future, it is useful to ask whether it can play a modest role in satisfying teachers' varied needs, encouraging meaningful dialogue between teachers and administrators, and promoting community support for the schools. In most school districts, the answer to this question will be an emphatic "no." But in a few districts the answer could be a tentative "yes." We hope that our work provides some clues to the types of districts where an answer of "maybe" makes sense and what types of merit pay plans hold some promise.

There is one final theme in our evidence that seems to apply to districts both with and without merit pay: improving teachers' performance through evaluation. If evaluation is to contribute to the goal of helping teachers improve, it must be carried out by skilled and knowledgeable supervisors in an atmosphere that rewards honesty and cooperation. When teachers who conceal their failings receive higher pay than those who do not, the atmosphere for useful evaluation and advice is poisoned. If supervisors are to engage in a productive dialogue with teachers, they must act in a way that is consistent with the sustained nature of their relationship with teachers. Evaluation is a repetitive sequence which creates expectations, memories, and sensitivities that can either contribute to improved performance or, if treated insensitively, undermine it. It was the goal of merit pay's advocates to put the power of money into the evaluation process as a way to improve teachers' performance. That goal is misguided. But the broader lesson—that school administrators must work to create relationships with teachers in which evaluations contribute to improvement, change, and cooperative problem solving—is one that must not be forgotten even after the pressures for merit pay dissipate.

References

Alchian, A. A., & Demsetz, H. (1972). Production, information costs, and economic organization. *American Economic Review, 62,* 777–795.

Bacharach, S. B., Lipsky, D. B., & Shedd, J. B. (1984). *Paying for better teaching.* Ithaca, NY: Organizational Analysis and Practice.

Calhoun, F. S., & Protheroe, N. J. (1983). *Merit pay plans for teachers: Status and descriptions.* Arlington, VA: Educational Research Service.

Coltham, J. B. (1972). Educational accountability: An English experiment and its outcome. *School Review, 81,* 15–34.

---

[6] See, for example, *Small Grants for Teachers* (n.d.).

Erickson, D. A. (1982). Disturbing evidence about the "one best system." In R. B. Everhart (Ed.), *The public school monopoly* (pp. 393–422). Cambridge, MA: Ballinger.

Evendon, E.S. (1918). *Teachers' salaries and salary schedules in the United States, 1918–19.* Washington, DC: National Education Association.

Freeman, R. B., & Medoff, J. L. (1984). *What do unions do?* New York: Basic Books.

Gramlich, E., & Koshel, P. (1975). *Educational performance contracting.* Washington, DC: Brookings Institution.

Hanushek, E. (1981). Throwing money at schools. *Journal of Policy Analysis and Management, 1,* 19–41.

Hirschman, A. O. (1970). *Exit, voice, and loyalty.* Cambridge: Harvard University Press.

Johnson, S. M. (1984). Merit pay for teachers: A poor prescription for reform. *Harvard Educational Review, 54,* 175–185.

National Catholic Education Association. (1985). *The Catholic high school: A national portrait.* Washington, DC: Author.

National Education Association. (1923). *Report of the salary committee, teachers' salaries and salary trends in 1923.* Washington, DC: Author.

National Education Association. (1928). Practices affecting teacher personnel. *Research Bulletin, 6.* Washington, DC: Author.

Pencavel, J. H. (1977). Work effort, on-the-job screening, and alternative methods of remuneration. In R. Ehrenberg (Ed.), *Research in labor economics* (Vol. 1, pp. 225–258). Greenwich, CT: JAI Press.

Porwoll, P. J. (1979). *Merit pay for teachers.* Arlington, VA: Educational Research Service.

Seiler, E. (1984). Piece rate vs. time rate: The effect of incentives on earnings. *Review of Economics and Statistics, 66,* 363–375.

Small grants for teachers. (n.d.). Pittsburgh: Allegheny Conference on Community Development.

U.S. Department of Education. (1984). *The nation responds: Recent efforts to improve education.* Washington, DC: Author.

Williamson, O. E. (1975). *Markets and hierarchies: Analysis and antitrust implications.* New York: Free Press.

Wise, A. E., Darling-Hammond, L., McLaughlin, M. W., & Bernstein, H. T. (1984). *Teacher evaluation: A study of effective practices.* Santa Monica: Rand Corporation.

The research on which this paper is based was supported by the Institute for Finance and Governance, School of Education, Stanford University. We would like to thank Katherine Jamentz, Patrick Murnane, and Niall Nelson for able research assistance; and Chris Argyris, Estelle James, Susan Johnson, Charles Lindblom, Giandomenico Majone, Richard Nelson, Robert Pollak, David Stern, Dvora Yanow, and participants in workshops at Boston University, Harvard University, and the University of Pennsylvania for helpful comments on earlier drafts. We would especially like to thank Edward Pauly, who read several drafts of the paper and provided many important ideas.

Teacher Unions in Schools: Authority and Accommodation

SUSAN MOORE JOHNSON

Does collective bargaining standardize school practices, formalize relationships between principals and teachers, and reduce faculty commitment to meeting the needs of students? Susan Moore Johnson's study of teacher unions in six school districts addresses these questions, describing the variation in enforcement of contract provisions at both district and school levels. She concludes that labor relations among the districts vary in response to and enforcement of specific contract provisions. More importantly, labor relations at the school level vary widely within districts, influenced by such non-contractual factors as administrative leadership, staff allegiance, and student needs.

Thirty-nine years after negotiation of the first teachers' contract, controversy persists over the impact of collective bargaining on public education. Advocates contend that teacher unions are reforming the schools; critics argue that they are laying waste to them.[1] The one point of agreement is that the effects of collective bargaining are both big and important. Stephen K. Bailey characterized the popular and professional debates: "Few issues in the field of American education have been more controversial in the past two decades than the rise of teachers' unions. Struggles over appropriate bargaining agents, what issues are negotiable, grievance procedures, the right to strike, and even the underlying compatibility of unions and the educating profession have divided faculty, outraged administrators, politicized schools and colleges, entangled the courts,

---

[1] Over two decades ago, Myron Lieberman set forth both sides of the case in *Education as a Profession* (Englewood Cliffs, N.J.: Prentice Hall, 1956), pp. 334–353. More recently, Marshall O. Donley, Jr. predicted favorable outcomes from collective bargaining: "Where will all this collective bargaining lead? In the long run, it will lead, among other things, to fewer strikes by teachers, greater professionalism of educators, higher teacher morale, an enlarged role in the school for the teacher, and higher salaries for school personnel." See his *Power to the Teacher* (Bloomington, Ind.: Univ. of Indiana Press, 1976), p. 207.

By contrast, a recent feature story about education in *Newsweek* magazine reviewed prevailing criticisms about the effects of teacher unionism: the "unseemingly blue collar image," the prevalence of strikes, the "demeaning" effects of collective bargaining on teacher professionalism, and the unions' protection of incompetents. "The unions," it said, "are the source of considerable friction within and without the profession." Dennis A. Williams, "Teachers are in Trouble," *Newsweek*, 27 April 1981.

Myron Lieberman and Albert Shanker continue the polarized debate in Myron Lieberman, "Teachers Bargaining: An Autopsy"; and Albert Shanker, "After 20 Years Lieberman's Vision is Failing," *Phi Delta Kappan*, 63 (1980), pp. 231–236.

Harvard Educational Review   Vol. 53   No. 3   August 1983, 309–326

and roiled public opinion."[2] Although public attention has been drawn to the expansion of teacher unionism, until recently there has been scant empirical research to inform public opinion about its effects.[3] The popular press regularly implies that collective bargaining is standardizing schooling, undermining principals' authority, and diverting teacher loyalties.[4] Such views, however, are shaped more by dogma than data. Anyone familiar with the labor practices of even a few districts knows that negotiations, contract language, and administrative practices are remarkably diverse. District level labor relationships are variously collaborative, cooperative, or contentious. Union officers are aggressive in one district, cautious in another; school district officials variously seek confrontation with or support from their teachers.[5]

It is not so apparent, though, that labor practices vary within districts as well. Because rules, procedures, and hierarchy are prominent under collective bargaining, one might well expect to find that contracts are fully enforced, that work practices are indeed standardized, and that principals are rapidly becoming neutral functionaries who routinely apply the contract's rationalized procedures to the technology of schooling.

My prior experience in schools, however, challenged these assumptions. First, I saw many district office policies lie unheeded in the filing cabinets of schools, and my previous research about performance-based layoff practices illustrated that, once negotiated, implementation of these practices was at best uncertain.[6] I knew that school districts are not the hierarchical, "tightly coupled" systems they would have to be if contracts were to be fully and literally implemented in all schools.

Second, I knew that principals vary in administrative style and effectiveness. Some enforce rules; others don't. Some command faculty loyalty; others foster dissent. How these principals work and how they are regarded by staff might well influence the union's activity and the role of the contract in schools.

Finally, my teaching had taught me that schools are quite different from factories. The process of education is poorly defined, and the responsibilities of teachers and administrators are broad and diffuse. While hierarchical on paper, the relationship between teachers and administrators is in many ways reciprocal and their work interdependent. Because schools are designed to educate children rather than to manufacture widgets, teachers hold different views than many laborers about the character and social value of their work.

---

[2] Bailey, Foreword in *Faculty and Teacher Bargaining*, ed. George W. Angell (Lexington, Mass.: Heath, 1981), p. ix.

[3] The research that is available centers largely on salary scales rather than school practices. A small number of empirical studies do examine the organizational effects of collective bargaining. These include: Charles T. Kerchner and Douglas Mitchell, *The Dynamics of Public School Collective Bargaining and Its Impacts on Governance, Administration and Teaching* (Washington, D.C.: National Institute of Education, 1981); Lorraine McDonnell and Anthony Pasal, *Organized Teachers in American Schools* (Santa Monica, Calif.: Rand Corporation, 1979); Charles A. Perry and W. A. Wildman, *The Impact of Negotiations in Public Education: The Evidence from the Schools* (Northington, Ohio: Jones Publishing, 1970).

[4] See, for example, Williams, "Teachers are in Trouble," pp. 78–84.

[5] Throughout the text, the terms "teacher unions" and "unionism" will be used to refer to the National Education Association and its affiliates as well as to the American Federation of Teachers and its affiliates. While the sample sites were drawn from both organizations, no conclusions can or should be made about the national affiliates on the basis of this small sample.

[6] Susan Moore Johnson, "Performance-Based Staff Layoffs in Public Schools: Implementation and Outcomes," *Harvard Educational Review*, 50 (1980), 214–233.

For all of these reasons, I decided to study collective bargaining from the perspective of the schools rather than the negotiating tables. I followed collective bargaining into offices, classrooms, and corridors to explore its effects on schools and those who work there. I was investigating a number of related questions: Does collective bargaining standardize school practice? How prominent is the union in schools? Is the contract fully or only partially enforced to meet the needs of the schools? Does collective bargaining formalize relationships between principals and teachers? Does it change teachers' attitudes toward their work or commitment to their schools? What administrative constraints accompany collective bargaining, and how do principals respond to those constraints?

I found no simple, unequivocal answers to these questions, and the following discussion explores the complexity and ambiguity of the findings. Overall, however, the school-site effects of teacher unionism proved to be far less extreme, uniform, and unmanageable than many suppose.

The Method

I selected a diverse sample of six districts so that I might consider collective bargaining in a range of settings.[7] I wanted to consider districts with expanding resources and enrollments as well as those experiencing decline, and I sought to understand labor practices in the context of both cooperative and adversarial relationships. The sample districts, which have here been assigned fictitious names, vary in size, controlling labor statutes, American Federation of Teachers/National Education Association affiliation, regional location, urban/rural/suburban character, racial and ethnic composition, enrollment and economic trends, experience with strikes, and strength and complexity of the contracts. Table 1 summarizes these district features.

The school districts, which were recommended by state educational agency administrators, union leaders, community leaders, and other school officials, were selected sequentially to ensure that the balance of variables in the sample would be maintained. I requested entree into eight districts; two refused my request, and the remaining six make up the final sample.

Data collection, which extended from July 1979 to November 1980, proceeded similarly in each district. Two hundred eighty-nine interviews of this study were semi-structured, and they varied in length from thirty minutes to two hours. I conducted in-depth interviews with all central office administrators and union leaders who were identified locally as relevant to the research. On their recommendations, I selected a group of principals varying in age and experience, sex, school level and location, labor attitudes, and administrative style. The number of principals interviewed in each district ranged from two to seventeen, depending on the size of the district.[8]

On the basis of these interviews with principals, I chose three to five schools in each district that represented the range of grade level, location, administrative style, and

---

[7] The methodology for this study is explained in detail in the full study report: Susan Moore Johnson, *Teacher Unions and the Schools* (Cambridge, Mass.: Institute for Educational Policy Studies, 1982).

[8] In Northwood, where there were but two schools, I interviewed both building principals. In Metropolis, I interviewed 17 of the 279 principals. The percentage of principals interviewed in each district are: Metropolis, 6 percent; Shady Heights, 36 percent; Plantville, 50 percent; Northwood, 100 percent; Vista, 58 percent.

TABLE 1
Characteristics of Sample School Districts

District	Region	Type	District Size	Economy	Student Composition	Union Affiliation	Union Strength	Bargaining History	Labor Relationship
Plantville	Northeast	Urban	9,800 students 600 staff 14 schools	Declining	Predominantly white	99% AFT	Moderate	7 years 0 strikes	Cooperative
Shady Heights	Northeast	Suburban	18,000 students 1,200 staff 28 schools	Declining	Predominantly white	81% AFT	High	14 years 4 strikes	Cooperative
Vista	Southwest	Suburban/ Consol- idated	17,500 students 1,200 staff 19 schools	Expanding	White Hispanic[a]	80% NEA	Low/ moderate	12 years 0 strikes	Adversarial
Metropolis	Northeast	Urban	240,000 students 13,000 staff 279 schools	Declining	62% black 32% white 6% Hispanic	95% AFT	Very high	15 years 4 strikes	Adversarial
Mill City	Midwest	Urban	17,000 students 1,000 staff 23 schools	Declining	Predominantly black	65% NEA	Low/ moderate	14 years 3 strikes	Cooperative
Northwood	Northwest	Rural	850 students 75 staff 2 schools	Stable	Predominantly white	80% NEA	Moderate/ high	10 years 0 strikes	Conciliatory

[a]A small percentage of the students at Vista were Hispanics; exact figures were not available.

union activity within the district. With the assistance of the principals and union building representatives, I selected a sample of seven to fifteen teachers, which represented the diversity within the school on a number of variables: grade, subject, sex, union views, support of or opposition to the principal, degree of involvement in school activities. I repeatedly asked those interviewed whether the sample was "balanced and representative of the teachers in the school." I supplemented the sample with additional teachers who were recommended during the course of data collection.

I spent one or two full days in each of twenty schools and interviewed from 5 percent of the staff in the largest high school to 66 percent of the staff in the smallest elementary school. In addition, I informally observed classrooms, corridors, cafeterias, main offices, teachers' rooms, and after-school activities. I attended several faculty meetings and one school board meeting when labor issues were on the agenda.

Qualitative research of this sort necessarily sacrifices breadth of investigation for depth. The samples of districts, schools, and respondents were selected to represent the range of sites and individuals involved in educational labor relations. It must be left to the reader rather than to tests of statistical significance to determine whether these findings are plausible, generalizable, and instructive.

Differences between Districts

The six districts had negotiated notably different contracts, and the six unions varied in their aggressiveness in enforcing what they had negotiated. For example, Metropolis, a large urban district in the Northeast, had a well-established and militant union that had bargained a strong and detailed contract and maintained an adversarial relationship with the district administration.[9] By contrast, in Northwood, a northwestern rural district, the union was strong but had nurtured an intentionally cooperative relationship with the administration and negotiated a teachers' contract of only modest strength.[10] Therefore, as might be expected, there were discernible differences from district to district in the overall effects of the contracts and the unions on schools.

The difficulties of school administration that followed from collective bargaining generally increased with the strength and complexity of the contract and with the aggressiveness of the local union. Principals in Metropolis maneuvered around many constraints. Frequent seniority-based transfers, rigid class size limits, a short work day for teachers, and prohibitions against assigning supervisory duties combined to make effective school management in Metropolis more difficult and uncertain. By contrast, principals in Vista, a suburban district in the Southwest, could manage their schools with few serious contract restrictions and rarely encountered challenges by the union. A Vista principal compared his current job to a similar one he had held in a strong union district: "The difference is that there I would have to think, 'How am I going to get this done?' Here, I can simply say, 'I'm going to get this done,' and do it."[11]

---

[9] For example, the Metropolis contract called for strict seniority-based layoffs and transfers, a uniform class size limit, and well-paid extracurricular positions for teachers to assume on a voluntary basis. Seven full-time union staff members monitored contract compliance, and approximately 250 grievances were filed annually.

[10] The Northwood contract, which includes binding arbitration, also calls for performance-based layoffs and mandatory extracurricular participation. Class size limits are not specified. Only one grievance had been filed since the advent of collective bargaining.

[11] Personal interview with Vista principal, 8 Jan. 1980.

What had been bargained, how it was being interpreted and administered by district officials, and whether it was being enforced by the local union did, therefore, make a difference. There were discernible differences among districts in the effects of the contracts and the unions on the schools.

Differences within Districts

There were also extensive variations in labor relations practices from one school to the next within the same district. Standardization of work practice, generally assumed to be one of the outcomes of collective bargaining, had not been achieved in the schools studied.[12] In fact, school site labor practices and labor relationships were quite particularistic.

All contract provisions were theoretically of equal weight, but few were actually complied with and enforced throughout the schools of any district. Those contract provisions that were fully implemented—seniority layoffs and transfers, class size limits, and duty-free lunch guarantees—were both highly valued by teachers and enforceable.[13]

Teachers considered seniority-based layoff and transfer provisions to be their protection against arbitrary job loss or transfer. One Mill City teacher expressed the views of many teachers: "It's not very fair if you have a job for a long time. You work and you work and you work and you expect that that kind of loyalty will provide some stability over time in your position. It's not fair if then you are taken out of that job and put in another school. . . . If [teachers] cannot work for the stability of their positions, then they really have nothing to work for."[14] Some teachers believed that such provisions might eventually compromise the educational program by, for example, assigning teachers to classes for which they are not well qualified. However, in this study there was no instance in which teachers waived seniority rights for the sake of students.

Similarly, class-size limits were also known to protect jobs. As one teacher from Plantville said, "I would initiate a grievance about the issues that are closest to me; for example, if somebody tried to take advantage of the class-size limitations. I realize that class size is tied to class assignments and, unless we watch closely, some other teacher's job would eventually be on the line."[15] Teachers generally insisted that negotiated class-size limits be honored unless temporary adjustments would not jeopardize any staff jobs. These provisions were closely monitored in the four districts with declining enrollments, but occasionally abridged in Vista, where enrollments were expanding rapidly.[16]

The guarantee of a duty-free lunch, provided for in all the sample contracts, was the third type of contract provision that was fully enforced. Teachers were adamant that their negotiated right to eat lunch alone be honored and often contended that the assurance of a duty-free lunch implied immunity from cafeteria duty at any time. In the case

[12] Charles T. Kerchner, "The Impact of Collective Bargaining on School Governance," *Education and Urban Society*, 2 (1979), 182.

[13] Salary scales were also fully enforced. This discussion addresses only non-wage contract provisions.

[14] Personal interview with Metropolis teacher, 3 Dec. 1979.

[15] Personal interview with Plantville teacher, 20 Sept. 1979.

[16] Northwood had no negotiated class-size limits.

of these few, fully implemented provisions, contract language did determine practice, and the variation in school site practices within any district was slight.

While these contract provisions were closely enforced and the variation within any district was slight, there were many other contract provisions that were not fully implemented. In some cases, these provisions addressed issues that were important to teachers but could not be readily enforced with the grievance procedures. These included assurances of equitable treatment, standards for student discipline, and guarantees of adequate building security or maintenance. For example, poorly heated classrooms aggravated many teachers but were not regarded by union members as contract violations to be remedied through formal procedures. Similarly, although teachers were often dissatisfied with discipline standards and practices, they rarely relied on their contracts to improve the situation. They were, for the most part, resigned to pursuing such concerns informally, outside the contract, even when those issues had been formally negotiated. Consequently, such provisions were weakly implemented in all schools.

Finally, there were many contract provisions that were variably implemented within the same district — enforced in some schools, ignored in others, and informally renegotiated in yet others. They addressed such issues as supervisory duties, the length and frequency of meetings, the use of preparation periods, and the role of the building committee. For example, five contracts limited the frequency and length of staff meetings, but the actual meeting schedules varied widely from school to school within any district. In most schools, principals reportedly called fewer meetings than the one per week that most contracts permitted. However, in one Vista school, a newly appointed principal routinely called two or three meetings a week and had never been opposed by his staff.[17] A Shady Heights principal reported that he sometimes called an extra meeting: "Occasionally things come up — something that I have to get to them fast, something about a new program that is coming. And so I call a meeting at that time and there is no problem."[18] One Plantville principal reportedly had been forced by the union to reschedule two meetings because he had not provided the required forty-eight hours' notice.[19] Yet, in another Plantville school, the principal said that he occasionally called a meeting with only a day's notice by explaining to his staff, "I know this is not according to the contract, but it would be mutually beneficial if we all met." The teachers, he said, accepted this because he did not "call meetings for the sake of calling them."[20]

In some instances, a school's staff informally readjusted a contract provision to fit the needs of its school. For example, all contracts assured teachers twenty-five to forty-five minutes of preparation time each day. In Metropolis, where a dispute arose over how that time could be used, an arbitrator ruled that, in the absence of explicit contract language, individual teachers could use the time as they saw fit. Most did, and many principals made no effort to influence them for fear of formal grievances. However, at some Metropolis schools the faculty and administration mutually planned to use the time for schoolwide responsibilities in addition to preparation — supervisory duties, grade-level planning meetings, or inservice training.

[17] Personal interview with Vista principal, 8 Jan. 1980.
[18] Personal interview with Shady Heights principal, 9 Aug. 1979.
[19] Personal interview with Plantville principal, 27 June 1979.
[20] Personal interview with Plantville principal, 28 June 1979.

School by School Variation

The overall effects of collective bargaining at any particular school were unique to that site, and there was diversity among schools, even in the smallest district. There were schools where the contract was very prominent and other schools within the same district where teachers and principals did not mention it. There were schools where the contract was rigorously enforced and schools where teachers knowingly bent it for the good of the school. There were schools with many contract grievances and schools with none. There were schools where most teachers did little more than the contract required and other schools where teachers went well beyond its minimal requirements. There were schools where labor relations were hostile and schools where labor relations were cordial. The following two schools in the large urban district of Metropolis illustrate dramatic differences in administrative style, union assertiveness, contract prominence, and the level of teacher services.

Metropolis High School #1

The labor relationship in this high school was adversarial, with the principal and union building representative engaged in open, hostile conflict.[21] The principal reported that there was a union emphasis on being able to say, "I caught you"; the building representative called labor-management relations "abominable." Teachers said that the principal deliberately forced grievances; the union had filed five grievances about school-site practices within a year. Although teachers did not fully support the building representative, they did insist that the contract be closely policed, and they very rarely bent its provisions to meet the needs of the school. For example, teachers assumed no supervisory responsibilities since their contract required none.

The principal, who characterized his administrative style as "democratic, with blends of dictatorial," reported that he found the meet-and-discuss requirements of the contract burdensome; teachers charged him with being "aloof, brusque, and arbitrary." One teacher stated, "He manages the building inefficiently and arbitrarily, making almost all decisions himself, from placing personnel to setting the bell schedule." Teachers reported that colleagues pressured them not to volunteer for extra duties or activities because of the principal's authoritarian stance toward them. One explained, "The idea is 'Don't give in to him.' " Teachers expressed strong dissatisfaction with the overall organization of the school and blamed the administration for problems of discipline and disorder. For example, after a teacher had been stabbed by an intruder and several staff members thought the principal might have done more to make the building secure, he responded that such problems should be "collective concerns." Relationships between teachers and the principal were typified by distance, distrust, and blame.

Metropolis High School #2

The union organization in another Metropolis high school was quite strong, but the labor relationship in the school was exceptionally cooperative.[22] The principal, said to be "firm and decisive" and to "go by the book with the contract," actively pursued a close

[21] All data for the description of Metropolis High School #1 were gathered during personal interviews with the principal and teachers in this school on 23 Oct. 1980 and 6 Nov. 1980.

[22] All data for the description of Metropolis High School #2 were gathered during personal interviews with the principal and teachers of this school on 23 Oct. 1980 and 5 Nov. 1980.

working relationship with the building representative and building committee. He said: "The building committee becomes a resource that I can call for assistance in administering the school. . . . Their involvement in this committee leads to their acceptance of responsibility for the school. . . . The faculty here have a commitment to this school. We have an understanding that this is *our* school, and not *my* school, or *his* school." Teachers approved of this cooperative venture, the building representative explained: "The building committee serves as an advisory committee for Mr. _____ and he serves as a consultant for the advisory committee." One teacher reported, "Here the principal and faculty get along. I have seen schools where that relationship is hateful."

Teachers also reported being very satisfied with school discipline, order, and security. The principal was said to be visible: "He's in the hallways. He's checking the bathrooms. He's observing what's going on in the school. He's not sitting in his office, and the teachers know that he knows what's happening." One teacher said, "He's a strong principal and an extremely good disciplinarian. He is completely supportive of the faculty and staff, and he runs a very tight ship." Another said, "This guy means business."

The contract, while respected and adhered to by the administration, was occasionally bent for the school. The principal said, "Teachers in this school don't make an issue of class size unless they're really choked." In order to maintain advanced math and language courses which had small enrollments, teachers agreed to teach combinations of small and large classes, thus complying with the class-size averages but not with individual classroom limits. One teacher explained, "We have to give and take." No teachers reported pressure to refrain from volunteer activities, and there were reports that such participation was common. As the building representative explained, "Teachers feel part of it here."

The role of the contract and the relationship between the principal and teachers differed in these two schools. Teachers in the first were considerably less flexible in responding to school needs, teacher-administrator relationships were more formalized, and practices were more rule-bound than in the second school. These differences persisted even though the same local union represented these teachers and the same contract defined their working conditions.

Other intra-district differences were not always so extreme. Two elementary schools in Plantville, a small urban district in the Northeast, illustrate less dramatic but equally important variations.

Plantville Elementary School #1

The principal of this elementary school was a strong advocate of teacher unionism but believed that the principal should set the standards for the school: "The teachers," he said, "will go along — contract or no contract."[23] One teacher described the principal: "He's not an anti-union principal. His father was a union man and he's pro-teacher, unless you mess things up. Then you'll have to answer to him. He's a strict principal. He likes a tight building." This principal had firm expectations about the performance of his staff. He required teachers to begin supervising the school at 8:20 A.M., fifteen minutes before the beginning of their contractually defined work day, and he assigned

---

[23] All data for the description of Plantville Elementary School #1 were gathered during personal interviews with the principal and teachers of this school on 17 Aug. 1979, 20 Sept. 1979, and 21 Sept. 1979.

teachers to supervise the school yard at the end of the day. Neither was required by contract. He monitored the after-school help that teachers provided for students by requiring weekly reports of conferences held. He ran a system of staggered lunches that assured teacher supervision of the cafeteria and playground — an unusual arrangement in the district. Although the schoolwide average on class size was enforced, students were grouped by ability so that classes varied considerably in size within the school, sometimes exceeding the contractual limits.

The teachers, all union members, reported being very satisfied with the school and its administration. One said, "He is extremely organized. He knows how to delegate authority. He has high expectations, but he's as supportive as he can be." There had been no transfer requests in four years, and one active union member said, "I would do anything in my power to stay in this building." However, teachers agreed that incompetent staff wouldn't last in the school, "They wouldn't be working for Mr. _____ if they didn't do the job. They'd be transferred out. He puts too much pressure on people he's dissatisfied with." Teachers expressed considerable regard for the principal's leadership and tolerant acceptance of his extra demands. One said: "The loyalty here is to him rather than to the union. If he told us to stay late, why everyone would. People help him out and he's good to others in response. I guess that's not quite kosher as far as the contract's concerned, but we do it." The contract had low prominence in the school, and the building representative reported having a good working relationship with the principal, against whom no grievances had ever been filed. A teacher explained, "Because there is this personal relationship between the principal and the teachers, things do not get grieved here that would be grieved in another building. Those kinds of things would be considered nit-picking here."

Plantville Elementary School #2

The principal of this elementary school was also a strong union supporter, but he assumed a laissez-faire stance toward the teachers, the school, and the union.[24] One teacher said, "He's extremely casual and unauthoritarian. He lets us do our own thing. He's totally permissive. He makes absolutely no demands on us." Another said, "He likes to kick issues under the rug and hopes that they'll go away." The principal was reluctant to monitor the arrival and departure times of teachers, commenting, "I don't like to be a police officer. They say I'm too easy on them." The staff expressed concern about two teachers who were not doing their jobs: "They're never made to toe the line by the principal."

The teachers, all union members, were not active in the union, and the building committee did not function. The issues that concerned teachers in the school — lack of administrative direction, late deliveries of supplies, lack of staff influence over school policies, and tolerance of incompetent teachers — were not perceived to be union issues. As one teacher said, "You simply can't file a grievance about not getting your crayons on time."

Teachers had organized lavatory and recess supervision on their own but believed that the building also should have been supervised before school. Some teachers initiated ex-

[24] All data for the description of Plantville Elementary School #2 were gathered during personal interviews with the principal and teachers of this school on 28 June 1979, 27 Sept. 1979, and 28 Sept. 1979.

tracurricular activities, and the principal reportedly neither opposed nor supported such efforts. One staff member said, "The teachers in this building would like more consistent direction, but don't get me wrong, we don't want to manage the building. We want to be able to teach." As one teacher said, "There's no serious contention in this building. . . . It's more an issue of omission than one of commission."

Labor relations did not differ as dramatically at these two Plantville schools as they did at the Metropolis schools described earlier. For instance, in these two Plantville schools grievances were rare, and the principal and building representative were said to cooperate. Yet there were important differences in administrative leadership, the role of the contract, and teacher services. Both Plantville principals respected the contract, but the first asked teachers to go beyond it for the good of the school. They complied. The second principal pursued a cautious course, asking no more of teachers than they were obliged to give. Teachers approved of the first principal's direction, but expressed dissatisfaction with the second principal's lack of leadership, however contractually correct it might be.

As these examples from Metropolis and Plantville suggest, differences in principals' administrative styles appeared to be central in determining the character of the school site labor relationship, the prominence of the contract, and the level of teacher services at the school site. One might legitimately question what other factors influence these outcomes — for example, the level and location of the school, history of building labor relations, style of the building representative, or prevailing union sentiments of staff. Such variables were not controlled in this study, but two schools presented the opportunity to consider their importance when the principalship changed, while other factors such as location, union strength of the staff, and the economic level of students remained constant. A brief account of what happened in each of these schools will illustrate the apparent importance of the principal.

Vista High School

Under a previous administrator, Vista high school had floundered; labor relations were strained.[25] One teacher described the problem: "[The previous principal] was authoritarian, but he was never in control of the faculty or the students. We were afraid of him. He was shouting and slamming all the time. The association and the principal were in constant battle. Department meetings with him were very difficult. Nobody could really figure out what he wanted. . . . We didn't have control of anything. Students would leave the campus; they wouldn't be in classes. It was general confusion." Ten grievances were filed in one year against this principal. One teacher describing the labor relationship said, "It was war."

By contrast, this principal's replacement was characterized as taking "a problem-solving approach to things." One teacher said, "He's very innovative and doesn't come to the teachers with a decision but with a problem. And he gets things done." Another teacher said, "The principal makes decisions that have to be made. He's strong, and there's a good feeling about him." The principal was said to be very active and visible in the school. Student absenteeism, which had been the highest of any high school in the state,

---

[25] All data for the description of Vista High School were gathered during personal interviews with the principal and teachers of this school on 10 Jan. 1980, 13 Feb. 1980, and 14 Feb. 1980.

improved dramatically. Teaching performance was observed and evaluated. One staff member said that more teacher evaluations had been done by Christmas "than five administrators had done in five years." Morale among teachers was reportedly very high. Under the new administration, the building representative, who had initiated grievances the previous year, assumed broad administrative responsibilities for student attendance. A teacher said that the labor relationship changed from being "below average and poor" to "above average and good." No new grievances were filed, and teachers reported voluntarily accepting various supervisory responsibilities for the good of the school.

Shady Heights High School

A new principal, described by teachers as "very professional" and "authoritarian" replaced another whom they agreed had been a failure.[26] One teacher characterized the former principal's shortcomings: "The previous principal was an inconsistent disciplinarian. He was particularly concerned about what couldn't be done. He had a 'hands tied' mentality. He had a buddy approach to dealing with the faculty. . . . He ruled by granting favors. He did things like eliminating the sign-in/sign-out sheet for teachers. He disciplined infrequently and indiscriminately both students and teachers. There were a lot of problems in the building; students were late to class; there was a lot of noise in the corridors; students would come to class unprepared to learn."

When the new principal arrived, teachers were impressed by his purposefulness and were inclined to support him. One teacher said, "People took him very seriously. He met minimal resistance from the faculty. They were dying to have someone come in and do what he did." He quickly reinstated checks on teachers' performance. Staff members were required to sign in and out and received letters of reprimand if they were late more than three times. Teachers were required to be in their homerooms when the bell sounded, to stand in the corridors between classes, and to formally supervise the halls before, during and after school. The principal expected them to go beyond the requirements of the contract, and his demands were not grieved even though this was a school with a strong union organization, and the principal was thought by some to be anti-union. As one teacher said, "He hates the union, but he knows how to work with people. He's very sharp, and he's always prepared. . . . He doesn't break the contract, nor does he make the ridiculous demands that principals do in some other schools."

Teachers reported that the changes had restored order to the school; virtually everyone believed the reforms had been productive. One teacher said: "The morale and performance of teachers have gone up since he has been principal. People no longer take days off, just to take days off. People have accepted the new rules for the sake of the building." Another teacher summarized her satisfaction, "You have to do the classroom job because now the conditions are good and the school is running well."

These two examples underscore what the others have suggested—that the levels of teacher service, the enforcement of the contract, and the quality of labor relations were subject to considerable influence by the principal.[27] Intra-district variations were un-

---

[26] All data for the description of Shady Heights High School were gathered during personal interviews with the principal and teachers of this school on 14 Aug. 1979, 4 Oct. 1979, and 5 Oct. 1979.

[27] Others have found the role of the principal to be central in successful school programs. See, for example, Paul Berman and Milbrey McLaughlin, *Implementing and Sustaining Innovation*, Vol. VIII of *Federal Programs Supporting Educational Change* (Santa Monica, Calif.: Rand Corporation, 1978), pp. 30-31; Ron-

mistakable. Teachers in some schools assumed extra supervisory responsibilities, used preparation periods for inservice training, attended extra meetings, reallocated student assignments within the school, and volunteered for extra activities. Teachers in other schools cut corners on the work day, refused noninstructional duties not included in the contract, and insisted on literal enforcement of teacher observation procedures. There was, of course, variation between these extremes.

The School Organization and Unionism

While the popular view may be that teacher unions closely monitor the implementation of their contracts and force principals to standardize practices in conformance with negotiated provisions, this study does not confirm that view. The principals' formal authority had been constrained by the collective bargaining agreements, but the power that principals exercised varied greatly from school to school. Contract provisions were found to be differentially implemented; some were closely enforced and some were not.

What accounted for this variation? What enabled principals to exercise extensive powers despite their contractual restrictions? What permitted the contract to be variously enforced, ignored, abridged, bent, or violated? What is it about schools, teachers, and principals that produces these differences?

Three characteristics of the school as an organization seem particularly important in explaining these outcomes. These include the interdependence of teachers and administrators, the breadth of teacher concerns that extended well beyond the contract, and teacher ambivalence about unions. Each of these will be explored.

Interdependence. While it may be true that principals once could wield considerably more power than they can now, that power never really was absolute, largely because of the decentralized character of schooling. Classrooms are cellular; teachers are the street-level bureaucrats; and principals simply cannot closely inspect the work of their staff.[28] Teachers have always successfully reserved certain important powers for themselves. The principals may have ordered the books, but the teachers taught the lessons — they decided how to use those books. The principals may have taken attendance at faculty meetings, but teachers decided whether to listen or participate. Covert insurrection was always a teacher's option in responding to the powers of the principal. Moreover, whatever the principal's powers, he or she could not run the school alone.[29]

Even before collective bargaining, the relationship of teachers and principals was highly interdependent.[30] The success of each depended, in part, on the cooperation of the other. Teachers could not be effective in their classrooms without fair and balanced

---

ald Edmonds, "Effective Schools and the Urban Poor," *Educational Leadership,* 37 (1979), 15-24; Donald R. Moore, Arthur Hyde, Kathy A. Blair, Sharon M. Weitzman, *Student Classification and the Right to Read* (Chicago: Designs for Change, 1981), p. 115.

[28] Dan C. Lortie, *Schoolteacher: A Sociological Study* (Chicago: Univ. of Chicago Press, 1975); Richard Weatherly and Michael Lipsky, "Street-Level Bureaucrats and Institutional Innovation: Implementing Special Educational Reform," *Harvard Educational Review,* 47 (1977), 171-197; Seymour B. Sarason, *The Culture of the School and the Problem of Change* (Boston, Mass.: Allyn and Bacon, 1971).

[29] Seymour Sarason writes, "The tendency to think in terms of, and to over-evaluate, the power of the principal is no less mistaken in the case of principal than it is when we think of the power of the President of our country." (*The Culture of the School,* p. 119).

[30] Lortie likens the relationship between teachers and principals to that between vassals and lords during medieval times: "The Superordinate is expected to use his power to protect and help those of lesser rank; they, appropriate deference and respect." (*Schoolteacher,* p. 200.)

class assignments, while principals could assure order in the school only if teachers upheld administrative rules and policies. Principals had to be attentive to teacher interests if they were to command teacher loyalty. The principal and teachers, like the family to which they are often compared, informally negotiated ways of working together that served their mutual interests. To be sure, some of those families were repressive, some of the principals dictatorial, and some of the teachers cowed. But in general, norms of teacher-administrator reciprocity took precedence over narrow rules and definitions of responsibilities.[31]

Collective bargaining, teacher unions, and contracts have entered public education in the context of this interdependence. One Shady Heights principal explained how he relied on reciprocal relationships with teachers to manage his school: "I want safety first. I don't want kids hurt and I don't want their clothes torn. Then secondly, I want teaching going on all the time. Teachers like that. They like to be able to use their time to teach. They like me to support them in that. And when they're teaching all the time and making me happy, then they know that if they need something I'll help them out. If they have to leave for a special medical appointment, then I'll go in and take their class."[32]

Teachers in this study relied on their principals for many things that made successful teaching possible — a balanced teaching load, a manageable selection of students, adequate text and supplies, and the maintenance of order in the school. And principals, who face expanded responsibilities with declining resources, were increasingly dependent on the professional commitment and good will of teachers to make their schools work.

Teachers' Concerns. While it may be appropriate to speak of *union* priorities when considering district-level labor issues, it is necessary to speak of *teacher* priorities at the school site. For in this setting, union affiliation is but one of the teachers' concerns. The relationship between teachers and principals extends well beyond the relationship of labor and management, and in order to comprehend the complexity of that relationship, it is necessary to consider the breadth of teacher concerns.

Through a variety of interview questions, teachers were asked about what they needed and wanted in their work. Eleven concerns emerged repeatedly.[33] They sought salaries that would enable them to live comfortably and the job security they believed was due them in exchange for accepting positions of public service. They wanted to be assigned a reasonable number of students and classes, and they wanted to reduce or eliminate nonteaching duties, which they regarded as a misuse of their professional time. They sought uninterrupted non-teaching time during which they could relax and catch up on work. They wanted equitable treatment, resented favoritism, and sought assurances that decisions such as transfers and assignments would be made in orderly, fair ways. They expected to have a modest amount of influence over school policies and practices, particularly those affecting their classrooms. They liked to be consulted, and wanted the opportunity to initiate change, but did not seek large-scale responsibility for school-site matters; their attention centered on their classrooms.

---

[31] Lortie, *Schoolteacher*, pp. 201-202.

[32] Personal interview with Shady Heights principal, 9 Aug. 1979.

[33] Because of the method by which data were gathered, it is not possible to rank order these responses. However, there was remarkable consensus among the 189 teachers interviewed about what they wanted in their work.

Student discipline and safety from intruders were also among the frequently mentioned concerns of teachers, who believed that order in their classrooms depended, in part, on the overall order of the school. Teachers often spoke about the lack of parental support and public regard for their work. They wished parents would emphasize the value of schooling with their children, monitor homework, endorse teachers' expectations for good behavior, and respect teachers' expertise. Finally, they wanted to work with effective principals, administrators who not only assured the order, security, and maintenance of the school, but who also provided direction, leadership, and high standards for student and teacher success. Such administrators were said to be visible, active and principled; they expected teachers to be so as well.

Some of the issues which concern teachers could be addressed by collective bargaining; some could not. Many of the teachers' concerns had been dealt with in the contracts of this study, and bargaining had helped them achieve their ends. However, certain very prominent teacher concerns were not negotiable, including guarantees of parental support, public regard, and administrative leadership. Principals who administered schools effectively under collective bargaining were attentive to these concerns as well as those addressed by the contract.

Teacher Views of Unionism. While unionized teachers are often portrayed as fervent and pugnacious in their pursuit of higher wages, job security, and improved working conditions, the teachers in this study were ambivalent about teacher unionism. Throughout the entire study, very few regarded themselves as union members who single-mindedly enforced the contract in their schools. Respondents were pleased that collective bargaining had improved their salaries, limited the size and number of their classes, and tempered administrative abuse. But they were also uneasy about its effects on their professional status, the quality of their relationships with administrators, and on the competence and performance of their peers. Even though union membership levels were high and teachers in several districts overwhelmingly supported strikes during periods of strained negotiations, many teachers reported having strong reservations about both the notion of unionism and the conduct of their local organization.[34]

There were many teachers who regretted the necessity of collective bargaining. As one teacher stated: "I'm an idealist and I would like to believe that it would not be necessary, that these things could be settled without a formal organization, but I think that it's probably unrealistic at this time."[35] There were other teachers who firmly believed that virtually all educational gains were union accomplishments that would be swept away if it were not for the continued presence and vigilance of the union. As one Vista teacher said, "Without a union, we'd be nowhere."[36] While there was overwhelming, if sometimes reluctant, agreement among teachers in all sample districts regarding the continued necessity of collective bargaining for teachers, few teachers reported full satisfaction with the contract or the action of their organization.

[34] R. Theodore Clark, Jr. explains teachers' ambivalence about being union members: "Teaching is a profession, and professional employees, at least in this country, tend not to desire unionization unless it is necessary for defensive reasons. It should come as no big surprise then that many teachers and would-be teachers embrace collective bargaining with less than total enthusiasm. Moreover, the highly adversarial nature of collective bargaining in public education, including strikes, picketing, and name-calling, is hardly designed to enhance the reputation or attractiveness of the teaching profession." See his "Commentary" in *Faculty and Teacher Bargaining,* ed. George W. Angell (Lexington, Mass.: Heath, 1981), p. 89.

[35] Personal interview with Mill City teacher, 15 Dec. 1979.

[36] Personal interview with Vista teacher, 12 Feb. 1980.

Some teachers were dissatisfied with the cost and the politics of their state or national affiliate. There were teachers in each district who were unhappy with the adversarial relations and the "excessive concern for contract compliance" that accompanied collective bargaining. Some repudiated the blue collar image of unions—pickets, mobs, confrontation—that they considered incompatible with professionalism. One union member said: "I intensely dislike teachers' unions. My big fear in life is that my obituary will be headlined, 'AFL-CIO Member Dies.' I consider unions to be blue collar, not professional organizations. I think that they have no place in education."[37]

One of the most frequently voiced dissatisfactions of both active and inactive union members was that unions, in meeting their obligation to fairly represent all teachers, overly protect poor teachers. One Metropolis respondent argued this way: "They no longer should have to defend the riff-raff. When they first organized, it was important for teachers to see that the Federation was strong and that they would defend people. But now they're plenty large. They could police their own instead of defending some teacher who can't teach himself out of a paper bag."[38]

In all districts, some teachers criticized their union's pursuit of high salaries and reduced duties at the expense of well-maintained buildings, adequate supplies and equipment, and inservice training. As one Metropolis teacher said, "There's too much emphasis on 'me.' "[39]

Most teachers focused on one or two points of dissatisfaction that were offset by points of agreement. Few expressed total disapproval, just as few voiced unconditional acceptance. Collective bargaining was viewed as a useful and necessary means to achieve narrow objectives rather than a cause deserving constant and unconditional commitment. At the district level, where the voice of one teacher might be inaudible, teachers accepted the necessity of pursuing their interests collectively. However, at the school site, where teachers were known individually and where they had the opportunity to act on their own behalf with administrators, they were far less likely to stress their union identities.

As the study progressed, it became apparent that teachers' decisions to ally with others as union members, to define teacher interests in opposition to administrative interests, and to pursue problems through formal procedures depended largely on their views of their principals. In most schools, if the principal was attentive to the broad range of teacher interests and was effective in supporting instruction, teachers were likely to endorse administrative priorities, overlook occasional contract violations, avoid formal grievance procedures, and bend the contract in the interests of the school. As one Mill City teacher said, "If we have to bend it to make survival easier, then we'll do it."[40]

Conclusion

The picture of labor relations at the school site that emerged from this study had few fixed and many flexible features. Certain contract provisions, once negotiated, were fully implemented and limited the principal's control over faculty composition, the allo-

---

[37] Personal interview with Plantville teacher, 21 Sept. 1979.
[38] Personal interview with Metropolis principal, 20 Oct. 1980.
[39] Personal interview with Metropolis teacher, 18 Nov. 1980.
[40] Personal interview with Mill City teacher, 15 Dec. 1979.

cation of students to classes, or the supervision of the cafeteria. Other provisions, however, were reinterpreted and informally renegotiated at the school site where such factors as teacher interests, educational consequences, administrative leadership, and staff
allegiance were balanced and counterbalanced. Principals could manage their schools
well in even the strongest union districts, but very restrictive contracts put great demands on their time, ingenuity, and resourcefulness.

There was considerable discrepancy between rules and practice. Identical contract
language did not prevent strikingly different outcomes even within schools of the same
district. Notably, such deviations were usually endorsed, even initiated, by the teachers
on whose behalf the contract had initially been negotiated. As collective bargaining
agreements were not fully enforced and contract provisions were modified by teachers
and principals, the union's objectives were only partially realized. But the schools were
changed. Principals worked amidst new constraints. Teachers gained more attention for
their concerns.

Those who predicted that teacher unionism would transform the schools into hostile,
rigid institutions expected that teachers would pursue their self-interests narrowly, that
they would aggressively enforce the contract provisions negotiated on their behalf, and
that traditional educational values — flexibility, responsiveness, cooperation — would be
abandoned for conformity, confrontation, and formality. Such commentators discounted the reciprocal school setting, the independence of teachers, and the day-to-day
realities of school work.

It was important to the teachers of this study that principals respect and honor their
contracts, but they also allowed for flexibility, amendment, and mistakes when the principal's actions were believed to be responsible, well-intentioned, and in the interests of a
good school. They accepted authoritarian as well as democratic administrators and
were critical of laissez-faire principals who relinquished too much power. They were tolerant, and often respectful, of principals who held high standards, monitored teacher
performance, and expected more of teachers than the contract required.

Teachers in this study did not want to run the schools, but they were prepared to support a principal who demonstrated that their schools could be run well. For most teachers, being part of a good school took precedence over union membership or close enforcement of the contract. As one Metropolis administrator observed, "Teachers like to
be part of a winning team."[41]

---

[41] Personal interview with Metropolis district administrator, 9 July 1980.

This article is taken from a larger work to be published by Temple University Press. I am grateful to the
Ford Foundation for supporting this research and to David K. Cohen, David Kuechle, and, particularly,
Jerome T. Murphy for their helpful critiques of earlier drafts.

Fidelity in Teaching, Teacher Education, and Research for Teaching

NEL NODDINGS

Viewing fidelity from the perspective of an ethic of caring, Nel Noddings explores how this virtue might be moved from the periphery to the center of educational work. She argues that such a reorientation would not undermine, but rather enhance, the quality and depth of teaching, learning, and research. She urges, further, that fidelity to persons be taken as the proper measure and guide for the implementation of educational reform.

Fidelity is an interesting word. It connotes, on the one hand, a state or quality of faithfulness and, on the other, exactitude or a high degree of accuracy. Both meanings will figure in the present discussion because when we are reflectively faithful to someone or something, we try to refine or fine-tune our faithfulness. In this conjunctive sense, we are in *good faith* when we know to what or to whom we are faithful, when we have reflected on the reasons and emotions involved in our faithfulness, and when we are committed to fresh affirmations of faithfulness at ever finer and truer levels.

In ethics, it is not surprising that mention of fidelity most frequently arises in discussions of friendship or marriage. Henry Sidgwick observed that "it is natural to us to admire fidelity in friendship and stability of affections, and we commonly regard these as most important excellences of character."[1] But he goes on to note that services done out of a sense of fidelity rather than affection are often, and properly, rejected by the "refined person." He observes that "in relations of affection we often praise one party for offering what we rather blame the other for accepting."[2] Sidgwick's comment is symptomatic of a general weakness in traditional ethics. It is supposed that an ethically motivated deed involves something taken from one person (albeit voluntarily) and given to another. The generous person gives from a sense of duty; the sensitive receiver either refuses the gift or incurs a debt.

Both in Sidgwick's utilitarian ethics and in Kantian ethics, fidelity to individuals is derived from fidelity to principle. Fidelity to persons, then, is seen as a possible

---

[1] Sidgwick, *The Methods of Ethics* (1907; rpt. Indianapolis and Cambridge: Hackett, 1981), p. 258.
[2] Sidgwick, *The Methods of Ethics*, p. 259.

Harvard Educational Review   Vol. 56   No. 4   November 1986, 496–510

duty (one of many), and the question naturally arises whether, in Sidgwick's words, it is "a positive duty." We can certainly agree with him that most of us would prefer to be treated well by another out of regard rather than duty, and much current philosophical debate centers on this issue.[3] But perhaps fidelity is too narrowly defined here; indeed, it may even be the case that such narrow definition is inevitable in ethical systems that isolate moral agents from their actual relations and place abstract "positive duties" on them. In Kantian ethics, we are obliged to act out of duty, and fidelity to persons might well be required if we have made promises that imply it. In utilitarian ethics, there is some doubt about the status of fidelity, because the principle of benevolence requires us to consider whether fidelity (or anything else) will produce happiness. In both systems, however, it is clear that fidelity in a larger sense serves as the principal part of a moral axiom: One owes fidelity to duty or to the utilitarian principle.

From an alternative perspective — that of an ethic of caring[4] — fidelity is not seen as faithfulness to duty or principle but as a direct response to individuals with whom one is in relation. Natural caring — the sort of response made when we want to care for another — establishes the ideal for ethical caring, and ethical caring imitates this ideal in its efforts to institute, maintain, or reestablish natural caring. From this perspective fidelity may be interpreted as a precondition for subjectively satisfying relations and a continuing condition for their maintenance. Thus fidelity is attached to particular persons and particular relations, and it remains so attached. Persons guided by an ethic of caring do not ask whether it is their *duty* to be faithful (whether promises have been made or utilities may be in conflict); rather, for them fidelity to persons *is* fidelity; indeed, fidelity is a quality of the relation and not merely an attribute of an individual moral agent's behavior or character. As both parties contribute to a dyadic relation, both maintain fidelity and both are involved in the refinement of skills that build relational competence, or what I refer to here as "high fidelity."

It may well be that an ethic of caring grows more naturally out of women's experience than men's. Jane Austen noted (through one of her characters) that *constancy* was more likely to be practiced by women than by men,[5] and constancy is clearly fidelity to the quality of relation — to a way of being that supports affection and steadfastly promotes both the welfare of the other and that of the relation. It is important to recognize that fidelity is not, on this account, owed by law or principle (it is not a duty), and if the quality of a relation is destroyed so also is the obligation to maintain the relation. As Carol Gilligan has repeatedly pointed out, a relation involves at least two parties and is characterized by distinctive forms of reciprocity,[6] but it may well be that women take greater responsibility than men for

---

[3] See, for example, Bernard Williams, *Ethics and the Limits of Philosophy* (Cambridge: Harvard University Press, 1985); Marcia Baron, "The Ethics of Duty/Ethics of Virtue Debate and its Relevance to Educational Theory," *Educational Theory, 35* (1985), 135–150.

[4] See Carol Gilligan, *In a Different Voice,* (Cambridge: Harvard University Press, 1982); Nel Noddings, *Caring: A Feminine Approach to Ethics and Moral Education* (Berkeley: University of California Press, 1984).

[5] Alisdair MacIntyre cites Austen's *Mansfield Park* and *Persuasion* in his *After Virtue* (Notre Dame, IN: Notre Dame University Press, 1984), p. 242.

[6] Gilligan, *In a Different Voice*. Refer also to tapes of a symposium and conversation from the annual meeting of the Association for Moral Education, Ontario Institute for the Study of Education, Toronto, 8–9 Nov. 1985.

relations. In her work, as well as mine, the "different voice" expressing an ethic of caring is more likely to be female than male, but the reason for this is to be found in culture and experience. No claim is made for a necessary connection to nature.

The caring attitude as a moral attitude is gaining in respectability, and as it continues to do so we might predict that women will no longer feel rationally inferior in living by it nor will men fear being demeaned and shamed for adopting it. Daniel Maguire, for example, welcomes the "feminization of God and ethics," suggesting that all human beings will benefit from a heightened moral sensitivity. He remarks, "Because the experience of women has given them certain advantages in their moral perceptivity, their exclusion from most centers of power in most civilizations has impoverished the species."[7] Maguire certainly does not mean that women are morally better than men. In the same article, he is careful to note that "our sisters are not without sin,"[8] but he sees clearly that a feminine ethic (one arising out of female experience) has the potential to enrich moral life for all of us.

What I want to do in the remainder of this paper is to show how an ethic of caring — an ethic that has fidelity to persons and the quality of relations at its heart — may be applied to issues in teaching, teacher education, and research on teaching. A discussion of this length cannot, obviously, be comprehensive, but by reflecting briefly on three vast domains, it should reveal both the power to guide ethical conduct as envisaged by Maguire and the constancy or unity extolled by Austen.

Fidelity in Teaching

There are longstanding arguments in education over fidelity, although they are rarely referred to in that way. Joseph Junell points to one of these controversies when he asks, "To what part of man does public education owe its first obligation?"[9] Junell feels that we make a great error when we give our fidelity to training the rational intellect at the expense of affect and emotion. In agreement with Junell, one might argue further that when we give our fidelity to the training of intellect, fidelity to persons once again becomes derivative. John Gardner, for example, has argued that persons who cannot, or choose not to, achieve academic excellence must find other arenas in which to excel, and one might infer from his arguments that the school owes them nothing but an equitable opportunity to achieve academically.[10] From the perspective of an ethic of caring, however, development of the whole person is necessarily our concern. As Milton Mayeroff has pointed out, caring involves promoting the growth of those for whom we care,[11] and teaching requires caring for the individuals we teach. Aristotle said of the teacher-learner relationship that it is a "moral type of friendship, which is not on fixed terms: it makes a gift, or does whatever it does, as to a friend."[12] Further,

[7] Maguire, "The Feminization of God and Ethics," *Christianity and Crisis*, 25 March 1982, pp. 59–60.

[8] Maguire, "Feminization," p. 62.

[9] Junell, *Matters of Feeling: Values Education Reconsidered* (Bloomington, IN: Phi Delta Kappa Educational Foundation, 1979), p. 2.

[10] Gardner, *Excellence: Can We Be Equal and Excellent Too?* (New York: Harper, 1961).

[11] Mayeroff, *On Caring* (New York: Harper & Row, 1971).

[12] Aristotle, *Nichomachean Ethics*, Book VIII, chap. 2.

Aristotle says, we wish for our friends that they should be good persons, and we wish this for their own sakes. Thus teaching requires our fidelity to persons.

Fidelity to persons does not imply that academic excellence, the acquisition of skills, or the needs of contemporary society should be of no concern. To suppose, for example, that attention to affective needs necessarily implies less time for arithmetic is simply a mistake. Such tasks can be accomplished simultaneously, but the one is undertaken in light of the other. We do not ask how we must treat children in order to get them to learn arithmetic but, rather, what effect each instructional move we consider has on the development of good persons. Our guiding principles for teaching arithmetic, or any other subject, are derived from our primary concern for the persons whom we teach, and methods of teaching are chosen in consonance with these derived principles. An ethic of caring guides us to ask, What effect will this have on the person I teach? What effect will it have on the caring community we are trying to build?

This way of thinking and speaking has almost disappeared from formal educational discourse. It occurs on the fringes of the educational research community, in almost embarrassed whispers. While there is a growing reaction against single-minded calls for excellence and technical proficiency, it is a disgruntled response cast largely in the language of liberal ideology.[13] That is not to say that it is wrong or unwelcome but, rather, to note its source and predict yet another swing of the pendulum of power. With its ascent to the liberal tip of the arc, we can expect a renewed emphasis on equality and diversity (and this we might label "good"), but we can also expect a proliferation of agencies, bureaucratic regulations, and specialized jobs (and this we might label "not so good"). A liberal counter-reform will not revolutionize education, because it will not challenge the fundamental premises of masculine intellectualism: abstractionism and consequentialism. To challenge these, we need a language of relation that guides our thinking in concrete situations. It is heartening to hear occasional mention of "compassion" and "caring" in reform recommendations, but one fears that these terms are not central enough to the positions in which they occur to make a lasting difference in schooling.[14] We simply have not learned to use the language of relation comfortably outside the private domain, and yet it is clearly possible — and, I would argue, imperative — to do so.

A specific example may help here. The following example is not profound in its subject matter, but in its very ordinariness may serve to illustrate how pedagogical thinking is guided by fidelity to persons. Ms. A, a math teacher, has expressed concern about students who are falling behind. Several of them have failed a test on factoring, and she is trying to decide whether to provide retests for these students. She thinks aloud:

> *Ms. A:* Surely I have to do something. It is irresponsible to allow these kids to go on to algebraic fractions when they can't factor. But lots of their classmates already have got it. Maybe I can just proceed, do a little extra remediation, and see if they

[13] Among the liberal dissenters, see: Ernest L. Boyer, *High School: A Report on Secondary Education in America* (New York: Harper & Row, 1983); Shirley Brice Heath, *Ways with Words* (New York: McGraw-Hill, 1983); and Theodore R. Sizer, *Horace's Compromise: The Dilemma of the American High School* (Boston: Houghton Mifflin, 1984).

[14] See, for example, Sizer's comments in *Time*, 10 Oct. 1983, p. 66; on caring and community service, see Boyer, *High School*.

do better on the fraction test. No, that won't do. The bad grade on this test is itself a handicap. It makes them feel scared and hopeless. They need time to learn more and a chance to improve their position. I'll have to give retests.

Devil's Advocate (D.A.): So will anyone fail? Don't you owe the institution a fair reporting on who's good at math and who isn't?

Ms. A: Of course I owe the institution something. I owe it students who have learned as much as their effort and mine can achieve but also students who have regard for this school and schooling in general — who feel supported by the school and who will, in turn, support it. In the long run both individual student and institution are served by this choice.

D.A.: But is it fair to the students who passed the first time?

Ms. A: I'm not sure fairness is the right criterion here. This isn't a *contest*. Why should there be winners and losers? Those who pass the first time don't lose anything — they don't have to prepare for a retest. Someday they may need the opportunity themselves.

D.A.: But aren't you encouraging dependency? You're protecting them from competition and failure. You're reducing their suffering. Remember what Nietzsche said about suffering: "How deeply one can suffer almost determines the order of rank."[15] Perhaps life is, as the Greeks saw it, *agon* — a contest.

Ms. A: Ha! Remember that we get "agony" from *agon*. I have no desire to induce suffering in my students. I am not trying to produce heroes. I am trying to educate community-builders — people who will be faithful to each other — people who will have a sense of efficacy, a belief that their own effort coupled with that of others can achieve something.

It is clear that Ms. A recognizes an obligation to the institution, that she wants her students to learn mathematics and to be responsible members of a community, but she does not detach these goals from the relational situation in which she identifies them. She does not set them apart and ask to which she owes her "fidelity," her first duty. Her fidelity is her way of being in relation with each of her students. Her thinking is ordered by it: "Given that my fidelity is to these persons, my students, what are my obligations to X (X = {institution, community, mathematics, . . . }) and how best can I meet them?"

This way of thinking does not force a choice between individual goals and social goals as aims of education; rather, it conditions a teacher's way of thinking about both. For such a teacher, self-actualization is not entirely a matter of individual choice and the pursuit of individual achievement; thus, it is not best facilitated by permissiveness or unconditional acceptance.[16] Since the self is a relational being, it is actualized by ever-increasing fidelity in relation. The self is surpassed, but not in the Nietzschean sense; that is, the self does not grow more individually powerful, more cruel in the pursuit of highly valued goals, more unlike the human beings it seeks to dominate. Rather, the self is surpassed in relation, in the realization of interdependence and the joy of empowering others. One whose fidelity is part of his or her relations cannot, for example, be "hostile even to the people he

---

[15] Friedrich Nietzsche, *Nietzsche Contra Wagner*, in *The Portable Nietzsche*, ed. Walter Kaufmann (New York: Penguin Books, 1959), p. 679.

[16] The permissive view is well expressed in A. S. Neill, *Summerhill* (New York: Hart, 1960); acceptance is described by Carl Rogers, *Freedom to Learn* (Columbus, OH: Merrill, 1969).

loves and the institutions in which he grew up."[17] Nor can such persons simply accept the people they love and their institutions as they present themselves. Mere acceptance of a flawed self does not lead to self-actualization, and acceptance of a faulty institution, as John Dewey said so clearly, destroys the legitimacy of any rationales for socialization. For Dewey, and for me, socialization can be synonymous with education if the practices to which people are socialized are truly representative of defensible ideals. To induce the habit of inquiry and reflection, for example, would be to educate and also to socialize, if the society genuinely valued inquiry and reflection.[18]

Fidelity as a way of relation requires *confirmation* rather than mere acceptance or hostility:

> When we attribute to the cared-for the best possible motive consonant with reality, we confirm him; that is, we reveal to him an attainable image of himself that is lovelier than that manifested in his present acts. In an important sense, we embrace him as one with us in devotion to caring. In education, what we reveal to a student about himself as an ethical and intellectual being has the power to nurture the ethical ideal or to destroy it.[19]

It is this striving for the best in ourselves and in those with whom we interact that marks self-actualization, and a community that embraces this view of fidelity has a strong rationale for socialization, for it is not asking for fidelity to institutions as they are but as they might realistically be at their best. Further, fidelity is never given first to either self as individual or to institution, but to the others with whom we are in relation and to the relations by which we are defined.

An ethic of caring is, clearly, phenomenological in its method. In formal phenomenology, where interests are largely epistemological, we try to uncover the structures of consciousness and its objects. In ethical phenomenology, we are concerned not only with our own consciousness (that of the subject) but also with that of the one we encounter; the "object" of consciousness is a subject, another consciousness. It is not true that an ethic of caring has no use whatever for principles or utilities, but these are not primary in the ethic, and they do not dictate method. The central method of ethical caring is a faithful search for understanding of the subjective aspects of experience. Ms. A illustrates the quest for fidelity in her thinking aloud; she wants her students to learn the next topic in mathematics, but she is also concerned with the effect of their recent poor grades. ("It makes them feel *scared* and *hopeless*.") She recognizes an obligation to the institution but defines it in terms of the persons she will turn out ("students who have *regard* for this school — who feel supported by the school and who will, in turn, *support* it"). She rejects the notion of life as a contest even though she wants students to have a sense of efficacy and to achieve. ("I am not trying to produce heroes. I am trying to educate community-builders.")

[17] Friedrich Nietzsche, *Schopenhauer as Educator*, trans. James W. Hillesheim and Malcolm R. Simpson (Chicago: Regnery, 1965), p. 45.
[18] For a discussion of the conditions under which education and socialization may properly be construed as synonymous, see Dewey, *Democracy and Education* (1916; rpt. New York: Free Press, 1966), esp. pp. 83, 87, 301.
[19] Noddings, *Caring*, p. 193.

Her method reveals potential conflicts of fidelity but resolves them by steady adherence to a particular view of fidelity — fidelity as a way of being in relation. Further, it illustrates the quest for competence, or high fidelity. By reflecting on matters of principle and utility but casting her reflection continuously in the service of caring and relation, she fine-tunes her own ethical and pedagogical thinking. Problems do not disappear as a result of this way of thinking and being, but many false dichotomies *do* disappear, and every educational recommendation is screened through reflection on these questions: What effect will it have on the present relation? What effect will it have on the development of this person as a caring person? What effect will it have on our community of caring?

Fidelity in Teacher Education

Since teacher education involves teaching, the sort of thinking already discussed applies to it as well. It is tempting to suppose that, if caring is central to teaching, we must strive to produce caring teachers and then, of course, prove that we have done so. It should, indeed, be our goal in all of education to produce caring, moral persons, but we cannot accomplish this purpose by setting an objective and heading straight toward it. Rather, we approach our goal by living with those whom we teach in a caring community, through modeling, dialogue, practice, and confirmation.[20] Again, we see how unfamiliar this language has become. For the past few years, the blame for massive perceived failure in our schools has fallen on teachers and students, mainly on teachers.[21] They must be brighter, more knowledgeable, more willing to change in whatever direction authority prescribes. We rarely ask how things might be changed so that teachers can accomplish the work they see as *teaching*, nor do we ask what this work is; nor do we ask how teacher educators might best educate people who are average in academic capability but superior in social commitment.

It is often assumed by those in teacher education that their first duty is to the children of the land. Often, indeed, preservice teachers are treated rather harshly by professors who claim "to care about the children" who will be taught by the new teachers. (Administrators, too, often behave this way, and not infrequently we praise them for it.) A utilitarian ethic encourages this kind of thinking, seeking to produce an optimum level of good. From this perspective, it may be justified to make a few people suffer if the result will be happiness and success for many more. In the name of children we raise standards, tighten selection procedures, increase would-be teachers' workloads, create new and tougher tests. Even in a Kantian ethic, we may find ourselves serving the new rules rather than the persons we teach, because our duty is to be faithful to laws and promises.

But the young people learning to teach were once the children we claim to care about and, in an ethic of caring, they must still be the direct objects of caring. Fur-

---

[20] Noddings, *Caring*, chap. 8.

[21] For the effects of this continual blaming teachers, see Sara Freedman, Jane Jackson, and Katherine Boles (Boston Women's Teachers' Group), "Teaching: An Imperiled 'Profession,'" in *Handbook of Teaching and Policy*, ed. Lee S. Shulman and Gary Sykes (New York: Longman, 1983), pp. 261–299.

ther, perhaps the best way to ensure that they will treat children as we want them to be treated is to demonstrate, in our own teaching, how teachers convey their caring. Thus, modeling is central in teacher education.

Once again, potential conflicts of fidelity arise. In all this talk of fidelity to persons, of the modeling of caring, and of producing moral persons, do we not run the risk of producing incompetent and lazy people? Should we not be concerned with higher standards and achievements? The apparent conflicts suggested by these questions are, at bottom, not real. When our fidelity is a way of life, unshakable in its caring for the people under our gaze, we can look at each of these other admirable goals and ask what they mean, how they serve the purposes of community and personal growth, and how best we can achieve them without betraying the persons to whom we will remain faithful.

When we act as models of caring, for example, we may also model a host of other desirable qualities: meticulous preparation, lively presentation, critical thinking, appreciative listening, constructive evaluation, genuine curiosity. An ethic of caring gives us an anchor to throw out when we are in danger of drifting away from persons and relations. Hence, while we do not necessarily reject the goals of reform, we do not accept them uncritically; nor do we aim straight at them over the heads of those whom we teach. We do not place our students at the service of the goals but, rather, we examine the goals reflectively to see how they may be constructively interpreted to serve the caring community.

Another example may help. All teachers are faced with the ordeal of grading. It is sometimes thought that fuzzy-feeling, permissive, and "caring" teachers simply "give" good grades to keep everyone happy. They contribute to something called "grade inflation." Those who give their fidelity to standards complain that grades no longer discriminate sufficiently between the excellent and the merely good, between the good and the barely adequate, and so on. The solution proposed, then, is usually tougher grading. Tougher grading is sometimes even proposed in the name of caring: If we care about our students, it is argued, we will push them to do their best.

Ms. A considers. She sees the potential conflict but begins with different concerns. She wants students to learn to evaluate their own motives and their own work. She believes, with Dewey, that students must be involved in construction of the purposes that guide their learning.[22] There are ways, she thinks, for them to earn legitimately high grades if they wish to do so. She negotiates with her students. Stating openly and in broad terms what things must be accomplished if she is to certify successful completion of her course, she then asks students what they will undertake. Together, specific objectives and tasks are constructed. Ms. A helps her students to achieve the cooperative goals set forth. In such a program, many students will earn A's. Others will earn less, often by conscious choice, for Ms. A makes it clear that students need not love her subject nor strain industriously at it to be considered worthy and attractive persons. Does this course of action betray the institution, lower standards, or coddle the students? On the contrary, Ms. A thinks that it *sustains* the institution by making its purposes real, that

---

[22] Dewey, *Experience and Education* (1938; rpt. New York: Collier Books, 1963), p. 67.

it gives meaning to talk of "standards," and that it encourages honesty and self-understanding in her students.

Another component of moral education and hence, by necessity, of teacher education, is dialogue. If teachers are to engage their own students in dialogue, they must learn what dialogue is and how it is conducted. Teacher-education programs have long been easy captives of fads, which, while in fashion, are treated as gospel. Teachers today learn how to plan the five-step lesson, use assertive discipline, and write behavioral objectives. It is, perhaps, all well and good to learn these things, but to insist that teachers actually use them and to evaluate teachers on their use, contradicts many of the goals we espouse in our talk of reform. The object of teacher education from a caring perspective is not to produce people who will do their duty as it is prescribed or faithfully use the means deemed likely to achieve discrete learning goals but, rather, to produce people who will make autonomous decisions for the sake of their own students. In this form of teacher education, we offer ideas and strategies (fads and all) as material to be analyzed, discussed, critiqued, and considered. It is possible that some thoughtful student teachers will reject entirely some of the methods to which we expose them on the grounds that they violate their own ethical sense of what it means to teach. Such an outcome is always a potential of genuine dialogue. If we are serious about critical thinking as an educational goal and if we believe that education is essentially a moral enterprise, then true dialogue must become an integral part of our interaction in schools at all levels.

A third component in the moral education of teachers is practice. Practice teaching is a universal part of teacher training, but not every such program satisfies the requirements of practice from the perspective of caring. Practice in teaching should be practice in caring.[23] There is an attitude to be sustained and enhanced as well as a set of skills to be learned. By working with master teachers whose fidelity is to persons, new teachers will have the opportunity to learn that this fidelity induces a drive for competence, more and deeper learning, responsible experimentation with instructional arrangements, considered suggestions for structural changes in the school, and the exercise of imagination in resolving conflicts. All of this is guided by fidelity as a way of being, and no goal is allowed to become detached and pursued merely for its own sake.

In the best of practice-teaching situations, new teachers would observe their professors, master teachers, and novice colleagues working together in fidelity. They would be part of a community in which people simultaneously care for each other and strive for the supreme level of competence that I have called "high fidelity."

All current plans for the reform of teacher education say something about both practice teaching and the professional hierarchy into which the new teacher will fit. It is useful to look at these proposed hierarchies through an ethic of caring. Consider a recommendation of the Holmes Group that there be three levels of teachers: instructors (who will not be fully credentialed and may only teach for five or so years), professional teachers (fully credentialed), and career professional

---

[23] In this area, nurse educators seem to be ahead of teacher educators; see Jean Watson, *Nursing: Human Science and Human Care* (Norwalk, CT: Appleton-Century-Crofts, 1985).

teachers (fully credentialed teachers with advanced credentials and responsibilities).[24] Unless great care is taken in defining the roles of professionals and career professionals, the distinction may well be invidious. If, for example, professionals play the part of general practitioners and stay in the classroom full time while career professionals spend part of their time in the classroom and part in special activities such as curriculum development, should the latter receive more pay? Why? As ethicists working in a framework of caring, we would want to ask each such planning group what effect their recommendations will have on the caring community. Similarly, ethicists like Lawrence Kohlberg would want to press questions about effects on the "just community";[25] these questions, however, are somewhat easier to answer than ours because they fit into traditional frameworks and depend upon deductive thinking. Their concerns and ours might overlap, but there would almost certainly be important differences—the just community is not necessarily a caring community. If all the criteria for advancement are unambiguously and publicly laid out, and if all teachers have access to the necessary resources, we might conclude that the new arrangements are indeed just. But if the effects include dissension among teachers, an increase in adversarial relations, and a greater separation between those at the top of the educational hierarchy and the students at the bottom, then the new arrangements must be considered threatening to a caring community. These are matters to be considered as the recommendations for reform are made ready for implementation.

The last major component of teacher education in this model is confirmation. As I have said in another place, "Confirmation, the loveliest of human functions, depends upon and interacts with dialogue and practice."[26] It plays a significant role in every moral relation and at every level of education. As we work, talk, and debate together, we begin to perceive the ethical ideals that each of us strives toward. Then we are in a position to confirm—to help the other to actualize that best image. The image that we cooperatively bring forth will not be a clone of ourselves, and cloning should not be our purpose.

It seems odd to talk of teacher education in terms of modeling, dialogue, practice, and confirmation instead of content, selection of students, exit tests, and credentials. All of these must be considered, of course, but their consideration in isolation from frameworks that describe the kind of communities we intend to build, the sort of people we want to produce, and the ways in which we will interact can only perpetuate the malaise now widely felt in education.

Research for Teaching

From the discussion so far, one might suppose—if one were bent on misunderstanding and had a gift for caricature—that the solution of education's problems lies rather simply in our being nicer to each other. This interpretation has always posed a special problem for women and, indeed, for any who have espoused fidelity to persons as the beginning or wellspring of ethics.[27] It has been held by think-

---

[24] *Tomorrow's Teacher: A Report of the Holmes Group* (East Lansing, MI: The Holmes Group, 1986).
[25] See Kohlberg, *The Philosophy of Moral Development*, Vol. 1 (San Francisco: Harper & Row, 1981).
[26] Noddings, *Caring*, p. 196.
[27] See Nel Noddings, "In Search of the Feminine," *Teachers College Record, 87* (1985), 195-204.

ers of considerable stature, and even by Immanuel Kant, that women are some-how naturally nice, but that their nice nature is spoiled by "laborious learning or painful pondering."[28] Recommendations on caring are, then, often dismissed as the affectionate musings of people who do not really understand the realities. It is, therefore, imperative to say and to show that caring is a rational way of being in the world and that it is neither destroyed by painful pondering on matters of pedagogy, policy, or research, nor does it eschew these. On the contrary, while an ethic of caring cannot provide specific answers to ethical or educational ques-tions, it can provide steady, rational guidance in the form of questions to be asked and directions to be taken.

In educational research, fidelity to persons counsels us to choose our problems in such a way that the knowledge gained will promote individual growth and maintain the caring community. It is not clear that we are sufficiently concerned with either criterion at present. William Torbert, for example, has noted that edu-cational research has been oddly uneducational and suggests that one reason for this may be the failure of researchers to engage in collaborative inquiry.[29] There is a pragmatic side to this problem, of course, but from an ethical perspective, the difficulty may be identified as a failure to meet colleagues in genuine mutuality. Researchers have perhaps too often made *persons* (teachers and students) the ob-jects of research. An alternative is to choose *problems* that interest and concern re-searchers, students, and teachers, and I will mention several of these a bit later. Such research would be genuine research *for* teaching instead of simply research *on* teaching.

When teachers are the direct objects of our research, we run the risk of wrong-ing them as persons. When we assign teachers randomly to instructional strategies that they will implement, for example, we suppose that the strategies themselves are somehow instrumental in producing student achievement. We rarely ask about teacher *commitment* to either the strategies or the students, and yet it is recog-nized (in another compartment of the research brain) that teachers are or ought to be autonomous professionals who make decisions for the benefit of their stu-dents as persons — not simply for their students' achievement. To suppose that teachers are irrelevant except for the instructional strategies they employ is surely to wrong them as persons. We also wrong teachers when we make judgments about them or their work that they could not anticipate from the original descrip-tion of our research — judgments that they are unreflective, sexist, or racist, in-competent in their subjects, entrenched in mediocrity. I am not claiming that such judgments should not be made by the persons authorized to evaluate teachers (al-though even then the judgmental stance is usually unproductive), but I am raising an ethical question about whether such judgments should be made by researchers whose access to data is granted by the very people so judged.

In recent years there has been a general increase of interest in the ethical prob-lems of research. The growing popularity of qualitative methods, for example, has

---

[28] See Kant, *Observations on the Feeling of the Beautiful and Sublime.* The relevant quotation appears in Hilde Hein, "Woman — A Philosophical Analysis," in *Philosophy of Women,* ed. Mary Briody Ma-howald (Indianapolis: Hackett, 1983), p. 344.

[29] Torbert, "Why Educational Research Has Been So Uneducational: The Case for a New Model of Social Science Based on Collaborative Inquiry," in *Human Inquiry,* eds. Peter Reason and John Rowan (New York: Wiley, 1981).

prompted some researchers to suggest that Kantian ethics might be more appropriate to fieldwork than the utilitarian ethics so widely used in large-scale experimental and survey research, because the nature of the researcher-subject interaction differs substantially.[30] I am not going to argue that different ethics may be appropriate to different domains (this sort of thinking has consigned women's ethical thinking to the private domain for centuries), but it is clear that different situations press different sorts of problems on us. When we encounter our research subjects face to face, we are forced to deal with them as autonomous beings, and so our ethical problems are, by the very nature of our working relationship, different from those engendered by research in which we never encounter the living subject as individual. In qualitative research, we often chat with our subjects, share food and coffee breaks, and generally build trusting relationships. Indeed, the fieldwork situation is so different from experimental research that Margaret Mead said, "Anthropological research does not have subjects. We work with informants in an atmosphere of trust and mutual respect."[31]

Fieldworkers in the past, however, were somewhat protected from the ethical problems in education that arise today. They worked primarily with people in other places and cultures, and a considerable part of their work was necessarily aimed at building mutual trust. The atmosphere of mutual trust is both facilitated and complicated in situations where fieldworkers and host people are *not* "mutually alien";[32] when the host people are professionals working in the same global profession (education), expectations of professional respect and genuine mutuality arise quite naturally. An unfavorable report from a friendly and apparently knowledgeable researcher hurts doubly. The hurt is aggravated by a feeling of betrayal: this person, with whom a relation of trust has been established, has said these dreadful things.

Problems of fidelity arise with special force in qualitative research on teaching. Researchers sometimes find themselves torn between honoring the relation of trust upon which their access was predicated, and their perceived responsibility to a clientele that supports, evaluates, and depends upon public education. A Kantian interpretation of fidelity makes it our duty to tell the truth no matter what the consequences (being sure, of course, that it *is* the truth); a utilitarian interpretation demands fidelity to the principle of optimizing good outcomes over bad. An interpretation from the ethic of caring, however, reminds us that fidelity means faithfulness to persons and the expectations established in relation.

This kind of thinking arouses considerable indignation in some researchers. What are we supposed to do, they ask, if we go into a classroom to study, say, questioning patterns, and find out in the course of things that a teacher is downright incompetent? Should we be "faithful" to the teacher's trust and conceal our evaluation? Notice how the second question is phrased; it suggests that to be faithful to the teacher's trust we must conceal our evaluation.

[30] See Joan Cassell, "Harms, Benefits, Wrongs, and Rights in Fieldwork" (pp. 7–31), and also Murray L. Wax, "Research Reciprocity Rather than Informed Consent in Field Work" (pp. 33–48), in *The Ethics of Social Research*, ed. Joan E. Sieber (New York, Heidelberg, Berlin: Springer-Verlag, 1982).

[31] Mead, "Research with Human Beings: A Model Derived from Anthropological Field Practice," *Daedalus 98* (1969), 371.

[32] For a discussion of such research under the typical conditions wherein researcher and subjects are "mutually alien," see Wax, "Research Reciprocity," p. 36.

But logic allows us to split the two conditions:

1. We must be faithful to the teacher's trust.
2. We must conceal our evaluation of incompetence.

An ethic of caring takes (1) as elemental — our fidelity is to persons. But we are not necessarily constrained to accept (2). Many decisions on (2) are compatible with an ethic of caring. We might, for example, face the teacher with our concerns and seek his or her justification for the behavior we have labeled incompetent. Both the teacher's and our own interpretations might appear in the final report, but nothing irrelevant to the stated purpose of research would appear there without the teacher's consent. Either (or both) of us — teacher and researcher — might learn from the other in genuine dialogue; our original interpretation might be altered, or the teacher's subsequent behavior might be changed. These outcomes do not exhaust the possibilities, but they illustrate the kind of thinking required. Colleagues, like friends, do not simply report or tell on each other's errors. As Aristotle advised us, true friends or colleagues "may even be said to prevent it [error]."[33]

As we struggle with ethical problems in research and try to resolve them through collegial caring, other problems arise. Are we now doing research, or something else? Those who worry that the research project may be destroyed or turned into "development" sometimes advocate other solutions to the problem of fidelity. One such solution advocated by Lee Cronbach and his associates is to prepare multiple research reports, giving information to each interested party on the basis of a need and right to know.[34] But does this practice solve ethical problems or make them worse? Multiple reports in education, as in medicine, may properly be used to address technical problems. Physicians, for example, typically cast their reports to patients in language different from that used with colleagues, and the language of a technical report published in a research journal is properly different from that used in a popular adaptation for laypersons. But the *substance* must be the same. Similarly in education, it would seem downright unethical to give teachers innocuous reports of their performance and then pull out all the stops in a "vivid rendering" for research colleagues. Further, researcher and teacher are part of one profession; the teacher can read the dissertation or technical report if he or she is determined to do so, and the resulting pain could be excruciating.

Another possible solution to the problem of wronging subjects through our report writing has been suggested by Ernest House: "Another approach [an alternative to board reviews of write-ups] would be to arrange for negotiations over the data between the researchers and people researched."[35] House himself fears that this move raises the "spectre of censorship," but insists that something must be done to protect subjects at the report-writing stage because "review of instruments prior to data collection is simply an inadequate safeguard."[36]

---

[33] *Nichomachean Ethics*, Book VIII, chap. 10.

[34] Cronbach and associates, *Toward Reform of Program Evaluation* (San Francisco: Jossey-Bass, 1980).

[35] House, "Critique of Campbell and Cecil's Proposal: Subjects Need More Protection," in *The Ethics of Social Research*, ed. Joan E. Sieber (New York, Heidelberg, Berlin: Springer-Verlag, 1982), p. 123.

[36] House, "Critique," p. 123.

From the perspective on fidelity that I have been taking, concern over censorship begs a deeper question. To whom do these "data" belong? These are not data on inanimate objects or unreflective animals. In qualitative research, the data are not even simple responses given to a researcher who asks a specific question. The data are, in an important sense, mutually constructed by researcher and subjects, and so a genuine question arises over ownership of data and over whose interpretations should be included in any written reports.

When we think this way, we are led to examine the entire program of research on teaching. Teaching is a constitutively ethical activity. It is a "moral type of friendship" in which teachers and students work together to construct and achieve common ends. Those who enter classrooms become part of this ethical activity. If improvement of teaching is the avowed aim, it may be that researchers will have to rethink the role they play in classrooms. Consideration of ethical questions that threaten the whole mode of present research does not—even on the strictest interpretation—signal "an end to research." There are many, many problems that are congenial to collaborative inquiry:

- the area of small-group learning (for example, how groups should be constituted for various purposes, what problems or topics are best tackled in small groups, length of engagement and frequency of meetings for groups of various ages, usefulness of various materials and their production and refinement)

- genuine implementation studies in which researchers, teachers, and students, all fully informed, work together toward faithful implementation (the result might be a descriptive report of how implementation is best accomplished)

- teaching strategies not randomly assigned to teacher-subjects but consciously studied, tried out, and comonitored by researchers and teachers

- curricular studies in which teachers, students, and researchers cooperatively evaluate and revise materials

The list is limited only by time, space, and imagination. As items are proposed, fidelity to persons guides our selection: What will be the effects of this inquiry on the persons involved and on the caring community?

Conclusion

We live in an age of calls for reform in education. Much of the language used in these calls is mere rhetoric; the air is filled with cries for "excellence," "higher standards," "tougher grading," and the like. "Curiously absent," says Catherine Cornbleth, "is serious consideration of the intended meaning of the called-for excellence, the purpose(s) of public schooling, the content of the courses to be required for high school graduation, the processes of teaching and learning, and the possibility of organizational or structural changes to improve schooling."[37] The debate, Cornbleth suggests, has deteriorated to ritual guided by technical rationality.

Any ethicist would shudder at the thought of discussing education without discussing values and matters of the spirit. Even the two traditionally great ethical

[37] Cornbleth, "Ritual and Rationality in Teacher Education Reform," *Educational Researcher 15*, No. 4 (1986), 6.

systems—Kantian and utilitarian—are used infrequently in contemporary calls for reform and, even when they are used, can be too easily invoked in the service of ritual and technical rationality. I have argued that an ethic of caring is appropriate and useful for an examination of teaching, teacher education, and research for teaching. Such an ethic takes fidelity to persons as primary and directs us to analyze and evaluate all recommendations in light of our answers to questions concerning the maintenance of community, the growth of individuals, and the enhancement of subjective aspects of our relationships.

In the discussion of teaching, I tried to show how a primary fidelity to persons might guide the thinking of teachers. In the section on teacher education, I offered a model that might help teacher educators to include matters that lie at the very heart of teaching. Finally, in a brief look at research on teaching, I suggested that too little attention is presently given to matters of community and collegiality and that such research should be reconstrued as research *for* teaching.

It may be that the kind of thinking illustrated here—characterized, I hope, by both coherence and constancy—arises more naturally out of women's experience than men's. Maguire has suggested that women's experience has led them to be "less seducible by abstractions," more in touch with the affective component of moral judgment, and more closely associated with children, and hence "with the moral rhythms of minimally corrupted human life."[38] Men affected by the experience of macho-masculinity have, in contrast, suffered from "an anti-communitarian hierarchical proclivity," "a disabling abstractionism," and a "proneness to violent modes of power."[39] Clearly, not all men have been radically infected by macho-masculinity; many disavow it. But in our entire culture, both male and female thinking have been affected by it.

These modes of thinking can change. Today, women are learning (and modifying) the traditional ways of thinking in the disciplines. Men are learning to care more directly for children. In the realms of ethics and education it may be time to study, express, analyze, and teach a feminine way of being in the world.[40] At the very least, this way of thinking should be used to enliven and deepen the current debate on educational reform.

[38] Maguire, "Feminization," p. 61.
[39] Maguire, "Feminization," p. 63.
[40] See Jane Roland Martin's argument for revising the ideal of educated persons to include the feminine: "Bringing Women into Educational Thought," *Educational Theory 34* (1984), 341–354; also her *Reclaiming a Conversation: The Ideal of the Educated Woman* (New Haven and London: Yale University Press, 1985).

PART 5

Critical
Reviews

The Professor and the Practitioner Think about Teaching

MARUE ENGLISH WALIZER

THE PRACTICE OF TEACHING
by Philip W. Jackson. *New York: Teachers College Press, 1986. 159 pp. $18.95, $9.95 (paper).*

> In the opinion of fools it is a humble task,
> but in fact it is the noblest of occupations.
> — Erasmus

Philip Jackson was one of the first educational researchers to pay serious attention to teachers' own comments on their work and to what they did in classrooms. One of his great insights in *Life in Classrooms* (1968) was his call for a different kind of research that would "move up close to the phenomena of the teacher's world" (p. 159). Since that time, research on teaching has increased dramatically. In *The Practice of Teaching*, his new collection of essays, Jackson delves more deeply into some issues he raised in *Life in Classrooms*. He develops his earlier intuition that teaching is a far more complex activity than most people, even teachers themselves, often realize. The epigraph above, which appears at the beginning of his book, establishes the oppositions of the argument and lets us know which side the angels are on. Ready to join those ranks, I was somewhat surprised by the philosophical detachment that shapes these essays. Ironically, the discussion in this book is far more removed from the classroom than Jackson's earlier work.

Let me state my biases right here so the reader may put my comments in perspective. A book by Philip Jackson with this direct a title was bound to capture my attention. After twenty years of teaching in public high schools, I returned to graduate school five years ago to begin a doctoral program in education. Within weeks I realized that, for all my teaching experience and two degrees in English literature, I was having a serious language problem. *Life in Classrooms*, which I read during my first year's course work, consoled me with the knowledge that the problem was not purely personal. Jackson had articulated my central concern:

> Generalizations about the characteristics of children or about the merits of an educational theory are being continually tested, as the teacher considers them, against the qualities of the particular students with whom she is working and the specific constraints of her classroom. As might be expected, this degree of specificity greatly in-

Harvard Educational Review Vol. 56 No. 4 November 1986, 520–526

hibits the easy translation of theory into practice and serves to increase the difficulty of communications between the teacher and others with more abstract interests. (1968, p. 147)

But I was also angry. Jackson had pondered the responses of classroom teachers to researchers' inquiries about their work and had described teacher talk as revealing a "conceptual simplicity" which he characterized under four aspects: "(1) an uncomplicated view of causality; (2) an intuitive, rather than rational approach to classroom events; (3) an opinionated, as opposed to an open-minded, stance when confronted with alternative teaching practices; and (4) a narrowness in the working definitions assigned to abstract terms" (1968, p. 144).

To his credit, Jackson recognized that this conceptual simplicity often stood in contrast to the complexity of what teachers did in the classroom. Understanding that teachers' language differed from researchers', he speculated that the simple and intuitive thinking reflected in teachers' language might be required (and thus excused?) by the nature of the work. Nonetheless, teachers' intelligence came off as inferior to the abstract, rational thinking of researchers. I was not happy to be condemned to simplemindedness and narrowness by work I love. Moreover, this reading contradicted the way my colleagues and I function with each other and with students. So I began to ponder, looking for another perspective, a different way of examining teacher language and thinking. I looked forward to Jackson's latest thoughts on the issue.

This question of language and communication continues to bedevil an educational community still divided into two fairly distinct cultures: those who do educational research and develop theory in universities and those who work in elementary and secondary schools. The two groups not only speak different languages but have very different epistemological interests. Jackson's current essays tackle this problem by asking what role the university in general and the school of education in particular can legitimately play in the education and development of teachers. Six independent but related chapters explore the kind of knowledge needed to teach, attitudes about teaching, what it means "to teach," the uncertainties inherent in the work, and the nature of changes in teaching practice over the generations. Finally, Jackson reviews the debate between conservative and liberal schools of educational thought and rechristens the two camps "mimetic" and "transformative" education. In an energetic attempt at intellectual treaty-making, he sees them as differing more in emphasis than in kind.

In his first chapter, "On Knowing How to Teach," he revisits some issues considered in *Life in Classrooms*: Why is teaching so often described in simplistic terms when careful observation reveals it is an extremely complex activity? How do we describe and define teaching activity from the perspective of the knowledge required to teach? Is there a "common epistemic base" that everyone who hopes to teach must have and how might this knowledge be acquired? In trying to identify that base, Jackson is really asking whether the formal training of teachers is a valid enterprise or merely a requirement perpetuated by the prevailing power structure in education. It is a good question, one you would hear discussed quite heatedly were you to ask it in any faculty lounge. Jackson first examines some popular arguments for alternate forms of training, such as life experience, apprenticeship, on-the-job training, and peer collaboration. He then considers the role of common sense and memory in providing informal kinds of teacher education. Finally, he makes the case for formal training in certain areas such as organizing particular kinds of knowledge for teaching, dealing with the increasingly diverse identities and cultures of students, understanding child development, and teaching to higher levels of intellectual development. Respectfully, in the last sentence, Jackson defers to teachers themselves for their judgment of the university's role in teaching much of this. Obviously, he hopes that we will have found his argument both fair and persuasive enough to take his course and to read on. But I was left wondering whether he had asked any experienced teachers what they believed they needed to know. What about *their* epistemological interests?

In his chapter, "How to Talk to Teachers," Jackson, with some glee, defends his profession by chiding one of its giants, genial William James. James's lectures, *Talks to Teachers*, delivered in 1892, were immensely popular at the time, and they still provide useful insights. In them James advises the Cambridge teachers not to be "too docile" in accepting the pronouncements, "more mystifying than enlightening," of those in authority (James, 1899/1958, p. 23). Jackson takes issue with James's criticizing educationists for being vague and condescending to teachers while secretly doing the same thing himself. As evidence that James was, in fact, rather contemptuous of the teachers he was addressing, Jackson quotes a letter James wrote in 1897. Although he accuses James of "mystifying" as much as the worst experts, he acknowledges that James's language in the lectures, while "not the most profound of his writing," is "rich, all the same, in metaphor and anecdote —infused with wisdom and enlivened with good humor" (p. 31), serving primarily to delight the audience then and the reader now.

Jackson's reason for reviewing the lectures is to learn from James's success in talking to teachers. Yet he misses an important point in James's language. It is not merely practical and concrete; in its use of metaphor and anecdote, it is also complex, imaginative, and suggestive of multiple meanings. It may, in fact, appeal to a different kind of cognitive structure that is more natural to teachers. As I learned long ago in studying literature, style is not mere form; it is substance. Jackson relates James's more popular style to the problem of relating theory and practice, which Jackson wants to redefine as putting theory "into practitioners" rather than into practice (p. 50). But that language portrays practitioners as being akin to blank disks waiting to be programmed; it fails to consider how they think about their work. If Jackson wants to know how to talk to teachers, he might reconsider the epistemological underpinnings of James's style and its appeal to teachers.

Jackson finally forgives James and sees him as "ministering" to the Cambridge teachers, "comforting, illuminating, even inspiring—a balm for weary souls" (p. 51). That overlooks some very substantial material in James's lectures: the chapters on habit, on native reaction, on the association of ideas. Granted, most of these lectures by James were drawn from the earlier *Principles of Psychology* (1890), pruned of its technical language and condensed for this teacher audience, but that makes them neither less complex nor less substantial. The teachers apparently thought them useful. Moreover, James was asserting what neo-Marxist critics would come to much later: that the "deskilling" of the profession was underway and that teachers should beware of "experts" spouting jargon and clothed in advanced degrees. As even Jackson admits in his last chapter, it is still good advice.

In his chapter, "The Uncertainties of Teaching," Jackson dissects an issue also raised in his earlier book. This leads him to an insightful analysis of the function of questioning and testing as methods for reducing uncertainty. His account clearly sets forth the strengths and the pitfalls of these processes, the mixed motives that shape teachers' decisions to use or to forego these methods, and the problems created by asking the student for knowledge that the teacher feels responsible for having imparted. Jackson devotes much space in this chapter to analyzing the uncertainties in the learning model described as "knowledge reproduction," which relies heavily on memory and recall. Yet this is far less complex in its cognitive expectations than, for example, Dewey's model of knowledge transformation which deals with such questions as "how the knowledge in question is being used by the learner, how it relates to what was learned before, how it becomes personalized by being translated into the learner's own language, how it becomes applied to new situations and so forth . . . and encompasses levels of mental functioning that customarily fall under the rubrics of 'judgment' and 'understanding' " (p. 71). Jackson realizes that this model of knowledge increases the level of teacher uncertainty dramatically. That aspect, far more interesting to me, is not considered in detail until his last chapter. Many teachers will recognize and affirm the propositions Jackson develops in this chapter, but find little that adds to their ability to deal with the ambiguities they face each day.

In "Real Teaching," Jackson joins the heirs of James, the analytic philosophers of education, to consider what we really mean by the term "teaching." The conceptual definition is important to university professors because the arguments often shape the kind of research that gets proposed and approved. The analysis is useful to teachers because it sheds light on the values implicit in their beliefs and activities. Jackson examines four philosophical approaches to an analytical definition of teaching: the generic model of Smith (1961), the epistemological model of Green (1964; 1968, pp. 36–37), the consensual definition of Scheffler (1960), and an evolutionary model based on work of Toulmin (1980, p. 38). After appreciating the strengths and elucidating the problems in each approach, Jackson opts for Toulmin's evolutionary model, which allows for a changing definition of what counts as teaching. Although it is an academic's discussion, not really designed for teachers, the essay raises an important point about how teachers think and how researchers address that issue.

Jackson recalls from a conversation held with nursery school teachers years earlier that some of those teachers believed one had to "think like a teacher" in order to behave like one. His recollection serves to reintroduce the question of what it means "to think like a teacher" and develops a position that owes a good deal to the educational ethnographic research of the last decade. (Jackson deserves much credit for the increase in this research approach, which he called for in *Life in Classrooms*, 1968.) Teaching is never really "seen," Jackson notes; it is always "read," that is, interpreted in a way that is inevitably shaped by the assumptions of the observer. Since all descriptions of teaching are interpretations, the question for observers is how to lay bare the thinking that shapes the described behavior.

Teacher thinking is a new item on the research agenda, appearing for the first time as a chapter by Clark and Peterson in the third (1986) edition of the *Handbook of Research on Teaching.* The topic once again harks back to Jackson's earlier insight that researchers and teachers think quite differently about the work of teaching. If we are finally getting around to attending to that difference and trying to clarify how teachers do indeed think (there seems to be little debate about how the researchers think), we have Professor Jackson to thank. The difference is quite distinct; having worked in both worlds now, I am beginning to understand how radically the structure and organization of thought and experience differ (as Jackson noted), and that the nature of the work of each group accounts to a large degree for that difference (as James, drawing on his theory of habit and the association of ideas, would surely have told us had we asked). I have no doubt that the complexity of teacher thinking will be explored more fully by a different research approach than we have yet seen. The assumptions about the quality of teachers' thinking are still to be questioned, but work in this area is beginning.

In the chapter, "The Future of Teaching," Jackson uses a different context to examine these two different learning models and their conceptions of knowledge. He traces their history and practice in two long-standing traditions of educational thought: the subject-centered and the child-centered approaches. He then identifies changes in educational practice over the generations in terms of two goals: the search for a "pain-free pedagogy" and the desire for increased self-governance of students. Reviewing the debate over the relative power of internal development and external formation, Jackson places the changes that have occurred in teaching practice over generations in the context of larger societal changes. He also realizes that going overboard on these goals can undermine learning rather than enhance it, and so calls for a reasonable blend of the two approaches, noting that the differences are often more those of degree rather than kind.

The final chapter, "The Mimetic and the Transformative: Alternative Outlooks on Teaching," takes a more ambitious and useful look at the "opposing" schools of conservative and liberal thought considered in the previous chapter and picks up the issue of alternate conceptions of knowledge alluded to earlier. Jackson sees these two opposing schools of thought as two traditions of educational methodology which he rechristens the "mimetic" and the "transformative." Mimetic knowledge is described by the theory of knowledge reproduction. "The key idea is that some kinds of knowledge or skill can be doubly possessed, first by the teacher alone (or the writer of the textbook or the computer program), then by his or her student" (p. 119). The practice of mimetic teaching is therefore defined as the transmission of this knowledge. The alternative "transformative" model portrays the teacher as trying to effect change in the student, using personal modeling, "soft" suasion, and narrative as primary teaching methods. Transformative teaching is an overtly moral and philosophical undertaking, seeking to stimulate change in the student through the Socratic methodology of discussion, demonstration, and argumentation.

Interestingly, Jackson remarks in a footnote (p. 130) that the two different teaching modes seem to parallel the two models of paradigmatic and narrative thought structure recently described by Bruner (1986). It occurs to me that this in turn parallels the different kinds of thinking and language used by researchers and teachers, respectively. Researchers are trained in the model of paradigmatic thinking to look for general laws and to observe the standards of validity and replicability inherent in that model. Practitioners, on the other hand, tend to think in terms of specific cases and to make decisions about practice and judgments of individuals based on comparisons with previous, similar experiences. This cognitive process has been explored by Schön (1983) in *The Reflective Practitioner*. My own experience suggests that this is much closer to the way in which teachers think about their work. Ask a teacher how he or she teaches a concept or handles a classroom problem; at some point in the response you will likely get the story of a particular class or student. This kind of response is usually dismissed as anecdotal, useful as an example but of secondary importance. Nonetheless, Bruner (1986) says we know "precious little" about this form of thinking although it is a distinctly different way of constructing experience and has "its own criteria of well-formedness" (pp. 11–13). These two different modes of thinking may help to explain the difficulty researchers and teachers experience in communicating with each other effectively.

Near the close of this last chapter, Jackson, somewhat unhappily, observes that the mimetic model of teaching appears ascendant in current educational practice. The emphasis on marketable skills, on standardized testing, on mastery, competency, and accountability highlight the "hegemony of the 'scientific spirit' " in research and testing. While admitting to a preferential bias for the "scientific" (paradigmatic) in his own approach, Jackson wisely worries about the signs of a mimetic takeover in educational practice and is pessimistic about the possibilities of turning this process around. Yet he hopes for a balance, believing that the tension between the two orientations can be resolved "at the individual level, within the confines of a single classroom" (p. 145).

A recent article in the *Washington Post* will encourage him. Emily Feistritzer (1986), director of the National Center for Educational Information, writes that her survey for the Carnegie Foundation found that teachers think "that the main purposes of education today are to 'teach students reasoning and analytical skills' and 'to help students develop sound character' " (p. C1 ff.). Now that sounds as though many teachers value both the better aspects of the paradigmatic as well as the transformative approach. And, in the classroom, the last word still belongs to the teacher.

Jackson has carefully presented his perspective on some persistent and disturbing debates that continue to absorb the educational community. He has alerted us to some dangers and suggested their sources, and he has discussed ways to address them. In doing so, he has not forgotten the myriad issues that the classroom teacher contends with every day. But given his genuine and sincere concern for teachers in the classroom, why has Jackson chosen to write only theoretically about teaching as an abstraction? After *Life in Classrooms* (1968), I anticipated a much closer look at the complexities of classroom teaching. This book is actually a discussion of the *concept* of practice: it does what university faculties traditionally have done. Jackson has moved farther from the frontline to make his current commentary.

These essays leave me uncertain whether Jackson has heeded his own advice from *Life in Classrooms*. What in this book has Jackson learned from teachers themselves? Only one anecdote about a conversation with nursery school teachers indicates that he has talked at any length with practitioners or considered teachers' own insights on their work. He may have drawn on such conversations, but the voices of teachers and their perpectives on their experience are not audible here. Teachers, though they write very differently than researchers, can certainly be reflective and informative about their practice. A pleasurable perusal of the books of Ashton-Warner (1963), Paley (1979, 1981), or Wigginton (1985) will demonstrate the diverse ways that practicing teachers discuss their experience. These teachers tell readers about what happens in their classrooms and what they think and feel about their students, their fellow teachers, their superiors, the parents, and the whole range of experiences that teaching school entails. They are quite analytic in a very concrete sort of way, fashioning their points in selected experiences which they choose to share with their readers. In discussing topics like what kind of knowledge is required to teach or alternative approaches to teaching, the perspectives of practicing teachers surely are significant material to consider.

Jackson's method in exploring these issues about teaching continues to respond to the epistemological interests of the researcher, not the teacher. He has not asked the teachers what counts as knowledge for them; he has not examined how they test and revise their beliefs; he has not asked what experiences for them have been most educational. What thinking processes do teachers develop during their lives in classrooms? I believe that, although these are qualitatively different from and, in Bruner's words, "irreducible" to the researchers' model of thinking, they are quite valid and valuable on their own terms. Talking to teachers about practice in ways meaningful to them may depend on recognizing, respecting, and describing this alternative model. Jackson could put his considerable skill to work to that end. Maybe next time. The real sequel to *Life in Classrooms* is still to be written.

Despite my chagrin at what he has not done, I do value what Jackson has provided in these essays. He has the courage to remain undogmatic in his analysis at a time when the bureaucracy is proclaiming hundreds of commandments with the verve of Moses coming down from the mountain. Jackson demonstrates his respect for teachers (although from the distance of the podium) as well as his appreciation of the complexities of teaching. Most teachers will recognize and affirm his insights as I do, even as they find them still a bit "abstract." But I cannot honestly say this is a book for those who practice teaching. I have been distressed by the resentment I hear in conversations with classrooms teachers, now once again being asked, by the newest Carnegie report (Carnegie Forum, 1986), to take more courses, with no assurance that the courses will be better or the time spent more fruitful. Most teachers continue to regard education courses as fairly useless, and *The Practice of Teaching* does not make the case that the professor has learned to talk *with* teachers as well as *to* them. I wish Jackson had heeded his own advice from his earlier book and given the teachers some space. He remains more in the lecture hall with James than he may want to admit, certainly nifty company in its own way, but not what Jackson said he had in mind.

The Practice of Teaching is a book for those who have not had much teaching experience and want to understand more about the underlying complexities and contradictions embedded in practice. These essays provide insights for those outside the classroom, many of whom formulate so much of our current educational policy. That seems a particularly useful role for the university professor to play. It is highly appropriate for Jackson to aim his commentary at departments of education, state legislatures, and like-minded organizations. It would be a blessing on all our houses if the testers and the technocrats and the policymakers in the federal and the state legislatures could develop some of the same appreciations and comprehensions that Jackson has, as they consider more resolutions about education for the twenty-first century.

References

Ashton-Warner, S. (1963). *Teacher.* New York: Simon & Schuster.

Bruner, J. (1986). *Actual minds, possible worlds.* Cambridge: Harvard University Press.

Carnegie Forum on Education and the Economy. (1986). *A nation prepared: Teachers for the 21st century.* The Report of the Task Force on Teaching as a Profession. New York: Author.

Clark, C. M., & Peterson, P. L. (1986). Teachers' thought processes. In M. C. Wittrock (Ed.), *Handbook of research on teaching* (3rd ed., pp. 255–296). New York: Macmillan.

Feistritzer, E. (1986, June 22). What teacher crisis? They're happy, well-paid. *Washington Post.*

Green, T. (1964) Teaching, acting, and behaving. *Harvard Educational Review, 34,* 507–524.

Green, T. (1968). A typology of the teaching concept. In C. J. B. Macmillan & T. W. Nelson (Eds.), *Concepts of teaching: Philosophical essays* (3rd ed., pp. 28–62). Chicago: Rand McNally.

Jackson, P. W. (1968). *Life in classrooms.* New York: Holt, Rinehart & Winston.

James, W. (1890). *Principles of psychology.* New York: Holt.

James, W. (1958). *Talks to teachers on psychology: And to students on some of life's ideals.* New York: Norton. (Original work published 1899)

Paley, V. G. (1979). *White teacher.* Cambridge: Harvard University Press.

Paley, V. G. (1981). *Wally's stories.* Cambridge: Harvard University Press.

Scheffler, I. (1960). Teaching. In *The language of education* (pp. 60–75). Springfield, IL: Thomas.

Schön, D. (1983). *The reflective practitioner: How professionals think in action.* New York: Basic Books.

Smith, B. O. (1961). A concept of teaching. In B. O. Smith & R. H. Ennis (Eds.), *Language and concepts in education* (pp. 86–101). Chicago: Rand McNally.

Toulmin, S. (1980, April 3). The charm of the scout. *New York Review of Books.*

Wigginton, E. (1985). *Sometimes a shining moment: The foxfire experience.* Garden City, NY: Anchor Press/Doubleday.

Feminist Scholarship
and Women's Studies

NANCY JO HOFFMAN

FEMINIST SCHOLARSHIP: KINDLING IN THE GROVES OF ACADEME
by Ellen Carol DuBois, Gail Paradise Kelly, Elizabeth Lapovsky Kennedy,
Carolyn W. Korsmeyer, and Lillian S. Robinson. *Urbana: University of Illinois
Press, 1985. 240 pp. $19.95.*

FOR ALMA MATER: THEORY AND PRACTICE OF FEMINIST SCHOLARSHIP
edited by Paula A. Treichler, Cheris Kramarae, and Beth Stafford. *Urbana:
University of Illinois Press, 1985. 466 pp. $32.50.*

LEARNING OUR WAY: ESSAYS IN FEMINIST EDUCATION
edited by Charlotte Bunch and Sandra Pollack. *Trumansburg, NY: The Crossing
Press Feminist Series, 1983. 336 pp. $12.95.*

RECLAIMING A CONVERSATION: THE IDEAL OF THE EDUCATED WOMAN
by Jane Roland Martin. *New Haven: Yale University Press, 1985. 218 pp.
$21.50.*

WOMEN'S WAYS OF KNOWING: THE DEVELOPMENT OF SELF, VOICE AND MIND
by Mary Field Belenky, Blythe McVicker Clinchy, Nancy Rule Goldberger,
and Jill Mattuck Tarule. *New York: Basic Books, 1986. 248 pp. $19.95.*

That roar which lies on the other side of silence. — George Eliot[1]

If a visitor from another planet were to arrive on these shores at this moment asking, "What is women's studies," she might be told with confidence, "Read the five
books listed above, and you will know." Indeed, these books tell an accurate and
inspiring story of the rise of a new field of study. A brief version of the narrative
goes something like this: Because of the civil rights movement, the rise of the New
Left, the publication of *The Feminine Mystique*, and the anti-war movement, feminism was reborn in the United States almost two decades ago. At first it was a
grass-roots movement drawing educated women into small, informal discussion
groups in which they began to explore "that roar on the other side of silence,"
claiming for the first time a vocabulary with which to express their questions about
personal life — sexuality, childcare, marriage and relationships, women's educa-

---

[1] George Eliot, *Middlemarch* (New York: Penguin Books, 1871–72).

Harvard Educational Review Vol. 56 No. 4 November 1986, 511–519

tion, and work. These new feminists quickly came to question public and institutional inequalities and to connect them with the politics of personal life. By the early 1970s a nationwide and well-organized political movement had been born, drawing its inspiration from the civil rights movement, but asking, with veils newly drawn back, its own urgent questions: What is women's history? Who are women writers? Why does psychology think we all belong to one role, one place? Why have we tolerated knowing so little about ourselves? As early as 1973 Jane Howard could write quite accurately, "I have hardly found a [woman] of late, of any age or station, who has not to some degree been affected by the new wave, the inescapable tidal wave, of feminism."[2]

In institutions of higher education, women's studies emerged after black studies as a response to often vociferous requests for a curriculum dealing with students' issues of identity and culture. Housed on the peripheries of institutions, the early women's studies programs took their location as symbolic; they faced at once out toward their communities of origin where women lacking access to education might be organized as feminists, and inward where, as Paula Treichler points out in "Alma Mater's Sorority: Women and the University of Illinois, 1890–1925," they presided over the intellectual nourishment of their brothers (pp. 15–61). For many feminist educators and scholars, this balancing act persists today: work in community organizations and technical assistance projects is as much the rule as are forays to request women's studies majors, graduate programs, faculty development projects, or tenure for feminist teachers. Over the years, however, the work of activists in women's studies has made room in academia for an explosion of fine and varied scholarship on women. Increasingly an acceptable specialty, the study of women has engendered a National Women's Studies Association, 40 academic centers for research on women, several scholarly journals, and about 500 academic programs. Today, one need not leave either the campus or one's discipline to find colleagues interested in research on women.

From my perspective, the best of women's studies activism and scholarship demands simultaneously an open commitment to feminist social change beyond the campus *and* a transformation of intellectual paradigms. However, the five books under review here, each passionate and revolutionary in its way, do not all meet that criterion. Indeed, it is difficult for me to admit that *Women's Ways of Knowing*, the book that could make the greatest difference in our practice of teaching women students, acknowledges neither the political nature of its own conclusions nor the political movement that gave legitimacy to women's learning as a field of study. What ought one to make of such a truth? In the first section of this essay, I review each book on its own terms. Subsequently, I suggest both problems and ironies facing women's studies teachers and scholars as their movement is broadened and put to use by people who, while sympathetic with it, have participated neither in community activities to fight women's oppression nor in the building of the on-campus women's movement. I have arranged the books reviewed below to reflect a continuum from the "praxis-minded" *Learning Our Way*, ringing with voices of committed feminist organizers, to *For Alma Mater* and *Kindling in the Groves*, which describe and demonstrate "transformed" scholarship, to *Reclaiming a Conversation*

---

[2] Howard, *A Different Woman* (New York: Dutton, 1973), p. 27.

and *Women's Ways of Knowing*, which remain within the traditional boundaries and proprieties of academic research.

Begun in 1977 as the documentary history of Sagaris, an independent, collectively-run summer school for women, *Learning Our Way* documents the politics of creating healthy educational environments for women. With its frank and sometimes painful descriptions of putting new visions into practice, this book has an honesty often missing from writing about the implementation of new ideas. It devotes equal time to feminist education within existing institutions and to alternative structures for feminism. Its authors, many well known for their activism, have been on the barricades, struggling to live and work by feminist principles. One essay chronicles the New Right attack on the Women's Studies program at Long Beach State University in California; another details the evolution of a white woman's antiracism group in Los Angeles.

Three essays in this book present in outline the agenda for work on women's issues over the last five years. Florence Howe's 1981 essay describes the new feminist scholarship on women as "transformational"—changing the shape of research so that "all the human race, not just a small segment of it," is included (p. 107). She lists ten major areas in which formidable bodies of knowledge must be developed, including, for example, the "still chaotic area of biological/psychological sex differences"; (p. 103) and "an understanding of women in the work force through history, in the present, and crossculturally . . . " (p. 104). Charlotte Bunch's "Not by Degrees: Feminist Theory and Education" sets out a model for developing theory that includes not only a description of what exists and an analysis of why, but also a vision of what *should* exist, and a hypothesis about how to change "what is" to what should be—the steps usually ignored by those claiming to be creating value-neutral knowledge. Nancy Schniedewind's "Guidelines for a Teaching Methodology in Women's Studies" empirically describes methods and processes for the feminist classroom, actually giving concrete advice about sharing classroom leadership, fostering collaborative projects, and the like.

Kindling in the Groves and *For Alma Mater*[3] demonstrate that much of the research Howe called for in 1981 has indeed been going on. *Kindling in the Groves*, a seamless, collaborative study of women's issues in five disciplines—anthropology, education, history, literature, and philosophy—is an imaginative and rigorous work of synthesis. For many years, Xeroxed, mimeographed, and printed course outlines and bibliographies of women's studies research in disciplines and specific problem areas circulated among feminist teachers; next came comprehensive works using single disciplines to feminist ends.[4] *Kindling in the Groves*, however, focuses on the disciplines themselves, a new contribution. The authors compare the ways disciplines cluster to solve problems, and explain how and why some disciplines are more likely to change because of feminism than are others. They argue convincingly that work on the relations between private and public domains, a key concern of feminists, is necessarily highly interdisciplinary, while work on sex discrimination and affirmative action best draws on the traditional methods in philosophy and political theory.

[3] Not to be confused with Helen Horowitz's *Alma Mater: The Design and Experience in the Women's Colleges from their Nineteenth-Century Beginnings to the 1930s* (New York: Knopf, 1984).

[4] A fine example is the philosopher Alison M. Jaggar's comprehensive work, *Feminist Politics and Human Nature* (Rowman & Allanheld, 1983); *Reclaiming a Conversation* is a second example.

The framework of the core chapters is elegant and simple; the authors take women's oppression and women's liberation to be the projects underlying all feminist scholarship, either implicitly or explicitly, but they assert that no single view prevails. Indeed, their characterization of the conflicting schools of thought among feminists should provide teachers with fresh questions to pose for their students as well as with an interesting critique of male-dominated scholarship. For example, on the question of the origins of women's oppression, the authors assert that "most social scientists . . . have not been concerned with the first causes of undesirable human institutions. As strict empiricists, they have considered questions of origin impossible to investigate and, as functionalists, they have treated them as unimportant" (p. 91). According to the authors, this is not true for feminists, who locate the origins of women's oppression in one of three realms: (1) in economic conditions following Marx and Engels; (2) in women's childbearing capacity after Simone de Beauvoir and Shulamith Firestone; or (3) in a separate structure of sexual and gender relations, as proposed by anthropologist Gayle Rubin, drawing on the work of Marx, Engels, Lévi-Strauss, Lacan, and Freud. The authors ask similarly probing and fundamental questions about scholarship on liberation, and provide ample documentation for each topic discussed.

In their concluding chapters, the authors sum up the effects of feminist research on the disciplines by presenting a systematic survey of the inclusion of work on women in the major refereed journals in their five disciplines. Among their findings is that "education . . . is especially prone to isolate work on women in special issues," and that "virtually no attention is paid to women or to gender difference in research that is not specifically devoted to women" (p. 183).

Kindling in the Groves makes no claim to developing new theory. *For Alma Mater*, on the other hand, with its essays ranging from linguistics to propaganda to hormones, exemplifies all that is new, and demonstrates the vibrancy and urgency of the best feminist scholarship. As the authors of *Kindling in the Groves* assert, feminist scholarship often "expands, modifies, . . . and . . . even overturns" traditional assumptions of the disciplines (p. 157). Many of these essays do "overturn," among them Gail Paradise Kelly's article on research about women's education in the Third World and Judith Hicks Steihm's study of the impact on men of the integration of women into the military academies. Kelly observes that because the expansion of education in the Third World in the 1970s did not have the significant economic development impact predicted, some governments cut back on educational expenditures, calling women's education a "bad risk" because some women's educational outcomes were less valued than men's. But, she argues, one must look at the assumptions underlying those programs. Most assumed a bifurcation between private and public spheres of action, relegated women to the private sphere, and then asked how education improves the family, not how the educational needs of women as individuals might best be met. When women are at the center of research, then one will ask, How does education change the impact of marriage, reproduction, and child-rearing on women's roles in society? Does education allow women to obtain greater power in both spheres?

Somewhere between the synthetic work of *Kindling in the Groves* and the transformational work of *For Alma Mater* lies Jane Roland Martin's *Reclaiming a Conversation*, several excellent chapters of which have appeared previously in the *Harvard*

Educational Review and elsewhere.[5] Martin's re-reading of several key texts on the ideal of education exemplifies the superimposition of current feminist values and vision on scholarship of the past; this kind of theorizing—which Bunch advocates and that *Kindling in the Groves* demonstrates—is rare in philosophy. In brief, Martin re-reads Plato, Rousseau, Wollstonecraft, Catherine Beecher, and Charlotte Perkins Gilman, asking each for responses to the questions: What constitutes a proper preparation for citizenship and for the reproductive processes of society? To whom should such preparation be extended? Martin asserts that each seldom gives only a partially satisfying answer. If Wollstonecraft, for example, argues in defense of women that they should receive the same education and rights as men, she leaves women still carrying out the "domestic and nurturant tasks" for which they are untaught (p. 93). Beecher adds to the ideal the necessity to teach women a serious discipline of "domestic economy," and from her, Martin urges women to claim a right to preparation for nurturance along with the right to citizenship.

The power of Martin's argument lies not in a sentimental assertion that men and women alike should be caring and nurturant, but in a logic that says neither family nor state can exist and improve without an education combining both traditionally male and traditionally female virtues. Such an education requires changes. As she argues in her concluding chapter, "We must . . . build nurturing capacities and an ethic of care into the curriculum itself" (p. 197).

Until recently work on the content, method, and process of women's education has been experiential and documentary—in the spirit of *Learning Our Way*. With the publication of *Women's Ways of Knowing*, however, the accounts of what works with women students have given way to sustained and systematic study of how women learn. With this book, we move from the realm of the feminist teacher's description and the student's report to the use of experiential accounts for building of theory. This path-breaking and very moving study is filled with the voices of women—old, young, middle-aged, black, white, Hispanic—telling in myriad ways what was important to them about life and learning. Based on hours of interviews with 135 women in formal institutions—a prestigious women's college, a co-educational college, an urban community college, an "early" college (grades 10–12 and the first two years of college), and an alternative urban high school—and in several "invisible colleges" (human service agencies supporting women in being parents), this book proposes a model of women's intellectual development. Happily, the model coincides in large measure with the anecdotal evidence, and confirms in part the ideal proposed by Martin in *Reclaiming a Conversation*—that the qualities one learns from mothering and in the family form one legitimate and significant strand in the education of both women and men.

Because of the new ground that it turns, *Women's Ways of Knowing* rightly needs a review of its own. Here I can only suggest the contribution it makes to teachers who, because of it, might work more sensitively and effectively with women students. Revising the epistemological positions identified by William Perry in *Forms*

---

[5] See Jane Roland Martin, "Sophie and Emile: A Case Study of Sex Bias in the History of Educational Thought," *Harvard Educational Review*, 51 (1981), 357–372 and "Feminist Scholarship and Women's Studies," *Harvard Educational Review*, 52 (1982), 137–148.

of Intellectual and Ethical Development in the College Years[6] on the basis of what they heard from women, Belenky and her colleagues developed five major categories of women's knowing. These perspectives—the authors do not have evidence of "stagelike" or sequential ordering—include:

> silence, a position in which women experience themselves as mindless and voiceless and subject to the whims of external authority; received knowledge, a perspective from which women conceive of themselves as capable of receiving, even reproducing knowledge from the all-knowing external authorities but not capable of creating knowledge on their own; subjective knowledge, a perspective from which truth and knowledge are conceived of as personal, private, and subjectively known or intuited; procedural knowledge, a position in which women are invested in learning and applying objective procedures for obtaining and communicating knowledge; and constructed knowledge, a position in which women view all knowledge as contextual, experience themselves as creators of knowledge, and value both subjective and objectives strategies for knowing. (p. 15)

Among the many conclusions in *Women's Ways of Knowing* that will ring true to feminist teachers is the book's strong recommendation that for many women "connection" must be made a precondition for learning. The only way for women to understand an idea is not to doubt it, to "knock it down" or "take it apart" as men tend to do, but to understand the experience of the person to whom the idea belongs and to share her experience. Speaking of the knowledge that begins in empathy in Simone Weil's "attentive love"; or Sara Ruddick's "maternal thinking"; or in Barbara McClintock's capacity "to hear what [the corn] has to say to you," the authors of *Women's Ways of Knowing* propose that for women, "confirmation and community" are preconditions for intellectual development. Unfortunately, connection with the learner and belief in her capacities are not the mode in most of higher education. Indeed, these researchers acknowledge frankly that a rural public health clinic, run on the connected teaching model, provides "more clearly, consistently, and sincerely than any other institution we sampled . . . confirmation that [the] women [clients] could be trusted to know and to learn" (p. 195).

Women's Ways of Knowing is divided into two sections. The first develops the categories of knowing; the second asks what the categories mean in the context of family and school. While more speculative in tone than the first section, the second is equally as courageous. This is a book in which one feels that the authors have listened carefully to their subjects and permitted themselves to be changed deeply by what they heard. Reminiscent of Paulo Freire's injunction that teachers begin with content "problematized" by learners, they conclude with a plain question about women's learning. "In considering how to design an education appropriate for women, suppose we were to begin by simply asking: What does a woman know?" (p. 198).

---

[6] Perry, *Forms of Intellectual Development in the College Years* (New York: Holt, Rinehart, and Winston, 1970). From hours of in-depth interviews with male Harvard students, Perry developed a scheme for describing the intellectual growth of students as they progress through a series of epistemological positions. In brief, the key positions are dualism ("there are right/wrong or good/bad answers and authorities know them"); multiplicity ("everyone has a right to her opinion and mine is as good as anyone's"); relativism ("truth is relative and depends on context"); and finally, commitment ("despite the relativism of truth, I must decide and act on my decisions").

As one long associated with women's studies — the first West Coast women's studies conference was held on my front lawn in Santa Barbara, California, in 1970 — I hear several ironies in the question asked by Belenky and her colleagues. While *Women's Ways of Knowing* is indeed a powerful book, it proceeds — at least in its second section — as if neither the women's movement nor women's studies had already changed educational practice, an omission equally characteristic of *Reclaiming a Conversation*. For example, while both books cite a passionate and moving speech about women's education given in 1978 by the poet Adrienne Rich, who argues that higher education is about "how men have perceived and organized their experience, their history, their idea," neither book acknowledges the extent to which contemporary feminists have built a body of knowledge and practice to correct this omission. Indeed, none of the authors notes that Rich herself is a consummate practitioner of "connected" scholarship, the origins of which are at least partially in the women's movement. In an essay in *On Lies, Secrets, and Silence*, Rich describes her attempt, years in the making, to read Emily Dickinson as she was meant to be read. She travels to Dickinson's home. Here is the passionate rigor of feminist scholarship: "For months, for most of my life, I have been hovering like an insect against the screens of an existence which inhabited Amherst, Massachusetts, between 1830 and 1886. . . . Here [in Dickinson's bedroom] I become again, an insect, vibrating at the frames of windows, clinging to the panes of glass, trying to connect."[7]

Further, if these researchers had looked within the very institutions they studied, they would have seen examples of "connected education" in woman-centered classrooms both within women's studies programs and elsewhere. Such examples would have strengthened their case and would have given more significance to an almost casual remark in *Women's Ways of Knowing*: "It should come as no surprise that the courses most often mentioned as powerful learning experiences were . . . courses in feminist theory, which helped women translate their ideas from the darkness of private experience into a shared public language"(p. 203). At least since the early seventies, "feminist pedagogy" has been a major subject of concern to movement-oriented academic women. Indeed, feminist teachers have developed a new genre of essay which describes the dialectic between intellectual inquiry and personal experience in the classroom. The recently published *Gendered Subjects*, for example, compiles two decades of writing about feminist teaching, including essays with such titles as "The Politics of Nurturance," "Staging the Feminist Classroom," and "Toward a Pedagogy of Everywoman's Studies."[8] The achievement of *Women's Ways of Knowing*, then, is not the invention of the concept of "connected" education, but the systematic and empirical justification of it as a mode suited to women students.

I point out these omissions not to diminish *Women's Ways of Knowing* or *Reclaiming a Conversation*, but as a way of assessing the progress of women's studies as a field and a practice. From one perspective, the absence of attention to feminist ac-

---

[7] Adrienne Rich, *On Lies, Secrets, and Silence: Selected Prose, 1966–1978* (New York: Norton, 1978), pp. 158–161.

[8] Margo Culley and Catherine Portuges, eds. *Gendered Subjects: The Dynamics of Feminist Teaching* (New York: Routledge & Kegan Paul, 1985).

tivism or women's movement politics in these books is cause for optimism — as a category of legitimate study, "woman" has entered the mainstream. From another perspective, however, if scholars as sensitive to the educational climate as Martin and Belenky and her colleagues do not explore women's studies as a forerunner of the changes they envision for the educational system, they only confirm the slow pace of feminist transformation in the academy. Despite the proliferation of new scholarship on women and the institutionalization of women's studies programs, most students still graduate from institutions of higher education without studying feminist practice or theory (which includes with increasing frequency the study of race and class issues as well). The introductory courses that compose the core of general education are largely taught from texts which in their newest editions may mention Elizabeth Cady Stanton or the concept of sex-role stereotyping, but do nothing to provide a serious answer to the question, What would research be like that includes the whole of the human race, not just the male segment of it?

In the last several years, recognizing the perils of ghettoizing women's studies, faculties have begun to formulate strategies to transform the content and approach of entire institutions. In rare instances, faculties have had the political power and acumen to require a women's studies course, or a course on race and gender, as part of general education. But far more prevalent are faculty development models designed to integrate women's studies into the "mainstream" curriculum. These include strategies as diverse as providing financial incentives to encourage discipline-based faculties to incorporate new material on women into their courses, to the transformation of curriculum materials and even the knowledge bases of the disciplines by experts who then "train" interested faculty members in the new approaches.[9]

In general, the goal of integration projects has been to "help faculty in traditional disciplines to use the key research findings, fresh perspectives, and transforming insights which arise from the new scholarship on women."[10] (The material in *For Alma Mater*, for example, would be useful in such an endeavor.) The encouraging news is that, to date, several hundred institutions have undertaken projects. But such efforts also pose dilemmas of which the "integrationists" are well aware. I note three of greatest significance. First, some administrators have embraced the integration movement as a means of phasing out unruly and contentious women's studies programs; without a strong base of operations, women's studies is likely not to survive. Second, with support from women of color in various disciplines and from black studies departments, women's studies is beginning to develop multicultural perspectives and methods. Johnnella Butler of Smith College has argued, however, that women's studies ought not to represent its perspective to the rest of the academy until it has transformed itself.[11]

Third, and most important for this review, is the quality of "mainstream" transformation itself. Betty Schmitz observes that critics of the integration movement fear that "the least radical scholarship may be selected for faculty development

[9] See Betty Schmitz, *Integrating Women's Studies into the Curriculum, A Guide and Bibliography* (New York: Feminist Press, 1985); and Marilyn Schuster and Susan Van Dyne, "Placing Women in the Liberal Arts: Stages of Curriculum Transformation," *Harvard Educational Review, 54* (1984), 413–428.

[10] Peggy McIntosh, "Directory of Projects: Transforming the Liberal Arts Curriculum Through Incorporation of the New Scholarship on Women," *Women's Studies Quarterly, 11*, No. 2 (1983), 23.

[11] As cited by Schmitz in *Integrating Women's Studies into the Curriculum*, pp. 6–7.

seminars precisely because it is the most acceptable. . . . "[12] Project designers are tempted understandably to present skeptics with scholarship that appears to be neutral information, fresh content for a syllabus rather than a questioning of the values and perspectives by which one lives. Transformational scholarship, by contrast, acknowledges at least the following: that however "objective" in presentation, all scholarship represents the frame of mind of the knower, her or his "reading" of the world; that gender, race, and class are lenses as powerful as historical moment and cultural context; and that women's studies is fundamentally a political venture. These may be pills too strong for most faculty to swallow, at present.[13] Not only may radical scholarship be lost, but feminist pedagogy as well. Indeed, in several projects I describe elsewhere, designed to integrate material about women and minorities into the curriculum, planners ignored almost entirely the precepts of feminist education.[14] They used a lecture or formal seminar format, paid little attention to interracial dynamics, and did not attempt to connect with the experience of their professor participants.

The five books under review here expose some differences in what I call the "integrationist" and "women's studies" approaches. The "integrationist" books, *Reclaiming a Conversation* and *Women's Ways of Knowing*, boldly overturn traditional readings of accepted works and perspectives on their discipline's own terms (the modification of Perry's five stages of development, for example, into five categories for women). Their authors identify themselves with disciplines and departments. Neither book places its recommendations for educational change within the politics of our sex/gender system. As I noted at the outset, neither book recognizes the political nature of its own conclusions. Neither asks such a politically charged question as, What shifts in the structure of power within academia would have to take place if both sexes were to learn about nurturance *and* citizenship, or if women were to claim classroom time to speak from personal experience? In contrast, the authors of *Kindling in the Groves* and *Learning Our Way* always keep politics fully in view. They write out of the perspectives developed in women's studies programs. The *Kindling in the Groves* authors all participated in the building of the Buffalo Women's Studies college where they put their rather formidable scholarly talents to the service of understanding the sources of women's oppression and changing them. In the program and in the book, they worked collectively—this despite their knowing that reward and recognition within academia, as well as their own ingrained habits of thought, depended on solitary contemplation. The commitment to work collectively is not ornery political "correctness," but is rather the result of a shared connection to a political women's movement which they see as "the lifeblood of feminist scholarship, not its tragic flaw" (p. 8).

Martin asks how the philosophy of education might be remade to tell the story of educational ideals for women, while DuBois and her colleagues would ask how feminists seeking to articulate educational ideals might utilize the disciplines, and

---

[12] Schmitz, *Integrating Women's Studies*, p. 6.
[13] Respect for subjectivity is on the rise, however, through such continental movements as hermeneutics and deconstruction which do recognize, though not always sympathetically, the power of gender.
[14] Nancy Jo Hoffman "Black Studies, Ethnic Studies, and Women's Studies: Reflections on Some Collaborative Projects," *Women's Studies Quarterly*, *14*, Nos. 1 and 2 (1986), 49–53.

what have the disciplines contributed to women's liberation or oppression? These are quite different questions. I do not want to suggest that *Reclaiming a Conversation* or *Women's Ways of Knowing* are the "less feminist" works or the less valuable ones because they do not spring from holistic conceptions of women's studies as a field or embrace overt politics, but rather to suggest that they are more valuable in combination with the more radical, political vision and practice found on the margins of academia. The question facing women's studies and feminist scholarship in the next decade is, then: How can the radical and transforming vision of women's studies programs and research centers be extended into the heart of academia?

Reading, Writing, Teaching: Classroom Teachers Discuss Literature on the Teaching of Writing

JOSEPH W. CHECK
DENISE BURDEN
PETER GOLDEN

The editors of HER *became interested in the literature on the teaching of writing when what seemed like a deluge of recent contributions began crossing our desks. After some thought and discussion, we approached the staff of the Boston Writing Project (BWP), a program of the Institute for Learning and Teaching at the Boston campus of the University of Massachusetts, and asked them to assemble a panel of teachers to review some notable works of this burgeoning literature. We requested that the panel also assess the relationship between the literature and actual teaching practice.*

The BWP is one local site of the curricular phenomenon called the National Writing Project, a network of 141 sites in 47 states. [1] *Like all the other sites, including the famous Bay Area Writing Project on the West Coast, the BWP conducts intensive summer institutes and in-service programs in the teaching of writing for teachers of all subjects and levels, kindergarten through college.*

The panel assembled by the BWP for this review included sixteen teachers and administrators from urban and suburban schools. Their oral and written comments inspired the essay which opens this review. Following the essay is a collection of short reviews written by members of the panel. The works reviewed here were selected with advice from directors of other National Writing Project sites across the country.

We are in the midst of an explosion of literature on the teaching of writing. Happily, it is an explosion that provides us with much more than mere quantity. Nearly ten years have passed since *Newsweek*'s cover story "Why Johnny Can't Write" gave nationwide visibility to the issue of writing in our schools and colleges.[2] In that time, a steady stream of books and articles has appeared describing the processes of experienced and inexperienced writers from primary grades

---

[1] James Moffett recently called the National Writing Project "the best curricular movement I know of"; see his "Hidden Impediments to Improving English Teaching," *Phi Delta Kappan, 67* (1985), 50–56.

[2] Merrill Sheils, "Why Johnny Can't Write," *Newsweek,* 8 Dec. 1975, pp. 58–65.

Harvard Educational Review   Vol. 55   No. 4   November 1985, 464–477

through college. As one measurement of that growth, the number of listings under "composition" in the catalogue of the National Council of Teachers of English (NCTE) has increased from nearly nothing to eleven full pages. In addition, basic research on composing and classroom contexts for writing is now a vigorous and respected arm of educational inquiry.

An important characteristic of this growth is the emergence of a number of publishers committed to improving the teaching of writing by collaborating with teachers and researchers to develop high-quality resource books. Publishers such as Boynton-Cook, Heinemann, Teachers and Writers Collaborative, and NCTE have done much to insure that the flood of materials goes beyond "writing process" textbooks, workbooks, how-to books, and traditional college-composition rhetorics.

For a group of classroom teachers the thought of evaluating this burgeoning literature was both intriguing and intimidating. How could we do justice to the breadth of the task and yet maintain the classroom teacher's point of view? We reasoned that the ultimate purpose of books on composition is to teach students to write better by helping their teachers to instruct better. Thus in our discussion we explored, as a group of practitioners, the relationship between our professional reading and the improvement and renewal of our classroom practice.

At the outset it became obvious that many in the group did not regard themselves as people who kept up with their professional reading. There was a near-universal feeling that the pressures of everyday teaching and the demands of personal and family life leave little or no time to pick up a book or article and give it the attention it deserves. At the same time, everyone in the group seemed to be familiar with a variety of recently published material in the field, or with information and ideas from such publications. By exploring this seeming contradiction, we began to clarify the paths along which new professional ideas reached us as writing teachers.

Our discussion was guided by questions which seemed simple and obvious: How does reading about writing fit into our professional life? How do we decide what to read? How do we evaluate what we read? How do we incorporate ideas from a book or article into practice? Has any one author or book had a profound effect on our teaching of writing? The discussion of these questions lasted several hours; the transcript ran to fifty-nine pages. What follows is a distillation of the most striking points, interspersed with quotations to transmit the flavor of the discussion itself.

> I find if I'm not taking courses I will not make the effort to look for books that deal with writing unless I want to do a fun activity that's different from what I normally do. I'll go look for some writing activity . . . but that's as far as I go.

> I find I read more and more, but I read less and less about writing. I think there's only so much you can say about writing, although I read the *English Journal* because the department gets it. There are about three or four people in the department that sort of share articles about writing if they have come across something.

> Does anybody steer things your way?

> A group within the department does.

> Yes, and also the principal. . . . If he comes across an article on writing in something he gets, he'll mimeograph it and put it in the box.

> I have a great department head who sends me articles all the time. All my reading about writing has been done either as part of the Boston Writing Project or because my department head has sent articles, and because of the workshop I took this summer on writing to learn.

Our discussion suggested that for committed writing teachers, an intricate and ongoing relationship exists between reading and teaching. It is a relationship characterized by change, growth, and distinct types of reading undertaken for specific purposes at specific times. We began to discover that good writing teachers are avid readers with diverse needs and interests, for whom there is no "steady state" relationship between reading and teaching.

Teachers may develop a prolonged, intense interest in a single author — usually a writing "guru" such as James Moffett or Donald Graves — early in their careers or at a professional turning point. Such an interest may originate in a graduate course, in-service program, or summer institute where there is time for both reflective reading and conversation with people who share an interest in writing. Then, having had this original experience, teachers may return to the trusted author or book as a touchstone when they need to change their practice as a result of assignment to a new grade level or new school, or some other change in their lives.

On a day-to-day level, other forms of reading complement and improve practice. Faced with a specific difficulty in a class or with a student, a teacher will search for a specific solution. It frequently comes from a collection of classroom-tested writing activities, a suggestion from a colleague, a handout at a workshop, or a presentation at a conference. It will be used on a trial basis before becoming part of a teacher's permanent repertoire.

The same teacher, at the same time, may be engaged in other reading related to writing but not directly applicable to the teaching of writing. Books such as Eudora Welty's *One Writer's Beginnings*, Zora Neale Hurston's *Dust Tracks on a Road*, and Dorothy Farnam's *Auden in Love* were mentioned in our discussion because they answer the writing teacher's need to learn about the growth and development of professional writers.[3]

> Even though I am teaching third grade, I would prefer to read a biography of a poet and then internalize that, even though it does not directly apply to teaching something in the third grade. . . . I just finished *Auden in Love*. I'm always looking for coincidences, and just coincidentally, when he was in England before he came to this country, Auden was teaching at a lower level, and he supervised a student publication called *The Badger* for kids. And suddenly I realized that this poet, one of the great poets of the twentieth century, was involved with publishing children's writing, and thought it was very important. It was much more stimulating for me to look at this coincidence than to just read something in an educational journal, because Auden's experience really happened.

In general, we came away from our discussion with a greatly widened definition of professional literature. If this is reading which directly affects how and why

---

[3] Welty, *One Writer's Beginnings* (Cambridge: Harvard University Press, 1984); Hurston, *Dust Tracks on a Road: An Autobiography* (Urbana: University of Illinois Press, 1984); and Farnam, *Auden in Love* (New York: Simon and Schuster, 1984).

teachers teach writing, good teachers place an extremely wide range of items in this category, not just books about the teaching of writing:

> I realized when I talked about writing that it referred to how writers write rather than how teachers teach writing, or what you do in your classroom. If I pick up something, even in pleasure, about writing, I bring it to the classroom somehow. It isn't so technical.

Through our discussion, we identified three broad types of reading that affect our practice: literary works, theory and research about writing, and how-to books. The first is represented by *Auden in Love, One Writer's Beginnings, Dust Tracks on a Road*, and various pieces of fiction, poetry, and journalism. Our group saw this as professional reading in two senses: it is by or about successful professional writers, and it aids teachers in the performance of their duties.

The second and third categories are types of professional reading in the traditional sense. In the second, teachers take on a "big book," like James Britton's *The Development of Writing Abilities* or Shirley Brice Heath's *Ways with Words* as a conscious project, usually making time for serious reflection on specific implications the reading has for their teaching.[4] They often revise their teaching strategies as part of the reading process.

The third type of professional reading consists chiefly of articles, handouts, and chapters or sections from how-to books on writing that meet immediate classroom needs. They are normally short, practical, and may or may not be related to a larger conceptual or research base for teaching writing.

In the first type the essential reading relationship is dualistic: the teacher meets the text. In types two and three the relationship is triangular, encompassing teacher, text, and a context which gives rise to and shapes the reading. A wide variety of contexts were mentioned in our discussions, including graduate courses, in-service programs, summer institutes, conference presentations, informal discussions among a small group of colleagues, and ongoing suggestions from an administrator who screened professional literature and passed on selected articles to faculty.

There is, of course, cross-fertilization among the three types of reading here identified. For an individual teacher at a particular moment, all three may be going on, or none. Over time, good teachers of writing seem to be involved in all three and to engage in a sort of longitudinal dialogue among the types, going through phases which cross and recross the lines between theory and practice.

Our discussion suggested strongly that over time this interrelationship between the various types of reading is a key element in the periodic renewal and recommitment that teachers require. Writing teachers in particular benefit from this interrelationship and apply it to their classroom practices because it mirrors the cross-disciplinary nature of writing.

The fact that two of the three types are context-dependent underscores the importance of school organization. In a well-administered, financially stable school

---

[4] Britton, *The Development of Writing Abilities* (Urbana, IL: National Council of Teachers of English, 1975), pp. 11–18; Heath, *Ways with Words: Language, Life, and Work in Communities and Classrooms* (New York: Cambridge University Press, 1983); see also Harold Rosen's essay review of this book on pp. 448–456 in this issue of *HER*.

system, networking, administrative "steering," and meaningful in-service programs actively promote professional growth. On the other hand, in school systems undergoing financial and administrative crisis, peer networks which support professional reading can be destroyed by teacher reassignments and layoffs. Administrators who have previously screened and steered appropriate literature to teachers may find their positions eliminated or become so engulfed by additional duties that they give up this function. In addition, opportunities for in-service training may decrease as school budgets become tighter. There is no doubt that the administrative stability and relative financial health of a given school system can play a strong role in promoting excellent teaching of writing.

The role played by the school context can be illustrated by three typical answers given by teachers in our group to the question: How does the climate or atmosphere in your school affect your attitude toward professional development?

> I find little community in our school. The principal is negative in his approach — he forces things down people's throats. He feels he knows everything.

> I'm ambivalent. Teachers are encouraged to share in a dictatorial, insensitive approach, leaving them defensive, shy, and uneasy. I have to plan how and with whom I share.

> I am one of thirty-five members of the English Department of a comprehensive high school with a student body of three thousand. The department includes bilingual and reading specialists. . . . In this climate, one can adopt almost any attitude or select one's atmosphere by one's choice of faculty lounge — the social activists, the rebels, the scornful, the concerned, the turned-off and tuned out. But the potential is always available. Our department head is supportive and encouraging in the introduction of new ideas.

What implications do the points raised by our discussion have for evaluating the explosion in writing literature? The growth of literature on writing is to be celebrated as much for the contexts in which it has grown, and the possibilities for professional growth it has opened for both university scholars and classroom teachers, as for the excellence of many individual studies within the field. Rapid growth in writing literature has been encouraged by growth in networks between practitioners and researchers that make theory, research, and models of successful practice accessible to teachers. The involvement of all educational levels in this process has opened dialogue on larger professional issues such as restructuring the school day to allow more time for writing, restoring a balance between reading and writing, and looking at writing in contexts such as critical literacy and the ethnography of language development. Extensive school/university collaborative networks, of which the Writing Project is one example, have given classroom teachers an opportunity to become creators as well as sophisticated consumers of professional literature.

We have selected for review titles which are illustrative of some point raised in our discussion or some aspect of the "explosion of literature in writing" that we think is particularly significant. We wanted to show, for example, that a climate has been created in which a researcher like Donald Graves feels it appropriate and important to speak of the relationship between his research and his own growth as a writer, and a teacher such as Marian Mohr can speak with authority as a researcher of her own classroom. We felt it essential to demonstrate that there is excellent material available for teachers from kindergarten through college, for teachers in need of proven practical strategies and those seeking deeper philosophical and research grounding, and for teachers who need to sustain themselves by keeping a foot in both worlds, that of teaching and that of literary and professional writing. One of the central realizations we came to as a result of our discussion was that each of the books selected for review could be, for the right teacher at the right time in the right context, a "notable work" on the teaching of writing.

Contributors to the Discussion:

Denise Burden, *Boston Writing Project, University of Massachusetts, Boston*

Joseph W. Check, *Boston Writing Project, University of Massachusetts, Boston*

Stephen Driscoll, *New Horizons Academy, M. L. King Middle School, Boston*

Jean Gibran, *Hurley Elementary School, Boston*

Peter Golden, *Boston Writing Project, University of Massachusetts, Boston*

Jacqueline Harris, *Fenway School, Boston English High School*

Rosalind W. Hoey, *Trotter Elementary School, Boston*

Jane Kreinsen, *Braintree High School*

Joseph P. McDonald, *Watertown High School*

Thomas Moore, *Wachusett Regional High School*

Paul Moran, *Austin Preparatory School, Reading*

Lois Osmer, *Lincoln Elementary School, Brookline*

Ann Phillips, *Runkle Elementary School, Brookline*

Joyce Simms, *Mather Elementary School, Boston*

◆ ◆ ◆

REVISION: THE RHYTHM OF MEANING by Marian M. Mohr. *Upper Montclair, NJ: Boynton/Cook, 1984. 248 pp. $9.50 (paper).*

Teaching students to revise may be the most avoided, least understood task that writing teachers face, and until now no comprehensive, classroom-based treatment of the subject for secondary school teachers has been available. *Revision* fills this need. It can help teachers at all levels understand the revision process in all its complexity and teach it successfully to their students.

As sources for her text, Marian Mohr uses the writing and comments about writing of her students (ranging from ninth grade to college freshmen), her own writing and comments, her study of the drafting processes of professional writers, and revision research. She weaves these varied voices into an effective, illustrative whole. The book's nine chapters cover topics such as "The Goals of Revision," "Assigned Writing," "The Writer in the Writing," and "Active Revision," and are enriched by Mohr's technique of juxtaposing the fresh voices of students discovering their own revision processes with the comments of experienced writers engaged in the same processes. She studies working drafts of writers such as Mark Twain, Richard Wilbur, and John Updike, as well as her students' own exploratory, rough, and final drafts. For the reader, this technique provides a convincing demonstration of two of Mohr's contentions which have important implications for the classroom: "Students revise as professional writers do" and "all writers will revise most of the time if given the opportunity" (p. 236).

Mohr's book explores these implications and provides a comprehensive guide to teaching revision that includes sample assignments, principles for constructing effective assignments, classroom management strategies, and time management strategies. Two brief closing chapters present her eight major conclusions about revision, a model of revision, and a look at the model in the classroom. Her bibliography of revision resources includes carefully selected and annotated listings under four headings: experienced writers discussing their revision processes, revised drafts of experienced writers, revision research and theory, and teaching revision.

JOSEPH W. CHECK
Boston Writing Project
University of Massachusetts, Boston

◆ ◆ ◆

PERSONAL FICTION WRITING: A GUIDE TO WRITING FROM REAL LIFE FOR TEACHERS, STUDENTS & WRITERS by Meredith Sue Willis. *New York: Teachers & Writers Collaborative, 1984. 208 pp. $9.95 (paper).*

For teachers who are constantly faced with students who claim, "I have nothing to write about," Meredith Sue Willis has put together a volume of practical writing exercises. As a writer and a teacher, her basic assumptions are that all students can learn to compose and all writers have real experience and vision to share.

Willis presents 355 classroom activities to help students develop a series of entries which they may expand to longer pieces. These activities, or ideas, as she refers to them, are not traditional lesson plans but rather stimuli to motivate students to want to write. One such assignment suggests that students "make as precise a word portrait as possible of any adult you know" (p. 36). I tried this with reluctant high schoolers, as part of an intended longer piece about families that relocate, and found it to be a good strategy. Not only did we have fun as a class putting together a group portrait of an adult we all knew, but I also found that when the students wrote their pieces individually, they took great care in the adjectives they chose and in the overall quality of their work.

These activities are based on what Willis has learned through participation in group discussions, children's writings, and talks with classroom teachers. They have been tested with classroom populations and range in grade-level appropriateness from first grade through college-level or adult classes. They are designed to fit into a forty-five to sixty-minute instructional period. Writing ideas are categorized under the following chapters: describing places, people, and action; writing dialogue and monologue; and creating structure.

Each writing assignment is followed by examples from students' papers as well as by excerpts from literature. Willis must be applauded for selecting passages from a wide variety of authors, many of whose work contributes to an ethnically diverse content. Willis critiques the student writing and excerpts, and explains how each piece illustrates the theme of the particular chapter.

This book of writing ideas can be a terrific resource for the classroom teacher as well as the novice writer. Willis does not go into detail about classroom management or a teacher's response to student writing, but she does include notes on revision in an appendix.

DENISE BURDEN
Boston Writing Project
University of Massachusetts, Boston

◆ ◆ ◆

THE WRITING WORKSHOP, VOL. 2 by Alan Ziegler. *New York: Teachers and Writers Collaborative, 1984. 230 pp. $9.95 (paper).*

In this book, Alan Ziegler continues his case for a supportive yet challenging writing workshop model as a staple of any curriculum designed to address the crisis in writing skills among schoolchildren. His first volume was concerned with the creation of a comfortable writing atmosphere and the involvement of students in the writing process; this second volume answers the question, What are we supposed to write today?

The opening activities are designed to get student writing off the ground in a nonthreatening way. Not only can these activities be introduced and completed in less than thirty minutes, they also allow time for sharing and introduce approaches that will be useful in later assignments.

The orientations sequence discusses seven sources writers draw on for their ideas, including emotion, experience, observation, and communication, with suggested activities to tap each source. These activities provide students with a wide range of writing experiences which can be combined to form different designs for future writing.

This section is followed by a catalogue of sixty assignments designed to introduce students to an array of popular writing topics, some of which may be connected with other areas of study or the writer's previous experience. The assignments are amply illustrated by examples of both student and adult papers, and each idea is accompanied by suggestions for ways to present it to a class. Included in this section are assignment ideas such as interviews, poems, free writing sessions, rituals, metaphors and similes, and observation. Although most of the activities contained herein are adaptable to all grade levels, the author does warn that teachers of the lower elementary grades will have to "pick and choose." The assignments offered are not necessarily to be used verbatim or in sequence but as pure and simple inspiration to students.

JACQUELINE HARRIS
Fenway School
Boston English High School

◆ ◆ ◆

A RESEARCHER LEARNS TO WRITE: SELECTED ARTICLES AND MONOGRAPHS by Donald H. Graves. *Portsmouth, NH: Heinemann, 1984. 208 pp. $10.00 (paper).*

Although Donald Graves presents extensive research on the teaching of writing in primary grades, much of what he says can be applied to upper grade levels as well. He shows teachers how to be researchers in their classrooms, thus benefiting themselves and their students. Several of his articles depict ways to follow children's development closely by showing charts detailing procedures and phases of individual case studies. He encourages teachers to be participants in the writing process, to develop and learn by facing the same problems as their students.

The articles collected here range in date from 1973 to 1983. Each is introduced by Graves with a pithy reevaluation of his style and "voice" as it has changed during the twelve years he has been publishing his research. These introductions are written as if Donald Graves is in a writing conference with the reader, and they give excellent insight into the personal side of professional research writing by elaborating on the struggles the author has had with the development of his own writing.

A focal point of this book is discussion of teacher-learner writing conferences conducted one to one by the teacher with each student, in order "to elicit information from children rather than issue directives about errors on their papers" (p. 49). In Grave's view, writing conferences between teachers and students are essential. He demonstrates what a writing conference entails, why it is the key element in the teaching of writing, and how it can be as short as forty-five seconds, yet productive for both student and teacher. He also discusses unassigned writing periods as a good time for teachers to move around the group, conducting mini-conferences. Graves states that "an environment that requires large amounts of assigned writing inhibits the range, content, and amount of writing done by children" (p. 35).

Though this book is full of practical suggestions concerning conferences, case studies of children's growth, and the keeping of research journals by teachers, Graves is not a believer in hard and fast rules. His final chapter, "The Enemy is Orthodoxy," asks the writing teacher to be flexible enough in teaching to accommodate the child's developmental level and dispense with ideas that are not working; to listen and "let the children teach us what they know" (p. 193). He asks teachers to write every day, even short journal entries, so that the process is always fresh, the awareness of difficulties always present, and the truth about good teaching always clear — so that it is "a process of discovery in its own right" (p.193).

ROSALIND W. HOEY
Teacher, Grades 4–5
Trotter Elementary School, Boston

◆ ◆ ◆

DUST TRACKS ON A ROAD: AN AUTOBIOGRAPHY, 2nd ed. by Zora Neale Hurston; edited and with an introduction by Robert E. Hemenway. *Urbana: University of Illinois Press, 1984. 348 pp., $9.95 (paper).*

This new edition of Zora Neale Hurston's autobiography, the first since the book's original publication in 1942, contains complete versions of several chapters which had been severely cut in the original edition. Hemenway's introduction locates this enigmatic work in the context of its time and its author's major fictional and ethnographic works while providing significant biographical information — for example, the fact that census records have revealed that Hurston was probably ten years older than she claimed. These ten missing years in her autobiographical sequence make her life story more puzzling than ever. In many instances, *Dust Tracks* leaves us wondering if we are reading autobiography or fiction, concealing much of what we want to know about Zora Neale Hurston even as it claims to reveal. In Hemenway's judgment, the book "presents an image of its author that fails to conform with either her public career or her private experience" (p. ix).

Dust Tracks is stylistically rich and contains a wealth of anecdotes, insights, and analyses of two of Hurston's worlds — the rural black South that was both home and her central subject in a lifetime of novelistic and ethnographic study, and the educated, literary, Northern world to which her early road out of the South led her. Frequently, her story presents the collision between these two worlds as she herself experienced it.

Readers, especially teachers, who come to this book after first encountering Hurston's best-known novel, *Their Eyes Were Watching God*, will learn a great deal about the richness, variety, sophistication, and creativity of oral language, and about its central importance to all aspects of community life. The strength and subtlety which control of a rich, evocative language gives are evident throughout the book, both in her own style and in the tales she tells. One of the book's appendices contains a piece Hurston wrote in Haiti in 1937 entitled "My People, My People!" In it she sets forth a series of ways to define "her people," including this one: "If he hunts for six big words where one little one would do, that's My People. If he can't find that big word he's feeling for, he is going to make a new one. But somehow or other that new-made word fits the things it was made for. Sounds good, too. . . . When you find a man chewing up the dictionary and spitting out language, that's My People" (p. 298). In a sense, though Zora Hurston is the subject of this book, the transforming power of language is its true heroine.

JOSEPH CHECK
Boston Writing Project
University of Massachusetts, Boston

◆ ◆ ◆

CONTEXTS FOR LEARNING TO WRITE: STUDIES OF SECONDARY SCHOOL INSTRUCTION by Arthur N. Applebee, with contributions by Judith A. Langer, Russel K. Durst, Kay Butler-Nolin, James D. Marshall, and George E. Newell. *Norwood, NJ: Ablex, 1984. 224 pp. $27.50, $17.95 (paper).*

The second report on the National Study of Writing in Secondary Schools, conducted by Arthur N. Applebee and a team of researchers from Stanford University and the University of California at Berkeley, concentrates on students' writing skills as well as changes that occur when writing is used as a tool for exploring new ideas.

With grants from NIE, Applebee and his team spent three years conducting an in-depth examination of the most frequently used textbooks in a variety of subjects. They also conducted a longitudinal study of the writing process of representative students over sixteen months. In addition, they explored two other issues of concern: the role that knowledge of a subject plays in students' composing processes and the uses of writing as an aid to learning.

Each of the book's eleven chapters has an introduction, an extensive description of methodology, and a conclusion summarizing its findings, while the last chapter summarizes the findings of the study as a whole. The findings reveal two disturbing conclusions: textbook writing experiences are, for the most part, narrow and limiting, and only 12 percent of the exercises in composition textbooks required writing even a paragraph. The primary audience for student writing was the teacher, the writing requested was very restricted (fill in the blanks, short answers, and word choices), and over 97 percent of the extended writing exercises were designed to test previous knowledge. In short, the textbooks' "underlying philosophy of writing assignments is one of the transmission of knowledge rather than interpretation of knowledge" (p. 36).

The case studies revealed that 88 percent of the student writing was intended to be informational, yet the instruction about the assignments only described the final form the pieces were to take. Revision occurred most frequently when students addressed a wider audience for a greater purpose or worked on the papers for more than a class period. Yet most of the writing assignments had few such characteristics.

Applebee also examined the writing-as-process method of teaching composition. He found that since most writing asked for a demonstration of learning, the content and final form were what counted. Therefore, students found the writing process irrelevant to the final product, often short-circuiting a teacher's well-intentioned process techniques. In many classrooms, writing-process technique fails because it does not fit into current teaching goals. This finding, Applebee believes, "requires a reassessment of the purposes for asking students to write at all" (p. 187).

PETER GOLDEN
Boston Public Schools and Boston Writing Project,
University of Massachusetts, Boston

◆ ◆ ◆

RHETORICAL TRADITIONS AND THE TEACHING OF WRITING by C. H. Knoblauch and Lil Brannon. *Upper Montclair, NJ: Boynton/Cook, 1984. 171 pp. $9.95 (paper).*

Rhetorical Traditions and the Teaching of Writing attempts to provide writing teachers with a philosophical basis for the implementation of student-centered writing workshops. C. H. Knoblauch and Lil Brannon find the philosophical justification for the approach they advocate in the writings of Descartes, Locke, Kant, and Coleridge, who emphasize discourse as a process of continuous learning, constituting both "the means of learning and the shape of knowledge, so that creating discourse is equivalent to coming to know" (p. 52). According to Knoblauch and Brannon, this is precisely the antidote required for the prescriptive, skills-based approach to composition which they feel reflects a widespread misconception about Aristotelian and Ciceronian rhetoric.

The authors are convinced that the only path to mastery in writing lies in frequent practice and constant revision, and that any classroom practice which fails to demonstrate this belief is ultimately harmful because, at best, it projects a mixed message to the student and compromises the student's sense of the value of the work. As they put it: "Writing is the making of meaning, first, last, and always; it is other things only because it is this. Writing is the expression of human intelligence and imagination, not merely a convenient packaging of preconceived thought, and certainly not a mere social grace or job skill" (p. 60).

Knoblauch and Brannon argue passionately that the art of teaching writing has been denied the respect to which it is entitled and that part of the reason for this slight is the lack of a solid philosophical base for the work of practitioners. This volume attempts to remedy that lack by linking an appreciation of modern rhetoric, with its emphasis on "the process of composing more than the features of completed text" and concepts such as "writing to learn," "coherence," and "revision" (p. 4) with classroom practices which successfully apply these concepts. They make their case forcefully, and while their mistrust of both traditional approaches to composition and middle-of-the-road "smorgasbord" curricula may offend some, this is a work worthy of the attention of all teachers of writing.

PAUL MORAN
Austin Preparatory School, Reading

♦ ♦ ♦

COURSES FOR CHANGE IN WRITING: A SELECTION FROM THE NEH/IOWA INSTITUTE edited by Carl H. Klaus and Nancy Jones. *Upper Montclair, NJ: Boynton/Cook, 1984. 296 pp. $9.50 (paper).*

The "courses" of the title represent the work of the remarkable Institute on Writing at the University of Iowa. Begun in 1977 on a grant from the National Endowment for the Humanities, the Institute invites the heads of writing programs at various colleges and universities to spend six months in Iowa City engaged in what James Britton in his introduction to this volume calls "a strenuous study of theory—rhetorical, linguistic, psychological, and more" (p. v). The purpose of such study is to inform an effort by these Institute Fellows, sanctioned by their deans, to fashion new writing courses specifically tailored to their home institutions. The volume is a sampler of this work: descriptions of sixteen writing courses designed primarily for beginning undergraduates, plus four programs designed to foster faculty commitment to the teaching of writing across the disciplines.

Each course is described by its developer in an essay plus an extensive syllabus detailing specific assignments and methods. The format seems calculated to be practical without being prescriptive, to paste a warning label on what otherwise seems a simple teaching template: "Danger—this course was cut for a very specific purpose." The essays which constitute this label are at once theoretical and personal. That is, they seek to link the peculiarities of the course approach to broad concerns and findings in the exploding scholarship of teaching writing, but they also describe the particular circumstances, and quite often the passionate conviction, that defined and animated the development of the course.

One might imagine that the value of this volume to teachers of composition, especially on the high school level, would reside in its assignment ideas and other practical teaching tips. I believe, however, that its greater contribution may be its capacity to provoke in us a better notion of *course*. Klaus suggests in his introduction that the great diversity in the courses is a product of attempts to fit them to a matching diversity of institutional contexts. Of course, this must be true. But I think it is true as well that the courses reflect a similar diversity of interests and styles among their designers and teachers, and this is where I sense a special value. In effect, the volume encourages a notion of *course* as grounded in the individual teacher's perspective on how to learn and on what should be learned, as well as in the student's learning needs. There is a profound implication in this action for schools lately grown manic in pursuit of curricular standardization. Some curricular idiosyncracy may be a good thing, may in fact give good teaching its fire, especially in a domain like writing, which Klaus aptly calls "profoundly personal . . . profoundly social" (p. xvii).

JOSEPH P. McDONALD
Watertown High School, Watertown

◆ ◆ ◆

C. S. LEWIS LETTERS TO CHILDREN edited by Lyle W. Dorsett and Marjorie Lamp Mead, with Foreword by Douglas H. Gresham. *New York: Macmillan, 1984. 120 pp. $9.95.*

Among children, Clive Staples Lewis is known and remembered for his classic *The Chronicles of Narnia* rather than for his extensive writings on theology and literary criticism. *C. S. Lewis Letters to Children*, a slim volume of almost one hundred carefully selected letters, shows how the creator of the world behind the wardrobe corresponded with children and analyzed their writing. Lewis's generous replies to his youthful fans' letters make it clear that his "students" benefited from an ongoing "correspondence course" run by a genuinely involved master. The letters also reveal Lewis's personality and much about his writing process. He comments on juvenile bouts with chicken pox, literary illustrations, math marks, and most especially poems and stories. He seriously considers the vocabulary and style of young writers. "The content of the poem is good," he assures one faithful correspondent, "but the verse creaks a bit" (p. 81).

The book covers the period from 1944 to Lewis's death in 1963 and will interest parents, teachers, and students who believe in children's writing. Lewis advises on language usage, admits to symbolism in the Narnia series, and muses about reality and fantasy. Taken as a whole, the letters provide a glimpse of a special world in which Oxford Fellows dreamed up imaginary universes for weary mid-twentieth century wayfarers. Readers of all ages will receive special insights into the world of lions and ents, and into other worlds created by Lewis's colleague and friend, J. R. R. Tolkien.

The book includes a brief reminiscence by Douglas Gresham, Lewis's stepson, a biographical sketch, and an essay on his childhood. The editors have also included an annotated bibliography of Lewis's works for children.

Though writer-in-residence programs at the elementary and secondary school level are a relatively recent phenomenon, *Letters to Children* shows that respecting children's writing is not a recent invention. These precise lessons in answering young people guilelessly and credibly stand as a model of the best in writer-student interaction.

JEAN GIBRAN
Teacher, Grade 3
Joseph J. Hurley School, Boston

RECLAIMING THE IMAGINATION: PHILOSOPHICAL PERSPECTIVES FOR WRITERS AND TEACHERS OF WRITING by Ann E. Berthoff. *Upper Montclair, NJ: Boynton/Cook, 1984. 320 pp. $11.50 (paper).*

Reclaiming the Imagination is a collection of articles about knowing, or how we make sense of the world. Ann Berthoff has selected articles from longer pieces written by philosophers, scientists, and artists such as Ernst Cassirer, L. S. Vygotsky, Kenneth Burke, and Rudolph Arnheim. The selections, which Berthoff says enlarged her understanding of the composing process, are not about composing but rather about modes of thinking, knowing, perceiving, and communicating.

Berthoff believes that constant dialogue between theory and practice, between philosophers and teachers, is critical for both groups. Because these pieces elucidate the dialectical nature of thought and language, I believe they will influence teachers.

In my own reading of this book, I found myself returning to Berthoff's earlier book, *The Making of Meaning*, for guidance in establishing more specific links between theory and practice.[1] It is a more accessible entry to her thinking, while *Reclaiming the Imagination* is a book for those who wish to explore the sources of these important ideas about teaching and learning.

ANN PHILLIPS
Teacher, Grades 4 and 5
Runkle Elementary School, Brookline

---

[1] Berthoff, *The Making of Meaning: Metaphors, Models, and Maxims for Writing Teachers* (Upper Montclair, NJ: Boynton/Cook, 1981).

Empty Promises

HARVEY KANTOR

ROBERT LOWE

SCHOOLING AND WORK IN THE DEMOCRATIC STATE
by Martin Carnoy and Henry M. Levin.
Stanford: Stanford University Press, 1985. 307 pp. $32.50.

In 1976 Martin Carnoy and Henry Levin published a collection of essays titled *The Limits of Educational Reform*.[1] The central theme of those essays was the futility of using schools to eliminate poverty or to equalize income and occupational status. Pointing to the persistence of poverty despite the expansion of a universal system of compulsory schooling, Carnoy and Levin argued that the history of school reform provided little support for those who claimed that education would equalize opportunity. Those interested in doing so, they advised, would do far better to focus their attention on the economic system that generates inequality.

Why was education so ineffective an instrument of economic reform? Along with Samuel Bowles and Herbert Gintis, Carnoy and Levin argued that the answer lay in the structural correspondence between the social relations of the school and the social relations of the workplace.[2] The schools, they said, were an integral part of the capitalist system; they mirrored the needs of capitalist production. Schools taught the norms and values of hierarchical work organizations and socialized students differentially according to their class and race, channeling black and working-class students into jobs at the bottom of the occupational hierarchy and white middle- and upper-class students into positions at the top of the occupational hierarchy. Indeed, far from liberalizing opportunity, they concluded, the educational system functioned primarily to reproduce the inequalities inherent in the capitalist system of production.

This analysis usefully challenged many commonly held conceptions about school and work. In particular, it provided a valuable corrective to the widespread liberal belief that schools function independently of the workplace and that educational reform can, by itself, overcome the inequalities of economic life in capitalist society. But the notion that schools function like factories also had a number of shortcomings. As both Marxist and non-Marxist scholars were quick to point out, it underestimated how politics shaped educational structures and overlooked the

[1] Carnoy and Levin, *The Limits of Educational Reform* (New York: McKay, 1976).
[2] Bowles and Gintis, *Schooling in Capitalist America* (New York: Basic Books, 1976).

Harvard Educational Review   Vol. 57   No. 1   February 1987, 68–76

influence of ideology on school processes. Consequently, despite its important contributions, the theory of economic reproduction failed to explain how the demand for labor is translated into specific educational policies or why school outcomes sometimes conflict with the needs of production.[3]

Carnoy and Levin's new book, *Schooling and Work in the Democratic State*, addresses these issues by examining the connection among educational policy, the state, and capitalism. The authors argue that schools reproduce capitalist inequality. But in contrast to their previous work, they dispute both the idea that school structure and practice are determined solely by the relationships of production and that educational reform is unlikely, if not impossible, without prior economic change. They contend that the connection between school and work is also shaped by the democratic values of equal rights and opportunity, and that past struggles for equal education have sometimes effectively countered the economic forces attempting to dominate the schools. The result, they say, is a school system that serves the needs of the economy but is more democratic and equitable than the workplace and other institutions in American society.

The key to this revised analysis lies in Carnoy and Levin's conceptualization of the school as a state institution. Most writing on education and work, they believe, is informed by either pluralist or Marxist theories of the state, though these views are seldom made explicit. Implicit in pluralist theory is the assumption that government and education are intended to serve the public interest. In this perspective, the state has no underlying purpose or connection to production; it is an autonomous institution that exists to reflect the consensual expression of individual wills registered by the electorate through political parties and interest groups.[4]

By contrast, Marxist or class perspective theories of the state begin with the assumption that the state does not represent the common good, but is the political expression of the dominant class and functions to preserve its interests. Precisely how this happens is a matter of considerable debate among Marxist and neo-Marxist scholars. Some argue that the class bias of the state is due to the upper-class origins of its leaders. Others maintain that the state is an instrument of the dominant class because in a capitalist society it must reflect the nature and requirements of the capitalist mode of production. Still a third formulation argues that the state is independent of capital and labor, yet functions to smooth out the process of capital accumulation, since it depends on economic growth for its own survival. All agree, however, that the state functions to reproduce the forces and relations of capitalist production.[5]

Carnoy and Levin are critical of all these formulations, although they are considerably more sympathetic to class perspectives than to pluralist theories. In their view, pluralist theories ignore the connection between political and economic

---

[3] For a review of some of these criticisms, see Madeline Arnot and Geoff Whitty, "From Reproduction to Transformation: Recent Radical Perspectives on the Curriculum from the USA," *British Journal of Sociology of Education*, 3 (1982), 93–103.

[4] See, for example, Robert Dahl, *A Preface to Democratic Theory* (Chicago: University of Chicago Press, 1956).

[5] For a review of recent Marxist theories of the state, see David Gold, C. Lo, and Erik Olin Wright, "Recent Developments in Marxist Theories of the State," *Monthly Review*, 27, 28 (1975), 29–43, 36–51; and Martin Carnoy, *The State and Political Theory* (Princeton: Princeton University Press, 1984).

power and the perpetuation of classes from one generation to the next. Class perspective theories, on the other hand, link economic and political power. They expressly recognize that economically powerful groups have been able to use the state to retain their dominance. But, Carnoy and Levin argue, these theories are overly deterministic, since they focus almost exclusively on the role of the state in the reproduction of capitalism and fail to account adequately for the democratic nature of the liberal state.

Building on these class perspective theories, Carnoy and Levin construct an alternative theory that attempts to incorporate what they label the "democratic dynamic" into an analysis of how economic power relations influence the structure and practice of the state. The state, they say, is more than an instrument of the ruling class: although it attempts to reproduce capitalist economic relations, in doing so it also incorporates subordinate classes. Consequently, state policy is marked by contradiction, since even as the state seeks to serve the interest of the dominant class, it is forced to compromise with dominated groups. In other words, the state, in this view, is an arena of struggle in which capitalists try to reproduce their hegemony, and dominated groups push to expand their rights and opportunities.

This social conflict theory of the democratic capitalist state provides the framework for Carnoy and Levin's analysis of school and work. They argue that because schools are public institutions, they reflect the conflicts that arise from the state's efforts to reproduce capitalist social relations. On the one hand, the schools aim to train workers for the hierarchical structure of capitalist production but, on the other hand, they are pressured by social movements — such as the civil rights and women's movements — for greater equality of access, resources, and curriculum. Schools are not, therefore, independent of the needs of the workplace, but neither do they respond simply to dominant class definitions of what and how much schooling should be provided. Although they train workers for capitalist production, as public institutions serving the state they also generate practices that conflict with the production of efficient workers.

Carnoy and Levin attempt to demonstrate the reproductive dimension of the school-work relationship through an ethnographic study that examines how educational processes in two first-grade classrooms in California (in a lower-middle-class and an upper-middle-class school) differentially socialize students according to their parents' occupational roles. In the lower-middle class school the teacher tended to encourage the development of traits required for jobs at the bottom of the occupational ladder. The chief method of classroom control was external (the teacher directed activities by commanding students to obey rules); opportunities for verbal self-expression ("show-and-tell") were infrequent; and greater stress was placed on completing assignments than on the quality of the work done. By contrast, student-teacher interactions in the upper-middle-class school were characterized by the qualities necessary to obtain managerial and professional positions. The dominant form of control was internal (teachers encouraged students to "use good judgment" and to "be your own teacher"); every day began with at least ten minutes of show-and-tell; and the teacher emphasized that cognitive work mattered (by tutoring individual students and requiring that sloppy work be redone). In this way, Carnoy and Levin conclude, the schools function to reproduce the unequal relations of production and the division of labor in capitalist society.

The reproductive process, however, is only one part of the story. More important, Carnoy and Levin maintain, are three types of contradictions that are associated with the democratic nature of schooling and that generate outcomes at odds with the needs of the workplace. One type of contradiction results in struggles over school spending. Since schooling is public, they argue, the state is subject to pressure from working-class and minority groups for increased school spending. But such demands frequently conflict with the state's capacity to enhance capital accumulation, resulting in conflict between capital and labor over state spending on education.

The second type of contradiction creates an overexpansion of education relative to the availability of suitable jobs in the labor market. Carnoy and Levin point out that possession of educational credentials has become increasingly necessary for access to good jobs. Together with traditional notions of democracy in education, this has made schooling appear to many to be the chief route to social mobility. Yet this has also produced an expansion of enrollments beyond the economy's need for educated labor. The result is thought to be underutilization of educated labor, which, they say, produces unhappy, frustrated workers who behave in ways contrary to the requirements of efficient production.

The final type of contradiction arises out of the correspondence process itself. As schools have come to correspond structurally to the workplace, Carnoy and Levin contend, they have also incorporated many of the conflicts associated with work. Just as workers are alienated from their jobs because they are excluded from decision making, students are alienated from schools dominated by teacher-centered instruction. So, too, class and racial resistance occurs at school, as it does at work. Some students openly defy school norms and standards; others consider success in school a betrayal of their peers; and still others simply drop out in the classroom, resisting passively by not listening, withholding their enthusiasm, and not completing assignments.

Carnoy and Levin conclude that these conflicts will eventually generate efforts to reform both the workplace and the school. At the workplace, they say, managers will attempt to reduce worker dissatisfaction and raise productivity by redesigning work and increasing worker participation. Initially, these efforts will consist of reforms such as job rotation, flexible scheduling, and incentive pay plans that seek to increase worker satisfaction without relinquishing managerial control of the labor process. But the frustrations of overeducated and unfulfilled workers, they predict, will also push management to institute more fundamental changes —including cooperative work groups and worker councils—that give workers greater say in such matters as production schedules, work assignments, and work methods, without jeopardizing managerial control of products, prices, and marketing.

Whatever happens at the workplace, however, work reform by itself will not be enough to assimilate dissatisfied workers. As in the past, Carnoy and Levin argue, school reforms will also be necessary. The precise nature of these reforms, they say, will depend on political circumstances. Given the current emphasis on the social reproductive dimensions of schooling, successful reforms will likely be those that correspond to workplace reforms. In their view, reforms that inadequately address the sources of worker discontent and alienation, such as career education and "back-to-basics" programs, are likely to fail. Those reforms oriented to cooperative, participative work relationships will rise in importance. These include programs such as group decision making and peer training which, Carnoy and Levin say, will impart the skills and habits required by the team approach to production that will become necessary to satisfy disgruntled workers.

Several aspects of this analysis are noteworthy. In contrast to their earlier argument that the organization of the workplace chiefly determines the structure and practice of schooling, Carnoy and Levin now recognize that schools are shaped by political and ideological forces as well as economic ones. Indeed, what makes their analysis significant is not just that it acknowledges noneconomic forces; by focusing on the state, it also helps to explain why the economy does not strictly determine educational practice, and to indicate under what circumstances noneconomic forces may be influential.

Just as important, by considering the school within the larger social conflicts that exist within liberal capitalist society, Carnoy and Levin counter recent trends in educational research. During the last decade, there has been considerable interest among both Marxist and non-Marxist scholars in how teachers and students behave in classrooms.[6] This has produced several detailed studies of classroom life, some of which show that students and teachers do not conform mindlessly to school norms and procedures. But these studies have also tended to isolate the classroom from the political demands and economic constraints of the wider society.[7] By contrast, Carnoy and Levin usefully remind us that an analysis of educational policy, the state, and capitalism is indispensable for understanding the conditions under which teachers and students work.

Unfortunately, Carnoy and Levin's analysis also exhibits difficulties that seriously weaken their argument. One of the most troubling is their treatment of class, race, and state policy in education. For the most part, they simply lump blacks, workers, and other oppressed groups who seek equality in education into a broad social movement that opposes those interested in using education to reproduce the conditions of the workplace. But this analysis obscures the quite different educational demands that these groups have made on the state. Indeed, largely because of their historically different relationship to the state, white workers and blacks have been on opposite sides of educational conflicts instead of uniting to pressure the state for more democratic schooling.

Ira Katznelson and Margaret Weir make this particularly clear in their book *Schooling for All.*[8] Because working-class people in the United States were granted access to schooling (along with the franchise) without prolonged political struggle, working-class educational politics by and large have been issue-specific. Consequently, ever since the mid-nineteenth century, working-class educational demands have been relatively easy to satisfy within the educational system. By

---

[6] For examples in the Marxist tradition, see Michael Apple and Lois Weiss, eds., *Ideology and Practice in Schooling* (Philadelphia: Temple University Press, 1983). On non-Marxist research on teachers and classrooms, see Merlin C. Wittrock, ed., *Handbook of Research on Teaching*, 3rd ed. (New York: Macmillan, 1986), esp. Secs. 2, 3.

[7] On this point, see Arnot and Whitty, "From Reproduction to Transformation," p. 102; and Andy Hargreaves, "Resistance and Relative Autonomy Theories: Problems of Distortion and Incoherence in Recent Marxist Analyses of Education," *British Journal of Sociology of Education*, 3 (1982), 107–126.

[8] Katznelson and Weir, *Schooling for All: Class, Race, and the Decline of the Democratic Ideal* (New York: Basic Books, 1985), chap. 7.

contrast, because of their historical exclusion from educational services and policy-making, educational demands of blacks have gone beyond specific issues to evoke fundamental questions of citizenship that have been difficult to accommodate within existing institutional structures. One result is that black protest has been threatening both to school officials who wished to maintain traditional patterns of educational decisionmaking and to relatively advantaged working-class whites. A more accurate historical survey of the relationship between blacks and whites with respect to educational concerns would document the way white schools often prospered as a result of the systematic impoverishment of black ones.[9]

Carnoy and Levin, however, are sensitive to the ways different groups in recent years have viewed the politics of state spending on education. Although the authors focus on the class dimensions of conflict over school spending, they also point out that in the last decade pressure to reduce school expenditures has come not just from businessmen interested in using the state to enhance capital accumulation. Rather, they indicate that some businessmen today favor higher educational expenditures because they desire a better trained work force, while certain segments of the working class (particularly unionized workers in the private sectors) resist increases in educational spending because they oppose paying higher taxes. Even in this instance, however, the authors do not explicitly acknowledge that this situation pits segments of the white working class against blacks and women, who have benefited most from the expansion of employment opportunities in the public sector. Although they point to the impact of spending reductions on state employment, they generally attribute tax resistance to "middle-class voters," thereby minimizing genuine conflicts of interest that divide white working-class males, blacks, and women.

A good part of the difficulty in specifying the relations between social groupings stems from the authors' failure to sustain their analysis with any concrete consideration of the development and implementation of educational policy. They say repeatedly that the connection between school and work reflects the balance of power between those interested in using school to reproduce the conditions of the workplace and those interested in greater equality. They seldom specify, however, how educational policy is shaped by the interplay of educational interest groups or the political power of social movements. Consequently, they generally fail to account for distinctions that have differentiated groups from one another in the struggle for more democratic schooling.

The problem with this analysis is not only that the authors overlook how groups differently situated in the social structure have viewed the formation of educational policy. Equally troubling is their failure to consider sufficiently how the state shapes and is shaped by the power of social movements. For all intents and purposes, they treat the state as an open space in which oppressed groups struggle more or less successfully for rights and opportunities. Yet this is hardly an adequate conception of how the state responds to social demands. Although Carnoy and Levin are certainly correct in asserting that the state is not just an instrument

[9] See, for example, Horace Mann Bond, *Negro Education in Alabama: A Study in Cotton and Steel* (New York: Atheneum, 1969; originally published, 1939); and Louis R. Harlan, *Separate and Unequal, Public School Campaigns and Racism in the Southern Seaboard States, 1901-1915* (New York: Atheneum, 1969).

of the ruling class, neither is it simply an arena for struggle. As Frances Fox Piven and Richard Cloward have pointed out, the state also helps to structure social conflict by making efforts to define the content of proposed reforms in ways that minimally disrupt existing institutional arrangements.[10]

Perhaps nowhere was this more evident than in the federal government's response to demands for equal educational opportunity in the 1960s and early 1970s. During these years, U.S. leaders responded to pressure from social movements by enacting an unprecedented series of laws and programs designed to increase access and expand opportunities for those previously neglected by the educational system. But they also defined these new programs in ways that were consistent with established institutional procedures. Thus, even though programs such as the Elementary and Secondary Education Act of 1965 provided badly needed funding for some urban schools and produced some measurable gains in educational attainment for disadvantaged students, they did not require major changes in the organization and practice of schooling. Rather, the new initiatives by and large sought to increase access while maintaining a competitive, class-stratified school system, thereby accommodating demands for greater equality in education without altering the fundamental principles on which the schools are based.[11]

Increased access was no small victory, of course, particularly for black Americans. Moreover, as Carnoy and Levin point out, in today's political climate, even those gains are in jeopardy and must be defended. Nevertheless, the political history of educational reform in the 1960s presents a more ambivalent and contradictory picture of state-sponsored reform than the authors' social conflict theory of the state admits. If it is not inevitable that the state will attempt to co-opt discontent mainly by extending already established procedures to new groups, this possibility certainly deserves more consideration than the single paragraph Carnoy and Levin devote to it.

An appropriate analysis requires more careful scrutiny not only of the political context that shapes the formation and implementation of educational policy but also of the effects that the decentralized nature of school governance has on popular political activity. Nowhere, for example, do Carnoy and Levin consider how the local character of educational decisionmaking influences the pattern of popular politics. Yet the structure and tradition of local control has had a large impact on social movements, for it tends to focus discontent about the nature of work and inequality on educational rather than economic issues. Even in the 1960s, when popular protest raised fundamental questions about the nature of opportunity in U.S. society, the structural arrangements of school governance helped to direct discontent into educational channels and away from economic reform.[12]

The redirecting of discontent by the school system hardly means that educational politics will be free of conflict. On the contrary, largely because schools are locally controlled and thereby appear to be more accessible to popular influence

---

[10] Piven and Cloward, *Poor People's Movements* (New York: Pantheon Books, 1977), chap. 1.

[11] See, for example, Ann Bastian, Norm Fruchter, Marilyn Gittell, Colin Greer, and Kenneth Haskins, "Choosing Equality: The Case for Democratic Schooling," *Social Policy, 15* (1985), 34–51.

[12] On this point, see Frances Fox Piven and Richard A. Cloward, "Social Policy and the Formation of Political Consciousness," in *Political Power and Social Theory*, Vol. 1, ed. Maurice Zeitlin. (Greenwich, CT: JAI Press, 1980), pp. 117–152.

than large corporations and other institutions in American society, educational politics will frequently be highly contentious. But since local government has little control over those institutions in which economic decisions are made, those conflicts are unlikely to have more than a marginal impact on the crucial decisions that shape the relationship between education and the workplace.

Although Carnoy and Levin correctly argue that school processes sometimes conflict with the needs of production, the existence of conflict between school and work hardly guarantees by itself the democratic outcomes they anticipate. They are surely right, for instance, when they say that the overexpansion of education relative to the demand for educated labor produces frustration at the workplace. But making education and work more cooperative activities, as they predict will happen, is only one possible response to worker dissatisfaction.[13] Given the current balance of political and ideological forces, it seems that the crisis of overeducation will generate efforts to tighten the link between school and work by intensifying the competitive nature of schooling as much as by implementing reforms aimed at making the school a more egalitarian institution. In fact, many current reforms, such as the imposition of higher standards for high school graduation, point in this direction.

So, too, it is difficult to dispute that many minority and working-class youth feel alienated from school and contest the ideological messages conveyed in the classroom. Yet this by no means prevents schools from reproducing the inequitable relations of capitalist production. On the contrary, the studies of resistance that Carnoy and Levin cite, such as Paul Willis's study of working-class boys in an English comprehensive school, suggest that the disdain working-class youth feel for education actually reinforces the school's reproductive function since it hardens into a rejection of all forms of mental labor.[14] In Willis's study, the "lads" defy the school only to trap themselves in menial jobs. Thus, the school ultimately succeeds in channeling them into class-determined positions, though Carnoy and Levin fail to acknowledge this outcome.

Indeed, contrary to the authors' assertion that the reproductive function of schooling violates the democratic values schools are entrusted to teach, the hierarchical relations of school have in most instances proven to be quite compatible with its role in preparing students for life in a liberal capitalist democracy. For instance, Carnoy and Levin imagine that the school curriculum presents students with "a version of their history which stresses the fight against injustice" (p. 149). Jean Anyon, among others, however, has uncovered persuasive evidence to the contrary. In her examination of widely used history texts, she shows clearly that

[13] Nor will such measures, if implemented, necessarily produce radical change. Without a corresponding shift in power relations, they might just as plausibly be seen as an attempt to adjust workers to the changing relations of capitalist production as an effort to alter them. Indeed, the history of twentieth-century labor relations suggests that the former is more likely. See, for example, David Brody, *Workers in Industrial America: Essays on the Twentieth Century Struggle* (New York: Oxford University Press, 1980), chap. 2; Stuart Brandes, *American Welfare Capitalism, 1880–1940* (Chicago: University of Chicago Press, 1976); and Loren Baritz, *The Servants of Power: A History of the Use of Social Sciences in American Industry* (Middletown, CT: Wesleyan University Press, 1960).

[14] Willis, *Learning to Labor: How Working Class Kids Get Working Class Jobs* (Farnborough, Eng.: Saxon House, 1977); also see Jean Anyon, "Social Class and School Knowledge," *Curriculum Inquiry*, *11* (1981), 3–42.

such books reflect the interests of dominant groups. Far from liberating students to participate in the struggle for a more democratic society, she concludes that "textbook history illustrates one way of imposing beliefs and constraining choice."[15]

Carnoy and Levin also point to student rights as evidence that the school's commitment to democracy conflicts with its reproductive function. But student rights in schools are no more subversive of hierarchy than are textbooks. Not only does reliance on teachers for grades impede freedom of expression, but teachers and administrators freely define the boundaries of appropriate comment by students and punish transgressors with suspensions or expulsions. Students do not participate in hiring and firing teachers; they can rarely choose which instructors will teach them; and they have little say in what and how instructors teach, or in how instructors will evaluate them.

Of course, savvy parents can occasionally manipulate school policies and procedures in ways that work to the advantage of individual students. And powerful social movements, like the black struggle in the 1960s, can for a time make schools more responsive to those who have been denied equal opportunity. Generally, though, public education is *for* the public rather than *by* it. At bottom, schools train the young for life in a society whose democratic values harmonize with social and economic inequality. Equal opportunity, not economic democracy, stands at the core of the democratic ideology in the United States.

While schools are not impervious to change, the foregoing discussion raises serious doubts about the contradictions in education that Carnoy and Levin perceive. Their sanguine notion that contradiction is likely to produce democratic schools that overcome class and racial divisions relies on faith rather than hard analysis. Although the authors contend that study of the past informs their optimism, their inquiry never goes beyond vague formulations about the relationship between social struggle and educational change. By leaving this fundamental relationship unclear, the authors create a misleading sense that greater democracy requires neither programs nor actors.

Carnoy and Levin certainly have developed a potentially useful framework for understanding how schools operate in a society that is both capitalist and democratic, but in the absence of serious dialogue between theory and history, such a framework remains suppositional. The reader is simply left with a promise of more democratic schools and a more democratic economy. Ironically, the book ends with a faith in progressive change that strikingly resembles the perspective of mainstream educational scholars that Carnoy and Levin have criticized so effectively in the past.

---

[15] Anyon, "Ideology and U.S. History Textbooks," *Harvard Educational Review,* 49 (1979), 383. On history texts, also see Frances Fitzgerald, *America Revised: History Schoolbooks in the Twentieth Century* (New York: Vintage Books, 1980); and on the conservative persuasion of nineteenth-century schoolbooks, see Ruth Miller Elson, *Guardians of Tradition: American Schoolbooks of the Nineteenth Century* (Lincoln: University of Nebraska Press, 1964).

The authors wish to thank Nicholas Burbules for his comments on an earlier draft of this article.

The Voices of Communities
and Language in Classrooms

HAROLD ROSEN

WAYS WITH WORDS
by Shirley Brice Heath.
Cambridge: Cambridge University Press, 1983. 448 pp. $49.50, $17.50 (paper).

The reputation of Shirley Brice Heath's book will have marched triumphantly ahead of this review, not, I hasten to add, because of a voguish novelty in its content, not because it is ethnography-on-the-doorstep, but rather because it represents a unique blend of cultural-linguistic analysis with a resolute intention to intervene positively in the world she describes. We have not been short of analyses in the human sciences which purport to offer, and on occasion actually provide, illumination to teachers. Heath's huge endeavor to present the texture and meaning of the daily goings-on and of the talk, as we say, of "ordinary folk" is complemented by a readiness, notoriously rare, to work alongside teachers in the construction of programs and practices. These are then informed by an awareness of the language and culture she has come to know as "ethnographer learning." For all her expertise she stays a learner, offering the teachers and students ways of understanding but also learning from them.

Trackton and Roadville are the two small communities at the heart of Heath's study. They are, you might say, exotic little places as remote—culturally speaking—from the lives of most contemporary city dwellers or farming communities as the Trobriand Islands described by Bronislaw Malinowski.[1] Why, then, should we follow with the closest attention the inhabitants' daily doings on porches or in the plaza, and eavesdrop on their chatter? We must admit that we often have a voyeuristic taste for scenes from the lives of those who in space, time, or culture seem distantly bizarre. There are academic studies which pander, wittingly or unwittingly, to these desires in peeping-Tom mainstreamers. Heath's book, however, is never in danger of being one. Heath proposes that (a) there are more Roadvilles and Tracktons than we recognise and know about, even if they are a stone's throw away, and (b) that schools which address themselves to formulating a culture-sensitive curriculum must be, in a sense, ethnographic centers. Her

[1] Malinowski, *Coral Gardens and Their Magic*, Vol. 2 (London: Allen & Unwin, 1935).

book, then, is no travelogue for the fireside but a sharp challenge to everyone concerned with schooling, teachers in particular.

Heath is a rare figure, an academic who does not see her role as a chastener
of the ignorant. We do not have to hear yet again how teachers have got it all
wrong, are victims of their cultural prejudices, and are irredeemably class-bound,
linguistically naive, and politically impotent. She operates amongst them as a colleague who shares their dilemmas and strategies. It can be put very simply: she
is not seeking the accolades of the academy but intends, when her ethnography
is put to work, to help students to learn.

Back then to Roadville and Trackton in the Piedmont Carolinas. We might
have called these two tiny collections of houses industrial villages. Almost — for
they lack the communal amenities we associate with the term "village," except for
churches, which are shown to play a major role in the people's lives. Trackton is
black and Roadville is white. They are both dependencies of the textile mill, the
major source of employment for these working-class people. They are both off the
beaten track and some way from Gateway, a small town which Heath sees as the
embodiment of mainstream values. Until she takes us fully into their lives, the
people and their towns seem fragile, marginalized in a society which has passed
them by. Vulnerable encampments, microghettos. It is here — in these towns and
in Gateway — that Heath installs herself with the solid advantage that she grew up
in Piedmont and has personal acquaintances in both Roadville and Trackton. *And
she pursues her work for ten years:* watching infants grow up and enter school and get
jobs; witnessing marriages, departures, deaths. Ten years, I say again, from 1969
to 1978.

In an uncompromising prologue, Heath lays out the context and theoretical
starting-points of her study. The context was the concern felt by "black and white
teachers, parents, and mill personnel," about communication, the "effects of the
preschool home and community environment on the learning of those language
structures and uses which were needed in classrooms and job settings" (p. 2). At
this point, let me pause to say that the citation of the "concern" felt by certain significant people does not make clear whether Heath subscribed to that view or is
merely tendering it for the record. I had the same difficulty at certain critical
points in the text. The concern of millowners baffles me, too, for right down at
the end of the book we are told that the mill offers "almost no opportunities to
write, few chances to read, and almost no occasions when their uses of oral language are critical for success" (p. 365).

Heath sets out, nevertheless, to satisfy a "need for a full description of the primary face-to-face interactions of children from community cultures other than
[the] mainstream one" (p. 3) which would meet the above concerns and in the end
"help working-class black and white children learn more effectively" (p. 4). At this
stage in the text certain terms begin to glow provocatively. I take it that here
"working class" is being contrasted with "mainstream." What then does "mainstream" imply? Middle class? There is the suggestion here of a norm. Sure
enough, tucked away in the notes to a later chapter is an attempt to face up to
the difficulty (p. 391, n. 2), but it raises more questions than it answers: What
are the *fundamental* determinants of class? How do the practices of everyday life relate to them? Who are the "middle class" and to what extent is it a homogeneous

stratum? Yet her allegiance is clear and explains how it was that she became, through her collaboration with teachers, an "associate, colleague, aide, and some-time-coauthor of curricular materials" (p. 4).

The aspirations are familiar enough—more effective learning by students through deeper understanding of the culture by teachers—yet we know these aspirations have been repeatedly challenged; mainstream school culture has been criticized as promoting shoddy or even pernicious values; it has been contended that schools are class institutions which internally regulate their diet for different clients; it has been said that mainstream culture does not exist, for there is no such homogeneous thing in our society, and so on. The relationship between schools and jobs is never a simple one, and the proposition that certification and high test scores will lead into the Promised Land is a plain and painful delusion. I think Heath knows all this and is content at the outset to pretend a certain innocence. The key lies in her tart and brief rejection of certain bleak, radical views at the very end of the book:

> It is easy to claim that a radical restructuring of society or the system of education is needed for the kind of cultural bridging reported in this book to be large scale and continuous. I have chosen to focus on the information and bridging skills needed for teachers and students as individuals to make changes which were for them radical, and to point to ways these cultural brokers between communities and classrooms can perhaps be the beginning of larger changes. (p. 369)

Heath is no political innocent: she has read her Bowles and Gintis (see p. 369, n. 5), and much more besides; and she may be reassured, because at a period of intense attack from the Right on the best hopes of schools, teachers, and students (recorded in a moving section of the epilogue), it no longer looks so radical to join in the attack.[2]

Moreover, Heath makes clear that she has rejected totally the well-known scientific model of "experiments" and research design. Instead she offers a record of "the natural flow of community and classroom life over nearly a decade. . . . actual processes, activities, and attitudes involved in the enculturation of children in Roadville and Trackton" (p. 8). It should be noted that Gateway gets nothing like the "thick description" which is lovingly devoted to Trackton and Roadville (the ratio is approximately seven to one, the townspeople getting one chapter of twenty-six pages). Perhaps the assumption is that her most likely readers all swim in the mainstream one way or another, or have at least gazed at it long enough from the bank, but it does raise some problems. More of that later. For the moment let us emphasize that she is content to let her case rest in the hands of her readers, who must be the judges of how scientific her work is. This reviewer-reader's assessment is that, if anything, she might have probed further, in her own chosen manner, certain aspects of the lives of the communities which for me remain shrouded in mystery. But before pursuing that, I have to say without equivocation that I applaud her stance. Whether the research watchdogs bark or not, I cannot imagine anyone honestly concerned with the complex interpretation of

---

[2] See, for example, Henry Giroux's *Theory and Resistance in Education* (Portsmouth, NH: Heinemann, 1983).

community, language, and schooling who would not choose to become caught up in the fates of the infants, young people, and old folk who are brought to life with deep but unsentimental respect in her text. No research training of any type could by itself produce her eye and her voice. These must emerge from values which we are left to deduce less from explicit intellectual propositions than from our perceptions of her conduct. I defy any reader to exorcise Heath from her account, to distinguish the dancer from the dance. The result is not an egocentric display but a subtle refusal to disappear behind the foliage of research lingo. She openly acknowledges a role, openly intervenes, and finally goes for total immersion in a bold collaboration with teachers and students. The "neutral observer" becomes a sorry figure in comparison. Listen to the infants of Trackton talking to Heath about some wooden blocks she had brought for them to play with and we get a glimpse of how involved they are with her: " 'Dese Shannon's blocks?' 'You buy dese?' 'Can I keep dese?' 'What you do wid 'em?' 'How'd dat git dere/*pointing to the glue/?*' " (p. 107).

One more insistence: the book represents an unwavering case for looking at the social and cultural context in a particular kind of way rather than constructing an edifice of discrete data ("input," as she says witheringly). We know about context these days. A lot of people vote for it. We know too the acrimonious battles fought in the field of linguistics (compare Halliday to Chomsky).[3] It seems almost strange that Heath should have to underline its importance. However, her warm acknowledgement of Dell Hymes as her teacher should remind us that, as he has so persuasively argued, only a profound awareness of who and what our students are and the accommodation of that awareness in the ways schools conduct themselves can take us forward.[4] But there are those who bitterly dispute this idea. Here in Britain there are those who argue that it is none of our business. Schools must deliver the national culture, whatever that is, to students, whoever they are. For Heath, culture includes history. Obvious again? Not at all. There are sociological studies, including sociolinguistic studies, which assume that the working class has no history, that it is no more than "the murmur of societies," "a multitude of qualified heroes who lose their names and faces while becoming the mobile language

---

[3] See M. A. K. Halliday, *Language as Social Semiotic* (London: Edward Arnold, 1978); and Noam Chomsky, *Language and Reponsibility* (Sussex: Harvester Press, 1979).

[4] For a rich elaboration of Dell Hymes's ideas, see Hymes, *Language in Education: Ethnolinguistic Essays* (Washington, DC: Center for Applied Linguistics, 1980); and Hymes, *Ethnolinguistic Study of Classroom Discourse*, Final Report to the National Institute of Education (ERIC, 1982. ED 217–710). The thesis he elaborates is summed up in the latter document:

> Educational linguistics requires a theoretical groundwork of its own. What is now called "theoretical linguistics" leaves out of account too much of what educational linguistics must consider. The teacher interpreting the verbal behavior of children must take into account intonation, classroom context, personal histories, community background. The teacher must always take into account abilities, means, and intentions that can be operating in the context in question. This set is likely to be less than the formally imaginable ideal set of the language as a whole, on the one hand, and is likely to include possibilities not taken into account by the formal models. (p. 22)

Hymes also provides an example very relevant to Heath's approach: "Narrative behavior, the telling of stories in class that seem disorderly to us because of our own assumptions about narrative order, may actually express an order of its own, coming from another set of cultural understandings as to what it is to report experience, tell a story, make a speech, and the like" (p. 23).

of calculations and rationalities."[5] Teachers, schools, curricula have histories too. Heath is as good as her word. Her book begins with a history of workers in the mills of Piedmont. Yet this readiness to inscribe history into ethnography creates its own vulnerability.

Rich and intimate as it is, Heath's description cannot be total; telling how it is means telling how it seems through a prism which foregrounds the significant and does not register what seems insignificant. Consider this: "Any reader who tries to explain the community contrast in this book on the basis of race will miss the central point of the focus of culture as learned behavior and on language habits as part of that shared learning. Children in Roadville and Trackton came to have different ways of communicating, because their communities had different social legacies" (p. 11).

I was distressed by this evasion, especially as it runs counter to some of the deepest *implicit* awarenesses of the book. A second reading (my first was almost uncritically rapturous) revealed a persistent refusal to confront the issue of race. I do not trust Heath's apparent naivete; at best it is an astute calculation of political possibilities. Throughout the text we are made aware that Roadville is white and Trackton is black. Why bother? Yes, indeed, communities have different social legacies. A major component of this legacy must be the experience of racism and *its continued existence.* Why has Heath chosen to warn us off? Black English is the expression and negotiation of black experience. Racism does no more than lurk in the shadows of this text, raising questions which are not posed by Heath. The historical chapter firmly announces, "The Civil Rights Movement forced the breaking of the color barrier on hiring, and blacks began to assume production line jobs in the mills" (p. 27). In the rest of the book there is scarcely a whiff of the continuation of that struggle. Are Trackton people so "lumpen" that none of their "ways with words" are affected? One way of cleansing the book of such awkward considerations is to avoid (a) analyzing talk in black and white encounters and (b) probing further the implications of what momentarily pops up in the text. From the description of Gateway, homogeneously "mainstream," there peeps out the existence of black suburbs. Suddenly we hear someone in Roadville declaring, "When the niggers (pause) uh, the blacks, you know, started comin' in, I knew that wasn't for me. I wasn't ever gonna work for no nigger" (p. 39). These almost subliminal moments make one aware of a kind of self-denying ordinance or self-censorship operating in the ethnography.

By the same token, Heath's history tells how "workers began to show signs of an independent and unbiddable spirit when strikes claimed the lives of some of their leaders" (p. 25). Does nothing of that remain in either Roadville or Trackton? Apparently not. In speaking of Trackton, Heath writes that "they do not themselves take part in any aspect of the political process . . ." (p. 62). Of white Roadville no such comment is made, though it seems to apply equally. For them "the sun shines on the chimneys of the mill" (p. 47). On the job in both Roadville and Trackton, "workers look for no reasons for the task, nor do they give their opinion of the role of their task in the whole. . . . The topics of their talk rarely

---

[5] See Michel De Certeau, "On the Oppositional Practices of Everyday Life," *Social Text, 1* (1980), 3–43.

include their work" (p. 365). I find it odd, but it is perhaps true. Are they union-ized or not? Do they never talk about their working conditions and attempt to change them? Is it all harmony, or resignation? Do blacks and whites occupy the same kinds of posts, and is this never a theme of anyone's conversation? What is the significance of the fact that "most households [in Trackton] have a double por-trait of Coretta and Martin Luther King" (p. 55)?

Gateway's townspeople, we are told, are mainstreamers divided into two groups — "old-timers" and "newcomers." From thousands of miles away I remain skeptical. I cannot believe they are all economically and professionally successful, that there are no sharp divisions and clashes based on ethnicity and class. Nor can I envisage a town of 50,000 inhabitants without its "lower orders" — garage me-chanics, truck drivers, workers in small enterprises, street cleaners, hospital em-ployees, school ancillary staff, minor government employees, and so forth.

I have a feeling that there is a calculated strategy behind this, for, as I have indi-cated, Heath is highly conscious of these matters and how they have been debated. Yet she treads very warily round them. The reason eludes me. The book is far, far richer ethnographically than, for example, Paul Willis's *Learning to Labour,*[6] but far weaker politically. However, nothing I have said would lead anyone to be in doubt about the unique qualities of this book. Indeed, I suspect that it is con-structed in order to provoke my kind of response.

Let us now see how Heath imposed order on what must have been one of the most daunting piles of accumulated material ever to have confronted a researcher at the moment of writing-up. Part 1 begins by taking us into the two communities, sampling their day-to-day living and their notions of "getting-on." Armed with this awareness, we are led into a presentation of "learning how to talk" in Trackton and "teaching how to talk" in Roadville, which simultaneously compares early lan-guage development in the two communities and enlarges our view of how life is conducted. It is a credit to Heath that there is no way of summarizing the density of her descriptions. All is alive and enacted. But at carefully selected moments a very legible signpost appears. In black Trackton, for example, "babies are in the midst of nearly constant human communication. . . . which flows about them" (pp. 74, 75). In white Roadville: "At both individual and group levels, the belief in and practice of using 'the right word' help structure the cognitive patterns which children draw of the world, i.e. what they come to know, and their notion of how to show what they know. Rigidly prescribed oral performance . . . is the way to prove learning" (p. 144).

Yet it is the voices, scenes, and episodes which command our attention and stir our thinking. In what for me is the most memorable transcript in the book, Annie Mae of Trackton, "the community cultural broker," delivers her sociolinguistic analysis and language development curriculum:

> He gotta learn to *know* 'bout dis world, can't nobody tell 'im. Now just how crazy is dat? White folks uh hear dey kids say sump'n, dey say it back to 'em, dey aks 'em 'gain 'n 'gain 'bout things, like dey 'posed to be born knowin'. You think I kin tell Teegie all he gotta know to get along? He just gotta be keen, keep his eyes open, don't he be sorry. Gotta watch hisself by watchin' other folks. Ain't no use

[6] Willis, *Learning to Labour* (Westmead, Eng.: Saxon House, 1977).

me tellin' 'im: 'Learn dis, learn dat. What's dis? What's dat?' He just gotta learn, gotta know; he see one thing one place one time, he know how it go, see sump'n like it again, maybe it be de same, maybe it won't. He hafta try it out. If he don't he be in real trouble; he get lef' out. Gotta keep yo' eyes open, gotta feel to know. (p. 84)

Whatcha *call* it ain't so important as whatcha *do* with it. That's what things 'n people are for, ain't it? (p. 112)

I can see myself and others interpreting that text, knowing that in the process I am telling Annie Mae what she means, and in the stiff cadences, our stock-in-trade, losing its nuances and fervor.

Compare the do-it-yourself Headstart program of white Roadville as Peggy sees it.

I figure it's up to me to give 'im a good start. I reckon there's just some things I know he's gotta learn, you know, what things are, and all that. 'n you just don't happen onto doin' all that right. Now, you take Danny 'n Bobby, we, Betty 'n me, we talk to them kids all the time, like they was grown-up or something, 'n we try to tell 'em bout things, 'n books, 'n we buy those educational toys for 'em. (pp. 127–128)

Always, Heath by her uncanny ear makes her choices jump from the page at you, and the invitation is to understand before we rush to deliver verdicts or pigeonhole complex utterances in neatly polarized concepts (restricted/elaborated; universalistic/particularistic).

The story continues. We move on to consider oral traditions in Roadville and Trackton and then literate traditions. I shall single out one central aspect of oral traditions — narrative — and let it stand as a paradigm for all that is best in this book. Since I hold that narrative is a touchstone of oral tradition, I believe that Heath's account should become a point of reference for all discussion of spontaneous oral story telling.[7] Moreover, Heath's work on literacy in the community was being cited widely before the appearance of this book.[8]

In Roadville there are criteria for story telling which establish a clear framework, firmly excluding some possibilities and making very clear the principles of inclusion. Stories must be accounts of actual events, free from hyperbole, "an expression of social unity, a commitment to maintenance of the norms of the church and of the roles within the mill community's life" (p. 150). Above all, they require a moral or summary message. The induction of children into story telling constitutes a dramatic apprenticeship to this tradition: "Children in Roadville are not allowed to tell stories, unless an adult announces that something which happened to a child makes a good story and invites a retelling. When children are asked to retell such events, they are expected to tell non-fictive stories which 'stick to the truth' " (p. 158).

Fictive stories are lies. Roadville stories are moral episodes, and the monitoring of their narrations ensures that the model is thoroughly learned.

---

[7] See Rosen, *Stories and Meanings* (Sheffield, Eng.: National Association for the Teaching of English, 1984).

[8] See, for example, "Protean Shapes in Literacy Events," in *Spoken and Written Language: Exploring Orality and Literacy*, ed. Deborah Tannen (Norwood, NJ: Ablex, 1982).

Sue: Why did you drop your eggs? What did Aunt Sue tell you 'bout climbing on
  that thing?

Wendy: We better be careful.

Sue: No, 'bout eggs 'n climbing?

Wendy: We better not climb with our eggs, else 'n we'd drop 'em. (p. 158)

To turn to Trackton's stories is to enter another narrative universe. In Trackton,
"Good story-tellers . . . may base their stories on an actual event, but they creatively fictionalize the details surrounding the real event, and the outcome of the
story may not even resemble what indeed happened" (p. 166).

Stories do not contain didactic highlighting to guide or control moral conduct.
The stories must be dramatic, and therefore storytellers frequently resort to dialogue, which in itself opens up a source of mimicry, humor, narrative point. The
free expression of feeling generates word-play and word-artistry which Heath is
quick to pounce on (see twelve-year-old Terry's tale on p. 181 in which fantasy
and reality are inextricably intertwined). She sums up her detailed examination
and comparison with a bold contrast: "In short, for Roadville, Trackton's stories
would be lies; for Trackton, Roadville's stories would not even count as stories"
(p. 189). All this is laid out beautifully and delicately for us: the participants, the
settings, the microdramas of the tellings and their subtexts. To all this are added
some very detailed inspections of the storyteller's art in both communities,
rounded off with a more general and distanced view. However, to demur a little
again, there is no attempt to tell us *why* such divergent cultural practices have
arisen, nor to see their roots in the social and economic experience of the narrator.
Black and white again?

Part 2 is the knight's move, for it contains an account of the collaboration between the author and the schools, a maneuver of high risk not only in its execution
but even more in its being recorded here in cold print. The project, as I have indicated, is "to make accessible to teachers an understanding of the differences in language and culture their students bring to their classrooms" (p. 265), and then to
engage in the development of programs and practices in the light of that understanding. The goal is success in school for everyone. Heath recounts in detail the
endeavors of the teachers. It would be easy to dismiss much of what the teachers
do as familiar curriculum practice—familiar, that is, to anyone conversant with
the curriculum reforms of the last twenty years—for example, what came to be
regarded as "good practice" before the current fierce dismantling process got under
way. Mrs. Gardner, having been allocated a class of nineteen black first-grade students designated potential failures, opens up her classroom and engages in her
now-despised "activity methods." Her children tell stories and there is lots of talk.
That old standby, the grocery store, is set up in another class. In a fifth-grade science class, consisting again of black boys with a low reading level, an ethnographic
project on local agricultural practices is mounted, involving the youngsters in
work in the community. To say we've heard all this before is to miss the point.
It is the nature and consequences of the process of change which are significant,
and if they include reinventing the wheel (a much maligned practice!), so be it.
The contrast is between, on the one hand, teachers and students actively engaged
in changing their ways of learning and teaching and, on the other, uniform pro-

grams emanating from above which presume that teachers are mere docile trans-
mitters and that learners are uniform and culture-free in their needs. I feel it both
irrelevant and impertinent, therefore, to scrutinize closely the language teaching
described in this section. In any case, there are better things to do than snigger
at one teacher's enthusiasm for topic sentences or another's insistence on "a school-
accepted format" (p. 320) for written work. But, of course, this puts Heath in a
difficult position. She too rejects the role of judge and jury, but her respect for the
teachers and children leaves us to guess, though not without clues and nudging,
where her preferences lie. The science-cum-ethnography project is described with
scarcely concealed delight, but it includes amongst its goals the mastery of "the
language of science" and making "acceptable scientific statements" (p. 325). It
would appear that this includes, "avoid telling stories about their knowledge: be
able to discuss an item or event for its own sake, not in terms of their direct experiences with it" (p. 325). Do those suspect goals receive Heath's imprimatur? I give
her the benefit of the doubt, for she must know the philosophical and linguistic
debate on these matters. I never understand what it means to do something for
"its own sake." And what has Heath been doing for the previous three hundred
pages but telling stories about her knowledge, and not for their own sake but for
ours?

Picking her way judiciously through the innovations, Heath makes very clear
that the teachers did not see themselves as launching basic changes in content, nor
abandoning established classroom methods (basal readers, for example). The criteria for "school success" in the end remain unchanged, and the core of mainstream
values is not tampered with: "students learned to share the goals and methods of
the classroom" (p. 340). There is not a hint that black and white students in the
Carolinas studying in the same classrooms might raise some tricky issues in history and social studies and in the job-getting aspects of some of their work. What
Heath has chosen to do is to present all that seems most positive in the teachers'
work and to imply that ethnicity did not affect the basic processes. Yet, the introduction of teachers — and, later, students — to ethnographic ways of studying sur-
reptitiously their own and their community's practices does in fact erode the old
curriculum. New *ways* of learning constitute new learning. How else can one begin? As Heath observes, "Students now provided information for the teacher to
question — the reverse of the usual classroom practice of the teacher presenting the
information and questioning students on their knowledge" (p. 342). Furthermore,
she offers: "Critical in the thinking of these teachers was that their approach was
not a remedial one designed for poor learners. Instead, they felt that the attention
given to different ways of talking and knowing, and the manipulation of contexts
and language benefited all students" (p. 355).

The principles do not in themselves constitute a complete apparatus for changing the role of language in the curriculum, but they have a huge potential if pushed
to their logical conclusion. They could be extended into a critical examination of
the language of textbooks or the ways in which communities are linked to and
shaped by influential forces in society, including the ways in which language is
used in the media, by politicians and others, to affect daily lives. Finally, there
is the question of how Roadville and Trackton students are to develop their own
voices so that they can articulate a critical view of society and act more powerfully

in it. Ethnography cannot by itself achieve these ends. To assert this is not to diminish the courageous work of the teachers; it is only to sketch out its essentially initiatory character and its vulnerability.

And vulnerable it proved to be. In a sad but all too familiar phrase, we learn that "in the Piedmont of today, the methods used by these teachers have all but disappeared" (p. 356). The bureaucracy of tests has taken over and, as one teacher says, "there's no joy left in teaching now" (p. 359). This defeat is known on both sides of the Atlantic. To reverse it requires acting outside the classroom.

Heath writes in her last pages of "a recognition and a drive to use language as a source of power," but an indication of limits she sets herself is registered in the way that the sentence tails off into a circumscribed notion of power and its source: "for access to and maintenance of expanded types and places of work" (p. 363). The source of the power is much more than the job market.

In the end, teachers can defend successfully the enclaves they have constructed only if they have won the parents and community to their methods and can invoke their support in sustaining them. And those are "ways with words" which have to be learned too. They constitute the language of political participation. If all of us do not learn this way with words, we shall go on placing wreaths on the tombstones of projects all over the world, overcome with sadness and impotence.

Whatever we do or fail to do in resisting the conversion of our schools into brutally frank machines for social control, in the end thousands of teachers must encounter millions of students daily in classrooms. Heath's book suggests to us a new way of looking at that encounter. Ethnographers are the heroes of her text. There are other kinds of heroes whom we need to acknowledge, but that should not prevent us from saluting the ethnographers — and Shirley Brice Heath in particular.

Notes on Contributors

ALMA FLOR ADA is Professor in the School of Education at the University of San Francisco. Her chief professional interests lie in bilingual education as an instrument of social change, adult literacy, the empowerment of minorities, and children's literature. She is the author of *Hagamos Caminos*, a Spanish-language reading series, and editor in chief of the *Journal of the National Association of Bilingual Education*.

WILLIAM C. AYERS is Instructor in the Department of Curriculum and Teaching, Teachers College, Columbia University. His major professional interests are early childhood education and teacher education. He is book review editor of *Day Care and Early Education* and a contributor to the literature on learning and early education.

ARTHUR S. BOLSTER, JR. is Professor Emeritus of Education, Harvard University. From 1979 to 1982 he was director of the Harvard–Framingham State College collaborative project for training teachers in higher education. His current interests lie in teaching and teacher development. Among his published works are *Advancing Truth* (1954) and *The Clinical Professorship in Teacher Education* (1967).

DEBORAH P. BRITZMAN is Assistant Professor of Education in the School of Education and Human Development, University Center, the State University of New York, Binghamton. She includes multicultural education, teacher education, and methodology in critical pedagogy among her current professional interests.

DENISE S. BURDEN is Codirector of the Boston Writing Project at the University of Massachusetts, Boston, and teaches at its College of Public and Community Services. Her major professional interests are teaching writing, curriculum development, teacher training, and the impact of culture on writing. Recent articles include "Developing Student Writing Curriculum for Culturally Diverse Classrooms" (1986) and "Writing Projects and Literacy Education: Report on an Experiment" (in press).

PENELOPE BUTLER was librarian at the Bureau of Study Counsel, Harvard University, at the time she assisted in research for the article by Kiyo Morimoto.

JOSEPH CHECK is Director of the Boston Writing Project at the University of Massachusetts, Boston and is also a member of the advisory board of the National Writing Project and of the executive board of the Massachusetts Council of Teachers of English. He is author of "Real World Meets Writing Process," *National Writing Project* (1987).

DAVID K. COHEN, formerly Professor of Education and Social Policy at Harvard University, is the John A. Hannah Distinguished Professor of Education and Social Policy at Michigan State University. A specialist in social policy, the politics of education, and the nature of teaching and administrative practice, he is coauthor with Arthur G. Powell and Eleanor Farrar of *The Shopping Mall High School: Winners and Losers in the Educational Marketplace* (1985).

SELWYN R. CUDJOE is Professor in the Department of Black Studies at Wellesley College. His major professional interest is in literacy and political theory, with special reference to the Caribbean and Afro-Americans. He has recently completed and submitted for publication a literary study on the work of the novelist V. S. Naipaul.

LISA D. DELPIT is Assistant Professor of Reading, Language, and Literacy in the College of Human and Rural Development at the University of Alaska, Fairbanks. Her present professional interests include various aspects of multicultural education. She has written and lectured widely on reading, language, and cultural identity.

ELEANOR DUCKWORTH is Associate Professor of Education at Harvard University, with a special interest in teacher education, curriculum, and how people learn. Faculty sponsor of the Harvard Teacher Network, and a former student translator and colleague of Jean Piaget, she is author of a number of articles on teaching and learning. Her book, *The Having of Wonderful Ideas and Other Essays on Teaching and Learning*, will appear in 1987.

CORA LEE FIVE is a teacher at the Edgewood School in Scarsdale, New York, where she serves also as mentor to teachers who are newcomers in her district. Her particular interest is the connection between reading and writing, a subject on which she has lectured throughout the country. She is the author of "Children Recreate History in Their Own Voices," in *Breaking Ground*, edited by Hansen, Newkirk, and Graves (1985), and "Joy in Learning: A Teacher Investigates Her Own Learning Process," *Language Arts* (1986).

CLARE FOX, who has taught high school English in Tucson, Arizona, now lives in Somerville, Massachusetts, where she is pursuing her career as a writer.

SOPHIE FREUD is Professor of Social Work at the Simmons College School of Social Work. She is also on the faculty of the Harvard University Extension School, where she teaches a course on the psychology of women. Her current focus is in human developmment, the psychology of women, and clinical interventions.

HENRY A. GIROUX, Professor of Education and Renowned Scholar in Residence at Miami University in Ohio, is interested in the sociology of education, cultural studies, curriculum theory, and public philosophy. His most recent books include *Ideology, Culture, and the Process of Schooling* (1981, 1984), and *Education under Siege*, with coauthor Stanley Aronowitz (1985). His forthcoming books are *Education and the Public Sphere: Schooling for Democracy* and, with Peter McLaren, *Schooling and the Politics of Culture*.

PETER GOLDEN is Codirector of the Boston Writing Project, University of Massachusetts, Boston. Prior to joining the Project, he taught secondary English in the Boston public school system.

MAXINE GREENE is Professor of Philosophy and Education and William F. Russell Professor in the Foundations of Education at Teachers College, Columbia University. Critical philosophy and aesthetic education are among her major professional interests. Her writings include *Teacher as Stranger* (1973), *Landscapes of Learning* (1980), and *The Dialectic of Freedom* (in progress).

JUDITH GREGORY, Coordinator of Gap Mountain Permaculture, is also a cofounder of Land Trust at Gap Mountain in Jaffrey, New Hampshire. Her interests include religion, ecology (permaculture), and issues of feminism and gender, as well as the connections among them. She has written numerous articles for *The Catholic Worker*, of which she is an associate editor. Her essay, "Remembering Dorothy Day," appeared in *America* (1981).

NANCY JO HOFFMAN is Acting Assistant Dean for Academic and Student Services at the Graduate School of Education, Harvard University. She is on leave from the College of Public and Community Service, University of Massachusetts, Boston, where she is Professor of Humanities. Her research focuses on women writers, interracial collaboration, and women's education. She is the author of *Women's "True" Profession: Voices from the History of Teaching* (1981) and *Spenser's Pastorals* (1979), as well as editor with Florence Howe of *Women Working: Stories and Poems* (1979).

KATHE JERVIS teaches at the Center School, an alternative public middle school in Manhattan sponsored jointly by Community School District 3 and Fordham University. In addition to her teaching, she edits *Pathway: A Forum for Progressive Education*. This article is a chapter from a book in progress which continues the narrative of Karen's P.S. 135 classroom.

SUSAN MOORE JOHNSON is Assistant Professor of Education at Harvard University and Director of the Boston-Harvard School Development Project. Her current professional interests are teacher policy and the implementation of reforms, and the school as a workplace. Among her recent writings are *Teacher Unions in Schools* (1984) and, with Niall Nelson, "Teaching Reforms in an Active Voice" (*Phi Delta Kappan*, 1987).

HARVEY KANTOR, Assistant Professor in the Department of Educational Studies at the University of Utah, is conducting research on education and liberal reform in the post-World War II period, with a particular focus on the 1960s. He is coeditor with David Tyack of *Work, Youth, and Schooling: Historical Perspectives on Vocationalism in American Education* (1982) and author of *Learning to Earn: Work, School, and Vocational Reform in California, 1880–1930* (in press).

MAGDALENE LAMPERT, Associate Professor of Teacher Education, Michigan State University, and teacher of fifth grade mathematics, Spartan Village School, East Lansing, Michigan, is also currently a Spencer Fellow, National Academy of Education. She is concerned with teacher education, the development of meaningful mathematics curricula for children in the middle grades, and the analysis of the nature of teachers' work.

MAGDA LEWIS is a doctoral candidate at the Ontario Institute for Studies in Education and is Adjunct Professor in Queen's University, Toronto. Her present work in progress is a feminist critique of the social construction of national identity. She has also published works on native images in children's books.

DANIEL P. LISTON is Assistant Professor of Education in the Department of Education at Washington University in St. Louis and a Spencer Fellow, National Academy of Education. His current professional interests focus on teacher education and teachers' work, and on explanatory and ethical examinations of Marxist theories of schooling. He is author of *Capitalist Schools? Explanation and Ethics in Marxist Studies of Schooling* (1987).

ROBERT LOWE, Associate Director of the Educational Opportunity Program, Marquette University, is interested in race, class, and equality of opportunity from a historical perspective. He is coauthor with David Tyack and Elizabeth Hansot of *Public Schools in Hard Times: The Great Depression and Recent Years* (1984).

ANNE MARTIN teaches kindergarten at the Lawrence School in Brookline, Massachusetts, and is cochairperson of the Boston Laboratory for Teachers. Her major professional concerns are classroom teaching, writing about children in the classroom, and providing editorial assistance to other teachers who are writing about their teaching experiences. A recent collection of such writing, to which she also contributed, is *Speaking Out: Teachers on Teaching* (1986).

JOSEPH P. McDONALD, Clinical Professor of Education at Brown University, works with the Coalition of Essential Schools at Hope High School in Providence, Rhode Island. He wrote the present article while teaching in the Watertown High School in Massachusetts, where he was lead teacher in the interdepartmental studies program.

PETER L. McLAREN is Assistant Professor in the Department of Educational Leadership at Miami University, Ohio. His research has a multidisciplinary focus that includes critical ethnography, the sociology and anthropology of education, and critical pedagogy. He is author of *Cries from the Corridor* (1980), *Schooling as a Ritual Performance* (1986), and the forthcoming *Schooling for Empowerment*, and coauthor with Henry A. Giroux of *Schooling and the Politics of Culture* (in press).

DANIEL MEIER teaches first grade at the Park School in Brookline, Massachusetts. His professional focus is on relationships between reading and writing and talking, literacy development in poor children, and writers and writing communities. He is a student in the Writing Program at the Bread Loaf School of English, Middlebury College.

MARGARET TREECE METZGER teaches English at Brookline High School in Massachusetts, and is particularly interested in working with new teachers. She is presently finishing a textbook for a new writing curriculum which emphasizes the connection between writing and thinking. Her work is featured in Ernest Boyer's *High School*.

KIYO MORIMOTO is Lecturer on Education at Harvard University, a consultant on education for the Danforth Foundation and the Lilly Endowment, and former director of the Bureau of Study Counsel, Harvard University. His principal interests are in psychological and study counseling, and in the exploration of the process of learning.

RICHARD J. MURNANE is Associate Professor of Education at Harvard University. His areas of professional interest include teacher labor markets and the determinants of school effectiveness. He is author of numerous articles investigating the economic roots of education, among them "How Enrollment Declines Affect per Pupil Expenditure Levels in Public School Districts" in *Perspectives in Local Public Finance* (1985) and "An Economist's Look at Federal and State Education Policies" in *American Domestic Priorities*, edited by John M. Quigley and Daniel L. Rubinfeld (1985).

NEL NODDINGS, Professor of Education at Stanford University, has a special interest in feminist ethics and epistemology and in problem solving in mathematics education. She is a frequent contributor to scholarly journals and is author of *Caring: A Feminist Approach to Ethics and Moral Education* and, with Paul J. Shore, *Awakening the Inner Eye*, both published in 1984.

VIVIAN GUSSIN PALEY is a teacher at the University of Chicago Laboratory Schools. Her professional interests include teaching young children and writing about their lives in the classroom. She is the author of *Wally's Stories* (1981), *Boys and Girls* (1984), *Mollie is Three* (1986), and *Bad Guys Don't Have Birthdays* (forthcoming).

HAROLD ROSEN is Emeritus Professor of Education at the University of London Institute of Education and currently Visiting Professor and Leverhulme Senior Research Fellow at the Open University. He is concerned with narrative theory and its educational significance and, more broadly, language in education. He is author of *Stories and Meanings* (1985), coauthor with Connie Rosen of *The Language of Primary School Children* (1972), and, with Tony Burgess, of *The Languages and Dialects of London Schoolchildren* (1985).

PHILIP SBARATTA is Chairperson of English and Communications at North Shore Community College in Beverly, Massachusetts. His professional focus is on the teaching of writing, particularly of the composition process itself, on the·connection between reading and writing, and on management in higher education. He is a frequent contributor to college journals and bulletins.

IRA SHOR is Professor of English at the College of Staten Island, City University of New York, a former Guggenheim Fellow, and the 1986 Chancellor's Scholar in Residence, CUNY. He cites as his chief interests critical pedagogy, the work of Paulo Freire, and the politics of reform. He is coauthor with Paulo Freire of *A Pedagogy for Liberation* (1987); and author of *Culture Wars: School and Society in the Conservative Restoration, 1969–1984* (1986), and of *Critical Teaching and Everyday Life* (1987), which is now in its third edition.

LEE S. SHULMAN is Professor of Education and Affiliated Professor of Psychology at Stanford University. His research centers on the process of reasoning and practice in two professions: teaching and medicine. He is also conducting research on teacher assessment to support the efforts of the emerging National Board of Professional Teaching Standards, both activities funded by the Carnegie Corporation. He is coeditor with Gary Sykes of *The Handbook of Teaching and Policy* (1983). He is currently studying the knowledge base of teaching under a grant from the Spencer Foundation.

ROGER I. SIMON is Associate Professor in the Department of Curriculum, Ontario Institute for Studies in Education, Toronto. His major professional interests lie in critical pedagogy and cultural studies.

DONALD W. THOMAS, Chairman of the English Department at Brookline High School in Massachusetts, maintains a professional interest in interdisciplinary studies, semiotics, and educational reform. His teaching career has taken him to a number of high schools, including Comprehensive High School in Nigeria. He is the author of a series of books, the most recent of which is *Semiotics 4: Language in the Making* (1983).

MARUE ENGLISH WALIZER is a teacher in the Wilton High School in Connecticut. From 1984 to 1986, while on sabbatical, she served as Senior Adviser in the Freshman Dean's Office of Harvard College. Now returned to her teaching post at Wilton High School, her chief professional interest is teaching and research on teachers' thinking in narrative forms. She is coauthor of *Adam, Where Are You?* (1968), a novel used as a high school ethics text.

MARGARET V. YONEMURA is Professor of Education at the University Center, State University of New York, Binghamton. Concerned with exploring the limitations of stage theories on professional development of students in early childhood education programs, she has been a frequent contributor to the literature on the education of children and is the author of *A Teacher at Work: Professional Development and the Early Childhood Educator* (1986).

KENNETH M. ZEICHNER, Professor in the Department of Curriculum and Instruction, University of Wisconsin, Madison, is also a senior researcher working with the National Center for Research in Teacher Education in the United States. He is engaged primarily in the study of teacher education, with particular interest in how teachers learn to teach; his articles on these subjects have been published widely in this country and abroad.

Index